The Preservation of Art and Culture in Times of War

The Oxford Series in Ethics, National Security, and the Rule of Law

Series Editors Claire Finkelstein and Jens David Ohlin

Oxford University Press

About the Series

The *Oxford Series in Ethics, National Security, and the Rule of Law* is an interdisciplinary book series designed to address abiding questions at the intersection of national security, moral and political philosophy, and the law. It seeks to illuminate both ethical and legal dilemmas that arise in democratic nations as they grapple with contemporary national security imperatives. The series also seeks to create a synergy between academic researchers and practitioners as they focus on common problems in national security theory and practice. The aim of the series is ultimately to advance thinking about how to protect and augment the rule of law in the context of contemporary armed conflict and national security.

The book series grew out of the work of the Center for Ethics and the Rule of Law (CERL) at the University of Pennsylvania. CERL is a nonpartisan interdisciplinary institute dedicated to the preservation and promotion of the rule of law in twenty-first century warfare and national security. The only Center of its kind housed within a major research university, CERL draws from the study of law, philosophy, and ethics to answer the difficult questions that arise in times of war and contemporary transnational conflicts.

The Preservation of Art and Culture in Times of War

Edited by

CLAIRE FINKELSTEIN, DEREK GILLMAN,
AND FREDERIK ROSÉN

OXFORD
UNIVERSITY PRESS

OXFORD
UNIVERSITY PRESS

Oxford University Press is a department of the University of Oxford. It furthers the University's objective of excellence in research, scholarship, and education by publishing worldwide. Oxford is a registered trade mark of Oxford University Press in the UK and certain other countries.

Published in the United States of America by Oxford University Press
198 Madison Avenue, New York, NY 10016, United States of America.

Library of Congress Cataloging-in-Publication Data
Names: Finkelstein, Claire, editor. | Gillman, Derek, editor. |
Rosén, Frederik, editor.
Title: The Preservation of Art and Culture in Times of War / Edited by: Claire Finkelstein, Derek Gillman, and Frederik Rosén.
Description: New York, NY : Oxford University Press, [2022] |
Series: Ethics national security rule law series | Includes index. |
Identifiers: LCCN 2021033612 | ISBN 9780197610565 (hardback) |
ISBN 9780197610589 (epub) | ISBN 9780197610572 (updf) | ISBN 9780197610596 (online)
Subjects: LCSH: Cultural property—Protection (International law)
War (International law)
Classification: LCC KZ6535 . P74 2021 | DDC 344/.094—dc23
LC record available at https://lccn.loc.gov/2021033612

DOI: 10.1093/oso/9780197610565.001.0001

1 3 5 7 9 8 6 4 2

Printed by Integrated Books International, United States of America

Note to Readers

This publication is designed to provide accurate and authoritative information in regard to the subject matter covered. It is based upon sources believed to be accurate and reliable and is intended to be current as of the time it was written. It is sold with the understanding that the publisher is not engaged in rendering legal, accounting, or other professional services. If legal advice or other expert assistance is required, the services of a competent professional person should be sought. Also, to confirm that the information has not been affected or changed by recent developments, traditional legal research techniques should be used, including checking primary sources where appropriate.

(Based on the Declaration of Principles jointly adopted by a Committee of the American Bar Association and a Committee of Publishers and Associations.)

Table of Contents

Preface

On February 24, 2022, Russia invaded the sovereign nation of Ukraine, and for a third time in the past century, Europe was plunged into war. As of the time of this writing, the conflict between Russia and Ukraine rages on, with few signs that the conflict will abate any time soon. The inability of the Russian military to swiftly take control of Ukrainian territory, unlike when Russia invaded Crimea in 2014, has been due in part to a forceful international response in defense of Ukraine. Vladimir Putin's evident frustration with the ineffectiveness of the Russian military campaign turned quickly to a punitive stance toward Ukraine: If Ukraine will not be part of Russia, it must cease to exist. The result has been a criminal campaign against the Ukrainian people, against Ukrainian life, against the Ukrainian language, and against anything that would signify that Ukraine is a separate country with a distinct history and culture of its own.

This book was originally inspired by a similar campaign against culture waged in the Middle East during the Global War on Terror. As we commemorated the twentieth anniversary of that war during the fall of 2021 and the impact of twenty years of war on all aspects of the international security environment, we were reminded of the degree to which wars of aggression are all too often attacks on culture, on a way of life that is anathema to the attackers. And in that sense, the campaigns waged by the Taliban, Al Qaeda, and later the Islamic State of Iraq and Syria (ISIS) achieved at least part of their objectives. In the space of a few short hours, starting in the early morning hours of September 11, 2001, U.S. culture was transformed dramatically and irrevocably: the United States pivoted from focusing on how to avoid international armed conflict with rogue nations to an overwhelming focus on fighting non-state actors waging a jihad against not only Western democracy, but liberal culture as well. Ironically, the United States and Western Europe have now come full circle. After more than two decades learning how to fight violent non-state actors, we are once more honing our skills on the challenges of international armed conflict.

Twenty years of fighting Middle East terrorism, however, has revealed the complexity of armed conflict against violent non-state actors on many levels, especially against the backdrop of profound differences in culture, both between East and West, but also among the many different cultures and religious communities within the Middle East. In a world in which tolerance is not a value, ideological differences present an existential threat to one's own way of life. It is not by accident that Al Qaeda chose to target the World Trade Center—the ultimate symbol of capitalism and economic might—as part of its aim to reject American hubris and cultural supremacy. But it also why in 2001, Mullah Muhammad Omar, the leader of the Taliban, issued a decree ordering the elimination of all non-Islamic statues and sanctuaries in Afghanistan, including the famous Bamiyan Buddhas.

The destruction of the Bamiyan Buddhas was an iconic act that came to symbolize the sheer brutality and intolerance of the Taliban almost as much as their intentional destruction of human life. Similar to the attack on so-called "degenerate art" on the part of the Nazis, or the burning of thousands of books, the destruction of the Buddhas became a symbol for the lack of humanity that characterized the Third Reich. Fortunately Nazi greed and the desire to ridicule German intellectual and artistic life led the Nazis to preserve, rather than destroy, some of the finest visual art of the twentieth century, though the art was separated from their rightful owners, often never the be returned to them or their descendants who sought the return of their property after the war. Similarly, ISIS's plunder of Syria and Northern Iraq of its great treasures to provide funding for their murderous activities destroyed cultural heritage in another way—by destroying archeological areas and separating objects from the cultures and contexts that were their intended homes.

Attacking culture has been a part of war for as long as there has been military conflict, just as controlling religious and cultural practices and places has been a preferred tool of political repression and a challenge to individual autonomy since time immemorial. As the German poet Heinrich Heine wrote in 1823, "Dort wo man Bücher verbrennt, verbrennt man auch am Ende Menschen."[1]

The greatest challenge the West has confronted in the face of this war of ideology is how to address the threat posed by illiberal worldviews that produce violent extremism, while adhering to the rule of law that forms the core of western liberal culture. How do we fight a violent *jihad* oriented towards the destruction of our way of life, against an enemy that seemingly knows

[1] "There where books are burnt, so too in the end shall men burn" (trans. mine).

no legal constraints, without losing our own integrity and humanity in the process? Thus far the United States and its allies have failed to answer this question. What should be clear is that addressing the challenges posed by the preservation of art, culture, and artistic expression in other cultures in the context of armed conflict is a critical part of that integrity.

A substantial body of international and domestic laws prohibit the destruction and misappropriation of cultural heritage, but achieving global adherence to those laws is a significant challenge. In a deeper sense, the protection of cultural heritage is also the protection of a critical human right, a right that some regard as more precious than life itself. The UN Universal Declaration of human rights recognizes cultural and artistic rights as an aspect of personal freedom. Article 18 recognizes "the right to freedom of thought, conscience and religion." Article 19 recognizes "the right to freedom of opinion and expression," which includes the "freedom to hold opinions without interference and to seek, receive and impart information and ideas through any media . . ." Article 22 talks about "cultural rights indispensable for . . . dignity and the free development of . . . personality," and Article 27 recognizes "the right freely to participate in the cultural life of the community, to enjoy the arts and to share in scientific advancement and its benefits." These provisions sit uneasily with the libertarian orientation of the Anglo-American approach to liberty, which sees liberty as "*freedom from,*" rather than "*freedom to,*" as Isaiah Berlin once wrote. At the same time, the United States in recent years has experienced a cultural revolution in its relationship to its own past, particularly relating to its shameful glorification of figures from the Confederacy, such as Robert E. Lee, the general who led the South's military insurrection against the Union, and whose statute, image, and name one could find, until very recently, adorning the public spaces or educational institutions of numerous Southern towns and cities. Consistent with this was the conspicuous presence, until very recently, of Confederate flags flying next to the American flag in front of the state houses of so many American cities in the South.

In the North, it was common to find tribute paid to many figures who are becoming increasingly controversial, such as Thomas Jefferson, who famously owned slaves and even impregnated one of them, Sally Hemmings; or Christopher Columbus who has come under new scrutiny as a purveyor of prejudice and cruelty against indigenous peoples. Even Woodrow Wilson has been demoted from his vaunted position in US educational institutions, with the result that statues have been removed and schools renamed to strip them of the perceived taint of the post-Civil War period known as Reconstruction. Yet these same symbols, and public opposition to their display, have come to galvanize the extreme right wing of the US Republican Party. The members of Q-Anon and other right wing groups who broke into the U.S. Capitol Building in an attempt to halt the peaceful transition of power to a duly elected president were armed with confederate flags and Nazi paraphernalia. Insurrectionists wore tee shirts prominently displaying the logo "Camp Auschwitz," mixed in with Swastikas and other symbols of bigotry and hate.

How, then, shall we assess the cultural, historical, political, or aesthetic value of a statue, a flag, a work of art, or even an image painted or tattooed on the human body? Under what circumstances should we defend historical and cultural preservation and under which eschew it? Those who would laud the value of a work of art or cultural artifact as based in part on its identity as a repository of human memory might yet reject its preservation where such symbols become an organizing mantra for illiberal political leaders and racist or otherwise prejudiced ideologies. Was UNESCO right to designate the Auschwitz concentration camp a cultural heritage site, to ensure that we never forget its horrors, despite the fact that thousands of white supremacists also fight for its preservation as a shrine whose ideology they believe worth defending and reviving the world over?

The chapters in this volume grapple with some of the most fundamental tensions that inhere in the foundations of democracy, a system of government predicated on the task of protecting and preserving a culture organized around free expression in a society of profoundly conflicting and opposing values. Such a project may seem doomed to failure from the outset. Yet history has proven in myriad ways that there simply is no acceptable alternative. It is hard to avoid the conclusion that a culture that insists on stamping out or even suppressing dissent and threats to its own basic values cannot hope to preserve those same values.

The challenges surrounding the preservation of cultural heritage are critical to address, both in their philosophical and theoretical dimensions, and in their practical manifestations. Can we confidently argue that the Bamiyan Buddhas are worth preserving, when we also reject the preservation of a massive mural of Saddam Hussein in Bagdad; a statue of white supremacist Cecil Rhodes; the iconic Mount Rushmore celebrating four of America's Founding Fathers, ironically built on land seized from indigenous peoples; a statue of Winston Churchill, rendered controversial by the latter's colonialist views regarding Indian independence; and Nathuram Godse, Gandhi's assassin, whom Hindu nationalists are now honoring with statues; or the dozens of monuments to the confederate insurgents who fought to preserve the most abhorrent practice in U.S. history, namely the slave trade? Is cultural preservation an end in itself or is it an instrumental good that helps to secure other things we value, such as community, memory, and religious identity? If an end in itself, is that end outweighed or defeated when that preservation is connected with political oppression and illiberal ideologies? Is the controversy surrounding the preservation of cultural heritage ultimately an echo of classic debates over democracy and freedom of speech, namely that democracy requires us to preserve cultural heritage at the same time that it may not survive if we do? If the preservation of cultural heritage ultimately does play a critical role in preserving democracy, what priority should be placed on that enterprise, especially when it occurs, as it often does, in the context of armed conflict where we may seem to have to choose between preserving lives or preserving art, when we cannot always preserve both? Is the preservation of cultural heritage at odds with the need to protect the homeland, or should it be understood as playing an ineliminable role in realizing that aim?

This volume grew out of a conference organized by the Center for Ethics and the Rule of Law (CERL) at the University of Pennsylvania in conjunction with the Penn Cultural Heritage Center at the Penn Museum in 2017. Much has changed since that time. In particular, the Western world is no longer steeped in battle with Al Qaeda or ISIS, and the archaeological sites held captive for ransom and constant terrorist destruction of the cultural icons of Northern Iraq and Syria have (mostly) been returned to their previous protected status. Yet it seems we have come full circle, for with the withdrawal of U.S. and allied troops from Iraq and Afghanistan and the takeover of Afghanistan by Taliban rule, will cultural heritage once more come under threat in Afghanistan? And if so, is the international community prepared to defend international law and confront the perpetrators over its destruction or exploitation? The question is of course broader than just the current conflicts in the Middle East. It has become a perennial part of many struggles for political independence and plays out in different theaters of war across the globe.

The questions addressed in the original 2017 conference are thus likely to remain with us as long as there are cultures left to preserve and wars left to fight. The following chapters will attest that the answers to the hardest questions regarding culture and war can best be sought through a rich, interdisciplinary conversation of the many complexities they raise. To address them requires the combined efforts of philosophers, historians, archaeologists, lawyers, members of the armed forces, and many others. While the chapters we have assembled offer no common conclusions, the debate and discussion that emerge will both enrich our understanding of the challenges surrounding cultural heritage preservation and help identify a range of answers to the questions here posed.

Acknowledgments

The editors wish to thank the Penn Museum and the Penn Cultural Heritage Center for the collaboration in the original 2017 conference from which this volume emerged as well as the Penn Middle East Center and the Office of the Provost of the University of Pennsylvania for its support. In addition, the editors owe a debt of gratitude to Ashley Fuchs for her dedicated assistance preparing the manuscript for publication.

List of Contributors

James Barry is a Research Fellow at the Alfred Deakin Institute at Deakin University, Australia. An anthropologist by training, he specializes in ethnolinguistic and religious minorities in Iran and their relationship with Iranian national identity. His book *Armenian Christians in Iran: Ethnicity, Religion and Identity in the Islamic Republic* is available through Cambridge University Press (2018).

Jos van Beurden is an Affiliated Researcher of the Vrije Universiteit, Amsterdam. He specializes in colonial cultural collections and restitution issues. Among his publications are *Ongemakkelijk Erfgoed—Koloniale collecties en teruggave in de Lage Landen* (Inconvenient Heritage—Colonial collections and restitution in the Netherlands and Belgium) (Walburg Pers 2021) and the pioneering *Treasures in Trusted Hands—Negotiating the Future of Colonial Cultural Objects* (Sidestone Press 2017).

Mark A. Drumbl is the Class of 1975 Alumni Professor at Washington and Lee University, School of Law, where he serves as Director of the University's Transnational Law Institute. His research and teaching interests include public international law, global environmental governance, international criminal law, post-conflict justice, and transnational legal process. He is the author of *Reimagining Child Soldiers in International Law and Policy* (Oxford University Press 2012); *Atrocity, Punishment, and International Law* (Cambridge University Press 2007); and co-editor of the *Research Handbook on Child Soldiers* (Elgar 2019).

Claire Finkelstein is the Algernon Biddle Professor of Law and Professor of Philosophy at the University of Pennsylvania and a distinguished research fellow at the Annenberg Public Policy Center (APPC) as well as a senior fellow at the Foreign Policy Research Institute (FPRI). She is the Founder and Faculty Director of Penn's Center for Ethics and the Rule of Law. An expert in the law of armed conflict, military ethics, and national security law, she is a co-editor (with Jens David Ohlin) of *The Oxford Series in Ethics, National Security, and the Rule of Law* and a well-published author in the areas of national security and democratic governance. Professor Finkelstein is a frequent radio, broadcast, and print commentator.

Helen Frowe is a Professor of Practical Philosophy and Knut and Alice Wallenberg Scholar at Stockholm University, where she directs the Stockholm Centre for the Ethics of War and Peace. Her research focuses on permissible harming, particularly harming in self-defense and war. She is the author of *Defensive Killing* (Oxford University Press 2014) and *The Ethics of War and Peace: An Introduction* (Routledge 2015), and co-editor of *The Oxford Handbook of Ethics of War* and *How*

We Fight: Ethics in War (Oxford University Press 2018). She is currently co-directing the AHRC-funded project on the protection of cultural heritage in war.

Derek Gillman is a Distinguished Teaching Professor, Art History and Museum Leadership, and Executive Director, University Collections and Exhibitions, Drexel University. He was president of the Barnes Foundation from 2006–2013 and, prior to that, of the Pennsylvania Academy of the Fine Arts. He is author of *The Idea of Cultural Heritage* (Cambridge University Press, 2nd edn, 2010), a board member of the International Cultural Property Society, an emeritus member of the Association of Art Museum Directors, and a consulting scholar in the Asian Section of the University of Pennsylvania Museum.

Martin Hamilton is a Senior Analyst at the National Operations Department of the Swedish Police Authority and a former lecturer at the Centre for International and Operational Law of the Swedish Defence University in Stockholm. He holds a PhD in International Law from the University of Kent, UK. His thesis is entitled "Cultural Genocide in International Law: A Normative Evolution?"

Kristin Hausler is the Dorset Senior Research Fellow and Director of the Center for International Law at the British Institute of International and Comparative Law in London (UK). She is a consultant on cultural heritage matters, and has provided training on cultural heritage to armed groups and police forces. She has taught courses on cultural heritage law and policy at Georgetown University, the University of Florida, the University of Geneva, and Leiden University, among others.

Benjamin Isakhan is a Professor of International Politics and Founding Director of "Polis," a research network for Politics and International Relations, in the Alfred Deakin Institute at Deakin University, Australia. He is also an Adjunct Senior Research Associate in the Department of Politics and International Relations at the University of Johannesburg, South Africa.

Andrzej Jakubowski is an Assistant Professor at the Institute of Legal Studies of the University of Opole and at the Institute of the Polish Academy of Sciences in Warsaw, Poland. He serves as chair of the Committee on Participation in Global Cultural Heritage Governance of the International Law Association and a mediator at the UNESCO Intergovernmental Committee for Promoting the Return of Cultural Property to its Country of Origin or its Restitution in Case of Illicit Appropriation (ICPRCP). He is the author of *State Succession in Cultural Property* (Oxford University Press 2015).

Duncan MacIntosh is a Professor of Philosophy at Dalhousie University, where he served as department chair, and a member of the Executive Board of the Center for Ethics and the Rule of Law. Professor MacIntosh is a widely published author who works in metaethics, decision and action theory, metaphysics, philosophy of language, epistemology, and philosophy of science. Most recently he has focused on philosophical issues in the rule of law and national security.

Derek Matravers is a Professor of Philosophy at the Open University and a Senior Member of Darwin College, Cambridge. He is the author of *Introducing Philosophy of Art: Eight Case Studies*, *Fiction and Narrative*, and *Empathy* (Routledge 2012), among other works, and has published numerous articles on aesthetics, ethics, and the philosophy of mind. He is the editor, with Paloma Atencia-Linares, of the *British Journal of Aesthetics* and is currently co-directing the AHRC-funded project on just war theory and cultural heritage in war at the Stockholm Center for the Ethics of War and Peace.

Carsten Paludan-Müller is an archaeologist who has held leading positions within museums and heritage management in Denmark. From 2003 to 2017 he was the general director of The Norwegian Institute for Cultural Heritage Research. He has worked as an expert with the Council of Europe, the European Commission, ICOMOS, Anadolu Kültür, the Norwegian MFA, and the World Bank.

Victoria Reed is the Sadler Curator for Provenance at the Museum of Fine Arts, Boston. She holds a BA in liberal arts from Sarah Lawrence College and an MA and PhD in art history from Rutgers University. Since 1997 she has been conducting provenance research in American art museums. Dr. Reed has lectured widely and published extensively on matters related to provenance research, including the issue of Nazi-era looting and restitution.

Frederik Rosén is the director of the Nordic Center for Cultural Heritage and Armed Conflict and an Adjunct Associate Professor at the Department of Cross-Cultural and Regional Studies at the University of Copenhagen and has published widely on international security and the law of armed conflict. He is a leading international expert on military challenges related to cultural heritage and has directed several NATO projects on the topic.

Laurie W. Rush is an Archaeologist who works for the US Army at Fort Drum, NY. She is a fellow of the National Science Foundation and the American Academy in Rome. Dr. Rush was the military liaison for return of Ur to Iraqi stewardship and represented the Department of Defense for heritage issues in Kabul and across the Middle East. She is a board member of the US Committee of the Blue Shield and co-author of the book, *The Carabinieri TPC: Saving the World's Heritage* (Boydell Press 2015).

Ricardo A. St. Hilaire is an attorney in the area of international cultural heritage law, with a focus on transnational antiquities trafficking. He is the founder and executive director of Red Arch Cultural Heritage Law & Policy Research and authors the *Cultural Heritage Lawyer* blog. He serves as a presidential appointee to the Cultural Property Advisory Committee.

Elizabeth Varner is the Director of the National Coast Guard Museum, an Attorney, Arbitrator, and an Adjunct Professor at Indiana University Robert H. McKinney School of Law. She is the chair of the American Alliance of Museums' Curatorial

Ethics Subcommittee and on the American Bar Association's Art and Cultural Heritage Steering Committee; the board of the US Committee and the Standing Legal Committee for the International Council of Museums. She formerly served as president of the Lawyers' Committee for Cultural Heritage Preservation, and faculty for American Arbitration Association and John Hopkins University Graduate Museum Program.

List of Abbreviations

AA	Archaeological Administration
ACLS	American Council for Learned Societies
AML/CFT	anti-money laundering/countering the financing of terrorism
ANF	Al-Nusrah Front for the People of the Levant
ANSAs	armed non-State actors
AQIM	Al Qaeda in the Islamic Maghreb
ARPA	Antiquities Act and the Archaeological Resources Protection Act
ASOR CHI	American Schools of Oriental Research Cultural Heritage Initiatives
ASSMT	Analytical Support and Sanctions Monitoring Team
BSA	Bank Secrecy Act
CASD	Centre for Advanced Studies in Defense
COPs	Command Outposts
CP/FT	cultural property/financing of terrorism
CPIA	Cultural Property Implementation Act
CPK	cultural peacekeeping
CPP	cultural property protection
DEIC	Defense Environmental International Cooperation
DOD	Department of Defense
DOJ	Department of Justice
DOS	Department of State
ECA	Educational and Cultural Affairs
EPIC	Emergency Protection for Iraqi Cultural Antiquities Act
EU	European Union
Europol	EU Agency for Law Enforcement Cooperation
FATF	Financial Action Task Force
FDD	Foundation for Defense of Democracies
FOBs	Forward Operating Bases
GTAs	graphic training aids
HAS	Historic Sites Act of 1935
HQN	Haqqani Network
IAATPA	Illicit Art and Antiquities Trafficking Prevention Act
IACs	international armed conflicts
ICC	International Criminal Court
ICCROM	International Centre for the Study of the Preservation and Restoration of Cultural Property
ICOMOS	International Council on Monuments and Sites

ICPRCP	Intergovernmental Committee for Promoting the Return of Cultural Property to its Countries of Origin or its Restitution in case of Illicit Appropriation
ICRC	International Committee of the Red Cross
ICTY	International Criminal Tribunal for the former Yugoslavia
IHL	International Humanitarian Law
IMCOM	Installation Management Command
INTERPOL	International Criminal Police Organization
IS	Islamic State
ISIL	Islamic State of Iraq and the Levant
ISIS	Islamic State of Iraq and Syria
JALLC	Joint Analysis and Lessons Learned Centre
KLEs	Key Leader Engagements
LOAC	Law of Armed Conflict
MENA	Middle East North Africa
MFA	Museum of Fine Arts, Boston
MFAA	Monuments Fine Arts and Archives
MFA&A	Monuments, Fine Arts, and Archives
ML/TF	money laundering/terrorist financing
NAGPRA	Native American Graves Protection and Repatriation Act
NCMM	National Commission for Museums and Monuments
NHPA	National Historic Preservation Act
NIACs	non-international armed conflicts
OG	Operational Guidelines
OTP	Office of the Prosecutor
PPICPA	Protect and Preserve International Cultural Property Act
RBCM	Royal British Columbia Museum
RMA	Rijksmuseum Amsterdam
ROTC	Reserve Officer Training Corps
SAA	Society for American Archaeology
STOP Act	Safeguard Tribal Objects of Patrimony Act of 2019
STORM Act	Stop Terrorist Operational Resources and Money Act
TD	Treasury Directive
TOC	transnational organized crime
UDHR	Universal Declaration of Human Rights
UK	United Kingdom
UN	United Nations
UNDRIP	United Nations Declaration on the Importance of Indigenous Peoples
UNIDROIT	International Institute for the Unification of Private Law
UN ECOSOC	United Nations Economical and Social Council
UNESCO	United Nations Educational, Scientific, and Cultural Organization
UNODC	United Nations Office on Drugs and Crime

UNSC	United Nations Security Council
UNTOC	United Nations Convention against Transnational Organized Crime
US	United States
USSR	Union of Soviet Socialist Republics
WHC	World Heritage Center

Introduction

Cultural Heritage and Armed Conflict: Preserving Art While Protecting Life

Frederik Rosén

One evening in 2019, the cathedral of Notre-Dame in Paris caught fire while I was at a conference in NATO Headquarters in Brussels on war and cultural heritage. We had just started dinner as the messages started ticking in. Our immediate thought was that this was an arson attack by jihadists. It was not. No evidence of foul play has been found, but conspiracy theories of jihadist involvement live on. But the world would not have been surprised if the fire had been an attack. It would have followed the current global trend in which belligerents destroy and misappropriate cultural heritage, including places of worship, to stir up rage and antagonisms, as we have seen most recently in conflicts in, among other places, Afghanistan, Syria, Iraq, Mali, Yemen, and Ukraine.

The rise of cultural heritage as a security issue has led states and international organizations to strengthen old, and build new, political and legal mechanisms for protecting, safeguarding, and managing issues related to cultural heritage in connection with conflicts. Accordingly, the title of our conference at the NATO Headquarters was "NATO and Cultural Property. Embracing New Challenges in the Era of Identity Wars." At the core of the responses stands the recognition that cultural heritage matters increasingly to international security. Sometimes cultural heritage embodies a value for societies so strong that its destruction may precipitate destabilization, an eruption of violence, or even a fatal erosion of cultures and cultural groups. It may be exploited for domination and as a tool of provocation. It may be used to display power, to draw up contours of security communities, and to mobilize action. Cultural heritage has simply become a material frontier in conflict and war.

Frederik Rosén, *Introduction* In: *The Preservation of Art and Culture in Times of War*. Edited by: Claire Finkelstein, Derek Gillman, and Frederik Rosén, Oxford University Press. © Oxford University Press 2022.
DOI: 10.1093/oso/9780197610565.003.0001

This volume seeks to deepen our understanding of this evolving nexus between cultural heritage and security in the twenty-first century. It provides the reader with a collection of chapters that aims to open up new horizons for thinking about the relationship between cultural heritage, security, and international law. It responds to the change from viewing the protection and preservation of cultural heritage in times of conflict as a matter of the value of artifacts and sites in isolation, to a matter of safeguarding identity and the survival of both the individual and the collective. Coming from a variety of disciplines and perspectives, the chapters examine a complicated set of relationships between, on the one hand, deliberate violence to cultural heritage in times of conflict; and, on the other, basic societal values, legal principles, protection, and security concerns.

Nations and communities identify with their cultural heritage because it articulates their sense of belonging to a distinctive place, group, or cause. It includes relics, buildings, monuments, places, landscapes, and intangible practices that people care for, to such an extent that they may be willing to sacrifice privileges or even their lives to preserve and protect them. In 2006, Samuel P. Huntington envisaged, "In the coming decades, questions of identity, meaning cultural heritage, language, and religion will play a central role in politics," alluding to the shift in association and antagonism among the countries he analyzed in his 1992 book, *The Clash of Civilizations and the Remaking of World Order*.[1] Looking at current world politics and the changing role of cultural heritage in war and conflict, we see how Huntington's prediction materializes in front of our eyes. Russia staked claims to cultural entitlement and a "historical homeland" to legitimize the illegal annexation of Crimea, and cultural heritage issues have played an integral role in the development of the subsequent conflict.[2] Serbia's objectives with regard to Kosovo stand on claims to ownership over and access to cultural heritage. In fact, one of the three main reasons why NATO sustains its mission in Kosovo is unresolved issues with regard to ownership of cultural heritage sites.[3] Hence, the two most destabilizing European territorial conflicts in recent times both involve a cultural heritage dimension. This is not to mention the

[1] Samuel P Huntington, *The Clash of Civilizations and the Remaking of World Order* (Simon and Schuster 1992).

[2] Kateryna Busol, "Crimea's Occupation Exemplifies the Threat of Attacks on Cultural Heritage" (Chatham House, 4 February 2020) <https://www.chathamhouse.org/expert/comment/crimea-s-occupation-exemplifies-threat-attacks-cultural-heritage> accessed 4 September 2020

[3] Frederik Rosén, "NATO and Cultural Property: Embracing New Challenges in the Era of Identity Wars" (Nordic Center for Cultural Heritage and Armed Conflict 2018).

Cyprus conflict, and, a little further to the East, the Israeli-Palestinian conflict, where, besides self-determination, issues related to cultural heritage and places of worship stand at the heart of the conflict. China has mapped cultural heritage sites in the South China Sea to support its maritime claims and argued that "archaeological findings prove that the Chinese people is the real owner of South China Sea Islands."[4] State actors systematically and strategically erase cultural heritage of minority groups, from Turkey to Myanmar, as a means of asserting dominion, repressing those groups, and reconfiguring the cultural dimension of the geopolitical space.

Non-state armed groups and terrorist organizations, including the Taliban in Afghanistan, ISIS in Syria and Iraq, and Ansar-Dine in Mali, partly gained their notoriety from dramatically destroying cultural heritage. Recently, even the US President explicitly threatened an adversary state with the bombing of its major cultural heritage sites.[5] In addition, wherever conflicts entail a breakdown of law and order, the systematic looting of archaeological sites mushrooms, often driven by international organized criminal networks, enabling non-state armed groups including terrorist groups to make a profit. Looting and the illicit trafficking of artifacts plays a new and complex role in conflict economies, as recognized by a number of UN Security Council resolutions, even if the factual basis of this link remains to be determined.[6] It is beyond the scope of the current volume to address national issues related to collective memory, public spaces, and contested historical monuments. In the United States, however, protests for racial equality following the killing of George Floyd[7] and evidence of COVID-19's disproportionate effect on minority communities spurred a dramatic toppling of controversial statues and Confederate monuments. Even if not within the context of an armed conflict, these topplings warrant discussion here as part of a global pattern of perceiving cultural objects at the center of social antagonism and conflict. There is hence a link between the topplings of 2020 and the dispute over the Theodore Roosevelt statue outside the American Museum of Natural History

[4] Embassy of the People's Republic of China in the Republic of the Philippines, "Archaeological Findings Prove That Chinese People Are Real Owner of South China Sea Islands" (Embassy of the People's Republic of China in the Republic of the Philippines, 15 June 2016) <http://ph.china-embassy.org/eng/sgdt/t1372445.htm> accessed 4 September 2020.

[5] Lara Jakes, "Defenders of History Take Aim at Trump's Threat to Strike Iran's Cultural Sites" (*The New York Times*, 5 January 2020).

[6] Matthew Sargent and others, "Tracking and Disrupting the Illicit Antiquities Trade with Open Source Data" (The RAND Corporation 2020).

[7] Audra D. S. Burch, Amy Harmon, Sabrina Tavernise and Emily Badger, "The Death of George Floyd Reignited a Movement. What Happens Now?" (New York Times, April 20 2021).

in New York[8] and the acceptability of historical statues and monuments in many other countries. The role of statues as political statements encourages reflection on power and domination as well as on the very idea of cultural heritage. To be sure, those who saved artifacts from vandalism and destruction during the French Revolution did so on the premise that some artifacts had a cultural value that superseded their political and symbolic freight. This idea that cultural value can be separated from political power stands central to the dilemma of balancing the politics of sites and objects that are important to collective memory, including monuments and statues.

The possibility of such a separation and value-neutrality of cultural objects from political power remains highly contested. As Duncan Macintosh argues in his chapter in this volume, the political dimension of monuments that symbolize disgraced ideologies, no matter how important they are to collective memory and heritage, may well override any moral or legal imperative to protect them as cultural heritage.

I. Cultural Heritage and International Security

Altogether, in the last three decades, cultural heritage has become increasingly "conflict prone," suffering systematic exploitation, attacks and destruction by belligerents, notably non-state actors and terrorist organizations, but also state actors. Such acts are often intentional and based on well-planned strategies for inflicting harm on groups of people and communities, and typically involve publicity campaigns that exploit the speed and global reach of social media as well as the transnational and global character of contemporary conflicts. Destruction of an ancient site in a remote desert in the Middle East may spur instant emotional reactions in communities thousands of kilometers away, hurting adversaries and mobilizing support among followers.

The international community recognizes this developing situation. With reference to ISIS' destructions in Syria and Iraq, the former Secretary-General of the United Nations, Ban Ki-Moon, claimed in 2016, "The large-scale,

[8] Sinclaire Devereux Marber, "Bloody Foundation? Ethical and Legal Implications of (Not) Removing the Equestrian Statue of Theodore Roosevelt at the American Museum of Natural History" (2019) Columbia Journal of Law and Arts 85; Paul Cooper, "What to Do with a Heinous Statue. Lessons for Trump from post-Nazi Germany and post-Soviet Eastern Europe" (*Foreign Policy*, August 17 2017) <https://foreignpolicy.com/2017/08/17/what-to-do-with-a-heinous-statue-trump-confederate-robert-e-lee-nazi-soviet/> accessed 4 September 2020.

systematic destruction and looting of cultural sites . . . highlights the strong connection between the cultural, humanitarian and security dimensions of conflicts and terrorism."[9] Ban Ki-Moon's statement echoes a comment made by the former UNESCO Director-General, Irina Bokova, in 2015 as she presented at a roundtable on terrorist financing organized by the British think tank for defense and security, the Royal United Services Institute (RUSI): "It is not often that a Director-General of UNESCO is invited to speak about heritage and culture with security experts." The Director-General added, "This says something about the nature of conflicts today, when culture has moved to the center of the battlefield."[10] Congruently, the NATO Secretary-General's Annual Report for 2019 states that "The protection of cultural property and common heritage has been a core NATO value since its foundation in 1949. As an essential aspect of the security environment, cultural property and its protection can constitute an important element in strategic, operational and tactical considerations"[11]; a statement indicating how NATO recently broadened its view on cultural property from a matter of the Law of Armed Conflict (LOAC) to a broader security issue. NATO recognizes cultural heritage can be used as a tool of hybrid warfare and that attacks on cultural heritage may impact on societal resilience and indicate an attempt to undermine national unity or identity.[12]

Concerns about cultural heritage have now clearly migrated beyond the cultural sphere to sectors dealing with peace and security. We have progressed from seeing conflict-related destruction of cultural heritage just as a "cultural tragedy" to understanding it also as a "security issue." It is a shift from protecting cultural property from the harms of war for the sake of cultural property itself to viewing it as closely connected to the broader peace and security agenda: from the protection of civilians and the financing of

[9] "Report of the UN Secretary-General on the threat posed by ISIL (Da'esh) to international peace and security and the range of United Nations efforts in support of Member States in countering the threat" (United Nations, 29 January 2016) 4 <https://www.un.org/sc/ctc/news/2016/06/03/report-of-the-secretary-general-on-the-threat-posed-by-isil-daesh-to-international-peace-and-security-and-the-range-of-united-nations-efforts-in-support-of-member-states-in-countering-the-t/> accessed 4 September 2020.

[10] UNESCO Director-General Irina Bokova (Royal United Services Institute 2015). <https://en.unesco.org/news/struggle-against-cultural-cleansing-security-imperative> accessed 4 September 2020

[11] "The NATO Secretary General's Annual Report 2019" (NATO, 20 January 2020) 77 <https://www.nato.int/nato_static_fl2014/assets/pdf/2020/3/pdf_publications/sgar19-en.pdf>.

[12] Frederik Rosén, "NATO and Cultural Property: A Hybrid Threat Perspective" (Nordic Center for Cultural Heritage and Armed Conflict 2021).

terrorism over issues related to societal resilience and post-conflict reconciliation of territorial conflicts and hybrid warfare.

A range of mutually reinforcing developments shape this agenda, including the advancement of new norms and laws related to cultural heritage in armed conflict as well as more generally; the transnationalization and globalization of conflicts, and the ensuing turn to cultural belonging and group identity rather than nation-state borders to demarcate security communities; the urbanization of warfare and the rise of asymmetric and hybrid forms of warfare; developments in global social media; and the rapidly evolving transnational market for illicit antiquities, enabling armed groups to more easily profit from looting and trafficking antiquities. Hence, while not entirely new *in kind*, conflict-related violence against cultural heritage today implicates a new and "modern" power base and involves new legal, political, and moral complexities for states as well as civil society, including museums and collectors.

The surfacing in international politics of the concept of "cultural cleansing," referring to the idea that it is possible to erase cultural groups by erasing their cultural heritage, stands as the most dramatic expression of this development. As stated by Irina Bokova in connection with the adoption of United Nations Security Council Resolution 2347 for the Protection of Cultural Heritage, "the deliberate destruction of heritage is a war crime, it has become a tactic of war to tear societies over the long term, in a strategy of cultural cleansing."[13] The intended destruction of cultural heritage during armed conflicts may, from the view of applicable international law, certainly constitute a war crime. Yet labeling it "cultural cleansing" places such acts, at least rhetorically, in the group of the most serious international atrocity crimes, viz genocide, war crimes, and crimes against humanity.[14] As some commentators claim, such crimes may trigger a responsibility on the part of the international community to act and, if necessary, even to intervene with military force.[15]

[13] UNESCO Director-General Irina Bokova, "Maintenance of International Peace and Security: Destruction and Trafficking of Cultural Heritage by Terrorist Groups and in Situations of Armed Conflict" (United Nations Security Council 2017).

[14] See Rome Statute of the International Criminal Court (adopted 17 July 1998, entered into force 1 July 2002) 2187 UNTS 3 (ICC Statute).

[15] James Cuno, "The Responsibility to Protect the World's Cultural Heritage" (2016) Brown Journal of World Affairs 97; Thomas G Weiss and Nina Connelly, "Protecting Cultural Heritage in War Zones" (2019) Third World Quarterly 1.

Whether the destruction of cultural heritage could be regarded as a most serious war crime that triggers a responsibility to intervene analogous to, or as a part of, the contested international principle of "Responsibility to Protect" (R2P) remains disputed. Yet the political effects of invoking the concept of "cultural cleansing" has aided some members of the public in seeing attacks on cultural heritage as a critical human security issue. The concept indicates how destruction of cultural heritage today is viewed as intimately connected with fundamental human rights and the broader agenda about armed conflicts and the protection of civilians.[16] In addition, the linkage at a high level of abstraction by some international organizations and leading scholars of the concept of cultural cleansing with R2P tells us something about the value ascribed to cultural heritage as a constitutive dimension of society. In that regard, it is worth mentioning that the drafters of the 1948 Convention on the Prevention and Punishment of the Crime of Genocide[17] planned to include cultural heritage destruction within the convention; hence, the concept of "cultural cleansing," with its link to mass atrocity crimes, is not without a historical trajectory.

II. Cultural Heritage in the Midst of Armed Conflict

If it is possible to severely delimit or even destroy a cultural group by destroying what the group regards as its cultural heritage, then cultural heritage must be understood not only to comprise historically fascinating, aesthetically appealing, and scientifically interesting items and sites, but also to be a key constituent of societies. If the glue and meaning of our collective and individual lives depend on our particular cultures, it may not be possible to divorce the idea of cultural heritage from the very idea of being human. This viewpoint echoes G.W.F. Hegel's understanding of the inextricable relationship between personhood and property[18] to which some of the authors of the present volume subscribe. To them it follows that protecting cultural heritage becomes inseparable from protecting society

[16] UNESCO, "Expert Meeting on the Responsibility to Protect" (UNESCO 2016) <http://www.unesco.org/new/en/culture/themes/armed-conflict-and-heritage/governance-and-meetings/conferences/expert-meeting-responsibility-to-protect/> accessed 4 September 2020.

[17] Convention on the Prevention and Punishment of the Crime of Genocide (opened for signature 9 December 1948, entered into force 12 January 1951) 78 UNTS 277 (Genocide Convention).

[18] See Blake Wilson, "Personhood and Property in Hegel's Conception of Freedom" (2019) 11 Pólemos.

itself. In that regard it is worth noting that recent ideas of cultural heritage and its role in society have been strongly influenced by constructionism and the idea of nations as "imagined communities." These approaches fit well with how the dominant idea of cultural heritage and its concepts in international law distinguish cultural heritage on the basis of a value-laden selection and nomination. In well-organized museums, every piece of the collection has been evaluated and assessed; every UNESCO heritage site involves a political nomination.

Acknowledging that cultural heritage is highly political and derives value from processes of evaluation within specific cultures (which will share *categories* of value with many other cultures) certainly throws us into a vortex of perspectives and arguments about the "constructed" nature of cultural heritage. Yet, to reduce cultural heritage to human decrees, to insist that discourse and human practice create its meaning, ignores the material and "tactile" dimension of cultural heritage. The recent academic critique of the prevailing dualist notion in social science and humanities that discourse creates the meaning of the material world appear highly relevant to our topic:[19] At the surface, discourse theory speaks well to cultural heritage, including its legal concepts and their insistence on collective values and sentiments. But it cannot account for the significance and power of the material itself—its historical uses and previous meanings, aesthetics, physical location, and practical functions in society. Therefore, it is argued, we need to overcome this idea of a separation between thing and meaning, concrete and abstract, physical and mental, medium and message, and instead to refocus on the materiality of cultural life and the entangled and mutually constitutive relationship between culture and cultural heritage.[20] While human life and "stones" may look separable to some eyes, in practice, personhood and property entwine, from private lives to national identity. Humans are tactile animals who live in and through physical space by interpreting, assigning meaning to, and using things, objects, and places.

One of the consequences of this line of thinking is that physical space and geography become important dimensions for considering cultural heritage. As Carsten Paludan-Müller considers in his chapter, cultural heritage reflects a strong link among cultural/ethnic groups, territory, and history. It is simply

[19] See Bjørnar Olsson, *In Defense of Things: Archaeology and the Ontology of Objects* (AltaMira Press 2013).

[20] Tracy Ireland and Jane Lydon, "Rethinking Materiality, Memory and Identity" (2016) Public History Review 1.

difficult to speak about national territory and state borders without speaking about cultural heritage. Similarly, it is difficult to speak about cultural groups and societies without speaking about what they regard as their cultural heritage as a territorial anchorage. Therefore, Paludan-Müller argues, cultural heritage is also about geopolitics. Seeing the geopolitical link between identity, society, territory, and cultural heritage makes it clear that cultural heritage easily becomes politicized and drawn into conflicts as markers of friend and enemy and territorial belonging and ownership. Belligerents who seek to dominate adversaries by removing or destroying—openly violent or discreetly—cultural heritage with the aim of transforming collective memory and identity in relation to a certain geographical space may be viewed as geopolitical engineers. Their acts aim at transforming emotional-material bonds between cultural groups and physical territory.

The geopolitical perspective on the developing role of cultural heritage in contemporary conflicts echoes what some scholars recently identified as "the new geopolitics,"[21] which is "a product of a twenty-first century preoccupied with the symbols of power and the natural audience for that display: the people."[22] It is a geopolitics that is connected to the crisis of the international liberal order, the political refutation of the "coldness" of its institutions and formalism, and the turn toward the "warmth" of the symbolic and the emotional as the foundation of political association and antagonism. That was, I believe, Huntington's prediction about the rise of identity and "heritage" politics. And with that, cultural heritage becomes geopolitical reference points and an issue and sometimes frontier in internationally security. It becomes a vulnerability that must be protected as one element in the broader protection of society and territories.

III. The Heritage-Security Nexus and the Ethics of Protecting Cultural Heritage

The paradigmatic change in how we think about cultural heritage in international law and security affects a large range of societal institutions and sectors. Some of the authors use the term "heritage-security nexus"

[21] Vibeke Schou Tjalve, *Geopolitical Amnesia: The Rise of the Right and the Crisis of Liberal Memory* (McGill-Queen's UP 2020).

[22] ibid 151.

to refer to this new framing of cultural heritage protection as a broader security issue, a concept that joins the recent family of "nexus"-concepts, coined to describe cross-sectoral challenges and cooperation in order to understand and address a complex problem (the "development-security nexus," the "climate-security nexus," the "migration-security nexus," etc.). International legal instruments that were previously dedicated just to protecting cultural heritage against looting and illicit cross-border trade have today become instruments in curbing the financing of terrorism, and thus the protection of society. In NATO, cultural property protection lies within the NATO Human Security Unit in the Office of the NATO Secretary-General, along with protection of civilians' issues. Leading military powers, including the United States and the United Kingdom, have scaled up their focus on the topic. Museums have become active partners in global security governance.

One noteworthy result of the securitization and enhanced military focus on cultural heritage is the foregrounding of the dilemma between protecting cultural heritage and protecting civilians and soldiers alike. The 2014 film *The Monuments Men* drew public attention to this dilemma but underscored that we ought not to risk human lives for the sake of preserving art and cultural artifacts. One of the real monuments men, who was deployed to Italy during the Second World War to rescue art from the Nazi havoc, became frequently cited for stating, "No work of art is worth the life of a single boy, but risking your life to fight for a cause is absolutely worth the effort."[23] Yet, as described by the present author in his chapter, we also hear the opposite. One famous exponent of that position was the British diplomat Harold Nicolson, who in 1944 argued that "the loss of even the most valid human life is ultimately less disastrous than the loss of something which in no circumstances can ever be created again."[24]

The question of protecting heritage or saving lives is, however, a more complex matter than deciding whether it may sometimes be appropriate to sacrifice human lives to save a World Heritage site. Any state activity to protect cultural heritage during armed conflicts requires resources that could be used to protect vulnerable groups. How can we justify routing funds to secure archaeological areas in the midst of a humanitarian crisis? And any

[23] Rose Pacatte, "'The Monuments Men' Wonders: Is Art Worth a Life?" (*National Catholic Reporter*, 2014) <https://www.ncronline.org/blogs/ncr-today/monuments-men-wonders-art-worth-life> accessed 15 June 2020.

[24] Harold Nicolson, "Marginal Comments" (*Spectator*, 25 February 1944).

employment of uniformed personnel to safeguard cultural heritage in volatile environments involves a risk to their lives. Any proportionality assessment, as required by LOAC, weighing the protection of cultural heritage with military objectives and necessity considerations will involve a compromise with military effectiveness that may entail direct or indirect risk or danger to civilians or soldiers.

The ultimate question, then, is how an enhanced focus on the meaning and role of cultural heritage in armed conflicts may translate into a willingness and justification on the part of states to put the lives of soldiers and civilians at risk to protect and safeguard it. This includes setting military priorities and objectives that accommodate protection considerations, such as routing funds for protecting museums and their collections instead of educating and feeding children in refugee camps and, more generally, using taxpayers' money for this cause.

The question is whether such weighing and the implied justification of priorities and possible direct or indirect infliction of harm is ipso facto immoral due to what many consider a fundamental ethical incommensurability between human lives and nonhuman objects. Philosophy has only most recently started to grapple with this issue. What is certain is that beyond *The Monuments Men*'s simplistic portrayal of a trade-off between art and lives lies a deeply complex subject and series of choices, one that belies the suggestion that cultural heritage preservation, national security, and military necessity represent conflicting goals. Accordingly, the place of cultural heritage in armed conflict, and related choices and dilemmas, have grown increasingly prominent and complex—morally, politically, and legally, which raises new questions about the moral and political foundation of our legal frameworks and practices for addressing crimes against cultural heritage as elements of international security.

What is at stake when cultural heritage issues overlap or merge with security priorities? While analyses of various cultural aspects of armed conflicts, such as ethnicity, religion, and ideology, are well developed by a number of academic disciplines, including security studies, these fields remain largely silent on the role of the materiality of culture. Further, the recent "cultural turn" in military affairs still considers primarily the immaterial dimension of culture in conflict zones and generally does not consider its material manifestations. For examinations of the topic one has to look to other disciplines, such as heritage studies, architecture, archaeology, art history, anthropology, and, not least, public international law. The main body of literature dealing with cultural heritage and armed conflict mostly takes a protection-focused perspective that uncritically applies the rules of protection found in the 1954 Hague Convention and its protocols.[25] The discussions of fundamental values tend to be kept separate within academic contexts and do not interact much with the debates about international law and security. This book aspires to take the first step in bringing together interdisciplinary perspectives on international law and security and thereby inspire discussion of cultural heritage that goes beyond the separate disciplines of international law and heritage studies.

IV. What is Cultural Heritage?

To lay the groundwork for the chapters that follow, we must identify the concepts of cultural heritage and cultural property. International organizations, as well as academics, often use these concepts interchangeably but when speaking about objects today lean toward using the technically viewed broader concept of cultural heritage. Since the late 1980s, we have seen a growing tendency to use the concept of cultural heritage also in international law, yet the concept of cultural property remains in full use. Therefore, what may appear to be a confusing oscillation between concepts, even at the international level, represents a fairly recent development in international law as it relates to the debate about cultural heritage/property.[26] Thus, the authors in this book sometimes use the expression "cultural heritage" to refer to the movable and immovable objects that LOAC identify as "cultural property."

What exactly are the kind of objects and places we speak about when we speak about cultural heritage/property? It is here worth recalling the definition of cultural property in the 1954 Hague Convention, Article I, "Definition of cultural property":

[25] Convention for the Protection of Cultural Property in the Event of Armed Conflict (adopted 14 May 1954, entered into force 7 August 1956) 249 UNTS 215 (Hague Convention of 1954). See also its protocols: Protocol to the Convention for the Protection of Cultural Property in the Event of Armed Conflict (adopted 14 May 1954, entered into force 7 August 1956) 249 UNTS 215; Second Protocol to the Hague Convention of 1954 for the Protection of Cultural Property in the Event of Armed Conflict (adopted 26 March 1999, entered into force 9 March 2004) 2253 UNTS 172 (Second Protocol to Hague Convention of 1999).

[26] Lyndell Prott and Patrick O'Keefe, "'Cultural Heritage' or 'Cultural Property'?" (1992) International Journal of Cultural Property 30.

> For the purposes of the present Convention, the term "cultural property" shall cover, irrespective of origin or ownership:
> (a) movable or immovable property of great importance to the cultural heritage of every people, such as monuments of architecture, art or history, whether religious or secular; archaeological sites; groups of buildings which, as a whole, are of historical or artistic interest; works of art; manuscripts, books and other objects of artistic, historical or archaeological interest; as well as scientific collections and important collections of books or archives or of reproductions of the property defined above;
> (b) buildings whose main and effective purpose is to preserve or exhibit the movable cultural property defined in sub-paragraph (a) such as museums, large libraries and depositories of archives, and refuges intended to shelter, in the event of armed conflict, the movable cultural property defined in sub-paragraph (a);
> (c) centers containing a large amount of cultural property as defined in sub-paragraphs (a) and (b), to be known as centers containing monuments.

Under this definition, the concept of cultural property is both broad and difficult to delimit. The Geneva Conventions Additional Protocol I[27] and II[28] further complicate what is considered cultural property from the per spective of LOAC. By adding the protection of "historic monuments, works of art or places of worship, which constitute the cultural or spiritual heritage of peoples," the protocols expanded the common interpretation of "places of worship" in the 1954 Hague Convention from religious buildings representing a cultural value to places that hold contemporary reverence value. It has been argued that the Protocols merely reiterate the definition of the 1954 Hague Convection. Either way, places of worship, including temples, synagogues, mosques, churches, cemeteries, and holy trees and hills, clearly fall under the same international legal protection regime as archaeological sites and museum collections. The idea of "cultural heritage in conflict" thus involves, at least from a legal perspective, not only artifacts but also places of worship. Debates about terrorist attacks on cultural and symbolic places and places of worship—from the attacks on the World

[27] Protocol Additional to the Geneva Conventions of 12 August 1949, and Relating to the Protection of Victims of International Armed Conflicts (Protocol I) art 85.

[28] Protocol Additional to the Geneva Conventions of 12 August 1949, and Relating to the Protection of Victims of Non-International Armed Conflicts (Protocol II) art 16.

Trade Center in New York in 2001 to the Mosque in Christchurch, New Zealand, in 2019—should thus be understood alongside debates regarding looting and illicit trafficking of Middle Eastern antiquities, and questions of post-conflict repatriation of artifacts. Digital archives containing material with heritage value may also enjoy protection under the 1954 Hague Convention and its protocols, thus pushing our topic into the domain of digitalization and cyberwarfare. Clearly, our topic is extremely broad in terms of relevant objects to consider.

The other critical vector for the definition of cultural heritage regards the question of when an object or place qualifies as cultural heritage for the purpose of recognition and protection under international law. When may an object be "moved" into the legal category of cultural heritage and thus enjoy legal protection? No laws contain objective criteria for distinguishing the status of an object on the basis of an object itself. In other words, international law pertaining to cultural heritage/property don't identify intrinsic value. LOAC identifies cultural property not by recording bricks, stones, and objects, but through observing that they are collectively ascribed some additional cultural value beyond their (mere) practical function.

This lack of a priori definition leaves us with two sets of fundamental questions. Firstly, what parameters and concepts of value should be applied when assessing the heritage value of objects? Secondly, what kind of knowledge and expertise is required to make such assessments? This is where the question of value starts to get really tricky. The debates stretch between a cosmopolitan or universalist position and the "cultural stance," which emphasizes local values and sentiments, as discussed by Helen Frowe and Derek Matravers in their chapter, which insists that objects of cultural heritage derive their value from their specific context.

International law straddles both positions. On the one hand, the 1954 Hague Convention's concept of "cultural heritage of *every people*" (emphasis added) embodies a norm of local ownership, viz cultural heritage matters to all people, but more so at the local level. Furthermore, this general local interest in cultural heritage provides a universal basis for protecting it, enshrining the value all people seem to ascribe to their respective cultural heritage. The preamble to the convention marries this connection between the local and global by stating, "Damage to cultural property belonging to any people whatsoever means damage to the cultural heritage of all mankind." On the other hand, international law also embraces a cosmopolitan version of the "cultural heritage of all mankind." The preamble of the 1972

World Heritage Convention states that "Considering that parts of the cultural or natural heritage are of outstanding interest and therefore need to be preserved as part of the world heritage of mankind as a whole,"[29] hence subscribing to a notion of value that spreads it out to all people of the world whatever (local) people holds the juridical ownership over the concerned object or place. This position is also considered valid by many scholars due to the conflation of certain strands of European thought from the late eighteenth to the mid-twentieth centuries.

The question of which kind of knowledge and expertise should be applied to identify cultural heritage and its value similarly ranges from a cosmopolitan vision of expert-based criteria for value assessments and the "cultural stance" position, insisting on the primacy of local and contextual value regimes, however those are understood. The cosmopolitan approach is underpinned by agreements about the value of objects, which emerge from the world's vast range of cultural practices. The cultural stance subscribes to a relativistic culture-focused approach to uncover local socially embedded values. The two approaches are not mutually exclusive and can be employed alongside one another.

The critical questions that should be asked from the perspective of cultural heritage protection is (a) how to define the threshold of value that triggers the recognition of a given object as a legal object enjoying protection under international law, and at the same time as an object with moral standing; (b) how to define the criteria for assessing value from the view of law and morality; and (c) how to apply threshold values and assessment criteria to real-world objects and places, thus enabling us to consider cultural heritage in our political and bureaucratic matrixes for prioritizing the assignment of governmental resources, including military affairs. In our present volume we have not taken on the task of offering threshold values for considering something as cultural heritage; nor is our task to find new ways of calculating the value of cultural heritage. Rather the collection of chapters offers reflection, analyses, and case studies that illustrate the fundamental ambivalence on the part of scholars and policymakers about the meaning and value of cultural heritage. The chapters must therefore be viewed, as acknowledged by most authors, as written on essentially contested ground.

29 UN Educational, Scientific and Cultural Organization (UNESCO), Convention Concerning the Protection of the World Cultural and Natural Heritage, 16 November 1972.

V. A Preview of the Chapters

The book is divided into three parts, each of which addresses different aspects of our topic. The first part, *The Value of Cultural Heritage*, considers the question of cultural heritage and value on various levels and in various contexts, ranging from moral philosophy to norms of customary international law. The second part, *Legal and Security Aspects of Cultural Heritage Preservation*, examines the impact of the securitization of cultural heritage on the legal regulation of cultural heritage in armed conflict. The third part, *Healing the Past: Repatriation of Stolen Art and Culture*, addresses repatriation and rebuilding in the aftermath of wrongdoing toward cultural heritage, as well as considering heritage destruction as a means of geopolitical engineering.

Derek Gillman opens Part I by offering his own understanding of heritage. He then outlines long-standing tensions between the cosmopolitan and the particular, before moving to a broader consideration of value. Using examples from, among other places, Beijing, Bamiyan, and Madrid, in order to illustrate his thoughts about where value lies in works of art, buildings, historic sites, and other cultural phenomena, Gillman proposes that we engage with cultural material through a limited number of widely held intrinsic values. In this way he hopes to bring us closer to what is at stake in our discussions about heritage and conflict.

Helen Frowe and Derek Matravers further reflect on the tension between the cosmopolitan and the particular by asking what should happen to cultural heritage that has been damaged or destroyed in war. They describe how the last twenty or thirty years have seen a marked shift in heritage and conservation studies away from an object-centered focus on cultural heritage to what we can call the *cultural stance*: the view that, in thinking about protection and conservation, the local cultural meanings of objects are more relevant than their physical integrity. In other words, the value of cultural heritage objects is viewed as flowing primarily from local sentiments and attitudes. This shift, they argue, bears important implications on the question of whether we should leave damaged cultural property in its damaged state or reconstruct it, minding that reconstruction comes with a wish to erase some aspect of the history of the object, and thus must be considered an intended destruction of its recent record.

A challenge we face is how to weigh the value of human lives against "stones" when considering the protection of cultural heritage in armed conflicts. The dilemma forms part of the LOAC, which obliges military commanders to sometimes apply the rule of proportionality to situations involving cultural heritage. This restrictive obligation constrains operational flexibility and firepower and thereby unavoidably implies a possible compromise to the safety of soldiers and civilians alike. Continuing the reflections from the first two chapters, my chapter argues that applying the principle of proportionality presupposes an actual value assessment of cultural heritage. Yet the cultural stance position, which today largely dominates the politics of cultural heritage, not only makes it practically impossible to establish such value for the purpose of making proportionality assessments. It also hinders the elaboration of an analytical perspective on this notable contemporary protection dilemma. In fact, my chapter argues, unresolved fundamental issues of value haunt the international cultural heritage protection regime and severely undermine its effectiveness.

Duncan Macintosh scrutinizes another fundamental distinction in the international legal protection of cultural heritage, which is the notion that cultural heritage is always good and, per definition, should be protected. He argues that we need to re-examine the view that the theft of, trade in, and destruction of art and cultural artifacts in time of war are evils, and that they are ought to be thought of as war crimes. The international protection regime for cultural heritage mirrors in essence the international rules protecting civilians in armed conflict. Whereas the regime for the protection of civilians stands on a firm and non-derogable right to life, cultural heritage is political and open to interpretation. Accordingly, what some groups consider cultural heritage may for others be symbols of wrongdoing and evil and thus, Macintosh argues, could be regarded as legitimate targets.

Adding further historical depth to the international norm against destroying cultural heritage, Martin Hamilton's chapter offers a historically informed analysis of how heritage destruction almost was adopted as a legal dimension of the gravest human atrocity, genocide, in the 1948 Convention on the Prevention and Punishment of the Crime of Genocide. The preparatory drafts contained the concept of "cultural genocide," covering acts by which one group of people strived to eradicate another cultural group by destroying its cultural heritage. Hamilton analyzes the concept of cultural genocide in the preparatory work for the Genocide Convention and the reason why cultural genocide ultimately was left out. He then relates it to how international law, both at its normative and enforcement levels, deals with the concept of cultural genocide today: especially in the context of deliberate and systematic targeting and destruction of cultural heritage in armed conflict.

In that way, Hamilton offers an important addition to the most recent efforts by UNESCO and others to frame certain systematic forms of heritage destruction as "cultural cleansing," a concept that borrows from the original concept of cultural genocide.

The second part of the book, *Legal and Security Aspects of Cultural Heritage Preservation*, commences with Kristin Hausler and Andrzej Jakubowski's chapter, which focuses on the changing role of international heritage law in a time where cultural heritage increasingly is viewed as a security issue. For instance, addressing the trafficking in cultural objects has firmly become part of the UN counterterrorism efforts and the work of the UNSC toward the maintenance of international peace and security, including stabilization and resilience. To frame their inquiry, they analyze the emergence of the "heritage-security nexus" as a new priority on the international protection agenda with a focus on the threats associated with the illicit trade of cultural objects originating from conflict-ridden territories.

Ricardo Hilaire continues the analysis of the "heritage-security nexus" in a national context, namely how the new security-based thinking about cultural heritage and its elevation to a higher spot on the list of public policy objectives has come to be expressed in US law. By examining a range of cases from the Afghanistan War to congressional focus in 2017–19 on money laundering and cultural heritage, Hilaire identifies an "emergent cultural property protection paradigm" in US law, and he concludes that the goal of heritage preservation will continue to be mixed with national security priorities that target global terrorism and transnational crime. The "heritage-security nexus" is therefore expected, he argues, to guide the US State Department's consideration of future bilateral agreements covering cultural property import controls and to direct congressional lawmakers and federal authorities as they focus on cultural property and money laundering.

In the following chapter, Elizabeth Varner focuses on a critical aspect of IHL, specifically the concept of military necessity as the exception to the general rule against attacking cultural heritage in armed conflict. In that regard, Varner analyzes the likely customary international law status of certain crucial elements of the Second Protocol to the 1954 Hague Convention. She finds that even states that are not party to this international legal instrument may be obliged to comply with these obligations. What may look like a technical finding about international law, however, needs to be viewed in the broader field of value and norms related to cultural heritage and its protection in armed conflict. As customary international rules indicate value in the form of a mix of state attitudes and practices, Varner's chapter provides us with important information about the consolidation of a global value-infused norm against destroying cultural heritage in armed conflicts.

The international regulation of cultural heritage in armed conflict has become increasingly politicized because of its contested understanding of value, which invites conflicting perspectives as well as provides space for new developments. Mark Drumbl explore a recent trend in this area, which is the deployment of international judicial institutions to prosecute offenders of international heritage crimes. The Statute of the International Criminal Court, the "Rome Statute," prohibits as a war crime the intentional direction of attacks against buildings dedicated to religion, education, art, and science, which are not military objectives in international and non-international armed conflicts. Court practice will develop international criminal law in the area but also more generally affect the interpretation of the war crime of intentional attacks on cultural property within international law and thus involve at least a juridical detailing of the "value base." As explained by the authors, it is vexing, from a legalist perspective, that the term "cultural" entered the lexicon of ICC proceedings even though it is absent from the actual language of the prohibited crime in the Rome Statute.

Courts act in response to alleged crimes. Yet those states who wish to comply with their international humanitarian law obligations and avoid the risk of creating permissible environments for crimes need to invest in resources to make international law an operational reality. The 1954 Hague Convention has suffered from a great deal of ignorance from states themselves. One of the few states that has picked up the ball, however, is the United States. In her chapter, Laurie Rush, a cultural resource manager within the US Army, shares experiences with, and perspectives on, cultural property protection from the vantage point of her almost twenty years working with cultural property protection programs within the US Department of Defense and the US Military. Considering the lessons from US deployment of missions in areas rich with cultural heritage, including NATO-led missions, it becomes clear that the strategic military relevance of considering cultural property protection during missions points to the strong value of cultural heritage for host nation populations as well as for the international community.

The first two chapters of Part III, *Healing the Past: Repatriation of Stolen Art and Culture*, focus on stolen antiquities. As reports of theft and looting from Iraq and Syria made international headlines, the art world has again been forced to address the long-standing question of how to prevent plundered antiquities from circulating on the market and entering museum collections, as well as how to address artifacts removed from their places of origin or owners during conflicts. As Victoria Reed shows in her chapter, today is not the first time that museums have confronted this problem: the looting of cultural heritage during World War II was so vast that the process of identifying and returning it continues to this day. Taking the Boston Museum of Fine Arts as a case study, Reed examines the extent of its curators' knowledge of wartime theft and looting. She considers why the broad awareness of looting was, in many cases, insufficient to change the ethos of collecting and preventing the acquisition of stolen heritage. We must understand how and when, Reed argues, the process of due diligence failed in postwar America if we wish to apply the lessons learned to the situation in the Middle East.

Jos van Beurden focuses on the question of repatriation and differing attitudes toward looted cultural heritage. He suggests that if cultural heritage embodies a universal value immune to political agendas, we should expect a certain neutrality in the politics of repatriation. However, as van Beurden notices, this is far from the case, a situation that demonstrates different approaches to the ethics of cultural heritage. Van Beurden plunges into this issue by comparing the ways countries and claimants deal with Nazi-looted art works and how former colonizers and former colonies deal with their turbulent past. He finds a certain global agreement about how to deal with Nazi-looted art, but much less so when it comes to colonial objects. This difference, van Beurden argues, provides us with an inroad for reflecting on the intricate politics involved in ascribing value and building protection regimes for cultural heritage.

James Barry and Benjamin Isakhan bring Frowe and Matravers's reflection on values and the reconstruction of war damaged heritage to Syria and Iraq, where ISIS undertook an aggressive iconoclastic campaign and dramatically destroyed key heritage sites. In response, the international community has launched several initiatives to reconstruct damaged sites and prevent future damage. Through empirical studies, Isakhan and Barry explore the intersection between international and local understandings of the value of heritage. They find that the failure to truly understand the complexity of assigning value to heritage in the context of international interventions ultimately undermines the broader mission to foster stability and promote peace, and can fuel the propaganda machinery of Islamist groups such as ISIS.

Finally, Carsten Paludan-Müller offers a novel helicopter perspective on our topic by exploring how cultural heritage relates to space, territory, and conflict on a global to local scale through time. Evidently, cultural heritage constitutes a strong symbolic link between cultural/ethnic groups, territory, and history. Therefore, Paludan-Müller argues, geopolitics, which focuses on the relationship between politics, geography, and cultural/ethnic groups, comes into view as a natural perspective for exploring this dimension of cultural heritage. During the twentieth century, geopolitics became a dominant perspective within international politics and war studies to understand the global distributions of power, space, and nation-states. Yet as the nation-state fades as the primary organizer of identity and territorial belonging due to the increasingly identity-driven and transnational character of contemporary security communities, cultural heritage (re)emerges as a crucial reference for mooring collective identities to geography. Paludan-Müller both inscribes our topic into classical disciplines studying international conflicts as well as provides us with a critical perspective on why cultural heritage is often purposefully destroyed during conflict, and why its eventual reconstruction, and good-willed efforts to remedy wrongs and heal the past, may or may not help post-conflict reconciliation. It is all about global order.

* * *

The overall picture emerging from the chapters indicates the arrival of an era where objects and places of significant cultural value, viz. cultural heritage, increasingly will occupy a central place in politics, security, and violent conflicts. Concurrently, the ambivalent value of cultural heritage will continue to cause ethical and public policy challenges. The situation as a whole is new and it contains both liberal and post-liberal elements. Liberal, because the general framing of cultural heritage draws heavily on norms, attitudes, and visions of state and society growing out of the enlightenment and the twentieth-century's liberal world order. Post-liberal, because the current crisis of the liberal order, with its rise of identity-based geopolitics, a growing sensitivity toward cultural markers and new transnational forms of societal order and organizations, thrusts ahead a focus on cultural heritage as references for associations and antagonisms. The reader is therefore urged to reflect on the chapters and their cross-cutting themes and issues as a product of our particular time and its struggles about the relationship between culture, community, and territorial belonging. Why do we have these debates now? What can they, and the issue of cultural heritage in relation to violent conflicts more broadly, tell us about the times we are living through? Is what we see a blip on the historical screen, or a part of the coming of age of a new world order?

PART I

THE VALUE OF CULTURAL HERITAGE

1

Preserving Valuable Objects and Sites, in Times of War and at Other Times

Derek Gillman

I. Introduction

History and heritage overlap, but they are different. While numerous countries have a long-standing consensus about what history is, both as a subject and discipline (methodological approaches aside), the idea of cultural heritage is relatively modern. It was formulated in response to the French Revolution by the Anglo-Irish conservative politician Edmund Burke, who framed transmission of the English Constitution and customary law as an "entailed estate."[1] There is now an industry in heritage, which has only grown since Robert Hewison first chronicled it in the 1980s, and a field of study in which conservation features large, whether of individual buildings, whole towns, landscapes, and other sites.[2] As Frederik Rosén notes in his chapter, one outcome of postwar efforts to define heritage within internationally binding legal instruments is that they embrace almost every tangible and intangible cultural product, across time and geography (it might be more efficient to list what is not included). So, as a guide to readers of the present volume, here is this author's working definition of the concept with regard to a particular culture or nation: *an aggregate of cultural (e.g., ritual, performing, literary, visual, culinary, sporting, educational) practices, products, and institutions deemed worthy of being preserved and handed down.*

In nations that have numerous ethnicities and religions, and a diverse range of cultural practices, disputes must inevitably arise around what is worthwhile. Moreover, with whose heritage a particular cultural thing or site is most closely associated can be contestable, on which I reflect in section V

[1] Derek Gillman, *The Idea of Cultural Heritage* (2nd edn, CUP 2010) 82–89, 176.
[2] Robert Hewison, *The Heritage Industry: Britain in a Climate of Decline* (Methuen 1987).

Derek Gillman, *Preserving Valuable Objects and Sites, in Times of War and at Other Times* In: *The Preservation of Art and Culture in Times of War.* Edited by: Claire Finkelstein, Derek Gillman, and Frederik Rosén, Oxford University Press.
 DOI: 10.1093/oso/9780197610565.003.0002

with regard to the great Buddhas at Bamiyan, Afghanistan, where Buddhism has been absent for a thousand years. Cultural practices and products are frequently common to more than one nation or cultural group—the Buddhist Diamond Sutra for example, which for many centuries has been studied across East and South-East Asia. A ninth-century Chinese illustrated copy of the text is especially important, being the world's earliest dated printed book.[3] Aggregating valuable practices and products at the international level creates a "heritage of all humankind," discussed in section II.

"Cultural property" is often used synonymously for cultural heritage, although some resist it. Since property is a long-established domain of law, domestically and internationally, the term is more comfortable to lawyers, giving a "thingness" to heritage. It is a useful term to distinguish products that have only monetary value, like a run-of-the-mill washing machine, from those that have value *in addition* to the economic.[4] Lyndel Prott and Patrick O'Keefe prefer cultural heritage to cultural property because they believe the latter term encourages disputants to see valuable manifestations of culture as more than merely chattels or real property.[5] For philosopher Kwame Anthony Appiah, ownership is indeed the wrong model here, but for a different, cosmopolitan concern, about expansive rights-based claims to cultural material, "the traditional products and practices of a group—its songs and stories, even its secrets—are not best understood as its property, or made more useful by being tethered to their putative rights."[6] Intellectual property law can be brought to bear on some but not all examples of intangible heritage, since it evolved to deal with the products of specific authors and institutions, rather than long-standing cultural practices.

Mapping the boundary between "historical" and "cultural" narratives is beyond the scope of this chapter. Even if an important narrative is demonstrably mythical, it will likely have a role in certain practices and thus be considered worthy of transmission; individuals, however, have no obligation to

[3] From the repository at Dunhuang, Gansu province, brought to England by Marc Aurel Stein and held by the British Library. For a discussion of political issues surrounding the inscription of shared intangible heritage on UNESCO's Urgent Safeguarding List, see Sarah Sargent, "'Fractured Resemblances': Contested Multinational Heritage and Soft Power" (2020) 27 (1) International Journal of Cultural Property 97.

[4] Mindful that if the washing machine survives for a hundred years or more it may be valued for its historic interest.

[5] Lyndel V Prott and Patrick J O'Keefe, "'Cultural Heritage' or 'Cultural Property'?" 1992 (1) International Journal of Cultural Property 307. For a discussion of cultural things as more than "mere chattels," see Gillman (n 1) 103–05. Definitional problems of "cultural property" are addressed by Frederik Rosén in his chapter.

[6] Kwame Anthony Appiah, *The Lies That Bind: Rethinking Identity* (Liveright 2018) 208.

assert its historical accuracy.[7] People frequently gather around certain events and persons, factual or mythical, as key components of their heritage. One such is the Declaration of Independence of the American colonies from Britain, celebrated on 4 July. The championing of liberty and equality is central to America's story of itself, whereas the task of better understanding the new nation's involvement in the slave trade has traditionally fallen to historians. Yet, following the May 2020 death of George Floyd under the knee of Minneapolis police officer Derek Chauvin, many Americans are now scrutinizing and challenging public narratives about their country, and the ways in which their history has been taught. Memorials to Confederate leaders erected after the Civil War as figures of virtue have recently been removed, or toppled, as symbols of vice.[8] Internationally, protests against racism and colonialism accelerated the taking down, officially and unofficially, of monuments to slave traders and empire builders.

In Britain, there had long been discussions about removing John Cassidy's sculpture of Edward Colston from the center of Bristol, from which in June 2020 it was dragged to and toppled into the city's harbor. This protest might have played out differently had the plinth's 1895 text celebrating Colston as one of city's "most virtuous and wise sons" been augmented more briskly by a plaque noting his preeminent role in the seventeenth-century slave trade out of Bristol, one of Britain's principal transatlantic ports. Colston's bronze was recovered from the water and moved to storage, alongside the rope that pulled it down and protest banners, pending recontextualized display within a museum. Underlining contests between divergent cultural narratives, journalist Tom Wall noted that, in response to a poll conducted by the *Bristol Post*, 61% of the ten thousand respondents supported the statue's removal and the elimination of Colston's name from many streets, institutions, and landmarks, while a third of the readers wanted no change.[9] Simon Schama agrees

[7] Aside perhaps from that imposed by peer pressure.

[8] A number of print and web journals have recently scrutinized identity in the southern United States by writing about attractive regional traditions in parallel with the histories of slavery, segregation, and massive income disparity; see Richard Fausset, "Southern Magazines, Easy Pleasures and Hard Questions" *New York Times* (New York, 5 September 2017); see also Caroline Randall Williams, "You Want A Confederate Monument? My Body Is a Confederate Monument" *New York Times* (New York, 28 June 2020).

[9] Tom Wall <www.theguardian.com/uk-news/2020/jun/14/the-day-bristol-dumped-its-hated-slave-trader-in-the-docks-and-a-nation-began-to-search-its-soul> accessed 14 June 2020. The idea for an additional, contextualizing plaque was proposed in 2018 by Bristol City Council's Principal Historic Environment Officer, see Roger Ball <www.brh.org.uk/site/articles/the-edward-colston-corrective-plaque> accessed 13 June 2020. Colston Hall, the city's largest concert venue, was renamed Bristol Beacon in September 2020.

with relocation to museums, "Let them disappear, then, but not into canals, ponds or rubbish dumps, since arbitrary acts of destruction shut down debate quite as much as uncritical reverence. Better, surely, to relocate them to museums where, properly curated, they can trigger genuine debate and historical education."[10] This is an approach that I support: recontextualizing them in museums will expand knowledge of the history of slavery and is an argument for keeping them.

Views about where control of, access to, and narratives about cultural material properly reside, as well as about rights of ownership and representation, have recently been inflected by a greater sensitivity to the effects of empire. Decolonization has firmly entered museum practice in Europe and America, moving to display cultures more equitably. Attention is being paid to the framing of stories; to the roles of museums as collectors within the larger context of European maritime expansion and colonial rule; and to clarifying the histories of objects taken under duress, particularly those from Africa, Asia, and Central and South America. Some were spoils of war, claimed at the time as retribution, for example, bronzes from the Oba's Palace in Benin, which are widely dispersed across European and American museums, with the largest holdings at the British Museum and the Ethnologisches Museum Berlin, and objects from the Yuanmingyuan, the Old Summer Palace in Beijing.

In section II, I review debate between those who propose that important matters of cultural discourse remain with originating and local cultures—the nationalist/particularist view—and those who incline to a worldview, in the spirit of Immanuel Kant's utopian great federation of states.[11] The debate was initiated around the restitution of cultural things but it does affect the present volume, insofar as decisions need to be made about the safe storage, conservation, and restoration or replication of sites and objects damaged by warfare. Who speaks for a culture, what is said about it, and who "owns" it, are different according to time and place.[12]

[10] Simon Schama, "History Is Better Served by Putting the Men in Stone in Museums" <https://www.ft.com/content/1117dfb6-8e51-46ec-a74b-59973a96a85a> accessed 15 June 2020; see also Richard J Evans, "The History Wars" <www.newstatesman.com/2020/06/history-wars> accessed 18 June 2020.

[11] On the recent rise of nationalist rhetoric in Britain and the USA, see Jeff McMahan <https://www.newstatesman.com/politics/2020/10/how-britain-and-us-became-trapped-nationalism-decline> accessed 2 October 2020.

[12] In general, cultural narratives are liable to be contested in liberal democracies but tightly controlled under tyrannies.

Whether we use cultural property or heritage, the sheer range of material under discussion eludes simple definition, its amorphousness decreasing clarity about how best to act in the field of war. Rosén wonders how the law can even adjudicate between the value of material things and the value of human life, and thus asks how commanders on the ground can be expected to make rational judgments about balancing military objectives and the preservation of heritage? What guidance should they be given about negotiating the value of human lives—including those under their command—alongside the worth of cultural things? Certainly to many people human life is preeminent: perhaps because of their religion; perhaps because of the emphasis on life within their customary laws; perhaps because of human rights conventions (individuals are ends rather than means); or perhaps because they feel life trumps other values, logically or intuitively (within the realm of philanthropy, medical charities in the United States raise more than arts charities).[13]

Prima facie it seems obvious that heritage should be preserved, yet one contributor to this volume, Duncan MacIntosh, finds grounds for allowing buildings and objects to be destroyed under certain exceptional circumstances. His position suggests that beneath the question of *how* cultural heritage is best preserved during times of war must lie reasons *why* it should be preserved, and under what circumstances. The argument of this chapter is that we should seek the answer in value, since the commonality between all cultural properties is that some group values them.[14] This demands of us a discussion of values, intrinsic and instrumental. In section III, I discuss the list of seven incommensurable basic values proposed in 1980 by the legal philosopher John Finnis (while disagreeing with a recent revision to it). Which of these we foreground will be a personal choice, mediated by the degree to which our autonomy is constrained by social and political pressures. At an abstract level, the battlefield dilemma is how optimally to balance desirable outcomes that allow engagement with value. For example, how to secure the safety of individuals (because one values life), while also protecting, as much as possible, valuable works of art and architecture, and archaeological sites (because one values knowledge, aesthetic experience, etc.)? Finnis's values are transnational but engagement with them is local, giving us another way to think about cosmopolitanism and particularism.

[13] Health charities in America raise about twice that of arts and humanities charities <https://grahampelton.com/giving-usa-2020> accessed 1 July 2020.

[14] Individuals within the group do not need to be contiguous; they could, for example, be geographically spread co-religionists.

II. The Cosmopolitan and the Particular

Attitudes toward the preservation of cultural heritage have been framed by a long-standing tension between the cosmopolitan and the particular, focused during the past four decades on restitution of cultural objects and human remains, and recently also on decolonizing museums. In the context of this volume, that tension lies in the control of cultural objects and sites in war zones, and the extent to which outside interest in their preservation by alien governments, NGOs, academics, etc., is legitimated by an argument that all cultures are components of a larger world heritage.

Here one can hardly ignore commentary on, and contribution to this debate by the Stanford-based legal scholar John Henry Merryman. In Merryman's eyes, claims to material objects associated with particular nations and cultural groups sharply differentiate cosmopolitan and particularist approaches.[15] His liberal cosmopolitan thesis was that certain goods, including preservation, are challenged by the desire to maintain particular, often national, heritages. He was generally (but not always) scathing about assertions by nation-states that in order to remedy past wrongs, important cultural properties should be restituted and embedded within regional heritage. In defending his version of cosmopolitanism, Merryman proposed a hierarchy of key instrumental considerations that should govern policy toward cultural property, listing preservation, truth, and access in descending order "If we don't care about its preservation, it isn't, for us, a cultural object."[16] The logic here is that the elevation of the instrumental value of preservation is grounded in intrinsic values such as truth (or knowledge). The distinction is that intrinsic (or basic) values are good in themselves, whereas instrumental values fulfill a purpose. Black letter law is purpose driven, and practicing lawyers will see merit in his focus on preservation: in times of war and in the face of immediate danger, most would agree the instrumental goal of preservation both of people and cultural things should be front of mind. Balancing instrumental values is something that most of us do, in small or large ways, most of the time. Courts across the world do it constantly. Yet to build *general* cultural policy around the exigency of wartime situations is too quick, and the following sections discuss the role of intrinsic values, which provide important reasons for doing what we do.

[15] Gillman (n 1) 41–49, 174–79.

[16] 'John Merryman, *Thinking about the Elgin Marbles: Critical Essays on Cultural Property, Art and Law* (2nd edn, Wolters Kluwer 2009) 160.

Having ranked preservation above truth, Merryman had only a cautious regard for archaeologists, who place a premium on contextual knowledge and the proximity of artifacts to their original archaeological or architectural sites. He cast cosmopolitanism and particularism (or nationalism) as "two ways of thinking." In *The Idea of Cultural Heritage*, I made the case for mapping this topology onto a parallel one in contemporary political philosophy: between liberal cosmopolitans and liberal culturists like Will Kymlicka, the latter seeing local cultures as a crucial framework for individual choice making.[17]

Those who argue that the cosmopolitan concept of world heritage trumps claims of particular peoples have at least four legs upon which to balance their stool: first, the 1954 Hague Convention (for the Protection of Cultural Property in the Event of Armed Conflict), which addresses "the cultural heritage of all mankind" that Merryman saw as exemplifying cultural internationalism (in contrast to the nationalism he perceived in the 1970 Convention on the Means of Prohibiting and Preventing the Illicit Import, Export and Transfer of Ownership of Cultural Property);[18] second, a lineage of universalist thinking about culture that reached maturity in the aftermath of World War II;[19] third, a modernist approach valorizing form, which, it should be noted, was abetted by the arrival in Europe of often uncontextualized African, Pacific, and Asian objects from British, French, and German colonies and campaigns;[20] and fourth, the evolution of museums and related institutions that commit to researching and displaying diverse cultures. Champions of the cosmopolitan, ambassadorial role of encyclopedic museums include Neil McGregor, former director of the British Museum; and James Cuno, president of the Getty Trust, the latter recalling his first introduction to the Louvre's "wondrous universe of its encyclopedic collection, and how it made me feel, in my own small way . . . a part of it, with the dividers of time and space suddenly collapsed, non-existent: the diverse, interrelated cultures of antiquity no longer distant."[21]

[17] Gillman, *The Idea of Cultural Heritage* (n 1) 180–81.
[18] ibid 42–45.
[19] Well articulated by two German Jewish philologists who had settled in America, Leo Spitzer and Erich Auerbach.
[20] Eg linear rhythm, mass, space, light, and color, adumbrated by Roger Fry, "An Essay in Aesthetics" (1909) in JB Bullen (ed), *Vision and Design* (OUP 1981) 23–24; see also Derek Gillman, "Albert Barnes and the Rejection of History" (2014) 158 (2) Proceedings of the American Philosophical Society 107.
[21] James Cuno, *Who Owns Antiquity? Museums and the Battle over our Ancient Heritage* (Princeton UP 2008) 160.

In contrast, the belief that particular heritages take precedence over the "heritage of all mankind" draws upon a conviction that individuals find greater meaning and well-being in the local than the universal. Particularism emerged in the late eighteenth century, first and richly formulated by J.G. von Herder, who influenced G.W.F. Hegel's view that language and customary practice bind peoples.[22] Particularist arguments for restitution have, for the most part, been based upon moral claims deriving from group rights, the justification of which are not always jurisprudentially obvious (in the case of human remains, that knot is quickly cut by political action). Jurist John Moustakas argues that group personalities are substantial, and that nations and cultural groups possess personality (grouphood) in like manner to an individual. The capacity of qualifying groups to take on personhood at law is well established, but he insists on more than legal role playing. For Moustakas, a trinity of people, ancestors, and objects satisfies a basic need for identity while also symbolizing shared values.[23] Whether we agree with him or not, it cannot be controversial to assert that an individual's sense of identity is strengthened through attachments to particular groups and/or places. Hence, as a construction, "cultural heritage" can cover both the culture of a people and the culture of a place, often overlapping. Alasdair MacIntyre argues that morally significant lives only make sense within the complex interlocking practices of particular cultures, from which individuals create their own narrative trajectories.

At heart, the tension between cosmopolitanism and particularism reflects the pull between individuals and their communities. Strong forms of particularism within cultural groups and states, for example, in communist nations and theocracies, demand that individuals subordinate their actions to social norms and narratives; in contrast, liberalism insists that individuals must have the autonomy to revise and/or reject them.[24] Cosmopolitan approaches toward heritage encourage active engagement with other cultures, and an appreciation of how much cultures borrow (often eliding the fact). As Jeremy Waldron observes, "Humans are curious and adventurous animals . . . And they report back what they have found out about the ways in which others

[22] Gillman (n1) ch 2; and Appiah (n 6) 82 ff. The internet presents challenges for languages that lack a written form, see Frances Jenner on the Guaraní language spoken by a majority of Paraguayans, "Can This Indigenous Language Thrive in a Digital Age?" <www.sapiens.org/language/guarani-digital> accessed 3 September 2020.

[23] John Moustakas, "Group Rights in Cultural Property" (1989) 74 Cornell Law Review 1179.

[24] Including forms of liberalism which understand individualism as a socially embedded phenomenon, such as Kymlicka's liberal culturalism.

live (and trade and fight etc.)"[25] Particularism in heritage debate focuses on return, on restoration of the status quo ante, and on policing perimeters. At stake here, aside from claims to title at law, are moral claims on proprietary objects and intangible practices that are deemed to belong to a culture.

Well reflecting these tensions between cosmopolitanism and particularism is a set of mid-eighteenth-century zodiac animal waterspouts taken from a Versailles-style fountain at the Yuanmingyuan, the earlier and grander of two Qing dynasty summer palaces in Beijing. The fountain fronted the Haiyantang, Hall of Calm Seas, within a suite of late Baroque buildings at the northeast corner of the grounds, an exotic feature designed for the Emperor Qianlong by two Jesuits at his court, painter Giuseppe Castiglione and hydraulic engineer Michel Benoist. An Italian and a faithful servant of the Jesuit Order, Castiglione was more than both of those. During his half-century residence at the capital, he produced a unique body of work that reconciled the cunning of European illusionism and the materiality of Chinese painting, amalgamating two technically quite different practices—one culturally indigenous and the other imported.[26] Cast in bronze by palace craftsmen to Castiglione's designs, the twelve heads were removed in 1860 during the second Opium War when the palace was looted by an Anglo-French army whose military mission was to coerce the court into ratifying treaties that further opened Chinese ports and allowed unrestricted trade in Indian opium. Provoked by the execution through torture of twenty members of his negotiating delegation, among whom was the correspondent from the London *Times*, the British commander, Lord Elgin, was intending to retaliate by burning down the fifteenth-century Forbidden City but was persuaded by his French counterpart, Baron Gros, to settle instead for the Yuanmingyuan, of which only marble ruins from the European halls remain. Submission to the Western powers during the nineteenth and early twentieth centuries undergirds much of today's nationalist sentiment in China, and so the seven Yuanmingyuan heads that have reappeared in recent years became a lightning rod for such sentiment, with all of them returning to China.[27]

25 "What Is Cosmopolitan?" (2000) 8 (2) The Journal of Political Philosophy 232.

26 The *Shanghai Daily* (Shanghai, 15 May 2016) opined that his magisterial 1728 handscroll *One Hundred Horses*, a national treasure in Taiwan, is "among the top 10 masterpieces of traditional Chinese painting."

27 A considerable literature exists on the Yuanmingyuan and its aftermath; see Derek Gillman, "The Old Summer Palace and the Rhetoric of National Treasures" (2019) 5 (2) Santander Art and Culture Law Review 233.

Although similarly imagined sets of twelve zodiacal figures survive from first-millennium CE tombs, the Yuanmingyuan's was designed by a European. Ai Weiwei has asked whether it is right for these zodiacal heads to be described as Chinese national treasures because of foreign involvement in their production—not least by Qianlong whose ancestors invaded and occupied China, establishing the Manchu Qing dynasty in 1644. Following a canceled Christie's sale in 2009 of the rabbit and rat heads from Yves Saint Laurent's collection, when the Chinese buyer refused to pay on patriotic grounds, the artist created a larger-than-life-size bronze set of the Castiglione spouts, modeled partly on the originals and partly from imagination. In a video released in 2010, which includes footage of protests against the sale, he remarks about the set, "It was designed by an Italian, made by a Frenchman, for a Qing dynasty emperor, which is actually somebody who invaded China. If we talk about national treasure, which nation are we talking about?"[28] Irony is a frequent component of Ai's practice and in making this and a smaller gilt-bronze edition, he was recognizing the unusual valorization of a set of objects designed by foreigners for an occupying power.

Twenty-first-century decolonization efforts by museums are beginning, slowly, to create an important zone wherein the benefits of cultural exchange, historical and present, are recognized alongside an acknowledgment of numerous inequities of economic and military power that permitted, if not encouraged, objects precious to particular cultures to rest in other countries. In sections III and IV, I propose that what *should* move us to preserve culturally valuable things and sites, in times of war and peace—including those in which we personally have no interest—is recognizing the importance to peoples across the world of basic values, which are incommensurable.

III. Values and Valuing

Within *The Idea of Cultural Heritage*, I made the case that a list of seven basic values drawn up by John Finnis in 1980 was helpful in approaching cultural property issues, not because I regarded him as having the final say on valuation but because as broad categories they seemed to capture important

[28] <www. Zodiacheads.com> accessed 1 November 2018.

categories of valuing. The values are incommensurable, not rankable as Merryman ranked the imperative of preservation over truth and access.

Finnis's list of basic values was knowledge, life, play, aesthetic experience, sociability (friendship), practical reasonableness, and "what we summarily and lamely call 'religion.'"[29] In 2011 he offered a revised version, still of seven.[30] Aesthetic experience was dropped as a self-standing value, now included under knowledge, and play was re-described as skillful performance. The previous encapsulation of the value of life "corresponding to the drive for self-preservation" was now divided into two values: bodily life and marriage. The latter, grounded by Finnis in Aristotle and Roman Catholic orthodoxy, is defined as the sexual association between a man and woman. I reject this formulation, which sees value only in heterosexual marriage. In addition, I find it helpful to maintain the separation of aesthetic experience and knowledge, about which will be talked about later in the chapter, and thus will keep to the 1980 list.

That these values are embedded in cultures is recognized by Finnis, who notes that we encounter them as "part of a cultural heritage, even before we understand them as goods."[31] For many, such values will be understood through specific instantiations, for example, the religion into which one was born, a personally favored sport for play, and familiar works for aesthetic experience. Finnis regarded the seven as foundational, suggesting that "[countless] other objectives and forms of good will be found, on analysis, to be ways or combinations of ways of pursuing (not always sensibly) and realizing (not always successfully) one of the seven basic forms of good, or some combination of them."[32] Indeed, it is often the case that we engage with several of these values simultaneously; religious ritual, for example, might well include knowledge, aesthetic experience, play, and friendship. They are not incompatible with John Rawls's primary liberal goods, instrumentally required for citizens to be free and equal persons; Finnis however locates equality and distributive justice *within* his value of practical reasonableness.[33]

29 John Finnis, *Natural Law and Natural Rights* (Clarendon 1980) 86–90.

30 John Finnis, *Reason in Action: Collected Essays Volume 1* (OUP 2011) 244, n 25.

31 John Finnis, *Moral Absolutes: Tradition, Revision, and Truth* (The Catholic University of America Press 1991) 42; I am grateful to Frederik Rosén for this reference.

32 Finnis (n 29) 90.

33 Rawls's liberal goods are "[B]asic rights and liberties . . .; freedom of movement and free choice of occupation . . .; powers and prerogatives of offices and positions of responsibility . . .; income and wealth . . .; the social bases of self-respect" *Political Liberalism* (Columbia UP 1996) 180–81. Finnis (n 29) 165–77.

The precise contour of these lists is less important for my purpose here than the recognition that there seems to exist a relatively small number of common categories, or domains, of human valuing.[34] Finnis was explicit about this: "My present concern is the universality of those basic value judgments that are manifested not only in various moral requirements and restrictions but also in the many forms of human culture, institutions and initiative."[35] I agree with him that certain categories/forms of value appear to be universal, and that most individuals on the planet have the capacity to engage, in some way, with those he describes. Before considering basic values in the context of cultural property, let me recognize present doubts about the rightness of firmly separating intrinsic/basic values and instrumental values.

The seven may have evolutionary or biological roots. Valuing life, friendship, religion, and play help deal with the inescapable—death, decay, oblivion, danger, competitors, and the unfamiliar in general—and Finnis notes wryly that H.L.A. Hart itemized only one universally recognized, indisputable end: survival.[36] Joseph Raz also challenges foundational schemes, "For example, some friendships and some religions or aesthetic experiences are without merit at all. Good friendships are good, and good religious experiences or lives are good, but not all friendships nor all religious experiences or religious lives, one is inclined to say, derive any value from being friendships or from being religious."[37] There are certainly bad social, religious, and political practices in the world, as there are bad works of art and architecture. That certain instantiations are without merit does not mean that the categories themselves are without merit.

Advocates for the arts often speak about them as good *in themselves*. Yet many aspects of engagement that we regard as intrinsically valuable can, at the same time, credibly be seen as instrumentally so. It may be that my own engagements with aesthetic experience, affected by the lottery of my personality, class, education, etc., lead me to think of them as intrinsically valuable; however, as I analyze them, their intrinsic nature seems to slide away. That does not, I think, make them of less value. Preservation of things with which we engage for aesthetic experience is instrumentally good, in the service of an intrinsic value. No particular damage has been done to the project of

[34] Unless by using the values "religion" and "aesthetic experience" we commit to meaning only "good religion" or "good aesthetic experience," which is obviously problematic.
[35] Finnis (n 29) 84.
[36] ibid 82; Hart was Professor of Jurisprudence at Oxford.
[37] Rawls (n 33) 180–81, n 8; Joseph Raz, "Value: A Menu of Questions" in John Keown and Robert P George (eds), *Reason, Morality and Law: The Philosophy of John Finnis* (OUP 2013) 13–23.

understanding heritage by setting aside sharp divisions of values into basic and instrumental, with the caveat that at the intrinsic level they are incommensurable. The innumerable engagements of people across the world with aesthetic experience, knowledge, play, friendship, and religion are not devalued by their being re-described as instrumental rather than intrinsic, or as both instrumental *and* intrinsic. And what makes a cultural practice or a cultural product valuable? Surely engagement with the values of knowledge, of friendship, of aesthetic experience, of religion, etc. In aggregate, cultural practices form cultures, and cultural practices that are valuable in themselves also embed values within genres and particular instantiations (e.g., in the genres of Chinese bamboo painting, European history painting, American bluegrass music, etc., and in instantiations like Pablo Picasso's *Guernica*).

At the national level, value plays a key role within import and export regimes. In Britain, permission to export culturally significant work is controlled by a committee that assesses works against three criteria, the second and third of which are based, respectively, on the value of aesthetic experience and the value of knowledge (while the first, the value of "our history and national life," represents an aggregate of values, especially of knowledge, religion, sociability, and play).[38] The value of knowledge is particularly interesting in the case of works of art and architecture, where we deal with two forms of knowledge. The first is knowledge required for connoisseurly ranking, that is, extensive familiarity with individual works produced in a particular practice and genre; the second form is historical and contextual knowledge, including the motivations and declared intentions of the producer/s. It can be extremely awkward, indeed inappropriate, to detach contextual knowledge from aesthetic value. *Guernica* was painted immediately after Nazi planes bombed the town in April 1937 to accelerate Spanish submission to fascist rule and could, theoretically, be valued just for knowledge about Picasso's contribution to Spanish Republican resistance—the circumstance of its commission, its display in Paris at the 1937 World's Fair, and subsequent tours—without considering his remarkable pictorial achievement. Alternatively, this celebrated painting could be appreciated for its aesthetic form alone. To do one or the other would serve neither viewer nor artist. Separation of these values rarely occurs in practice: visitors to the Reina Sofia in Madrid will, one hopes, experience both its aesthetic value and its larger

[38] Gillman (n 1) 141–50.

historical context.[39] Besides contextual knowledge associated with specific works, there is, of course, contextual knowledge of sites and excavations, a defining feature of the modern profession of archaeology.

Engagement with value depends on our preferences, and preferences are subject to change. Frank Furness (1839–1912) is presently regarded as among the most creative architects to have worked in America. Nonetheless, a number of his Philadelphia buildings were taken down during the twentieth century by developers and planners who derogated the entire genre of Gothic Revival, and thought his buildings bad. Nobody involved in allowing their decay or destruction could argue that Furness lacked design skills, even if they greatly disliked the way in which he applied them. Value emerges over time through an often ragged and rarely unanimous consensus among socially embedded communities of valuers, national or transnational, who judge and rank instantiations of value within practices, and more specifically within genres.[40] Discussing the integrity of sets, jurist Paul Bator offered this observation on consensus, "Some things are much more beautiful or interesting if seen as part of a given complex, some only a little. Consensus about the 'how much' may be difficult to find; consensus about whether this factor should be determinative in a given case even harder."[41]

The key role of imagination in creating highly valued cultural products was first promoted within the English-speaking world by Samuel Taylor Coleridge, for whom it "dissolves, diffuses, and dissipates" in order to recreate.[42] In visual, literary, and performing practices, imagination brings into being, not always consciously, new associations and ideas, images and metaphors, interpretations and styles, and forms and rhythms. It is manifest in innumerable ways, from the eighth-century subtleties of Du Fu's tightly regulated poetry to Picasso's startling *Tête de taureau* (Bull's Head)—constructed in 1942 from a bicycle seat and handlebars—about which the artist said, "It came to me before I had a chance to think."[43] Is my focus on imagination here

[39] Kirk Pillow discusses such a division between aesthetic appreciation and knowledge with regard to *Guernica* in *Sublime Understanding: Aesthetic Reflections in Kant and Hegel* (MIT Press 2000) 55–56, as I did in *The Idea of Cultural Heritage* (n1) 136–37.

[40] For the link between values, standards of excellence, and genres, see Joseph Raz, *The Practice of Value* (R Jay Wallace ed, Clarendon Press 2003) 131–38.

[41] Paul Bator, *The International Trade in Art* (Chicago University Press 1983) 22.

[42] For Coleridge, specifically the "secondary imagination," see Gene M Bernstein, "The Recreating Secondary Imagination in Coleridge's 'The Nightingale'" (2000) 48 (2) ELH 339.

[43] *Tête de taureau* is in the Musée Picasso, Paris; photographs from 1940 showing a bicycle seat mounted on the wall of Picasso's Royan studio slightly dent his assertion of spontaneity, see Ann Temkin and Anne Umland, *Picasso Sculpture* (MoMA 2015) 187.

attributable only to European Romanticism? I think not, since the contribution of imagination to poetry was recognized in China by the late fifth century.[44] Yet imagination in itself cannot warrant an aesthetically valuable work, which also requires skill.[45] At the same time, millions of surviving pieces of art and architecture demonstrate considerable visual skills while reusing established tropes and techniques; they are worth preserving, although they cannot be described as especially creative. For example, we can engage with the aesthetic value of a brilliantly executed Chinese eighteenth-century blue and white porcelain vessel in early Ming dynasty style, and engage for the information it provides about elite taste in the Qing dynasty, and, if analyzed, about ceramic recipes at that point in time. Its design and technical elements are nevertheless broadly subordinate to innovations of the fourteenth and fifteenth centuries, knowledge about which is needed to make sense of the vessel. Absent that, its contribution to the practice of Chinese ceramics will be exaggerated. I should note, parenthetically, that at law the bar for originality is fairly low. In English law the exercise of labor, skill and/or judgment has long been sufficient to confer copyright, although in 2012 a court aligned the "trusty triumvirate"—as Emily Gould and Alexander Herman call it—with a more compressed continental notion of "the author's own intellectual creation."[46]

Since very accurate replicas of works of art can now be produced, especially of works on paper but in other media also, here is a thought experiment.[47] Suppose it was feared that *Guernica*'s public display made it vulnerable (for whatever reason) and so, as a precautionary measure and with

[44] In his annotated translation of Liu Xie's *Wenxin diaolong*, Vincent Yu-chung Shih renders *shensi* 神思 as imagination; see *The Literary Mind and the Carving of Dragons: A Study of Thought and Pattern in Chinese Literature* (Chinese University Press 1983) 298–99. From the Tang dynasty on, painters deemed to demonstrate *shen* were ranked by critics at the highest level; see Susan Bush and Hsio-yen Shih, *Early Chinese Texts on Painting* (Harvard UP 1985) 75–76, where *shen* is translated as inspired.

[45] For the visual arts, skills in design and technique, and for certain practices also in performance (eg East Asian calligraphy and painting which demands disciplined coordination of arm, hand and fingers); such skills embrace natural ability, acquired technique, and the effective application of technical knowledge.

[46] *Temple Island Collections Ltd v New English Teas*; see Emily Gould and Alexander Herman, "Copyrights in Photographs of Paintings: The UK Approach, the Impact of European Jurisprudence and the Prospects in a Post-Brexit World" (2017) 2 *Art, Antiquity and Law* 159.

[47] A new International Center for Cave Art at Montignac reproduces paintings from the Lascaux Cave complex, which for conservation reasons the public can no longer access. A related and interesting question, beyond the scope of this discussion, is about where value lies in unauthorized prints and multiples, since falsification and manipulation diminish the value of knowledge; the first to discuss the value of multiples was Walter Benjamin in 1936, see *The Work of Art in the Age of Its Technological Reproducibility, and Other Writings on Media* (Belknap Press 2008).

appropriate labeling, the Reina Sofia placed on display a copy so exact that a connoisseurly eye could not distinguish it from Picasso's original. In that case, aesthetic experience of the copy should, prima facie, be identical to that of the original. What makes engaging with this *Guernica* substantively different is that, unlike the eighteenth-century porcelain vessel, which is derivative but self-standing, the replica is a technical exercise whose aesthetic value lies *entirely* in Picasso's original work. In the following paragraphs I concentrate on three values—aesthetic experience, knowledge, and religion—since these have the most bearing on the valuation of cultural objects and sites.

To think further about value, we move to a religious image in the British Museum: a Chinese marble sculpture of Amitabha Buddha, dated 585, carved for the Chongguang temple at Hancui village in Hebei province.[48] Amitabha is a major deity in Mahayana (Great Vehicle) Buddhism, presiding over the Pure Land paradise into which the faithful may be reborn. In 1935–36 the almost six-meter-high figure was lent to the *International Exhibition of Chinese Art* held at Burlington House, London, by CT Loo, one of the two principal international dealers in Chinese art at the time. Loo then presented the sculpture to the Chinese government, which in turn gifted it to the British Museum to commemorate the exhibition. This transfer of title was executed against a background of ever-increasing encroachment by Japan on mainland China, and given its size and weight the Buddha was not an easy object to return.[49] Displayed within the north staircase, the British Museum's architecture demands that visitors circle the Amitabha as they climb or descend, echoing the circumambulation of early worshippers. A few Buddhist visitors will undoubtedly venerate the sculpture, but most who engage with it more than fleetingly will do so for the value of aesthetic experience and/or knowledge (connoisseurly and/or contextual).

Communities of valuers ascribe and revise degrees of value to tangible things and intangible practices, with "community" understood here to be individuals and institutions subscribing to the same or similar sets of norms and expectations. China's gift of the Amitabha was generous indeed and we can fairly ask—the political situation notwithstanding—why the Chinese government chose to act so, as opposed simply to placing it on long-term loan? One reason may lie in the relatively low esteem in which, until recently, sculpture was held by Chinese connoisseurs and historians; before 1980

[48] Hancui no longer exists, see Derek Gillman, "General Munthe's Chinese Buddhist Sculpture" (1996) IV The Buddhist Forum 112–13, n 67.

[49] The Second Sino-Japanese War broke out in July 1937.

Chinese archaeological and antiquities journals only rarely included articles dedicated to the subject. At different times and in different cities, members of China's literati circles wrote extensively about how best to evaluate the visual arts—genres, styles, and individuals and their works—and it is reasonable to say, in general, that hierarchies were different to those of Europe. This goes for roles as well as works. In Europe, respect for the *role* of painter evolved during the High Renaissance. In China, respect for the role of calligrapher came in the early first millennium CE. Hard-won mastery of the flexible writing brush was admired, yet it generally conferred status just on those who were educated. The point here is that engaging with aesthetic experience is complex, since our engagement may be as much with the actor (e.g., in the role of calligrapher or painter) as with a work itself. From the eleventh century until the latter part of the last century, calligraphy and painting ranked as the premier fine arts, alongside ancient bronzes, prized especially for cast inscriptions carrying information valuable both to history writing and epigraphy, whereas architecture and sculpture were regarded as artisan activities. Buddhism was a foreign import with no connection to pre-imperial antiquity, and connoisseurs evinced little interest in its sculpture as fine art or in the names of makers, even though pieces from the Wei and Tang dynasties sometimes carried long donor-centered inscriptions on their bases (as the British Museum Amitabha Buddha has).[50] Dismissal of Buddhist sculpture as art did not affect it as a vehicle of religion, since gods have lives for those to whom their actions are real.[51] Buddhist, Daoist, and Confucian-oriented images permeated the fabric of social and political life in China, the pantheons of the latter two echoing national and regional administrative structures in the mundane world. Many individuals managed to hold Confucian and Buddhist tenets in their minds without cognitive dissonance, moving between two sources of authority that often confronted each other.[52]

Religion is the focus of many anxieties about heritage, being embedded in communities and within a wide variety of community-based practices to which people are committed, tying together ancestors and descendants,

[50] One exception is the record of the names of three seventh-century sculptors who led work at the Fengxian temple, a major imperially sponsored project at Longmen, Henan province; Craig Clunas, *Art in China* (2nd edn, OUP 2009) 104.

[51] See Gillman (n 1) ch 4, s 1.

[52] Two sets of official institutions, institutional rules and conventions, beliefs about the nature of death and of the soul, and practices related to social responsibilities. Appiah notes equivalent dual allegiances among the Asante (n 6) 66–67. Despite its focus on political order, Confucianism greatly valued engagement with the dead, indeed it was predicated on relationships between ancestors and descendants.

gods and supplicants, and in certain societies also rulers and subjects.[53] It governs conventions for burials, memorial services, the care of tombs, and the treatment of human remains and relics, as well as those for the creation and care of images, and other objects used for worship and ritual. However, if we do not personally respect certain practices, and we personally do not approve of their practice—just as the eleventh-century statesman and literatus Ouyang Xiu respected neither Buddhism nor Buddhist practices—do we have reasons not to allow them to decay? Not all practices are good just because they are culturally practiced. Liberals believe that a key ground for curtailing illiberal practices is the requirement to treat individuals as ends not means, even if the means is claimed to be cultural survival of a community. This has a different ground from suppressing so-called bad practices in order to sustain an opposing ideology—as Ouyang Xiu wished to suppress Buddhism during the Northern Song dynasty.[54]

Because the West has valued sculpture since antiquity, and Buddhism has played a far greater role in Japanese social life during the last millennium than it has in China, private and institutional collectors from Europe, America, and Japan seized upon the mass of sculptural material that flooded from warlord-controlled north Chinese provinces to the Beijing market.[55] This not only allowed Westerners to begin building a corpus of connoisseurly knowledge but such work was also received in Europe and America within a modernist discourse about the universal qualities of great art, championed by Roger Fry, Laurence Binyon, Osvald Sirén, and Albert Barnes.[56] For avant-garde connoisseurs in London in the mid-1930s who subscribed to formalism, the Amitabha Buddha offered an exceptional instance of rhythm and vitality (the values of aesthetic experience and play). On the other side of the globe, when the Amitabha's smaller accompanying Guanyin (Kannon) figure entered the Tokyo National Museum, Japanese visitors surely engaged, additionally, with the value of religion.[57] It is inconceivable that in 1936 the Chinese government would have gifted to the British Museum one of the

[53] Sometimes so strongly imposed by peer pressure that they are coercive.

[54] If he could be asked, Ouyang Xiu might argue that foot binding helped maintain the Confucian social order and that liberalism, like Buddhism, is just another misplaced ideology.

[55] For an account of Americans involved in the market between the Boxer Rebellion and the Japanese Occupation, see Karl E. Meyer and Shareen Blair Brysac, *The China Collectors: America's Century-Long Hunt for Asian Art Treasures* (Palgrave Macmillan 2015).

[56] See Derek Gillman, "The Reception of Chinese Buddhist Sculpture in the West" (1998) 38 Art Bulletin of Victoria 7.

[57] 2.5 m high, Important Cultural Property. Acquired in China in 1915 by the Norwegian collector Johann Munthe and sold to Baron Kawasaki in Kobe; see Gillman (n 48) 112–13, n 68.

major paintings in the Burlington House show, as they gifted the Amitabha. Tastes have changed in China during the last forty years and museums now have galleries dedicated to Buddhist sculpture.

In 1850, the zodiacal waterspouts at the Yuanmingyuan were valued differently to the way they are in Beijing today. Then, accessible only to those permitted within the palace grounds, they were likely perceived as no more than finely made decorative fittings, but the heads are now regarded as sculptures in themselves, are Class One cultural relics, and, importantly, are associated with the humiliation of China by Western powers during the second half of the nineteenth century, with the rat and rabbit exhibited in a prominently featured gallery at the National Museum of China, *The Road to Rejuvenation* (*Fuxing zhi lu*), where they symbolize the instrumental value of national self-determination.

IV. Heritage and Vulnerability

Calls for the return of valuable cultural things are sometimes accompanied by statements about the harm caused by their absence, as, for example, when Beijing's Cultural Heritage Bureau told state media that the 2009 Christie's Paris auction of the Yuanmingyuan rat and rabbit heads had "harmed the cultural rights and national feeling of the Chinese people."[58,59] In making the case that woundedness justifies collective rights to cultural things (the grounds for which I have questioned),[60] John Moustakas helpfully draws attention to the linkage between heritage and vulnerability, which I emphasize in the following passage with italics:

> The absence of works representing an "irreplaceable cultural heritage" is psychologically intolerable . . . [T]he toppling of Jerusalem's Wailing Wall would *wound* the spirit of world Jewry, Lord Elgin's removal of the Parthenon Marbles *injures* Greek groupness by having emasculated the greatest of all Greek art—the Parthenon. By destroying the Greeks' mana, the embodiment of their highest humanistic hopes and a measure of their

[58] This section formed part of a paper first read at the American Academy in Berlin in 2013, through the generosity of Marina Kellen French, and published in *Yichan* (*Heritage*, Nanjing UP 2019) vol 1, 3. I am grateful to Professor Wang Xiaokui of the Southern University of Science and Technology, Shenzhen, for permission to reproduce it here.

[59] Gillman (n 27) 239.

[60] Gillman (n 1) 190–93.

existence, Lord Elgin *harmed* Greek grouphood by irreparably diminishing an integral part of the celebration of "being Greek."[61]

In "Valuing," the first essay of Samuel Scheffler's *Equality and Tradition*, the author suggests that "valuing something makes one vulnerable to feelings and emotions of many different kinds," and that "value-dependent vulnerability is apt to be greatest when the things that one values are themselves things that can fare well or poorly, can be in good and bad condition, or can flourish or be damaged or destroyed."[62] Thus, valuing any particular thing, person, or phenomenon, involves a susceptibility to experience a range of context-dependent emotions regarding it. That certainly seems right for works of art, architecture, sites, cities, etc., and for the cultural practices that sustain them. A key element of value, then, would be the emotional vulnerability to which we expose ourselves when we engage in the act of valuing something that is subject to loss or decay, or to success or failure. With respect to our present concerns about cultural property, is Scheffler's observation about the relationship between emotion and value banal, even if philosophically interesting? Why would that be the case? It would be banal if, for example, knowing the passion and heat generated by debate over the Elgin marbles, we then merely observe that debates about cultural properties generate emotion. But Scheffler clearly is saying something different here, about the significant correlation between the degree to which we value something and the degree to which we feel vulnerable to losing it in some way. To illustrate this, we can propose that even if the Parthenon had not been damaged under the Ottomans, and even if elements of the sculpture had not been removed to England and Germany, those who value early Greek temples—whether Greek or not—would still be emotionally vulnerable to damage to the temple structure, or to the separation of its elements.

What makes Scheffler's proposition not banal, at least to me, is that value and vulnerability are linked not only after the fact of loss, decay, and destruction, but before it. The vulnerability of something we value also makes us vulnerable. Look for example at a situation where a massive Tiffany mosaic designed by Maxfield Parrish was threatened with removal from the Curtis Publishing Center in Philadelphia to a casino in Las Vegas owned by the American entrepreneur Steve Wynn. *The Dream Garden* had gone mostly

[61] Moustakas (n 23) 1195–96, emphasis added.

[62] Samuel Scheffler, *Equality and Tradition: Questions of Value in Moral and Political Theory* (OUP 2010) 15–40.

unnoticed for decades, but when the proposed sale was announced in 1998, there was a considerable outcry in the local press, one artist declaring that it was as much part of Philadelphia's cultural history as the Sistine Chapel frescoes are of Rome's.[63] Hence, one measure of how much we value a particular cultural object is the degree to which it makes us feel emotionally vulnerable, whether we were previously aware of it or not.

Should we maintain awareness of our vulnerability with respect to an object or person? It is certainly not a bad thing—if it protects against the loss, decay, or damage to an object or to a human relationship. On how many million occasions has a partner within a long-term relationship said to the other, "You take me for granted"? That all-too-common remark reminds us that one way by which we maintain the value of our friendships is to protect them against becoming withered. Indeed, recognizing the value of another person to us, and our vulnerability to the loss of that relationship in our lives, implies that both of us shall benefit by not taking the other for granted. That is true for the conservation and maintenance of objects, and of buildings. The entire conservation field has become much more geared to preventative work, as distinct from just remedial treatment. It is surely a fact that unless we live in an earthquake zone, or a war zone, most of us do not walk around constantly worrying about potential damage, decay, and loss to buildings or objects.

One can see why cosmopolitan writers might take a hard line on the apparent carelessness of national or regional caretakers who allow cultural property to accumulate in poorly conditioned museum stores. Such stewards may well value those things, and they may care *about* them, but they cannot, for various economic reasons, care *for* them. This leads to another of Scheffler's thoughts, that the terms "valuing" and "caring," while closely related, are not interchangeable. It seems more natural, he writes, to say that one values one's friend's sense of humor than to say one cares about it.[64] To value something is to feel that it is worthy or valuable, whether instrumentally or intrinsically. So the question I ask myself is, how does proposing this integral linkage between value and emotional vulnerability deepen our understanding of cultural things, or affect policy toward them? What does acknowledgment of a link between value and emotional vulnerability add to an otherwise singular focus on value?

[63] Gillman (n 1) 160.
[64] Scheffler (n 63) 25.

It offers a believable explanation for the passions with which we associate debates over cultural property, and especially the moral claims to such things as the Parthenon sculptures or the bust of Nefertiti in the Neues Museum, Berlin. If, as Scheffler argues, value and emotional vulnerability are linked then, in the case of works to which people attach very high value, emotional vulnerability would be correspondingly high. Moustakas says this when he talks about the injury to Greek "groupness." If the Wailing Wall were toppled, many Jews would be horrified and some traumatized. Would it matter by what it was toppled? Supposed it was toppled not during a war, like the Mostar bridge, or by a terrorist act, but by an earthquake. Then some orthodox Jews would likely imagine this to be an act of retribution or warning by God. They might be deeply wounded not just because of the loss of the surviving temple wall, but also because of the belief that this was an expression of divine anger directed toward them. Others would be deeply saddened, although not angry in the way they would be if it had a human cause. Moustakas implies that he is concerned not so much by divine intervention, or natural disaster, but by human agency. This is illustrated by the tragedy of 9/11, which made the entire United States profoundly angry, and many others in the world; the anger was especially caused by the loss of three thousand lives, and to a lesser degree by the attack on a highly prominent symbol of New York's commercial centrality.

Particular people will be emotionally wounded by the loss of the Wailing Wall and the Statue of Liberty, whether caused by natural or human agency, but angry only if this loss is caused by other people, either willfully or by negligence. We should separate woundedness from anger. What is common in both circumstances—natural disaster or human agency—is emotional vulnerability, a manifestation of the valuing of those structures. The emotional tenor of the debate about cultural property is both explained *and* excused. Indeed, people are properly excused in expressing deep hurt or anger over cultural objects because of this link between emotional vulnerability and value. I do not believe that it is banal to point this out, since Merryman complained about the intensity of nationalist debate. And while we all realize that nationalism and patriotism can be artificially created and manipulated, there are real reasons behind the passions in this arena, reasons generated by the link between value and emotion. No evidence tells us that something we value intrinsically will make us more emotionally vulnerable than something we value instrumentally. The point I want to make is that emotional vulnerability, a crucial aspect of value, becomes a ground for moral claims to cultural property. Decolonization moves within museums have focused particularly on objects taken in the nineteenth century, during periods of colonial rule and military occupation, where legal claims to good title conflict with such moral claims. Scheffler's observations on the relationship between value and emotion seems to be useful here and should not be dismissed lightly.

In concluding this section, let me return to the distinction made before between valuing and caring. Basic values themselves are not vulnerable, as individual objects, sites, and practices can be, yet they are worthy of care, not least in the field of war where carelessness about the values of knowledge and aesthetic experience can have irrevocable consequences. As Appiah affirms:

> Values aren't a birthright: you need to keep caring about them . . . The values that European humanists like to espouse belong as much to an African or an Asian who takes them up with enthusiasm as to a European . . . They are ours only if we care about them. A culture of liberty, tolerance, and rational inquiry: that *would* be a good idea. But these values represent choices to make, not tracks laid down by a Western destiny.[65]

V. Responsibility Toward Values and the Avoidance of Destruction

Looting, as at the Yuanmingyuan, and ideological iconoclasm are rooted differently. Iconoclasm calls for the destruction of things of value that represent conflicting beliefs, thereby amplifying a particular ideological position. In the cases of Islam and Judaism, foundational worldviews are challenged by religious reverence for sculptures of deities.[66] Thus the two monumental Buddhas at Bamiyan, Afghanistan, blown up by the Taliban in 2001, should long have been problematic for local residents since Central Asia has been Muslim for a millennium. David Joselit argues that the Taliban and ISIS have "skillfully spectacularized" such acts through videos designed to attract maximum outrage in the West and solidarity among sympathetic partisans. He quotes Jamal Elias, an historian of Islamic culture, who understands them as re-enactments of prophetic tradition, conceived to contrast the destruction

[65] Appiah (n 6) 211.

[66] Yet orthodox practitioners of both religions fully embrace things of aesthetic value in the literary arts, and in the visual arts through excellent design and calligraphy.

of material images with the loss of human life in Middle Eastern and Central Asian wars.[67]

Because of their remarkable ambition the Buddhas were unmissable: the taller figure, datable to the early seventh century, was almost ten times the height of its Chinese near contemporary, the Amitabha at the British Museum.[68] As much as residents of the Valley may have deplored the destruction of these preeminent landmark figures, the Buddhas could possess no religious value for them. The sculptures must, however, have contributed to their understanding of the role that Bamiyan played as a place of pilgrimage and commerce on the Silk Route, and the empty niches continue to contribute as a locus of memory. For those living in the vicinity of the Valley, the Buddhas therefore represented the value of knowledge—with respect to the history of their region, reaching far back in time when different social and political forces operated—and likely also the value of sociability, since the figures were a large and familiar part of the community's environment.[69] As survivors of a Buddhist past they were unique and their loss is deeply felt; no one can now engage with them aesthetically except through photographs.[70] There is a third set of stakeholders here, engaged with the value of religion. When discussions take place, as they have, about whether to reconstruct or restore the Buddhas within the empty niches at Bamiyan,

[67] David Joselit, *Heritage and Debt: Art in Globalization* (MIT Press 2020) 195–96.

[68] Prior to their destruction they were the second and third largest Buddhist sculptures in the world. The larger figure may have represented Maitreya Buddha; see Kosaku Maeda, "Mural Paintings along the Road" in Kazuya Yamauchi, Yoko Taniguchi, and Tomoko Uno (eds), *Mural Paintings of the Silk Road: Cultural Exchanges between East and West* (Archetype Publications 2006) 23–25. The upper faces were long missing, but in their original form were probably gilt copper hammered over carved wooden blocks that rested on the stone chins, see Deborah Klimburg-Salter, *The Kingdom of Bāmiyān: Buddhist Art and Culture of the Hindu Kush* (Instituto Universitario Orientale and Instituto Italiano per il Medio ed Estremo Orienta 1989) 87–92. The smaller, earlier Buddha dates from the mid-to-late sixth century, see Catharina Blänsdorf, Marie-Josée Nadeau, Pieter M Grootes, Matthias Hüls, Stephanie Pfeffer, and Laura Thiemann, "Dating of the Buddha Statues–AMS 14C Dating of Organic Materials" in ICOMOS (ed), *The Giant Buddhas of Bamiyan: Safeguarding the Remains* (Hendrik Babler Verlag 2009) 231–36. For information about the painted surfaces see Anna Lluveras-Tenorio, Roberto Vinciguerra, Eugenio Galano, Catharina Blänsdorf, Erwin Emmerling, Maria Perla Colombini, and Leila Birolo, "GC/MS and Proteomics to Unravel the painting history of the lost Giant Buddhas of Bāmiyān (Afghanistan)" <www.doi.org/10.1371/journal.pone.0172990> accessed 28 June 2020.

[69] A thirteenth-century Persian geography text describes "something marvelous" at Bamiyan, see Minoru Inaba, "The Narratives on the Bāmiyān Buddhist Remains in the Islamic Period" in Blain Auer and Ingo Strauch (eds), *Encountering Buddhism and Islam in Premodern Central and South Asia* (de Gruyter 2019) 75–96.

[70] Seven hundred and fifty Buddhist cave temples survive at Bamiyan, about fifty of which still have sections of early murals, see Yoko Taniguchi, "Issues of Conservation for the Bamiyan Buddhist Mural Paintings" in Yamauchi, Taniguchi, and Uno (n 69) 144–45.

is it not appropriate that the millions of practicing Buddhists in Asia should have a voice, perhaps through the World Buddhist Sangha Council?[71]

But how to appeal to potential iconoclasts who are acting rationally within the framework of their particular ideologies? How are ideologically reasonable arguments for iconoclastic action effectively to be countered, aside from military, political, or economic threat? Clearly an appeal to the value of religion will not work, since iconoclasm reasons that opposing ideologies are enshrined within vulnerable objects and sites, and to attack them pushes back on the enemy. To destroy a valuable part is to attack the whole, as ISIL intuited. One must remain hopeful that within potentially iconoclastic groups, religious and political, there will in fact be influential individuals to whom other values matter.

There are also gray zones between war and peace, which may involve states' violence toward their own citizens, ethnic cleansing, and political revolutions.[72] Early in the Chinese Cultural Revolution, on August 18 1966, a group of Red Guards made clear their intention to enter the Palace Museum the following day, having been inflamed by Mao Zedong and Lin Biao in Tian'anmen Square. At Zhou Enlai's order the Palace gates were sealed and a unit of the Beijing Garrison Command dispatched to mount guard. On August 19, in the face of demands and shouts for eradication of the "four olds," the doors stayed locked, as they would for the next five years.[73] If Zhou's intention was clear—to use his power as Premier to save the early Ming dynasty site and its imperial collections—what might have been his motives for doing what he did that day? Another official might have let everything go: on ideological grounds that art created under feudal conditions did not deserve to be saved, and on pragmatic grounds that for a decade Mao had led the charge against conservatism (and conservation).[74] At a moment in Beijing when it was felt that history was turning and that "old ideas, cultures, customs and habits" had to be debunked, this would have been a rational position to take. I suspect that what drove Zhou to act was an urgent instrumental need to preserve the uniquely important site from a fate not dissimilar to the

71 James Janowski argues for their restoration, given how much of the original material survives, "Bringing Back Bamiyan's Buddhas" (2011) 28 (1) Journal of Applied Philosophy 44.

72 For example, during Kristallnacht, a year prior to the outbreak of World War II, the Gestapo focused on the burning of German synagogues.

73 Xie Yinming and Qu Wanlin, "'Wenhua da geming' zhong shei hubao le gugong" (19 January 2007) Zhongguo gongchandang xinwen 3.

74 Wang Jun, *Beijing Record: A Physical and Political History of Planning Modern Beijing* (World Scientific 2011) 332–36.

Yuanmingyuan, and surely also a massive obligation to the values of history (knowledge) and aesthetic experience which, as much as anywhere on the planet, were embedded within the Palace and its collections. Zhou likewise issued an order in December 1968 that the Beijing Observatory, re-equipped by the Jesuit Ferdinand Verbiest in the 1670s, should similarly be protected.[75] Despite his obvious allegiance toward revolution, he was profoundly disturbed by the new level of chaos that Mao unleashed in 1966 and acted to protect not only sites but also key members of China's revolutionary elite.[76]

Ronald Dworkin believed that we should "count ourselves as trustees for protecting the richness of our culture," which captures the sense of responsibility I imagine Zhou Enlai felt that day at the Palace Museum.[77] When iconoclastic acts are threatened we must hope that, in the spirit of Zhou, individuals in positions of power will act, because by caring about values (e.g., of knowledge, aesthetic experience, and religion) cultural sites and objects might be preserved. From a liberal pluralist perspective, perhaps the last hope against the destruction of culture by ideological iconoclasts is that there are those among them willing at least to protect the value of historical knowledge.

During times of peace, private property rights can often conflict with public interest in the built environment, the past seeming to oppose progress.[78] During the second half of the twentieth century, numerous valuable civic structures were taken down, one infamous example being the Beaux-Arts headhouse above New York's Pennsylvania Station railroad tracks, demolished in 1963 to make way for the Madison Square Garden entertainment and sports complex. Another such removal occurred in Beijing during the early years of the People's Republic: twin brick reliquary pagodas built for the Linji Chan Buddhist masters Haiyun Yinjian (1203–57) and his disciple Ke'an, abbots of the Daqingshou temple. Standing just to the west of the Forbidden City, these Yuan dynasty structures were a feature of Beijing's skyline for seven centuries until it was decided that the western expansion of Chang'an Avenue trumped their existence. The situation was a familiar one, of modernization in tension with preservation. In 1950, Liang Sicheng,

[75] ibid 402.

[76] Gao Wenqian, *Zhou Enlai: The Last Perfect Revolutionary* (Peter Rand and Lawrence Sullivan trs, Public Affairs 2008) 134 ff.

[77] Ronald Dworkin, "Can a Liberal State Support Art?" in *A Matter of Principle* (Harvard UP 1985) 229.

[78] On codes that cover the preservation of buildings and historic sites, ranging from the very stringent to the libertarian, see Gillman (n 1) 155–65.

then Vice-Director of the Beijing City Planning Commission as well as the country's leading architectural historian, wrote to Zhou Enlai arguing that the center of government should be moved westward, preserving the palace and its precincts. Liang also vehemently opposed plans to dismantle Beijing's inner and outer walls in order to improve the city's traffic flow and facilitate construction of the new metro system. His widow recalled him saying this about the pagodas, "In advocating protection of this ancient city, I definitely did not mean that nothing in it must be changed. But why must the two towers standing side by side in Twin Pagoda Qingshou Temple on West Chang'an Avenue be torn down . . . Why not preserve the towers and turn the area into a small park?" Liang's arguments were to no avail, and the pagodas were first excavated and then demolished in 1954, as were the city walls themselves over the next decade and a half.[79] The site is now under Chang'an Avenue itself, and the Beijing Book Building sits over the original temple precinct. Chinese temples have regularly been rebuilt, carrying forward the spirit of vulnerable originals, so perhaps replicas of the Twin Pagodas might be built? But for what purpose, other than "pastness"?[80]

The intention of this chapter has been to focus on underlying reasons why people care about what we call heritage—cultural practices, objects, buildings, and historical sites. These reasons are present at times of war and in peacetime. Over the centuries, innumerable places that would now be designated as heritage sites have been adapted, diminished or destroyed, often for rational reasons such as the need to modernize. Joseph Raz argues that in destroying works of art we are "blind to one of the values which gives life a meaning."[81] We should strive to preserve historical sites and works of art, because through them we engage with values—the values of aesthetic

[79] The last remaining temple buildings were also demolished in 1954, along with the pagodas, see Jun (n 75) 154, 252, 255. Daqingshousi was built in the early 1160s as the first imperial Chan Buddhist temple at the Jin dynasty capital, located just north of the city walls, see Derek Gillman, "The imperial luohans of Zhongdu and the reassertion of Chan (Zen) Buddhist influence in north China" (2013–14) 78 Transactions of the Oriental Ceramic Society 41. Unlike the Jin city itself (razed by the Mongols), Daqingshousi was incorporated in the newly constructed Yuan dynasty city, and the twin pagodas, nine and seven stories high, were erected within the temple's grounds. A painted stone memorial sculpture of Haiyun excavated prior to demolition is displayed at the Capital Museum, not far from the site.

[80] If constructed with attention to thirteenth- century architectural style they could convey to tourists the sense of "pastness" that Cornelius Holtorf regards as a desideratum of historicizing rebuilding projects, as undertaken, for example, in Dresden's Neumarkt, razed during WWII, see Cornelius Holtorf, "Perceiving the Past: From Age Value to Pastness" (2017) 24 (4) International Journal of Cultural Property 497.

[81] Joseph Raz, *The Morality of Freedom* (Clarendon Press 1986) 212–13.

experience, knowledge, and religion among them. Since many battles are fought on territory unfamiliar to one side, commanders should *at the least* provide appropriate information to their troops about all notable sites and objects of value in the field, drawing on the expertise of regional museums and antiquities authorities wherever possible.

2

The "Cultural Turn" and the Reconstruction of Heritage

Helen Frowe and Derek Matravers

I. Introduction

What should happen to cultural property that has been damaged or destroyed in war? Should it be preserved as monument to war, removed to make way for new constructions, or rebuilt as it was prior to the damage? The devastation of cultural property in areas of armed conflict, not least in the Middle East, has brought these questions to the forefront of the international cultural property protection agenda. This chapter addresses some of the neglected considerations when deciding whether cultural property should be left in its damaged state or restored to its original state before the damage was inflicted.[1] The argument consists of three parts. First, we review the current debate with respect to how decisions with respect to cultural property should be made, revealing at least two different approaches. Second, we argue that the answers reached according to each approach will be likely to conflict with one another. Third, we explore a possible defense for one of these answers.

II. Approaches to Heritage Conservation

Until recently, heritage conservation was governed by what we call *the object-centered stance*—an approach that focuses on the integrity of the object. Such a stance aims to preserve two different values. The first, which we call *age*

[1] The literature in this area distinguishes between restoration and reconstruction. See, for example, *The Burra Charter* (first published 1979, Australian ICOMOS 2013) 1.7 and 1.8 <https://australia.icomos.org/wp-content/uploads/The-Burra-Charter-2013-Adopted-31.10.2013.pdf> accessed 25 August 2020. The arguments in this chapter apply to both; hence we will not distinguish between the terms.

Helen Frowe and Derek Matravers, *The "Cultural Turn" and the Reconstruction of Heritage* In: *The Preservation of Art and Culture in Times of War*. Edited by: Claire Finkelstein, Derek Gillman, and Frederik Rosén, Oxford University Press.
 DOI: 10.1093/oso/9780197610565.003.0003

value, in accordance with the writings of Austrian art historian Alois Riegl, is the value grounded in the authentic marks of the object's age.[2] Protecting age value rules out removing or repairing such marks as well as taking steps to protect the object from decay. If the object is protected, the marks will manifest an age younger than the object, thus rendering the marks inauthentic. The second, which, following Riegl, we call *historical value*, involves preserving the maximum informational value of an object for future study. Preserving historical value can conflict with preserving age value since the former is ensured only by stopping the object's decay which, in turn, undermines its value as a source of information.

The locus of value in the object-centered stance is the object itself—that is, the value is not to be construed as indexed to any particular group. This does not imply neglecting provenance or sidelining the rich particularities of the object's origins; facts of this sort will contribute to the object's historical value. It means, rather, that the value of the object is, to quote the preamble to the 1954 Hague Convention, part of "the cultural heritage of all mankind."[3] That is, the object-centered stance dovetails neatly with the "cosmopolitan" approach to heritage conservation—as discussed by Derek Gillman in his contribution to this volume. As Gillman says, within the cosmopolitan approach museums have evolved to be the custodians of such values. As the conservation of objects can involve preserving one value at the expense of another, difficult decisions need to be made. The object-centered stance brought about the rise of "conservators," trained professionals best equipped to ensure the integrity of the object.[4]

Over the past four decades or so, there has been a marked shift away from this object-centered stance to what we call the *cultural stance*: the view that, in thinking about conservation, the cultural meaning of objects is more relevant than their physical integrity. The reasons for this shift are both political in nature and a reaction to the perceived absence of good philosophical foundations for the object-centered stance. We make no comment on the cogency of these reasons—for that, readers are referred to Gillman's

[2] See Alois Riegl, "The Modern Cult of Monuments: Its Essence and Development" in Nicholas Stanley-Price, M. Kirby Talley Jr, and Alessandra Melucco Vaccaro (eds), *Historical and Philosophical Issues in Conservation and Development* (The Getty Conservation Institute 2016).

[3] *The 1954 Hague Convention or the Protection of Cultural Property in the Event of Armed Conflict* (UNESCO 1954) <http://www.unesco.org/new/en/culture/themes/armed-conflict-and-heritage/convention-and-protocols/1954-hague-convention/ accessed 25 August 2020.

[4] For an overview, see Salvador Munoz-Vinas, *Contemporary Theory of Conservation* (Routledge 2005).

paper.[5] Instead, the aim of this chapter is to tease out the implications of this shift for debates regarding what should be done with damaged or destroyed heritage.

The shift to the cultural stance is understood, in part, as a heightened sensitivity to the perspectives of indigenous populations following the decline of colonialism. There is hostility to the practice of "encyclopaedic museums" acquiring pieces from poorer countries and removing them for display as part of their collections—usually in Europe or America. This has dovetailed with a skepticism about the very notion of non-relational value. It is thought to make no sense for an object to simply have value, independent of any valuer. Rather than the locus of value being the object, the value is construed as a two-place relation: the value of the object for someone or other. That is, if the object has value at all, that value is socially constructed. Given that this social construction occurs in some social realms (or cultures) rather than others, this view suggests that the object can be understood and possibly appreciated only in relation to those social realms. We can see this in the shift from a focus on objects (usually described as "monuments") in the early Charters and Conventions to the kind of stance taken in the preamble to the 1970 Convention on the Means of Prohibiting and Preventing the Illicit Import, Export and Transfer of Ownership of Cultural Property: "[C]ultural property constitutes one of the basic elements of civilization and national culture, and that its true value can be appreciated only in relation to the fullest possible information regarding its origin, history and traditional setting."[6]

The view that the value of heritage is socially constructed and, therefore, can be understood only from the point of view of "its origin, history, and traditional setting" paints a very different picture of museums' responsibilities. Rather than being repositories of objects whose value is given and of concern to all humanity, certain cultures will bear an epistemological and value relation to those objects not borne by other cultures. Insomuch as museums are the stewards of those objects and concerned with their interpretation and value, a prima facie case is established for those cultures having a special

[5] The arguments are considered at greater length in Derek Gillman, *The Idea of Cultural Heritage* (CUP 2010). See also the papers in Alison Richmond and Alison Bracker (eds), *Conservation: Principles, Dilemmas, and Uncomfortable Truths* (Routledge 2011).

[6] *Convention on the Means of Prohibiting and Preventing the Illicit Import, Export and Transfer of Ownership of Cultural Property* (UNESCO 1970) <http://portal.unesco.org/en/ev.php-URL_ID=13039&URL_DO=DO_TOPIC&URL_SECTION=201.html> accessed 25 August 2020. Thanks to Frederik Rosén for pressing us to clarify this paragraph.

interest in objects to which they stand in that relation. Consequently, certain cultures claim the right to being stakeholders in those objects.

The cultural stance raises problems to be solved in both theory and practice. First, there is the issue of identifying which, if any, cultural group is a potential stakeholder for a particular object. The obvious candidate is the originator culture (the culture that created the object) or, failing that, the successor to the originator culture. The answer to this might be obvious when the originator culture is still flourishing; however, identifying a successor culture can be more problematic.[7] As an example, Nigeria claims the surviving works of art from the Nok culture as part of its national patrimony. The basis for this claim is that the land occupied by the Nok, whose culture flourished from 1500 BCE to 500 CE, is located in modern Nigeria. That, however, is not necessarily a reasonable basis for identifying modern Nigeria as the "successor culture."[8] Even if the right groups are identified, the question remains as to whether this is sufficient for being a stakeholder—that is, what rights over an object are conferred by having a special cultural interest in it? James Young has argued for a "cultural significance principle": that "the basis of a culture's claim on cultural property can simply be the great value that some property has for members of that culture."[9] Important though these problems are, solutions to them are beyond the scope of this chapter.

III. Implications of the Cultural Turn

The shift from the object-centered stance to the cultural stance within heritage and conservation studies has had enormous implications for decisions regarding cultural property that has been damaged or destroyed during conflict. This can be seen by a cursory examination of several key conservation documents on the treatment of buildings and sites. The Venice Charter, an

[7] A further complication, which we will ignore here, is the view that for most significant cultural property the successor culture is all mankind, which effectively collapses the distinction between the object-centered stance and the cultural stance. See James Cuno, Who Owns Antiquity?: Museums and the Battle ver Our Ancient Heritage (Princeton UP 2008).

[8] "We don't know whether Nok sculptures were commissioned by kings or commoners; we don't know whether the people who paid for them thought of them as belonging to the kingdom, to a man, to a lineage, to the gods. One thing we know for sure, however, is that they didn't make them for Nigeria." Kwame Anthony Appiah, *Cosmopolitanism: Ethics in a World of Strangers* (Penguin 2007) 119.

[9] James O. Young, *Cultural Appropriation and the Arts* (Blackwell 2008) 88. For a more skeptical view, see Gillman (n 5) 188–95.

influential document published in 1964 by the International Council on Monuments and Sites (ICOMOS), reflects the object-centered stance, focusing on preserving the epistemological value of the physical material: "the intention in conserving and restoring monuments is to safeguard them no less as works of art than as historical evidence."[10] The Burra Charter, which has grown in significance since its publication in 1979, changes the focus to the relation between the heritage and relevant cultural groups. The following excerpt is indicative of the general tenor of the Charter.

> Groups and individuals with *associations* with the *place* as well as those involved in its management should be provided with opportunities to contribute to and participate in identifying and understanding the *cultural significance* of the place. Where appropriate they should also have opportunities to participate in its conservation and management.[11]

The approach manifest in the Burra Charter has become the orthodox mainstream view, which is aptly demonstrated by recent reactions to one of the most dramatic assaults on cultural heritage—the destruction of parts of Palmyra by ISIS. Although, as we write, the war in Syria is ongoing, some have turned their minds to the question of what should be done about the damage wreaked by ISIS once hostilities have ceased. Adopting the cultural stance, we would expect to look to "groups and individuals with associations with the place" to find the stakeholders who will decide upon a course of action. Current writing on this issue argues for the establishment of procedures to allow "all stakeholders to participate freely and openly" and identifies the key stakeholders as "the Syrians—who were born in, and lived, and participated in constructing Palmyra's fame throughout history."[12]

Although the cultural stance clearly has a bearing on decisions pertaining to damaged or destroyed heritage, it arguably falls short of determining the correct course of action. This is because the cultural stance aims to identify

[10] *International Charter for the Conservation and Restoration of Monuments and Sites (The Venice Charter)* (ICOMOS 1964) 3 <https://www.icomos.org/charters/venice_e.pdf> accessed 25 August 2020.

[11] *The Burra Charter* (first published 1979, Australian ICOMOS 2013) 26.3 <https://australia.icomos.org/wp-content/uploads/The-Burra-Charter-2013-Adopted-31.10.2013.pdf> accessed 25 August 2020. By "place" is meant "elements, objects, spaces and views" (1.1).

[12] Nour A. Munawar, "Reconstructing Cultural Heritage in Conflict Zones: Should Palmyra Be Rebuilt?" (2017) EX NOVO: Journal of Archaeology 2: 33–48. See also Elly Harrowell, "Looking for the Future in the Rubble of Palmyra: Destruction, Reconstruction, and Identity" (2016) Geoforum 69: 81–83.

who it is that should take the decision—namely, those to whom the culture is appropriately tied. It does not have an obvious bearing on *which decision those stakeholders should take*. This apparent lack of guidance in the cultural stance helps explain the current confusion surrounding whether or not to reconstruct damaged heritage sites and artifacts.

The confusion arose from the approach taken by UNESCO's World Heritage Committee (WHC)—the body charged with overseeing decisions concerning heritage—appearing to contradict the Burra Charter recommendations. The Operational Guidelines for the WHC are unpinned by an adherence to the object-centered stance:

> In relation to authenticity, the reconstruction of archaeological remains or historic buildings or districts is justifiable only in exceptional circumstances. Reconstruction is acceptable only on the basis of complete and detailed documentation and to no extent on conjecture.[13]

Reconstruction sits uneasily with the object-centered stance with respect to both age value and historical value. It obscures the age value by removing the appearance of the object's age. Furthermore, it obscures the object as a source of knowledge by making the object appear, superficially at least, as what it is not. With that being said, when decision-making is guided by the cultural stance and the stakeholders are consulted they sometimes favor reconstruction.[14] Thus, despite their own guidelines, there has been and continues to be WHC support for significant reconstruction projects. Such confusion has led to accusations of "ad hoc decision-making by the WHC," along with a plea for "new guidance."[15]

[13] <https://whc.unesco.org/en/guidelines/> accessed 20 August 2020. Quoted in Nicholas Stanley-Price, "The Reconstruction of Ruins: Principles and Practice" in Alison Richmond and Alison Bracker (eds), *Conservation: Principles, Dilemmas, and Uncomfortable Truths* (Routledge 2011) 33.

[14] In "Syrian and Iraqi Opinion on Protecting, Promoting, and Reconstructing Heritage after the Islamic State" in this volume, Benjamin Isakhan and James Barry provide an excellent example of the rich variety of views a properly conducted stakeholder consultation will reveal—including nuanced views about the desirability of reconstruction. See also Eva von Engelberg-Dockal and Hans Rudolf Meier, "Traditional Rebuilding in Germany after the Second World War" in John Bold, Peter Larkham, and Robert Pickard (eds), *Authentic Reconstruction: Authenticity, Architecture and the Build Environment* (Bloomsbury 2017). This collection also contains case studies of reconstruction projects supported by the WHC.

[15] Christina Cameron, "Reconstruction: Changing Attitudes" (*The UNESCO Courier*, 2017) <https://en.unesco.org/courier/july-september-2017/reconstruction-changing-attitudes> accessed 31 March 2018.

The fact that the cultural stance seems to identify only who should make the decision, rather than which decision should be made might make these conflicting recommendations look to be a clash between expert opinion opposed to reconstruction and unreasoned populism in favor of something "faked" but familiar. The familiar, however, might be a perfectly reasonable option. For example, there are occasions when the view of the stakeholders in favor of reconstruction has had an instrumental basis, such as the effects of income and tourism on the postwar economy. We shall now argue that there is at least one argument in favor of restoration that does not have such an overtly instrumental basis. Contrary to appearances, the cultural stance is not merely a means of deciding who should make the decision as to what happens to damaged or destroyed heritage, but also provides some guidance regarding which decision should be made.

IV. Two Views Within the Cultural Stance

The stakeholders for some piece of cultural property can stand in at least two different kinds of relation to that property. The first kind of relation holds when there is some practice within the stakeholder culture regarding how the object should be treated; that is, the justification for treating the object in a particular way only makes sense as a justification from the standpoint of that culture. The cultural stance holds that, all things being equal, this justification should be respected.[16] Call this the *practice-based view.*

The following example illustrates this view. The National Museum of the American Indian holds that it will advance its mission "in consultation, collaboration, and co-operation with Native peoples."[17] The museum has a collection of pots produced in the past by the Zuni people. In accordance with its mission, the museum decided to return the pots to the Zuni Pueblo on long-term loan. The project was planned and managed along with representatives of the Zuni, in particular Eileen Yatsattie, "a well-known and respected traditional potter."[18] If the museum had embraced the object-centered

[16] The "all things being equal" clause is itself difficult to cash out. It is designed to allow respect for culturally specific justifications to be overridden when, for example, those justifications are immoral (whatever that might mean in the culturally neutral sense that is required for the clause to work).

[17] Marion A. Kaminitz, W. Richard West Jr, Jim Enote, Curtis Quam, and Eileen Yatasattie, "Conservation, Access and Use in a Museum of Living Cultures" in Alison Richmond and Alison Bracker (eds), *Conservation: Principles, Dilemmas, and Uncomfortable Truths* (Routledge 2011) 198.

[18] ibid 201.

stance, various safeguards would have been put in place to protect the physical integrity of the object, including encasing the pots in plastic bags during transport. This safeguard, however, ran counter to the treatment advocated by the stakeholder culture; Yatsattie requested that the pots not be put in bags because "the pottery is considered to be living ancestors of the Zuni."[19] In this instance, there is a certain cultural practice (regarding the pots as living ancestors) that provides a justification for not transporting them in plastic bags (it would suffocate the ancestors). We can assume this is not the museum's justification for not transporting the pots in plastic bags; rather, its justification is that the stakeholder culture has this justification and that the culture's justification should be respected.

When the stakeholder culture stands in this kind of relation to cultural property, identifying the stakeholders may reveal a cultural practice that will dictate how the property should be treated. In the case of museum artifacts, this may result in a decision to reconstruct. For example, a New Zealand museum has in its collection a Maori eel trap that had fallen into a state of disrepair. The initial reaction of the museum, taking an object-centered stance, was to place the net in long-term storage. This struck the appropriate balance between preserving the object's age value and maximizing its epistemological value for future researchers. The relevant stakeholder group, however, identified a cultural practice which resulted in the decision being changed.

> Boxed storage was considered inappropriate for an object that is viewed as *taonga*, objects, places or activities to which Maori attribute qualities of power, fear and ancestral authority and this led to a new conservation proposal. The museum's Maori Advisory Committee (MAC) stated a preference for "repair and display in a manner that recognised its cultural value [to representatives of the originator culture]." This meant that the "damaged appearance of the eel net was clearly not fitting." This led to the implementation of an interventive treatment. The net was surface-cleaned and humidified in order to make it flexible enough to re-align the misshapen mesh; tears and breaks in the mesh were closed and secured with Japanese paper and "conservation grade" adhesive. In-fills, made by a Maori weaver in the same knotting technique but in "conservation grade" materials, were adhered to fill remaining voids in the mesh.[20]

[19] ibid 203.
[20] Dinah Eastop, "The Cultural Dynamics of Conservation Principles and Reported Practice" in Alison Richmond and Alison Bracker (eds), *Conservation: Principles, Dilemmas, and Uncomfortable*

The Maori cultural practice justified the view that the net should be reconstructed so as to exhibit a "sound, cared-for, and valued appearance."[21] In this case, identifying the stakeholder gave access to a set of reasons which led to the decision to reconstruct. The aforementioned examples are of museum artifacts, although there are cases where an existing cultural practice dictates what should happen to buildings and complexes. Consider, for example, the Ise shrine, an important Shinto shrine in Japan. The cultural practice of the stakeholder culture is to destroy and rebuild significant parts of the shrine every twenty years, effectively settling any question that might arise concerning the appropriateness of reconstruction.[22]

Thus far, we have focused on the first kind of relation between a culture and the relevant cultural property in which a practice within the stakeholder culture dictates how the object should be treated. The second kind of relation exists when there is no culturally specific practice to justify a particular course of action. The examples that concern us—such as the damage to Palmyra by ISIS—are more usually of this sort. In this case, identifying the stakeholders seems to be only a way of allocating responsibility for making the decision, not determining the correct decision. As we will argue, even in cases of this second sort, there is a link between the status of being a stakeholder and the grounds for making one decision rather than another. The argument will have three components. Firstly, we will argue if a group is unjustly harmed by the damage to or destruction of its cultural heritage, then it constitutes an injustice to that group; secondly, that the correct response to such an injustice is some form of compensation; and finally, that the structure of compensation provides a basis for arguing in favor of reconstruction. Call this the *injustice-based view*.[23]

Truths (Routledge 2011) 156. The original quotations are from C Smith and H Winkelbauer, "Conservation of a Maori Eel Trap: Practical and Ethical Issues" in D Saunders, JH Townsend, and S Woodcock (eds), *The Object in Context: Crossing Conservation Boundaries* (London, IIC 2006).

[21] Eastop (n 20) 157.

[22] Byung-Chul Han, *Shanzhai: Deconstruction in Chinese* (MIT Press 2017) loc. 696.

[23] Both views can apply to the same stakeholders concerning the same piece of heritage if they have been unjustly harmed by its damage or destruction, and if there is a cultural practice as to how it should be treated.

V. Injustice

We focus here on cases in which one group (let us call them "the destroyers") intentionally and unjustifiably damages or destroys another group's (the stakeholders) highly valued items of cultural property. Our claims extend to all cases in which damage to or destruction of cultural property unjustly harms the stakeholders, assuming that a harm is unjust if the stakeholders have not forfeited their usual rights over the property in question.[24] For example, our claims apply to cases in which heritage is justifiably destroyed because its destruction is unavoidable in pursuit of some justified military objective. With that being said, our claims do not apply to cases in which intentionally destroying heritage is justified because, for example, the existence of the heritage itself constitutes or causes unjust harm to some group. In such cases, damaging or destroying it would not be an unjust harm. This may be the case with heritage that celebrates a past or present injustice to some group—say, a monument lauding a genocide or expressing admiration of slavery.[25] It is not sufficient to justify destroying the heritage on the sole basis that the destroyers *believe* the existence of the heritage constitutes or causes a harm to some group. If that were sufficient, then those who follow some all-encompassing conception of the good, which does not recognize the legitimacy of any competing conceptions, would not be committing an injustice in any act of iconoclasm motivated by their conception of the good.[26] Thus, we are presupposing certain basic liberal claims: there is a plurality of conceptions of the good and those who hold one conception of the good should not impose their values on those who do not hold that conception

[24] Our argument is focused on reparative justice, however there is a clear extension to issues of distributive justice. The global poor are unjustly harmed in that they are unable to maintain that which they value in their environment. We thank Cécile Fabre for raising this point. We also grant that, given that future members of a group are stakeholders in its cultural property, it is plausible that destruction of property usually constitutes an unjust harm even if current members of the group forfeit their rights to their property (for example, by using a cultural building as a weapons cache).

[25] For a defense of the view that Confederate statues ought to be removed because of the harm they cause, see (Timmerman Forthcoming). For exploration of other justifications for removing certain types of cultural heritage, see Joanna Burch-Brown, "Is It Wrong to Topple Statues and Rename Schools?" (2017) Journal of Political Theory and Philosophy; Helen Frowe, "The Duty to Remove Statues of Wrongdoers" (2019) Journal of Practical Ethics; Derek Gillman, "Preserving Valuable Objects and Sites, in Times of War and at Other Times" in this volume.

[26] The Taliban Edict on Images, issued shortly before the destruction of the Bamiyan Buddhas includes the following: "All statues and non-Islamic shrines located in different parts of the Islamic Emirate of Afghanistan must be destroyed. These statues have been and remain shrines of unbelievers and these unbelievers continue to worship and respect them. God almighty is the only real shrine and all fake idols should be destroyed." Quoted in Finbarr Barry Flood, "Between Cult and Culture: Bamiyan, Islamic Iconoclasm, and the Museum" (2002) The Art Bulletin 655.

of the good. The fact that some cultural heritage does not fit into the destroyers' conception of the good does not, in itself, justify their damaging or destroying it. Their doing so would constitute an injustice to the stakeholders for that cultural property.

Attending to the fact that this destruction is an act of injustice enables us to look at our problem in a new way. First, we can equate the extent to which a group is a stakeholder in the fate of the heritage with the extent to which that group was wronged by its damage or destruction. This seems to be the fundamental moral issue for which issues such as the population's geographical proximity merely stand proxy. It also advantageous that being a stakeholder comes in degrees; this is a more desirable consequence than some group being the sole determiners with no other group's views being considered.

VI. Compensation

The precise aims and nature of compensation are contested. We will assume here the plausible view that compensation ordinarily forms part of an appropriate response to injustice.[27] If the damage or destruction of cultural property is an injustice, then the stakeholders are owed compensation. This raises two questions: Who owes the compensation and what form should the compensation take? We should first distinguish between two types of costs a wrongdoer might be liable to bear in light of their wrongdoing. The first involves making good the harm that results from or constitutes the relevant injustice. The second involves bearing costs related to the injustice itself. For the purposes of this paper, we restrict ourselves to the former—the appropriate ways by which a harm could be made good.

It is widely accepted that those who wage unjust wars owe compensation and reparation to those who have been wronged by that war.[28] In the cases discussed here, however, this is often impossible to obtain from the relevant

[27] Luke Moffett, Dacia Viejo, and Robin Hickey have recently argued that international law in this area should shift its focus from preservation, prosecution, and punishment to reparations for loss and damage. In doing so, they have done valuable work in thinking through the role a regime of reparations could play (Luke Moffett, Dacia Viejo, and Robin Hickey, "Shifting the Paradigm on Cultural Property and Heritage in International Law and Armed Conflict: Time to Talk about Reparations?" (2019) International Journal of Heritage Studies). This paper, although more narrowly focused, is in sympathy with their view.

[28] Pietro Sullo and Julian Wyatt, "War Reparations" in *Max Plank Encyclopedia of International Law* (Max Plank Foundation for International Peace and the Rule of Law 2015). Benjamin Isakhan and James Barry discuss stakeholders' view of this question in their contribution to this volume.

group. (It is difficult, for example, to see how the stakeholders of Palmyra could claim compensation from ISIS, which is not a legal entity and lacks legal assets or resources from which compensation might be paid.) In such cases, there will be a variety of options for distributing the costs stemming from the injustice. One option is that the harm the stakeholders suffer is not made good. They are simply left as victims of an unjust harm with no compensation being offered. Alternatively, if the stakeholders have the resources, it may be in their best interest to make good the damage themselves (we will discuss what this amounts to below). For example, if the damaged or destroyed heritage are objects of national significance, restoring them may be part of an attempt to shore up a sense of national identity. Clearly, such a project is not morally or politically neutral and the assessment of its worth is, in part, a valuation of the establishment of that cultural identity.[29] If the stakeholders lack the resources and it is still thought important that the harm is made good, then we must move from an "offender pays" principle to an "ability to pay" principle.[30] Consequently, states or interstate institutions would be likely to bear the costs of making good the harm.[31]

The form the compensation should take allows us to close the gap between the practice-based view and the injustice-based view the stakeholders bear to cultural property. With the practice-based view, identifying the stakeholders necessitates an identification of cultural practices that determine what should be done with the damaged or destroyed cultural heritage. With the injustice-based view, identifying the stakeholders means identifying some unjustly harmed group that is entitled to compensation. The gap will be closed if the appropriate form of compensation implies some particular course of action with respect to the damaged or destroyed heritage.

In his classic paper on the topic, Robert Goodin argues that "compensation" (he uses the term to cover only what is owed to make good the harm) should take the form of the wronged party receiving "the equivalent" of what they had before. He then describes "two kinds of equivalence." The first is "means replacing compensation" in which "the idea is to provide people

[29] The concert by the Mariinsky Symphony Orchestra (from St Petersburg) in the Roman Amphitheatre, which followed the expulsion of ISIS from Palmyra—an event attended by Vladimir Putin (by video link), representatives from the Assad regime, and the Russian and Syrian military, has set the pattern for reconstruction efforts in that country.

[30] Simon Caney, "Climate Change and the Duties of the Advantaged" (2010) Critical Review of International Social and Political Philosophy.

[31] Clearly this is an instance where it is important to distinguish making good the harm from compensating for the wrong done. Only the perpetrators themselves owe the latter.

with equivalent means for pursuing the *same* ends" (he calls this "compensation1"). The second is "ends-displacing compensation" in which people are compensated "not by helping them pursue the same ends in some other ways, but rather by helping them to pursue some other ends in a way that leaves them subjectively as well off overall as they would have been had they not suffered the loss at all" (he calls this "compensation2").[32] This distinction is succinctly captured in the following example. I value my way of life that involves tending my garden. This is unjustly taken away from me. I can then be compensated either by my way of life tending my garden being restored (compensation1) or by being given another way of life, provided I would be as happy as I would have been had I not suffered the unjust loss (compensation2).

Goodin has two arguments for the superiority of compensation1 over compensation2.[33] Recall, the cases in question are those in which people did not choose to lose something they valued for the sake of compensation—they were forced to lose it. Hence, the issue is whether, having been so forced, the better compensation is being put back where they were or being put back in a situation they would have regarded, antecedently, as of equal value. Goodin points out two drawbacks with the latter. First, even if the loss is replaced by something as good, the replacement good might not fit in with existing plans and projects as well as the replaced.[34] The second is simply a matter of autonomy; people did not choose to be deprived of something even if what they get in return is something they regard as of equal value. What they would have chosen in some hypothetical situation is neither here nor there.

What light does this reflect on the official policies of states and international organizations with respect to reconstruction? Compensation given to a stakeholder group will be for the purposes of ameliorating the unjust harm done to that group. Given that compensation1 is superior to compensation2, it is reasonable, all things being equal, for the group to favor the restoration of the means to pursue the same ends as were pursued before the harm was done. Among those ends will be to dwell in the same environment and enjoy the same relations with the built or natural environment. The structure of

[32] Robert Goodin, "Theories of Compensation" (1989) OJLS 60.

[33] ibid 66–70. Adam Slavny argues for a related distinction between "negating" and "counterbalancing" corrective duties. Like Goodin, he takes the first of these to be a superior form of compensation (Adam Slavny, "Negating and Counterbalancing: A Fundamental Distinction in the Concept of Corrective Duty" (2014) Law and Philosophy).

[34] One might wonder what promises were made to those forcibly moved out of sites such as Palmyra and Petra to free the sites of a modern urban context.

compensation makes it reasonable for a group to want restored to them those objects that supported their way of life, thus enabling them to walk around that which they used to walk around and interact with that with which they used to interact. The decision to opt for restoration, when it is favored, is not simply an untutored preference; it is defensible within the framework of the appropriate kinds of compensation for unjust harms.

Stakeholders are free to opt for compensation in either form, and there will be scenarios in which opting for compensation2 would be appropriate.[35] If the pursuit of some set of ends is thought dispensable, it would be understandable for a group to pursue some other set of ends. There are historical examples of bomb damage being taken as an opportunity to change the community's way of life or restructure some part of a town. The parts of Manchester destroyed by the 1996 IRA bomb were not reconstructed, but rather regenerated with different and better buildings.[36] It might also be that compensation2 could fund projects that would stimulate the local economy (although this raises difficult questions concerning stakeholders who may not benefit from a resurgent local economy—those most wronged by the heritage being damaged or destroyed may, for example, have been displaced).[37] Our claim is only that there is something in the structure of compensation that is available to help the stakeholders, all things being equal, decide what should be done.

Such a conclusion, however, runs into an obvious problem. Goodin himself contrasts objects that can be replaced (such as a production-line car or a five-pound note) with objects that cannot: "works of art, keepsakes, historical landmarks and natural wonders are all irreplaceable in so far as what we value about them is intrinsically bound up with the history of their creation."[38] If what has been lost cannot be replaced, then, whatever their desires, the stakeholder group cannot have the means to the ends it had prior to the unjust harm restored to it. These considerations can be used to support seemingly incompatible conclusions. The first is that we need to go for compensation2 because the restoration of the status quo ante and, therefore,

[35] Moffett, Viejo, and Hickey (n 27) 8.

[36] According to the *Financial Times*, it was "the bomb that backfired. The IRA tried to wound Manchester 20 years ago and jolted awake a sleeping giant instead" (Andrew Bounds, "Manchester's Remarkable Rise From the IRA Rubble" (2016) Financial Times).

[37] See, for example, Bujar Demjaha, "Post-Conflict Urban Reconstruction of Bazaars in Gjakova and Peja, Kosovo" in John Bold (ed), *Authentic Reconstruction: Authenticity, Architecture and the Built Heritage* (Bloomsbury 2017).

[38] Goodin (n 32) 65.

compensation1 is impossible. The second is that we need to go for compensation1 given that nothing could be equivalent to the object's value, rendering compensation2 impossible.

The arguments support the claim that, all things being equal, the stakeholders should get compensation if they ask for it. The problem is that all things are not equal: compensation is not available; they cannot be provided with the means to the same ends as they had previously. The implication is that the stakeholders should get *the closest possible substitute for what has been lost*. This brings us to the critical question: Is the restoration of damaged or destroyed heritage, so that it is as close as it can get to the status quo ante, the closest possible substitute for what has been lost?

It is easy to think not. With their actions, the destroyers deprive the stakeholders of something that has existed continually since it was built (we set aside here the difficult question concerning continuity in the face of replacement of parts over time). That property of the object cannot, by hypothesis, be restored. Regardless of how much the citizens of Warsaw wanted their ancient town center restored, what was restored was not, at least in any simple sense, an ancient town center. Nonetheless, it would be an error to argue that, because of this, the citizens of Warsaw were not compensated at all. A detailed examination of those things that can and cannot be restored is needed properly to address this issue.

VII. Problems With and Limits to Restoration

Restoration, by its nature, aims at counterfactual dependence: it should have the properties it has only because the original object had those properties. In other words, the nature of what is put in place of the damaged or destroyed heritage is determined by the nature of what was there before. This is why the WHC holds that "reconstruction is acceptable only on the basis of complete and detailed documentation." If we do not know what was there before, reconstruction is impossible. Furthermore, "what was there before" will not, in the cases that interest us, indicate only one state of affairs. The historic center of Warsaw, for example, has been around since 1408, with an incredibly destructive fire in 1607 and subsequent periods of development. The decision as to which period to aim at in a restoration will be guided by several considerations, including what we know about what was there in the past and whether the restored heritage will serve whatever purposes it is designed to serve. For example, Warsaw was restored to its eighteenth-century glory because that period was most extensively documented. Its eighteenth-century appearance had largely survived up until the destruction; hence, in electing to prioritize that period, the Poles were also restoring its prewar appearance. A sensible pragmatism, however, also prevailed. Various nineteenth-century buildings and "buildings immediately outside the walls, and buildings of poor quality without documentation, were not reconstructed." This meant that the resulting town plan "appeared more open and lofty."[39]

Thus, the urban layout, the "footprint" of the buildings, and the appearance of the buildings can all be reconstructed.[40] Historical value, that is, the epistemological value of the site, can also be reconstructed by following a strict counterfactual dependence, including methods of construction, materials, and careful record keeping. If there are plenty of practical limits to reconstruction, there is also one important theoretical limit: age value cannot be reconstructed. Above we claimed, following Riegl, that age value "involves respecting the marks of an object's usually significant age." Reconstruction cannot do this. It can either reconstruct the object in pristine condition (as was done with the "House of Blackheads" in Riga) or reconstruct the object complete with the look of age—a reconstructed patina. Neither solution is wholly satisfactory: in the former, what is reconstructed is not what was taken away but, at most, something in the history of what was taken away; in the latter, the patina, by definition, is not something that can be reconstructed. At most we can get the *look* of patina—a constant visual reminder of the fabrication of age value.

In addition to the irreplaceability of age value, the act of reconstruction is paradoxically an act of destruction. The desire to reconstruct is the desire to wipe out some aspect of the history of the object—to make the world as if it never happened. To that extent, it is a willful destruction of the recent record. For some, this provides a sufficient argument against reconstruction. For example, in 1969 an American bomb reduced the largest temple tower (the A1 kalan) in the Vietnamese complex of Mỹ Sơn to rubble. According to Elizabeth Scarbrough,

[39] Ingrid Appelbom Karsten, "Reconstruction of Historic Monuments in Poland after the Second World War - the Case of Warsaw" in John Bold (ed), *Authentic Reconstruction: Authenticity, Architecture and the Built Heritage* (Bloomsbury 2017) 59.

[40] "The oldest part of Warsaw, the historic center situated along the River Vistula, can be seen today as it was before—as a symbol of Warsaw—as Bellotto painted it [between 1770 and 1780]" ibid 59.

> The conservation community decided not to reconstruct the A1 kalan at Mỹ Sơn, and I believe this was the right decision. What remains is the bomb crater—a ghost of a ruin. An important question conservationist ought to ask themselves is what story does this site tell? Ruins are valued in part because they evoke the importance of age-value, the endurance of human effort through time. This is no longer true for A1, which stood inviolate for a thousand years only to be inexorably changed in a matter of seconds. The crater at A1 speaks to the wanton destruction of historic sites like these to make some political point. This is just one story A1 tells, but it is an important one in my view.[41]

For Scarbrough, all events that happen to an object are part of the "story they tell." To "reverse" some event is to tell an incomplete story. A culture may well want that story told—a story of how elements of their culture were wantonly destroyed. By contrast, they may not want that story to stand: a concern to compensate for an injustice may manifest itself in a desire for injustice to be reversed. They may seek a path of restoration so that they do not continue to suffer the injustice of having to do without that which was unfairly taken from them. In such cases, the desire for compensation following an injustice is the desire to have the objects restored to them, rather than telling the story of their damage or destruction.

[41] Elizabeth Scarbrough, "War and Ruins" (2017) Philosopher <https://politicalphilosopher.net/2017/03/24/featured-philosopher-elizabeth-scarbrough/> accessed 23 October 2018.

3

Mission Impossible

Weighing the Protection of Cultural Property against Human Lives

Frederik Rosén

I. Introduction

Should we risk human lives to save cultural property in war? May the protection of cultural property be reasonably weighed against the protection of human lives? Could it, according to the key perspectives guiding our interpretation of the use of force in war, be considered morally acceptable to impose risk upon or even sacrifice human lives to save cultural property? Might a concern for cultural property lead to estimating collateral damage, namely a calculus of unintended but perhaps foreseen collateral harm to individuals, in the course of safeguarding, protecting, or minimizing damage to sites and objects?[1] Such questions arise repeatedly when discussing the protection of cultural property in armed conflict. We thus see an emerging, yet still embryonic debate about "saving lives or saving stones."[2] This chapter contributes to this debate by scrutinizing the conceptual framework for casting this apparent ethical dilemma, which has a legal norm in the form of the Law of Armed Conflict (LOAC) principle of proportionality. As of 2020, 134 states signed on to the 1954 Hague Convention for the Protection of Cultural Property in the Event of Armed Conflict (from now, "1954 Hague Convention")[3] and thereby obligated themselves to take cultural property

[1] See Frederik Rosén, *Collateral Damage: A Candid History of a Peculiar Form of Death* (Hurst Publishing 2016).

[2] Eric Hatala Matthes, "Saving Lives or Saving Stones? The Ethics of Cultural Heritage Protection in War" (2018) 32 Public Affairs Quarterly 67.

[3] Convention for the Protection of Cultural Property in the Event of Armed Conflict (adopted 14 May 1954, entered into force 7 August 1956) 249 UNTS 215 (Hague Convention of 1954). See also its protocols: Protocol to the Convention for the Protection of Cultural Property in the Event of Armed Conflict (adopted 14 May 1954, entered into force 7 August 1956) 249 UNTS 215; Second Protocol to the Hague Convention of 1954 for the Protection of Cultural Property in the Event of Armed Conflict

Frederik Rosén, *Mission Impossible* In: *The Preservation of Art and Culture in Times of War*. Edited by: Claire Finkelstein, Derek Gillman, and Frederik Rosén, Oxford University Press. © Oxford University Press 2022.
DOI: 10.1093/oso/9780197610565.003.0004

into account when planning and conducting military operations. The 1977 Additional Protocols to the Geneva Conventions contain similar constraints on military force.[4] And according to another author in this volume, the LOAC principle of proportionality as it applies to cultural property has attained the status of Customary International Law (CIL). Several branches of international law thus require military commanders to apply proportionality assessments when using military force on, or in the immediate vicinity of, cultural property. It also obliges them to abstain from using cultural property for military purposes unless required by military necessity.

The LOAC principle of proportionality, however, does not specify what kind of issues and values that may be considered when assessing the proportionate and necessary use of force in a given situation. It is therefore a moral decision to accept or reject to weigh the protection of lives against the protection of cultural property when applying the principle of proportionality. The common position rejects such a weighing. The argument is that the value of human life stands above any other precept, without exception. Yet we also see the opposite position. For instance, the famous British diplomat and intellectual, Harold Nicolson, argued that "the loss of even the most valid human life is ultimately less disastrous than the loss of something which in no circumstances can ever be created again."[5]

From an operational perspective, the military dilemmas arising from encountering cultural property during operations moves beyond combat situations. It could be about a commander's decision to change the route of a military convoy to avoid driving through an ancient part of a town, even if this may not be optimal for troop protection, or may trigger force escalation. Also consider the deployment of uniformed personnel to safeguard sites: NATO sustains its troop deployment in Kosovo to protect cultural property, and while it is not currently an area of armed conflict, NATO troops still guard flashpoint prone places and thereby risk attracting fire. Such peacetime deployments fall outside the scope of LOAC and its rule of proportionality, but they indicate a broader agenda for weighing military involvement in the protection of cultural property against the risk to human lives. Having

(adopted 26 March 1999, entered into force 9 March 2004) 2253 UNTS 172 (Second Protocol to Hague Convention of 1999).

[4] Marina Lostal Becerril, "The Meaning and Protection of "Cultural Objects and Places of Worship" Under the 1977 Additional Protocols" (2012) 59 Netherlands International Law Review 455.

[5] Harold Nicolsen, "Marginal Comments" (Spectator, 25 February 1944).

cultural property among the legal and normative factors to consider when using military force inevitably compels commanders to weigh the protection of human lives, soldiers, and civilians alike, against the protection of cultural property. No matter how we turn and twist this dilemma, it will eventually present us with human life considerations. This makes a compelling case for initiating a serious endeavor to clarify the nature of the dilemma, which remains surprisingly underexamined in the academic literature.

This chapter will therefore discuss the dilemma of weighing cultural property protection against the protection of human lives within the parameters of the philosophical and legal principles of proportionality and military necessity. My aim is not to articulate a moral argument for or against destroying or protecting cultural property. Rather, the chapter surveys a series of preliminary problems one must consider before setting out a moral framework around harm to cultural property in armed conflict. As the decision to include or not the dilemma of "saving lives or saving stones" in proportionality assessments remains a moral one, the chapter will draw its framework from the just war theory literature. I start out by suggesting five reasons why just war theory has omitted cultural property from its repertoire of concerns and moral dilemmas. Next, I juxtapose what is conventionally seen as the ultimate concern of just war theory, that is, human beings and their right to life and liberty, with the class of objects identified as "cultural property" in order to suggest it as a possible new concern of just war theory. However, as we shall see, the more we speculate on the constitution of value and moral quality of cultural property in the context of the ethics of war discussions, the clearer it becomes that an analytical just war theory perspective on "weighing lives against stones" appears to be a mission impossible.

II. The Lacking Just War Theory Perspective on Cultural Property

Scholars have recently launched critical blows to the just war theory tradition. One scholar concludes, "Just war theory is a dead letter. It was never more than a theory and at its worst it was a lie, a deadly lie. It promised at least the possibility of war without sin, war without criminality, war without guilt or shame, war in which men would risk their lives but not their souls or their humanity."[6] True, the concerns that originally sparked off philosophizing by

[6] Robert Emmet Meagher, *Killing from the Inside Out: Moral Injury and Just War* (Cascade Books 2014) 129.

Augustine and Thomas Aquinas, which formed the roots of just war theory, were not about the killed but rather about whether the killer's breaking of God's Sixth Commandment, "thou shalt not kill," would hurl his soul to heaven or to hell. To carve out a moral space for warfare and the act of killing, and thus save the souls of kings and their soldiers, early just war theory scholars elaborated exceptions to the divine rule against killing. As famously argued by Augustine, "They who have waged war in obedience to the divine command, or in conformity with His laws, have represented in their persons the public justice or the wisdom of government, and in this capacity have put to death wicked men; such persons have by no means violated the commandment, 'Thou shalt not kill.' "[7]

While critics worry that just war theory promises a war without shame, thus opening a moral door for atrocities, we may also move up a level on the ladder of abstraction and view it as a scholarly conversation that has come very far in mapping out moral dilemmas related to the use of force in war. Whether promising salvation or mapping complexity, whether evading or detailing moral liability, whether legitimizing wars or bracketing them, the just war theory tradition presents us with the main philosophical framework for identifying and debating the morality of waging and fighting wars, with all the limitations such a project is doomed to face. Just war theory is today "widely invoked by policy makers and members of the military, shapes the development and implementation of new weapons and tactics, informs new programs for military ethics training, and serves as the basis for international humanitarian law."[8]

Though addressing a wide range of old and new ethical issues of warfare, just war theory remains somewhat silent on the issue of cultural property. This is surprising. In the past hundred years, we have seen a growth in international norms, laws, and state practices, including large national and international cultural sector programs, which recognize the value of cultural property;[9] and state practices, including large national and international cultural sector programs, which recognize the value of cultural property. As part of this development, we have also seen an increasing focus on cultural property preservation and protection during armed conflict. The detailed

[7] Saint Augustine, *The City of God* (The Modern Library 1993) 27.

[8] Marcus Schulzke, *Just War Theory and Civilian Casualties: Protecting the Victims of War* (CUP 2017) 4.

[9] The concepts of cultural property and cultural heritage are today used interchangeably. I choose "cultural property" to emphasize that the focus of this article is movable or immovable objects.

international regulation of this part of LOAC actually preceded the detailing of civilian protection in the Additional Protocols to the Geneva Conventions by more than twenty years. Debates over the 1948 Genocide Convention[10] even considered whether to include the intended, systematic destruction of cultural property as a means of destroying populations as the crime of "cultural genocide." This indicates the significance ascribed to cultural property and its assumed connection to the safety and security of populations and nations as well as a growing societal interest in a dimension of warfare, which scholars consider as old as warfare itself. Altogether, history, not least that of the twentieth century, has provided plenty of occasions and inroads for elaborating a perspective from moral philosophy on the morality of targeting, destroying, or protecting cultural property in war. If cultural property is as important to communities and humankind as is claimed by leading voices and agencies of the international community, as well as in academic scholarship; if the practice of attacking the kind of objects we today call cultural property has been a part of warfare throughout history; and if it can be used as a weapon of war to attack individuals and destroy cultures, then why have the philosophical treatments of war only recently started to take an interest in the ethics of cultural property protection?[11] I will, in the following, suggest five reasons for why this deficit can be viewed as a result of underlying conceptual strains rather than coincidence or ignorance.

A. Explanation One: Fundamental Incommensurability

The first reason I will suggest is that cultural property is no easy fit for the just war theory tradition, which stands on two pillars: a notion of the fundamental and equal right of individual human beings to life and liberty, and a general moral principle against the infliction of death and suffering on human beings. With these anchor points, just war theory sets out to explore under which exceptional circumstances war may create a moral necessity that momentarily overrides these general principles against killing or depriving individuals of their liberty, including the infliction of harm or risking the lives of soldiers and civilians. But overriding the principle against

[10] Convention on the Prevention and Punishment of the Crime of Genocide (opened for signature 9 December 1948, entered into force 12 January 1951) 78 UNTS 277 (Genocide Convention).

[11] Matthes (n 2) 67.

killing does not mean also overriding the notion that human beings are fundamentally equal. Whatever kind of military necessity applies to a given case, the pillars remain as the substructure for identifying moral dilemmas and theorizing about them.

This traditional position makes it difficult to apply just war theory thinking to "nonhuman" objects and sites: a difficulty clearly observable, for instance, in the attempt to develop just war theory approaches to the environment.[12] We may also note that, as will be discussed later in this chapter, today's concept of cultural property encompasses a very wide range of objects that makes it even more difficult to insert "cultural property" as a generic concept in just war theory equations. We may therefore assume a certain hesitancy toward exchanging the familiar principal concern of just war theory, the human being, with nonhuman, and inherently ill-defined and unstable objects, such as cultural property, which immediately raises complex questions about the object itself and its moral standing.

B. Explanation Two: Ethical Incommensurability

We see a general attitude in the post-Enlightenment West, as well as among moral philosophers, that the value of human life always stands above the value of "things." If this position is accepted, the conventional use-of-force-dilemmas about killing in self-defense, risking the lives of soldiers to save the nation or civilians, or accepting loss of civilian lives as "collateral damage" cannot apply to cultural property. If it is believed that protecting cultural property can never create a moral ground for killing or risking civilian or uniformed lives, then it cannot spark any life and death dilemmas.

Theoretically speaking, this position is premised on a supposed ethical incommensurability between cultural property and the human body, the ultimate humanitarian reference: their apple and pear quality, it is believed, prevents us from viewing them as part of the same moral system. In other words, the fundamental difference between human life and cultural property presents us with an unbridgeable ethical boundary that makes it nonsense to even consider a weighing of "cultural property" against human life. From this

[12] Marcus Hedahl, Scott Clark, and Michael Beggins, "The Changing Nature of the Just War Tradition: How Our Changing Environment Ought to Change the Foundations of Just War Theory" (2017) 5 Public Integrity 429, 437.

position, the mere suggestion of a dilemma of saving human lives or saving stones comes across as an immoral proposition because it implies compromising the exclusive value of human life. As no God-given rule dictates this position, we must however still view it as a matter of how we weigh values. Many, if not most wars have been fought and many lives sacrificed for objects in the nonhuman realm, including natural resources and territory. If such values may outmaneuver the value of human life, then why not cultural property? We must here acknowledge the tradition of separating *jus in bello* and *jus ad bellum* questions, that is, the just use of force in the course of war and the just resort to armed force to start a war, respectively. While the proportionality rule of LOAC takes no interest in whether the war was started on legal or illegal grounds, just war theory questions the moral rightness of this dualistic conception of the law of armed force by arguing that *jus in bello* considerations are subjected to *jus ad bellum*. Still, the strong tradition in the theory of warfare legally and morally to separate the nonhuman values and interests underpinning the resort to armed force with the acts of killing in war as "two distinct normative universes"[13] may also have contributed to this view that killing in war and values associated with inanimate objects form separate moral schemes.

C. Explanation Three: A New Phenomenon

While belligerents' destruction of what we today call cultural property historically runs as deep as war itself, the discussion thereof, including its morality, lacks historical depth. Only occasionally did the fathers of just war theory, including Jakub Przyluski,[14] Hugo Grotius,[15] and Emer de Vattel,[16] mention cultural property in their writings. Contemporary scholars writing on cultural property and war often tag these names to add historical depth to their topic, but mentioning them carries little weight, because we see no elaborations of moral dilemmas or ideals concerning things as we see with issues related to, for instance, the moral implications of killing enemy soldiers, targeting noncombatants, and the right to wage war as self-defense.

[13] Carsten Stahn, "'Jus ad bellum,' 'jus in bello' . . . "jus post bellum"?—Rethinking the Conception of the Law of Armed Force" (2006) 17 European Journal of International Law 921, 925.

[14] Jakub Przyłuski, *Leges seu Statuta ac privilegia Regni Poloniae omnia* (1553).

[15] Hugo Grotius, *The Rights of War and Peace* (1625).

[16] Emer de Vattel, *Le Droit des Gens, ou Principes de la Loi Naturelle, appliqués à la Conduite et aux Affaires des Nations et des Souverains* (1725).

Before the 1954 Hague Convention, we did not have a legal definition or any established international norms of "cultural property" that grouped places of worships, archeological areas, historical buildings, museums, libraries, and paintings within the same category of objects. The Convention contains the first mention of "cultural property" in international law. And within two decades we get a legal concept of "World Heritage," as defined in the Convention Concerning the Protection of the World's Cultural and Natural Heritage, which was adopted by the General Conference of UNESCO on November 16, 1972.

The law, so to speak, came before a philosophical or cultural definition of the objects: the law constituted cultural property as a separate category of objects with a special legal standing. This is what lawyers call progressive lawmaking (as a contrast to codifying already existing norms), and it raises the question of how the relatively new legal standing (following twentieth-century developments in law) of objects categorized as "cultural property" may alter their moral standing, from being objects of significant cultural value to also being legal objects. Because, as legal philosophers have argued, a certain moral obligation to follow the law may apply regardless of the content of the law. Therefore, on top of ethical incommensurability as obstacles for a just war theory approach, we must also consider the implications of progressive lawmaking on moral reasoning and the conceptual newness of "cultural property" as a legal category.

D. Explanation Four: The Morality of Destroying Cultural Property Is Not a Biblical Topic

Our concept of cultural property and its normative, institutional, and legal frameworks and related intellectual debates is very much a modern phenomenon. It postdates by some two thousand years the earliest surviving written accounts of the Ten Commandments with its divine law against killing. What is more, the Bible, the key driver of early Christian just war theory doctrines, offers no insight for viewing the destruction of cultural property as a moral dilemma. Yet, the biblical texts burgeon with historical and sacred places that would qualify as cultural property, and they thematize collective emotional attachment to them as well.

The most famous is the story of Moses's destruction of the golden calf, the paradigmatic allegory of iconoclasm in the Abrahamic religions. Cases of biblical destruction of places of worship include Solomon's temple; Sodom and Gomorrah (Book of Genesis); and the story of King Josiah's systematic demolition of sacred places as part of his reform (Book of Kings 2), which, according to one scholar, "literally cleaved the space in which the Mosaic distinction could be drawn." Like the Taliban's destruction of the Buddhas in March 2001, Josiah's rites of violence served to rid the land of what Mullah Omar referred to as "the gods of infidels."[17] Another example, may be found in the oft-quoted First Letter of St. Paul to the Corinthians, which specifies that "If anyone destroys God's temple, God will destroy that person; for God's temple is sacred, and you together are that temple."[18] Yet this passage is usually interpreted as an account of the Christian community and the human being as the temple of god, the carrier of God's spirit—not any physical temple or place of worship.

My point is that the Bible offers no thematization of sin, guilt, or liability arising out of demolishing sacred places and icons in the way it does with killing. Rather, the biblical narratives suggest a moral good in sometimes destroying objects we today identify as cultural property and contain numerous injunctions to do so. Seemingly, unlike killing, such destruction did not call for consideration of moral consequences. This may explain why the early moral philosophers, strictly preoccupied with biblical themes, appear indifferent to the question of possible moral implications of destroying the kind of objects we refer to as cultural property.

E. Explanation Five: Few Military Examples

A final suggestion I will give for the lack of a just war theory focus on cultural property is that we have few historical examples of wars started by or being fought over disputes about cultural property. We have a limited number of examples where military force has been engaged with the purpose of conquering or protecting cultural property. And military rules of engagement seldom, if ever, sanction the use of armed force to protect cultural property. The current difficulty of the international cultural property protection community to convince defense organizations about the relevance of developing policy, doctrine, and capacity on cultural property protection indicates the

[17] Lauren Monroe, *Josiah's Reform and the Dynamics of Defilement: Israelite Rites of Violence and the Making of a Biblical Text* (OUP 2011) 1.

[18] First Letter of St. Paul to the Corinthians 3:17.

topic's low priority in the history of war fighting. Military combat, with its implied idea of necessary human sacrifices for the cause of the war, rarely springs from cultural property issues. Hence, cultural property does not in practice spur the kind of moral dilemmas that commanders face on an everyday basis when it comes to weighing the loss of human lives against military necessity. The military issues we see today with cultural property and mobilization are a most recent development.

* * *

These five reasons offer some answers to the question why just war theory never embarked on discussing cultural property as a moral issue for warfare. It may explain why Michael Walzer's book *Just and Unjust Wars*, accepted by leading scholars as providing the standard statement of topics and views for just war theory, did not even mention cultural destruction. Even though it invokes plenty of historical examples, including siege warfare, and is set against the backdrop of World War II and its massive and intended destruction of cultural property, it is silent on this issue. Had Walzer included just half a page on cultural destruction, it would likely have triggered elaborations by his numerous scholarly commentators. The international legal regulation of cultural property in armed conflicts thus developed without a corresponding debate in moral philosophy. Looking at the extensive debate about killing civilians in war that accompanies the international legal protection of civilians and soldiers alike, we see a lacuna.

F. A Modern Phenomenon

As already indicated, we have good reasons to view the current role of cultural property in conflicts as a modern phenomenon. The drivers of this development include the twentieth-century's proliferation of norms, laws, and institutions related to cultural property on both the national and international level, combined with the recent rise of identity-driven, asymmetric, urbanized, hybridized, and globalized conflicts, which together have fundamentally altered the global politics of cultural property in conflicts.[19] The transnationalization of armed struggles, and the weakening of national

[19] Frederik Rosén, "NATO and Cultural Property: Embracing New Challenges in the Era of Identity Wars" (Nordic Center for Cultural Property and Armed Conflict 2017) 13 ff.

borders as the principal demarcation of antagonisms and enmity, elevates culturally important places and objects into material references for security communities. But historically viewed, it is a most recent concern. While the ethics of cultural property and its moral dimensions in the context of war do have historical intellectual seeds, these seeds did not grow into trees before the twentieth century. This critical observation suggests that cultural destruction should be viewed not as a "neglected topic" of just war theory, but as a new topic and set of concerns with a new ethical agenda: the question of war, cultural property, and value, as we discuss it today, with all its complexity, is new. In the following pages, the chapter will inspect the challenges of building an ethics in war agenda around the topic of cultural property.

III. Cultural Property as a New Object of Just War Theory

If cultural property is a topic new to just war theory, then how should we approach it? First of all, we may notice that cultural property stands among a range of new topics of just war theory. Those scholars taking revisionist positions have theorized about new moral questions produced by changes in warfare and weapon technologies and argued that the standard scheme of just war theory endures notable difficulties with accommodating moral reflection on, for instance, hybrid and asymmetric warfare; new weapon technologies such as lethal autonomous weapon systems;[20] drones;[21] cyber; information warfare on social media;[22] and the natural environment, including cultural landscapes.

Compared to these topics, cultural property stands apart in several ways. First, except for the environment, these new topics concern new methods or technologies of warfare while the fundamental humanitarian concern for the rights-bearing human being remains unchanged. In contrast, the topic of cultural property introduces into legal and moral discourse a concern for a new category of objects of moral value. Second, "cultural property" is

[20] Michael C Horowitz, "The Ethics & Morality of Robotic Warfare: Assessing the Debate over Autonomous Weapons" (2016) 145 Daedalus 25; Thomas W Simpson and Vincent C Müller, "Just War and Robots' Killings" (2016) 66 The Philosophical Quarterly 302.

[21] Marcus Schulzke, *The Morality of Drone Warfare and the Politics of Regulation* (Palgrave Macmillan 2017).

[22] Mariarosaria Taddeo, "Information Warfare and Just War Theory" in Luciano Floridi and Mariarosaria Taddeo (eds), *The Ethics of Information Warfare. Law, Governance and Technology Series* (Springer 2014).

a category of objects demarcated and thoroughly regulated by the LOAC, something that sets it apart from the environment, which the LOAC hardly consider.[23] Third, even when considering larger constructions and sites, like the Louvre in France or Palmyra in Syria, cultural properties are physical, specifiable objects with relatively clear parameters for determining degrees of damage. Increasingly, scholarly approaches from all disciplines include intangible cultural heritage in their concept of cultural property. This will be addressed later as the "cultural turn" in cultural heritage studies, involving collective sentiments and emotions, something that sets cultural property further apart from the above-mentioned new topics of just war theory.

Fourth, damage to cultural property objects entails no direct nor secondary effects to the physical well-being of individuals, the immediate stability of society, or other living creatures or fauna. If damage to cultural property creates such harm, it is because the damaged object includes critical infrastructure functions—for instance, a historical building hosting a hospital, stock market, computer servers, or the like—or because its destruction produces fear and anxiety. Yet from an analytical perspective, these dimensions need to be kept separate from the concerns related to cultural property.

Then what happens when we identify "cultural property" as a new subject of protection in just war theory? This will lead us to ask when cultural property may be legitimately targeted, or what level of necessity must exist to override existing legal protections compared with the value of the cultural property object in question? Under what circumstances would it be permissible to risk soldiers' lives to safeguard cultural property? How do we weigh cultural property protection against other forms of protection? Should states expect their soldiers to take additional risk or risk civilian lives to safeguard cultural property? Is it morally legitimate to kill someone who destroys cultural property?

What happens, I argue, is that we immediately face a set of interrelated challenges in attempting to identify real moral dilemmas, specifically these: (1) the falseness of the "humans-are-apples-and-cultural-properties-are-pears" account; (2) the layers of value challenge related to the innumerable forms and values of the wide array of cultural property objects identified by international law; (3) the local ownership paradigm of the "cultural stance" related to definitions of the value of cultural property objects; (4) consequentialism and cultural property crimes; and (5) the lack of a victimology

[23] See Britta Sjöstedt, *The Role of Multilateral Environmental Agreements* (Hart Publishing 2020).

describing and theorizing what kind of harm the victims of crimes against property would incur. The following section will discuss these challenges.

A. The Falseness of the "Apple and Pears" Account

The "apple and pears" perspective on saving cultural property versus saving human lives asserts that these cannot be weighed against each other because of their fundamentally incommensurable value. I will argue that this framework is false, but for slightly different reasons than are usually offered. As already mentioned, just war theory is interlinked with natural rights thinking, which views human beings as morally equal by nature. As put by the philosophers Helen Frowe and Seth Lazar: "Every decent person now believes that all persons are created equal."[24] There is a lot going on in this sentence: every decent person (there are also non-decent people) now (it has been different before) believes (we speak about belief and not an a priori fact) that all persons are created (by the fact of being born) equal (same fundamental value). The statement, in my view reflects the first step of the dominant argument in just war theory tradition: that by virtue of being born human—the fact of their singular naked life—and before being anything else, all human beings are of equal value.

The second step is the assertion that human beings therefore enjoy equal fundamental rights by this mere fact of being human, "Our right to life and liberty is a big deal. They are directly connected to our passion of moral status, indeed, may even be constitutive of it. We cannot surrender or lose these rights except when we do something that warrants such a severe fate."[25] Put in a different way by the philosopher Graham Parson, "The theory of discrimination [in just war theory] . . . is derived from a theory of justice that places the value of the private individual above that of political society."[26] Or as another scholar puts it, "non-combatants immunity remains a core value of just war theory, perhaps even the core value."[27] *Wherever and whoever these noncombatants are*, we may add.

[24] Helen Frowe and Seth Lazar, *The Oxford Handbook of Ethics of War* (OUP 2018) 29.
[25] Seth Lazar, "Evaluating the Revisionist Critique of Just War Theory" (2017) 146 Daedalus 113, 119; Schulzke (n 8) 31 ff.
[26] Graham Parson, "The Dualism of Modern Just War Theory" (2017) 45 Philosophical Quarterly of Israel 751, 751.
[27] Schulzke (n 8).

The dominant value position of just war theory (at least for its "decent" positions) is this idea of fundamental value and fundamental rights, which is not open to political negotiation, applying equally to soldiers and civilians, but which is also something that may be put aside under exceptional circumstances. This position is taken by both traditionalists and revisionists. We may view it as a value-based ("decent people believe") position that separates the rights-bearing agent, ultimately represented in the form of the passive and naked human body, from human agency, namely politics. In other words, human beings possess human rights by virtue of being human rather than being a member of a group or a society.

I am not offering my own stance here on whether human beings come with an inherent moral right to be considered equal, in terms of moral standing and rights. My task is merely to identify a dominant position within intellectual theories that reflect on the morality of warfare. This position, anchored in a notion of a fundamental and indivisible value of the human being, provides the bedrock for just war theory. It organizes the theoretical system and enables commensurability between elements, examples, and arguments; it makes it possible to weigh combatant and civilian lives against each other, across the globe, and formulate and employ general principles such as "it is forbidden to [inflict] harm on noncombatants either as an intended end or as means to an end. In other words, noncombatants have the right not to be deliberate targets of attack."[28] It makes it possible to theorize about in what kind of exceptional situations military necessity may override their equal right to life; and it makes it possible to elaborate paradigmatic dilemmas and solutions that may be applied to situations across time and space—all this without first clarifying in what ways a fundamental comparability may apply to these situations.

Starting from there, just war theory sets out to explore under which circumstances military necessity may override soldiers' right to life, namely when may soldiers kill soldiers, when may commanders risk their soldier's life (to protect cultural property for instance), when may the safety of civilians and civilian infrastructure be compromised, and so on. Without going into the conceptual quagmire of the notion of state sovereignty, this corresponding idea of all states being essentially equal in terms of a formal state sovereignty also forms the backbone of the *jus ad bellum* debates.

[28] Richard J Arneson, "Just Warfare Theory and Noncombatant Immunity" (2006) 39 Cornell International Law Journal 663, 664.

The inversion of the equal value of life position would be to put the value of political society over the private individual—a position we associate with the hallmark of fascism or communism. Just war theory could not endure that. Injecting a collectivist or fascist notion of the individual would simply explode its theoretical template, as any consideration of moral agency and wrongs would require an assessment on a case-by-case basis of the value of each individual life. It would destabilize entirely statements like "noncombatants have the right not to be deliberate targets" because there would not be a class of "noncombatants" to toy with academically, but rather a horde of individuals with different values and rights (that would need to be established before reflecting on noncombat immunity for particular individuals) that would affect proportionality assessments. In order to elaborate theoretical schemes and moral positions, just war theory would actually have to come up with a general clarification of how to calculate the value of each separate individual. In the absence of a practical theory for a divisibility of the value of human life, just war theory would be all at sea.

In comparison, cultural properties are not in and of themselves rights-bearing objects, as the human body is. Rather, as noted in the introduction to this book, lacking the intrinsic value of life its designation rests, per definition, on its ascribed cultural value and use. It hence derives its moral value not from its being in and of itself, but from the agency of human beings in the form of value assessments and nominations, and how they act toward it. The concept of cultural property, as a concept of international law, embraces a wide category of movable and immovable objects and places, including monuments, museums, archives, archeological sites, historical buildings, art and book collections, and places of worship,[29] such as churches, mosques, cemeteries, holy rocks and trees, and so on. Within each of these general subcategories of objects, we see an innumerable variety of objects and associated values. Most recently, we have seen a well-developed critique in heritage studies of the conventional separation of natural and cultural heritage,[30] opening another possible new dimension to our repertoire. It would be hard for just war theory to sustain a separation if some authorities on cultural heritage/property dismiss it.

In sum, the legal concept of cultural property provides us with a very loose identification of a vast list of objects. International law regulating cultural

[29] 1977 Additional Protocols to the Fourth Geneva Conventions, art 53.

[30] Rodney Harrison, "Beyond 'Natural' and 'Cultural' Heritage: Towards an Ontological Politics of Heritage in the Age of the Anthropocene" (2015) 8 Heritage and Society 24.

property in armed conflict states that certain objects enjoy projection as cultural property, but it says very little about how to establish this value. Apart from recognition on UNESCO's World Heritage Lists—which really is about political nomination—international law offers no procedure for identifying the relative value of cultural property. Altogether, the radical heterogeneity of cultural property stands in stark contrast to the just war theory notion of the moral equality of human beings and their indivisible right to life and liberty. The value of cultural property appears radically divisible: without any further comparison, it presents the just war theory tradition, theoretically viewed, with the same challenge as does a fascist notion of the collective value of human beings.

The challenge for developing a just war theory perspective on cultural property is therefore not about the difficulty of weighing apples (human lives) against pears (cultural objects). While we do see a relatively clear-cut apple in the form of human beings and their moral value, cultural property presents us with a large and heterogenous category of objects associated with such diverse values that we do not even see a pear to weigh against.

To develop a just war theory perspective on cultural property therefore requires the expansion of a tradition of theorizing that stands on relatively stable ground, which is the notion of the human being and its indivisible right to life and liberty, to a category of essentially heterogenous objects. It is about employing concepts that refer to a concrete object of defined value and innumerable objects of various values, respectively, in the same equation. Therefore, any abstract dilemma between saving human life and saving cultural property is simply void. There can be no meaningful general discussion of saving cultural property at the expense of human lives.

Still, the question can be recast. We may ask whether we could imagine a situation where the value of a concrete object is higher than the right to life of a human being. An affirmative answer to that question implies that there could be a particular situation that presents us with a dilemma between saving human life and saving cultural property. However, in the absence of a philosophical methodology that identifies the exact value of cultural property, that question would hardly provide us with an opening for developing a general theory. In contrast, when weighing human lives against human lives, the dilemma will always be there due to the deep-rooted notion of the fundamental moral equality of human beings.

These reflections on the challenges of considering cultural property within moral debates about the morality of killing in war also raises the question whether the legal definition of cultural property provides enough conceptual ground for moral reasoning. Law can create legal objects: for instance, cultural property. But just as law does not make a moral right, law does not necessarily create objects with a moral value. What the international legal concept of cultural property seems to do for moral philosophy is to establish a link to a thematic area in international law and its related debates, as well as to indicate that cultural property, as a certain class of objects with moral significance, may exist independently of international law. If we did not have the 1954 Hague Convention, then how would our debate on objects and places of significant cultural value have looked today? Would we ever consider discussing attacks on a mosque within the same legal protection regime as cyber-attacks on historical digital archives?

B. A Layer of Value, Collective Values, and Wronging Groups

The position that cultural property lacks inherent value is not a child of post-structuralism. Rather, it is the international legal scheme for regulating cultural property (separate from the numerous domestic regulatory schemes). The 1954 Hague Convention distinguishes cultural property and is mindful of this agreed-upon collective value assessment that human beings add to certain sites and objects. It is the extra "cultural" value added to a civilian-use historical building that augments its value from being a civilian object already protected by the Geneva Conventions to also enjoying protection under the 1954 Hague Convention and its Protocols. It is the extra cultural value added to the historical building that houses, say, a branch of the defense intelligence agency which requires military targeteers and planners to weigh its value as a military target against its value as a cultural property site. Normative attitudes and sentiments form this "extra value" that constitutes cultural property as a separate class of moral objects. One person's dearest private goods cannot qualify. The collective dimension needs to be there.

Now, ethics is always relational, requiring "the other." It is about the moral conduct of behavior in light of how an activity may affect others. For our thinking about cultural property in war, the concept of cultural property as socially constituted objects means that the ethical relation is not between the perpetrator and the object. It is between the offender and the group of individuals forming the collective that holds dear the object in question. The ethical relation goes through the objects to other persons; the object becomes a medium, a pathway. The ethics, as an exploration of moral principles, of cultural property destruction and preservation must therefore start from the fact that wrongdoing per definition is about wrongdoing toward a group, if not the whole of humankind. That is why cultural property can work as an effective "weapon." One private person may attack an entire global collective by attacking its cultural property. And that group may be composed of individuals with varying interests and emotional dispositions for experiencing loss and agony—in both present and coming generations.

C. Cultural Property and the Cultural Turn

The 1954 Hague Convention obliges its member states to elaborate inventories of national cultural property as well as mark it for the purpose of ensuring protection. Yet such lists may be political in nature; they can therefore indicate but not substantiate the value of cultural property for the purpose of theorizing their moral status in war. And while a list may guide the application of international law, it offers little guidance for a value assessment to inform proportionality assessments during military operations. The same applies to other objects and sites abstractly identified by the 1954 Hague Convention and its Protocols, as well as the Geneva Conventions, as enjoying protection as cultural property, including places of worship.

But is such guidance necessary? Are commanders in the field not in any case left to pragmatic decisions? They are. Yet military organization also offers a range of decision-making support tools including Rules of Engagement, operational documents (directives, doctrines, handbooks), as well as digital collateral damage estimation tools informed by the extensive historical and contemporary debates on the threshold for acceptable civilian casualties. Without going into the procedural steps of proportionality assessment, it should suffice to note that all these mechanisms, if based on LOAC principles, imply an equal value of human life approach. Their application as a means to fulfill international legal obligations requires no ad hoc value assessment of its object of protection.

As a stark contrast, if not an actual inversion of this paradigm, cultural property and its recent conceptualization according to international law requires the assignment of a practical value assessment to each concrete situation.

Certainly, the universal value of cultural property is an established international norm broadly reflected in UNESCO's policies and conventions. For instance, the World Heritage Convention employs the concept of "Outstanding Universal Value" and the 1954 Hague Convention that of "the cultural heritage of all mankind." However, in addition to this cosmopolitan approach, the 1954 Convention also recognizes a local ownership approach. As stated in the Convention's preamble, "Being convinced that damage to cultural property belonging to any people whatsoever means damage to the cultural heritage of all mankind, since each people makes its contribution to the culture of the world." In other words, the sum of local heritage of any people adds up to a universal "heritage of mankind." In that way the Convention may be viewed as bridging the cosmopolitan or object-focused approach to cultural property with a local or "cultural stance" approach. The "Western" cosmopolitan approach to cultural heritage taken not least by UNESCO has been challenged by many former colonized countries. We also hear a swelling critique of this approach from academics and lay commentators alike, as well as a more general turn within international politics toward local ownership-based approaches to issues such as international development aid and conflict resolutions.

At the heart of the critique of the universalist approach to cultural heritage/property lies a reality: a notion of the difficulty, if not impossibility of assessing "from the outside" the value of objects, that is, how particular individuals and communities ascribe value to these objects.[31] Out of the wide range of objects that international law regards as[32] relevant for just war theory to consider as cultural property, only a few of them hold the status of recognized UNESCO World Heritage Sites. And even if UNESCO and the international community at first see no value in say a stone in a remote valley of Afghanistan, that stone may, from the perspective of international law, qualify as a cultural property object if the stone functions as an important reference for local mythology.

The insistence on local group interest and collective emotions and attitudes as the basis of ethics raises the question of just who is entitled to nominate cultural property for the purpose of international legal protection, and moral philosophizing with respect to just war theory. As no generally applicable

[31] For a discussion of the idea of universal cultural heritage and its critiques, see Sophia Labadi, "UNESCO, Cultural Property, and Outstanding Universal Value" (Rowman & Littlefield 2015).

[32] Roger O'Keefe, "The Meaning of "Cultural Property" under the 1954 Hague Convention" (1999) 46 Netherlands International Law Review 26.

parameters exist for establishing this value, the answer must be the stakeholder community, however large. Realism tells us that no theory enables us to schematize such objects, a priori, for the purpose of classifying cultural property according to their different values—we cannot spot value from the air, so to say. You can see a human being and hence their value (which is the same as your own) from afar, but while cultural property may even be seen from the moon (Great Wall of China), its value always escapes the eye.

A main argument in the field of heritage studies is that identifying cultural property is a cultural act in itself; and that is the point of the "cultural turn" in heritage studies, proponents of which would argue that the principle of "local ownership" must apply to any establishment of value for the purpose of proportionality assessments in connection with military decisions. The cultural turn in understanding the value of cultural heritage may in principle apply a narrow or very wide geographical scope of "local." What matters from this perspective is not so much the territorial stretch but that those who possess a heritage interest in an object are recognized and considered as the stakeholder community for defining its value—not an expert committee in an international organization or similar.

To push the implications of the cultural turn one step further: our "objects" of concern are not material objects as such, but the underlying and constitutive emotions and attitudes that qualify an object as cultural property. Therefore, the question becomes how patterns of collective emotions that constitute objects as cultural property may fit into the analytical perspectives of just war theory. To identify something to "weigh" human lives against, we must first identify those who define cultural property, and how the object in question matters to them. We cannot weigh abstractions but must depend on empirical reports of what people feel about an object. Instead of weighing stones against lives, nonhuman objects against humans, we are asked to weigh intangible sentiments, attitudes, and patterns of collective identity, at a particular time in history.

Presumptions about the value of cultural property have changed over time. Temporality must be central to any appreciation of its value. As mentioned in the beginning of this chapter, the development of twentieth-century legal norms, intellectual entrepreneurship, and societal changes have contributed vastly to our contemporary idea of, and value ascription to, cultural property. We cannot discard the possibility that this will change in the future. Cultural property may lose the attention and legal protection it enjoys today. At least, its meaning and value will change over time. If the "real" object of concern is not the tangible object or site but a constantly transmuting constellation of group interests and collective emotions and attitudes, we must find a way to assess this social dimension of cultural property as a precondition for developing an analytical just war theory perspective on the topic or for employing the LOAC principle of proportionally during military operations.

From an academic perspective, ethnographic fieldwork, with its slow-moving qualitative interviews and observations, stands as the preferred method to acquire knowledge about such matters. Before contemplating protection and proportionality, before contemplating trade-offs between risk to human lives and protection of cultural property, legal advisors and just war theorists alike, need, in principle, to go to the field and conduct an ethnographic field study of how stakeholders feel about the place or object in question. Such extensive empirical requirements effectively stop most philosophizing; for military commanders and their legal advisors, it creates an unworkable operational challenge for international law. The purpose is not to make that recommendation, but to illustrate the theoretical and operational consequence of today's dominant cultural stance-approach to cultural property in the LOAC and academy.

D. Consequentialism and Cultural Property Crimes

Unfortunately, our problems do not end there. If, hypothetically, we succeeded in assessing the relative value of a cultural property object vis-à-vis human life it would only take us half the way to where we are ready to insert its value into our analytical matrix of necessity and proportionality. While international law may see a crime in the mere breaking of rules, regardless if the act inflicts any harm, moral philosophy requires a concept of the harm inflicted on others. At least, the moral dimension of complying or not with legal obligations is a different topic than the morality of wronging others. To discuss moral action, we need a concept of wrongdoing and the kind of harm that flows from it. Something needs to get out of balance. We need to identify a consequence, an injury that gives rise to reflections on how the wrongdoing may be remedied and the balance re-established. In other words, we need a notion of inflicted harm and injury, namely the consequence to individuals and communities of losing cultural property.

What kind of harm and injury, then, may flow from the destruction of cultural property? Who gets hurt, how, where, when, and how much? It follows from the definition of cultural property as a collective value that its loss must be a collective loss. The answer to the "who gets hurt" is not a singularity, a person, but a multitude: destruction of cultural property must be viewed as a loss of an object that is expected to bring value in the future to everyone belonging to the wronged group. Even persons who did not experience the destruction, or may never learn about, may be considered harmed or injured and thus victims due to the possible damage to the community of which they are members. And as the loss of cultural property may affect future generations, as it is believed it can, victims may not even be born, and may never know about the earlier loss and how it affects their own contemporary life.

This long-term rationality for cultural property protection can be found in the UNESCO Declaration on the Responsibility of the Present Generations Towards Future Generations, adopted on November 12, 1997, which "requires that present generations take care to preserve the cultural diversity of humankind. The present generations have the responsibility to identify, protect and safeguard the tangible and intangible cultural heritage and to transmit this common heritage to future generations."[33] Even if not necessarily adopting this broad perspective, a key concern of the international legal protection of cultural property is not to prevent instant agony that a group may feel over the loss of an object, but rather the consequence to collective memory and cultural practices. It therefore clearly implies a concept of injury and victimhood that embraces a long-term perspective. As an example of a long-term perspective, let us notice how observant Jews still mourn the loss of the temples in Jerusalem. The temples are remembered by an annual fast day in Judaism, Tisha B'Av, indicating a 2,000–2,500 years perspective on the consequence of destroying cultural property on "future generations."[34]

Long-term consequences constitute a tricky issue for the LOAC, which in principle considers only immediate harm arising from combat situations. The rationale for omitting long-term consequences was to preclude strategic arguments about military necessity being confused by proportionality equations aiming at some aloof future goal. In other words, the rationale was to disallow collateral damage estimations at the highest strategic level because this would be practically unmanageable from the perspective of law, and therefore weaken the legal protection of soldiers and civilians alike.

[33] UNESCO Declaration on the Responsibility of the Present Generations Towards Future Generations (adopted 12 November 1997) art 7.

[34] Thanks to Derek Gillman for this point.

As noticed by the International Committee of Red Cross in their review of Customary International Law on the principle of Proportionality, the expression "concrete and direct"[35] military advantage was used in the Geneva Conventions Additional Protocol 1 in connection with the principle of proportionality to indicate that the advantage must be "substantial and relatively close, and that advantages which are hardly perceptible and those which would only appear in the long-term should be disregarded."[36]

Recently, the humanitarian community explored options under LOAC for considering harmful effects beyond the isolated combat operation, arguing that such effects can be detrimental to civilians and therefore need to be considered in the assessment of proportionality in the use of force. In a review of LOAC and state practice related to what they call "reverberating effects" (i.e., collateral effects that are only expected to materialize in the long term), Ian Henderson and Kate Reece find that indirect effects, namely harm to civilians, need to be considered but with an important qualification: "To meet the legal threshold for collateral damage, the indirect effects must be, as a minimum, more than speculative or a mere possibility."[37] Still, as noticed by Henderson and Reece, the obligation to include long-term effects in proportionality tests appears weak and contested. Overall, with an eye to possible future developments, we can conclude that the LOAC related to proportionality still considers combat-related, instant injuries, and harm to civilians and civilians' objects primarily within a short-term perspective on harm.

By contrast, the rules against destroying cultural property exclusively stand upon a long-term perspective on harm. The 1954 Hague Convention takes no interest in the destruction of cultural property designed to inflict instant terror in the hearts and minds of civilians. The regulation of terror campaigns and the psychological harm they aspire to inflict falls under a different set of legal and moral issues not associated with the question of cultural property destruction. For instance, Article 13(2) of the 1977 Additional Protocol II prohibits "acts or threats of violence the primary purpose of which is to spread terror among the civilian population."

The 1954 Hague Convention thus sets an entirely different agenda for proportionality assessments than the parts of the LOAC related to civilians.

[35] Protocol Additional to the Geneva Conventions of 12 August 1949, and Relating to the Protection of Victims of International Armed Conflicts (Protocol I) arts 51, 57.

[36] ICRC, IHL Database, Customary IHL, Rule 14. Proportionality in Attack.

[37] Ian Henderson and Kate Reece, "Proportionality under International Humanitarian Law (IHL): The 'Reasonable Military Commander' Standard and Reverberating Effects" (2018) 51 Vanderbilt Journal of Transnational Law 835, 855.

While the long-term perspective remains highly challenging if not unmanageable from a purely legal perspective, a philosophical account would need to involve a consequentialist perspective that considers value in terms of what may be lost and the kind of harm and injury the loss of cultural property may entail with a view to the future.

The debates about "cultural genocide" offer the strongest concern with regard to long-term effects. The associated term "cultural cleansing" was recently foregrounded in international politics when UNESCO used it to describe ISIS's destruction of cultural property in Syria and Iraq as part of its strategy to establish their Caliphate. History reveals that mass atrocities, including ethnic cleansing and genocide, are often accompanied by systematic destruction of cultural property to exterminate the cultural survival of the targeted group. Yet it has been debated whether systematic destruction of cultural property can be considered an act of "cultural cleansing" independent of human atrocities. The idea of the dependency of cultural groups on the material anchorage of culture in the form of cultural property still stands. It derives from this idea that cultures and cultural groups may disintegrate if they lose their material anchorage. As mentioned before, the international community aspired to include systematic attacks on cultural property directed against a cultural group in the Convention on the Prevention and Punishment of the Crime of Genocide from 1948. Yet such disintegration is not believed to be an instant cultural atomization following destruction. It is a creeping, long-term effect on collective sentiments, emotions, and social cohesion created by the loss of communal reference objects.

The concept of "cultural cleansing," the idea that cultures may be severely diminished or even destroyed by demolishing their material expressions, appears intuitively correct and historical examples come to mind. Yet, no systematic empirical research exists to substantiate such a causal effect. No systematic studies have assessed the anticipated long-term consequences of such destruction to social cohesion in cultural groups. We do not have a clear account of who the victims might be, and how they and their group and society might be affected. We do not have a qualified notion of loss, harm, and injury. Regardless of what we feel is right or true, we are left with anecdotal evidence. We therefore lack a clear account of the actual consequences to individuals and communities of losing cultural property. In other words, we lack an empirically informed victimology (the study of crime victims and victimization) of cultural property crimes. The proposed consequences of destruction and loss of cultural property therefore remain "speculative or a mere possibility." If we follow Henderson and Reece's account, the effect on individuals and groups of losing cultural property, as well as the gains from preserving it, remain too unclear to meet the minimum threshold for including them in collateral damage estimations under the LOAC.

We thus see a gap between the identification of cultural property—and its claimed value for the purpose of making proportionality assessments in relation to the use of force and the identification of the consequences of losing cultural property. Can these two dimensions be separated at all? Are they not both fundamental to a value assessment? It is tricky. A group of people may believe that the destruction of an object means the end of the world, and therefore consider its protection an entirely valid reason to start a war and sacrifice all their daughters and sons in one last battle. And they may lose the object, only to see the sun rise again as if nothing happened. Religious cults throughout time and geography developed rituals as substitutes for sacred objects and places. The loss of the object may be remedied by reconstructing it or replacing it with something else. A cucumber instead of an ox. Therefore, it is erroneous to equate the estimated value of an object with the feared harm of losing that object. We have no mirror ball available to measure the future societal effects of destroying cultural property.

IV. Conclusion

We are left with many unresolved questions, but one stands out as particularly important. Can the effects of cultural property destruction ever be included in calculations of proportionality? Can we theorize in any meaningful way about proportionality and military necessity with regard to taking or risking lives to protect cultural property? Without a victimology of crimes against cultural property, how can we identify victims, wrongdoings, and moral liability? The overall finding of this chapter is that the fundamentally contested or simply indefinable value of objects and sites identified by international law as "cultural property" hinders in several ways the elaboration of a general perspective on this notable contemporary protection dilemma. By "general perspective," I mean an agreed-upon theory for identifying and comparing cases for the purpose of discussing moral and legal rights and wrongs—similar to the extensive debates about the morality and legality of killing in war.

The more we speculate about the constitution of value and moral quality of cultural property, the clearer it becomes that an analytical just war theory perspective on "weighing lives against stones" appears to be a mission impossible. Not because ethical considerations necessarily place the value of human life above cultural property. But because cultural property per definition presents us with a radically heterogenous concept and unresolved if not irresolvable issues of valuation and victimhood. We simply cannot elaborate a deontological position on cultural property. That would go against international law as well as the dominant academic understanding of cultural property as a cultural matter. Any attempt to establish value for the purpose of developing an analytical perspective contradicts the legal and philosophical concepts underpinning today's notion of cultural property and is bound to attract charges of reification.

Things have not become easier over the years. Since the drafting of the 1954 Hague Convention, our idea of cultural property has developed profoundly. Namely, the change from a foremost focus on objects toward values embedded in the local cultural context forms a significant shift, which the interpretation and implementation of the 1954 Hague Convention struggle to accommodate. Yet, as the Convention obliges states to apply the principle of proportionality to cultural property, it also implies a dilemma between saving stones and saving lives and an obligation to sort out the meaning and issues of this dilemma.

We are therefore presented with a "baby in the bath water" problem: Should we decline to discuss the principled moral implications of intentionally destroying or protecting cultural property in times of war because of conceptual problems? Because we agree we do see a baby. While cultural property is a fundamentally heterogenous concept and the process for identifying the value constituting cultural property remains essentially contested, there is a general agreement that *there is cultural property* and that it matters greatly to many people. Cultural property sometimes comes with amazingly strong emotions. It can start wars. And a large number of states committed themselves under the 1954 Hague Convention and its Protocols to adhere to the general LOAC principles of proportionality and military necessity. In fact, as has been argued, these principles, as they apply to cultural property, may even be considered rules of Customary International Law, binding states that are not members of the Convention. Treaties and Customary International Law confirm the values we ascribe to cultural property and the relevance of applying the proportionality test. To deny the relevance of reflecting on the moral implications of targeting, destroying, or protecting cultural property in war would be to refuse that special value and social power. Furthermore, that would call for arguments against the comprehensive norm development on cultural property and the idea that it constitutes a separate moral and legal category of objects. So, there we stand: not between stones and human lives, but between a rock and a hard place.

4

Weaponizing Culture

A Limited Defense of the Destruction of Cultural Heritage in War

*Duncan MacIntosh**

I. Introduction

It is widely thought that the theft of, trade in, and intentional destruction of art and cultural artifacts in time of war are inherently immoral, and that it is right that these actions be treated as war crimes, which, indeed, they currently are.[1] As Mark Drumbl also argues in this volume, however, oppressive cultures have their heritage and cultural artifacts too, in the form of monuments, sites of worship, and so on; and for the oppressed, these things may be awful reminders of their subordination, and may even perpetuate it.[2] In the United States, Confederate monuments would be examples.[3] In Canada, statues of the founding prime minister of Canada, Sir John A. MacDonald, have come to have this status, because of his role in oppressing and suppressing rebellions of the indigenous peoples of

* For helpful comments, my thanks to Sheldon Wein, LW; my fellow participants in the conference for which this essay was originally prepared (especially Richard Leventhal and Kathy Peiss); and students in my classes at Dalhousie University. Special thanks to Frederik Rosén and Claire Finkelstein, whose written comments changed my thinking on a number of matters, and who saved me from many mistakes. (They *tried* to save me from many more.) Finally, thanks to Ashley Fuchs for her meticulous editing.

[1] For the history of treaties, conventions, and so on, cumulating to the idea that cultural property theft and destruction ought to be seen as illegal and prosecutable in war and other forms of armed conflict, see Patty Gerstenblith, "The Destruction of Cultural Heritage: A Crime against Property or a Crime against People?" (2016) 15 The John Marshall Review of Intellectual Property Law 336–93.

[2] Mark Drumbl, "The International Criminal Court and Cultural Property: What Is the Crime?" in this volume.

[3] See the American Historical Association Statement on Confederate Monuments (August 2017) <https://www.historians.org/news-and-advocacy/aha-advocacy/aha-statement-on-confederate-monuments> accessed 9 September 2020.

Duncan MacIntosh, *Weaponizing Culture* In: *The Preservation of Art and Culture in Times of War.* Edited by: Claire Finkelstein, Derek Gillman, and Frederik Rosén, Oxford University Press. © Oxford University Press 2022. DOI: 10.1093/oso/9780197610565.003.0005

Canada who existed there before colonial conquest.[4] I shall suggest that, since cultural objects can be both tools and symbols of unjust oppression, their theft and destruction ought to be seen as appropriate when this would be a means of overcoming oppression. Whatever current law may say, in these instances, it would be morally inappropriate to count such acts as war crimes.

I shall also make an additional point, one in reaction to what is currently permitted as means of war fighting. At present, it is legal to fight wars by such methods as one soldier killing another (under the principle of combatant immunity), and even by military maneuvers that result in death to civilians (as collateral damage), provided that such death is either unforeseen; or if foreseen, unintended and justifiable by principles of necessity and proportionality. These things are legal even though the theft and destruction of cultural property are not. I find this bizarre given that killing seems worse than property destruction and theft. I therefore further argue that, where possible, it would be better for conflicts to be fought using threats and acts of cultural property destruction rather than by the killing of soldiers and by other actions that may be expected to involve collateral killing of innocent civilians. The same goes for the theft of artifacts when used systematically as part of a war effort, such as to finance operations.[5]

In the course of defending these proposals, I shall respond to the standard objections to using theft and destruction of cultural property as a method of warfare, including objections premised in the assumed transcultural, timeless value of these objects and in the conceptual assimilation of their theft or destruction to an obviously objectionable kind of genocide.

[4] See Tristin Hopper, "Here Is What Sir John A Macdonald Did to Indigenous People" (*National Post*, 28 August 2018) <https://nationalpost.com/news/canada/here-is-what-sir-john-a-macdonald-did-to-indigenous-people> accessed 9 September 2020.

[5] Claire Finkelstein pointed out to me that in current ways of war fighting and conducting other violent conflicts, cultural property destruction is used more as a kind of magnifier of the effects of fighting by means of violence against persons. In these terms, she suggests that, when the oppressed seek to destroy cultural property in the name of justice, the protection of such property can in effect likewise be a magnifier, a magnifier of violence done to the oppressed, and of their cultural oppression. I agree with all of this. I am proposing, however, that the destruction of cultural property can also be a kind of stand-alone method of fighting, that it ought not to be seen as a war crime when used to combat oppression, and that it would be a better state of affairs if conflicts were conducted by means of cultural property destruction than by the killing of people.

II. The Standard Arguments Against Cultural Heritage Destruction or Theft

Looting and illicit trade in cultural artifacts from conflict zones is objected to on various grounds: it incentivizes theft from and desecration of archeologically significant sites; it results in undocumented removal of artifacts from their historical sites, making their scientific investigation more difficult;[6] it deprives nations and peoples of their cultural heritage;[7] and it allows terrorists to finance their operations by sale of artifacts on the black market.[8]

The intentional destruction of cultural artifacts in war is also generally disapproved of.[9] In the case of occupying armies, such actions are condemned on grounds of being militarily gratuitous, or worse, self-defeating, interfering with winning hearts and minds. The unintended but foreseen destruction of such artifacts by army action is objected to on similar grounds—better to take extreme care against military clumsiness in respecting the objects around which cultures are organized.[10] When destruction is engaged in by terrorists with political motivation, it is condemned for obliterating cultures in a way that is comparable to the genocide of a people. Destruction of cultural property is also objectionable for being destructive of the archeological record and therefore of the scientific value of these things, and for being aesthetically injurious. The theft and destruction of cultural artifacts comprise, therefore, unjustifiable harms to people, to cultures, and to scientific and aesthetic value. And

[6] On these first two points, and as exemplified in the case of Syria, see Emma Cunliffe, "Damage to the Soul: Syria's Cultural Heritage in Conflict" (*Global Heritage Fund*, 2012) 10–18 <http://ghn.globalheritagefund.com/uploads/documents/document_2107.pdf> accessed 10 September 2020; Patty Gerstenblith, "Controlling the International Market in Antiquities: Reducing the Harm, Preserving the Past" (Summer 2007) 8 Chicago Journal of International Law 169–95.

[7] Irina Bokova, "Culture on the Front Line of New Wars" (2015) 22 (1) Brown Journal of World Affairs 289–96, especially 292–93.

[8] Amr Al-Azm, "The Pillaging of Syria's Cultural Heritage" (*Middle East Institute*, 22 May 2015) <https://www.mei.edu/publications/pillaging-syrias-cultural-heritage> accessed 10 September 2020.

[9] See Richard Goldstone, "The War Crime of Destroying Cultural Property" (*International Judicial Monitor*, Summer 2016) <http://www.judicialmonitor.org/summer2016/globaljudicialperspective.html> for many good examples of war fighting by means of destroying cultural property, and for some of the standard rationales against this—eg, its demoralizing effect and its affront to human dignity.

[10] Laurie Rush, "Working with the Military to Protect Archaeological Sites and Other forms of Cultural Property" (2012) 44 (3) World Archaeology 359–77.

so they are actions worth the risk of loss of life to prevent, meriting the status of war crimes.

There are some extant arguments for exceptions to these views: on some rare occasions the destruction of cultural artifacts may be regrettably necessary to some valuable military or humanitarian end, or their preservation may be too costly in lives and materiel. There are also exceptions to be made when trade in artifacts encourages the discovery and protection of items that would otherwise be forgotten or damaged in war, or will result in repatriating items to their originating people or nations as part of the unwinding of colonialism, or will bring about the restoration of stolen property after war. Trading in cultural objects by museums is also sometimes defended, since the presentation of these items by museums creates a majestic exhibition of human creativity through history and allows a wider audience to appreciate their beauty and significance—a consideration that may in some cases countermand the argument for repatriation. For instance, James Cuno, president and CEO of the J. Paul Getty Trust, one of the world's most powerful art institutions, argues that we should aspire to cultural cosmopolitanism, representing all cultures in various museums rather than repatriating cultural artifacts to their native sites, the latter being a problematic nationalistic idea.[11]

For some sorts of cultural objects, namely, curios, there is simply not much objection to their trade. After all, they are large in number, well-understood archeologically, and not particularly essential to the identity of any extant culture. In this case, why not permit the activity as something that contributes to the economy by providing employment and that allows the indulgence of the tastes of collectors? Further, there are situations where regulating trade would fetishize these artifacts in ways unhealthy for their originating populations. Finally, in some cases, the improbable odds of implementing successful regulatory practices make the game not worth the candle.

Despite these considerations, the dominant if not sole attitude is that theft and intentional destruction of cultural property constitute inherently bad actions.

[11] See James Cuno, "Culture War: The Case against Repatriating Museum Artifacts" (November/December 2014) 93 (6) Foreign Affairs 119–24.

III. When Cultural Artifacts are Oppressive and Hegemonic

The foregoing positions both undersell and oversell the meaning of cultural artifacts in certain ways; therefore, we need to reconfigure the debate in starker terms. My main argument is that, like the cultures that create them, some artifacts have oppressive and hegemonic effects (e.g., when they represent and valorize mass atrocities). When this is the case, they should be fair game for targeted destruction in war by those peoples whom they oppress.

Art and cultural objects are infrastructures and transmitters of cultures. Cultures, in turn, are partly comprised of rules for the distribution of goods and for the assigning of entitlements. This is why cultures matter, morally and politically, and it is also one of the reasons their artifacts matter. Cultures that disentitle some of their people are understandable targets for the discontented. The destruction of oppressive cultural infrastructure, along with direct hostilities against ordinary members and agents of oppressing cultures, provide methods of combat and redress for the disentitled when the methods approved of within civilization have failed. To these people, typically members of minority cultures, the memes, art and artifacts of the cultures that oppress them are weapons against them. And the destruction of these things is a counter-weapon. Indeed, for people without much power in civilization, this is often their only counter-weapon.

War is often due to a clash of cultures over who is entitled to what. Since each culture's artifacts can constitute symbols of contested and often oppressive negative value to the other, far from being an evil or something rightfully classed as a crime, sometimes the theft or destruction of cultural artifacts is morally appropriate.

Consider Nazi architecture, art, costumes, and literature. There is a strong case that the combating of Nazism required the destruction of its cultural artifacts, and that their preservation would have been the continuation of Jewish oppression. There is more than just hate speech; there are also such things as hate architecture and monuments. Thus, there could have been no well-founded objection had Jewish resistance fighters blown up a Nazi statuary and edifices in World War II. Moreover, had there then been a market for Nazi memorabilia, there would have been a case for theft of and trade in its artifacts as a means of financing the resistance to the Nazi agenda. The opposite, however, would be true of Nazi destruction of Jewish cultural objects to advance the Nazi agenda, and of theft of Jewish memorabilia by Nazis to finance that agenda—both would be wrong sorts of actions.

Confederate monuments in the United States are further examples of cultural artifacts that would be understandable targets in overcoming oppression. As the American Historical Association says:[12]

> The bulk of the [building of Confederate monuments] took place not in the immediate aftermath of the Civil War but from the close of the 19th century into the second decade of the 20th. Commemorating not just the Confederacy but also the "Redemption" of the South after Reconstruction, this enterprise was part and parcel of the initiation of legally mandated segregation and widespread disenfranchisement across the South. Memorials to the Confederacy were intended, in part, to obscure the terrorism required to overthrow Reconstruction, and to intimidate African Americans politically and isolate them from the mainstream of public life. A reprise of commemoration during the mid-20th century coincided with the Civil Rights Movement and included a wave of renaming and the popularization of the Confederate flag as a political symbol. Events in Charlottesville and elsewhere indicate that these symbols of white supremacy are still being invoked for similar purposes.[13]

A related, plausibly just pretext for theft of and trade in cultural artifacts would be this. Suppose some artifacts were constructed on the backs of oppressed peoples. An example would be where one race has profited from the enslavement of another, as in the United States. Another example would be where one religion has dominated another, securing for its members greater rights, freedoms, and wealth at the expense of practitioners of other religions, something exemplified in the different balances between, for example, Sunni and Shia Muslims in different countries in the Middle East.[14] Yet further,

[12] The American Historical Association Statement on Confederate Monuments (August 2017) <https://www.historians.org/news-and-advocacy/aha-advocacy/aha-statement-on-confederate-monuments> accessed 9 September 2020.

[13] On the Charlottesville reference see Meghan Keneally, "What to Know about the Violent Charlottesville Protests and Anniversary Rallies" (*ABC News*, 8 August 2018) <https://abcnews.go.com/US/happen-charlottesville-protest-anniversary-weekend/story?id=57107500> accessed 9 September 2020. Keneally writes: "On Aug. 12, 2017, a 'Unite the Right' rally in Charlottesville turned deadly when a 20-year-old Ohio man allegedly accelerated his car into a crowd of counter-protesters, killing 32-year-old Heather Heyer and leaving 19 others injured, five critically . . . Charlottesville had been in a months-long battle over what to do with a statue of Gen. Robert E. Lee, who led the Confederate army during the Civil War."

[14] See "Sunnis and Shia: Islam's Ancient Schism" (*BBC News*, 4 January 2016) <https://www.bbc.com/news/world-middle-east-16047709> accessed 11 September 2020. For extensive documentation

perhaps more contestable examples, would be in the relations between the Christian West and the Muslim Middle East, especially as expressed in conflicts over control of resources in the Middle East, and as continuing conflicts dating back to The Crusades. Also suppose it is the rebellion by the enslaved or dominated peoples that is the occasion of war. Then these people seizing the artifacts of the oppressor culture (religious artifacts, venerated cultural objects) and selling them to finance their war of liberation is arguably morally defensible. Such motivation is claimed by some of those looting and selling cultural artifacts in Syria, for example.[15]

In the Nazi art and the Confederate monuments cases, it seemed defensible to destroy cultural products for their in effect legitimizing the unfair treatment of a group of people. A rather different scenario that makes it problematic to universally condemn the politically motivated, strategically targeted destruction of cultural artifacts is when a given culture's artifacts compete for space with possibly morally superior artifacts, as in occupying contested ground in competing myths of the primal right of the peoples who created these artifacts to the land on which they have been constructed. If one culture has better title to this ground than the other, arguably they have a right to destroy the intruder's artifact and replace it with one of their own. There may well be examples in the Israel-Palestine conflict. Suppose Jewish settlers build a synagogue on land whose ownership is contested by followers of Islam. One can imagine the impulse to destroy the synagogue and replace it with a mosque as being part of the contesting of these claims. (I take no side here on that conflict.)

Sometimes an item may have both the status of being a cultural artifact and of being something materially part of oppression. For example, arguably the Twin Towers, while icons of architectural achievement in the West, were also the site of financial transactions by businesses in the petrochemicals industry, some of which have extensive interests in Middle Eastern oil, and the defense industries, some of which profit from sales to US-supported regimes in the Middle East. And some Muslim factions in the Middle East see US actions there as illegitimate, as in effect kleptocratic, and has having the result

of these asymmetries and their effects in the Middle East, see generally Sarah Chayes, *Thieves of State: Why Corruption Threatens Global Security* (New York, WW Norton & Company 2015).

[15] See Terrence K Kelly, James Dobbins, Barbara Sude, and Ben Connable, "Knowing the Enemy: Understanding the Islamic State and Principles for Defeating It" (The Rand Corporation 2017) <https://www.rand.org/pubs/perspectives/PE200.html> accessed 11 September 2020.

of oppressing Muslim people—taking their rightful oil wealth and coercively determining their destinies. Under that description it could seem that the destruction of the Twin Towers was a just assault on an unjust culture by means of assault on one of its central cultural artifacts.[16]

The justice of the attack in this case is of course contestable. Nevertheless, the general point remains that it is doubtful whether we can decide that the destruction of a given piece of cultural property by an agent of one side in a conflict is bad without first deciding which side in the conflict is just. Sometimes it will be morally permissible for oppressed peoples and their allies to destroy some artifacts, as in the Nazi case. But sometimes preservation of cultural artifacts will be morally appropriate, as in saving indigenous art from erasure by the cultures that have sought to conquer indigenous peoples. (There is much more to say, case by case, about who has rights and duties to do what here, how much human risk and material the parties involved should undertake, what the rights and duties of bystanders would be, and so on.[17]) More generally, the question of the status of the destruction of artifacts should depend on whether the effects of their existence are morally good or bad. This could, in some cases, require the preservation of an artifact of an unjust and oppressive culture—for instance, if its preservation would have good effects by virtue of being a cautionary example. The preservation of Nazi death camps could be such a case—more later on.

Given that cultural artifacts can be oppressive and hegemonic, the dominant attitude that theft and intentional destruction of cultural property constitute inherently bad actions appears to be flawed. The truth is more complex. Sometimes theft and trade of one culture's items should be encouraged as a way of helping another culture overcome unjust oppression, or as a way of safeguarding items of a just culture that would otherwise be lost; sometimes theft and trade should be forbidden for being an aid to an oppressing culture. Sometimes we would be right to protect certain artifacts, those under attack from oppressive cultures. Sometimes we do evil if we would protect certain artifacts, oppressive artifacts that would be well destroyed.

[16] See Chayes (n 16) 183. Chayes writes: "Perhaps Al Qaeda's main intent was not to kill a large number of Americans so much as to visit a spectacular symbolic punishment upon the manifestations of what it saw as a criminal kleptocracy that controlled the most powerful instruments of force on earth."

[17] For a start on this complex issue, see Helen Frowe and Derek Matravers, "Conflict and Cultural Heritage: A Moral Analysis of the Challenges of Heritage Protection"(J Paul Getty Trust Occasional Papers in Cultural Heritage Policy, No 3, Getty Publications 2019).

There will be cases, however, where even some oppressive cultural objects should be preserved for their historical or aesthetic value, provided they can be prevented from having their toxic effects. One way this might be achieved is by removing the objects from the situation where they are oppressive and recontextualizing them with the benefit of critical analysis and historical and political perspective in museums. There, the artifacts can be surrounded in symbols that reveal them as morally problematic. If the objects are to remain in situ, however, a similar effect might be achieved by affixing of plaques, or by the artifacts being broadly condemned. Ensconcing these objects in museums, giving them context with plaques, and condemning them in public discourse, are a bit like isolating a computer virus: we prevent something from having its designed effect—in the case of cultural artifacts we prevent them from transmitting hate, or from perpetuating in-group out-group distinctions. Thus just because an artifact has a tainting past or a problematic political consequence now does not mean it must permanently have it. Just as there can be negotiations between cultures to attain a moral rapprochement in morally asymmetrical conflict, cultural artifacts can be recontextualized so their transcultural value comes to be the most salient fact about them. And this may make their preservation permissible. In some cases, their preservation may be a good thing not for their aesthetic value, or for their being part of the historical record, but because it is *morally* required that we keep these things around as warnings and reminders. (Think of the UNESCO resolution mandating preservation of Nazi concentration camps from World War II.[18]) While the continued existence, or at least omnipresence, of some of these things might seem tantamount to hate speech, there would be some of the usual arguments from defenses of free speech for preserving them: we need to know these ideas are out there in order to continually evaluate them and continually refute them for those who encounter them for the first time.[19]

Creating safe contexts for these objects will often be controversial. This is due again to (and further proof of) art and cultural artifacts having the power of weapons, so that their destruction or preservation, their theft or safeguarding, can be powerful means of war. Suppose a given artifact valorizes one of the sides in a conflict. Then people who take different sides on the substantive matter of the conflict will likely now reprise that conflict in

[18] See *Resolution adopted by the General Assembly on the Holocaust Remembrance*, A/RES/60/7 (1 November 2005) < http://undocs.org/A/RES/60/7>.

[19] My thanks to LW for suggesting many of the points in this paragraph. The classic defense of free speech is John Stuart Mill, *On Liberty*.

disagreements about what to do with the artifact. Think of the controversies over whether or how to preserve commemorative statues of people who were both founders of cities and oppressors of Black or indigenous peoples in the United States and Canada. Should these statues remain where they are, or does respect for the oppressed require that they be destroyed or put in museums? If plaques are to be affixed, giving the proper history of the statues and the persons they represent, which side gets to write the plaques?

IV. Theft and Destruction of Cultural Artifacts as a Better Means of Warfare than Killing

I suggest, further, that the threat of theft and destruction of cultural artifacts can be a more humane means of leveraging toward victory in war than threats to debase, damage, or destroy human life. Therefore, such theft and destruction ought not necessarily to be conceived as war crimes. Instead these actions should be seen as a more ideal, more humane form of warfare than that form which involves taking the lives of soldiers. Indeed, it would be a happy fantasy to imagine a war fought only by violence against things, not people. True, some killing is likely inevitable. For wars are only over when people stop fighting, and some people will stop fighting only when they are dead. A sociological factor to consider in deciding whether one's side in a given conflict can be advanced by attacking cultural property instead of people would be whether this will really advance the war effort, or only make one's opponent fight harder. Still, it would seem to be ideal to displace the locus of destruction onto inanimate things so far as possible.

We designate classes of actions war crimes when they are so evil that we especially want to disincentivize them. Well, do we really want to disincentivize combat by means of theft of, trade in, or destruction of cultural artifacts? Do we want to disincentivize it compared to, say, killing? Surely we would rather have wars be conducted by theft and destruction of cultural artifacts.

In what follows I will discuss seven different objections to this proposal, seven arguments for why the theft and destruction of cultural artifacts should be a war crime when ordinary killing premised on combatant immunity or military proportionality of harm is not: (a) They are worse crimes. (b) They are not worse crimes but there is less good justification for engaging in them, and greater risk of them being engaged in for nonpolitical reasons, so engaging in them should be more punished. (c) The people who typically engage in them do not have the same sort of authorization to do these things as people who engage in killings, perhaps because they tend to be non-state actors who therefore do not have the authorization of a state for what they do. (d) The crimes are ones more able to be deterred by being counted as war crimes than would be the deterring of, say, killing. For example, killing might be thought of as passion motivated and therefore not deterrable by having war-crime status, while theft is more coldly engaged in and therefore deterrable. (e) The crimes are, by virtue of their nature, redressable by being considered war crimes in a way that killing is not—property stolen can be restored to its owner, while a life taken is permanently lost. (f) They are crimes which cannot be addressed in any other way than by seeing them as war crimes while killing is not like this. (g) They are crimes for which, as a matter of *real politick*, greater agreement about doing something about them is possible, perhaps because, in many conflicts, all sides benefit from the preservation of cultural artifacts no matter who prevails.

I shall moot these objections in no particular order in the following general discussion. I begin with two items that can be quickly disposed of. About (d), that killing is motivated by passion and therefore not deterrable, while stealing and trading are done coldly and therefore are deterrable, I would point out that some killing in war is perfectly cold and calculated and to that degree deterrable; and some theft and trade of objects is motivated by passion. About (e), that property can be restored to its owner but killings cannot be undone, therefore the former should be a war crime, the latter not, I suggest that killings can be compensated for, whether by just retribution—a life for a life, for example—or by the murderer owing a conciliatory payment to the bereaved. So killing can be treated as a redressable crime.

Now on to matters needing more discussion. First, are theft and destruction of cultural property greater crimes than killing? Arguably not. Things should matter less than lives, so if anything should be a war crime, it should be the taking of life, not the destruction or theft of property. Things can in some sense have greater value than lives. The insured value of a building might be twenty million dollars, the insured value of a life one million. But it does not necessarily follow that someone who destroys a building has done something twenty times worse than someone who takes a life. In any case, it would be consistent with the proposal to make theft a war crime that someone who steals or destroys something worth, say, fifty thousand dollars, something with much less insured value than a single human life, should be considered guilty of a war crime, while someone who takes a single human life would not be so considered; and this seems absurd enough.

There is a connection between this issue and the question whether destruction of cultural property ought to have comparable standing as a war crime to such other war crimes as rape. Even if both are bad, arguably the latter is worse. And if prosecutorial resources are limited, they should go to penalizing violations of persons, not destruction of artifacts. This issue was raised vividly when, in 2016, the International Criminal Court (ICC) convicted Ahmad Al Faqi Al Mahdi of intentionally directing attacks against religious and historic buildings in Timbuktu, Mali during the 2012 occupation by Ansar Dine and Al-Qaeda in the Islamic Maghreb. There ensued controversy over why crimes against artifacts were prioritized for prosecution over other crimes. For this was "the first case at the ICC arising from the 2012 Mali conflict . . . And it was the first time that the ICC had brought a war crimes charge against a defendant for the destruction of cultural sites."[20]

In their two commentaries on this issue,[21] Brian Daniels and Helen Walasek, respectively, argue that while it may seem problematic to have the destruction of cultural property prosecuted as a war crime while things like rape go unprosecuted, the destruction of cultural property should not be minimized, since it amounts to erasing the identities of peoples and should therefore be seen as analogous to the crime of genocide, which everyone agrees is an atrocity in all meanings of the term. As explained by Martin Hamilton in this volume, the drafters of the Genocide Convention planned to include the concept of cultural genocide in the Convention, but the concept was taken out just before the last draft.[22] Still, this supports the idea that even if we are right to insist that respect for persons should be primary in wartime, arguably part of respecting persons would be respecting the cultural edifices into which persons have poured their labor and money, edifices they have invested with symbolic value, and which support the social infrastructure within which they live their lives.

Among the many reasons there are for protecting such things, one is because sometimes surviving cultural property is the only means by which

[20] I quote from Brian I Daniels in Brian I Daniels and Helen Walasek, "Is the Destruction of Cultural Property a War Crime?" (*Apollo: International Art Magazine*, 28 November 2016) <http://www.apollo-magazine.com/is-the-destruction-of-cultural-property-a-war-crime/>.

[21] ibid.

[22] Martin Hamilton, "The Concept of Cultural Genocide" in this volume.

dispossessed peoples can reconnect to the aspects of their culture they need in order to overcome the trauma of cultural assault. The indigenous peoples of Canada, for example, have experienced generations of direct and vicarious trauma. They retain enough cultural memory to feel that it is natural for them to exist in ways not approved of by the conquering culture, but many of these people do not retain enough memory to feel strong and worthy in their differences from that culture. The only way they can rehabilitate is by accessing their languages, traditions, and art works, the very things their oppressors tried to obliterate. Once indigenous peoples have access to these items, they can see that their struggles are not their fault, but owe to them having valid impulses not honored by the conquering culture; their self-esteem can be restored by them seeing how they are descendants of a culture worthy in its own right, especially if it can be revived enough that the impulses toward living in certain ways, these people feel can find a context in which to be expressed and by which to be affirmed.[23]

Nevertheless, I would argue that a person's body and freedom should be protected over their material creations; for people can reorient their commitments to cultural objects in ways they cannot to their physical welfare and freedom. It would still seem true, therefore, that killing and rape should be prevented/prosecuted first, then the destruction and theft of cultural objects. So the former should have higher status as a war crime under international criminal law compared the latter.

It might be argued that a person's body and freedom should have priority only unless they would wish otherwise. I would reply that their wishing otherwise is only an argument if the person is in a position to competently wish otherwise, something made doubtful by their very preference for the preservation of a thing over preservation of themselves.

Of course there is much more to say about all of this. I shall now discuss it further in the context of a proposal to reimagine warfare as ideally fought not by the debasement and destruction of people, but by the theft and destruction of things.

[23] Thanks to Max Dysart and LW for discussion on this point. For a First Nations perspective on the matter see Daniel N Paul, *We Were Not The Savages* (3rd edn, Fernwood Publishing 2006). See also the Government of Canada Official Commission Review, *Honouring the Truth, Reconciling for the Future: Summary of the Final Report of the Truth and Reconciliation Commission of Canada* (The Truth and Reconciliation Commission of Canada 2015) < https://ehprnh2mwo3.exactdn.com/wp-content/uploads/2021/01/Executive_Summary_English_Web.pdf > accessed 20 May 2020.

V. Objections to Warfare by Means of Theft and Destruction of Cultural Artifacts

Many will object in principle to this means of warfare.[24] They will see it as approving of conduct that is and ought to be conceived as war crime. But why should the destruction of cultural artifacts be a war crime? Because it is an atrocity? Frederik Rosén has offered a victimology of cultural object destruction according to which the destruction inflicts harms beyond material damage, harms based in people's emotional relations to objects, their value attitudes.[25] This is of course right. But the destruction does not seem to rise to the level of atrocity exemplified in the mass slaughter of actual people. Calling cultural object destruction an atrocity seems too strong a claim when compared to such a paradigm. So when people say theft and destruction of artifacts ought to be a war crime, they do not mean that committing these acts would be atrocious. They just mean that such acts are not things for which you should be legally immunized from prosecution just because there was a war on.

But why not? After all, many of the people who do these things are arguably just soldiers doing what they are told. And why should even the masterminds be punished? After all, if artifacts have value, then their destruction is a kind of harm to the enemy in war; and why should it not be a permitted harm?

Maybe the argument is that it is gratuitous in war, that it is not justified by military necessity. But arguably anything that people would rather have us not do can be made into a weapon, a thing the doing of which and the threatened further doing of which might bring about the end of the war by inducing surrender. It can also be made into the kind of thing people would dread about war generally, something that might therefore dissuade people from war. That means the following argument should not necessarily be available: that I should get to sue for the return of my grandmother's art collection because its theft was gratuitous in the fighting of the war. For under the current proposal, it may not have been gratuitous. Theft can be a weapon of war. And how odd if after the war I can sue for the return of an art work, and

[24] We considered earlier the practical objection that, in a given case, deliberate destruction of cultural objects will not advance the cause sought, but will merely make one's opponent fight harder and so would be self-defeating. In this section, however, I am only interested in objections to the effect that warfare by cultural heritage destruction is wrong in itself, and so should not be used even if it would work.

[25] Frederik Rosén, "Mission Impossible: Weighing the Protection of Cultural Property against Human Lives in this volume.

prosecute its thief, but cannot bring a charge of murder against a soldier for killing someone dear to me (my soldier son, for example, or someone killed as part of collateral damage in an action justified as militarily necessary).

It is true that committing serious *gratuitous* harms in war ought to be a crime; and this would be an objection to permitting random looting or random destruction of art and cultural artifacts. But it would not always be an objection to targeted, strategic looting or destruction. For committing harms by stealing cultural property or by destroying cultural artifacts is not necessarily gratuitous. Not if, for example, it is necessary to advancing a just cause in a just war. To give a less problematic example of such a pretext, everyone allows that sometimes artifacts must be used as bastions from which to fight; and that sometimes these bastions must be destroyed in the course of justified fighting.

We sometimes see the destruction of artifacts as even more shocking than the destruction of persons. Indeed, the destruction of cultural artifacts has been described as a method of fourth-generation warfare intended to shock and demoralize.[26] Why such destruction has this effect is not clear. Perhaps we think of artifacts as innocent things, like children, so that their destruction is especially heinous. And yet artifacts have no sentience, so this analogy is not strictly accurate—the artifacts do not suffer in the course of being destroyed, and they do not care whether they are destroyed.

Another possibility is that their destruction has the symbolic value of representing the destruction of the civilization and people that produced them.[27] Since the destruction of artifacts is not inherently the destruction of people, however, nor of the totality of their culture, our reaction of outrage may be strictly out of proportion. This means that not only is this symbolic value not a good objection to such destruction; it actually provides an additional argument in favor of using artifact destruction as a method of warfare. For we can see such destruction as warfare by what I have elsewhere called moral pseudo-injury,[28] that is, by an action that seems to be an injury only to those who believe something demonstrably false, or not demonstrably true,

[26] Department of Defense, Cultural Property Protection—Theory, Part 1. Retrieved 31 March 2020.

[27] For some interesting reservations about whether cultural destruction and looting ought to be seen as a war crime, and as a basis for intervention under the idea of Right to Protect, see Frederik Rosén, "PAPER for UNESCO Expert Group Meeting on Cultural Heritage Destruction and R2P" (Paris, The Danish Institute for International Studies 26–27 November 2015).

[28] See Duncan MacIntosh, "PTSD Weaponized: A Theory of Moral Injury," paper mooted at the Center for Ethics and the Rule of Law conference, "Preventing and Treating the Invisible Wounds of War: Combat Trauma and Psychological Injury," University of Pennsylvania Law School (3–5 December 2015).

something characteristic, for example, of all religions. Destruction of something wrongly perceived to be important given false or indemonstrably true beliefs, for example, destruction of a religious artifact, is not really a harm, since the thing that would have to exist—a god—in order for it to be a harm, does not exist. (In truth, the artifact was not created or beloved by a god, nor bestowed on a people or commanded to be preserved by a god; it does not represent a god that specially deserved representing; destroying it does not disrespect a god.) This may make warfare by moral pseudo-injury morally superior to warfare by actual injury. And warfare by the destruction of cultural products mistakenly invested with meaning may therefore be a morally superior substitute for warfare by the destruction of persons.

Perhaps such injury is really more than just pseudo-injury, rising instead to the level of some kind of actual injury—after all, feelings get hurt, and so on. But even if this is true, such injury still does not, from a moral value perspective, seem as bad as physically maiming and killing people.

Demanding the preservation of art works and cultural artifacts in war is like advocating war fighting by the functional equivalent of a neutron bomb, a bomb that, notoriously, harms people with radiation, but minimizes blast, thus saving property. And demanding this before the prosecuting of rape crimes and more thoroughly criminalizing killing in war casts warfare into something with extremely unflattering materialistic motivations. Neutron bomb warfare has been universally condemned, in part for the reasons that it would make warfighting too tempting, and grotesquely cynical and clinical.

But this may give us another possible explanation for why some people seem to favor warfighting by killing over warfighting by theft and destruction of property. The explanation may, strangely, derive from notions of integrity in warfighting: we might think someone could not possibly have a stake in merely killing someone, therefore it must have been done for a higher cause. This is false, however; for one can have a passion for someone's death on absurd pretexts. Still, someone is more likely to have a personal stake in stealing property—they might derive personal advantage from it. So that method of warfare is prima facie more suspicious.

But what of the destruction of property? It is less obviously something that would typically be done for merely personal gain (unless venting rage counts only as a personal gain, something unlikely in the typical cases, where the rage is more political or religious). At any rate, cannot we distinguish between the thief getting something out of the theft and a nation-state or political movement getting something out of it in the course of legitimately conducting war? If so, we might purify this as a method of warfighting by taking steps to ensure that the thieving only advances legitimate political goals, and does not result in illegitimate profit, whether for individuals or states. For example, we might arrange for things stolen in war to be warehoused for some long period (much as we sometimes seal sensitive documents) so that they benefit nobody until enough time has passed that nobody illicitly profits. Would that not safeguard integrity? The distinction between doing something for personal gain—which is the motive of crime—and doing something to advance a political cause, is vital. The former is objectionable in war (crimes of desperation apart), the latter, a prima facie wartime justification for actions that in other contexts would be crimes.

One reason we do not want to damage public property generally in war is that it is needed for people's lives (think of civilian objects such as houses and critical infrastructure); and if we defeat people by destroying these things, we may wind up indirectly killing more people than necessary. Destroying their things will also cost us more later when we have to help survivors rebuild in the peacetime that follows. But these good issues are not the same issue as the destruction of artifacts that are significant purely aesthetically, historically or scientifically, not functionally.

Maybe then these items should be regarded as like soldiers in armed conflict, namely, as permissible targets during war; and maybe we should regard actions against them as ones afforded the usual combatant immunity—immunity from prosecution after cessation of conflict.[29] But are these not civilian objects, in contrast with, say, military buildings, army trucks, and so on? And is it not inappropriate to target civilian objects, just as it is inappropriate to target civilian persons? As we now think of how wars should be fought, this would be a correct scruple. But I am proposing that those cultural objects that symbolize and promote oppression should be regarded as fair game in war. When it comes to being oppressive, then, the civilian/military distinction seems less the relevant one. I am talking in the first

[29] How would we then distinguish between "combatant" cultural heritage and "civilian" cultural heritage, especially given that the combatant/civilian distinction is not usually seen as aimed at minimizing oppression so much as at protecting civilian populations? (Thanks to Claire Finkelstein for the question.) This is a subtle matter. When two countries set their armies at each other in war, it is expected that the armies will fight it out in ways minimizing hazards to the civilian populations of both countries. But when one group in effect sets its *culture* at "war" with a population, it may not seem that there is a corresponding civilian thing to protect. I may be stretching the metaphor here, but perhaps combatant heritage is heritage implicated in oppression, while civilian heritage is neutral on that matter. Or maybe civilian heritage is whatever heritage is the unjustly oppressed one. Either way I suggest that oppressive cultural objects are fair game.

instance about structures of symbolic significance, not critical infrastructure. Although I can imagine a structure being so symbolic and transmitting of oppression, that even if it is also a piece of critical infrastructure for that part of a population that is doing the oppressing, it should be permissible to target it. Maybe it is acceptable to blow up a power station built to look like the Fuhrer, especially if it will be quickly replaced with something more symbolically innocent.

VI. The Objection from Cultural Genocide

The greatest objection to systematic theft and destruction of cultural artifacts as a legitimate means of warfare is the idea that to destroy a culture's artifacts is akin to destroying a people, to genocide. That appears to be the basis for the almost universal abhorrence of the practice. As was mentioned earlier, this link almost found a legal form in the Genocide Convention.

We can certainly imagine situations in which the destruction of a culture is the destruction of a people, just as we can imagine depriving a person of their right to do all of the things they would ever want to do as equivalent to the destruction of that person. Destruction of a culture is by definition the destruction of a people in the sense that it means no people can be identified as of that culture, losing whatever value and capacity to function in various ways that the identification conferred. Moreover, it can have many of the same effects as the killing of a large number of people, for example the effect of making land available for exploitation—you do not have to kill the people on the land to have this, you just have to deprive them of their cultural sense of entitlement to it, for example, by kidnapping their children and indoctrinating them, the next generation of these people, into a different conception of property, or into thinking they are not entitled to be on the land, or do not deserve to live the way they wanted to live on it.[30] (Think again of the indigenous peoples of North America.) Achieving these sorts of effects is among the motives for destroying a culture.

I suspect, however, that in some cases the deployment of the objection that destruction of cultural property is a kind of genocide and so should not be permitted in war, is due to a contestable understanding of the relation between respect for a people and respect for their cultural products.

[30] Thanks to LW for this insight.

We may tend to identify a people with its artifacts, making us think that to destroy their physical culture is akin to the destruction of the people, of their souls. But a culture and its objects are only things that structure the lives of a given people at a given time and in a given circumstance. This culture and its objects are not essential to those persons. For persons have a pre-cultural and transcultural identity—pre-cultural in that all humans have certain characters and needs dictated by their species membership prior to specific enculturation, transcultural in that all cultures share certain features by dint of the roles cultures serve in expressing the former characters and meeting the former needs. And persons can adapt to and create different cultures as their circumstances change. Their adaptations are undertaken with a view to meeting the needs all people have—for food, water, shelter, meaningful relationships, physical safety, and so on—needs that can be satisfied by any number of specific forms of culture. To deny this is to make a kind of fetish out of given cultures, to treat them as more important and valuable than they really are, to make them false ends in themselves.

Moreover, the rights people have to their artifacts and to the culture that produces them are not absolute and are not unconditional. People have a natural right only not to be *unjustly* deprived of these things.

Not all means of their privation is unjust. Think of naturally caused fish migration making the culture of Canadian East Coast fishing villages economically unviable, the culture comprised of boat building, net weaving, the songs and lore of the sea that accompany these things, the expertise in fishing, the community bonds needed to mount fishing enterprises, the architectures that support seaside life, the traditions of property and the handing down of fishing licenses, the deriving of dignity from honest work on the sea. It is sad when these things lose their pretext, but it is not obvious that people have a right to this culture. It is not obvious that they would have a right to be subsidized in it, for example. Arguably instead they should retrain and move on to different work and a different lifestyle and culture. (If the cause was not natural, but instead environmentally damaging activity of another group, matters would be different, and the fishing community might have rights to prevent, stop, or be compensated for the damage caused by such activity. Likewise if, while the cause was natural, the community was part of an insurance scheme against natural disasters of this sort, something in fact true of the community in question here by virtue of the participation of Canada's Maritime provinces in Canadian Confederation, which transfers money from have to have-not provinces as the fortunes of member provinces vary with time. But these things must be arranged before there are such rights.)

Moving on to other cases of cultures being extinguished but not unjustly, think of a culture coming to an end not by violent conflict but by critical thinking and sound argument (the project conducted and informed by philosophical reflection), as happens when religious and superstitious culture is replaced by secular and scientifically informed culture. Again, this is not obviously unjust. It would be difficult to argue that the people to whom this is happening somehow have a right to repine in their ignorance, or to be forcefully protected from the inexorable advance of knowledge. Certainly the pre-enlightenment culture would have no right to impose their culture on others.

Yet another case would be the extinction of violent, aggressive cultures by justified counterstrikes from those whom such cultures unjustly attack, and from resolutions from within such unjustly aggressive cultures to reform themselves, obvious examples being the renunciation of the militaristic, expansionist cultures of conquest of Japan and Germany after World War II.

Relatedly, not all cultures, even prima facie, have a right of preservation—again, think of Nazi culture, its, art, monuments, hate speech, and its artifacts of oppression, like gas chambers and concentration camps.

Further, sometimes the perception of people being massively injured by the destruction of cultural artifacts is really the perception of what is only a moral pseudo-injury, which is, recall, something that seems to be an injury only to those who believe something demonstrably false, or not demonstrably true. Think again of religions. Properly seen, the theft and destruction of their "cultural property" is not much different from the theft and destruction of property simpliciter. It is not additionally a violation of the sacred; for if that concept is defined by the relation of the thing in question to a god, and if no god exists, then the concept's very intelligibility and applicability are questionable.

Matters are different, of course, if a culture has a handle on important moral truths, and if its artifacts' continued existence, and continued holding in that culture's hands, are necessary to the attainment of morally important ends. (Think of enlightened legal codes, the documents that incarnate them, the people who hold to them, and the good actions these people then do.) But in that case what makes the preservation of these things (e.g., the documents of enlightened law) important is not that they are cultural products. It is that they are the incarnations and means of the right and the good.

What counts as that is precisely what is often the matter being contested in times of war. It might be thought that, since it is difficult to adjudicate in conflict between cultures who has the good culture and who the bad, we should just protect all cultures and so all cultural property. I suggest, however, that while this might be good counsel for difficult cases, it is not good counsel for obvious cases. Moreover, it is the commonest thing for observers in a conflict to find it easy to take a side; and it is universal for those engaged in conflict to have strong views about which side is right—their own, of course. This leaves us with the question how best to advance the perceived good side in a conflict. I say it is generally better to fight by attacking things than people. Although I suppose it could in principle happen that immoral people have produced good cultural objects, and that in such cases it is the people who need to go (or be induced to transform), not the objects.

Finally, as a philosopher I believe that, however difficult, there are truths to discern about which side in a conflict is just. We would therefore be abdicating our duty to make a determination if we just said it is difficult and all objects should be protected. For that would be like saying it is too much trouble to serve justice. (I recognize that, just as the Red Cross preserves political neutrality and so is allowed to minister to injuries of civilians on both sides of conflicts, which is good, so there might sometimes be pragmatic justification for a given nation being neutral about which culture in a conflict is the good culture.)

VII. The Objection from the Supposed Transcultural, Trans-Political Value of Cultural Artifacts

Some people argue that, regardless of their political significance and moral consequences, the artistic products of a culture have a timeless value, whether sourced in inherent aesthetic qualities of the products, or deriving from their exemplifying human creativity and ingenuity, or from their documentary and scientific importance; and that they should therefore be protected from destruction in war.[31] But these factors may be of lesser importance than the issues already discussed. Thus even if an artwork as such does not occupy a position on the spectrum of morally evaluable items, the effects of its

[31] See eg Leila Amineddoleh, "Protecting Cultural Heritage by Strictly Scrutinizing Museum Acquisitions" (2014) 24 (3) Media and Entertainment Law Journal 729–81.

existence can be so evaluated; and if these are bad enough then the destruction of the artwork that is their cause might be warranted. If some artifacts are instrumental to the oppression of a people, why should those people be made to pay the price of having to endure this oppression for the sake of scientific inquiry or aesthetically distanced appreciation? As Alexander A. Bauer suggests, we must always ask for whom the preservation of cultural objects is good, and by what measure.[32] For example, some culturally significant objects were originally designed to deteriorate. Bauer gives this example: "the 'war gods' figures made by the Native American Zuni are meant to disintegrate among the elements in order to maintain balance in their lives."[33] Bauer also points out that sometimes the repatriation of artifacts is sought by groups problematically seeking "to control the discourse about their cultural legacy and suppress unwanted narratives about the objects."[34]

Powers not directly involved in conflicts must take caution in assessing whether the aesthetic value of cultural artifacts outweighs whatever arguments may be made for their destruction on grounds of them forming part of a context of oppression for one of the parties in the conflict. It is all too easy for us in the West, for example, who may think of the cultural artifacts in the Middle East as merely of aesthetic, historical, or scientific interest, rather than as tools of political oppression, to insist on their preservation, not noticing their political toxicity. I can make this point in a logically extreme way: as a high-status white man in the West, I have no culture. That is, my culture is invisible to me. Culture is that quaint thing that other people have. What I have is true views, good taste, and well-premised practices. Nevertheless, I like to visit with the quaint artifacts of other cultures.

I am parodying myself here; but we all tend to see our own cultures as privileged in this way and to look upon others with some condescension. This puts us at risk of making an aesthetical, scientific, or historical fetish of the artifacts of other cultures, and of putting those values above things that may well have greater value—for example, saving people from oppression by these objects. The aesthetic or scientific value the objects may have to humanity at large is at best a competitor value to the values of those directly involved in conflict; and it is not obvious that it should be decisive. Even if there is, say, scientific value in relics, it does not follow that policy around their

[32] Alexander A Bauer, "New Ways of Thinking about Cultural Property: A Critical Appraisal of the Antiquities Trade Debates" (2007–2008) 31 Fordham International Law Journal 690–724.

[33] ibid 701.

[34] ibid 710–11.

preservation and trade should be designed to maximize their accessibility to scientific scrutiny.

Arguably science is only one value they serve, and science should yield to other values. There is nothing that makes it preeminent, any more than a scientific interest in my body, say, should automatically trump my rights to control what happens in and to my own body. It is even disputable whether the scientific significance of artifacts has value independently of a culture's valuing that sort of thing, which certain antiquarian, illiberal, and Luddite cultures ostensibly do not (e.g., ISIL, Boko Haram). And even if there is such a thing as disinterested value, the value of a thing as viewed from nowhere, As Thomas Nagel has put it, other things would doubtless have that kind of value, too, things like political justice.[35] Scientific value would be merely one value among many, a value whose advancement might displace other, possibly morally more preeminent values. Besides, even were there an objective truth about such matters, and even if there were theoretical agreement about it, this could well separate from what people care about, and from what they are inclined to do. So regardless of whether these value questions are objective, subjective, or relative, people with a scientific interest in cultural artifacts should have to negotiate their preservation and access to them with stakeholders who have other values.[36]

I suspect there is a similar discussion to be had concerning those who would preserve even politically problematic cultural artifacts for their historical value. I would distinguish this from the motive of scientific value, which might want to preserve the object for its usefulness in inspiring sociological or anthropological generalizations. By contrast, when people want to preserve an object for its historical value, they do so from a love of history qua history: this thing matters because it was the product of this event that happened. And again, we can question whether love of history as a value should automatically trump, say, the value of escape from the oppression that this object may be perpetuating.

I would make a similar reply to those who claim to value artifacts not qua things, but qua carriers of meaning or narrative—for the role they played in the story of a person, a people, or a time, or for the story they tell or can

[35] Thomas Nagel, *The View from Nowhere* (OUP 1986).

[36] A claim, eg, that science is more important than justice, is said to be objective if it is possible for a given opinion to be wrong about it, subjective if its truth is just a matter of opinion or preference so that one cannot be wrong about it, and relative if its truth varies depending on the standpoint of the person making the judgment.

be used to tell. For again, we can imagine these values not holding for some people and being outweighed by other factors even for people who do hold those values. (I was surprised at the vehemence with which preservationist values were expressed by those people I met at the Center for Ethics and the Rule of Law conference, mentioned before, who are in the business of curating cultural objects—museum directors, art dealers, and so on—and who took umbrage to some of the suggestions in this paper. But I am not immune to their values. At one point we were invited to view five-thousand-year-old Mesopotamian cuneiform tablets. As I looked at these things, carefully lifted off of a rolling tray by a man wearing blue gloves, seeing these things as smaller than cell phones, and realizing how small therefore were the hands that used them, I found myself weeping.)

I have suggested that some parties in conflicts might be justified in destroying or stealing cultural artifacts, in part because the existence of these things is a harm to them, a part of their oppression, or because their existence yields a profit to others that is a consequence of the oppression of the former people. But America (and perhaps its Western allies) in this case, as in so many others, may have a special status. Just as many of the conflicts in which America finds itself are asymmetrical conflicts, conflicts with people vastly inferior to America in numbers, technology, organization, and situational advantage, so America may find itself in culturally asymmetrical conflicts, ones in which, while its culture and cultural artifacts oppress, or at least trouble, others, the reverse is not true: America is not harmed by the cultures it combats, only by the agents of these cultures. America is not, as a collection of persons and physical things, nor as a culture (i.e., as a prevailing set of ideas, practices, and institutions), existentially threatened by other cultures. America may therefore have a kind of duty of condescension: since it is not harmed by these things, it would be gratuitous for America to destroy or confiscate them; and so not even the doctrine of military necessity could justify it in doing these things—in America's case, there is no such necessity. Ironically, the very conceit that America is prone to about its own cultural exceptionalism and superiority can result in America having a duty to obey stricter limits than other cultures on how it fights wars. (For example, Matthew Thurlow complains that American military manuals on protecting cultural artifacts do not go far enough.[37])

[37] See Matthew Thurlow, "Protecting Cultural Property in Iraq: How American Military Policy

This itself raises interesting issues: Ought America to feel more threatened than it does by other cultures and their artifacts? Is it from a kind of moral obtuseness that it feels unharmed by them? Is this an instance of the opposite of moral pseudo-injury, namely, moral pseudo-non-injury? After all, America is often slighted in various cultures, perhaps in ways not obvious to America. This may be part of an explanation of why America is sometimes surprised by its being hated: because Americans do not see the problem they get ambushed by anger when it is too late easily to appease it.

I wonder too whether it is not hypocrisy to see cultural artifacts in other people's conflicts as inherently innocent things therefore needing protection. For we certainly do not so see them when we are in the gunsights of warfare by means of culture. It is just that, when it is happening to us, we cannot see it as mere clash of cultures. We see it as *war*. Think of the impulse to destruction of "un-American" cultural objects in America in the era of paranoia about the influence of that culture which is called communism.

So it is contestable (and contested by some of the parties in the conflicts that occasion this debate) that there is a transcultural, trans-political value to cultural artifacts; and the idea that there is such a thing may be a delusion of us in the West, a stance of privilege, and a condescension committed by people who see themselves as above the cultures and conflicts whose artifacts they prize and admire—an attitude that vanishes when we find ourselves embroiled in conflict with cultures who truly do threaten us, whence we righteously seek destruction of these cultures' artifacts. And even if there is such a transcultural, trans-political value, it should yield to more pressing political and moral concerns in wartime.

VIII. The Objection from Both Sides in a Conflict Having an Interest in Preserving Cultural Artifacts, Regardless of which Side Wins

Perhaps one idea behind the criminalization of deliberately destroying cultural artifacts in war from a political motive is that they have value for both sides, so both want these objects to survive in case they win and then get to exploit the objects. This idea is amenable to a game-theoretic analysis: since

Comports with International Law" (2005) 8 (1) Yale Human Rights and Development Journal 153–87.

each party would like to win the conflict, thence to have exclusive use of the cultural artifacts, but since all parties benefit from the artifacts after the war regardless of who wins (even if the losing party benefits a bit less), the parties are in a kind of Prisoner's Dilemma with each other about them. In a Prisoner's Dilemma, one party can do very well only if the other party does very poorly, but both can do quite well by making and keeping an agreement to cooperate and respect each other's interests, this shareable benefit sometimes called the cooperative surplus, while both will do quite poorly if both violate this agreement. If the relations between warring parties and cultural artifacts is as to the cooperative surplus sought in Prisoners' Dilemmas, there may be rationality to pledges to preserve artifacts, and so to laws that require punishment for their destruction. An example might be a part of a town in the Middle East with religious significance for two competing religious groups.

By the same token, however, if you want something, I can harm you by actually destroying it and can control you by threatening to destroy it. Ironically the argument that cultural artifacts are cared about by one or all sides, or that they have high intrinsic value, is an argument for both sides regarding them as potential military targets, not against. For to the degree that these things are seen as having value, to that degree the threat of their theft or destruction can be an effective extortion; and extortion, after all, is the very method of warfare.

Here we have the classic Deterrence Dilemma: Can it be rational to form and fulfill a threat to do something not only other-harming but also self-harming if the other does not comply with some demand? There is academic controversy about this (centered on the theories of David Gauthier[38]), but since at least some students of the issue think the answer is yes, let us assume the yes answer for the sake of argument. In that case, it can be leveraged in war: one side can win if it manages credibly to convert the situation from an Assurance Game (whose structure is that each of us will refrain from doing a thing harmful to us both if each of us can be sure the other will refrain) into a Deterrence Dilemma (whose structure is that one party threatens to do something harmful to both parties unless the other party gives a concession)—the threatener must only manage to present as sincere and therefore likely to fulfill the threat. Of course, the other party can reply likewise; and

[38] For an introduction to this debate, see Duncan MacIntosh, "Assuring, Threatening, a Fully Maximizing Theory of Practical Rationality, and the Practical Duties of Agents" (2013) 123 (4) Ethics 625–66.

if the reply is credible, then the two parties are in a Mexican Standoff (a situation where neither side can gain an advantage by means of threat) or a Game of Chicken (where each side has an incentive to veer off from its threat strategy in order to avoid the catastrophe of mutual defeat and so of self-defeat). In that event, both sides have an incentive to reconfigure the situation as a Prisoner's Dilemma and to solve it by seeing it as an Assurance Game, thereby to back off the other party and to preserve the object valued by both in the conflict.

But one problem with this sort of thinking is that it presumes cultural objects have value to both sides no matter who wins. This is not a relevant consideration for the most outrageous of the destroyers of cultural artifacts, namely, ISIL. ISIL does not have a stake in the preservation of cultural artifacts since it opposes them as idolatry. So there is not the Prisoner's Dilemma argument for nondestruction in that conflict.

IX. The Argument Against Theft and Destruction of Cultural Artifacts from their Uniqueness and Irreplaceability

It might be argued that stealing or destroying property is worse than killing for some less tangible reason than, say, the matter of its insurable replacement value. It might be, for example, that it destroys a culture or that it symbolizes a disrespect for a culture. But this would only be an argument because a culture matters to someone. Obviously cultures matter to those who participate in them, and this should count for something. But again, it is questionable whether it should count for more than the death of a person. (Remember, we are here debating whether destroying cultural objects should be a war crime when killing a person—a soldier—is not.)

Suppose someone destroys the central relic of some religion, meaning that this relic can no longer be the thing around which certain cultural practices rotate. Perhaps a copy of the relic could be built, but arguably this would result in a different and less good culture, one centered on the duplicate rather than the original. Imagine some people met regularly to reminisce about John F. Kennedy Jr. while passing around the quarter that was in his pocket when he was shot. Then someone destroys the quarter. One cannot pass around the original quarter anymore, and passing around a quarter just like the original, but that was never in J.F.K.'s pocket, would not be quite the same.

Now let us make the quarter something the size of a small village—some ancient ruins, for example—and let us make the number of people who participate in the culture the size of a small nation. Again, the destruction of this object might mean that a culture centered on some replacement object might in some sense be a different, maybe even less good culture.

Let us call such objects haecceity objects, objects which are such that their identity makes them necessarily unique—a copy of the object would not be able to play the same role as the original, because, say, of the object's singular place in history. Haecceity is a term from that sub-field of Philosophy called Metaphysics, and it refers to the essential this-ness of an object, meant as picking out whatever it is that distinguishes the object from all other objects. Not all objects are haecceity objects. The J.F.K. quarter apart, money has no haecceity—a given dollar bill is as good as another, and if one is damaged or destroyed, another will do just as well. This property of dollars—the complete value replaceability of one by another—is called fungibility. Many of us have haecceity values—we care about the necessary uniqueness of certain things in our cultures. Nevertheless, in certain contexts this can seem a kind of fetish, something that should yield to other things of greater value—saving life and saving the dignity of lives.

Haecceity values are dangerous things to hold since they make one less resilient—one can be harmed by the destruction of an object one sees as having haecceity in a way that one cannot be harmed if one regards the object as fungible and so replaceable. Of course, some would argue that one's experiences are necessarily less deep if they all revolve around only fungible objects. Do you love your life partner as much as you might if you regard them as fungible, that is, acceptably replaceable by a clone? I am sometimes tempted to conjecture that in the West, few objects are regarded as haecceity objects in comparison with the Middle East. This might be thought a good thing since no object in the West is hostage to destruction in the way some objects in the Middle East are. Yet perhaps the West pays a price in the form of experiencing less meaning. And of course the West/Middle East distinction may be the wrong way to go. Maybe the right contrast is between cultures that see themselves as having a long history versus cultures that see themselves as recent; or between cultures that see themselves as defined around a particular region of land or around an artifact, rather than as around certain social practices. And there is the interesting question whether some of these cultures are therefore in some sense better than others, or whether some are therefore better in some ways, others, in others.

At any rate, suppose we agree that destruction of artifacts is a kind of destruction of a culture, and so of a people: Does it follow that it is bad? Only insofar as the culture and its people are good, or at least not bad. And recall too that, in spite of the arguments of communitarians (who think that people cannot have an identity apart from their surrounding culture), it is too quick to identify people with their culture, as if the destruction of the latter is the destruction of the former; for culturally speaking, people are like Turing Machines: they are reprogrammable; and their new culture might satisfy their needs just as well as did the old. This is because, as we noted earlier, many of the needs of people are not culture relative and culturally generated. Instead the purpose of cultures is to serve the antecedent pre- or transcultural and common needs of people.

What of the case of the forcible deprivation of the culture of the children of indigenous peoples in Canada by their mandatory enrollment in the residential school programs of the last two centuries? This was obviously an evil; does it not therefore reduce to absurdity the claim that people can be non-problematically reprogrammed in their cultures? No. What the case shows, and what I certainly do not deny, is that sometimes such reprogramming has unjust pretexts, as in the case of colonialism; and it is sometimes done in unjust ways, unjust either in means (e.g., kidnapping), or in failing to provide those who get reprogrammed with the resources to flourish (e.g., due to them being deprived of the land they need for their traditional livelihoods, or due to them then having to live as second-class citizens among members of the conquering culture); sometimes it involves forcing people to live in ways they simply cannot adapt to given how long they have lived in other ways; and sometimes it amounts to reprogramming people into a worse culture. (Canada's indigenous peoples had a culture which may have been more sustainable as a consumer of resources, to name just one of its many virtues.)

But the opposite is also true: think of helping to socialize someone out of criminal gang culture, or out of adherence to a cult. And think of cases where people reprogram themselves, as when a refugee is accepted into a new country and decides to adopt its culture, to assimilate.

It can be reasonable to demand the destruction of a culture if that culture is evil. This may involve the destruction of that culture's artifacts. But this need not amount to the destruction of that culture's people. It need not involve their physical death, for example. And if it involves their reprogramming into a better culture, then if this be cultural genocide, not all cultural genocide is bad.

X. Conclusion

Let me place my argument alongside one of the most powerful statements of the argument for making the theft and destruction of cultural artifacts war crimes, a statement from former Director General of UNESCO, Irina Bokova.[39] Bokova vividly describes the strategy of terrorism:

> These attacks, the destruction, and the persecutions are part of the same global strategy, which I call "cultural cleansing," intended to destroy identities, tear apart social fabrics, and fuel hatred. Such acts of destruction cannot be decoupled from the killing of people, as violent extremists attack anything that can sustain diversity, critical thinking and freedom of opinion—schools, teachers, journalists, cultural minorities, and monuments. In this context, the protection of heritage is more than a cultural issue: it is a security necessity. We see, with the Islamic State group, how terrorists use such destruction as a tactic of war to paralyze and weaken the social defences of people, to attract and recruit foreign fighters across the globe as well as to promote a fundamentalist agenda. Illicit trafficking of cultural objects is also linked to the financing of terrorism . . . It is clearly stated in Article 8 of the Rome Statute of the International Criminal Court that the deliberate destruction of cultural heritage is a war crime, and should be assessed, documented, and investigated so that the perpetrators can be brought to justice in the future.

Bokova also identifies the manifesto of the extremists: "violent extremists say humanity is not a single community that shares values . . . world heritage does not exist . . . pre-Islamic heritage is idolatry . . . diversity is dangerous . . . tolerance and dialogue are unacceptable."

Bokova gives the arguments for what is bad about what is done from this manifesto, and for the responses needed to deal with it, including military responses, legal reform, and preemptive relocation of threatened objects.

Even though I object to viewing all theft and destruction of cultural property as war crime, I do not disagree with Bokova's analysis. But I do point out that the people she is objecting to have a position; they have independent motivations toward taking this position deriving, in some cases, from their

[39] Irina Bokova, "Fighting Cultural Cleansing: Harnessing the Law to Preserve Cultural Heritage" (Summer 2015) 36 (4) Harvard International Review 40–45.

own oppression; and Bokova leaves out that, if you really want to counteract all of this, you need to address the oppressions that have led to it.

Much of the standard positioning that I have been disputing on these issues can be saved by adding in the assumption that we know which side in a conflict is just, and we are speaking only of what is to be done to agents who act against the justice of that side. But here we must be careful. For wars are fought precisely in the disputing of that very matter. And we have our own biases in assessing a given conflict. We are virtually unanimous in treating the conflicts in the Middle East as involving people clearly in the wrong when, arguably, they are people legitimately fighting for righteous status against oppression. Sometimes even when they are in the wrong on a given issue, they may be justified in acting out some private anger or grievance.

No doubt some cultural artifacts have a political status so innocent that the standard arguments against trade in, theft of, and destruction of cultural artifacts go through regarding them. And maybe some artifacts simply are the common treasure of all humankind, and only persons evil or misguided could possibly make themselves the enemy of these objects.

But it would be a mistake to say that of all artifacts in all contexts. It is tempting to see those who would destroy cultural artifacts as madmen, enemies of all people, men who should be dealt with as mere criminals. But if someone is the enemy of all men, then he sees all men as his enemy; and we need to look at how someone could come to feel this way, how someone could come to think that so many of the manifestations of civilization and its history are evil, are oppressive to them. For some of these people, madness is the explanation—they are not in fact oppressed, they only think they are, if they think intelligibly at all. It may be thought that, for others, the explanation is that they believe the tenets of a religion that requires them to destroy anything Western and to kill anyone not allied to their faith. But this in turn would need explanation. For many of us hold religious views that would require extremes of action, and yet we do not so act. A religion may tell you to do a ridiculous thing, or ridiculously tell you not to do what is in reality an innocuous or perfectly wonderful thing. Whether you become a fundamentalist adherent and act on such instruction is another matter. Why have some chosen to act on the more ridiculous, violence-prescribing tenets of the fundamentalism in their religion? For most, the explanation is that they have not been able to secure a dignified life and a fair share of the benefits of civilization. And the explanations for that are not far to seek: racism, sexism, classism, oppression by dominant religions of non-dominant religions, tribalism, colonialism, Kleptocracy, and the rule of law or its perversions that have, sometimes unwittingly, sustained these things. Then there are the people in otherwise healthy societies who for individual reasons have discontents, and who are drawn to conflict as a way to express their anger. There are also people moved to join in conflict from solidarity with the less powerful peoples of the world, peoples who live in what are in effect apartheid polities, and so who are ruled by laws they do not have a full contribution in making. And there are people moved to violence by the idea of a great conflict between good and evil, an evil the inadequacies of their own lives lead them to posit as their cause.

My hope is that we will try better to understand these discontents, and that we will spend less of our effort on policing the preservation of cultural artifacts and art objects, and more on trying to redress the political inequities that lead to them being threatened. For if we do anything other than this, we are merely sustaining the apartheid that has birthed the violent expression of discontent. And we will thereby continue to sow the seeds which grow into violence against people and culture. This means we must, so far as possible, see these actions as political, not criminal, see them as actions of war, even when they are the actions of non-state actors. And this recommends the extension of combatant immunity to what would otherwise be seen as thieves and barbarous vandals.

5

The Concept of Cultural Genocide

Martin Hamilton

I. Introduction

Over the past years, the world has looked on in horror as the extremist militants of the Islamic State (ISIS) have set about vandalizing, smashing, and even bulldozing cultural antiquities that existed for thousands of years in the territory the jihadists controlled. In February 2015, a video was released showing members of ISIS deliberately destroying cultural property belonging to the Assyrian minority people in the city of Mosul in Northern Iraq. ISIS justified the destruction of the Assyrian's cultural heritage by accusing them of being polytheists.[1] In an interview with the American edition of the newspaper *The Guardian*, Mardean Isaac, an Assyrian writer and member of A Demand for Action, an organization dedicated to protecting the rights of the Assyrians and other minorities in Syria and Iraq, stated that "the Islamic State is ethnically cleansing the contemporary Assyrian populations of Iraq and Syria, they are also conducting a simultaneous war on their ancient history and the right of future generations of all ethnicities and religions to the material memory of their ancestors."[2] Iraq's Minister of Tourism and Artifacts, Adel Fahad al-Shirshab, referred to these systematic and calculated attacks on cultural heritage belonging to the Assyrian people as cultural genocide.[3] This, however, was far from the only case where the concept of cultural genocide has been evoked. The Chinese government has been accused of committing cultural genocide toward the Uyghur minority

[1] Kareem Shaheen, "Isis Fighters Destroy Ancient Artefacts at Mosul Museum" (*The Guardian*, 26 February 2015) http://www.theguardian.com/world/2015/feb/26/isis-fighters-destroy-ancient-artefacts-mosul-museum-iraq accessed 7 June 2020.

[2] ibid.

[3] Graham Bowley and Robert MacKeyfeb, "Destruction of Antiquities by ISIS Militants Is Denounced" (*The New York Times*, 27 February 2015) <http://www.nytimes.com/2015/02/28/world/middleeast/destruction-of-antiquities-by-militants-is-denounced.html?_r=0> accessed 7 June 2020. See also "ISIS Video of Mosul Museum Epitomizes Cultural Genocide" (posted by ARTCENTRON, 2 March 2015) <http://artcentron.com/2015/03/02/isis-artifact-destruction/> accessed 4 March 2015.

Martin Hamilton, *The Concept of Cultural Genocide* In: *The Preservation of Art and Culture in Times of War*. Edited by: Claire Finkelstein, Derek Gillman, and Frederik Rosén, Oxford University Press.
DOI: 10.1093/oso/9780197610565.003.0006

in China[4] as well as toward the Buddhists in Tibet.[5] Turkey's policies toward the Armenians,[6] the US' treatment of American Indians,[7] as well as Russia's state practice toward Jews in the nineteenth century[8] have all been labeled cultural genocide.

In recent years, we have seen growing academic interest in the concept in relation to the evolving roles of heritage in armed conflict.[9] At the heart of the concept of cultural genocide lies the idea that cultural groups may be destroyed by destroying the material expressions or "anchorage" of their culture. As noted by the academic literature, this is no new idea. In fact, the concept of cultural genocide was seriously considered for inclusion in the Convention on the Prevention and Punishment of the Crime of Genocide (1948), and thus almost received an international legal status as a most serious international crime. Accordingly, it appears paradoxical that the concept of cultural genocide today finds little treatment in the literature on genocide, cultural heritage, and international law and is usually considered a controversial concept in the political debate, which has experimented with the softer term "cultural cleansing."[10] Either cultures can be destroyed by destroying cultural

4 Azeem Ibrahim, "China Must Answer for Cultural Genocide in Court" (*Foreign Policy*, 3 December 2019) <https://foreignpolicy.com/2019/12/03/uighurs-xinjiang-china-cultural-genocide-international-criminal-court/> accessed 9 January 2020.

5 David Eimer, "Dalai Lama Condemns China's 'Cultural Genocide' of Tibet' (*The Telegraph*, 16 March 2008) <https://www.telegraph.co.uk/news/worldnews/1581875/Dalai-Lama-condemns-Chinas-cultural-genocide-of-Tibet.html> accessed 5 March 2020.

6 Peter Balakian, "Raphael Lemkin, Cultural Destruction, and the Armenian Genocide" (2013) 27 (1) Holocaust and Genocide Studies <https://doi.org/10.1093/hgs/dct001> accessed 7 June 2020.

7 See also Lawrence Davidson, *Cultural Genocide* (Rutgers UP 2012) 44–64; Jeffrey Ostler, "Genocide and American Indian History" (*Oxford Research Encyclopedia of American History*, 2 March 2015) <https://oxfordre.com/americanhistory/view/10.1093/acrefore/9780199329175.001.0001/acrefore-9780199329175-e-3?print=pdf > accessed 20 March 2020; Katherine Hamilton, "'It's Called a Genocide': The Strength of Language in U.S. Government Apologies to Native Americans" (*Cultural Survival*, 2 July 2019) <https://www.culturalsurvival.org/news/its-called-genocide-strength-language-us-government-apologies-native-americans> accessed 24 March 2020.

8 See also Davidson (n 7) 44–64; Konstantin Azadovskii and Boris Egorov, "From Anti-Westernism to Anti-Semitism: Stalin and the Impact of the Anti-Cosmopolitan Campaigns on Soviet Culture" (2002) 4 (1) Journal of Cold War Studies 66–80.

9 See also Marie Louise Stig Sørensen and Dacia Viejo-Rose, *War and Cultural Heritage: Biographies of Places* (CUP 2015); Dacia Viejo-Rose, "Destruction and Reconstruction of Heritage: Impacts on Memory and Identity" in Helmut Anheier and Yudhishthir Raj Isar (eds), *Heritage, Memory and Identity* (SAGE 2011) 53–69; Jean-Marie Henckaerts "New Rules for the Protection of Cultural Property in Armed Conflict" in Nout van Woundenberg and Lisbeth Lijnzaad (eds), *Protecting Cultural Property in Armed Conflict: An Insight into the 1999 Second Protocol to the Hague Convection of 1954 for the Protection of Cultural Property in the Event of Armed Conflict* (Martinus Nijhoff Publisher 2010); Thomas G Weiss and Nina Connelly, "Protecting Cultural Heritage in War Zones" (2019) 40 (1) Third World Quarterly 1–17.

10 Irina Bokova, "Fighting Cultural Cleansing: Harnessing the Law to Preserve Cultural Heritage" (2015) 36 (4) Harvard International Review.

heritage—or they cannot. Either we recognize a strong value relation between cultural heritage and cultural groups—or we do not.

This chapter scrutinizes this proposed value relation between cultural heritage and cultural groups through an examination of the concept of cultural genocide. The aim is to situate the concept of cultural genocide within this volume's discussion of value and cultural heritage and to introduce the highly topical thoughts underpinning the "almost-adoption" of the concept of cultural genocide in the Genocide Convention.

The chapter first examines the values underlying the original concept of cultural genocide, including the importance of cultural heritage for the survival of a people and the normative evolution of the concept of cultural genocide from its origins to the 1948 Genocide Convention, and analyzes the drafting of the Convention and the reason why cultural genocide was omitted. The second part of the chapter evaluates how international law, both at its normative and enforcement level, deals with the concept of cultural genocide today: especially in the context of deliberate and systematic targeting and destruction of cultural heritage in an armed conflict. Finally, this will be held up against the fact that we still lack a systematic account of the effects on cultures of losing the material expressions of their cultural heritage.

II. Culture and Genocide Throughout History

> The act of genocide is as old as humanity.[11]

Genocidal aspirations, understood as the intended destruction of a people, always included aspirations to eradicate the tangible and intangible culture of a group. In the Old Testament, we find multiple accounts of groups that intentionally sought to destroy other groups through mass killing, indicating that such acts were common and accepted.[12] In the book of Genesis, God decides to "destroy all flesh, wherein is the breath of life, from under heaven; and everything that is in the earth shall die,"[13] with the exception of Noah, his family, and the nuclear of animal life. Further, as God decides that

[11] Jean-Paul Sartre, "On Genocide" in Richard A Falk, Gabriel Kolko, and Robert Jay Lifton (eds), *Crimes of War* (Random House 1971) 534.

[12] David Moshman, "Conceptions of Genocide" in Dan Stone (ed), *The Historiography of Genocide* (Palgrave Macmillan 2008) 82.

[13] *Holy Bible*, King James Version, Genesis 6:17.

the Israelites are to be the holy people and should remain apart from their neighbors, God declares the destruction of the Amalekites for opposing the Israelites when they came up from Egypt by ordering the Israelites to "utterly destroy all that they have, and spare them not; but slay both man and woman, infant and suckling, ox and sheep."[14]

The intention was, as Professor of Educational Psychology at the University of Nebraska David Moshamn points out, not to win a war and set terms for a peace, but to "destroy a nation, including its people, and take its place."[15] According to this account, the drivers of violence are social identity, national values, and the view that destroying another nation's value and social identity secures and strengthens one's own national value and social identity—a form of cultural genocide that stands alongside, if not underpins physical and biological genocide.

This concept is further illustrated in the New Testament against the Israelites. After the crucifixion of a rabbi known to history as Jesus Christ, the small dissident movement that surrounded him separated from the main body of Judaism, and in the fourth century, their faith, now called Christianity, became the state religion of the Roman Empire. As the followers of Jesus gradually separated from Judaism, they started to nurture a profound antagonistic attitude against their former faith and came to regard it as an ultimate enemy. The image of the Jews as antisocial Christ-killers is well rooted in the New Testament in which they are portrayed as an angry mob demanding the death of Jesus before the Roman court decides his fate. The Christians were now the Chosen People; if the Jews could not accept the arrival of the savior, something their own Bible had foretold, the covenants God had made with the Jews would no longer be relevant and subsequently, there would be no reason for Jewish law to exist or for the Jews as a people. Since the sole purpose of history was salvation, and the Jews had completed their role in historic salvation, their continued existence could only be seen as a threat and disruption. Therefore, for the early Christians, the disappearance of the Jews from history seemed to be a logical argument.[16]

The biblical narratives are of course disputed and, from a scientific point of view, unverified. They do, however, indicate what kind of themes and questions the authors and their societies grappled with. Based on the

[14] ibid, 1 Samuel 15:3.

[15] Moshman (n 12) 83.

[16] Lionel B. Steiman, *Paths to Genocide: Antisemitism in Western History* (Macmillan Press 1998) 3–7.

biblical accounts, we may conclude that utterances about acts aimed at eradicating another people have existed for at least three to four thousand years. Furthermore, we may conclude that biblical legitimizations of such acts find a historical parallel today, for instance in ISIS' claim that Allah has told them to eradicate all that are not belonging to the true faith of Islam.[17] In between, we see a steady stream of mass murder, torture, and public spectacle made, this time in the name of Christ, throughout Europe and the Middle East. These so-called Crusades of religious scarification of the Medieval Era produced an onslaught against the "unbelievers" of the Christian faith. And further east, Mongolian horsemen under the leadership of Genghis Khan laid waste to vast territories, exterminating entire nations by leaving nothing behind but bones, rubble, and fallow fields.[18] Through the physical killing and the destruction of material belongings, including agricultural land, all links to the original communities were erased. And with the material destruction went the cultural memories of the people, their civilization, and their social identity—all lost for eternity.

Altogether, historical accounts of the kind of acts we label as "genocide" indicate a strong relationship to cultural values. The cultural differences and the strong urge to protect one's own cultural and social identity are often the root of the genocidal act.

III. The Origin of the Legal Prohibition of Genocide

The modern legal origin against such acts can be found in the Peace Treaty of Westphalia of 1648. The normative evolution can thereafter be traced through peace treaties and international conventions, often as a reaction to the atrocities that occurred during previous conflicts. After World War I, the reaction against the crime of bringing about war and the atrocious acts that followed took a concrete expression. During the second plenary session of the Paris Peace Conference on January 25, 1919, efforts to set up an international tribunal for the trial of crimes committed by the Central Powers and their civil and military authorities took place. Under the name *Commission on the Responsibility of the Authors of the War and on Enforcement of*

[17] Amir Taheri, "The Ugly Attractions of ISIS' Ideology" (*New York Post*, 2 November 2014) <http://nypost.com/2014/11/02/the-ugly-attractions-of-isis-ideology/> accessed 5 January 2020.

[18] Eric S Margolis, *War at the Top of the World: The Struggle for Afghanistan, Kashmir, and Tibet* (Routledge 2001) 155.

Penalties, a body was created for the purpose of considering this question. The Commission's report used the expression "Violations of the laws and customs of war and of the laws of humanity."[19] According to William Schabas, some of these breaches came close to the criminal behavior now defined as genocide or crime against humanity and involved the persecution of ethnic minority groups.[20]

To our inquiry into the idea of cultural genocide, an interesting part of the Commission's report can be found under the rubric of "attempts to denationalize the inhabitants of occupied territory" in which the Commission cited some of the offenses committed by Bulgaria, Germany, and Austrian authorities in Serbia. Those offenses included prohibition of the Serbian language, which led to people being beaten for saying anything in Serbian; destruction of archives from the Serbian courts of law and churches; and closing of schools.[21] There were also examples of deliberate destruction of religious, educational, and historic buildings and monuments in Serbia and Macedonia, such as attacks against schools, monasteries, churches, and ancient inscriptions, all of which were instigated by Bulgarian authorities.[22] Even though the report might have referred to Section III of the Annex to 1907 Hague Convention IV, which codifies the rules applicable to the occupied territory of an army,[23] the report never explained the legal basis for qualifying these acts as war crimes. The 1907 Hague Regulations, however, only apply to the territory of an occupied belligerent, nothing else. Thus the Commission proposed the establishment of an international High Tribunal and urged "that all enemy persons alleged to have been guilty of offences against the laws and customs of war and the laws of humanity"[24] not to be included in any

[19] ibid.

[20] ibid.

[21] Paris Peace Conference (1919–1920) Commission on the Responsibility of the Authors of the War and on Enforcement of Penalties, *Violations of the Laws and Customs of War, Reports of Majority and Dissenting Reports of America and Japanese Members of the Commission of Responsibilities, Conference of Paris, 1919* (OUP 1919) 23.

[22] ibid 48.

[23] "Convention (IV) Respecting the Laws and Customs of War on Land: Annex Section III" (1907 Hague Convention IV, Annex Section III, 18 October 1907) in Adam Roberts and Richard Guelff (eds), *Documents on the Laws of War* (3rd edn, OUP 2002) 80–82.

[24] Paris Peace Conference (1919–1920) Commission on the Responsibility of the Authors of the War and on Enforcement of Penalties, *Violations of the Laws and Customs of War, Reports of Majority and Dissenting Reports of America and Japanese Members of the Commission of Responsibilities, Conference of Paris, 1919* (OUP 1919) 25; William A Schabas, *Genocide in International Law: The Crimes of Crimes* (2nd edn, CUP 2009) 22.

amnesty and that they be brought before either national tribunals or the proposed High Tribunal.[25]

It was at this time that international lawmakers started to focus increasingly on vulnerable groups, or "minorities," that could be identified by nationality, ethnicity, or/and religion. These groups would bear the brunt of the coming Nazi regime's persecution and ultimately set precedence for the future development of the law of genocide. These minority treaties were one of the forerunners of the legal system that deals with international human rights. They also contributed to Raphael Lemkin's pioneering work on genocide, which to a large extent is "the direct descendant of the minorities treaties of the inter-war years."[26]

A. Raphael Lemkin

Until World War II, the concept of genocide was, as stated by British Prime Minister Winston Churchill, a "crime without a name."[27] The man who, a few years later, would name the crime, place it in a global-historical context, and campaign for intervention and remedial action was a Jewish jurist named Raphael Lemkin. Lemkin was born in Eastern Poland, near the town of Bezwodene, and worked as a lawyer, prosecutor, and university lecturer in his native country. By the 1930s, Lemkin was a known international scholar in the field of international criminal law and had participated as a Rapporteur at the important Conferences on the Unification of Criminal Law. Being Jewish, Lemkin fled Poland in 1939 to neutral Sweden but later ended up in the United States as a professor at Duke University and later Yale University. Lemkin was a "norm entrepreneur" who worked tirelessly to promote legal norms directed against the crime of genocide, and as such he acted behind the scene as a consultant to the Secretary-General of the United Nations throughout the drafting of the Genocide Convention in 1948. John P. Humphrey noted in his diary that "[n]ever in the history of the United Nations has one private individual conducted such a lobby."[28]

[25] ibid.

[26] Schabas (n 24) 28.

[27] Adam Jones, *Genocide: A Comprehensive Introduction* (1st edn, Routledge 2006) 8.

[28] John P Humphrey, *Human Rights and the United Nations: A Great Adventure* (Transnational Publishers Inc 1984) 54.

The term genocide was created by Lemkin from two words: *genos*, which is ancient Greek for race, nation or tribe; and *caedere* or *cide*, meaning to kill or killing in Latin.[29] Lemkin proposed the following definition of genocide:

> [G]enocide does not necessarily mean the immediate destruction of a nation, except when accomplished by mass killings of all members of a nation. It is intended rather to signify a coordinated plan of different actions aiming at the destruction of essential foundations of the life of national groups, with the aim of annihilating the groups themselves. The objectives of such a plan would be disintegration of the political and social institutions, of culture, language, national feelings, religion, and the economic existence of national groups, and the destruction of the personal security, liberty, health, dignity, and even the lives of the individuals belonging to such groups. Genocide is directed against the national group as an entity, and the actions involved are directed against individuals, not in their individual capacity, but as members of the national group.[30]

The definition can be seen as quite narrow because Lemkin is referring to crimes directed against "national groups" and not against "groups" in general. It is, however, at the same time broad insofar as he contemplates acts aimed at destroying the cultural heritage and livelihood of the group within the concept of genocide and not just about the physical killing. As early as 1933, Lemkin proposed the recognition of two new international crimes, "vandalism" and "barbarity," in a report to the 5th International Conference for the Unification of Penal Law. Lemkin described *vandalism* to be "conceived as malicious destruction of works of art and culture because they represent the specific creations of the genius of such groups."[31] Lemkin argued that cultural objects belonged to humanity as a whole and, as a consequence, humanity as a whole has the obligation to protect it. *Barbarity* was to be "conceived as oppressive and destructive actions directed against individuals as members of a national, religious, or racial group."[32] It can therefore be argued that Lemkin was merging a "humankind value" with group and national value through cultural objects and cultural heritage.

[29] Raphael Lemkin, *Axis Rule in Occupied Europe: Laws of Occupation, Analysis of Government, Proposals for Redress* (2nd edn, The Lawbook Exchange 2008) 79; Schabas (n 24) 29.
[30] Lemkin (n 29) 79.
[31] ibid 91.
[32] ibid.

B. Axis Rule in Occupied Europe

Lemkin argued in his book *Axis Rule in Occupied Europe*, written during World War II and published in 1944, that genocide did not necessarily imply bodily killing. It could also consist of actions aimed at the destruction of the essential foundations of the life of a group and with the specific intention of annihilating that group.[33] "The objectives of such a plan would be disintegration of the political and social institutions, of culture, language, national feelings, religion, and the economic existence of national groups, and the destruction of the personal security, liberty, health, dignity, and even the lives of the individuals belonging to such groups. Genocide is directed against the national group as an entity, and the actions involved are directed against individuals, not in their individual capacity, but as members of the national group."[34] He defined several categories of genocide: Political, Social, Cultural, Economic, Biological, Physical, Religious, and Moral. Lemkin based his examples on the practice of the Nazis in occupied Europe and wrote:

Genocide is effected through a synchronized attack on different aspects of life of the captive peoples:

- in the political field, by destroying institutions of self-government and imposing a German pattern of administration, and through colonization by Germans;
- in the social field, by disrupting the social cohesion of the nation involved and killing or removing elements such as the intelligentsia, which provide spiritual leadership—according to Hitler's statement in Mein Kampf, "the greatest of spirits can be liquidated if its bearer is beaten to death with a rubber truncheon";
- in the cultural field, by prohibiting or destroying cultural institutions and cultural activities; by substituting vocational education for education in the liberal arts, in order to prevent humanistic thinking, which the occupant considers dangerous because it promotes national thinking;
- in the economic field, by shifting the wealth to Germans and by prohibiting the exercise of trades and occupations by people who do not promote Germanizm "without reservations";
- in the biological field, by a policy of depopulation and by promoting procreation of Germans in the occupied countries;

[33] ibid 79.
[34] ibid.

- in the field of physical existence, by introducing a starvation rationing system for non-Germans and by mass killings, mainly of Jews, Poles, Slovenes, and Russians;
- in the religious field, by interfering with the activities of the Church, which in many countries provides not only spiritual but also national leadership;
- in the field of morality, by attempts to create an atmosphere of moral debasement through promoting pornographic publications and motion pictures, and the excessive consumption of alcohol.[35]

Lemkin surprisingly lists mass murder of a people and the promotion of pornography and alcohol consumption side by side. Yet, Lemkin employs a logic that is clear in his explanation of what constitutes genocide. Genocide, according to Lemkin, does not simply mean the mass killing of a specific people, but can be brought about by various means.[36]

In the next part, Lemkin describes the different existing "techniques of genocide in various fields"[37] which, according to his analysis, includes political, social, cultural, economical, biological, physical, religious and moral genocide. He thus emphasizes the cultural dimension of what creates a society and identity. This view can be found in the trials following World War II.

After the war, an International Military Tribunal (IMT) was held in Nüremburg, Germany in which former Nazi leaders were indicted and tried for crimes against peace, crimes against humanity, and war crimes.[38] During the Nüremburg trial, several of the prosecutors used the term genocide in order to describe the atrocities that had been committed.[39] Genocide was also referred to as "the greatest crime of all."[40] Although the term genocide was not used in the final judgment of the Trial of the Major War Criminals,

[35] ibid xi–xii.

[36] Astrid Erll, "Cultural Memory Studies: An Introduction" in Astrid Erll and Ansgar Nünning (eds), *Cultural Memory Studies: An International and Interdisciplinary Handbook* (De Gruyter 2008) 2.

[37] ibid 82.

[38] Michael Salter, *US Intelligence, the Holocaust and the Nuremburg Trials: Seeking Accountability for Genocide and Cultural Plunder* (Brill 2009) 12–13.

[39] The French prosecutor, Champetire de Ribes, states, "[t]his is a crime so monstrous, so undreamt of in history through the Christian era up to the birth of Hitlerism, that the term "genocide" had to be coined to define it." As did the British prosecutor, Sir Hartley Shawcross, by stating "[g]enocide was not restricted to extermination of the Jewish people or the gypsies. It was applied in different forms to Yugoslavia, to the non-German inhabitants of Alsace-Lorraine, to the people of the Low Countries and of Norway." Trials of the Major War Criminals (*France v Goering*), 19 IMT 531 as quoted in Schabas (n 24) 39 and William A. Schabas, "Origins of the Genocide Convention: From Nuremburg to Paris" (2008) 40 (1) Case Western Reserve Journal of International Law

[40] Schabas (n 24) 36; Schabas (n 39).

Lemkin thought that the evidence produced at the Nüremburg trial gave full support for genocide.[41]

It is in Lemkin's home country of Poland, however, where we find more concrete links between genocide and attacks on cultural institutions within the trials and verdicts that followed the war. Poland set up their own Tribunal, the Supreme National Tribunal of Poland; and, in the case of Arthur Greiser, the Tribunal identified crimes committed against Poland, which included "Repression, genocidal in character, of the religion of the local population by mass murder and incarceration in concentration camps of Polish priests, including bishops; by restriction of religious practices to the minimum; and by destruction of churches, cemeteries and the property of the Church" and "equally genocidal attacks on Polish culture and learning."[42] The Tribunal further stated:

> The accused as the supreme authority in the Wartheland, acting with full powers granted to him by Hitler, in the opinion of this Tribunal committed crimes both from the point of view of the municipal, and international law. That is, he ordered, countenanced and facilitated, as is shown by the evidence, criminal attempts on the life, health and property of thousands of Polish inhabitants of the "occupied" part of Poland in question, and at the same time was concerned in bringing about in that territory the general totalitarian genocidal attack on the rights of the small and medium nations to exist, and to have an identity and culture of their own.[43]

Further, Amon Leopold Göeth, an Austrian Nazi, Captain of the SS, and commandant of the Nazi concentration camp at Płaszów, was found guilty by the Polish Supreme National Tribunal for "[t]he wholesale extermination of Jews and also of Poles had all the characteristics of genocide in the biological meaning of this term, and embraced in addition the destruction of the cultural life of these nations."[44]

[41] Raphael Lemkin, "Genocide as a Crime under International Law" (1947) 41 (1) American Journal of International Law 147.

[42] *Poland v Greiser* [1948] Supreme National Tribunal of Poland, *Law Reports of Trials of War Criminals: Selected and Prepared by The United Nations War Crimes Commission* (His Majesty's Stationary Office 1949) vol XIII, 112.

[43] ibid 114.

[44] *Poland v Göeth* [1946] Supreme National Tribunal of Poland, *Law Reports of Trials of War Criminals: Selected and Prepared by The United Nations War Crimes Commission* (His Majesty's Stationary Office 1949) vol VIII, 9.

IV. Cultural Genocide in the Travaux Préparatoires of the Genocide Convention

The Travaux Préparatoires of the 1948 Genocide Convention offers interesting insight into the concerns and intentions regarding the Convention. It shows that the concept of cultural genocide played a significant part in the drafting—to the extent that it almost derailed the Convention.

Raphael Lemkin described in *Axis Rule* the cultural aspects of genocide.[45] He especially described the atrocities in Poland where national monuments were destroyed and libraries, archives, museums, and galleries of art carried away. In 1939, the Germans burned the great library of the Jewish Theological Seminary at Lublin in Poland. This was reported by the Germans as follows:

> For us it was a matter of special pride to destroy the Talmudic Academy which was known as the greatest in Poland . . . We threw out of the building the great Talmudic library, and carted it to market. There we set fire t[o] the books. The fire lasted for twenty hours. The Jews of Lublin were assembled around and cried bitterly. Their cries almost silenced us. Then we summoned the military band and the joyful shouts of the soldiers silenced the sound of the Jewish cries.[46]

One of Lemkin's key points was that the destruction of a people often starts with attacks on their culture, particularly language and religious and cultural monuments or institutions. It could be argued the destruction of the Jewish Theological Seminary at Lublin was just that—the start of a destruction of a people—especially with the knowledge of the historical outcome during World War II.

The cultural aspect of genocide was in the foreground of the Travaux Préparatoires of the Genocide Convention from the beginning. In the proposed draft resolution relating to the crime of genocide by the delegation of Cuba, India, and Panama, the first paragraph reads:

> *Whereas* through history and especially in recent times many instances have occurred when national, racial, ethnical or religious groups have been destroyed, entirely or in part; and such crimes of genocide not only shook

[45] Lemkin (n 29) 84–85.
[46] ibid 85.

> the conscience of mankind, but also resulted in great losses to humanity in form of cultural and other contributions represented by these human groups.[47]

Echoes of this paragraph can clearly be seen in the beginning of UN GA Resolution 96 (I)[48] and is also reaffirmed in a note by the Secretary-General in which he asks the United Nations Economical and Social Council (ECOSOC) to draw up a preliminary draft convention regarding the crime of genocide.[49] On March 28, 1947, ECOSOC instructs the Secretary-General to "undertake, with the assistance of experts in the field of international law and criminal law, the necessary studies with the view to drawing up a draft convention in accordance with the resolution of the General Assembly."[50] The Division consulted three legal scholars: Professor Raphael Lemkin, (already mentioned), Professor Henri Donnedieu de Vabres from the University of Paris Law Faculty and former judge of the Nüremberg Tribunal, and the Romanian law professor Vespasian V. Pella, President of the International Penal Law Association.[51]

The Secretary began by proclaiming in the preamble that genocide "inflicts irreparable loss on humanity by depriving it of the cultural and other contributions of the group so destroyed."[52] The draft divided acts of genocide into three categories of which the third, entitled "Destroying the specific characteristics of the group,"[53] dealt with the crime's cultural aspects.

[47] UN Doc A/BUR/50, Annex 15, "Draft Resolution Relating to the Crime of Genocide, Proposed by the Delegations of Cuba, India and Panama" in Hirad Abtahi and Philipa Webb, *The Genocide Convention: The Travaux Préparatoires* (Martinus Nijhoff Publishers 2008) vol 1, 3.

[48] "Genocide is a denial of the right of existence of entire human groups, as homicide is the denial of the right to life of individual human beings; such denial of the right of existence shocks the conscience of mankind, results in great losses to humanity in the form of cultural and other contributions represented by these human groups, and is contrary to moral law and to the spirit and aims of the United Nations." A/RES/96 (I), "The Crime of Genocide" (11 December 1946) in Hirad Abtahi and Philipa Webb, *The Genocide Convention: The Travaux Préparatoires* vol 1, 34.

[49] UN Doc E/330, "The Crime of Genocide: Note by the Secretary-General" (12 March 1947) in Hirad Abtahi and Philipa Webb, *The Genocide Convention: The Travaux Préparatoires* vol 1, 35.

[50] Economic and Social Council Resolution 47 (IV), UN Doc E/325, "Crime of Genocide" (28 March 1947) in Hirad Abtahi and Philipa Webb, *The Genocide Convention: The Travaux Préparatoires* vol 1, 60.

[51] Schabas (n 24) 60; Nehemiah Robinson, "The Genocide Convention: Its Origins and Interpretation" (2008) 40 (1) Case Western Reserve Journal of International Law 2.

[52] UN Doc A/AC.10/42, "Committee on the Progressive Development of International Law and Its Codifications; Draft Convention for the Prevention and Punishment of Genocide (Prepared by the Secretariat)" (6 June 1947) in Hirad Abtahi and Philipa Webb, *The Genocide Convention: The Travaux Préparatoires* vol 1, 115.

[53] ibid 116.

"Cultural" genocide, according to the Secretary's draft, consists neither in the destruction of members of a group nor in restrictions of birth, but in the destruction by brutal means of the specific characteristics of a group.[54] This section on cultural genocide gave rise to conflicting views among the experts.

Lemkin argued that cultural genocide was more than just a policy of forced assimilation by moderate coercion involving, for example, "prohibition of the opening of schools for teaching the language of the group concerned, of the publication of newspapers printed in that language, of the use of that language in official documents and in court."[55] This policy of drastic methods aimed solely at the rapid and complete extinction of the cultural, moral, and religious life of a group of human beings. A racial, religious, or national group cannot continue to exist, Lemkin explained, unless it preserves its spirit and moral unity. The right to existence of such a group was not simply justified from the moral point of view, but also through the value of the contributions made by such a group to civilization in general. If the diversity of cultures were destroyed, it would be as disastrous for civilization as the physical destruction of nations. The means of cultural genocide, Lemkin added, "were criminal acts under municipal law and that hence there was no reason why they should not be included in the international crime of genocide."[56]

The other two experts, Professor Donnedieu de Vabres and Professor Pella, held that cultural genocide represented an "undue extension of the notion of genocide,"[57] reconstituting the former protection of national minorities which they argued was based on other conceptions. In the end, Lemkin's arguments won and cultural genocide was included in the draft.

The category on cultural genocide had five subcategories:

(a) *Forcible transfer of children to another human group*

The separation of children from their parents results in forcing upon the former at an impressionable and receptive age a culture and mentality different from their parents. This process tends to bring about the disappearance of the group as a cultural unit in a relatively short time.

[54] Secretary Draft E/447, "Draft Convention on the Crime of Genocide" in Hirad Abtahi and Philipa Webb, *The Genocide Convention: The Travaux Préparatoires* vol 1, 234.
[55] ibid 235.
[56] ibid.
[57] ibid 234.

The experts agreed that this point should be part of the convention on genocide; however, this is where their agreement stopped.

(b) *Forced and systematic exile of individuals representing the culture of a group*

The individuals to be covered under this part were considered to be chiefly scholars, writers, artists, teachers, educators, ministers of religion, doctors of medicine, engineers, lawyers, administrators, etc.

The cultural and moral life of a group is sustained by its members. If this is removed, the group is no more than an amorphous and defenseless mass. Its language is degraded to the rank of a dialect, and hence those using it are reduced to a position of inferiority, and the language has no longer any policy or social significance.

Lemkin suggested here the following wording: "systematic elimination of the individuals representing the culture of the group by acts of violence or infringement of personal liberty,"[58] however, this wording was deemed too complicated.

(c) *Prohibition of the use of the national language even in private intercourse*

This amounts to making the language illegal, even when used in the home or in private correspondence.

Lemkin proposed a different formulation: "prohibition, on threat of criminal punishment or violent measures, of the use of the national language even in private intercourse."[59]

(d) *Systematic destruction of books printed in the national language or of religious works or prohibition of new publications*

A religious linguistic national group cannot continue to exist if it relies on oral tradition only.

(e) *Systematic destruction of historical or religious monuments or their diversion to alien uses, destruction or dispersion of documents and objects*

[58] ibid 235–36.
[59] ibid.

> *of historical, artistic, or religious value and of objects used in religious worship*

Such measures are also directed at undermining the existence of a group of human beings.[60]

Both France and the United States supported the majority of the three experts in excluding the act of cultural genocide. The French government insisted that the definition of genocide should be "[l]imited to physical and biological genocide, for to include cultural genocide invites the risk of political interference in the domestic affairs of States, and in respect of questions which in fact, are connected with the protection of minorities."[61] The United States accepted the ideas of "physical genocide" and "biological genocide," but generally rejected the idea of "cultural genocide,"[62] stating:

> The United States is opposed to the inclusion of paragraph 3 of Article I, relating to "Destroying the specific characteristics of the group" by different means, except as to paragraph (a) "forced transfer of children to another human group."
>
> Paragraph (b) might be interpreted as embracing forced transfer of minority groups such as have already been carried out by members of the United Nations.
>
> Paragraphs (c), (d) and (e) relate generally to prohibition of the use of language, systematic destruction of books, and destruction or dispersion of documents and objects of historical or artistic value. The act of creating the new international crime of genocide is one of extreme gravity, and the United States feels that it should be confined to those barbarous acts directed against individuals which form the basic concept of public opinion on this subject. The acts provided for in these paragraphs are acts which should appropriately be dealt with in connection with the protection of minorities.[63]

[60] ibid.

[61] UN Doc A/401, Annex 3a, "Communications Received by the Secretary-General: Communication Received from France" (Paris, 7 October 1947) in Hirad Abtahi and Philipa Webb, *The Genocide Convention: The Travaux Préparatoires* vol 1, 383.

[62] UN Doc E/621, Annex, "Observations of the Governments of States Members and communications from non-governmental organizations on the Secretariat's draft Convention" Part 1 (3c) in Hirad Abtahi and Philipa Webb, *The Genocide Convention: The Travaux Préparatoires* vol 1, 526.

[63] UN Doc E/623, "Comments by Governments on the Draft Convention Prepared by the Secretariat" in Hirad Abtahi and Philipa Webb, *The Genocide Convention: The Travaux Préparatoires* vol 1, 538.

Some States favored retaining cultural genocide, such as the Lebanese representative who stressed the importance of cultural genocide, which, he argued, "impoverished the whole world,"[64] and expressed the hope that a prominent place would be given to it in the convention. The Soviet Union went one step further and insisted that "[t]he concept of physical destruction must embrace not only cases of direct murder of particular groups of population . . . but also the premeditated infliction on such groups of conditions of life aimed at the destruction of the group in question."[65] The Soviet Union stated:

> The concept of genocide must also cover measures and actions aimed against the use of the national language or against national culture (so-called "national-cultural genocide"), for example
> (a) the prohibition or restriction of the use of the national tongue in both public and private life: the prohibition of teaching in schools given in the national tongue;
> (b) the destruction or prohibition of the printing and circulation of books and other printed matter in the national tongues;
> (c) the destruction of historical or religious monuments, museums, documents, libraries and other monuments and objects of national culture (or religious worship).[66]

Venezuela took the opportunity to remind the other delegates that the General Assembly, through Resolution 96 (I) of December 11, 1946, had agreed that genocide deprived humanity of the cultural contributions of certain human groups. Venezuela therefore stressed the importance that the Convention should protect the cultural heritage of national groups against systematic destruction by the kind committed by the Hitler regime. The Venezuelan delegate continued to state that "[t]he cultural bond was one of the most important factors among those which united a national group, and that was so true that it was possible to wipe out a human group, as such, by destroying its cultural heritage, while allowing the individual members

[64] UN Doc E/SR.139, "One Hundred and Thirty-Ninth Meeting" (Lake Success, New York, 12 February 1948) in Hirad Abtahi and Philipa Webb, *The Genocide Convention: The Travaux Préparatoires* vol 1, 589.
[65] UN Doc E/AC.27/7, "Ad Hoc Committee on Genocide: Basic Principles of a Convention on Genocide" (7 April 1948) in Hirad Abtahi and Philipa Webb, *The Genocide Convention: The Travaux Préparatoires* vol 1, 696.
[66] ibid 697.

of the group to survive. The physical destruction of individuals was not the only possible form of genocide; It was not the indispensable condition of that crime."[67]

The Lebanese delegate noted that the complexity of the concept of cultural genocide clearly explained the attitude of the US representative who would rather base the Convention on the simpler concept of physical genocide.[68] Poland also stressed the importance of cultural genocide, since the country had suffered tremendously from that particular crime; however, the Polish representative felt that a distinction had to be drawn between cultural genocide and the physical extermination of a group of people, suggesting that the destruction of the cultural heritage of a group should be suppressed as a preparatory act to physical extermination.[69] The French representative also agreed on the importance of cultural genocide and took the opportunity to point out that France was "especially interested in the suppression of cultural genocide,"[70] but at the same time, also questioned if it should be included in an international convention due to the difficulties of agreeing on a definition.[71] The Chinese representative, however, agreed with the representative from Lebanon and felt that the cultural destruction of a group was tantamount in effect to the destruction of the group.[72]

The Chairman of the Ad Hoc Committee, John Maktos (also the US representative), felt that he needed to warn the Committee against an excessively wide extension of the concept of genocide, which, he felt, might possibly exceed the framework outlined by the General Assembly. "The fact," he continued, "which initiated the General Assembly resolution had been the systematic massacre of Jews by the Nazi authorities during the course of the last war, were the Committee to attempt to cover too wide a field in the preparation of a draft convention for example, in attempting to define cultural genocide—however reprehensible that crime might be—it might well run the risk to find that some States would refuse to ratify the convention or would give their signature only after a long period devoted to the study of the question."[73] In response, the Soviet Union stated that "[i]t was obvious

[67] UN Doc E/A.25/SR.5, "Ad Hoc Committee on Genocide: Summary Record of the Fifth Meeting" (16 April 1948) in Hirad Abtahi and Philipa Webb, *The Genocide Convention: The Travaux Préparatoires* vol 1, 726–27.
[68] ibid 728.
[69] ibid.
[70] ibid.
[71] ibid.
[72] ibid 729.
[73] ibid 727.

that the definition of genocide was not an easy task. That difficulty, however, should not lead the Committee to shirk its duty, but rather to redouble its efforts to find a formula embodying a unanimous solution of the question."[74]

The Committee decided by six votes to one that the principle of the suppression of cultural genocide should be inscribed in the draft convention.[75]

During the debate in the Ad Hoc Committee, the US representative suggested placing cultural genocide in a separate article, so as to "enable Governments to make reservations on a particular point of the Convention."[76] China did not agree and pointed out that legislative bodies could just as easily make reservations on parts of an article as on a whole; however, if making it a separate article would facilitate agreement among the members, China would not be opposed to that procedure.[77] But the Soviet Union remarked that "a Convention constituted a whole which could only be ratified or rejected in its entirety [and therefore] failed to understand the argument."[78]

The Soviet Union argued that it would not be "possible to isolate one of the elements constituting the crime in order to specify it in a separate article . . . It was essential to bear in mind that any prohibition of the use of a language, any destruction of cultural monuments, etc., did not necessarily constitute an act of genocide. They can only be so described if the acts were [the] result of a persecution carried out on racial, national or religious grounds."[79] Therefore, it should remain in the article defining the crime because, the Soviet Union argued, "it was an inseparable part of that definition."[80] France agreed with the United States and thought it would be easier for them to vote on the question of cultural genocide if it formed the subject of a separate article because cultural genocide and physical genocide were not exactly the same crime. If they were dealt with in two separate articles, it would avoid any confusion between them since their characteristics were quite different.[81]

With three votes to one with two abstentions, the Committee decided to insert the notion of cultural genocide in a separate article.[82] Since cultural

[74] ibid 729.
[75] ibid 731. The negative vote presumably was the United States.
[76] UN Doc E/AC.25/SR.10, "Ad Hoc Committee on Genocide: Summary Record of the Tenth Meeting" (16 April 1948) in Hirad Abtahi and Philipa Webb, *The Genocide Convention: The Travaux Préparatoires* vol 1, 837.
[77] ibid 838.
[78] ibid.
[79] ibid.
[80] ibid.
[81] ibid 839.
[82] ibid 842.

genocide now was covered in a separate article, the Soviet Union representative thought that such an article should be preceded by a general definition. After some debate, in which both France and the United States felt that cultural genocide should not be included in the decision of making genocide a new international crime, a committee, made up of China, Lebanon, Poland, the Soviet Union, and Venezuela, all of whom had been openly in favor of the concept of cultural genocide, were selected to prepare a new draft. After a few amendments made by Lebanon, the new article was adopted by five votes to two.[83] The new article read:

> In this Convention genocide also means any deliberate act committed with the intent to destroy the language, religion, or culture of a national, racial or religious group on grounds of the national or racial origin or the religious belief of its members such as:
>
> 1. Prohibiting the use of the language of the group in daily intercourse or in schools, or the printing and circulation of publications in the language of the group;
> 2. Destroying or preventing the use of libraries, museums, schools, historical monuments, places of worship or other cultural institutions and objects of the group.[84]

V. The General Assembly and its Sixth Committee

In the Sixth Committee,[85] cultural genocide once again gave rise to a discussion on whether such acts of genocide should be covered by the Convention. At its 83rd meeting the Committee decided, by 25 votes to 16, with 4 abstentions, not to include provisions relating to cultural genocide in the Convention.[86] The Soviet Union protested and proposed an amendment with

[83] UN Doc E/AC.25/SR.14, "Ad Hoc Committee on Genocide: Summary Record of the Fourteenth Meeting" (21 April 1948) in Hirad Abtahi and Philipa Webb, *The Genocide Convention: The Travaux Préparatoires* vol 1, 884–93.

[84] UN Doc E/AC.25/SR.1-28, Ad Hoc Committee Draft, Second Draft Genocide Convention, Prepared by the Ad Hoc Committee of the Economic and Social Council (5 April–10 May 1948).

[85] "The Sixth Committee is the primary forum for the consideration of legal questions in the General Assembly. All of the United Nations Member States are entitled to representation on the Sixth Committee as one of the main committees of the General Assembly." General Assembly of the United Nations, Sixth Committee (Legal).

[86] UN Doc A/760, "Genocide: Draft Convention and Report of the Economic and Social Council" (3 December 1948) in Hirad Abtahi and Philipa Webb, *The Genocide Convention: The Travaux Préparatoires* vol 2, 2024–25.

regards to the prohibition of cultural genocide. The amendment was rejected by 31 votes to 14, with 10 abstentions.[87] Venezuela also proposed an amendment prohibiting cultural genocide by adding a sixth paragraph to the list of punishable acts in Article II.[88] The Venezuelan representative stressed that a human group might "be destroyed not only by the physical extermination of its members, but also by acts which prevent it from maintaining its communal existence even if its members continued to exist physically. Thus the destruction of the place of worship of a religious group deprived that group of its reason for existence and led to its disappearance."[89] Venezuela also stated that their amendment was the result of detailed study which showed that "racial or religious hatred had always begun to show itself on the form of cultural genocide before it assumed the bloody aspect of mass murder."[90] If the General Assembly refused to include such factors mentioned, it would, Venezuela stated, "disappoint the hopes of some delegations who wished to condemn all forms of genocide and, in particular, cultural genocide."[91] At the end of the discussions, however, it was clear that other Member States did not share the Venezuelan desire. In order not to hamper the work of the Assembly, the Venezuelan delegation withdrew its amendment in hope that, at some future occasion, "the States parties to the convention would be prepared to be guided by experience and would support such an amendment, were it to be submitted again."[92]

In one of the final statements of the meeting, the Chinese delegation regretted that the concept of cultural genocide had been set aside since, "in certain aspects, it constituted a worse crime even than biological or physical genocide. It was less apparent and less brutal, but it was more extensive and more insidious since it was a means of depriving a whole people of its culture, its religion and even of its language."[93]

[87] UN Doc A/PV.179 in Hirad Abtahi and Philipa Webb, *The Genocide Convention: The Travaux Préparatoires* vol 2, 2078–79.

[88] UN Doc A/770, "Genocide - Draft Convention and Report of the Economic and Social: Venezuela: Amendment to the draft Convention on the Prevention and Punishment of Genocide proposed by the Sixth Committee" in Hirad Abtahi and Philipa Webb, *The Genocide Convention: The Travaux Préparatoires* vol 2, 2041.

[89] UN Doc A/PV.178, "Hundred and Seventy-Eighth Plenary Meeting" (9 December 1948) in Hirad Abtahi and Philipa Webb, *The Genocide Convention: The Travaux Préparatoires* vol 2, 2047.

[90] ibid.

[91] ibid.

[92] UN Doc A/PV.179, "Hundred and Seventy-Ninth Plenary Meeting" (9 December 1948) in Hirad Abtahi and Philipa Webb, *The Genocide Convention: The Travaux Préparatoires* vol 2, 2079.

[93] ibid 2078.

There was also a proposal to include cultural genocide in the Universal Declaration of Human Rights (UDHR),[94] which was drafted at the same time. Several European States proposed that an article should be added to the UDHR which would guarantee minorities a right to have their own schools, cultural or religious institutions, and be able to use their languages in the media, public assemblies, courts, and other state authorities. As with the inclusion of the cultural genocide article in the Genocide Convention, however, the United States was against an inclusion of the cultural genocide aspects. According to the United States, they had no minorities and insisted that minority rights be excluded from the UDHR because there were "no minority problems anywhere in the Western Hemisphere."[95] By being against the inclusion of cultural genocide in both the Genocide Convention and the UDHR, the United States clearly indicated that they would never agree to or negotiate for such an inclusion. This also became the viewpoint of the majority of the Western countries.

Instead of jeopardizing losing the legitimacy that the United States, Britain, France, and others major Western countries would give to the Genocide Convention, States like Venezuela and China agreed to take out the cultural genocide article from the Convention in hopes that, at some future occasion, States would be guided by experience and support an amendment to the Convention which included cultural genocide. Even though a lot of countries supported the ban of cultural genocide, the trend in postcolonial United Nations was shown to be the opposite. Many States were afraid that their actions may give rise to charges against them.

The Convention was signed on December 11, 1948, and opened for signature, in accordance with Article XI, until December 31, 1949, after which States could only accede to the Convention. It entered into force on January 12, 1951, and to this day has 41 signatories and 152 Parties.[96] The prohibition of genocide as embodied in the Convention was also accepted as part of customary international law, as affirmed in a report of the UN Secretary-General to the Security Council on May 3, 1993, concerning the establishment of the International Criminal Tribunal for the former Yugoslavia (ICTY).[97]

[94] UN Doc A/810, General Assembly Resolution 217 (III), UN GAOR, 3rd Session 71.

[95] Johannes Morsink, "Cultural Genocide, the Universal Declaration, and Minority Rights" (1999) 21 (4) Human Rights Quarterly 1009, 1019.

[96] For the current status on the Genocide Convention see <https://treaties.un.org/Pages/ViewDetails.aspx?src=IND&mtdsg_no=IV-1&chapter=4&clang=_en>.

[97] UN Doc S/25704, "Report of the Secretary-General Pursuant to Paragraph 2 of Security Council Resolution 808" (3 May 1993) 9.

It is clear that the question of cultural genocide gave rise to a full discussion. Those who supported the inclusion of cultural genocide in the Convention argued that there were two ways of suppressing a human group; firstly, by causing its members to disappear; and secondly by abolishing them, without making any attempts on the lives of the members of the group. According to this opinion, the Convention would fail to achieve its objective if cultural genocide were excluded. However, those who opposed the inclusion of cultural genocide argued that there was a considerable difference between physical genocide (including biological genocide) and cultural genocide. According to the "opposition," "only physical genocide presented those exceptionally horrifying aspects which had revolted the conscience of humanity."[98] From a practical point of view, they emphasized that the inclusion of cultural genocide in the Convention might prevent many countries from becoming parties to the Convention and therefore jeopardize its success.[99] It is clear that western European countries were worried about the implications of cultural genocide on their colonial practice and atrocities, while the USSR and Poland were ideologically and politically more sympathetic to the views of non-Western countries such as Republic of China. It was not just the colonial powers that were worried; Sweden, for example, noted that its conversion of the Lapps, indigenous people living in the northern part of Sweden, to Christianity made them liable to accusations of cultural genocide.[100]

VI. Cultural Genocide in International Law

The adoption of the Genocide Convention was a monumental historical moment. It marked a turning point in contemporary public international law not only for uniting the international community following the tumultuous events of World War II, but also for laying a foundation for a new common ethos: to once and for all put an end to the crimes of crimes. It was not, however, until the atrocities committed during the conflicts in Rwanda and

[98] UN Doc E/AC.25/W.4, "Ad Hoc Committee on Genocide: Portions of Report Adopted in First Reading" in Hirad Abtahi and Philipa Webb, *The Genocide Convention: The Travaux Préparatoires* vol 1, 1061.

[99] ibid.

[100] UN Doc A/C.6/SR.83 (Petren, Sweden).

former Yugoslavia that the Genocide Convention, as a legal instrument, was dusted off both nationally and internationally.

The definition contained in Article 2 of the Genocide Convention is generally recognized as the authoritative definition of the crime of genocide. The definition given in Article 2 is also part of customary international law and jus cogens.[101] The definition is reproduced almost word for word in many international instruments[102] and included in the legislations of many States.[103] Other countries have implemented parts of it in their national legislation. Israel, for example, has added "destroying and desecrating Jewish religious and cultural assets or values"[104] as a form of genocidal act. With this, Israel clearly underscores the importance of a people's cultural heritage and the value it holds for a people's survival.

The International Law Commission, in its Draft Code of Crimes against the Peace and Security of Mankind, decided that the wording of Article 2 of the Genocide Convention is exhaustive in nature. The Commission felt they needed to conform to a text widely accepted by the international community;[105] therefore, it seemed impossible to consider acts of cultural genocide as punishable crimes if they are unrelated to either physical or biological genocide. In particular, the Commission stated:

> As clearly shown by the preparatory work for the Convention on the Prevention and Punishment of the Crime of Genocide, the destruction in question is the material destruction of a group either by physical or by biological means, not the destruction of the national, linguistic, religious, cultural or other identity of a particular group. The national or religious element and the racial or ethnic element are not taken into consideration in the definition of the word "destruction," which must be taken only in

[101] *Reservations to the Convention on the Prevention and Punishment of the Crime of Genocide*, ICJ Advisory Opinion (28 May 1951) 15, 23; *Application of the Convention on the Prevention and Punishment of the Crime of Genocide (Bosnia and Herzegovina v. Serbia and Montenegro)* ICJ Judgment (26 February 2007) [161]; *Jean-Paul Akayesu* (Judgement) IT-96-4-T (2 September 1998) [495]; *Krstić* (Judgement, Trial Chamber) IT-98-33-T (2 August 2001) [541].

[102] Article 4 of the ICC Statues; Article 2 of the ICTR Statues; Article 4 of the ICTY Statues.

[103] For example, Germany, Austria, and the United Kingdom have mirrored Article 2 in their national legislation. See also John Quigley, *The Genocide Convention: An International Law Analysis* (Ashgate Publishing 2006) 16; Ben Saul, "The Implementation of the Genocide Convention at the National Level" in Paolo Gaeta (ed), *The UN Genocide Convention—A Commentary* (OUP 2009) 64–67.

[104] Nazis and Nazi Collaborators Punishment Law 5710-1950, *Laws of the State of Israel* (6 August 1963) in Sefer Ha-Chukkim No 404 (16 August 1963).

[105] UN Doc A/51/10, "Draft Code of Crimes against the Peace and Security of Mankind," Report of the International Law Commission on the work of its forty-eighth session (6 May–26 July 1996) 45.

> its material sense, its physical or biological sense. It is true that the draft Convention prepared by the Secretary-General at the second session of the General Assembly in 1947 and the draft convention of the prevention and punishment of the crime of genocide, prepared by the Ad Hoc Committee on Genocide, contained provisions on "cultural genocide" covering any deliberate act committed with the intent to destroy the language, religion or culture of a group, such as prohibiting the use of the language of the group in daily intercourse or in schools or the printing and circulation of publications in the language of the group or destroying or preventing the use of libraries, museums, schools, historical monuments, places of worship or other cultural institutions and objects of the group. However, the text of the Convention, as prepared by the Sixth Committee and adopted by the General Assembly, did not include the concept of "cultural genocide" contained in the two drafts and simply listed acts which come within the category of 'physical' or 'biological' genocide.[106]

This should prevent any interpretation regarding acts of cultural destruction from being considered a form of genocide. Nevertheless, as we will see in cases of the ICTY, the discussion on the inclusion was not finished.

A. Cultural Genocide at the International Criminal Tribunal for the Former Yugoslavia (ICTY)

Both the Genocide Convention and the Rome Statute of the International Criminal Court (ICC) constitute a benchmark in the progressive development of international law and international human rights law. Article 6 of the ICC Rome Statute, however, reproduces the text of Article 2 of the 1948 Genocide Convention since, at the time when the Rome Statute was adopted, the *Travaux Préparatoires* of the Genocide Convention were the principal source of interpretation of the definition.[107] So, even though more than 50 years divides the two treaties, little has changed in regard to how the crime of genocide is viewed within the treaty-based law.

[106] ibid 45–46.

[107] William A. Schabas, "Article 6 Genocide" in Otto Triffterer (ed), *Commentary on the Rome Statute of the International Criminal Court: Observers' Note, Article by Article* (2nd edn, CH Beck, Hart & Noms 2008) 144.

Although the International Law Commission made it clear that cultural genocide could not possibly be regarded within the definition of genocide, Judge Shahabuddeen, in his dissenting opinion in the Krstić case at the ICTY, set out a theory by which acts of cultural genocide would be considered within the definition of genocide. He explained that:

> It is the group which is protected. A group is constituted by characteristics—often intangible—binding together a collection of people as a social unit. If those characteristics have been destroyed in pursuance of the intent with which a listed act of a physical or biological nature was done, it is not convincing to say that the destruction, though effectively obliterating the group, is not genocide because the obliteration was not physical or biological.[108]

Even though Judge Shahabuddeen clearly acknowledged that cultural genocide was excluded from the Genocide Convention,[109] his concern was on the intent to destroy in which he stated: "The intent certainly has to be to destroy, but, except for the listed act, there is no reason why the destruction must always be physical or biological."[110] With this he meant that the destruction of culture may serve evidentially to confirm intent, being gathered from other circumstances, to destroy the group.[111] "In sum," he concluded, "I consider that the Statute is to be read to mean that, provided that there is a listed act (this being physical or biological), the intent to destroy the group as a group is capable of being proved by evidence of an intent to cause the non-physical destruction of the group in whole or in part."[112]

Judge Shahabuddeen reaffirmed what the Trial Chamber wrote in its judgment of the Krstić case a few years earlier. It stated that the intent to destroy in Article 4 also encompassed evidence relating to acts that involved cultural and other nonphysical forms of group destruction. The Trial Chamber based this on several declarations and decisions that had been adopted only years earlier.[113] One in particular was the Federal Constitutional Court of Germany which indicated in December 2000:

[108] *Krstić* (Judgment, Partially Dissenting Opinion of Judge Shahabuddeen) IT-98-33-A (2004) [50].
[109] ibid [51], [53].
[110] ibid [51].
[111] ibid [53].
[112] ibid [54].
[113] *Krstić* (Judgment) IT-98-33-T (2 August 2001) [577].

> the statutory definition of genocide defends a supra-individual object of legal protection, i.e. the social existence of the group [...] the intent to destroy the group [...] extends beyond physical and biological extermination [...] The text of the law does not therefore compel the interpretation that the culprit's intent must be to exterminate physically at least a substantial number of the members of the group.[114]

These reflections prompted the Trial Chamber to point out in their judgment that "where there is physical or biological destruction there are often simultaneous attacks on the cultural and religious property and symbols of the targeted group as well, attacks which may legitimately be considered as evidence of an intent to physically destroy the group. In this case, the Trial Chamber will thus take into account as evidence of intent to destroy the group the deliberate destruction of mosques and houses belonging to members of the group."[115]

Judge Shahabuddeen's views are also found in other Trial Chambers judgments. In the Blagojević case, the Trial Chamber acknowledged Judge Shahabuddeen's view on the intent to destroy,[116] and further reverberations can be found in the trial of Krajišnik in which the Trial Chamber indicated:

> "Destruction," as a component of the mens rea of genocide, is not limited to physical or biological destruction of the group's members, since the group (or a part of it) can be destroyed in other ways, such as by transferring children out of the group (or the part) or by severing the bonds among its members. Thus it has been said that one may rely, for example, on evidence of deliberate forcible transfer as evidence of the mens rea of genocide.[117]

This is further explained in a footnote to the paragraph:

> It is not accurate to speak of "the group" as being amenable to physical or biological destruction. Its members are, of course, physical or biological beings, but the bonds among its members, as well as such aspects of the group as its members' culture and beliefs, are neither physical nor biological.

[114] "Federal Constitutional Court, 2 BvR 1290/99, 12 December 2000, para (III)(4)(a)(aa)" as cited in *Krstić* (Judgment) IT-98-33-T (2 August 2001) [579].

[115] *Krstić* (Judgment) IT-98-33-T (2 August 2001) [580].

[116] *Blagojević* (Judgment) IT-02-60-T (17 January 2005) [659]–[660].

[117] *Krajišnik* (Judgement) IT-00-39-T (27 September 2006) [854].

> Hence the Genocide Convention's "intent to destroy" the group cannot sensibly be regarded as reducible to an intent to destroy the group physically or biologically, as has occasionally been said.[118]

With the earlier statement from the Trial Chamber and Judge Shahabuddeen's dissenting opinion, it could be argued that the conviction of General Krstić for aiding and abetting genocide with respect to the Srebrenica massacre indicates a norm change in the judicial interpretation of the customary law understanding of genocide, demonstrating a willingness to consider aspects of cultural genocide as part of the evidence of genocidal intent.

VII. Conclusion

It is clear that the main reason cultural genocide was not included in the Genocide Convention was self-interest. States were afraid that they might be accused of cultural genocide, which led them to force it out of the Convention instead of accepting responsibility for their actions. The fact that the 1948 Genocide Convention has not been updated or modified since its creation proves that States still act in the same manner today. The mirroring of the Genocide Convention's definition of the crime in both the International Tribunals and the International Criminal Court indicates the international community's reluctance to create a new interpretation of genocide.

So what does the future hold? It has been clearly established that there is no legal definition regarding cultural genocide; however, there is some light at the end of the tunnel for the concept of cultural genocide. By looking at the systematic destruction of cultural heritage belonging to a people as intent to commit genocide, the ICTY has invited a re-examination of the normative evolution regarding the concept of cultural genocide within international law.

Another milestone in the normative evolution regarding both genocide and the protection of cultural heritage (and arguably cultural genocide) is the unanimous vote by the European Parliament recognizing ISIS' systematic killing and persecution of religious minorities in the Middle East as genocide. This is the first time the body has recognized an ongoing conflict

[118] ibid [1710].

situation as genocide.[119] What makes this especially poignant is that the European Parliament has adopted the same approach as the ICTY in looking at the systematic destruction of cultural heritage belonging to a people as one aspect of intent to commit genocide.[120] This strengthens the argument regarding the future of the normative evolution of cultural genocide, namely that cultural genocide plays a subsidiary role in our present understanding of genocide and the destruction of a people's cultural heritage.

119 "European Parliament resolution on the systematic mass murder of religious minorities by the so-called ISIS/Daesh" (2016/2529(RSP)) RC\1085712EN.doc (3 February 2016).

120 ibid.

PART II

LEGAL AND SECURITY ASPECTS OF CULTURAL HERITAGE PRESERVATION

6

Combating Illicit Trade in Cultural Objects to Defend Peace and Security

Kristin Hausler and Andrzej Jakubowski

I. Introduction

Attacks against cultural heritage have become a major concern in the international peace and security agenda, considered alongside the proliferation of weapons of mass destruction or arms trafficking. Threats to peace are not only associated with the destruction and plunder of cultural property in armed conflict, but also with illicit excavations and antiquities trafficking that reportedly have become fundraising tools for terrorist groups and transnational criminal organizations.[1] This chapter analyzes the emergence of this heritage-security nexus as a new priority in the international protection agenda with a focus on the threats associated with the illicit trade of cultural objects originating from conflict-ridden territories. To this aim, it first scrutinizes the existing legal framework protecting cultural objects from looting during armed conflict. It then considers how the matter has evolved from a humanitarian law issue (the protection of cultural property) to one that is tied to the maintenance of international peace and security. In this latter regard, it outlines the growing concern of the UN Security Council (UNSC) in respect of cultural heritage, including the creation of legal obligations established under Chapter VII ("Action with Respect to Threats to the Peace, Breaches of the Peace and Acts of Aggression") of the UN Charter.[2] In particular, this chapter analyzes how the connection made between trafficking in antiquities and terrorism financing has strengthened the ways this

[1] See Ricardo A. St. Hilaire, "Cultural Property Protection in the Context of Counter Terrorist Financing: An Emerging Legal Paradigm" in this volume. See also Janet Blake, "Trafficking in Cultural Property: Where Cultural Heritage Law and the International Fight Against Transnational Organized Crime Coincide" in Anne-Marie Carstens and Elizabeth Warner (eds), *Intersections in International Cultural Heritage Law* (OUP 2020).

[2] (signed 26 June 1945, entered into force 24 October 1945) 1 UNTS XVI as amended.

Kristin Hausler and Andrzej Jakubowski, *Combating Illicit Trade in Cultural Objects to Defend Peace and Security*
In: *The Preservation of Art and Culture in Times of War*. Edited by: Claire Finkelstein, Derek Gillman, and Frederik Rosén,
Oxford University Press. © Oxford University Press 2022. DOI: 10.1093/oso/9780197610565.003.0007

form of illegal trade has been addressed at the global level. It then focuses on UNSC Resolution 2347 (2017),[3] "a historic milestone" in the international struggle to safeguard endangered heritage, and its implementation, referring to the recent report by the UN Secretary General dated November 17, 2017.[4] In that regard, the chapter explains how the heritage-security nexus has generated new forms of trans-sectoral, -institutional, and -border cooperation, which can best be described as multilevel (and multilateral) governance modalities of protection, as well as further opportunities for education and awareness building. Finally, the chapter seeks to conceptualize the notion of "cultural heritage security" by analyzing the linkage between the maintenance of international peace and security and a system of multilayered cultural heritage governance built on legally binding international obligations and voluntary policy commitments.

II. The Heritage-Security Nexus and Art Plunder

Art plunder has often been part of armed conflict, serving both as war booty and as a means or method of humiliation and conquest. Victorious forces have notoriously taken artifacts as war trophies from defeated enemies, which sometimes involved the destruction of monumental sites of great significance to the cultural identity of the conquered peoples. In ancient Rome, such plundering, though widely practiced, was considered different from ordinary war booty.[5] More recently, the destruction of the Royal Palace of Benin[6] and the Imperial Summer Palace of Beijing[7] as well as the pillage of their treasures provide additional examples of art plunder as part of colonial conquest. The practice of art plunder has affected both public and private collections; often it has involved looting of archaeological sites, thereby depriving objects of their historical context and erasing irrecoverable provenience information. During World War II, art plunder even became fully

[3] "Maintenance of International Peace and Security" (24 March 2017) UN Doc S/RES/2347.

[4] UN Doc S/2017/969.

[5] Margaret M Miles, *Art as Plunder: The Ancient Origins of Debate about Cultural Property* (CUP 2008) 82 ff.

[6] See eg Folarin Shyllon, "Unraveling History: Return of African Cultural Objects Repatriated and Looted in Colonial Times" in James AR Nafziger and Ann M Nicgorski (eds), *Cultural Heritage Issues: The Legacy of Conquest, Colonization and Commerce* (Brill-Nijhoff 2009) 161–63.

[7] See eg Derek Gillman, "The Old Summer Palace and the Rhetoric of National Treasures" (2019) 5 (2) Santander Art and Culture Law Review 233, 236–37.

institutionalized when the Nazis devised a systematically organized machinery of art looting across Europe.[8]

Although art plunder had been condemned in ancient times,[9] its normative prohibition took much time to crystallize.[10] It is only with the experience of the terrible wars of the twentieth century that the unlawful removal of cultural property in armed conflict became widely regarded as a violation of customary international law.[11] Yet cultural objects are still being looted and extracted from conflict-ridden territories. The case of Syria, where satellite imagery revealed an escalating numbers of illegal pits after the outbreak of the armed conflict, serves as the most dramatic recent example.[12] Moreover, antiquities from conflict zones regularly surface on the art market after having crossed several jurisdictions illegally, indicating a maturing organization of the illicit trade.[13] For example, the sale of antiquities originating from Yemen, such as statues or coins, has allegedly generated approximately one million U.S. dollars at auctions throughout the world since 2011.[14] Social media reportedly plays a critical role in the illicit trade of artifacts as well as in the planning of further illegal excavations.[15] While it may be partially

[8] International Military Tribunal (Nuremberg), Judgment of 1 October 1946, 70-1 <http://crimeofaggression.info/documents/6/1946_Nuremberg_Judgement.pdf> accessed 18 August 2021.

[9] Miles (n 5) 285 ff.

[10] See Wayne Sandholtz, *Prohibiting Plunder. How Norms Change* (OUP 2007).

[11] Jean-Marie Henckaerts and Louise Doswald-Beck, *Customary International Humanitarian Law*, vol 1 Rules (CUP 2005) 132–38; Elizabeth Varner, "Non-party Obligations Underlying the 1954 Hague Convention for the Protection of Cultural Property in the Event of Armed Conflict, Protocol II" in this volume. See also Zhang Yue, "Customary International Law and the Rule against Taking Cultural Property as Spoils of War" (2018) 17 (4) Chinese Journal of International Law 943. Note that pillage (in general) was already prohibited in The Hague Regulations concerning the Laws and Customs of War on Land, annexed to Convention Respecting the Laws and Customs of War on Land (1899 and 1907), Article 28.

[12] See eg Jesse Casana and Elise Jakoby Laugier, "Satellite Imagery-Based Monitoring of Archaeological Site Damage in the Syrian Civil War" (2017) 12 (11) PLoS ONE <https://journals.plos.org/plosone/article?id=10.1371/journal.pone.0188589> accessed 18 August 2021. See also Emma Cunliffe et al, "Satellite-Based Damage Assessment to Cultural Heritage Sites in Syria" (UNITAR 2014) <https://unosat.web.cern.ch/unitar/downloads/chs/FINAL_Syria_WHS.pdf> accessed 18 August 2021.

[13] See Daniel Kees, "ISIS the Art Dealer" (*The Regulatory Review*, 13 April 2020) <https://www.theregreview.org/2020/04/13/kees-isis-art-dealer> accessed 16 August 2021; also see Christine A Weirich, "Antiquities in a time of conflict: a crime script analysis of antiquities trafficking during the Syrian Civil War and implications for conflict antiquities" (2021) Crime Sci 10, 13

[14] Owen Jarus, "'Blood Antiquities' Looted from War-Torn Yemen Bring in $1 Million at Auction" (*Live Science*, 5 June 2019) <https://www.livescience.com/65641-yemen-blood-antiquities-investigation.html> accessed 19 August 2021.

[15] Steve Swamm, "Antiquities Looted in Syria and Iraq Are Sold on Facebook" (*BBC News*, 2 May 2019) <https://www.bbc.co.uk/news/world-middle-east-47628369> accessed 19 August 2021, citing the report by Amr Al-Azm and Katie A Paul, "How Facebook Made It Easier Than Ever to Traffic Middle Eastern Antiquities" (*World Politics Review*, 14 August 2018) <https://www.worldpoliticsreview.com/insights/25532/how-facebook-made-it-easier-than-ever-to-traffic-middle-eastern-antiquities> accessed 19 August 2021. See also Amr Al-Azm and Katie A Paul's full report, "Facebook's

explained by increased data collection and analysis, a significant growth in trafficking in cultural objects from conflict zones has been observed. According to INTERPOL, "[t]he black market in works of art is becoming as lucrative as those for drugs, weapons, and counterfeit goods."[16] Illicit operations are particularly concerned with antiquities and archaeological objects, often excavated and smuggled from conflict-ridden territories. According to UNESCO, the black market in antiquities, alongside the trafficking in drugs and arms, "constitutes one of the most persistent illegal trades in the world."[17] Some estimations suggest that up to 80 to 90% of antiquities on the global market come from illicit origins,[18] and that "their trade is often associated with other forms of organized crime, such as drug traffic and money laundering."[19]

Although the exact scale and value of trafficking in antiquities and archaeological objects remain difficult to assess given a lack of reliable data,[20] it is probable that the illicit trade in so-called "blood antiquities" also constitutes a source of terrorism financing, even if only marginal.[21] Although disputed and still poorly studied,[22] this alleged connection has nevertheless played a major role in the recent forefronting of attacks against cultural heritage as a

Black Market in Antiquities – Trafficking, Terrorism, and War Crimes" (June 2019) <http://atharproject.org/wp-content/uploads/2019/06/ATHAR-FB-Report-June-2019-final.pdf> accessed 20 August 2021.

[16] See <https://www.interpol.int/Crimes/Cultural-heritage-crime/The-issues-cultural-property> accessed 20 August 2021.

[17] "The Fight against the Illicit Trafficking of Cultural Objects the 1970 Convention: Past and Future" (15–16 March 2011) UNESCO Doc CLT/2011/CONF.207/6, 3.

[18] European Commission, "Impact Assessment Accompanying the document 'Proposal for a Regulation of the European Parliament and of the Council on the Import of Cultural Goods'" (13 July 2017) SWD(2017) 263 final, 12.

[19] UNESCO Doc C70/19/7.SC/8b (April 2019) [2]; see further Peter B Campbell, "The Illicit Antiquities Trade as a Transnational Criminal Network: Characterizing and Anticipating Trafficking of Cultural Heritage" (2013) 20 (1) International Journal of Cultural Property 113.

[20] Duncan Chappell and Kenneth Polk, "Unravelling the "Cordata": Just How Organized Is the International Traffic in Cultural Objects?" in Stefano Manacorda and Duncan Chappell (eds), *Crime in the Art and Antiquities' World. Illegal Trafficking in Cultural Property* (Springer 2011) 99.

[21] See Annelies Pauwels, "ISIS and Illicit Trafficking in Cultural Property: Funding Terrorism through Art" (*Freedom from Fear Magazine*, 1 November 2015) <http://f3magazine.unicri.it/?p=1098> accessed 20 August 2021. See also Matthew Bogdanos, "Thieves of Baghdad: And the Terrorists They Finance" in Noah Charney (ed), *Art Crime. Terrorists, Tomb Raiders, Forgers and Thieves* (Palgrave Macmillan 2016) 118.

[22] See in particular Matthew Sargent, James V Marrone, Alexandra Evans, Bilyana Lilly, Erik Nemeth, and Stephen Dalzell, *Tracking and Disrupting the Illicit Antiquities Trade with Open Source Data* (Homeland Security Operational Analysis Center operated by the RAND Corporation 2020) <https://www.rand.org/content/dam/rand/pubs/research_reports/RR2700/RR2706/RAND_RR2706.pdf> accessed 20 August 2021, which challenges the widely reported view that trafficking is a major source of terrorism financing.

matter of international peace and security, spurring a range of policies and practices aimed at combating this form of illicit activities. Before examining this emerging field, or "cultural property security paradigm," the following section outlines the international protection regime governing looting and the illicit trade in cultural objects.

A. Armed Conflict, Illicit Trade in Cultural Objects, and International Law

The international protection of cultural property from plunder or other unlawful removal in the event of an armed conflict involves two main groups of obligations: (1) to respect and secure cultural property in armed conflict, and to restore material appropriated and transferred in breach of the former obligations; and (2) to prosecute and punish the perpetrators of violations of the rules on the protection of cultural property.

1. Protecting Cultural Objects from Seizure and Loot in Armed Conflict

Armed conflict entails a breakdown in the rule of law and security in general, thus accentuating the risk of looting, which in turn can be used to fundraise to conduct hostilities. The law of armed conflict, or international humanitarian law (IHL), does not prohibit the trading in cultural objects per se. It does, however, prohibit the seizing or pillage of certain cultural objects as a consequence of the distinction first made in the eighteenth century between civilian and military objects.[23] In the nineteenth century, specific provisions protecting cultural objects were then incorporated in some non-binding instruments as well as within military manuals.[24] The adoption of the Hague Regulations (1899 and 1907) eventually prohibited parties to an international

[23] Sandholtz (n 10) 43–44.

[24] See eg the 1874 Brussels Declaration (Project of an International Declaration Concerning the Laws and Customs of War, adopted by the Conference of Brussels, 27 August 1874, as reprinted in 1 AJIL Supp (1907) 96–107); the 1880 Oxford Manual (Institute de Droit International, "Les Lois De La Guerre Sur Terre," 1880 [The Laws of War in Land] <https://www.uscbs.org/1880-oxford-manual.html> accessed 19 August 2021); the 1863 Lieber Code (The Instructions for the Government of Armies of the United States in the Field, General Order No 100, 14 April 1863 (the Lieber Code of 1863), art 34, art 35, art 36, art 38, in US Department of War, *The War of The Rebellion: A Compilation of the Official Records of the Union and Confederate Armies* (1902) 148), which applied to American troops and contained provisions affording a protected status to libraries, scientific collections, and art works. For a detailed analysis of these instruments see eg Yue (n 11) 971–76.

armed conflict from seizing "the enemy's property, unless such . . . seizure be imperatively demanded by the necessities of war."[25] They also forbid seizing "property of communes, that of religious, charitable, and educational institutions, and those of arts and sciences," including state property (which is to be treated as private property), as well as works of art and science, adding that such conduct "should be made the subject of proceedings."[26]

The 1949 Geneva Conventions do not contain any provision directly relating to cultural property, but their Additional Protocols (APs), adopted in 1977, protect cultural objects from direct attack in situations of international and non-international armed conflict, respectively, and prohibit their use in support of the military effort, which could, arguably, include their sale to finance military operations.[27] In addition, AP I specifically prohibits making cultural objects the subject of reprisals.[28] The two provisions contained in the APs to the Geneva Conventions, however, are not particularly detailed; thus, as a consequence of the vast looting operation put in place during World War II, the Hague Convention for the Protection of Cultural Property in the Event of Armed Conflict was adopted in 1954 (1954 Hague Convention),[29] along with its First Protocol (1954 Hague Protocol) focused on the return of cultural property from either occupied territory or the territory of another State Party.[30]

[25] Art 23(g) of the 1899 and 1907 Hague Regulations. The Hague Regulations refer to the instruments annexed to the Hague Conventions on the Laws and Customs of War on Land, which were part of a series of treaties adopted at two diplomatic conferences, first in 1899 and then in 1907. The Hague Convention IV respecting the Laws and Customs of War on Land and its annexed Regulations (adopted 18 October 1907, entered into force 26 January 1910) 208 Parry's CTS 77, largely confirmed the provisions contained in the II Hague Convention (1899) with Respect to the Laws and Customs of War on Land its annexed Regulations (adopted 29 July 1899, entered into force 4 September 1900) 187 Parry's CTS 429. The 1899 Hague Convention II, which remain in force for those States that have not become party to the subsequent regulations, has fifty States Parties, while the 1907 Hague Convention IV has thirty-six. Note that on 15 April 1935, after these Regulations were adopted, the Treaty on the Protection of Artistic and Scientific Institutions and Historic Monuments (Roerich Pact) was adopted (entered into force 26 August 1935) 167 LNTS 289. It is still in force for its ten States Parties, which include the USA and certain States of Latin America.

[26] Art 56 of the 1899 and 1907 Hague Regulations.

[27] Art 53 of the Protocol Additional to the Geneva Conventions of 12 August 1949, and relating to the Protection of Victims of International Armed Conflicts (Protocol I) (adopted 8 June 1977, entered into force 7 December 1978) 1125 UNTS 3 has 174 States Parties; and Art 16 of Protocol Additional to the Geneva Conventions of 12 August 1949, and relating to the Protection of Victims of Non-International Armed Conflicts (Protocol II) (adopted 8 June 1977, entered into force 7 December 1978) 1125 UNTS 609 which has 169 States Parties.

[28] Art 53(c) AP I.

[29] (adopted 14 May 1954, entered into force 7 August 1956) 249 UNTS 240. The 1954 Hague Convention counts 133 States Parties. For a commentary of the Hague Convention, see Kevin Chamberlain, *War and Cultural Heritage—A Commentary on the Hague Convention 1954 and Its Two Protocols* (2nd edn, Institute of Art and Law 2013).

[30] (adopted 14 May 1954, entered into force 7 August 1956) 249 UNTS 358. The 1954 Hague Protocol counts 110 States Parties.

Nearly half a century later, after the wave of cultural heritage atrocities committed during the wars of the 1990s, the Second Protocol[31] to the 1954 Hague Convention was adopted in 1999 to supplement a number of gaps observed in the practice of IHL in force and extend the protection of cultural property in non-international armed conflict (NIAC).[32] In addition to those of the Hague Regulations (1899 and 1907) generally recognized as part of customary international law, the International Committee of the Red Cross (ICRC) Study considers certain provisions of the 1954 Hague Convention and its Protocols as constitutive of customary international law (and thus binding on all States even if they are not party thereto), including the use of cultural property for military purposes and the respect for cultural property.[33]

The 1954 Hague Convention defines cultural property broadly, including "moveable" objects, such as "works of art; manuscripts, books and other objects of artistic, historical or archaeological interest; as well as scientific collections and important collections of books or archives," without providing further details such as age threshold for objects to qualify as "cultural property."[34] In accordance with the Convention, cultural objects that fall within its scope must also be considered "of great importance to the cultural heritage of every people."[35] It is difficult to implement this vague understanding of cultural property, since military personnel need to rapidly determine whether an object falls within the protection provided by the 1954 Hague Convention. In order to facilitate the identification of "cultural property," this treaty establishes a system of recognition through the display of a distinctive emblem, which may be affixed to an object to inform belligerents of its protected status.[36] There is no obligation, however, to display the emblem for cultural property under the general protection of the 1954 Hague Convention;

[31] (adopted 26 March 1999, entered into force 9 March 2004) 2253 UNTS 212. The Second Protocol counts eighty-two States Parties. For a commentary to this treaty, see Nout Van Woudenberg and Elisabeth Lijnzaad (eds), *Protecting Cultural Property in Armed Conflict—An Insight into the 1999 Second Protocol to the Hague Convention of 1954 for the Protection of Cultural Property in the Event of Armed Conflict* (Nijhoff 2010).

[32] Regarding its application in NIACs, see Art 22 of this treaty.

[33] The ICRC Study is published in Henckaerts and Doswald-Beck (n 11) 1 Rules, 127–38. See Rules 38–41.

[34] Art 1(a) of the 1954 Hague Convention.

[35] ibid.

[36] Arts 6, 10, 16, and 17 of the 1954 Hague Convention, and Art 20 of Regulations for the Execution of the 1954 Hague Convention. On the marking of destroyed cultural sites, see Jiří Hladík, "Marking of Cultural Property with the Distinctive Emblem of the 1954 Hague Convention for the Protection of Cultural Property in the Event of Armed Conflict" (2004) 86 (854) International Review of the Red Cross 379.

States Parties to this treaty may choose another means of identification (such as publication lists, mapping system, notification to opposing forces, etc.).[37]

During armed conflict, the 1954 Hague Convention requires States Parties to *respect* cultural property by refraining from exposing it to possible damage or destruction, such as by using cultural property in a manner likely to turn it into a military objective,[38] except in cases of "imperative military necessity,"—a difficult concept to apply in practice given its lack of clarity.[39] The inevitable insecurity in armed conflict renders looting likely; therefore, States Parties must also prohibit and prevent any form of pillage of cultural property.[40] They are themselves not permitted to requisition cultural objects from the territory of another State Party. A State Party, however, may house in its territory cultural objects of another State Party solely for safekeeping, but must return them at the cessation of hostilities.[41]

The UNESCO Committee for the Protection of Cultural Property in the Event of Armed Conflict, in reference to the Regulations for the Execution of the 1954 Hague Convention and 1954 Hague Protocol, explains that such "safekeeping" may involve the establishment of "safe havens for cultural property situated in States outside a conflict zone," that is, "a secure location where cultural property can be stored, maintained or even restored in certain cases."[42] Such "refuge storerooms" are intended to prevent cultural property "from suffering important damages, and partial or total destruction."[43] The secured cultural property must be returned once the danger is over.[44] It is also worth noting that IHL is generally binding on all parties to an armed conflict, including armed non-State actors (ANSAs).[45] Therefore, the rules

[37] There is an obligation to display the emblem for cultural property under special protection. In such cases, the emblem may even be displayed three times ("triple use").

[38] Arts 2, 3, 4(1), 7(1), and 7(2) of the 1954 Hague Convention. Also Rule 40 of the ICRC Study: Henckaerts and Doswald-Beck (n 11) 1 Rules, 132–35.

[39] Art 4(2) of the 1954 Hague Convention. As imperative "military necessity" is not defined further under the 1954 Hague Convention, it must be construed within the general rules of international humanitarian law (IHL). Note that the Second Protocol to the 1954 Hague Convention narrowed this exception; see Art 6.

[40] Art 4(3) of the 1954 Hague Convention. See also Rule 40(B) of the ICRC Study: Henckaerts and Doswald-Beck (n 11) 1 Rules, 132–35.

[41] See Part II of the 1954 Protocol to the 1954 Hague Convention.

[42] "Report commissioned by UNESCO on Decision of the Committee for the Protection of Cultural Property in the Event of Armed Conflict" (2017) UNESCO Doc. C54/17/12.COM/6, Annex 1 40.

[43] ibid.

[44] ibid 41. Andrzej Jakubowski, "International Protection of Cultural Heritage in Armed Conflict: Revisiting the Role of Safe Havens" (2019) 16 (2) Indonesian Journal of International Law 169, 173.

[45] See, in particular, Common Article 3 to the 1949 Geneva Conventions, and 1977 Additional Protocol II.

protecting cultural property in armed conflict also apply to non-state armed groups.[46]

In addition to its general protection system, the 1954 Hague Convention also provides for "special protection," effectively affording cultural property immunity from any acts of hostility.[47] This special protection, however, only applies to certain immovable objects under certain circumstances, although it does include refuges which shelter cultural objects originating from armed conflict.[48] The Second Protocol expanded this additional form of protection, introducing an "enhanced protection" regime applicable to any movable cultural property that is part of the "heritage of greatest importance for humanity."[49] States Parties need to request the inclusion of particularly important cultural heritage objects in the International List of Cultural Property under Enhanced Protection.[50] Only ten States registered their properties in this inventory to date, few of which include movable cultural property.[51]

Alongside obligations applicable in armed conflict, the 1954 Hague Convention requires States Parties to *safeguard* cultural property in times of peace "against the foreseeable effects of an armed conflict" by, for instance, developing inventories, preparing for the removal of cultural objects, and establishing competent safeguarding authorities.[52] States Parties must also incorporate cultural property protection in their military manuals, foster respect for cultural objects among its troops, and establish specialized personnel within the armed forces to deal with cultural property matters.[53] In

[46] See eg Art 19(1), 1954 Hague Convention, which states that in the case of a NIAC, "each party to the conflict" must respect cultural property. On the application of the rules protecting cultural property to ANSAs, see Kristin Hausler, "Culture Under Attack—The Destruction of Cultural Heritage by Non-State Armed Groups" (2015) 1 (2) Santander Art and Culture Law Review 117; Marina Lostal, Kristin Hausler, and Pascal Bongard, "Armed Non-State Actors and Cultural Heritage in Armed Conflict" (2017) 24 (4) International Journal of Cultural Property 407; Marina Lostal, Kristin Hausler, and Pascal Bongard, *Culture under Fire: Armed Non-State Actors and Cultural Heritage in Wartime* (Geneva Call 2018) <https://www.biicl.org/documents/10_cultural_heritage_study_final_highres.pdf> accessed 20 August 2021.

[47] Arts 8–9 of the 1954 Hague Convention

[48] Arts 8(1), 10, 16, and 17 of the 1954 Hague Convention. Note that in addition to placing cultural property under special protection on a permanent basis, it is also possible to transport cultural property under special protection; see Chapter III of the 1954 Hague Convention and Regulations for the Execution of the Convention.

[49] Art 10(a) of the Second Protocol.

[50] Art 27 of the Second Protocol.

[51] See <http://www.unesco.org/new/fileadmin/MULTIMEDIA/HQ/CLT/pdf/Enhanced-Protection-List-2019_Eng_04.pdf> accessed 31 August 2020.

[52] Art 3 of the 1954 Hague Convention, which provides that States Parties must take measures they consider appropriate, was strengthened by Art 5 of the Second Protocol, which lists the measures to be taken.

[53] Art 7 of the 1954 Hague Convention.

2016, UNESCO published its own military manual,[54] which specifies the rules of conduct of States Parties to the 1954 Hague Convention and its Protocols. The manual emphasizes how international law requires an occupying power to prevent all forms of theft, pillage, misappropriation, and vandalism of cultural property, including plunder of archaeological sites (on land and under water). These obligations not only refer to the acts of an occupant, but also to the duty of occupying forces to prohibit, prevent, and, if necessary, put a stop to the commission of such acts by others, including by organized criminal groups.[55]

The heritage-security nexus has cast a new light on these obligations, which now serves to protect heritage as such and combat the illicit trade in antiquities within the framework of maintaining international security. This shift has driven new practices, including various educational programs addressed to military commanders and civil experts assisting military forces. These include, inter alia, the International Training and Research Centre for the Economy of Culture and World Heritage in Turin, established by Italy under auspices of UNESCO;[56] the Centre for Advanced Studies in Defense (CASD) in Rome; the pilot training organized by Geneva Call on the protection of cultural heritage for armed groups; the newly established International Centre for Training and Research on Cultural Heritage in Danger in Wroclaw, Poland; as well as the training on First Aid to Cultural Heritage and Prevention of Illicit Trafficking in Times of Crisis for specialized police units, organized by the International Centre for the Study of the Preservation and Restoration of Cultural Property (ICCROM) and INTERPOL.

[54] Roger O'Keefe et al, *Protection of Cultural Property. Military Manual* (UNESCO 2016) <https://unesdoc.unesco.org/ark:/48223/pf0000246633> accessed 20 August 2021.

[55] ibid paras 185–94.

[56] See *Agreement between UNESCO and the Italian Republic regarding the establishment of an International Training and Research Centre on the Economics of Culture and World Heritage—ITRECH as a centre under the auspices of UNESCO (category 2)* (signed 16 February 2016) <https://whc.unesco.org/document/148967> accessed 31 August 2020; also *Memorandum of Understanding between UNESCO and the Italian Republic on the Italian National "Task Force in the framework of UNESCO's Global Coalition Unite4Heritage" for initiatives in favour of Countries facing emergencies that may affect the protection and safeguarding of culture and the promotion of cultural pluralism* (signed 16 February 2016) <http://itra.esteri.it/vwPdf/wfrmRenderPdf.aspx?ID=50858> accessed 20 August 2021.

2. The Prohibition of Trafficking in Cultural Objects Originating from Conflict-Ridden Territories

The prohibition of the plunder of cultural property in armed conflict, occupation, and trade in such material are not confined to the regime of the 1954 Hague Convention and its two Protocols. In fact, a number of other treaties and instruments protect cultural objects from being illegally removed from their place of origin. In particular, the UNESCO Convention on the Means of Prohibiting and Preventing the Illicit Import, Export and Transfer of Ownership of Cultural Property, adopted in 1970 (1970 UNESCO Convention), requires States Parties to protect cultural objects on their territory against looting and illicit export through preventive measures.[57] When there is a particular risk of pillage, such as during the onset of an armed conflict, this treaty foresees specific import and export controls.[58] In addition to providing for precautionary measures, the 1970 UNESCO Convention also seeks to strengthen cooperation between States Parties, with special regard to restitution as there is a duty to return an object which has been stolen or illegally exported upon request to its State of origin.[59]

In 2015, the Meeting of States Parties adopted Operational Guidelines for the Implementation of the 1970 UNESCO Convention (OG).[60] These detail the preventive measures that should be taken to combat trafficking such as cooperating with local communities in the protection of archaeological sites or even guarding them,[61] which may be difficult (if not impossible) during armed conflict. The OG also highlight that ignorance is a cause of trafficking; therefore, awareness raising and education are of paramount importance.[62] While UNESCO has established a Database of National Cultural Heritage Laws, States Parties must also ensure that their domestic rules pertaining to the transfer of cultural objects are publicized, particularly to the relevant stakeholders such as collectors, dealers, and museums.[63]

[57] (adopted 14 November 1970, entered into force 24 April 1972) 823 UNTS 231, counts 140 State Parties, with Yemen being the last State that ratified it in June 2019.

[58] Art 9 of the 1970 UNESCO Convention.

[59] Art 7(b)(ii) of the 1970 UNESCO Convention.

[60] Operational Guidelines for the Implementation of the Convention on the Means of Prohibiting and Preventing the Illicit Import, Export and Transfer of Ownership of Cultural Property (Paris, UNESCO 1970) <http://www.unesco.org/new/fileadmin/MULTIMEDIA/HQ/CLT/pdf/OPERATIONAL_GUIDELINES_EN_FINAL_FINAL.pdf> accessed 20 August 2021.

[61] ibid paras 46–47.

[62] ibid para 14.

[63] ibid para 31.

The system of the 1970 UNESCO Convention is supplemented by that of the Convention on Stolen or Illegally Exported Cultural Objects adopted by UNIDROIT (1995 UNIDROIT Convention).[64] While the former treaty sets out obligations vested in States and not applicable to private entities, the latter extends the obligation to return cultural objects to any possessor, who is in turn entitled to compensation if they can prove that due diligence was exercised when acquiring the object.[65] The 1995 UNIDROIT Convention relates to situations of theft, including illicit excavations and unlawful export, and thus comprises instances of unlawful removals from conflict-ridden and occupied territories. Yet this treaty does not foresee specific measures to address trafficking but rather focuses on its consequences.

a. *Import Restrictions and Protection of Cultural Property in Armed Conflict*

The 1970 UNESCO Convention covers both illicit export and import of cultural objects. While export restrictions are widely implemented at the national and regional levels, import controls have long been the weakest element of the protection system established by this treaty;[66] States Parties have rarely introduced legislative restrictions on imports of cultural objects, including those unlawfully transferred from conflict zones. Recasting the 1970 UNESCO Convention and the 1995 UNIDROIT Convention from cultural property protection to instruments of international security management exposed the need for further mechanisms. For instance, the need for more effective import controls have been addressed by a number of instruments adopted to protect cultural property in recent conflicts.[67]

Following the Iraq invasion in 2003, the UNSC adopted Resolution 1483, a UN Charter Chapter VII resolution binding on all UN members, stressing "the need for respect for the archaeological, historical, cultural, and religious heritage of Iraq" and calling on States not only "to facilitate the safe return to Iraqi institutions of Iraqi cultural property and other items of archaeological, historical, cultural, rare scientific and religious importance illegally re- moved from the Iraq National Museum, the National Library, and other

[64] (adopted 24 June 1995, entered into force 1 July 1998) (1995) 34 ILM 1322. This treaty counts forty-seven States Parties.

[65] Art 4(1) of the UNIDROIT Convention.

[66] See a series of studies in James AR Nafziger and Robert Kirkwood Paterson (eds), *Handbook on the Law of Cultural Heritage and International Trade* (Edward Elgar 2014).

[67] Sandholtz (n 10) 191–96.

locations in Iraq," but also to prohibit "trade in or transfer of such items."[68] This resolution fostered the adoption of import bans specifically concerned with cultural goods at the domestic level.[69]

The conflict in Syria prompted the adoption of similar security motivated measures, with the European Union (EU) being the first to enact a specific import ban with regard to Syrian antiquities in 2013.[70] Prompted by the Al-Qaeda Sanctions Committee,[71] the UNSC followed in 2015 with Resolution 2199, which prohibited the trade in Syrian antiquities.[72] Its adoption raised widespread awareness about threats associated with the black art market and strengthened both domestic regulatory machinery and cooperation through information sharing to counter the illicit trafficking in antiquities.[73] Given that not all armed conflicts have led to the establishment of international obligations aimed at curbing the trafficking in cultural objects originating from such contexts,[74] a recent European initiative has prompted the adoption of an import licensing system for objects at risk of trafficking. In 2019, the EU adopted a new regulation on the import of cultural goods to address the trafficking in cultural objects, citing instruments used to combat the financing of terrorism and thus linking the two issues (Regulation 2019/880).[75] The EU

[68] (22 May 2003) UN Doc S/RES/1483 para 7.

[69] On the implementation of this resolution in the USA, UK, and Switzerland, see Patty Gerstenblith, "From Bamiyan to Baghdad: Warfare and the Preservation of Cultural Heritage at the Beginning of the 21st Century" (2006) 37 (2) Georgetown Journal of International Law 215, 329–34, fn 158.

[70] Art 11(c) of the Council Regulation (EU) No 1332/2013 of 13 December 2013 amending regulation (EU) No 36/2012 concerning restrictive measures in view of the situation in Syria [2013] OJ L 335/3.

[71] See the Monitoring Team Report S/2014/815. Note that the Monitoring Team continues to engage with Member States regarding the collection of data on antiquities trafficking, as well as with the private sector. It has made additional recommendations to implement measures to stop asset generation from antiquities trafficking, see in particular S/2016/629 which was the basis for UNSC Resolution 2347 (2017).

[72] (12 February 2015) UN Doc S/RES/2199.

[73] Intervention of Irina Bokova (former UNESCO Director-General) at the UNSC briefing meeting, where she underlined that about 50 States have already strengthened their legislation and are sharing information to fight the illicit trafficking in antiquities; UN Doc S/PV.7907 (24 March 2017) 4.

[74] There has been no UNSC resolutions regarding the trade of cultural objects from Libya or Yemen for example, although UNESCO has encouraged States to adopt measures for objects originating from those countries. See the letter from the UNESCO Director-General, dated 18 May 2016, regarding the implementation of UNSC Res 2253 (17 December 2015) on sanctions for terrorist activities <http://unesdoc.unesco.org/images/0024/002448/244857e.pdf> accessed 20 August 2021.

[75] Regulation (EU) 2019/880 of the European Parliament and of the Council of 17 April 2019 on the introduction and the import of cultural goods [2019] OJ L 151/1; see Preamble, para 1, which cites the Council Conclusions of 12 February 2016 on the fight against the financing of terrorism <https://www.consilium.europa.eu/en/press/press-releases/2016/02/12/conclusions-terrorism-financing> accessed 18 August 2021; and the Communication from the Commission to the European Parliament and the Council of 2 February 2016 on an Action Plan for strengthening the fight against

sought to "prohibit the introduction into the customs territory of the Union of cultural goods unlawfully exported from third countries, with particular emphasis on cultural goods from third countries affected by armed conflict, in particular where such cultural goods have been illicitly traded by terrorist or other criminal organizations."[76] It applies to those cultural goods that are listed in its Annex (similarly to the 1970 UNESCO Convention or the 1995 UNIDROIT Convention) and falls within certain age and/or financial thresholds. While some objects must be more than 250 years old whatever their value, such as products of archaeological excavations or elements of historic monuments, others must only be more than 200 years old but reach a certain financial threshold, such as antiquities like coins which must be older than 200 years old and be valued at EUR 18,000 minimum per item.[77]

Regulation 2019/880 mainly requires those seeking to import cultural objects listed in its Annex to either obtain an import license for those objects most at risk or submit an importer statement, which amounts to a declaration.[78] In order to obtain a license, evidence must be provided with regard to the lawful export "from the country where they were created or discovered" (either in accordance with the applicable laws of that country or in the absence of such rules at the time). If no such evidence can be provided because either the country of origin cannot be reliably determined or the object in question was removed from its territory before the 1970 UNESCO Convention came into force (24 April 1972), then evidence of lawful exportation is needed from "the last country where they were located for a period of more than five years."[79] A limited number of exceptions to the license/statement system are provided in Regulation 2019/880, such as objects which will enter the EU territory in order to be exhibited or restored.[80] Nevertheless, some actors in art trade are concerned that the new regime, which will not be implemented in full before 2025, will generate a significant administrative and financial burden.[81]

terrorist financing and Directive (EU) 2017/541 of the European Parliament and of the Council, COM(2016) 50 final.

[76] Regulation 2019/880, Preamble, para 3.
[77] ibid Annex Part B.
[78] ibid arts 4–5.
[79] ibid art 4(4).
[80] ibid art 3(4).
[81] See Emily Gould, "The EU's Parting Gift to the Art Market" (*Institute of Art & Law*, 1 April 2019). The author cites the International League of Antiquarian Booksellers <https://ial.uk.com/the-eus-parting-gift-to-the-uk-art-market> accessed 201 August 2021.

b. Trafficking in Cultural Objects as a Transnational Crime

In the criminal justice sphere, the UN Convention against Transnational Organized Crime (Palermo Convention, or UNTOC),[82] which fosters international cooperation to effectively combat trafficking, contains a reference to "offences against cultural heritage and the growing links between transnational organized crime and terrorist crimes" in its Preamble.[83] In order to apply the Palermo Convention to the trafficking in cultural objects, the UN General Assembly adopted the International Guidelines for Crime Prevention and Criminal Justice Responses with Respect to Trafficking in Cultural Property and Other Related Offences.[84] Although non-binding, they are helpful for States to develop effective crime prevention and criminal justice policies, adopt legislation that implements the Palermo Convention, and strengthen cooperation mechanisms. Its forty-eight Guidelines (2014 UNGA Guidelines) cover the role of States in providing both legal and policy instruments to effectively address illicit trade in cultural material. Accordingly, they are first asked to introduce various preventive mechanisms. These include, inter alia, the creation of databases or inventories of cultural objects and contribution "to international data collection on trafficking in cultural property and related offences" within the schemes operated by the UN Office on Drugs and Crime (UNODC) and INTERPOL, which have also called for better data gathering at the domestic level.[85] Alongside the already well-established action by INTERPOL in the field of international cooperation in organized art crime[86] and other law enforcement agencies operating at the regional level, such as the EU Agency for Law Enforcement Cooperation (Europol),[87] the UNODC's role has been enhanced.[88] In 2016, a new assistance tool for the implementation of the 2014 UNGA Guidelines

[82] (signed 12 December 2000, entered into force 29 September 2003) 2225 UNTS 209.

[83] 10th recital.

[84] UNGA Res 69/196 (18 December 2014) UN Doc A/RES/69/196, Annex.

[85] ibid Guidelines 1 and 3(e).

[86] (n 16).

[87] See eg the successful Operation "Demeter," involving joint efforts by police forces from four EU Member States (Germany, Italy, Spain, United Kingdom), Europol and European Union Agency for Criminal Justice Cooperation (Eurojust) <http://art-crime.blogspot.com/2018/07/operation-demetra-trafficking-of.html> accessed 18 August 2021. For more information see < https://www.europol.europa.eu/crime-areas-and-trends/crime-areas/illicit-trafficking-in-cultural-goods-including-antiquities-and-works-of-art> accessed 20 August 2021.

[88] See the list of UN documents supporting UNODC's action in these matters <https://www.unodc.org/unodc/en/organized-crime/trafficking-in-cultural-property-mandate.html> accessed 20 August 2021.

was launched within the framework of the UNODC campaign against trafficking in cultural property.[89]

Importantly, the 2014 UNGA Guidelines also call on States to launch effective, inclusive mechanisms of cooperation with cultural institutions and the private sector, including internet providers and online traders, which should be encouraged to adopt codes of conduct regarding the acquisition of cultural objects.[90] This aspect has recently been supported by UNESCO[91] and the EU, pursuant to the European Parliament resolution on "Cross-border restitution claims of works of art and cultural goods looted in armed conflicts and wars."[92] The latter document calls for the creation of a central meta-database which would facilitate the exchange of information and provenance research.[93] Unsurprisingly, an important segment of the 2014 UNGA Guidelines details effective systems of criminal and administrative sanctions that States are called to effectively introduce to their domestic systems.[94] They are also called to provide mutual assistance in this regard, pursuant to new bi- and multilateral arrangements.[95]

At the European level, the Council of Europe adopted the Convention on Offences relating to Cultural Property in 2017 (Nicosia Convention) in order to harmonize the criminalization of trafficking in cultural objects at the national level and strengthen cooperation in combating criminal offenses relating to cultural property at the international level.[96] This treaty, however, is not in force as it has not yet reached the sufficient number of ratifications.[97] This ambitious treaty designed to prevent and struggle against offenses relating to tangible items of cultural heritage may never be binding due to profound differences between national cultural heritage law systems discouraging States from its ratification.[98]

[89] UNODC, "Practical Assistance Tool to assist in the implementation of the International Guidelines for Crime Prevention and Criminal Justice Responses with Respect to Trafficking in Cultural Property and Other Related Offences" (2016) <https://www.unodc.org/documents/organized-crime/Publications/16-05585_eBook_English_UPDATED.pdf> accessed 17 August 2021.

[90] 2014 UNGA Guidelines 5–8.

[91] See UNESCO Doc C70/19/7.SC/8b (2019).

[92] See Resolution of the European Parliament, "Cross-Border Restitution Claims of Works of Art and Cultural Goods Looted in Armed Conflicts and Wars" (17 January 2019) <http://www.europarl.europa.eu/doceo/document/TA-8-2019-0037_EN.html> accessed 18 August 2021.

[93] ibid paras 18, 26–28.

[94] 2014 UNGA Guidelines 13–31.

[95] ibid Guidelines 32–47.

[96] ETS no 221.

[97] It currently counts ten State signatories but only two States have ratified or accessed to it.

[98] In fact, the earlier (1985) European Convention on Offences relating to Cultural Property (signed 23 June 1985, not entered into force) ETS No 119 has not been ratified by any State.

Given that transnational crimes sometimes support terrorist activities, a link noted by the UNTOC, the International Convention for the Suppression of the Financing of Terrorism (CSFT)[99] must also be considered in the combat against the transnational crime of antiquities trafficking. Although it does not contain specific references to antiquities trafficking, the CSFT also applies to trafficked antiquities or proceeds from the art market when these funds are meant to support terrorist activities. Affirming that trafficking in cultural objects is a transnational crime, which may in turn contribute to finance terrorism, thus means that two of the most well ratified treaties, namely the Palermo Convention and the CSFT,[100] not only apply to this form of crime but also benefit from global support to address it. In addition to global efforts specifically aimed at tackling terrorism financing, legislation seeking to curb money laundering further strengthen the fight against trafficking in cultural objects. The EU's Fifth Money Laundering Directive of 2018 (Directive 2018/843)[101] specifically expands the EU's anti-money laundering legislative framework to art market operators, who will need to modify their practices particularly with cash transaction of €10,000 or more.[102] The application of anti-money laundering legislation to art dealers and auctioneers should further prevent the art market from being used to support terrorism financing, and thus work to minimize global security risks.

3. Shortcomings of the Existing Legal System

Notwithstanding these normative and policy developments, which increasingly reframe looting and illicit trade in cultural objects as a matter of international security, enduring implementation challenges render the regulatory framework mostly ineffective: illicit removal, transfer, and trafficking from conflict-affected areas remain major issues.

First, although international obligations to respect cultural property and return such materials unlawfully appropriated and transferred are widely accepted by the international community and recognized as stemming from customary international law, the actual determination of a

[99] (signed 9 December 1999, entered into force 10 April 2002) 2178 UNTS 197.

[100] The Palermo Convention counts 190 States Parties and the CSFT counts 189 States Parties.

[101] Directive (EU) 2018/843 of the European Parliament and of the Council of 30 May 2018 amending Directive (EU) 2015/849 on the prevention of the use of the financial system for the purposes of money laundering or terrorist financing, and amending Directives 2009/138/EC and 2013/36/EU [2018] OJ 156/43.

[102] Compare in the United States, the proposed Corporate Transparency Act of 2019 <https://www.congress.gov/bill/116th-congress/house-bill/2513> accessed 20 August 2021.

breach of such obligations (whether a given act can be considered unlawful) and the attribution of such a breach to a state (which is actually responsible) is not an easy task. In fact, state responsibility in this regard is often barred by the existence of military necessity, the lack of effective control of a territory, etc.

Second, most present-day armed conflicts are characterized by the involvement of non-state actors, thus raising challenging questions as to the effective control over archaeological sites, storages, and trafficking routes. The participation of non-state actors, such as armed groups and terrorist organizations, also raises questions as to the liability of such groups as collective entities for the breach of international obligations in respect of cultural heritage; at present, unless they become the State, they can only be held liable on the basis of individual criminal responsibility rather than a collective form of responsibility.[103] The most critical issue is perhaps the question of the existence itself of a non-international armed conflict, as it is not always straightforward to assess whether the threshold has been met for the rules applicable to armed conflict to apply and for attacks on cultural heritage to be considered as "war crimes."

Third, there are still many problems concerning the effective prosecution of cultural heritage crimes committed in armed conflict. These regard the issue of compliance by States with international obligations to introduce into their national legal systems adequate criminal and administrative sanctions for prosecuting the alleged perpetrators of heritage crimes. Moreover, national lawmakers are reluctant to harmonize catalogues and legal notions of offenses against cultural property, as evidenced by the low number of ratifications of the Nicosia Convention. In addition, there are a number of problems concerning the gathering and analysis of evidence of crimes committed in armed conflict, particularly against archaeological heritage.

Last but not least, effective information sharing is lacking, notwithstanding development of new technologies and constant calls on States by international organizations to build better channels of communication and cooperation.

[103] See Hausler (n 46) 140–42.

B. Trafficking in Cultural Objects as a Threat to International Peace and Security

Regardless of regulatory shortcomings, the aforementioned evolving international law framework has contributed to the gradual inclusion of cultural heritage in security sectors. Cultural heritage has been incrementally integrated within the frameworks of humanitarian, peacekeeping, security, and human rights policies and operations. This trend has been fostered and promoted by UNESCO as a new international agenda: "The role of culture for resilience, peace and security"[104] has developed since at least 2013, that is, the UN-UNESCO partnership in Mali, provided by the UNSC Resolution 2100.[105] In this regard, the engagement of the UN Security Council is pivotal. This UN organ, mandated to ensure peace and security,[106] determined that "the looting and smuggling of cultural property in the event of armed conflicts" constitute a threat to international peace and security.[107] As a result, it adopted Resolution 2347 in 2017, its first resolution dedicated exclusively to the trafficking (and destruction) of cultural heritage in situations of armed conflict. While the UNSC had already noted the risk posed by armed conflict to cultural objects, it had previously only done so in relation to specific conflicts.[108] As already noted, it had imposed import restrictions on two occasions with regard to Iraqi and Syrian objects. Resolution 2347 requests that States "take appropriate steps to prevent, and counter the illicit trade and trafficking" in cultural objects "where States have a reasonable suspicion that the items originate from a context of armed conflict."[109] It therefore goes beyond previous resolutions that were confined to certain specific armed conflict (Iraq and Syria) by expanding its request to any situation of armed conflict.

104 See <https://en.unesco.org/The-role-of-culture-for-resilience-peace-and-security> accessed 20 August 2021.

105 UNSC Res 2100 (25 April 2013) UN Doc S/RED/2100; see Sabine von Schorlemer, "Military Intervention, the UN Security Council, and the Role of UNESCO: The Case of Mali" in Carstens and Warner (n 1).

106 Art 24 of the UN Charter (signed 26 June 1945, entered into force 24 October 1945) 1 UNTS XVI, as amended.

107 In accordance with Art 39 of the UN Charter.

108 For more on the way the UNSC gradually affirmed cultural heritage protection as a matter of peace and security, Kristin Hausler, "Cultural Heritage and the Security Council: Why Resolution 2347 Matters" (*Questions of International Law*, 31 March 2018); Manlio Frigo, "Approaches Taken by the Security Council to the Global Protection of Cultural Heritage: An Evolving Role in Preventing Unlawful Traffic of Cultural Property" (2018) 101 (4) Rivista di diritto internazionale 1164.

109 UNSC Resolution 2347 para 8.

Importantly, Resolution 2347 identifies the risk of cultural objects being looted by terrorist groups and thus the possibility of it being used as a source of terrorism financing. Despite the growing role of the UNSC in countering terrorism since the 2001 September attacks on American soil, it did not expressly link international terrorism and trafficking in cultural objects immediately thereafter. It was only in 2014 that the UNSC expressed some concern at terrorists benefiting from transnational organized crimes including trafficking in artifacts.[110] Eventually, in 2015, it clearly affirmed the link between trafficking in cultural objects and terrorism when it noted that terrorist groups "are generating income from engaging directly or indirectly in the looting, and smuggling of cultural heritage items from archaeological sites, museums, libraries, archives, and other sites in Iraq and Syria, which is being used to support their recruitment efforts and strengthen their operational capability to organize and carry out terrorist attacks."[111] The alleged link between trafficking in cultural objects and terrorism resulted in the adoption of Resolution 2347 after the use of the illicit trade in antiquities to finance terrorism under the control of Abu Sayyaf, a now deceased high-ranking ISIL member, was duly noted.[112]

The connection between the trafficking in cultural objects and terrorism was raised again when the G7 countries signed the "Florence Declaration" in March 2017, calling for increased efforts against the illegal trafficking in cultural objects.[113] The Human Rights Council also made the connection between the illicit trafficking in cultural objects and the financing of terrorism, which is a threat to peace and security, adding that safeguarding cultural rights may thus contribute to fighting terrorism.[114] These objectives were reaffirmed by the meetings of the G20 countries in Hamburg in July 2019.[115]

[110] UNSC Res 2195 (19 December 2014) UN Doc S/RES/2195 Preamble.

[111] UNSC Res 2199 (12 February 2015) UN Doc S/RES/2199 paras 15–16. See also UNSC Res 2322 (12 December 2016) UN Doc S/RES/2322, Preamble.

[112] Ambassador Michele J Sison, US Deputy Permanent Representative to the United Nations, US Mission to the United Nations, "Explanation of Vote at the Adoption of UN Security Council Resolution 2347 on the Destruction and Trafficking of Cultural Heritage by Terrorist Groups and in Situations of Armed Conflict" (New York City, 24 March 2017).

[113] Joint Declaration of the Ministers of Culture of G7 on the Occasion of the Meeting, "Culture As An Instrument For Dialogue Among Peoples" (Florence, 30 March 2017) < http://www.g7.utoronto.ca/culture/culture-2017-en.html> accessed 19 August 2021.

[114] UNHRC, "Report of the United Nations High Commissioner for Human Rights on the Intersessional Seminar on Cultural Rights and the Protection of Cultural Heritage" (27 December 2017) UN Doc A/HRC/37/29. For more on the role of the Human Rights Council, see Kristin Hausler, "The UN Security Council, the Human Rights Council, and the Protection of Cultural Heritage: A Matter of Peace and Security, Human Rights, or Both?" in Carstens and Warner (n 1).

[115] See <https://www.consilium.europa.eu/media/23546/2017-g20-hamburg-action-plan-en.pdf> accessed 19 August 2021.

C. Strengthening the Global Response to Trafficking

In order to effectively address a crime that involves a variety of actors across borders, a comprehensive approach is necessary.

The first step is to tackle the problem at its source, that is, to limit opportunities for looters to take the objects through preventive measures. This is not only important to address the particular crime but also to safeguard the scientific value of cultural objects; once an archaeological object has been removed from its context, much of its scientific and cultural value is often lost forever. Therefore, where possible, sites that are rich in heritage must be protected from looters. When sites are inadequately protected, human lives are threatened: Khaled al-Asaad, the Syrian archaeologist and head of antiquities at Palmyra, was beheaded by the ISIS in 2015 after reportedly refusing to share the location of antiquities hidden for safekeeping.[116]

The protection of cultural sites and cultural objects in armed conflict has been integrated into armed forces in an inconsistent manner. Efforts are underway to formalize the participation of heritage experts within the military.[117] NATO's accredited Civil-Military Cooperation Centre of Excellence recommends two forms of training before deployment with regard to cultural property, including one that is country-specific.[118] In order to afford heritage sites and their artifacts adequate protection in situ, the UNSC has affirmed that the mandate of UN peacekeeping operations "may encompass, as appropriate, assisting relevant authorities, upon their request, in the protection of cultural heritage from . . . illicit excavation, looting and smuggling in the context of armed conflicts, in collaboration with UNESCO."[119] The UNSC had also extended the mandate of the UN peacekeeping mission in Mali (United Nations Multidimensional Integrated Stabilization Mission in Mali, MINUSMA) to "support for cultural preservation" by assisting the transitional authorities in protecting the heritage sites "as necessary and

[116] Kareem Shaheen and Ian Black, "Beheaded Syrian Scholar Refused to Lead ISIS to Hidden Palmyra Antiquities" (*The Guardian*, 19 August 2015) <https://www.theguardian.com/world/2015/aug/18/isis-beheads-archaeologist-syria> accessed 19 August 2021.

[117] See, for example, the establishment of a *Cultural Property* Protection Unit in the UK (2018) and of a Cultural Heritage Task Force with the US Army, in partnership with the Smithsonian, which is underway.

[118] NATO, Cultural property protection <https://www.nato.int/cps/en/natohq/topics_166114.htm> accessed 19 August 2021, where it states that in Afghanistan NATO forces contributed to the building of facilities to safeguard archaeological objects.

[119] UNSC Resolution 2347 para 19.

feasible."[120] Following deliberate attacks against cultural heritage by extremists, UNESCO launched the Global Coalition Unite4Heritage in 2015, a campaign that seeks to mobilize Member States, communities, and in particular young people to increase their efforts to safeguard cultural heritage.[121]

A Memorandum of Understanding was signed on February 16, 2016, between UNESCO and the Italian task force (ITF) regarding the establishment of the so-called "Blue Helmets for Culture" within the framework of UNESCO's Global Coalition Unite4Heritage. As trafficking in cultural objects is a transnational crime, the second step to successfully address it is to ensure that cooperation mechanisms are optimized both at the interagency and international levels. A number of cross-agencies initiatives have already been implemented. For example, in 2016, UNESCO and the ICRC signed a six-year Memorandum of Understanding in recognition of their complementary roles, the former with its expertise in cultural property protection and the latter with its operational presence in emergencies. The partnership agreement foresees information sharing between the two organizations with regard to cultural properties at imminent risk; it also provides for the ICRC's assistance in rescuing and evacuating cultural objects from conflict areas.[122] In 2017, UNESCO and the ICC signed a Letter of Intent in order to articulate a cooperation framework.[123] Since the ICC Statute (Rome Statute) gives jurisdiction to the Court for the war crime of pillage, cooperation between the two bodies may also impact the trafficking in cultural objects: the plunder of antiquities in war zones could be prosecuted before the ICC on a large scale.

Meetings were also organized in 2015 and 2016 by the Permanent Missions of Italy and Jordan with INTERPOL, UNESCO, and UNODC to draft suggested actions to combat trafficking, including increased cooperation between States and international organizations as well as the undertaking of studies to gather more data on trafficking routes and financial gains

[120] UNSC Res 2100 (25 April 2013) UN Doc S/RES/2100 para 16(f), to be read with para 17.

[121] See 38 C/Resolution 48, adopted by the Organization's 38th General Conference in November 2015. See also the website of the Unite4Heritage campaign <https://www.unite4heritage.org/> accessed 20 August 2021.

[122] Article I(v) and (vi), Memorandum of Understanding between UNESCO and the ICRC <https://www.icrc.org/en/document/cultural-property-protected-in-armed-conflict> accessed 19 August 2021.

[123] "International Criminal Court and UNESCO Strengthen Cooperation on the Protection of Cultural Heritage" (*UNESCO Press Release*, 6 November 2017) <https://en.unesco.org/news/international-criminal-court-and-unesco-strengthen-cooperation-protection-cultural-heritage> accessed 18 August 2021.

from trafficking.[124] In addition to suggested key actions to be taken at the international and national levels, this document also contains suggested action points specifically aimed at situations of armed conflict, including outreach activities.[125] Furthermore, the calls made by the UNSC in Resolution 2347, along with those made in earlier resolutions to address the financing of terrorism with antiquities trafficking, led to the integration of heritage personnel within police and customs authorities and the establishment of specialized units, or at least to the provision of training for police and customs officials. The development of databases on cultural objects identified as either missing or at risk of being trafficked further helps to address the issue by strengthening international cooperation between the relevant authorities and improve data collection.[126]

The report on the implementation of Resolution 2347 does not only consider the role of governmental authorities and international organizations but also non-state actors, including collectors, art dealers, auction houses, and online platforms as the "last line of defence against the sale of artifacts looted by terrorist organizations in conflict zones," and contemplates the establishment of "differentiated due diligence" for the various participants in the art market.[127]

III. Conclusion

The protection of cultural property in armed conflict against illicit trafficking has become one of the key issues in international efforts to combat terrorism and organized crime, despite insufficient data to affirm that trafficking in cultural objects is a key source of terrorism financing. This chapter explored and scrutinized the main elements of this process, integrating both legal and policy components. In this regard, it is evident that the normative and axiological weight of instruments and tools aimed at combating illicit trade in cultural objects have greatly changed. This change can arguably be observed in three different contexts.

[124] *Protecting Cultural Heritage—an Imperative for Humanity* (INTERPOL 2016) 13 <https://www.unodc.org/documents/publications/SRIUN_Protecting_Cultural_Heritage_2016.09.12_LR.pdf> accessed 20 August 2021.

[125] ibid 16.

[126] Report of the Secretary-General on the Implementation of Security Council, Resolution 2347 (2017) UN Doc S/2017/969 (17 November 2017) paras 12–18, 49–71.

[127] ibid paras 22–23.

First of all, at the rhetorical level, the trafficking in cultural objects and fight against such practices is claimed to be a serious threat to the core interests of all peoples and the fundamental values they share. The former UN Under-Secretary-General for Political Affairs, Jeffrey D. Feltman, noted that the protection of cultural heritage "is not only a cultural issue, it is also a security and humanitarian imperative," underlining that terrorist groups not only "exploit cultural sites to finance their activities" but also "[destroy and] traffic cultural heritage to undermine the power of culture as a bridge between generations and people of different backgrounds and religions."[128] This underlying axiological value was also noted in former UN Secretary General Ban Ki-moon's early statement, which referred to the protection of cultural heritage in terms of "political and security imperative" and called for it to be a "central component of peacebuilding and conflict resolution efforts and humanitarian and development policies."[129] Unsurprisingly, this rhetoric has been used constantly by UNESCO, as exemplified by the "Unite4Heritage" initiative. Moreover, the shift from heritage preservation to international security in policy underpinning new regulation and in initiatives aimed at implementing the "conventional" regulatory framework, namely the 1954 Hague Convention, the 1970 UNESCO Convention, and the 1995 UNIDROIT Convention, has added new value to heritage protection. This may be described as the securitization of heritage protection,[130] which today both supplements States' approach to modern diplomacy as well as their internal and external actions (an important element of soft power) and contributes to their political and territorial stability.[131] This "heritage-security" nexus is indeed observed at different levels of international law and policymaking, and vis-à-vis the growing threats to cultural heritage caused by terrorism, organized crime, and fundamentalism.[132]

[128] Intervention of Mr Feltman at the adoption of UNSC Resolution 2347, UN Doc S/PV.7907 (24 March 2017) 2–3.

[129] See Report on the International Conference, "Heritage and Cultural Diversity at Risk in Iraq and Syria" (Paris, UNESCO, 3 December 2014) 5 <http://unesdoc.unesco.org/images/0023/002325/232562e.pdf> accessed 19 August 2021.

[130] See Paolo Foradori, Serena Giusti, and Alessandro Giovanni Lamonica, "Reshaping Cultural Heritage Protection Policies at a Time of Securitisation: France, Italy, and the United Kingdom" (2018) 50 (3) The International Spectator 86, 86–87.

[131] Erik Nemeth, "Cultural Security: The Evolving Role of Art in International Security" (2007) 19 (1) Terrorism and Political Violence 19; Erik Nemeth, *Cultural Security: Evaluating The Power of Culture in International Affairs* (Imperial College Press 2014). See also Christina Luke and Morag Kersel, *US Cultural Diplomacy and Archaeology: Soft Power, Hard Heritage* (Routledge 2013).

[132] Mark V Vlasic and Helga Turku, "Protecting Cultural Heritage as a Means for International Peace, Security and Stability: The Case of ISIS, Syria and Iraq" (2016) 49 (5) Vanderbilt Journal of Transnational Law 1371.

The second level concerns the activity of the UNSC and the use of Chapter VII of the UN Charter for the purposes of cultural heritage protection as well as the fight against trafficking in cultural material as matters of international security and peace maintenance. This normative securitization undoubtedly constitutes the most important development in international law, demonstrating a paradigmatic shift in the legal governance of the art trade, from a net of national legislation and umbrella provisions of international cultural heritage law toward the area of global regulation, legitimized and justified by the protection of the core interests of all peoples.

The third level regards the current practice of States, international organizations, and other actors in implementing the binding UNSC resolutions, the non-binding resolutions of the UNGA, and the legal rules adopted by other entities within and beyond the UN system. In this latter context, the EU's new import regime is particularly significant as it embraces the other two dimensions. While highlighting the security aspects of the fight against trafficking in cultural property, it also refers to common values and the protection of human dignity.

Considering developments at these levels in tandem with increases in the value of the global art market, there shall be no doubt that the protection of cultural heritage against appropriation and removal in armed conflict is crucial for everyone's stability and security. The novelty of the new regime, however, may be explained through the consolidation of global concern and the global obligations to be vested in all members of the international community to cooperate to prevent trafficking and restore forcefully removed elements of cultural heritage to their rightful owners.

Addressing the trafficking in cultural objects has now firmly become part of the UN counterterrorism efforts and the UNSC's work toward the maintenance of peace and security. It can therefore benefit from efforts already undertaken at the global level to address other forms of transnational organized crime. Despite little evidence to assert trafficking in cultural objects as a major source of terrorism financing, the international developments made as a result of this alleged link, including calls for increased transparency in the art trade and better data collection in general, can only strengthen the combat against this form of trafficking which threatens the role of heritage in affirming cultural identity and supporting social cohesion.

7

Cultural Property Protection in the Context of Counter Terrorist Financing

An Emerging Legal Paradigm

Ricardo A. St. Hilaire

I. Introduction

Delta Force commandos raided an ISIS compound in eastern Syria in 2015, recovering a trove of military intelligence, hundreds of cultural objects, and digital photographs of artifacts readied for sale, all in the hands of the terrorist group's Antiquities Department chief. The seized evidence changed the way American policymakers, legislators, lawyers, and law enforcement think about cultural property. The discovery revealed how ISIS harnessed cultural objects to fuel its violence, which prompted authorities in the United States to take action, including filing an innovative court complaint that applied the powerful USA PATRIOT Act against the Islamic State of Iraq and Syria (a/k/a ISIS/ISIL/IS/Daesh). "The lawsuit marks the first time that the United States has filed an action to forfeit antiquities that are foreign assets of ISIL," announced the Department of Justice (DOJ) as it focused its attention on the security threat posed by ISIS.[1]

The forfeiture case exemplifies the brimming interest in the connection between transnational cultural heritage trafficking and terrorist financing, part of an emerging legal and public policy paradigm extending the focal point of cultural heritage protection from specialist discussions about preservation of cultural property—archaeological artifacts, antiquities, art, religious objects, ethnological material, monuments, manuscripts, and the like—to

[1] US Department of Justice, US Attorney's Office for the District of Columbia, "United States Files Complaint Seeking Forfeiture of Antiquities Associated with the Islamic State of Iraq and the Levant (ISIL)" (15 December 2016) <https://www.justice.gov/usao-dc/pr/united-states-files-complaint-seeking-forfeiture-antiquities-associated-islamic-state> accessed 28 October 2019.

Ricardo A. St. Hilaire, *Cultural Property Protection in the Context of Counter Terrorist Financing* In: *The Preservation of Art and Culture in Times of War.* Edited by: Claire Finkelstein, Derek Gillman, and Frederik Rosén, Oxford University Press.
 DOI: 10.1093/oso/9780197610565.003.0008

a broader concern for US national security, particularly terrorist financing. This new, security-based thinking is the product of the crosscurrents of heritage preservation, counter-transnational crime, and antiterrorism efforts, which together have lifted cultural property protection, particularly of antiquities and archaeological material from the Greater Middle East, to a higher public policy priority. From this context, a sitting American vice president spoke publicly about cultural artifacts funding ISIS terrorism, and congressional lawmakers voiced concern about a cultural property/financing of terrorism (CP/FT) nexus, both significant political moments because safeguarding cultural property principally had been viewed through the lens of heritage protection, not national security.[2] When lawmakers, for example, adopted the Antiquities Act and the Archaeological Resources Protection Act (ARPA), they did so as heritage preservation measures. When, in 2008, the United States ratified the 1954 Hague Convention for the Protection of Cultural Property in the Event of Armed Conflict, senators did so to protect monuments of world history, not to secure the homeland against enemies. But now, as UNESCO Director General Irina Bokova said, "attacks against culture are more than a cultural issue. This is a security issue."[3] Observing that "terrorist and criminal networks have looted and destroyed cultural heritage sites as well as trafficked cultural heritage to finance their operations," Assistant Secretary of State for Educational and Cultural Affairs (ECA) Marie Royce likewise described that "we have come to appreciate the direct impact cultural heritage work has on our safety and our security."[4] Meanwhile, according to House Committee on Foreign Affairs ranking member, Rep. Eliot Engel [D-NY-16], terrorists "use these artifacts to get money so that they can keep their war machine going, so that they can keep their killings going, so that they can keep their brutality going,"[5] which is why Congress passed the Protect and Preserve International Cultural Property Act (PPICPA).

[2] Safeguarding heritage has been approached from other perspectives, including controlling imports and exports, recovering stolen property, seizing contraband, and preventing genocide. This chapter's scope is limited to the protection of cultural property sourced from overseas as a national security objective, particularly antiquities and archaeological artifacts from the Greater Middle East.

[3] Irina Bokova, "Address at the Royal Institute of International Affairs: Roundtable 'Culture on the Frontline: Protecting Cultural Heritage in Conflict Zones'" (1 July 2015) <https://unesdoc.unesco.org/ark:/48223/pf0000233662> accessed 28 October 2019.

[4] Marie Royce, "Assistant Secretary Royce Speaks at the Smithsonian Institution" (11 December 2018) <https://www.youtube.com/watch?time_continue=37&v=C9ePLBdrJwU&feature=emb_logo&fbclid.=IwAR1xL1ZJIQMY5gR6eXj76n0rJbXmJ6IrswFQubhiRdGHTyg-ZJTn4TBmUTo> accessed 11 January 2020.

[5] 161 Cong Rec, Pt 6, p 8005, 1 June 2015 (statement of Rep. Eliot Engel).

Recognition of the CP/FT nexus, therefore, has translated into greater concern for heritage protection.[6]

This chapter chronicles the emergence of this cultural property protection paradigm in the United States, particularly exploring its flowering as ISIS blitzed toward Baghdad and expanded its territorial footprint (2014–2016). Also described are its cultivation following the 9/11 terror attacks and the ensuing wars in Afghanistan and Iraq (2001–2004), its fledgling roots (2005–2011), its budding during the Syrian civil war (2012–2013), and its ripening emphasis on money laundering (2017–2020).

II. Setting the Stage: Protecting Cultural Property with Heritage Preservation Laws

Commercial looting of archaeological artifacts brought heritage preservation to the attention of US lawmakers in the late nineteenth century. When President Theodore Roosevelt signed the Antiquities Act into law in 1906, proponents argued that artifacts on public lands were precious resources to be preserved, not uncontrollably unearthed and damaged. That is why the Act criminalized illegal artifact digging and vandalism with penalties that included a fine up to $500 and ninety days in jail, and it required the Secretaries of Interior, Agriculture, and the Army to issue permits for archaeological investigations "for permanent preservation in public museums."[7] Such preservationist thinking dominated the rationale behind successive cultural property legislation such as the Historic Sites Act of 1935 (HSA), making it national policy to protect historic sites, buildings, and objects;[8] the Archeological and Historic Preservation Act of 1960, which carried

[6] As this chapter was submitted for publication, RAND Corporation issued a report commenting that "[t]he illicit antiquities market has become an area of concern for policymakers. It is fueled by a well-documented rise in looting at archaeological sites and a fear that the proceeds of such looting may be financing terrorism or rogue states." Its authors opined that "journalists, researchers, and policy experts regularly inflate the importance of antiquities trafficking in funding for international terrorism and organized crime. Linking cultural property crimes to these high-profile law enforcement issues offers a means to bring funding and political attention to what has traditionally been an underrecognized issue. Unsubstantiated claims about the relationship among looting, weapons, drugs, and money laundering are common in both expert and popular publications, and inaccurate or exaggerated estimates of stolen items' value abound." Matthew Sargent, James V Marrone, Alexandra Evans, Bilyana Lilly, Erik Nemeth, and Stephen Dalzell, "Tracking and Disrupting the Illicit Antiquities Trade with Open Source Data" (RAND Corporation 2020) back cover, 10 <https://www.rand.org/pubs/research_reports/RR2706.html> accessed 27 August 2020.

[7] 16 USC §§ 431–433.

[8] 16 USC §§ 461–467.

out the aims of the HSA;[9] the National Historic Preservation Act of 1966, which created the National Register of Historic Places, state historic preservation offices, and the Section 106 process that assesses the impact of federally funded projects on historic properties;[10] the Archaeological and Historic Preservation Act of 1974, which amended the Reservoir Salvage Act of 1960 to preserve archaeology endangered by federally funded dams and reservoirs;[11] ARPA of 1979, protecting artifacts at least one hundred years old, requiring federal permits for their excavation on federal and American Indian lands, and imposing penalties on violators who illegally unearthed or trafficked archaeological resources;[12] and even the globally focused Convention on Cultural Property Implementation Act (CPIA), authorizing import restrictions on at-risk, foreign-sourced archaeological and ethnological materials.[13] The twenty-first century would reshape this paradigm.

III. Cultivating the Soil: 9/11 and Stolen Heritage (2001–2004)

The crime of terrorism gripped public consciousness after the deadly September 11, 2001, attacks destroyed the World Trade Towers, damaged the Pentagon, and led to the crash of United Airlines Flight 93 in a Pennsylvania field. Subsequent US military action against al-Qaeda and the Taliban in Afghanistan and Saddam Hussein's regime in Iraq sparked interest in the Taliban's destruction of ancient the Bamiyan Buddhas in central Afghanistan, the ransacking of the National Museum in Baghdad, and the widespread looting of archaeological sites in the two countries. Transnational antiquities trafficking also moved into the limelight with the publicized trial of well-known art dealer Frederick Schultz, charged in July 2001 with conspiring to receive stolen Egyptian antiquities. The case, at the time, was the latest in a sprinkling of dramatic cultural property prosecutions and civil forfeitures that unveiled the underworld of transnational heritage smuggling to a fascinated public.[14] Meanwhile, just one month prior to 9/11, a General

[9] 16 USC § 469 et al. The Archeological and Historic Preservation Act has been amended several times since its enactment on 27 June 1960.

[10] 16 USC §§ 470–470w-6.

[11] 16 U.C § 469 et al.

[12] 16 USC §§ 470aa–470mm.

[13] 19 USC §§ 2601–2613.

[14] *United States of America v Frederick Schultz*, 333 F.3d 393 (2d Cir. 2003).

Accounting Office report briefly flagged art and antiquities theft as a transnational crime.[15] Within this soil, the relationship between cultural property, transnational crime, and terrorism was cultivated.

Authorities did not make statements identifying a direct link between looted and trafficked cultural property and terrorism, but a confluence of public policy language wrapped the events of 9/11, transnational crime, stolen artifacts, and heritage protection into a single theme. Attorney General John Ashcroft's address to INTERPOL in 2003 helped mold this yet unrefined concept:

> The way we fight terrorism changed that day. . . . From the evidence that has emerged, there is a strong case to be made that the looting and theft of the artifacts [from Iraq's national museum] was perpetrated by organized criminal groups—individuals who knew precisely what they were looking for. . . . It is our goal to return parts of the Iraqi people's past.[16]

Against the backdrop of this nascent perspective, and amid the context of pursuing peace and security, the United Nations Security Council (UNSC), Congress, and various federal agencies pursued traditional heritage preservation strategies. The UNSC adopted a comprehensive resolution in May 2003 to address the conflict in Iraq—proposed by the United States, United Kingdom, and Spain—that instructed member states to ban the trade of Iraqi cultural property and to repatriate recovered stolen objects. Resolution 1483 invoked Chapter VII of the UN Charter, directing

> that all Member States shall take appropriate steps to facilitate the safe return to Iraqi institutions of Iraqi cultural property and other items of archaeological, historical, cultural, rare scientific, and religious importance illegally removed from the Iraq National Museum, the National Library, and other locations in Iraq . . . including by establishing a prohibition on trade in or transfer of such items . . . illegally removed.[17]

[15] US General Accounting Office, Report to the Honorable Ben Nighthorse Campbell, US Senate, "International Crime Control: Sustained Executive-Level Coordination of Federal Response Needed" (August 2001) 35.

[16] Prepared Remarks of Attorney General John Ashcroft, INTERPOL Meeting on Cultural Property Looting in Iraq, Lyon, France (6 May 2003) <https://www.justice.gov/archive/ag/speeches/2003/050603agremarksinterpolmeeting.htm> accessed 31 October 2019.

[17] S/RES/1483 (22 May 2003).

Washington lawmakers followed suit. In 2004, President George W. Bush enacted the Emergency Protection for Iraqi Cultural Antiquities Act (EPIC).[18] Sponsor Sen. Chuck Grassley [R-IA] touted the legislation's preservation aim, declaring that "it is very important that we in Congress remain mindful of the need to take steps to protect Iraq's cultural heritage."[19] Congress also established the Cultural Antiquities Task Force to respond to the looting.[20] In the executive branch, the State and Defense Departments monitored events in Iraq by deploying archaeologist Dr. John Russell to the country. From 2003–2004, he advised Iraq's Ministry of Culture to help restore the looted and damaged national museum and to document and preserve pillaged archaeological sites.[21] By 2008, the Department of State (DOS) exercised EPIC's authority to declare an emergency condition in Iraq, which authorized a US import ban on archaeological artifacts illegally taken from the nation since 1990.[22]

IV. Fledgling Roots: Revealing the Links Between Cultural Property, Terrorism, And Transnational Crime (2005–2011)

It is within the framework of preserving Iraqi heritage, enveloped by the milieu of antiquities looting and trafficking and the crime of terrorism, that the seed of cultural property's link to terrorism took root. Marine Colonel and Manhattan Assistant District Attorney Matthew Bogdanos alerted the public in 2005 about a link between the cultural property trade and fighting in Iraq. "Just as Taliban leaders in Afghanistan have begun to finance their activities through the opium trade, insurgents in Iraq have discovered a new source of income in antiquities," he penned in a *New York Times* op-ed.[23] Col. Bogdanos led a counterterrorism team to investigate the looting of the Iraq Museum, finding guns and antiquities mixed together. "In a series of

[18] Pub L No 108–429, Title III.

[19] 149 Cong Rec, Pt 11, p 15563, 19 June 2003 (statement of Sen. Chuck Grassley).

[20] Cultural Antiquities Task Force, ECA, US Department of State <https://eca.state.gov/cultural-heritage-center/cultural-antiquities-task-force> accessed 4 November 2019.

[21] John M Russell, "Efforts to Protect Archaeological Sites and Monuments in Iraq" in Geoff Emberling and Katharyn Hanson (eds), *Catastrophe! The Looting and Destruction of Iraq's Past* (The Oriental Institute of the University of Chicago 2008) 29–43.

[22] Import Restrictions Imposed on Archaeological and Ethnological Material of Iraq, 73 Fed Reg 23334–23342, 30 April 2008. The restrictions are codified at 19 CFR § 12.104j.

[23] Matthew Bogdanos, "The Terrorist in the Art Gallery" (*The New York Times*, 10 December 2005).

raids in June [2003] in northwest Iraq," he recounted that "marines arrested five terrorists in underground bunkers filled with automatic weapons, ammunition stockpiles, black uniforms, ski masks, night-vision goggles and 30 vases, cylinder seals and statuettes that had been stolen from the Iraq Museum."[24] Uncovering arms with artifacts prompted Bogdanos to call on governments to invest greater resources to track down pillaged cultural material. Equally riveting, the German news magazine *Der Spiegel* published a questionable short exposé in 2005 under the headline "Der Kunst als Terrorfinanzierung?" ("Art as Terror Financing"), which attracted widespread notice despite its reliability. Reportedly relying on information from Germany's Federal Criminal Police Office (BKA), the article claimed that the 9/11 hijackers may have funded their attacks by selling antiquities. The magazine wrote that principal hijacker Mohammed Atta approached a university professor in 2000 or 2001 about "ancient Afghan art with the aim of further education." *Der Spiegel* quoted the professor as saying that Atta "wanted to know where to market antiques." The professor purportedly referred Atta to Sotheby's auction house.[25] In contrast, a documentary crew in 2009 broadcast a more solid investigation called "Blood Antiques," which described a connection between the Taliban and the antiquities trade in Afghanistan and Pakistan.[26]

As the media reported ties between terrorism and antiquities, national security experts took a harder look at the connection between transnational organized crime (TOC) and terror. In 2006, the White House's *National Strategy for Combating Terrorism* outlined how terrorists relied on individual contributions, sham businesses and charities, fraud, extortion, and kidnap for ransom for funding.[27] Its *National Security Strategy*, issued four years later, amplified the severity of the risk posed by international traffickers on American security. "The crime-terror nexus is a serious concern as terrorists use criminal networks for logistical support and funding," warned the report, explaining that illegal trafficking networks were "expand[ing] dramatically in size, scope, and influence" and threatening the stability of nations, financial systems, and commercial markets.[28] The 2011 *Strategy to Combat Transnational Organized Crime* also described TOC's partnership

[24] ibid.
[25] "Kunst als Terrorfinanzierung?" (*Der Speigel*, 18 July 2005) 20.
[26] Peter Brems and Wim Van den Eynde, "Blood Antiques" (Journeyman Pictures 2009).
[27] The White House, *National Strategy for Combating Terrorism* (September 2006).
[28] The White House, *National Security Strategy* (May 2010) 49.

with terrorism. "In years past, TOC was largely regional in scope, hierarchically structured, and had only occasional links to terrorism. Today's criminal networks are fluid, striking new alliances with other networks around the world and engaging in a wide range of illicit activities . . . and providing support for terrorism."[29]

Gretchen Peters, a transnational crime researcher at George Mason University, connected the dots between cultural property, terrorist financing, and transnational crime. In 2010, Peters wrote that insurgents and terrorists in Afghanistan and Pakistan partnered with organized crime to fund militant operations.[30] Relying on the work of researchers located in these two countries, Peters concluded, "The Haqqani Network (HQN) appears to collaborate closely with the Pakistani Taliban and al-Qa'ida, both in terms of launching terror attacks and, specifically with the Pakistani Taliban, engaging in illicit activity. . . ."[31] Peters reported that one leader of the insurgency from Ghazni, Afghanistan, said that HQN donors included "businessmen who smuggle precious stones, sculptures and other historic artifacts [who] pay dues to the Taliban to avoid trouble on the road."[32]

Then the Syrian civil war erupted in March 2011.

V. Budding Awareness: Cultural Property for Guns (2012–2013)

Syria's civil war spawned renewed interest in the protection of cultural heritage during conflict and sparked attention to reported exchanges of guns for antiquities. Posted videos from Syria, a published list of Syrian cultural objects in jeopardy, and the release of a cautionary terrorist financing risk assessment joined eye-catching headlines about antiquities and guns. Together they formed the groundwork for the budding awareness of the CP/FT nexus. Starting in 2012, The Association for the Protection of Syrian Archaeology, a YouTube channel, vividly showcased industrial-grade cultural heritage destruction in Syria. One video reportedly showed illegal excavations at

[29] The White House, *Strategy to Combat Transnational Organized Crime: Addressing Converging Threats to National Security* (July 2011) 3.

[30] Gretchen Peters, *Crime and Insurgency in the Tribal Areas of Afghanistan and Pakistan* (Harmony Program, Combating Terrorism Center at West Point, 15 October 2010).

[31] ibid ii.

[32] ibid 36–37.

al-Rahba, the location of an ancient fortress.[33] In another film, a tractor drove through the site.[34] A subsequent clip depicted a large, parked excavator.[35] Responding to multiplying stories of widespread looting of Syrian artifacts, the museum community warned about the proliferation of illegal artifacts, and the International Council of Museums created a Red List spotlighting Syrian cultural objects at risk of plunder.[36] A Red List displays pictures of readily identifiable artifacts from a particular source country, illustrating the kinds of artifacts that may have been looted from archaeological sites, stolen from museums, or smuggled across borders. Also in 2013, the Financial Action Task Force (FATF)—an influential intergovernmental organization that identifies financial system threats and sets standards on anti-money laundering/countering the financing of terrorism (AML/CFT) efforts—acknowledged that the illegal trade in cultural property could fuel terrorist networks.[37] FATF published a risk report that listed cultural goods trafficking, antiquities counterfeiting, and illicit antiquities trading as categories to examine when assessing terror funding and money laundering. The report tagged auction houses and art and antiques dealers as businesses "that may be useful [to include] in building a list of the ML/TF [money laundering/terrorist financing] vulnerabilities. . . ."[38] The popular press too drew attention to threats associated with cultural heritage, pitching the theme that illegal digging was intermingled with gun buys. *Time* reported on a Syrian smuggler who used cultural property as currency to buy and sell arms. "We buy antiquities cheap, and then sell weapons expensively," boasted the trafficker in a 2012 interview. He claimed that the Free Syrian Army formed artifact looting gangs to finance the fight against President Bashar Assad.[39] An antiquities smuggler based in Beirut told the magazine that "he has seen an explosion in amateur diggers in Syria."[40] Additionally, CNN headlined

[33] "Al-Mayadin: Illicit Diggings at Qala't al-Rahba" (posted by Protect Syrian Archaeology, 23 August 2013) <https://www.youtube.com/watch?v=2zAioIu3S88> accessed 31 October 2019.

[34] "Deir Ezzor al-Mayadin: Pillage à Qasr al Rahba" (posted by Protect Syrian Archaeology, 20 July 2013) <https://www.youtube.com/watch?v=p2kPZwTaotQ> accessed 31 October 2019.

[35] "Deir Ezzor: Illicit Diggings at Qal'at al Rahba" (posted by Protect Syrian Archaeology, 30 November 2013) <https://www.youtube.com/watch?v=ylfFX5L35zc> accessed 31 October 2019.

[36] International Council of Museums, *Emergency Red List of Syrian Cultural Objects at Risk* (2013).

[37] Financial Action Task Force, *FATF Guidance: National Money Laundering and Terrorist Financing Risk Assessment* (February 2013).

[38] ibid 46, 48.

[39] Aryn Baker and Majdal Anjar, "Syria's Looted Past: How Ancient Artifacts Are Being Traded for Guns" *Time* (12 September 2012).

[40] ibid.

"Syrian Antiquities Looted for Gun Money," which described a Syrian rebel's attempt to sell an ancient manuscript for weapons.[41]

VI. Flowering Action: Law and Policy Responses to the Cultural Property/Financing of Terrorism Nexus (2014–2016)

ISIS dramatically expanded its footprint in Iraq in early 2014, conquering terrain filled with archaeological sites. The terror group reportedly controlled over thirty-four thousand square miles of land in Syria and Iraq in 2014.[42] By June 2015, DOS labeled ISIS a greater threat than core al-Qaeda, citing its "unprecedented seizure of territory in Iraq and Syria [and] the continued flow of foreign terrorist fighters worldwide to join ISIL."[43] And ISIS appeared to be winning. Although ISIS operated in the Middle East for a number of years under different names (e.g., Al-Qaeda in Iraq, Islamic State of Iraq), when it feverishly deployed truckloads of soldiers and equipment to Baghdad in June 2014, the terror group's raw violence and unbridled destruction beckoned widespread vigilance.[44] In 2015, President Barack Obama asked Congress for authorization to use force.[45] ISIS, meanwhile, had money. Commentators labeled ISIS "the wealthiest terror group in history,"[46] controlling oil, natural and human resources, and cash from plundered banks. Because evidence showed that the terrorists handled antiquities, authorities urgently began to scrutinize the reported CP/FT nexus—at least openly, since intelligence gathering and analysis is kept secret. From 2014 to 2016, mounting information

[41] Ivan Watson, "Syrian Antiquities Looted for Gun Money" (*CNN*, 7 April 2013) <https://www.cnn.com/videos/international/2013/04/07/syrian-antiquities-watson.cnn> accessed 31 October 2019.

[42] Editorial Research, "ISIS Fast Facts" (*CNN*, updated 4 December 2019) <https://www.cnn.com/2014/08/08/world/isis-fast-facts/index.html> accessed 6 December 2019.

[43] US Department of State, Bureau of Counterterrorism, *Country Reports on Terrorism 2014* (June 2015) 7.

[44] See "ISIS Fast Facts" (n 42) for a chronology of significant events.

[45] "Obama Urges Congress to Authorize Use of Military Force against ISIS" (*NPR All Things Considered*, 7 December 2015).

[46] Colin P Clarke, The Rand Corporation, "An Overview of Current Trends in Terrorism and Illicit Finance: Lessons from the Islamic State in Iraq and Syria and Other Emerging Threats," testimony before the US House of Representatives Committee on Financial Services Subcommittee on Terrorism and Illicit Finance, 7 September 2018, p. 4. See also Amr Al-Azm, testimony before the Task Force to Investigate Terrorism Financing on Preventing Cultural Genocide: Countering the Plunder and Sale of Priceless Cultural Antiquities by ISIS, 19 April 2016 ("ISIS is likely the wealthiest radical terrorist organization in contemporary history, with widely diversified sources of income").

pointed to cultural property financing ISIS. Compelling on-the-ground evidence, analyst reports, and congressional hearings roused unprecedented responses that included executive branch statements identifying and condemning terrorist funding tied to cultural property looting and trafficking; legislative proposals stifling ISIS's misappropriation of archaeological material; a court order forfeiting ISIS's loot; and US-backed efforts tackling CP/FT in the international arena.

A. On-the-Ground Evidence: Eyewitness Testimony, Satellite Imagery, and Seized Property

"In extensive conversations with those working and living in areas currently under ISIS control, we learned that ISIS is indeed involved in the illicit antiquities trade," wrote three scholars in a *New York Times* op-ed published in 2014. Dr. Amr Al-Azm and Dr. Salam Al-Kuntar, both Syrian-born archaeologists; and Dr. Brian Daniels, hailing from the Penn Cultural Heritage Center, returned from Turkey where they trained Syrians to protect their cultural heritage. The scholars learned from on-the-ground sources that "ISIS permits local inhabitants to dig at these sites in exchange for a percentage of the monetary value of any finds," explaining that this *khums* tax ranged from 20% to 50% or more. They also discovered that ISIS issued permits to experienced Iraqi looting crews, used heavy machinery to loot archaeological sites, and facilitated artifact smuggling from Syria to Turkey.[47]

Their report came on the heels of blockbuster information from *The Guardian*, circulating for two months and possibly unsubstantiated,[48] that Iraqi forces seized 160 ISIS flash drives containing the names of ISIS members and describing the organization's extensive finances. Sourced from an unnamed intelligence officer, the newspaper reported that antiquities accounted for part of ISIS's funding. The official was quoted as saying, "They had taken $36m from al-Nabuk alone [west of Damascus]. The antiquities there are up to 8,000 years old."[49]

[47] Amr Al-Azm, Salam Al-Kuntar, and Brian I Daniels, "ISIS' Antiquities Sideline" *The New York Times* (Op-Ed, 2 September 2014).
[48] For commentary on the article's claims, see Sam Hardy, "German Media Corroborates $36M Islamic State Antiquities Trafficking" (*Hyperallergic*, 28 November 2014).
[49] "How an Arrest in Iraq Revealed Isis's $2bn Jihadist Network" (*The Guardian*, 15 June 2014).

Videos and photos depicting rampant archaeological site looting appeared to bolster the testimony and claims. Protect Syrian Archaeology posted a number of films online that showcased the destruction, including one that documented looters using metal detectors at an archaeological site dating to 400 BC.[50] Moreover, the American Schools of Oriental Research Cultural Heritage Initiatives (ASOR CHI), a cooperative project with DOS that relied on satellites, in-country sources, and open-source data to investigate cultural property crimes in Syria and northern Iraq, collected satellite imagery of looting.[51] The images rapidly circulated among policymakers, academics, and the public because they indisputably exhibited hundreds of pockmarked sites and other tell-tale signs of commercial-grade archaeological theft. Secretary of State John Kerry praised the ASOR CHI team for its work at a press conference in New York in September 2014,[52] and pictures showing the destruction of sites at Dura Europos, Mari, and Tell Sheikh Hamad featured prominently on the DOS website.[53] Photos of cultural heritage destruction also were published in scholarly articles like "Ancient History, Modern Destruction," which recorded looters' pits—lots of them—in the zone where ISIS operated.[54] Authored by Geospatial Technologies and Human Rights Project, the article presented images from 2014 illustrating "looting on a massive scale . . . at Dura-Europos, with high-density looting . . . in the vast majority of the site enclosed by the ancient city wall."[55] Dura Europos is a town comprising heritage rooted in Greek, Persian, Roman, and other ancient traditions. Pictures showed holes dotting the city like a cratered moonscape. The disheartened authors remarked, "Inside the ancient city wall the

[50] "Idlib: Illicit Diggings at Tell Hizareen P.1" (posted by Protect Syrian Archaeology, 29 October 2014) <https://www.youtube.com/watch?v=tH-V81EEmlw> accessed 31 October 2019.

[51] Safeguarding the Heritage of the Near East Initiative, US State Department Cooperation Agreement NEA-PSHSS-14-001.

[52] John Kerry, Secretary of State, Remarks at Threats to Cultural Heritage in Iraq and Syria Event (22 September 2014) <https://2009-2017.state.gov/secretary/remarks/2014/09/231992.htm> accessed 31 October 2019.

[53] ECA, US Department of State website <http://eca.state.gov/cultural-heritage-center/syria-cultural-heritage-initiative/imagery-archaeological-site-looting> accessed 31 October 2019. The State Department posted the photos by at least 7 September 2014, according to the Internet Archive Wayback Machine.

[54] Geospatial Technologies and Human Rights Project, "Ancient History, Modern Destruction: Assessing the Status of Syria's Tentative World Heritage Sites Using High-Resolution Satellite Imagery" (December 2014) part 1. See also, eg, Jesse Casana and Mitra Panahipor, "Satellite-Based Monitoring of Looting and Damage to Archaeological Sites in Syria" (2014) 2 (2) Journal of Eastern Mediterranean Archaeology and Heritage Studies 128–51; Jesse Casana, "Satellite Imagery Based Analysis of Archaeological Looting in Syria" (September 2015) 78 (3) Near Eastern Archaeology 142–61.

[55] "Ancient History, Modern Destruction" (n 54) 7.

disruption was so extensive that counting of individual looting pits was impractical; the pits overlap so that it is impossible to distinguish one unique pit from another." Still, they reasoned that "looted areas beyond the city wall contain approximately 3,750 individual looting pits."[56] They observed that, in August 2011, "the soil at Dura-Europos is relatively undisturbed both inside and outside the walled city," but, by April 2014, the picture changed strikingly as "very high-density looting is present inside the ancient city wall, while portions of the archaeological site beyond the city wall have been covered with thousands of individual pits."[57] This startling aerial evidence exposed resolute efforts to plunder heritage, and ground photos taken by unnamed sources, who feared for their safety, further confirmed the fierce archaeological destruction.[58]

Foreign Policy published similar pictures for a popular audience. In "The Black Market Battleground," ASOR CHI academic director Dr. Michael Danti, characterized the scale of looting as "unprecedented," and Dr. Al-Azm noted that antiquities looting had evolved, saying, "They're hiring their own people, they're using a lot of earth-moving equipment—bulldozers, et cetera."[59] The publication presented the question of whether looted artifacts could be finding a path to America's shores, citing a survey that found that commodities, declared by importers to be antiques over one hundred years old from Syria, skyrocketed 133% between 2012 and 2013 after the start of the violence, raising suspicions about whether the imported goods actually were ancient archaeological artifacts stealthily disguised as benign "antiques" on customs entry forms.[60]

Information linking cultural property trafficking to terror also unfolded from an undercover CBS News investigation that found a dealer in Turkey selling an ancient mosaic looted from Apamea, Syria.[61] Correspondent Clarissa Ward reported that "there are multiple ongoing investigations into

[56] ibid 6.

[57] ibid 8.

[58] ibid 9.

[59] Justine Drennan, "The Black Market Battleground: Degrading and Destroying ISIS Could Take Place in the Halls of Auction Houses, Not the Pentagon" (*Foreign Policy*, 17 October 2014) <https://foreignpolicy.com/2014/10/17/the-black-market-battleground/> accessed 31 October 2019.

[60] ibid. See the original survey at Rick St. Hilaire, "Conflict and the Heritage Trade: Rise in US Imports of Middle East 'Antiques' and 'Collectors' Pieces' Raises Questions" (*Cultural Heritage Lawyer* blog, 6 October 2014) <https://culturalheritagelawyer.blogspot.com/2014/10/conflict-and-heritage-trade-rise-in-us.html> accessed 27 May 2020.

[61] "Following the Trail of Syria's Looted History" (*CBS This Morning*, 9 September 2015) <https://www.cbsnews.com/news/isis-looted-syrian-ancient-artifacts-black-market-us-and-europe/> accessed 11 October 2019.

ISIS looted artifacts that have reached the U.S," and ADA Bogdanos confirmed, "We have seen antiquities from ISIS-controlled countries wind up in the market."[62]

Most firmly establishing the CP/FT link was the recovery of critical material and intelligence from an ISIS compound in the al-Amr region of eastern Syria. On May 15, 2015, US Special Operations Forces executed a nighttime strike.[63] Soldiers seized at least seven hundred cultural objects[64] from Abu Sayyaf,[65] killed along with other ISIS fighters,[66] who "helped direct the terrorist organization's illicit oil, gas, and financial operations" according to the Defense Department.[67] Captured records revealed hundreds of millions of dollars in transactions.[68] The recovered trove included hard drives, thumb drives, DVDs, and papers.[69] Coins constituted over half of the retrieved cultural material. Some objects originated from the Mosul Museum.[70] Bronze coins bearing Greek, Latin, and Arabic inscriptions; silver dirhams; copper bracelets; gold dinars; cylinder seals; three manuscripts; an ivory furniture plaque; and more comprised the haul. Genuine articles appeared to have been mixed with reproductions, typical in the black market trade.[71] Court papers filed in a subsequent forfeiture case (discussed later in this chapter) recited

[62] ibid.

[63] Eg, Barbara Starr, Laura Smith-Spark and Ray Sanchez, "Abu Sayyaf, Key ISIS Figure in Syria, Killed in US Raid" (*CNN*, 17 May 2015) <https://www.cnn.com/2015/05/16/middleeast/syria-isis-us-raid/index.html> accessed 10 October 2019; "Army's Elite Delta Force Kills Top ISIS Official, Abu Sayyaf, in Daring Syria Raid" (*Fox News*, 16 May 2015) <https://www.foxnews.com/politics/armys-elite-delta-force-kills-top-isis-official-abu-sayyaf-in-daring-syria-raid> accessed 10 October 2019.

[64] US Embassy and Consulates in Iraq, Press Release, "The United States Repatriates Cultural Heritage Objects and Fragments to the Government of Iraq" (15 July 2015) <https://iq.usembassy.gov/united-states-repatriates-cultural-heritage-objects-fragments-government-iraq/> accessed 7 November 2019.

[65] This name is the *nom de guerre* of a man identified by authorities as Fathi Ben Awn Ben Jildi Murad al-Tunisi.

[66] Starr, Smith-Park, and Sanchez (n 63).

[67] Statement by Secretary of Defense Ash Carter on Counter-ISIL Operation in Syria (16 May 2015) <https://www.defense.gov/Newsroom/Releases/Release/Article/605506/> accessed 11 October 2019.

[68] "ISIS' Records Show Millions Raised by Antiquities Smuggling" (*CBS News*, 29 September 2015) <https://www.cbsnews.com/video/isis-records-show-millions-raised-by-antiquities-smuggling/> accessed 11 October 2019.

[69] Jonathan Landay, Warren Strobel, and Phil Stewart, "Exclusive: Seized Documents Reveal Islamic State's Department of 'War Spoils'" (*Reuters*, 28 December 2015) <https://www.reuters.com/article/us-usa-islamic-state-documents-group-exc-idUSKBN0UB0AW20151229> accessed 11 October 2019.

[70] ECA, US Department of State, "ISIL Leader's Loot" (25 July 2015) <http://eca.state.gov/cultural-heritage-center/iraq-cultural-heritage-initiative/isil-leaders-loot> accessed 1 November 2019.

[71] ECA, US Department of State, "ISIL Leader's Loot Photo Gallery" <https://eca.state.gov/gallery/isil-leaders-loot-photo-gallery> accessed 11 October 2019.

that Abu Sayyaf headed the Ministry of Natural Resources, Department of Antiquities, which claimed dominion over excavation sites. The seized evidence demonstrated that "ISIL generates a significant portion of its revenue from its control of territory and has established formal governance structures for extracting wealth from territory under ISIL control."[72] The ISIS leader exercised strict authority. "In one document, Abu Sayyaf issued an order to ISIL militants . . . [that] permitted a subordinate to dig for archaeological objects in ISIL territories, supervise others involved with excavating those objects, and arrest anyone who excavated in ISIL-controlled areas without authorization from the Antiquities Department," DOJ contended.[73] The department issued archaeological dig permits and taxed antiquities sales at twenty percent.[74] Additionally, "antiquities were cleaned and maintained in a manner consistent with the preparation for sale."[75] The prosecution of Abu Sayyaf's wife, Nisreen Bahar (a/k/a Umm Sayyaf), charged with contributing to the death of kidnapped American, Kayla Jean Mueller, revealed that Abu Sayyaf reported to ISIS leader Abu Bakr al-Baghdadi.[76] Court documents disclosed that American soldiers retrieved guns from the assault, later secured by the FBI.[77] Bahar confirmed that the residence housed "a large supply of firearms" and "was used to store large sums of U.S. currency that ISIL acquired through its oil and gas business and other illegal activities."[78] Altogether, the raid exposed ISIS's organization and operations, which directed the criminal misappropriation of cultural property to subsidize violence. The evidence "proves ISIS uses the illicit antiquities trade as an important source of revenue," Dr. Danti later told lawmakers.[79]

[72] Amended Verified Complaint for Forfeiture *In Rem*, *United States of America v One Gold Ring with Carved Gemstone, An Asset of ISIL Discovered on Electronic Media of Abu Sayyaf, President of ISIL Antiquities Department et al*, 16-cv-02442 (D.D.C. 2016) paras 8, 12.

[73] ibid para 13.

[74] ibid para 15.

[75] ibid para 10.

[76] Affidavit in Support of Criminal Complaint and Arrest Warrant, *US v Nisreen Assad Ibrahim Bahar a/k/a "Umm Sayyaf,"* 16-mj-63 (ED Va 2016) para 9.

[77] ibid para 13.

[78] ibid paras 20, 22.

[79] *Terrorist Financing: Kidnapping, Antiquities Trafficking, and Private Donations, Hearing Before the Subcommittee on Terrorism, Nonproliferation, and Trade of the House Committee on Foreign Affairs*, Serial No. 114–120, 114th Congress 60, 17 November 2015 (testimony of Michael D Danti, PhD).

B. Reports and Analyses

Published reports and analyses reinforced eyewitness testimony, satellite imagery, and the recovered ISIS cache that all pointed to a CP/FT nexus. The Congressional Research Service, for example, concluded that ISIS's "largest revenue sources appear (based on open-source information) to include . . . the sale of looted antiquities,"[80] arrestingly adding that "oil and antiquities can be smuggled and sold for considerable profit."[81] FATF, moreover, which flagged a CP/FT link in 2013, now devoted particular attention to cultural artifacts in a 2015 report that keenly observed, "ISIL's ability to earn revenue from the illicit sale of antiquities is contingent upon the presence of antiquities within territory where ISIL operates, knowledge of their existence, and ISIL's ability to recognize materials as artefacts and develop some estimation of their value."[82] FATF cautioned that "[r]eports on the smuggling of cultural artefacts by ISIL are limited, given that they are sold on the black market" and that "it might be impossible to show a direct link between the ISIL and the sale of a specific artefact."[83] Still, its analysis found that "ISIL makes money in two ways from antiquities, both through selling looted artefacts and taxing traffickers moving items through ISIL-held territory."[84] An assessment submitted to the UNSC in 2015 by the Analytical Support and Sanctions Monitoring Team (ASSMT) also confirmed this CP/FT tie as it discussed challenges to stopping illegal antiquities trafficking from funding both ISIS and Al-Nusrah Front for the People of the Levant (ANF).[85] ASSMT's report warned that "[t]he risk of terrorism financing is significant in the trading of illicit artefacts," but carefully conceded that "credible estimates related to the smuggling of antiquities by ISIL are currently unavailable."[86] Its report affirmed that ISIS "demands a fee for granting permits to looters and excavators and 'taxes' the antiquities excavated and smuggled" and that "[l]ooting and excavation are done using heavy machinery and more portable

[80] US Congressional Research Service, "Islamic State Financing and U.S. Policy Approaches" prepared by Carla E Humud, Robert Pirog, and Liana Rosen (10 April 2015) Summary.

[81] ibid 1.

[82] FATF, "Financing of the Terrorist Organisation Islamic State in Iraq and the Levant (ISIL)" (February 2015) 16–17.

[83] ibid 16, 17.

[84] ibid 17.

[85] UNSC, *Assessment by the Analytical Support and Sanctions Monitoring Team of the Impact of the Measures Imposed in Security Council Resolution 2199 (2015), Pursuant to Paragraph 30 of the Resolution: Chair's Summary* (25 September 2015) S/2015/739, para 7.

[86] ibid paras 6, 7.

metal detectors."[87] By 2016, a successive ASSMT report expressed that art and antiquities dealers doubted claims linking antiquities looting to significant ISIS funding, and the team found a lack of infrastructure and experience in the art and antiquities marketplace—with the exception of "more sophisticated market players"—to carry out AML/CFT checks to enforce sanctions.[88] This "strategic gap in counter-terrorism financing measures" worried the UN monitors.[89] The report, once again, accepted that "precise and official data [related to the illicit cultural property trade] . . . continue to be rare," but maintained that archaeological site looting was documented and that the taxing of antiquities and the management of looting and trafficking "clearly reflect the sustained expectation of profits."[90] Market players and scholars countered that these profits were small at the point of first sale, which necessitated "the trading of significant volumes of antiquities . . . if significant funds are to be generated," wrote the monitoring team.[91] A 2016 report by the UN Secretary-General, meanwhile, called out "[i]llegitimate sellers of such antiquities, who may have direct or indirect links with ISIL, [who] use social media platforms to find customers for illicitly obtained and exported artefacts"[92] and repeated that antiquities looting was a source of ISIS funding that threatened peace and security.[93] The report protested "[t]he online sale of Iraqi and Syrian antiquities [that] continues despite the worldwide prohibition on their trade, as set forth in Security Council Resolution 2199 (2015)" (discussed in a later section of this chapter).[94]

[87] ibid para 6.

[88] UNSC, *Challenges Business Entities Face in Implementing Security Council Resolution 2199 (2015): Report of the Analytical Support and Sanctions Monitoring Team Pursuant to Security Council Resolutions 1526 (2004) and 2253 (2015) Concerning Islamic State in Iraq and the Levant (ISIL) (Da'esh), Al-Qaida and the Taliban and Associated Individuals and Entities* (4 April 2016) S/2016/213, para 24.

[89] ibid para 25.

[90] ibid.

[91] ibid para 26.

[92] UNSC, *Report of the Secretary-General on the Threat Posed by ISIL (Da'esh) to International Peace and Security and the Range of United Nations Efforts in Support of Member States in Countering the Threat* (29 January 2016) S/2016/92, para 34.

[93] ibid para 16 (explaining ISIS "funds derive mostly from the exploitation of the natural and economic resources of the territories it occupies . . . as well as from bank robbery, extortion, confiscation of property, donations from foreign terrorist fighters and the looting of antiquities."). A subsequent report issued by the Secretary-General in May 2016 tempered the characterization of ISIS's involvement with cultural property. Citing the UN Assistance Mission for Iraq as the source, the report stated that "because ISIL has not conquered new territory in Iraq for some time, its ability to loot and sell fresh resources, assets or antiquities has been diminished." UNSC, *Report of the Secretary-General on the Threat Posed by ISIL (Da'esh) to International Peace and Security and the Range of United Nations Efforts in Support of Member States in Countering the Threat* (31 May 2016) S/2016/501, para 11.

[94] *Report of the Secretary-General*, 29 January 2016 (n 92) para 34.

C. Congressional Hearings

Influential congressional committees held groundbreaking hearings because of the heightened interest in ISIS and the CP/FT connection. Starting in November 2014, the powerful House Financial Services Committee discussed "Terrorism Financing and the Islamic State"[95] Dr. Matthew Levitt, former Treasury Deputy Assistant Secretary for Intelligence and Analysis, in a written statement to committee members, remarkably claimed, "Excavating and selling artifacts that date back to 9,000 BCE has provided ISIS its second-largest revenue stream after illicit oil sales." Levitt indicated that "[m]ore than a third of Iraq's 12,000 archaeological sites are under ISIS control" and that "[m]any of these [artifacts] are smuggled into Europe via Turkey, Iran, and Syria."[96] In April 2015, the committee's Task Force to Investigate Terrorism Financing further probed the relationship between antiquities trafficking and ISIS funding.[97] Rep. Michael Fitzpatrick [R-PA-8], chairman, voiced unease about the rise of ISIS: "It is estimated that the terrorist attacks of September 11, 2001, cost al Qaeda just $500,000 to plan and execute. Today, in 2015, the United States once again faces the specter of terrorism, this time from groups such as the Islamic State, which has a reported net worth of over $2 billion, the product of self-funding methods such as illicit oil sales, human trafficking, regional taxation, and antiquity dealing."[98] Juan Zarate of the Center for Strategic and International Studies and the Center on Sanctions and Illicit Finance at the Foundation for Defense of Democracies (FDD) agreed that "[t]he Islamic State runs a diversified war economy, from oil to the antiquities trade."[99] He insisted that there were "communities of interest [e.g., antiquities, wildlife, and human trafficking] who have information" who can partner with law enforcement and intelligence communities to "shut it down."[100] Seth Jones, director of the International Security and

[95] *Terrorism Financing and the Islamic State, Hearing Before the Committee on Financial Services, U. House of Representatives*, Serial No. 113–99, 113th Congress, 13 November 2014.

[96] Matthew Levitt, Fromer-Wexler Fellow and Director, Stein Program on Counterterrorism and Intelligence, The Washington Institute for Near East Policy, "Terrorist Financing and the Islamic State," testimony submitted to the House Committee on Financial Services, 13 November 2014.

[97] *A Survey of Global Terrorism and Terrorist Financing, Hearing Before Task Force to Investigate Terrorism Financing, Committee on Financial Services, US House of Representatives*, Serial No. 114–15, 114th Congress, 22 April 2015.

[98] ibid 1.

[99] ibid 9.

[100] ibid 37.

Defense Policy Center of the RAND Corporation, concurred that antiquities smuggling was an ISIS funding mechanism.[101] To solve this problem, Zarate testified that "you have to cut off the channels that they use to get money and antiquities to brokers in Turkey and Kurdistan," and, unlike how terror groups were defunded in the past, the United States physically needed to remove ISIS from its territory, from its oil, and from its other funding sources.[102] Jonathan Schanzer, FDD vice president, said as well that "[t]he Islamic State . . . continues to profit from the sale of oil and antiquities," specifying that illegal sales were going "through Turkish territory."[103] With regard to artifact buyers financing terrorism, Schanzer advised, "We have to figure out who these people are who are paying for the antiquities after these cities are being looted by the Islamic State."[104]

The subcommittee on Terrorism, Nonproliferation, and Trade, part of the influential House Committee on Foreign Affairs, continued the discourse on the CP/FT nexus in November 2015, which included a discussion about money laundering. John Cassara, former Treasury special agent, spoke about AML/CFT and referenced antiquities trafficking. Dr. Danti reprised testimony about satellite photos showing widespread archaeological site looting in Syria. The pair joined other witnesses as they explored the topic of "Terrorist Financing: Kidnapping, Antiquities Trafficking, and Private Donations."[105] In response to questions posed by Chairman Ted Poe [R-TX-2], Cassara, once a member of the Office of Terrorism Finance and Financial Intelligence, testified that terrorist groups "diversify just like any criminal organization does . . . —just like a good investor does, if you will. . . . So they use a wide variety of funding methods and laundering methods."[106] He explained that predicate crimes that generate illegal cash, including antiquities smuggling, powered terrorist financing. "You are talking real money here," stressed Cassara.[107] Danti upheld Cassara's view that "antiquities serve as instruments for money laundering."[108] Correspondingly, in written remarks, Danti expanded on the destructive picture of plundering and trafficking,

[101] ibid 13.
[102] ibid 14.
[103] ibid 11.
[104] ibid 22.
[105] *Terrorist Financing: Kidnapping, Antiquities Trafficking, and Private Donations*, Serial No. 114–120, 114th Congress.
[106] ibid 84.
[107] ibid.
[108] ibid 61.

emphasizing that "looting of archaeological sites represents the most frequently reported cultural heritage incident in Syria" and "that all major belligerents operating in the conflict zone engage in cultural property crimes; however, all lines of evidence indicate ISIS ranks as the most egregious and brazen offender."[109] Danti pressed that "more should be done now."[110] Answering a lawmaker's question, he detailed that "the primary trafficking points [for] antiquities coming out of Syria were Lebanon and Turkey, and from that point much of the material was going to Bulgaria and Greece and then with the objective of moving the material into the Schengen zone—the free border zone."[111] Danti contended that the evidence demonstrated that the "Islamic State is essentially new management taking advantage of existing looting networks and existing trafficking networks that predate the conflict period and they have essentially just encouraged additional—far more looting and trafficking of antiquities."[112] In fact, information collected by ASOR CHI substantiated that ISIS "has developed a highly organized approach to looting, trafficking and selling antiquities and other cultural property for funding."[113] Danti concluded that there was "no doubt that terrorists derive significant revenue from looted ancient antiquities and stolen cultural property," adjudging that "[t]his criminal activity has increased as other revenue streams such as oil have been targeted through air strikes or other counter measures."[114] Although Dr. Danti told lawmakers that "[w]e don't know the total dollar values of the illicit antiquities trade," he testified that "ISIS and other transnational criminal organizations certainly find it crucial to their operations. . . ."[115]

The Task Force to Investigate Terrorism Financing revisited the CP/FT link in April 2016 in a hearing titled "Preventing Cultural Genocide: Countering the Plunder and Sale of Priceless Cultural Antiquities by ISIS."[116] Experts supported earlier findings that ISIS licensed

[109] Michael Danti, Academic Director, American Schools of Oriental Research Cultural Heritage Initiatives, "The Finance of Global Terrorism Through Cultural Property Crime in Syria and Northern Iraq," testimony submitted to the House Committee on Foreign Affairs, Subcommittee on Terrorism, Nonproliferation, and Trade, 17 November 2015, p. 1.

[110] ibid 3.

[111] *Terrorist Financing: Kidnapping, Antiquities Trafficking, and Private Donations* (n 105) 81.

[112] ibid.

[113] ibid 60.

[114] ibid.

[115] ibid 61.

[116] Preventing Cultural Genocide: Countering the Plunder and Sale of Priceless Cultural Antiquities by ISIS, Hearing Before The Task Force to Investigate Terrorism Financing of the

archaeological site looting, imposed taxes on pillaged artifacts, and hired contractors to excavate cultural objects. Cultural property law professor Dr. Patty Gerstenblith countenanced the opinion that ISIS made money from antiquities crimes. In written remarks, she stated, "While there is still much that is uncertain about the details of the looting and trafficking in such objects, enough is known to conclude that the sale of cultural objects is providing a significant income stream to ISIL and other actors in the region." She conveyed that "[a]ll parties to [the Syrian] conflict, including both the Islamic State in Iraq and the Levant (ISIL) and the Assad regime, are participating in this destruction and are utilizing the sale of cultural objects through international channels to support their operations."[117] Dr. Al-Azm informed the task force that ISIS's Archaeological Administration (AA), operating under the Office of Resources, directed the harvesting of cultural property using "earth-moving machinery . . . to accelerate the digging and recovery process." AA held "a regular auction in the city of Raqqa dedicated to the sale of antiquities," he reported, noting that "[i]tems, which are not sold within the agreed time, stipulated by the licenses issued to looters and those acquired by ISIS cadres[,] are sold at the auction."[118] Yaya Fanusie, FDD director of Analysis Center on Sanctions and Illicit Finance, meanwhile, criticized federal officials for their disorganized response to the urgent national security problem, remonstrating, "Policymaking seems to be ad hoc, and coordination and intelligence sharing is lacking." "Despite the rise in antiquities looting [by ISIS], U.S. federal law enforcement has yet to indict anyone for supporting IS through the illicit trade," Fanusie decried, and "few sanctions have been applied to smugglers and buyers."[119] Gerstenblith agreed that prosecution "offers the opportunity to effectively interdict the trade and dismantle networks."[120] Fanusie openly wondered "who in the U.S. government is even

Committee on Financial Services, US House of Representatives, Serial No. 114-83, 114th Congress, 19 April 2016.

[117] Patty Gerstenblith, On Behalf of Herself and the US Committee of the Blue Shield, testimony submitted to the Task Force to Investigate Terrorism Financing of the Committee on Financial Services, US House of Representatives, 19 April 2016, p 2.

[118] Amr Al-Azm, Professor of Middle East History and Anthropology at Shawnee State University, testimony submitted to the Task Force to Investigate Terrorism Financing of the Committee on Financial Services, US House of Representatives, 19 April 2016.

[119] Yaya J. Fanusie, Director of Analysis Center on Sanctions and Illicit Finance, Foundation for Defense of Democracies, testimony submitted to the Task Force to Investigate Terrorism Financing of the Committee on Financial Services, US House of Representatives, 19 April 2016, p 8.

[120] Testimony of Patty Gerstenblith (n 117) 10. For a general critique of the government's failure to prosecute antiquities traffickers, see eg Rick St. Hilaire, "Cracking Down on Antiquities Trafficking

responsible for antiquities trafficking," and impressed on the task force that "[r]eform can only come about by declaring antiquities looting and cultural property crime a national security priority."[121]

D. Responses to the Evidence, Testimony, and Hearings

The photographic evidence, eyewitness accounts, seized material from Syria, expert reports, and congressional testimony, all outlining cultural property's financing of terrorism, ignited an extraordinary sequence of responses from the federal government's three branches and from US-backed international bodies.

1. Executive Branch

Executive branch leaders delivered remarkable public pronouncements about cultural property crime, manifesting the significant impact of the CP/FT paradigm on policymakers. A paramount moment unfolded during an event hosted by the Metropolitan Museum of Art in New York in September 2016 when Vice President Joseph Biden joined François Hollande for the French president's announcement of a heritage protection fund. The vice president described ISIS's sale of artifacts to fund terrorism and its attack on cultural diversity in the region.[122] Two years earlier, at the same venue, Secretary of State John Kerry told a crowd that the "[a]dministration [was] laser-focused on protecting the cultural heritage of countries all around the world," especially because "ancient treasures in Iraq and in Syria have now become the casualties of continuing warfare and looting." The secretary placed responsibility on terrorists, insisting that "no one group has done more to put our shared cultural heritage in the gun sights than ISIL."[123]

by Changing Homeland Security's 'Seize and Send' Policy" (*Cultural Heritage Lawyer* blog, 10 December 2012) <https://culturalheritagelawyer.blogspot.com/2012/12/cracking-down-on-antiquities.html>; Rick St. Hilaire, "Antiquities Trafficking Investigation Reveals Suspected Ties to Terrorism and Money Laundering—'Seize and Send' Outcome Flags Need for Special Prosecutors" (*Cultural Heritage Lawyer* blog, 30 September 2015) <https://culturalheritagelawyer.blogspot.com/2015/09/newly-obtained-documents-reveal.html> accessed 11 October 2019.

[121] Testimony of Yaya J Fanusie (n 119) 8.

[122] Rick St. Hilaire, "More on the French President's Cultural Preservation Fund" (*Cultural Heritage Lawyer* blog, 7 October 2016) <https://culturalheritagelawyer.blogspot.com/2016/10/more-on-french-presidents-cultural.html> accessed 11 October 2019.

[123] Sec John Kerry, Remarks at Threats to Cultural Heritage in Iraq and Syria Event (n 52).

Comments delivered by the Treasury Under Secretary for Terrorism and Financial Intelligence (TFI) buttressed these high-profile remarks from top White House officials and offered a rare public glimpse into the assessments made by law enforcement. Speaking at the Carnegie Endowment for International Peace, David Cohen, tasked with disrupting financial threats to national security, gauged that ISIS was unlike other terrorist organizations, which explained why looted cultural property had become so strongly tied to national security. "ISIL poses a different terrorist financing challenge," he said. "It has amassed wealth at an unprecedented pace, and its revenue sources have a different composition from those of many other terrorist organizations." Cohen judged that "ISIL derives a relatively small share of its funds from deep-pocket donors, and thus does not, today, depend principally on moving money across international borders."[124] He identified oil, kidnap for ransom, and extortion as its top fundraising tools, with oil extraction from Syria and Iraq yielding the largest amount of cash. Coming in fourth place was "a range of other criminal activities" that included "*looting and selling antiquities*."[125] He sounded the alarm that "ISIL threatens core U.S. interests" and "if left unchecked, could ultimately pose a direct threat to citizens of the United States and our allies outside of the Middle East."[126] Testifying on Capitol Hill, Cohen reiterated, "They rob banks, loot and sell antiquities, and steal livestock and crops."[127] If the TFI Under Secretary monitored cultural property, that meant it was a national security priority. Cohen doubtlessly brought this outlook with him to the Central Intelligence Agency when, in 2015, he became deputy director.

Other prominent executive branch officials joined the chorus when reacting to the 2015 military raid on ISIS's compound. US Ambassador to Iraq Stuart Jones declared that the recovery of artifacts revealed "indisputable evidence that Da'esh—beyond its terrorism, brutality, and destruction—is also a criminal gang that is looting antiquities from museums and historical sites and selling them on the black market."[128] Appearing on CBS News,

[124] US Department of the Treasury, Press Center, "Remarks of Under Secretary for Terrorism and Financial Intelligence David S Cohen at The Carnegie Endowment for International Peace, "Attacking ISIL's Financial Foundation" ' (23 October 2014) <https://www.treasury.gov/press-center/press-releases/Pages/jl2672.aspx> accessed 6 November 2019.

[125] ibid. (Emphasis added.)

[126] ibid.

[127] David S. Cohen, Under Secretary for Terrorism and Financial Intelligence, US Department of the Treasury, "The Islamic State and Terrorist Financing," testimony submitted to the Committee on Financial Services, US House of Representatives, 13 November 2014, p 4.

[128] US Embassy and Consulates in Iraq, Press Release, "The United States Repatriates Cultural Heritage Objects and Fragments to the Government of Iraq" (15 July 2015) <https://iq.usembassy.

Richard Stengel, Under Secretary of State for Public Diplomacy and Public Affairs, called the ISIS financing operation "systematic." It had receipts and an organizational chart. It operated globally. It relied on Facebook and the Dark Web. "It is a crime ring," he proclaimed.[129] Deputy Assistant Secretary Andrew Keller of the DOS Counter Threat Finance and Sanctions Bureau of Economic and Business Affairs, additionally, unveiled declassified documents verifying that ISIS organized a system to license archaeological site looting, traffic antiquities, and earn profits.[130] He disclosed an organizational chart depicting a "Diwan," or department, that oversaw the marketing, excavation, exploration, research, and administration of archaeological sites and antiquities; presented a letter dated November 2014 that identified Abu Sayyaf as the head of the Antiquities Division; and showed an example of an excavation license issued by the Diwan of Natural Resources, Antiquities Division. Receipts documented the collection of the 20% *khums*.[131] Robert Hartung, Deputy Assistant Secretary for Diplomatic Security and Assistant Director for Threat Investigations and Analysis Directorate, accordingly announced an unprecedented reward of up to $5 million dollars for information leading to the disruption of the illegal antiquities trade benefiting ISIS.[132] The FBI simultaneously cautioned dealers and collectors to be "careful trading Near Eastern antiquities, warning that artifacts plundered by terrorist organizations such as ISIL are entering the marketplace."[133]

2. Congress

While notable administration officials publicly addressed the CP/FT nexus, Capitol Hill evaluated legislation. Few proposed bills ever become law, but

gov/united-states-repatriates-cultural-heritage-objects-fragments-government-iraq/> accessed 7 November 2019.

129 "ISIS' Records Show Millions Raised by Antiquities Smuggling" (*CBS News*, 29 September 2015) <https://www.cbsnews.com/video/isis-records-show-millions-raised-by-antiquities-smuggling/> accessed 11 October 2019.

130 Andrew Keller, US Department of State, "Documenting ISIL' Antiquities Trafficking," presentation given at the Metropolitan Museum of Art (29 September 2015) <https://eca.state.gov/files/bureau/final_presentation_to_met_on_isil_antiquities_trafficking_for_das_keller_9.29.2015_.pdf> accessed 11 October 2019.

131 ibid.

132 Rick St. Hilaire, "Full Video: $5 Million Reward Announced at Conflict Antiquities Symposium Focused on ISIS Terror Funding" (*Cultural Heritage Lawyer* blog, 14 October 2015) <https://culturalheritagelawyer.blogspot.com/2015/10/full-video-5-million-reward-announced.html> accessed 11 October 2019.

133 "ISIL and Antiquities Trafficking: FBI Warns Dealers, Collectors About Terrorist Loot" (*Federal Bureau of Investigation News*, 26 August 2015) <https://www.fbi.gov/news/stories/isil-and-antiquities-trafficking/isil-and-antiquities-trafficking> accessed 11 October 2019.

legislators were able to pass the PPICPA. That statute, and lawmakers' consideration of several other unenacted bills, demonstrated Congress's seriousness about cultural property and the impact on national security.

Minority leader Sen. Harry Reid [D-NV] introduced comprehensive counterterrorism legislation titled Defeat ISIS and Protect and Secure the United States Act of 2015.[134] The text, in relevant part, offered the sense of Congress that the United States should "expand cooperation among G-20 and countries that are allies of the United States to strengthen the protection of antiquities and prevent ISIS from engaging in the theft, transport, and sale of cultural objects for the purpose of financing terrorism."[135] Meanwhile, in 2016, Sen. Robert Casey, Jr. [D-PA] introduced the Prevent Trafficking in Cultural Properties Act, following the bill's adoption by the House. The legislation hoped to advance a policy aimed at intercepting smuggled cultural property; disrupting trafficking networks, which included those trading in "stolen antiquities used to finance terrorism;" supporting federal cultural property prosecutions; and meeting American obligations under the 1954 Hague Convention, the 1970 UNESCO Convention on the Means of Prohibiting and Preventing the Illicit Import, Export, and Transfer of Ownership of Cultural Property, and the CPIA.[136] That same year, Sen. Mark Kirk [R-IL] introduced the Terrorism Art and Antiquity Revenue Prevention Act.[137] The TAAR Act intended to strengthen the National Stolen Property Act by targeting criminals who received, transported, or sold cultural property and set out to establish a database of cultural objects entering the United States from Iraq and Syria. Sen. Casey also introduced the STORM Act (Stop Terrorist Operational Resources and Money Act) in June 2016 to strike at ISIS financing and curb terror financing.[138] None of these bills reached the president's desk. But the PPICPA did.

Rep. Eliot Engel presented the bipartisan PPICPA to the House in November 2014. Committees that routinely review national security matters received the bill, including Foreign Affairs and Armed Services.[139] Bill cosponsor Rep. Chris Smith [R-NJ-4] vigorously articulated the CP/FT nexus underlying the proposal, exclaiming, "The fight to preserve our common

[134] S 2377, 114th Congress, 2015.
[135] ibid.
[136] S 3538, 114th Congress, 2016. See also Prevent Trafficking in Cultural Property Act, HR 2285, 114th Congress, 2015.
[137] S 3449, 114th Congress, 2016.
[138] S 3125, 114th Congress, 2016.
[139] HR 5703, 113th Congress, 2014.

cultural heritage, as well as to deny extremists such as ISIL resources from the sale of blood antiquities, is yet another front on the global war against terror."[140] Activating emergency import restrictions to prevent looted and smuggled Syrian heritage material from entering America's art and antiquities market was the legislation's primary goal, and it proposed the creation of a cultural property protection czar. "Today, ISIL and other terrorist organizations have found a lucrative source of revenue in artifacts they traffic out of areas of conflict," Engel stressed as he highlighted the interrelationship between heritage preservation, antiquities trafficking, transnational crime, and terrorist financing. "America must respond by denying terrorists and criminals the ability to profit from instability by looting the world of its greatest treasures."[141] Foreign Affairs Committee chairman Rep. Ed Royce [R-CA-39] told House members that the legislation directly addressed both heritage preservation and terrorist funding because "the looting of antiquities is big business for ISIS." He averred, "Experts estimate that the group has earned millions of dollars from the sale of stolen artifacts, which are often peddled by middlemen in old-fashioned markets or online. And unfortunately, buyers in the U.S. appear to be a primary end-destination for many of these pieces."[142] Although the PPICPA stalled in the 113th Congress, Rep. Engel resurrected the bill during the successive legislative session,[143] and Sen. Casey submitted it to the Senate in July 2015.[144] On May 9, 2016, President Obama signed the act into law.[145] The adopted statute reinforced traditional "core United States interests in" heritage preservation, namely:

> (A) protecting and preserving international cultural property;
>
> . . .
>
> (C) protecting sites of cultural and archaeological significance; and

[140] US Congressman Chris Smith, News Item, "Engel, Smith Offer Bill to Improve Cultural Preservation, Curb ISIL Funding" (14 November 2014) <https://chrissmith.house.gov/news/documentsingle.aspx?DocumentID=397716> accessed 1 October 2019.

[141] Committee on Foreign Affairs, US House of Representatives, Press Release, "Engel, Smith Offer Bill to Improve Cultural Preservation, Curb ISIL Funding" <https://foreignaffairs.house.gov/2014/11/engel-smith-offer-bill-improve-cultural-preservation-curb-isil-funding> accessed 1 October 2019.

[142] Committee on Foreign Affairs, US House of Representatives, Press Release, "House Combats ISIS's Trafficking of Antiquities," remarks of Rep. Ed Royce on the House floor (26 April 2016) <https://gop-foreignaffairs.house.gov/press-release/house-combats-isiss-trafficking-of-antiquities/> accessed 29 October 2019.

[143] Protect and Preserve International Cultural Property Act, HR 1493, 114th Congress, 2015.

[144] Protect and Preserve International Cultural Property Act, S1887, 114th Congress, 2015.

[145] Public Law No: 114-151.

(D) providing for the lawful exchange of international cultural property.[146]

Importantly, the law underscored the national security interest of "preventing and disrupting looting and illegal trade and trafficking in international cultural property, particularly exchanges that provide revenue to terrorist and criminal organizations."[147] From this point of departure, the statute called for emergency import controls on at-risk archaeological and ethnological material originating from Syria and for the establishment of an interagency coordinating committee, chaired by DOS, tasked "to protect and preserve international cultural property at risk from political instability, armed conflict, or natural or other disasters."[148] Unlike the four-year wait to publish emergency import restrictions covering Iraqi cultural material following EPIC's enactment, it took just three months to promulgate rules prohibiting US imports of Syrian artifacts like cylinder seals, ancient sculptures, and liturgical objects,[149] a stark illustration of the effect of the CP/FT paradigm shift.

3. Courts

The 2015 special operations assault on Abu Sayyaf's lair propelled the CP/FT issue into the judiciary when, in December 2016, the US Attorney's Office for the District of Columbia filed a civil forfeiture complaint seeking title to artifacts looted by ISIS.[150] The court, in November 2019, approved the request in the case of *U.S. v. One Gold Ring with Carved Gemstone, An Asset of ISIL Discovered on Electronic Media of Abu Sayyaf, President of ISIL Antiquities Department et al.*, which endorsed the application of one of America's most robust antiterrorism laws, the USA PATRIOT Act.[151] The objects forfeited in the case included an ancient Hellenistic/Roman gold ring, two ancient Roman gold coins, a Neo-Assyrian stone carving, and more.

President George W. Bush enacted the Uniting and Strengthening America by Providing Appropriate Tools Required to Intercept and Obstruct

[146] ibid §§ 2(4)(A), (C), (D).

[147] ibid § 2(4)(B).

[148] ibid § 2.

[149] Import Restrictions Imposed on Archaeological and Ethnological Material of Syria, 81 Federal Register 157, 15 August 2016, pp 53916–921.

[150] United States' Verified Complaint for Forfeiture *In Rem*, *US v One Gold Ring with Carved Gemstone et a.*, 16-cv-02442 (D.D.C.), 15 December 2016.

[151] Assistant US Attorneys Zia M. Faruqui, Deborah Curtis, and Brian P. Hudak represented the government. US Attorney Jessie K. Liu and asset forfeiture chief AUSA Arvind K. Lal headed the office.

Terrorism Act of 2001 after 9/11.[152] It decreed sweeping authority to deprive terrorists of a range of assets,[153] similar in scope to the Racketeer Influenced and Corrupt Organization Act's broad forfeiture provisions designed to dismantle organized crime.[154] When federal prosecutors inventively debuted this powerful antiterrorism statute to combat CP/FT—specifically 18 U.S.C. § 981(a)(1)(G)(i)—the court, by granting the government's petition, effectively ratified DOJ's national security approach to cultural property protection.[155]

Characterizing the prosecutors' complaint as "well-pleaded," Judge Thomas Hogan relied on the government's description of what was learned from the military raid to support judicial determinations that ISIS engaged in terrorism and that the defendant artifacts were "foreign assets of ISIL . . . affording a source of influence, as ISIL has and is engaged in planning and perpetrating federal crimes of terrorism. . . ."[156] The court unlocked § 981's formidable authority to order the surrender of the cultural property. Judge Hogan further declared that the DC federal district court retained the authority to forfeit items that were not actually in federal custody or in the country.[157] In this case, the defendant artifacts simply were depictions on digital photographs found in Abu Sayyaf's possession, whose "electronic media had a number of images of antiquities . . . prepared for marketing in order to sell the photographed items internationally."[158] The court opined that controlling law gave the DC court jurisdiction and venue, and its forfeiture order could "reach all property of terrorist organizations," encompassing property "which may never have touched the United States."[159] In fact, even before this pronouncement, the court in 2018 found probable cause to issue an arrest warrant for the defendant gold ring with carved gemstone that was located abroad, basing its decision on court rules governing asset forfeitures.[160]

[152] Pub L 107-56.
[153] 18 USC § 981(a)(1)(G)(i).
[154] 18 USC § 1963(a)(2)(D).
[155] Default Judgment and Order of Forfeiture, *US . One Gold Ring with Carved Gemstone et al*, 16-cv-02442 (D.D.C.), 7 November 2019, pp 4–5.
[156] ibid 4.
[157] ibid 2.
[158] Amended Verified Complaint for Forfeiture *In Rem*, *US v One Gold Ring with Carved Gemstone et al*, 16-cv-02442 (D.D.C.), 6 December 2017, para 31.
[159] Default Judgment and Order of Forfeiture, p 2 (citing 18 USC § 981(a)(1)(G)(i) and 28 USC § 1355(b)(2)).
[160] Warrant of Arrest *In Rem*, *US v One Gold Ring with Carved Gemstone et al*, 16-cv-02442 (DDC), 26 January 2018 (relying on Rule(G)(3) of the Supplemental Rules for Admiralty or Maritime Claims and Asset Forfeiture Actions).

Prosecutors sought the warrant because the ring had been sold by a "Syrian Antiquities Trafficker" and recovered in Turkey.[161] Ultimately, the effect of the court's final forfeiture order would empower US officials to claim title to all the defendant cultural artifacts as they surfaced in the marketplace.

4. International Bodies

The United States, as a leading member in the international arena, worked with the UNSC to combat the CP/FT nexus through adoption of Resolutions 2199, 2253, and 2322. Washington also cooperated with the G7. In February 2015, the UNSC unanimously passed Resolution 2199 to strangle terrorists' ability to raise money through cultural heritage trafficking and other criminal schemes like oil smuggling and kidnap and ransom, especially targeting ISIS's and ANF's fundraising efforts.[162] The resolution was adopted pursuant to Chapter VII of the UN Charter, which is focused on international peace and security. Ambassador Samantha Power, US Permanent Representative to the UN, expected that "by imposing a new ban on the trade in smuggled Syrian antiquities, this resolution both cuts off a source of ISIL revenue and helps protect an irreplaceable cultural heritage, of the region and of the world." The ambassador spotlighted how "the United States has sponsored the publication of so-called 'Emergency Red Lists' of Syrian and Iraqi antiquities at risk, which can help international law enforcement catch antiquities trafficked out of these countries."[163] In the paragraphs covering cultural heritage trafficking, the resolution expressly identified the UNSC's urgent security concern, declaring that it:

> *Condemns* the destruction of cultural heritage in Iraq and Syria particularly by ISIL and ANF . . .;
>
> *Notes with concern* that ISIL, ANF and . . . entities associated with Al-Qaida, are generating income from engaging . . . in the looting and smuggling of cultural heritage items from . . . Iraq and Syria, which is being used

[161] Government's Motion for Issuance of Warrant of Arrest *In Rem* and Supporting Memorandum of Law, *US v One Gold Ring with Carved Gemstone et al*, 16-cv-02442 (DDC), 6 December 2017, para 9.

[162] S/RES/2199 (12 February 2015).

[163] US Mission to the United Nations, Office of Press and Public Diplomacy, "Explanation of Vote by Ambassador Samantha Power, US Permanent Representative to the United Nations, at a Security Council Session on Threats to International Peace and Security Caused by Terrorist Threats" (12 February 2015).

> to support their recruitment efforts and strengthen their operational capability to organize and carry out terrorist attacks;
>
> . . . and *decides* that all Member States shall take appropriate steps to prevent the trade in Iraqi and Syrian cultural property.[164]

US Customs directly referenced Resolution 2199 when promulgating import regulations in 2016 targeting at-risk Syrian artifacts.[165] Further addressing security concerns was Resolution 2253, sponsored by the United States and Russia and adopted by the UNSC in December 2015, which intended to hold ISIS accountable by enhancing the Al-Qaeda terrorist sanctions framework.[166] The presence of finance ministers from member nations at the UNSC meeting, an unprecedented occurrence, accentuated the body's unanimous adoption of the resolution. US Treasury Secretary Jacob Lew remarked that "ISIL is a challenging financial target . . . [that] generates wealth from economic activity and resources within territory under its control."[167] The resolution identified antiquities as one of those resources.[168] UNSC Resolution 2322, approved the following year and backed by the United States, urged nations to enhance judicial cooperation to stem cultural property trafficking and other activities that assisted terrorists. The resolution expressed concern "at the growing involvement of terrorist groups . . . in the destruction and the trafficking in cultural property" and called for "broad law enforcement and judicial cooperation in preventing and combating all forms and aspects of trafficking . . . that benefit or may benefit terrorist or terrorist groups."[169] Cooperation with the international community, meanwhile, extended to the G7. When the United States gathered with the group of nations in May 2016, they published an action plan that aspired "to enhance efforts to hinder looting and trafficking of cultural property originating from regions under the control of terrorist groups."[170]

164 S/RES/2199 (n 162).

165 Import Restrictions Imposed on Archaeological and Ethnological Material of Syria, 81 Federal Register 157, p 53916.

166 S/RES/2253 (17 December 2015).

167 US Department of the Treasury, Press Center, "Remarks by Treasury Secretary Jacob J. Lew at the United Nations Security Council Meeting on Combating the Financing of Terrorism" (17 December 2015) <https://www.treasury.gov/press-center/press-releases/Pages/jl0306.aspx> accessed 1 October 2019.

168 S/RES/2253 (n 166) para 97.

169 S/RES/2322 (12 December 2016) 2, 5.

170 *G7 Action Plan on Countering Terrorism and Violent Extremism* (27 May 2016).

VII. Ripening Fruit: The Emphasis on Money Laundering (2017–2020)

Military pushback against ISIS in 2017 prevailed with the terrorist organization's expulsion from Mosul and the collapse of its capital in Raqqa. By the end of that year, Iraqi officials declared control over the border with Syria, and, by March 2019, Syrian Democratic Forces claimed victory over ISIS after wresting control of Baghuz. Pivotally, President Donald Trump announced in October 2019 that ISIS leader Abu Bakr al-Baghdadi had been killed in northwest Syria.[171] The CP/FT paradigm, which gained swift traction across all branches of government in conjunction with the terrorist group's rapid ascendancy and brutal ferocity, persisted in the waning years of ISIS's power, continuing to shape policy and deliberations. In March 2017, for example, the UNSC unanimously adopted Resolution 2347 that "*[d]eplores and condemns* the unlawful destruction of cultural heritage . . . as well as the looting and smuggling of cultural property from archaeological sites, museums, libraries, archives, and other sites, in the context of armed conflicts, notably by terrorist groups."[172] Co-sponsored by the United States, the resolution focused on cultural heritage protection in conflict situations, completing the circle of thinking about cultural property as fundamentally a discussion about preservation, but part of the wider context of national security, terrorism, and crime. Because ISIS allied itself with TOC and generated funds from cultural property, cultural heritage protection required the combination of targeting criminal and terrorist organizations as well as money laundering and corruption, implored Under-Secretary-General for Political Affairs Jeffrey Feltman.[173] Later, in June 2017, Rep. Stevan Pearce [R-NM-2] convened the Subcommittee on Terrorism and Illicit Finance to gather additional information about CP/FT.[174] A question still on the minds of some lawmakers was "how are funds related to these antiquities being used

[171] See "ISIS Fast Facts" (n 42) for a more complete chronology.

[172] S/RES/2347 (24 March 2017). See also Rick St. Hilaire, "US Supports UN Security Council Resolution Condemning Heritage Destruction by Terror Groups" (*Cultural Heritage Lawyer* blog, 25 March 2017) <https://culturalheritagelawyer.blogspot.com/2017/03/us-supports-un-security-council.html> accessed 11 October 2019.

[173] United Nations, Meetings Coverage, "Security Council Condemns Destruction, Smuggling of Cultural Heritage by Terrorist Groups, Unanimously Adopting Resolution 2347 (2017)" (26 March 2017) <https://www.un.org/press/en/2017/sc12764.doc.htm> accessed 11 October 2019.

[174] *Exploitation of Cultural Property: Examining Illicit Activity in the Antiquities and Art Trade, Hearing Before the Subcommittee on Terrorism and Illicit Finance of the Committee on Financial Services, US House of Representatives*, Serial No. 115-23, 23 June 2017.

to underwrite terrorist organizations?"[175] Dr. Daniels returned to Capitol Hill to attest, "There is now . . . compelling evidence that archaeological site looting is implicated in the financing of organized criminal activity and other terrorist networks," propounding "that these developments may represent a recent innovation and a restructuring of the overall antiquities and art trade."[176] To illustrate, Daniels explained that the "Italian Government confirmed that Daesh had expanded its organized looting activity into Libya as part of a collaborative enterprise with the Calabrian mafia."[177] But, he said, "to date, there has not been any really creative thinking about how we would address the issue of antiquities looting around financial crimes. And there hasn't been the kind of conversation about what laws or policies would actually look like at that nexus."[178] Rep. French Hill [R-AR-2] recommended that Treasury Secretary Steven Mnuchin discuss antiquities transfers when talking to the Gulf states about terror financing.[179] The following year the subcommittee conducted a "Survey of Terrorist Groups and Their Means of Financing" where political scientist Dr. Colin Clarke briefly testified about ISIS's diverse criminal funding portfolio, which included antiquities smuggling.[180] Yet the 2018 National Terrorist Financing Risk Assessment made no mention of cultural property, likely demonstrating that the perception of the CP/FT nexus was dimming in some quarters as ISIS diminished.[181] Notwithstanding, as officials looked "to defeat ISIS [in Libya] and protect U.S. security and economic interests,"[182] DOS signed a bilateral agreement in 2018 to restrict imports of Libyan archaeological and ethnological material in jeopardy of pillage, reinforcing emergency restrictions erected in 2017.[183]

[175] ibid 2, question presented by ranking member Rep. Ed Perlmutter's [D-CO-7].

[176] ibid 5.

[177] ibid 6.

[178] ibid 12.

[179] ibid 14–15. The congressman probably was recommending discussions with members of the Terrorist Financing Targeting Center (TFTC), created in May 2017 to combat terrorist financing networks. Members of TFTC include the United States, Bahrain, Kuwait, Oman, Qatar, Saudi Arabia, and United Arab Emirates.

[180] Colin P Clarke, Rand Corporation, "An Overview of Current Trends in Terrorism and Illicit Finance: Lessons from the Islamic State in Iraq and Syria and Other Emerging Threats," testimony submitted to the Subcommittee on Terrorism and Illicit Finance of the Committee on Financial Services, US. House of Representatives, 7 September 2018, p 5.

[181] US Department of the Treasury, *National Terrorist Financing Risk Assessment 2018*, pp 7–10.

[182] DOS, *Integrated Country Strategy—Libya* (14 August 2018).

[183] Memorandum of Understanding Between the Government of the United States of America and the Government of Libya Concerning the Imposition of Import Restrictions on Categories of Archeological and Ethnological Material of Libya (23 February 2018); Emergency Import Restrictions Imposed on Archaeological and Ethnological Material from Libya, 82 Federal Register 232, 5 December 2017, pp 57346–51.

Gripping news of terrorist connections to antiquities trafficking soon followed with a published report that Spanish police arrested two men for allegedly financing ISIS with looted Libyan artifacts.[184] Concerns about CP/FT, thereafter, hovered over war-ravaged Yemen,[185] and the United States established emergency import controls on at-risk Yemeni cultural property in 2020.[186]

Most significantly during this period, recognition of the CP/FT nexus ripened alongside debates about the relationship between art, antiquities, and money laundering. That is why, in the midst of the European Union's addition of art dealers and auction houses to AML/CFT compliance rules in April 2018,[187] Rep. Andy Barr [R-KY-6] brought the National Strategy for Combating the Financing of Transnational Criminal Organizations Act to the House floor.[188] Sponsored by Rep. David Kustoff [R-TN-08], the legislation sought to require the White House, Treasury Department, and relevant executive branch officials to assess the national security threats posed by TOC and craft a national strategy to secure financial networks. The bill called for the identification of industries that could be misused to facilitate money laundering, listing art and antiquities dealers by name.[189] Pointing to illegal money found in the art and antiquities sectors, Rep. Dan Kildee [D-MI-5] warned of "significant vulnerabilities . . . identified as major threats to our national security and the integrity of our financial system," insisting that "we know that the looting and trafficking in cultural heritage is a source of revenue that has funded ISIS' heinous activities, and we know that the opaque characteristics of the high-end art market and its lack of basic anti-money-laundering requirements make it a target for illicit funds."[190] The bill passed

[184] Georgi Kantchev, "Suspected Traders of Ancient Art Linked to Islamic State Are Detained" *The Wall Street Journal* (29 March 2018). *WSJ* called the arrest "the first publicly announced detentions by Western authorities working to dismantle the terrorist group's trade in plundered art."

[185] Tom Mashberg, "Yemen Asks US for Help to Curb Smuggling of Looted Ancient Artifacts" *The New York Times* (6 March 2019) <https://www.nytimes.com/2019/03/06/arts/design/yemen-united-states-looted-artifacts.html> accessed 4 June 2020 (reporting, "The Yemenis say they have strong evidence that their artifacts are being sold off by Houthi fighters and by terrorist groups like Al Qaeda in the Arabian Peninsula and the Islamic State, which infiltrated the country during its current turmoil.").

[186] Emergency Import Restrictions Imposed on Archaeological and Ethnological Material from Yemen, 85 Federal Register 26, 7 February 2020, pp 7209–14.

[187] Rick St. Hilaire, "New European AML/CTF Legislation Includes Art Dealers and Flags Cultural Artifacts Transactions" (*Cultural Heritage Lawyer* blog, 2 May 2018) <https://culturalheritagelawyer.blogspot.com/2018/05/new-european-amlctf-legislation.html#more> accessed 4 June 2020.

[188] National Strategy for Combating the Financing of Transnational Criminal Organizations Act, *Congressional Record*, Vol 164, No 39, 6 March 2018, p H1395.

[189] H.R. 4768, 115th Congress, 2018.

[190] *Congressional Record*, Vol 164 (n 187) H1396.

the House and moved to the Senate in the form of the CONFRONT Act.[191] The legislation stalled, but Rep. Kustoff reintroduced the measure in 2019, which remained pending as of June 2020.[192] Meanwhile, in March 2019, the House Subcommittee on National Security, International Development, and Monetary Policy convened a hearing under the banner of "Promoting Corporate Transparency."[193] Former FBI Special Agent and AML/CFT expert Dennis Lormel testified in certain terms that "[a]rts and antiquities have for a long time, quietly been a mechanism for hiding ill-gotten gains and serving as a money laundering tool. This was never more evident than with the theft and black market sales of art and antiquities from Iraq and Syria by the Islamic State to help support their terrorist organization."[194] Therefore, he advocated that Congress subject art and antiquities dealers to the Bank Secrecy Act, an important AML/CFT law.[195] Rep. Al Green [D-TX-9], chair of the Subcommittee on Oversight and Investigations, echoed these views on the House floor, avowing, "The United States of America should not allow ourselves to be the financier for those who perpetrate dastardly deeds in many countries around the world." Green accused Syria as a place where "you have terrorists who will take stolen artifacts, find a way to put them into commerce, and use that money to support terrorist activities."[196] He voiced lawmakers' sentiment that antiquities trafficking subsidizes terrorism,[197] a point of departure that advanced discussions on Capitol Hill about whether art and antiquities dealers should be included in the BSA. "We must find a way to close the loopholes that allow persons in this country to purchase these artifacts and allow that money to get back to those who would perform these dastardly deeds," demanded Green.[198]

[191] CONFRONT Act, S 2715, 115th Congress, 2018.

[192] CONFRONT Act, HR 1387, 116th Congress, 2019.

[193] *Promoting Corporate Transparency: Examining Legislative Proposals to Detect and Deter Financial Crime, Hearing Before the Subcommittee on National Security, International Development, and Monetary Policy of the Committee on Financial Services, US House of Representatives*, Serial No. 116-9, 13 March 2019.

[194] Dennis M. Lormel, President and CEO, DML Associates, LLC, testimony submitted to the Subcommittee on National Security, International Development, and Monetary Policy of the Committee on Financial Services, US House of Representatives, 13 March 2019, p 10.

[195] ibid. The BSA is formally called the Currency and Foreign Transactions Reporting Act of 1970. Its provisions are codified in multiple statutory sections and regulations. The bulk are found in 31 USC § 5311 et seq and in 31 CFR Chapter X.

[196] Acknowledging Lack of Transparency in Financial Transactions Poses a Threat to National Security, *Congressional Record*, Vol 165, No 45, 13 March 2019, p H2699.

[197] See Acknowledging That the Lack of Sunlight and Transparency in Financial Transactions Poses a Threat to Our National Security and Our Economy's Security and Supporting Efforts to Close Related Loopholes, H Res 206, 116th Congress, 2019.

[198] Acknowledging Lack of Transparency, *Congressional Record*, Vol 165 (n 196) H2699.

The BSA is potent. The statute establishes record keeping and reporting obligations as well as customer identification programs to flush out terrorist financiers and money washers. It is enforced by the Financial Crimes Enforcement Network (FinCen), the Treasury bureau tasked with tackling AML/CFT. Banks, casinos, high-value asset merchants, and cash-intensive sectors are subject to the BSA. Although art and antiquities sellers must file Internal Revenue Service Form 8300 like other businesses that accept \$10,000 + cash payments from customers, they are not compelled by the BSA to submit suspicious activity reports (SARS) to FinCen like dealers in precious metals, stones, or jewels; sellers of automobile, planes, and boats; real estate professionals; pawnbrokers; or travel agencies. Yet art and antiquities dealers and auction houses clearly have what the BSA looks for, namely "certain reports or records [that] have a high degree of usefulness in criminal, tax, or regulatory investigations . . . or in the conduct of intelligence or counterintelligence activities . . . to protect against international terrorism."[199] Because reputable art and antiquities sellers regularly transact business in an opaque marketplace and offer portable objects that can fetch high prices, the sector is attractive to money laundering and terrorist financing.[200] As early as 2012, the Basel Institute on Governance, an independent nonprofit, made an important observation repeated in 2018: "In comparison with other trade sectors, the art market faces a higher risk of exposure to dubious trade practices."[201]

To apply the BSA to art and antiquities dealers, Rep. Luke Messer [R-IN-6] introduced the Illicit Art and Antiquities Trafficking Prevention Act (IAATPA) in May 2018.[202] It faltered when the congressman lost his seat in midterm elections, but a bipartisan vote in 2019 on House Resolution 206, calling for sunshine on financial transactions and transparency in the antiquities trade, suggested that lawmakers still had an appetite for the idea.[203] The

[199] 31 USC § 5311.

[200] Rick St. Hilaire, "Money Laundering and the Trade in Cultural Property: Taking a Fresh Look at Federal AML/CTFs" (*Cultural Heritage Lawyer* blog, 25 January 2014) <https://culturalheritagelawyer.blogspot.com/2014/01/money-laundering-and-trade-in-cultural.html> accessed 13 November 2019. See also Rick St. Hilaire, "Shouldn't Art and Antiquities Sellers Be Subject to Anti-Money Laundering/Counter-Terrorist Financing Laws?" (*Cultural Heritage Lawyer* blog, 9 August 2016) <https://culturalheritagelawyer.blogspot.com/2016/08/shouldnt-art-and-antiquities-sellers-be.html> accessed 11 October 2019.

[201] Basel Institute on Governance, *Basel Art Trade Guidelines* (January 2012, reissued 2018).

[202] H.R. 5886, 115th Congress, 2018.

[203] Acknowledging That the Lack of Sunlight and Transparency in Financial Transactions Poses a Threat to Our National Security and Our Economy's Security and Supporting Efforts to Close Related Loopholes, H Res 206, 116th Congress, 2019 (introduced by Rep. Maxine Waters [D-CA-43].

resolution cautioned "that artifacts plundered by terrorist organizations such as the Islamic State of Iraq and the Levant are entering the marketplace."[204] The Antiquities Coalition, a nonprofit that assembled a Financial Crimes Task Force consisting of cultural property and AML/CFT professionals, endorsed it[205] and earned particular mention in the resolution's text.[206] It is along the lines of IAATPA and House Resolution 206 that Rep. Emanuel Cleaver [D-MO-5], joined by co-sponsors Rep. Steve Stivers [R-OH-5] and Rep. Carolyn Maloney [D-NY-12], introduced the COUNTER Act of 2019, which added antiquities sellers to the BSA's list of industries obligated to report suspicious financial activities.[207] This time, art dealers conspicuously were omitted without public explanation. The COUNTER Act passed the House in October 2019 as an amendment to the Corporate Transparency Act of 2019, sponsored by Rep. Maloney.[208] That bill sought BSA compliance for "a person trading or acting as an intermediary in the trade of antiquities, including an advisor, consultant or any other person who engages as a business in the solicitation of the sale of antiquities."[209] It also called on Treasury, FBI, the Attorney General, and Homeland Security to study "the facilitation of money laundering and terror finance through the trade of works of art or antiquities" in an effort to determine the scope of the problem and to understand which dealers could be exempted from regulation.[210, 211]

204 ibid.

205 Antiquities Coalition, "Multi-Stakeholder Initiative Launched to Combat Financial Crimes via Art and Antiquities: Allies from the Financial, Legal, Law Enforcement, and Art Market Communities Lay Roadmap for Action" (16 April 2019) <https://theantiquitiescoalition.org/initiative-launched-to-combat-financial-crimes/> accessed 13 November 2019. John Byrne, an AML/CFT specialist, also has become a leader supporting art and antiquities dealers' inclusion in the BSA. See eg John J. Byrne, *Illicit Funds in Terrorism* (AML RightSource 2019).

206 H Res 206 contained the language: "Whereas, according to the Antiquities Coalition, 'because the United States is the largest destination for archaeological and ethnological objects from around the world, the discovery of recently looted and trafficked artifacts in our country not only makes Americans and our institutions accessories to crimes, but also threatens our relations with other countries.'"

207 Coordinating Oversight, Upgrading and Innovating Technology, and Examiner Reform Act, HR 2514, 116th Congress, 2019.

208 HR 2513, 116th Congress, 2019.

209 ibid § 211(a)(3)(Z).

210 ibid § 211(b).

211 Since the submission of this chapter for publication, the National Defense Authorization Act became law in January 2021. That law, primarily concerned with military funding, contained national security measures to counter money laundering and illicit financial flows, mandating that company beneficial ownership information be collected and made available to FinCen and requiring antiquities dealers to file SARS with FinCen in accord with the BSA's reporting requirements. See Rick St. Hilaire, "Antiquities Trafficking Bathed in Sunshine: Disclosures of Shell Company Owners and Suspicious Financial Transactions May Be on the Horizon if the NDAA Becomes Law" (Cultural Heritage Lawyer blog, 5 December 2020, updated 1 January 2021).

The topic of art dealers re-emerged when the Senate Committee on Homeland Security and Government Affairs released an analysis of art's relationship to money laundering and terrorist financing. Titled "The Art Industry and U.S. Policies that Undermine Sanctions," the July 2020 investigative report urged lawmakers to add the high-end art market to the list of business sectors that must comply with the BSA, calling it "the largest legal, unregulated market in the United States."[212] "Given the intrinsic secrecy of the art industry," the authors concluded that "change is needed in this multi-billion-dollar industry."[213] To pierce through layers of artificially created shell companies designed to conceal illicit transactions, the report suggested that the Treasury Department find out the ultimate beneficial owners of these paper corporations to unmask criminals and their illegal business enterprises.[214] Such reforms, among others, were necessary because the combination of "[s]ecrecy, anonymity, and a lack of regulation create an environment ripe for laundering money and evading sanctions."[215]

Both the FBI's Art Crime Team (ACT) and Treasury, meanwhile, already trained their sights on fighting money laundering in the art market. "We have to prioritize the work that we're doing," explained ACT manager Tim Carpenter in 2020. "In 2014, the threat at the time was conflict area antiquities trafficking—that was a big concern for us and the US government. Today, we're more concerned about money laundering in the art market."[216] Treasury Deputy Secretary Justin Muzinich focused on the same target. He cautioned that "[a]rt and luxury goods dealers should be on alert to the schemes of money launderers who hide personal funds in high-value assets in an attempt to mitigate the effects of U.S. sanctions."[217] In December 2019, for instance, the Office of Foreign Assets Control designated Nazem Said Ahmad to the sanctions list, accusing him of washing money through an art gallery in Beirut that served as a front. Secretary Mnuchin expressed that "[t]his Administration will continue to take action against Hizballah financiers

[212] US Senate Committee on Homeland Security and Government Affairs, Permanent Subcommittee on Investigations, "The Art Industry and US Policies that Undermine Sanctions," Rob Portman, Chairman, and Tom Carper, Ranking Member (29 July 2020) 2–3, 10, 14.

[213] ibid 147.

[214] ibid 14.

[215] ibid 3.

[216] Megan Gates, "Have You Seen This Art?" (*Security Management*, ASIS International, May 2020) 47.

[217] US Department of the Treasury, Press Releases, "Treasury Designates Prominent Lebanon and DRC-Based Hizballah Money Launderers" (13 December 2019) <https://home.treasury.gov/news/press-releases/sm856> accessed 3 June 2020.

like . . . Ahmad . . . who . . . used money laundering and tax evasion schemes to fund terrorist plots. . . ."[218]

VIII. Conclusion

Cultural property looting and trafficking, terrorism, transnational crime, and money laundering have converged to form a law and policy paradigm that points cultural property protection toward national security. As attention to these constituent elements expand and contract over time, so too will the CP/FT paradigm blossom and wither, much in the same way that concern over CP/FT starkly flourished after ISIS militants exploded into public view in 2014, settled with the terrorist group's decline, and ripened with the growth of interest in the BSA and art and antiquities dealers. It is certain that the CP/FT tie, reinforced by unforgettable images of destroyed archaeological sites, will persist in the minds of law and policymakers so long as heritage preservation, counter-transnational crime, and antiterrorism occupy the American public policy agenda. For example, it is anticipated that continued recognition of the nexus will guide DOS's consideration of future cultural property agreements and will direct lawmakers' and federal agencies' efforts to tackle AML/CFT policy and enforcement. Indeed, the grave risks posed by terrorism to national security make it perilous for the White House, Congress, and law enforcement to ignore cultural property's misappropriation, which likely explains why DOJ continues to locate forfeited ISIS cultural property assets; why legislators and stakeholders continue to push for enactment of AML/CFT rules covering the antiquities trade; why customs officers vigilantly search for imports of archaeological material smuggled from Afghanistan, Iraq, Libya, Syria, and Yemen; and why Treasury and FBI officials sustain operations to dislodge illegal financial pipelines from terrorists, TOC, and the legitimate cultural property marketplace. Thus, heritage preservation remains grafted to national security, affording a measure of public policy precedence to international cultural property protection. President Trump's September 2019 appointment of former Cultural Property Advisory Committee member Robert O'Brien to the post of National Security Advisor perhaps exemplifies the pairing. Importantly, the paradigm's long-term credibility and longevity depend on additional intelligence gathering and

[218] ibid.

policymakers' sustained resolve to leverage actionable evidence. Solid information, similar to the secrets uncovered by the 2015 Delta Force raid, will need to be collected to demonstrate that terrorists—not just ISIS—finance their operations through antiquities sales. Other lawmakers, moreover, comparable to Reps. Engel (exiting Congress in January 2021) and Smith will need to muster support for successive bipartisan transnational heritage protection laws. Law enforcement, prosecutors, customs officers, and other authorities, additionally, will need to renew their commitments to support CP/FT solutions pursued by DOJ, ECA, Homeland Security, and Treasury, especially as AML/CFT strategies continue to cross-pollinate cultural property protection. In sum, expect cultural property protection to be spoken about in the context of national security in the coming years, but its importance as a national security priority will wax and wane as terrorist groups, particularly those operating in the MENA region, gain and lose power, money, territory, and influence.

8

Non-Party Obligations for Cultural Property in Armed Conflict under the 1954 Hague Convention, Protocol II

*Elizabeth Varner**

I. Introduction

The 1907 Hague Convention Respecting the Laws and Customs of War on Land (1907 Hague Convention);[1] the 1954 Hague Convention for the Protection of Cultural Property in the Event of Armed Conflict (1954 Hague Convention);[2] the 1977 Protocol to the 1949 Geneva Conventions (Geneva Conventions Protocol I (1977));[3] and the 1999 Second Protocol to the 1954 Hague Convention (Hague Convention Protocol II (1999))[4] advance the protection of cultural property in armed conflict. As these instruments have developed over time, so too have the protections afforded to cultural property.

* DISCLAIMER: This chapter is created in the author's personal capacity. The views expressed are the author's and do not necessarily reflect the views of the US government, Indiana University Robert H. McKinney School of Law, or any other associated entity. This chapter evolved out of the author's talk at a Lawyers Committee for Cultural Heritage Preservation panel with the Blue Shield. Much thanks to Dick Jackson for his insight.

[1] Convention Respecting the Laws and Customs of War on Land and its Annex: Regulations concerning the Laws and Customs of War on Land (opened for signature 18 October 1907, entered into force 26 January 1910) 187 CTS 227 (1907 Hague Convention). Given the parallels and relationship between the 1899 and 1907 Hague Conventions, only the 1907 Hague Convention will be discussed. See Hague Convention with Respect to the Laws and Customs of War on Land and its Annex: Regulations concerning the Laws and Customs of War on Land (adopted 29 July 1899, entered into force 4 September 1900) 187 CTS 429.

[2] Convention for the Protection of Cultural Property in the Event of Armed Conflict (adopted 14 May 1954, entered into force 7 August 1956) 249 UNTS 240 (1954 Hague Convention).

[3] Protocol Additional to the Geneva Conventions of 12 August 1949, and Relating to the Protection of Victims of International Armed Conflicts (adopted 8 June 1977, opened for signature 12 December 1977, entered into force 7 December 1978) 1125 UNTS 3 (Geneva Conventions Protocol I).

[4] Second Protocol to the Hague Convention of 1954 for the Protection of Cultural Property in the Event of Armed Conflict (adopted 26 March 1999, entered into force 9 March 2004) 253 UNTS 172 (Hague Convention Protocol II (1999).

Elizabeth Varner, *Non-Party Obligations for Cultural Property in Armed Conflict under the 1954 Hague Convention, Protocol II* In: *The Preservation of Art and Culture in Times of War.* Edited by: Claire Finkelstein, Derek Gillman, and Frederik Rosén, Oxford University Press. © Oxford University Press 2022. DOI: 10.1093/oso/9780197610565.003.0009

While some States, such as the United Kingdom, are Parties to the 1954 Hague Convention and both its protocols, others have ratified the 1954 Hague Convention but not the Hague Convention Protocol II (1999). This is significant as the Protocol came more than forty years after the 1954 Hague Convention and was intended to tighten the perceived loopholes or problematic aspects in the 1954 Hague Convention—chief among them being the concern over military necessity.

The Geneva Conventions Protocol I (1977) influenced the later Hague Convention Protocol II (1999), which opened for signature in 1999.[5] Many of the provisions in the Geneva Conventions Protocol I (1977) are considered international customary law, such that even if a State is not a Party to the Protocol it might be obligated to comply with provisions contained therein. As a result, some provisions in the Hague Convention Protocol II (1999) that were influenced by the 1977 Geneva Conventions Protocol I might be considered international customary law. In such a case, even if a State is not a Party to the Hague Convention Protocol II (1999), it might have obligations encapsulated in the Hague Convention Protocol II (1999).[6] Within this framework of inquiry, consider how the Hague Convention Protocol II (1999) modifies the obligations within the 1954 Hague Convention, particularly with respect to military necessity. If Hague Convention Protocol II (1999) provisions are customary international law, the State must comply with these customary international law obligations even if it is not a Party to the Protocol.

[5] See International Committee of the Red Cross, "Treaties, State Parties and Commentaries, Second Protocol to the Hague Convention of 1954 for the Protection of Cultural Property in the Event of Armed Conflict The Hague, 26 March 1999" <https://ihl-databases.icrc.org/applic/ihl/ihl.nsf/Treaty.xsp?action=openDocument&do cumentId=F0628265ED4F2118412567BB003E0B0C> accessed 19 March 2017.

[6] This chapter will start with the presumption that the Geneva Conventions Protocol I (1977) is customary international law and if the Hague Convention Protocol II (1999) provision fits within Geneva Conventions Protocol I (1977), it too is customary international law. Arguments abound, however, on what constitutes customary international law, but the threshold inquiry is generally States' actual practice and *opinio juris*. For a more nuanced discussion on how to determine if instrument provisions constitute customary international law, see Elizabeth Varner, 'The Art of Armed Conflicts: An Analysis of the United States' Legal Requirements towards Cultural Property under the 1954 Hague Convention' (2011) 44 Creighton Law Review 28. Rather than conducting an analysis of any one State however, this chapter will take a hybrid analysis of looking at international organizations' arguments and one State's—the United States'—Law of War manual to determine if provisions of the Hague Convention Protocol II (1999) are customary international law. Of interest, the Preface to the US Law of War manual specifies that the inspiration for the service-wide manual was in anticipation of the US' ratification of the 1977 Additional Protocols to the 1949 Geneva Conventions, which did not happen, to aid in their implementation. US Department of Defense, *Law of War Manual* (2016) (US LOW Manual) v. Moreover, the United States has indicated that its practice is consistent with Geneva Conventions Protocol I (1977). Brian Egan, "International Law, Legal Diplomacy, and the Counter-ISIL Campaign: Some Observations" (2016) 92 International Law Studies.

This chapter will focus on the Hague Convention Protocol II (1999) Article 6, Respect for Cultural Property, and, to a lesser degree, Article 7, Precautions in Attack, in order to analyze (1) interpretations of the Hague Convention Protocol II, Article 6, Respect for Cultural Property, which restricts the invocation of military necessity; (2) if the obligations in the Hague Convention Protocol II (1999), Article 6, Respect for Cultural Property, are customary international law; and (3) the extent to which States that have not ratified the Hague Convention Protocol II (1999), particularly the United States, might have obligations encapsulated in that article. This analysis will occur by evaluating Article 6 provision by provision.

> Hague Convention Protocol II, Article 6, Respect for Cultural Property, states:
>
> With the goal of ensuring respect for cultural property in accordance with Article 4 of the Convention:
>
> a. a waiver on the basis of imperative military necessity pursuant to Article 4 paragraph 2 of the Convention may only be invoked to direct an act of hostility *against* cultural property when and for as long as:
>   i. that cultural property has, by its function, been made into a military objective; and
>   ii. there is no feasible alternative available to obtain a similar military advantage to that offered by directing an act of hostility against that objective;
>
> b. a waiver on the basis of imperative military necessity pursuant to Article 4 paragraph 2 of the Convention may only be invoked to *use* cultural property for purposes which are likely to expose it to destruction or damage when and for as long as no choice is possible between such use of the cultural property and another feasible method for obtaining a similar military advantage;
>
> c. the decision to invoke imperative military necessity shall only be taken by an officer commanding a force the equivalent of a battalion in size or larger, or a force smaller in size where circumstances do not permit otherwise;
>
> d. in case of an attack based on a decision taken in accordance with sub-paragraph (a), an effective advance warning shall be given whenever circumstances permit.[7]

[7] Emphasis added.

II. Military Necessity

Provisions for military necessity are included in the 1954 Hague Convention, the Geneva Conventions Protocol I (1977), and the Hague Convention Protocol II (1999). Concerns with the concept of "military necessity" and how to properly interpret it have developed over time as demonstrated by the evolution of these instruments. Some States, such as the United States, which has only ratified the 1954 Hague Convention of the three instruments previously referenced, consider military necessity to be a foundational principle of the Law of War (LOW).[8] Others consider military necessity to be too ambiguous and a case of the exception swallowing the rule. These concerns and attempts to manage them are manifested in the Hague Convention Protocol II (1999).

A. What is Military Necessity?

General Dwight D. Eisenhower famously said in World War II:

> If we have to choose between destroying a famous building and sacrificing our own men, then our men's lives count infinitely more and the building must go. But the choice is not always so clear-cut as that. In many cases the monuments can be spared without any detriment to operational needs. Nothing can stand against the argument of military necessity. That is an accepted principle. But the phrase "military necessity" is sometimes used where it would be more truthful to speak of military convenience or even personal convenience. I do not want it to cloak slackness or indifference.[9]

As referenced in Eisenhower's quote, military necessity is a principle of the LOW. Military necessity justifies departures from what is normally allowed when the principle is incorporated into the LOW. The US Department of Defense LOW Manual states that military necessity is a "principle that justifies the use of all measures needed to defeat the enemy as quickly and efficiently as possible that are not prohibited by the law of war."[10] Other

[8] See US LOW Manual 52–57, 275–77.
[9] General Dwight D Eisenhower, Commander-in-Chief, US Army, "Memorandum Regarding the Protection of Historical Monuments in Italy" (29 December 1943). Emphasis added.
[10] US LOW Manual 52–57, 275–77.

foundational principles include those of proportionality and distinction/discrimination, which will be discussed later in this chapter.

Under the 1907 Hague Convention, property is not to be destroyed or seized unless there is imperative military necessity.[11] Pursuant to the 1954 Hague Convention, Article 4, Respect for Cultural Property, Parties must respect cultural property which "may be waived only in cases where military necessity imperatively requires such a waiver."[12] The Geneva Conventions Protocol I (1977), unlike the 1954 Hague Convention and the Hague Convention Protocol II (1999), is not exclusively focused on cultural property, but does contain Article 53, Protection of Cultural Objects and of Places of Worship. Notably, military necessity is not included within Article 53.

The International Committee of the Red Cross (ICRC) stated, "In 1977, Protocol I did away with this approach [ie cultural property can be attacked in case of 'imperative military necessity']. Henceforth, only military objectives—more clearly defined and more carefully selected—should be made the object of attack. It appeared self-evident that any improvement of the 1954 Convention should reflect this modern approach: cultural property is civilian property and it should not be attacked unless when it becomes a military objective."[13] The ICRC further clarified in the commentary to Rule 38, Attacks Against Cultural Property, that the threshold for the definition of cultural property in Geneva Conventions Protocol I (1977) was much higher and that there was no imperative military necessity waiver for attacking cultural property under Article 53.[14]

It is notable that Article 53 said, "without prejudice to the provisions of the Hague Convention for the Protection of Cultural Property in the Event of Armed Conflict of 14 May 1954, and of other relevant international instruments," suggesting that the absence of the term "military necessity" in the Geneva Convention Protocol I (1977), Article 53, does not override the 1954 Hague Convention provision on military necessity. It would be an odd result if civilian property under the Geneva Convention Protocol I (1977),

[11] 1907 Hague Convention, art 23(g).

[12] 1954 Hague Convention, art 4(2).

[13] International Committee of the Red Cross, "Treaties, State Parties and Commentaries, Second Protocol to the Hague Convention of 1954 for the Protection of Cultural Property in the Event of Armed Conflict The Hague, 26 March 1999" <https://ihl-databases.icrc.org/ihl/INTRO/590> accessed 22 February 2020. See Geneva Protocol I (1977), art 52.

[14] International Committee of the Red Cross, "IHL Database" <https://ihl-databases.icrc.org/customary-ihl/eng/docs/v1_rul_rule38> accessed 25 January 2020. Similar commentary exists for Rule 39, Use of Cultural Property for Military Purposes. ibid.

Article 52, which requires that only military objectives be attacked, was afforded more protection than cultural property. Typically, if an object or site does not fit within the threshold definition of cultural property, it could receive some protections as civilian or enemy property as seen in the 1907 Hague Convention.[15]

As in the case of the 1954 Hague Convention, Hague Convention Protocol II (1999), Article 6 uses the term "imperative" to modify "military necessity" such that there is an "imperative military necessity" exception to directing attacks against or using cultural property in a manner that would expose it to harm if the various parameters discussed are met. The ICRC Customary International Humanitarian Law (IHL) database includes the Hague Convention Protocol II, Article 6, restrictions in the explanation to Rule 38, Attacks against Cultural Property; and Rule 39, Use of Cultural Property for Military Purposes, specifically that the Hague Convention Protocol II "brings the Hague Convention up to date in the light of developments in international humanitarian law since 1954" and the Article 6 restrictions "clarify [the 1954 Hague Convention's] meaning" of imperative military necessity. The ICRC's IHL Rule 38 and Rule 39 both recognize imperative military necessity waivers to attacking or using cultural property in a manner that could damage it.

Consequently, it seems that imperative military necessity waivers to direct attacks against or use cultural property in a manner that would damage it are generally recognized; for attacks, however, imperative military necessity alone will likely not suffice, rather the cultural property would have to be a military objective. The United States agrees with the viewpoint requiring that an object be a military objective before there is military necessity to attack it, which will be discussed in the next section.

B. Directed Attacks and/or Use

Neither the Hague Convention Protocol II (1999), Article 6; the 1954 Hague Convention, Article 4, that the Hague Convention Protocol II (1999), Article 6, references; nor ICRC, Customary IHL permit attacks or hostilities against cultural property or use of cultural property that is likely to subject it to harm unless there is imperative military necessity.

[15] 1907 Hague Convention, art 23(g).

Hague Convention Protocol II (1999), however, further narrows the military necessity exception from that of the 1954 Hague Convention. For directed attacks, restrictions on imperative military necessity require that the cultural property is a military objective and there is no feasible alternative to obtain a similar military advantage. This echoes the Geneva Conventions Protocol I (1977), Article 53, which does not permit acts of hostility against cultural property, unless perhaps it has become a military objective under Article 52, nor use of cultural property in support of the military effort. The US DOD LOW Manual has noted that the "definition of military objective may be viewed as a way of evaluating whether military necessity exists to attack an object,"[16] showing that the United States considers that cultural property must be a military objective before military necessity justifies attacking cultural property.

For use of cultural property that is likely to expose it to destruction, the Hague Convention Protocol II (1999) includes an additional restriction that no other feasible choice is possible for a similar military advantage. One Party's use of cultural property can potentially generate another Party's justification to direct attacks against it. This is seen in the 1907 Hague Convention where cultural monuments are to be spared if they are not used for military purposes.[17] The US DOD LOW Manual notes that imperative military necessity can be invoked "when an enemy uses cultural property and its immediate surroundings to protect legitimate military targets, in violation of Article 4(1)."[18] Even if there is imperative military necessity that legally permits a waiver of the protection of cultural property, "as a matter of policy, decision-makers may still seek to refrain from harming cultural property."[19]

C. Military Objectives

As just seen, the Geneva Conventions Protocol I (1977), Article 52, and Hague Convention Protocol II (1999), Article 6(a)(i), require that cultural property be a military objective before it is attacked or acts of hostility are directed against it. The US Joint Publication 3-60, Joint Targeting, noted, "As long as buildings and monuments devoted to religion, art, charitable

16 US LOW Manual 210.
17 See also 1907 Hague Convention, art 27.
18 US Department of Defense, *Conduct of the Persian Gulf War: A Report to Congress* (1992).
19 US LOW Manual 277.

purposes, or historical sites are not used for military purposes, they may not be targets."[20] As a requirement of ICRC Rule 38, "Special care must be taken in military operations to avoid damage to buildings dedicated to religion, art, science, education or charitable purposes and historic monuments unless they are military objectives."

The definitions of a military objective in the Geneva Conventions Protocol I (1977);[21] the Hague Convention Protocol II (1999);[22] and the DOD LOW Manual[23] are similar with regard to the following key elements: (1) an object; (2) that by its nature, location, purpose, or use; (3) makes an effective contribution to military action; (4) and whose total or partial destruction, capture, or neutralization; (5) in the circumstances ruling at the time; (6) offers a definite military advantage.[24] While these definitions for a military objective focus on an object's "nature, location, purpose, or use," the Hague Convention Protocol II (1999), Article 6(a)(i), furthers the requirements by stating that the "function" of the cultural property must have made it into a military objective. Jiří Toman, in his commentary to the Hague Convention Protocol II, noted that the term "function" is a compromise between those who disputed that cultural property could ever inherently be a military objective (i.e., by its nature, location, or purpose) and others who were unwilling to restrict the definition of military objective to the object's use.[25] This "function" restriction on cultural property being a military objective might have increased the threshold for the invocation of military necessity in Hague Convention Protocol II (1999) more so than other instruments. The previously mentioned instruments' definitions of military objective would potentially permit some cultural property to be a military objective by virtue of its inherent nature, location, or purpose such as historic bridges and fortified sites (e.g., castles), especially those in advantageous locations (e.g., higher ground, sites that could control a passage). This, however, is subject to interpretation as some might consider "function" to be synonymous with the military advantage requirement discussed next.[26]

[20] US Joint Chiefs of Staff, *Joint Publication 3-60, Joint Targeting* (2013).

[21] Geneva Conventions Protocol I (1977), art 52(2).

[22] Hague Convention Protocol II (1999), art 1(f).

[23] US LOW Manual 206.

[24] See UNESCO, *Protection of Cultural Property Military Manual* (2016) 93 (stating that cultural "property will constitute a military objective only if its total or partial destruction, capture or neutralization, in the circumstances ruling at the time, offers a definite military advantage").

[25] Jiří Toman, *Cultural Property in War: Improvement in Protection, Commentary on the 1999 Second Protocol to the Hague Convention of 1954 for the Protection of Cultural Property in the Event of Armed Conflict* (UNESCO 2009) 107–09.

[26] Conversation with Dick Jackson, Professor of Law and DOD attorney (ret) (29 February 2020).

D. Feasible Alternative/Method to Obtain a Similar Military Advantage

In addition to requiring cultural property to be a military objective before attacks are directed against it, the Hague Convention Protocol II (1999) further narrows the military necessity exception in cases where attacks are directed against cultural property or where cultural property is used in a manner likely to cause damage. In both of these instances, the Hague Convention Protocol II (1999), Article 6(a)(ii) and (b), have similar language requiring that there be "no feasible alternative[s]" or not "another feasible method" "to obtain a similar military advantage." Consequently, the key terms involving feasibility and military advantage will be analyzed together.

1. Feasibility

Toman wrote that the Geneva Conventions Protocol I, Article 57(3) was the model for the Hague Convention Protocol II, Article 6(a)(ii) and (b) feasibility and military advantage requirements.[27] Both the Geneva Conventions Protocol I, Article 57(3), and the Hague Convention Protocol II, Article 6(a)(ii) and (b), contemplate alternative options for obtaining a similar military advantage that would result in less harm to protected objects. The strength of the language in the Geneva Conventions Protocol I, Article 57(3) (e.g., "when a choice is possible"), however, is more permissive than the language in the Hague Convention Protocol II, Article 6(a)(ii) and (b), which includes phrases such as, "there is no feasible alternative available to obtain a similar military advantage" and "no choice is possible between such use of the cultural property and another feasible method for obtaining a similar military advantage."[28]

The DOD LOW Manual further clarifies the US' understanding of feasibility. While the Hague Convention Protocol II's (1999) use of feasibility comes across as a strong barrier to attacking or using cultural property, the DOD LOW Manual clarifies that synonyms to the term "feasibility," albeit in discussions of precautions similar to that of Geneva Conventions Protocol I, Article 57, have included "[t]he words 'practicable,' 'reasonable,' 'due,' and 'necessary'" and that feasibility is more a matter of "due regard or diligence, not an absolute requirement to do everything possible."[29] Consequently, the

[27] Toman (n 26) 117–18.
[28] Hague Convention Protocol II (1999), art 6(a)(ii),(b).
[29] US LOW Manual 189–92.

United States likely interprets "feasibility" provisions as qualifying whatever obligations it modifies.

There are alternative views. J.M. Henckaerts, legal adviser in the Legal Division of the International Committee of the Red Cross and head of the project to update the Commentaries on the 1949 Geneva Conventions and the Additional Protocols of 1977, noted that this provision in Hague Convention Protocol II, Article 6, means that "when there is a choice between several military objectives and one of them is a cultural property, the latter shall not be attacked," such that military necessity will almost never justify attacking cultural property.[30] Scholar Roger O'Keefe noted that "attacking cultural property is a last resort."[31] Consequently, some interpret Hague Convention Protocol II, Article 6, "feasibility" language as a firm barrier to invocation of military necessity to attack or use cultural property in a manner that would damage it.

Upon delving deeper into "feasibility," it is apparent that "feasibility" is frequently associated with "precautions." For example, Geneva Conventions Protocol I, Article 57(3), is titled *Precautions in Attack*. The ICRC noted, "[t]he updating of the 1954 Convention in light of Protocol I also led to the inclusion of rules concerning precautions in attack that are found in Protocol I."[32] ICRC, Customary IHL, Rule 15, echoes Hague Convention Protocol II 7(b).

The placement of Geneva Conventions Protocol I, Article 57(3), and Hague Convention Protocol II, Article 6, is different within their respective texts. Geneva Conventions Protocol I, Article 57(3), is titled *Precautions in Attack*; while Hague Convention Protocol II, Article 6, is titled *Respect for Cultural Property*. This change in title is notable given that nearly every provision from Geneva Conventions Protocol I, Article 57, was incorporated and divided into either Hague Convention Protocol II, Article 6, *Respect for Cultural Property*, or Article 7, *Precautions in Attack*, suggesting that there was some intent behind the decision to split them. It is possible that the decision was to take the evaluation of military necessity out of the precautions section, which typically occurs after a valid military target is determined and applies to mitigate the effect, and move it to the actual targeting decision to

[30] Jean-Marie Henckaerts, "New Rules for the Protection of Cultural Property in Armed Conflict" (1999) International Review of the Red Cross 835.

[31] UNESCO (n 25) s 94.

[32] International Committee of the Red Cross, "Treaties, State Parties and Commentaries" <https://ihl-databases.icrc.org/ihl/INTRO/590> accessed 20 January 2020.

enhance the protection of cultural property. In practice, this typically happens in offensive attacks when there is time.[33] This change in placement, which allows analyses to occur earlier in the process, suggests heightened protections from that of the Geneva Conventions Protocol I. Consequently, it seems that Hague Convention Protocol II sets a higher bar for not attacking or using cultural property than does Geneva Conventions Protocol I.

The underlying obligations of the precautions are found throughout the LOW. The precaution sections in the DOD LOW Manual incorporate DOD principles such as distinction and proportionality, as well as concepts such as tailoring means and methods in the targeting process to minimize harm to civilian objects. The DOD LOW Manual, however, notes that the requirement of choosing a less damaging alternative in the Geneva Conventions Protocol I, Article 57(3), is not customary international law[34] nor is it an absolute obligation.[35] Given that Article 57 is more permissive than the Hague Convention Protocol II, Article 6(a)(ii) or (b), it is unlikely the United States would consider Article 6(a)(ii) or (b) customary international law or an absolute obligation.

2. Military Advantage.

Another key term in the Hague Convention Protocol II, Article 6(a)(ii) and (b) is "military advantage." The Geneva Conventions Protocol I (1977), Article 57(3), Precautions in Attack, and Hague Convention Protocol II (1999), Article 6, Respect for Cultural Property, (aii) and (b), all have provisions for "similar military advantage."

The DOD LOW Manual clarifies military advantage in terms of timing and scope. In regard to timing, the LOW Manual notes that the advantage need not be immediate. For scope of the military advantage, the DOD LOW Manual specifies that the advantage is not restricted to any part, such as the current mission, but can apply to a broader impact, such as the overall war strategy.[36] This is intriguing as presumptively the overall war strategy would include winning the hearts and minds of the local population or, at least, working to not antagonize them into impeding the war effort: damage or destruction of cultural property would most assuredly cause friction. The

[33] See US Joint Chiefs of Staff (n 21) noting that cultural property on the no-strike list are not valid targets.

[34] US LOW Manual 240.

[35] International Committee of the Red Cross, "Customary IHL Database, Rule 21, Target Selection" <https://ihl-databases.icrc.org/customary-ihl/eng/docs/v1_rul> accessed 19 March 2017.

[36] US LOW Manual 211–12.

broad scope of the interpretation of "military advantage" could result in an increased threshold for the invocation of military necessity and concomitant harm to cultural property, as seen perhaps in the No-Strike Lists. There has been concern, however, that "military advantage" within the definition of military objective is too limiting; the US' interpretation of "military advantage" includes targets that further war-sustaining capability, indicating some interpretations will be broader and necessarily reduce protections afforded to cultural property.[37]

III. Authorization Required to Invoke Military Necessity

Further restrictions on invoking military necessity include setting a rank that can invoke military necessity. The Hague Convention Protocol II (1999), Article 6(c), requires that "the decision to invoke imperative military necessity shall only be taken by an officer commanding a force the equivalent of a battalion in size or larger, or a force smaller in size where circumstances do not permit otherwise." Thus, the Hague Convention Protocol II (1999) establishes a level of responsibility, and floor for liability, for those that can invoke military necessity, albeit with a mitigating provision if circumstances require it. The burden and responsibility is limited to those higher in rank.

The Geneva Conventions Protocol I (1977), Article 57(2)(a), however, merely refers to "those who plan or decide upon an attack" and requires that they take precautions: target verification, means and methods, and proportionality. The 1954 Hague Convention did not specify an authorization level for general cultural property. The DOD Law of War Manual uses the generic term of "commander": battalion level of approval is not mentioned,[38] which is different from the Hague Convention Protocol II (1999). US targeting processes specify approval levels for special targets, which are typically included in classified rules of engagement.[39]

In practice, the authorization requirement in the Hague Convention Protocol II (1999), Article 6(c), is probably upheld in the United States under current targeting processes.[40] Benefits of requiring a higher level of command

[37] Toman (n 26) 116–17; Egan (n 7).

[38] But see US Joint Chiefs of Staff (n 21).

[39] ibid. Conversation with Dick Jackson, Professor of Law and DOD Attorney (ret) (29 February 2020).

[40] See US Joint Chiefs of Staff (n 21); Telephone Conversation with Geoffrey Corn, Professor of Law and Presidential Research Fellow at South Texas College of Law Houston (7 March 2017).

to authorize the attack include time, experience, resources to generate alternatives, and more information. The term "attacks," however, applies to offensive as well as defensive "acts of violence against the adversary."[41] Defensive attacks, in practice, do not require as high an authorization to protect troops given that there is less time and consequently less ability to conduct the inquiry as fully.[42] These issues are likely mitigated by the Hague Convention Protocol II (1999), Article 6(c), clause "as circumstances permit."

IV. Effective Advance Warning

The Hague Convention Protocol II (1999), Article 6(d), requires that "in case of an attack . . . an effective advance warning shall be given whenever circumstances permit." Advance warning requirements have been required in Geneva Conventions Protocol I (1977), Article 57(2)(c), and the ICRC considers this requirement to be part of customary international law.[43] The DOD LOW Manual recognizes that feasible precautions in conducting attacks to reduce the harm to protected objects include advance warning if circumstances permit. The DOD LOW Manual's interpretation of "effectiveness" for the advance warning is broad and case specific.[44] Nonetheless, it is likely the United States is already compliant with the Hague Convention Protocol II (1999), Article 6(d), requirements of effective advance warning, especially with the mitigating clause "whenever circumstances permit."

V. Conclusion: Obligations Under Hague Convention Protocol II, Article 6

There is much overlap between some provisions advancing the protection of cultural property in the Geneva Conventions Protocol I (1977) and that in the Hague Convention Protocol II (1999), Article 6, for the invocation of military necessity. If these instruments were exactly the same, however,

[41] Geneva Conventions Protocol I (1977), art 49(1).
[42] Telephone Conversation with Geoffrey Corn, Professor of Law and Presidential Research Fellow at South Texas College of Law Houston (7 March 2017).
[43] International Committee of the Red Cross, "Customary IHL Database, Rule 20, Advance Warning" <https://ihl-databases.icrc.org/customary-ihl/eng/docs/v1_rul_rule20> accessed 22 February 2020.
[44] US LOW Manual 237.

there would not be the ongoing query of whether the provisions of the Geneva Convention Protocol I (1977) generally considered customary international law require compliance with the Hague Convention Protocol II (1999), Article 6. The crucial differences between the Geneva Conventions Protocol I (1977) and the Hague Convention Protocol II (1999), Article 6, obligations are that the latter contains restriction on cultural property not being targeted unless it is a military objective by function; more stringent, no feasible alternatives to obtain a similar military advantage language; and higher level of approval.

Acceptance of obligations under the Hague Convention Protocol II (1999) by States that have not ratified the Hague Convention Protocol II (1999), Article 6, would depend on interpretation of the provisions. The United States probably already generally follows Article 6 under interpretations provided in the DOD LOW Manual, but would likely dispute more rigorous interpretations of Article 6. Given the US' participation in negotiations in the Hague Convention Protocol II (1999) and the similar provisions of the Geneva Convention Protocol I (1977) that were incorporated into the 1996 Protocol on Prohibitions or Restriction on the Use of Mines, Booby-Traps and Other Devices (1996 CCW Protocol), which the United States is a Party to, it is likely that the United States would have only agreed to its own interpretations of existing obligations under the Geneva Convention Protocol I (1977).[45] Moreover, key US participants have focused not only on restrictions in targeting, but rights thereof under the LOW, indicating that a restrictive interpretation is not likely.[46]

[45] Conversation with Dick Jackson, Professor of Law and DOD Attorney (ret) (29 February 2020). The Convention on Prohibitions or Restrictions on the Use of Certain Conventional Weapons Which May Be Deemed to Be Excessively Injurious or to Have Indiscriminate Effects (adopted 10 October 1980, entered into force 2 December 1983, amended 21 December 2001) 1342 UNTS 137.

[46] See Hays Park, "Rolling Thunder and the Law of War" (1982) Air University Review.

9

The International Criminal Court and Cultural Property

What Is the Crime?

*Mark A. Drumbl**

I. Introduction

This chapter examines the war crime of intentional attacks on cultural property and cultural heritage.[1] It does so through the lens of the policy and practice of the International Criminal Court (ICC). This is a fruitful lens for a number of reasons. The ICC Statute (the Rome Statute or simply the Statute)[2] prohibits as a war crime the intentional direction of attacks against buildings dedicated to religion, education, art, science or charitable purposes, historic monuments, hospitals, or places where the sick and wounded are collected which are not military objectives in international (IACs)[3] and non-international armed conflict (NIACs)[4]. What is more, the ICC's third

* Some sections herein draw from, though in places update Mark A. Drumbl, "From Timbuktu to The Hague and Beyond: The War Crime of Intentionally Attacking Cultural Property" (2019) 17 Journal of International Criminal Justice 77.

[1] For the purpose of the present chapter, the phrases "cultural property" and "cultural heritage" will be used interchangeably. We naturally recognize that uncertainty abounds within scholarship and practice about the overlaps, congruences, and differences—along with suitabilities—of each of these two terms. That said, we deploy them interchangeably. Contestations between the terms "cultural property" and "cultural heritage," however important, are dealt with elsewhere and are not a concern of this chapter, whose main goal is to set out the conceptual and semantic contributions of international criminal law, and the Rome Statute in particular. For more generalized discussion of the use of "property" and "heritage" see, inter alia, Manlio Frigo, "Cultural Property v Cultural Heritage: A 'Battle of Concepts' in International Law?" (2004) 86 International Review of the Red Cross 367; Janet Blake, "On Defining the Cultural Heritage" (2000) 49 International Journal & Comparative Law Quarterly 61; Lyndel V. Prott and Patrick J. O'Keefe, "'Cultural Heritage" or 'Cultural Property'?" (1992) 1 International Journal of Cultural Property 307. Please note that, unless otherwise stated, sources, including cases and materials, are up to date as of May 2020.

[2] Rome Statute of the International Criminal Court (adopted 17 July 1998, entered into force 1 July 2002) 2187 UNTS 3 (ICC Statute).

[3] ibid art 8(2)(b)(ix).

[4] ibid art 8(2)(e)(iv).

Mark A. Drumbl, *The International Criminal Court and Cultural Property* In: *The Preservation of Art and Culture in Times of War.* Edited by: Claire Finkelstein, Derek Gillman, and Frederik Rosén, Oxford University Press. © Oxford University Press 2022. DOI: 10.1093/oso/9780197610565.003.0010

conviction—that of Ahmad Al Faqi Al Mahdi (Al Mahdi), for conduct committed in Timbuktu, Mali—was entered solely on this charge.[5] Al Mahdi pled guilty and received a nine-year sentence. The ICC also has awarded reparations for the destruction of the shrines for which Al Mahdi had been convicted. The *Al Mahdi* case represents the first time that charges have been brought before the ICC for the war crime of intentional attacks on cultural property.[6] This means that the definitions, concepts, semantics, and vernaculars of international criminal law, as implemented through the ICC, become invoked in the quest to protect cultural property. This chapter will present, situate, and analyze this language. While beyond contemplation at the time *Al Mahdi* was decided, the responsive social distancing and lockdowns due to the COVID-19 pandemic, and concomitant burgeoning of virtuality, do challenge the ongoing "physicality" of cultural property as necessarily central to its existence and enjoyment. This chapter ends with a handful of reflections on this very recent development.

Although the term "culture" is not explicitly mentioned in the definition of the crime, Al Mahdi was prosecuted for conduct prosecutors and ICC judges characterized as attacks upon religious and historical buildings and broadly cast as targeting of "cultural property,"[7] a phrase that the 1954 Hague Convention[8] expressly invokes. On the one hand, it is somewhat vexing, from a legalist perspective, that the term "cultural" entered the lexicon of ICC proceedings even though it absents itself from the actual language of the prohibited crime in the Rome Statute. On the other hand, the use of the term "cultural property" as shorthand for the objects of the attack reveals the heart of the proceedings. The *Al Mahdi* case, moreover, forms part of a broader effort by the ICC Office of the Prosecutor (the OTP) to address cultural property crimes, which this chapter details along with other policy

[5] *Prosecutor v Ahmad Al Faqi Al Mahdi* (Judgment and Sentence) ICC-01/12-01/15 (27 September 2016). See also Marlise Simons, "Prison Sentence Over Smashing of Shrines in Timbuktu: 9 Years" *New York Times* (27 September 2016) <https://www.nytimes.com/2016/09/28/world/europe/ahmad-al-faqi-al-mahdi-timbuktu-mali.html> accessed 30 May 2020.

[6] See generally Mark S Ellis, "The ICC's Role in Combatting the Destruction of Cultural Heritage" (2017) 49 Case Western Reserve Journal of International Law 23, 24.

[7] *Al Mahdi* (n 7) [14].

[8] Convention for the Protection of Cultural Property in the Event of Armed Conflict (adopted 14 May 1954, entered into force 7 August 1956) 249 UNTS 215 (Hague Convention of 1954). See also its protocols: Protocol to the Convention for the Protection of Cultural Property in the Event of Armed Conflict (adopted 14 May 1954, entered into force 7 August 1956) 249 UNTS 215; Second Protocol to the Hague Convention of 1954 for the Protection of Cultural Property in the Event of Armed Conflict (adopted 26 March 1999, entered into force 9 March 2004) 2253 UNTS 172 (Second Protocol to Hague Convention of 1999).

developments and cooperation agreements between the OTP and the United Nations Educational, Scientific, and Cultural Organization (UNESCO). Moreover, a second accused from the Mali situation, Timbuktu Islamic Police chief Al Hassan Ag Abdoul Aziz Ag Mohamed Ag Mahmoud (Al Hassan), is in ICC custody and faces an array of charges that includes intentional attacks on cultural property.[9] An ICC pre-trial chamber confirmed charges in this case,[10] a trial chamber has been constituted at the end of 2019,[11] and the trial opened on July 14, 2020.[12]

With the *Al Mahdi* case conceiving offenses against cultural property as autonomous, rather than merely auxiliary, crimes,[13] the protection of cultural property by international criminal law has garnered growing attention from the international legal arena.[14] To be clear, the ICC is not the first

[9] See the developments of the case at <https://www.icc-cpi.int/mali/al-hassan> accessed 30 May 2020.

[10] *Procureur v Al Hassan Ag Abdoul Aziz Ag Mohamed Ag Mahmoud* (Rectificatif à la Décision relative à la confirmation des charges portées contre Al Hassan Ag Abdoul Aziz Ag Mohamed Ag Mahmoud) ICC-01/12-01/18, (13 novembre 2019) (available in French only). This decision was confirmed by the ICC appeals chamber in early 2020: *Prosecutor v Al Hassan Ag Abdoul Aziz Ag Mohamed Ag Mahmoud* (Judgment on the appeal of Mr Al Hassan against the decision of pre-trial chamber I entitled "Décision relative à l'"exception d'irrecevabilité pour insuffisance de gravité de l'affaire soulevée par la défense') ICC-01/12-01/18 OA (19 February 2020).

[11] *Prosecutor v Al Hassan Ag Abdoul Aziz Ag Mohamed Ag Mahmoud* (Decision constituting trial chamber X and referring to it the case of The Prosecutor v Al Hassan Ag Abdoul Aziz Ag Mohamed Ag Mahmoud) ICC-01/12-01/18 (21 November 2019).

[12] *Prosecutor v Al Hassan Ag Abdoul Aziz Ag Mohamed Ag Mahmoud* (Decision Setting the Commencement Date of the Trial) ICC-01/12-01/18 (6 January 2020). On April 23, 2020, the ICC Pre-trial chamber I issued a confidential decision partially granting the Prosecutor's request to modify the charges against the accused to include additional facts: *Procureur c Al Hassan Ag Abdoul Aziz Ag Mohamed Ag Mahmoud* (Version publique expurgée du Rectificatif de la Décision portant modification des charges confirmées le 30 septembre 2019 à l'encontre d'Al Hassan Ag Abdoul Aziz Ag Mohamed Ag Mahmoud, 23 avril 2020, ICC-01/12-01/18-767-Conf) ICC-01/12-01/18 (8 mai 2020) (available in French only). See also Press Release, "Al Hassan trial opens at International Criminal Court" (14 July 2020) <https://www.icc-cpi.int/Pages/item.aspx?name=pr1531> accessed 28 August 2020.

[13] See also Emily McGeorge, "Prosecution of Cultural Heritage Destruction: Framework, Precedents and Recent Developments in International Criminal Law" (2016) 3 Public Interest Law Journal of New Zealand 204, 227; Philippa Webb, "Foreword. Culture at the Frontline: Addressing Attacks on Cultural Heritage" (2016) 14 Journal of International Criminal Justice 1139; Paige Casaly, "Al Mahdi before the ICC. Cultural Property and World Heritage in International Criminal Law" (2016) 14 Journal of International Criminal Justice 1199.

[14] See ex multis: Roger O'Keefe, "Cultural Heritage and International Criminal Law" in Sébastien Jodoin and Marie-Claire Cordonier Segger (eds), *Sustainable Development, International Criminal Justice and Treaty Implementation* (CUP 2013) 120; Roger O'Keefe, "Protection of Cultural Property" in Dieter Fleck (ed), *The Handbook of International Humanitarian Law* (OUP 2013) 425; Waseem A Qureshi, "The Protection of Cultural Heritage by International Law in Armed Conflict" (2017) 15 Loyola University Chicago International Law Review 63; Federico Lenzerini, "The Role of International and Mixed Criminal Courts in the Enforcement of International Norms Concerning the Protection of Cultural Heritage" in Francesco Francioni and James Gordley (eds), *Enforcing International Cultural Heritage Law* (OUP 2013) 40; Andrea Carcano, "The Criminalization and Prosecution of attacks against Cultural Property" in Fausto Pocar, Marco Pedrazzi, and Micaela Frulli (eds), *War Crimes and Conduct of Hostilities* (Edward Elgar 2013) 78; Haydee J Dijkstal, "Destruction

judicial institution to turn to international criminal law to protect cultural property in armed conflict. The International Criminal Tribunal for the former Yugoslavia (ICTY) did so in the context of violence in Dubrovnik, Croatia;[15] the International Military Tribunal at Nuremberg indicted major war criminals for destruction of cultural monuments;[16] and in 1947 the French Permanent Military Tribunal found a civilian guilty of a war crime for destroying a statue of Jeanne d'Arc and a monument commemorating the dead of World War I.[17] The *Al Mahdi* case, however, is a breakthrough in awarding reparations to afflicted populations and in underscoring that the ICC conceptualizes such offenses as war crimes.

In Section II, this chapter sets out details of this war crime as codified in the Rome Statute: it provides for an analysis of the relevant provisions under the Statute and identifies their core features and rationale; additionally, it delivers a brief overview of the ICC for readers who may not be steeped in the details of international criminal law. Section III spells out the *Al Mahdi* proceedings as indicative of the operationalization of this substantive crime. Section IV examines the OTP's conceptualization of the crime, policy initiatives, and broader developments regarding the prosecution of this crime in the future. In Section V, this chapter assumes an interrogatory tone: What role, exactly, can international criminal law play in the protection of cultural property, in the definition of what is "culture," the scope (and beneficiaries) of "protection," and the development of a victimology of cultural property war crimes, namely, who exactly is harmed by them? Section VI concludes by

of Cultural Heritage before the ICC, The Influence of Human Rights on Reparations Proceedings for Victims and the Accused" (2019) 17 Journal of International Criminal Justice 391; Drumbl (n 2).

15 *Prosecutor v Miodrag Jokić* (Sentencing Judgment) IT-01-42/1-S (18 March 2004); *Prosecutor v Pavle Strugar* (Judgment) IT-01-42-T (31 January 2005). Jokić was sentenced to seven years' imprisonment; Strugar to eight years' imprisonment. See however *Al Mahdi* (n 7) [16] (noting that ICTY jurisprudence is of "limited guidance" in light of the fact that the crime in the ICTY Statute "does not govern 'attacks' against cultural objects but rather punishes their 'destruction or willful damage'").

16 *Trial of the Major War Criminals before the International Military Tribunal 14 November 1945–1 October 1946* (International Military Tribunal Nuremberg 1947) Vol I, 55–60, Indictment, Count Three (War Crimes), E (Plunder of Public and Private Property). One scholar notes that "[t]he [International Military Tribunal] held that confiscation and destruction of religious and cultural institutions and objects of Jewish communities amounted to persecution that was a crime against humanity": Ana F Vrdoljak, "The Criminalisation of the Intentional Destruction of Cultural Heritage" (2016) 14 <https://works.bepress.com/ana_filipa_vrdoljak/38/> accessed 30 May 2020.

17 United Nations War Crimes Commission, *Law Reports of Trials of War Criminals* (London 1949) Vol IX, 67, Case No 51, Trial of Karl Lingenfelder (11 March 1947). For a discussion on the evolution of cultural heritage crimes in international criminal law, see Anne-Marie Carstens, "The Swinging Pendulum of Cultural Heritage Crimes in International Criminal Law" in Anne-Marie Carstens and Elizabeth Varner (eds), *Intersections in International Cultural Heritage Law* (OUP 2020) 109.

summarizing but also by opening a window upon a broader conversation, to wit: What is the interplay between criminalizing the destruction of cultural property, on the one hand, and the promotion of transitional justice, on the other, predicated as it may be on resistance to cultures of oppression and impunity? While focusing on the practice and policy of ICC, this chapter also weighs in on questions regarding the more generalizable potentialities and limits of international criminal law when it comes to curbing crimes against cultural property in armed conflict (and beyond).

II. Law: The Rome Statute

A. The ICC and the Crime under Art. 8 of the Court's Statute

While early proposals for an international criminal court arose as early as in 1872,[18] the matter only reached the UN during the 1950s.[19] It was not, however, until Trinidad and Tobago's proposal to reinsert the issue in the UN General Assembly's agenda in 1989 that the drafting process was effectively triggered,[20] ultimately leading to the adoption of the Rome Statute and the establishment of the ICC in the following decade. The wording of art. 1 of the Statute shows that the Court has been conceived as (i) a permanent institution, (ii) with jurisdiction over the most heinous international crimes, and (iii) functioning in complementarity with national and domestic criminal *fora*.[21] The Statute regulates the Court's functioning in every respect and it represents the Court's most relevant enabling source.

According to art. 5 of the Statute, the jurisdiction *ratione materiae* of the ICC covers the crime of genocide, crimes against humanity, war crimes, and the crime of aggression.[22] Crimes against cultural heritage are subsumed under the cloak of war crimes.[23] In particular, arts. 8(2)(b)(ix)[24] and 8(2)

[18] James Crawford, *Brownlie's Principles of International Law* (OUP 2012) 678.

[19] Antonio Cassese, "International Criminal Law" in Malcolm D Evans (ed), *International Law* (OUP 2003) 721, 730. See also Malcolm Shaw, *International Law* (CUP 2008) 410.

[20] Crawford (n 20) 679.

[21] ICC Statute (n 4) art 1.

[22] ibid art 5.

[23] As *per* ibid art 8.

[24] The provision reads as follow: "2. For the purpose of this Statute, 'war crimes' means: . . . (b) Other serious violations of the laws and customs applicable in international armed conflict, within the established framework of international law, namely, any of the following acts: . . . (ix) Intentionally directing attacks against buildings dedicated to religion, education, art, science or charitable

(e)(iv)[25] address such offenses within the domain of IACs and NIACs, respectively.[26] The provisions are built upon other international instruments that dealt with this very issue *pendente bello*, and which, for such reason, did not necessarily adopt an international criminal perspective.[27] It is also noteworthy to mention that it is the ICC elements of crimes (not the Statute itself) which qualify such offenses as crimes targeting "protected objects," perhaps suggesting that we consider the law governing them as *lex specialis*.[28]

When identifying offenses against cultural heritage, respectively, in IACs and NIACs,[29] the two provisions employ the very same terminology.[30] In other words, the ICC Statute does not alter its definition of crimes against cultural heritage depending on the type of armed conflict at issue, namely,

purposes, historic monuments, hospitals and places where the sick and wounded are collected, provided they are not military objectives."

[25] The provision reads as follows: "2. For the purpose of this Statute, 'war crimes' means: . . . (e) Other serious violations of the laws and customs applicable in armed conflicts not of an international character, within the established framework of international law, namely, any of the following acts: . . . (iv) Intentionally directing attacks against buildings dedicated to religion, education, art, science or charitable purposes, historic monuments, hospitals and places where the sick and wounded are collected, provided they are not military objectives."

[26] Compare the provisions with Rule 156 of the ICRC Database on Customary IHL <https://ihl-databases.icrc.org/customary-ihl/eng/docs/v1_rul_rule156#Fn_5496F07B_00144> accessed 30 May 2020.

[27] See Hague Convention (IV) respecting the Laws and Customs of War on Land and its Annex: Regulations concerning the Laws and Customs of War on Land (adopted 18 October 1907, entered into force 26 January 1910) arts 27 and 57; Hague Convention of 1954 (n 10) arts 4, 9, 14, 19 and 28; Second Protocol to Hague Convention of 1999 (n 10) arts 6, 9, 12, 15, 22 and 38; Protocol Additional to the Geneva Conventions of 12 August 1949, and relating to the protection of victims of international armed conflicts (Protocol I) (adopted 8 June 1977, entered into force 7 December 1978) 1125 UNTS 3 (Additional Protocol I to the Geneva Conventions) arts 53, 85(4)(d), (5); Protocol Additional to the Geneva Conventions of 12 August 1949 and relating to the protection of victims of non-international armed conflicts (Protocol II) (adopted 8 June 1977, entered into force 7 December 1978) 1125 UNTS 609 (Additional Protocol II to the Geneva Conventions) art 16.

[28] William A Schabas, *The International Criminal Court: A Commentary on the Rome Statute* (OUP 2016) 267; *Prosecutor v Pavle Strugar* (Judgment) IT-01-42-A (July 17, 2008) [277]. See also *Prosecutor v Bosco Ntaganda* (Judgment) ICC-01/04-02/06 (8 July 2019) [1136], ft 3147 (distinguishing cultural objects from other protected objects).

[29] The distinction between international and non-international armed conflicts is complex and tangled. For the purpose of this chapter, suffice it to refer to the Geneva Conventions of 1949 common art 2 (Geneva Convention for the Amelioration of the Condition of the Wounded and Sick in Armed Forces in the Field, 75 UNTS 31; Geneva Convention for the Amelioration of the Condition of the Wounded, Sick and Shipwrecked Members of the Armed Forces at Sea, 75 UNTS 85; Geneva Convention relative to the Treatment of Prisoners of War, 75 UNTS 135; Geneva Convention relative to the Protection of Civilian Persons in time of War, 75 UNTS 287, all adopted 12 August 1949, entered into force 21 October 1950), for the former, and to the Geneva Conventions of 1949 common art 3 and to Additional Protocol II to the Geneva Conventions (n 29) art 2(1), for the latter. See also ICRC, Opinion Paper, "How is the term "Armed Conflict" defined in International Humanitarian Law?" (March 2008) <https://www.icrc.org/eng/assets/files/other/opinion-paper-armed-conflict.pdf> accessed 30 May 2020; Schabas (n 30) 228–35.

[30] For the drafting history of the provisions see Schabas (n 30) 268.

whether it is international or non-international in nature. With this *caveat* in mind, a joint scrutiny of the two articles follows herein.

B. Analysis of the Provisions

International criminal responsibility is assessed at the occurrence of a material and a mental element of the offense.[31] Conduct falls under the ICC crime against cultural property if four criteria (two of them pertaining to the actus reus and two of them concerning the mens rea) are met.

1. Actus Reus

> *The act must materialize the direction of an attack against buildings dedicated to religion, education, art, science or charitable purposes, historic monuments, hospitals and places where the sick and wounded are collected.*

This requirement is satisfied if an attack is simply directed against the enlisted buildings. Neither the Rome Statute nor the ICC elements of crime require any resulted damage.[32] In contrast with art. 3(d) of the ICTY Statute,[33]

[31] See, inter alia, Roger O'Keefe, *International Criminal Law* (OUP 2015) 122 *et seq*.

[32] Schabas (n 30) 268; but see *Strugar* (n 17), which required at least some actual damage. See, by contrast: Additional Protocol I to the Geneva Conventions (n 29) art 85(4)(d), (5). Compare the ICC Statute with the parallel Rules 38 and 40 of the ICRC Database on Customary IHL, which, on the one hand, require special care in order to avoid damage to buildings dedicated to religion, art, science, education or charitable purposes and historic monuments unless they are military objectives and prohibit attacks only against "property of great importance to the cultural heritage of every people" unless required by imperative military necessity; and, on the other hand, forbids, inter alia, the destruction or wilful damage to institutions dedicated to religion, charity, education, the arts and sciences, historic monuments and works of art and science. <https://ihl-databases.icrc.org/customary-ihl/eng/docs/v1_rul_rule38> and <https://ihl-databases.icrc.org/customary-ihl/eng/docs/v1_rul_rule40> all accessed 30 May 2020. See also *Al Hassan* (Rectificatif à la Décision relative à la confirmation des charges portées contre Al Hassan Ag Abdoul Aziz Ag Mohamed Ag Mahmoud) (n 12) [519].

[33] ICTY Statute (UN Security Council, Statute of the International Criminal Tribunal for the Former Yugoslavia, adopted by UN Security Council Resolution 827 of 25 May 1993) art 3(d) qualifies the "seizure of, destruction or wilful damage done to institutions dedicated to religion, charity and education, the arts and sciences, historic monuments and works of art and science" as violations of the laws or customs of war which the ICTY has the power to prosecute. Please note that the ICTY and the International Criminal Tribunal for Rwanda (ICTR) are no longer operating as they have been replaced by the International Residual Mechanism for Criminal Tribunals (IRMCT) <https://www.irmct.org/en/about> accessed 30 May 2020.

this certainly deserves a positive appraisal, as it allows for a more extensive safeguarding of cultural property.

> The buildings which are the object of the attack must not be military objectives..

The concept of "military objective" is one of the pillars of international humanitarian law. As enshrined under art. 52(2) of API to the Geneva Conventions, it encloses "those objects which by their nature, location, purpose or use make an effective contribution to military action and whose total or partial destruction, capture or neutralization, in the circumstances ruling at the time, offers a definite military advantage."[34] By contrast, civilian objects are identified *a contrario*, that is, by way of exclusion, as all property not falling under the category of military objectives.[35] The principle of distinction rests on this partition between civilian and non-civilian persons and objects.[36]

It is also relevant to note that the ICC elements of crime specify that "[t]he presence in the locality of persons specially protected under the Geneva Conventions of 1949 or of police forces retained for the sole purpose of maintaining law and order does not by itself render the locality a military objective."[37] In this regard, the international scholarship is divided on whether such buildings can be protected only if located not in proximity of military objectives.[38] In addition to the above, it might be relevant to point out that the Statute does not feature the exception of military necessity,[39] but only

[34] Additional Protocol I to the Geneva Conventions (n 29) art 52(2). Compare this provision with the definition under Rule 8 of the ICRC Database on Customary IHL: "In so far as objects are concerned, military objectives are limited to those objects which by their nature, location, purpose or use make an effective contribution to military action and whose partial or total destruction, capture or neutralization, in the circumstances ruling at the time, offers a definite military advantage." <https://ihl-databases.icrc.org/customary-ihl/eng/docs/v1_rul_rule8> accessed 30 May 2020. The provision has been mirrored in Second Protocol to Hague Convention of 1999 (n 10) art 1(f).

[35] See inter alia: Additional Protocol I to the Geneva Conventions (n 29) art 52(1) and Rule 9 of the ICRC Database on Customary IHL <https://ihl-databases.icrc.org/customary-ihl/eng/docs/v1_rul_rule9> accessed 30 May 2020.

[36] See, generally, Rule 1 and Rule 7 of the ICRC Database on Customary IHL <https://ihl-databases.icrc.org/customary-ihl/eng/docs/v1_rul_rule1> and <https://ihl-databases.icrc.org/customary-ihl/eng/docs/v1_rul_rule7> all accessed 30 May 2020.

[37] ICC, Elements of Crime (2011) 23, ft 45 and 36, ft 61.

[38] Schabas (n 30) 268; *Prosecutor v Tihomir Blaškić* (Judgment) IT-95-14-T (3 March 2000) [185]; *Prosecutor v Mladen Naletilić et al.* (Judgment) IT-98-34-T (31 March 2003) [603]–[605]; see also *Strugar* (n 17) [310].

[39] However, ICC Statute (n 4) art 31(1)(c) hints at some form of exception of military necessity. See also Micaela Frulli, "The Criminalization of Offences against Cultural Heritage in Times of Armed Conflict: The Quest for Consistency" (2011) 22 European Journal of International Law 203, 214.

applies the test of military objectives, perhaps allowing for a narrower scope of the exception.[40]

Along the same lines, in order to identify the protected categories, arts. 8(2)(b)(ix) and 8(2)(e)(iv) eschew a cultural-value test (which would be based upon the intrinsic cultural nature of the property),[41] in favor of a more teleological test (which qualifies property according to how it is used in practice).[42] In any event, the exception of military objectives remains nebulous.[43]

2. Mens Rea

The author must have intentionally directed the attack against the above-identified buildings.

That the author of an ICC crime must have perpetrated it with intent (i.e., a volitional element) and knowledge (i.e., a cognitive element)[44] is a feature of the whole statute, pursuant to its art. 30. Since the crime against cultural property does not entail any specific circumstance or consequence to have occurred, the mental element remains limited to the engagement in the conduct.[45] To some extent, this requirement must be read jointly with art. 32 of the statute, according to which mistakes of fact or law might be grounds for the exclusion of criminal responsibility if they negate the mental element required by the crime or, for the latter, as provided for in art. 33.

The author must have been aware of the factual circumstances that established the existence of an armed conflict.

The ICC elements of crime not only require the author to have intended the above-mentioned buildings to be the target of the attack but also to have been aware of the factual circumstances of the armed conflict.[46] In various instances, the ICC has stated that the accused must have had knowledge of

40 Ellis (n 8) 40–41; see Frulli (n 42) 215.
41 See, on the cultural value approach: Frulli (n 42) 204–12.
42 Yaron Gottlieb, "Criminalizing Destruction of Cultural Property: A Proposal for Defining New Crimes under the Rome Statute of the ICC" (2005) 23 Penn State International Law Review 857, 866.
43 See also ibid 866–67.
44 For an analysis see Schabas (n 30) 626–33.
45 ICC Statute (n 4) art 30(2)(a).
46 ICC Elements of Crime (n 40) art 8(2)(ix), 23, [3], [5]; art 8(2)(e)(iv), 36, [3], [5].

the existence of an armed conflict as an essential element of the crime.[47] The ICC elements of crimes are of aid in elucidating that the criterion does not require the perpetrator to have carried out a legal evalutation as to the existence of an armed conflict, nor, a fortiori, to have established its international or non-international character: it suffices that the accused has apprehended the occurrence of an armed conflict at the time when the act was carried out.[48]

III. The *Al Mahdi* Case

On September 27, 2016, an ICC trial chamber unanimously sentenced Al Mahdi to nine-years' imprisonment after convicting him of the war crime of intentionally attacking cultural property in Timbuktu, Mali. Al Mahdi pled guilty as a co-perpetrator and received the lowest sentence issued so far by the ICC. On August 17, 2017, the trial chamber issued its reparations order. It found Al Mahdi liable for 2.7 million euros for individual and collective reparations,[49] with only minor amendments being brought by the appeals chamber on appeal of the victims.[50]

In its judgment, the trial chamber described the conduct and crimes in considerable detail. In 2012, Al Mahdi jointly organized the destruction of structures (including mausoleums) of a religious and historical character in Timbuktu. An emblematic city, Timbuktu served as a trading *entrepôt* in the fifteenth and sixteenth centuries. It constituted a focal point for the spread of Islam in the region, housing libraries and manuscripts of great intellectual and spiritual renown. Acting in the name of fundamentalist Salafism, Al Mahdi destroyed shrines to Sufi saints situated above tombs.[51] Many were made of mud and brick. UNESCO had recognized all but one of these

[47] *Prosecutor v Germain Katanga et al* (Decision on the Confirmation of the Charges) ICC-01/04-01/07 (30 September 2008) [387]; *Prosecutor v Jean-Pierre Bemba Gombo* (Decision Pursuant to Article 61(7)(a) and (b) of the Rome Statute on the Charges of the Prosecutor against Jean-Pierre Bemba Gombo) ICC-01/05-01/08 (15 June 2009) [238]–[239], [263]–[264]; see Schabas (n 30) 237.

[48] ICC Elements of Crime (n 40) art 8, War crimes, Introduction, 13; Schabas (n 30) 237–38.

[49] *Prosecutor v Ahmad Al Faqi Al Mahdi* (Reparations Order) ICC-01/12-01/15 (17 August 2017).

[50] *Prosecutor v Ahmad Al Faqi Al Mahdi* (Judgment on the appeal of the victims against the "Reparations Order") ICC-01/12-01/15 A (8 March 2018) [97]–[99].

[51] Marina Lostal, "The Misplaced Emphasis on the Intangible Dimension of Cultural Heritage in the Al Mahdi Case at the ICC" (2017) 1 Inter Gentes - The McGill Journal of International Law & Legal Pluralism 45, 50 ("Timbuktu is sometimes referred to as the "City of the 333 (Sufi) Saints" . . . It also houses thousands of sacred manuscripts, many dating back to the 13th century . . . Sufism, one of the many different currents within Islam, is accused by followers of Salafism (the creed espoused by fundamentalist groups) of being polytheist").

structures as world heritage sites. Timbuktu indeed was inscribed on the World Heritage List in 1998.[52] Al Mahdi was charged solely in relation to his role in demolishing these shrines, and additionally the door of a renowned mosque (Sidi Yahia) and adjacent buildings, all of which constituted conduct falling under the auspices of Rome Statute art. 8(2)(e)(iv). The devotional sites he attacked have since been rebuilt with the help of foreign financial assistance.[53]

Armed violence became endemic in Mali beginning in January 2012. A complex situation arose. Armed groups took control of the north of the country following the retreat of official Malian forces. Among these armed groups were Al Qaeda in the Islamic Maghreb (AQIM) and Ansar Dine ("defenders of faith"). Al Mahdi was associated with Ansar Dine. These groups sought the establishment of an independent country, called Azawad, under the control of Ansar Dine. Between April 2012 and January 2013, AQIM and Ansar Dine "imposed their religious and political edicts on the territory of Timbuktu and its people . . . through a local government, which included an Islamic tribunal, an Islamic police force, a media commission and a morality brigade . . . called the *Hesbah*."[54] *Hesbah* enforced *sharia* and was tasked with "preventing, suppressing and repressing anything perceived by the occupiers to constitute a visible vice."[55]

Al Mahdi (also known as Abu Turab, his *nom de guerre*)—a teacher and an ethnic Tuareg—was born in Agoune in the region of Timbuktu and, at the time of his trial, was believed to be between thirty and forty years old.[56] He had received Koranic education since childhood and "belongs to a family recognised in his community for having a particularly high knowledge of Islam."[57] Although he was the head of the *Hesbah* until September 2012, he

[52] Convention for the Protection of the World Cultural and Natural Heritage (adopted 16 November 1972, entered into force 17 December 1975) 1037 UNTS 151 (also known as World Heritage Convention). For discussion of selection criteria and processes for the World Heritage List, which is established by this Convention, see section V(B) of this chapter (UNESCO and its Lists).

[53] *Al Mahdi* (n 52) [63] ("Since the attacks, UNESCO – together with other stakeholders – has rebuilt or restored each of the Protected Buildings"), [116]. See also Maev Kennedy, "Timbuktu's Historic Tombs Restored in Show of Confidence for War-Ravaged Mali" (*The Guardian*, 20 July 2015) <https://www.theguardian.com/world/2015/jul/20/timbuktus-historic-tombs-restored-in-show-of-confidence-for-war-ravaged-mali> accessed 30 May 2020.

[54] *Al Mahdi* (n 7) [31] (emphasis in original). For a poignant, painful, and utterly dignified cinematographic treatment of life in Mali under Ansar Dine in 2012 see *Timbuktu* (2014), a Franco-Mauritanian drama feature film directed by Abderrahmane Sissako.

[55] *Al Mahdi* (n 7) [33].

[56] ibid [9].

[57] ibid.

also reported to Ag Ghaly (leader of Ansar Dine) and Abou Zhed (governor of Timbuktu).

Al Mahdi had been arrested in Niger by French troops, from where he was sent to The Hague.[58] He reached a plea agreement with the OTP on February 18, 2016.[59] His trial was held between August 22 and 24, 2016.[60] In *Al Mahdi*, a total of eight victims participated in the trial proceedings.[61]

At trial, judges noted Al Mahdi's initial reluctance to demolish the mausoleums, a decision that had been made by his superiors.[62] While Al Mahdi believed that any construction over a tomb was prohibited by Islamic law, he initially recommended "not destroying the mausoleums so as to maintain relations between the population and the occupying groups."[63] Nonetheless, as time passed, he agreed to conduct the attack "without hesitation" when instructed, prepared a sermon dedicated to the destruction of the mausoleums, and "personally determined the sequence in which the buildings/monuments were to be attacked."[64] Al Mahdi was also well aware—for it was common knowledge—that mausoleums of saints and mosques of Timbuktu comprise "an integral part of the religious life of its inhabitants," are frequently visited, serve as places of pilgrimage, and "constitute a common heritage for the community."[65]

The sites were razed publicly and with great force. Security cordons protected the attackers. The door of the Sidi Yahia Mosque was "opened" with pick-axes that Al Mahdi had bought with *Hesbah* funds.[66] According to legend, that door had not been opened for 500 years. It guarded against the "evil eye."[67] Opening it would lead to the Last Judgment. Deriding these legends as "superstition," Al Mahdi explained to journalists that destruction of the doors was one way to eradicate idolatry and heresy, while also dispelling myths which *Hesbah* "fear[ed] will invade the beliefs of people . . . who,

[58] A single ICC judge issued his arrest warrant on 18 September 2015, ibid [1].
[59] ibid [3].
[60] ibid [7].
[61] ibid [6].
[62] For the argument that it remains unclear whether Al Mahdi is the "most responsible" for the crimes, see Milena Sterio, "Individual Criminal Responsibility for the Destruction of Religious and Historic Buildings: The Al Mahdi Case" (2017) 49 Case Western Reserve Journal of International Law 63.
[63] *Al Mahdi* (n 7) [36].
[64] ibid [37].
[65] ibid [34].
[66] ibid [38(viii)].
[67] Lostal (n 54) 49.

because of their ignorance and their distance from religion, will think that this is the truth."[68]

The OTP did not hesitate to qualify the crime as a war crime under the provision of art. 8(2)(e)(iv) of the ICC Statute.[69] The trial chamber explicitly (and approvingly) noted the OTP's specific decision not to charge Al Mahdi with the general crime, also proscribed by the Rome Statute, of attacking civilian property.[70] Judges differentiated the protection of cultural objects from generic protections offered to civilian objects (pillage). Following this rationale, it is exactly the specific feature of the intentional destruction of cultural property, "aimed at erasing the cultural identity and heritage of a population,"[71] which renders this very crime inherently serious in nature.[72] A focal aspect in the OTP analysis was played by the nonmaterial harm[73] which the attacks brought about, including the eradication of a culture's people, identity, and soul.[74]

Based on the admission of guilt and related facts, the three trial judges determined that Al Mahdi supervised the execution of the operations; collected, bought, and distributed the necessary tools; was present at all of the attack sites where he gave instructions and moral support; was responsible for justifying the attacks to journalists; and personally participated in the destruction of at least five sites.[75] Judges noted that nine of the sites were designated by UNESCO as important to international cultural heritage. Although these designations are supposed to protect cultural property, in the case of the Timbuktu shrines these designations may paradoxically have imperiled them. Al Mahdi, for instance, directly invoked the UNESCO protections as a reason to wreck one mosque: "Those UNESCO jackasses . . . they think that this is heritage. Does 'heritage' include worshipping cows and trees?" he said.[76]

[68] *Al Mahdi* (n 7) [38(viii)].
[69] See ex multis: *Procureur c Ahmad Al Faqi Al Mahdi* (Chef d'accusation retenu par l'Accusation contre Ahmad Al Faqi Al Mahdi) ICC-01/12-01/15 (17 Décembre 2015) (available in French only) [1], [23].
[70] *Al Mahdi* (n 7) [12].
[71] *Prosecutor v Ahmad Al Faqi Al Mahdi* (Public redacted version of "Prosecution's submissions on sentencing," 22 July 2016, ICC-01/12-01/15-139-Conf) ICC-01/12-01/15 (21 August 2016) [18].
[72] ibid [16]–[23].
[73] *Prosecutor v Ahmad Al Faqi Al Mahdi* (Public redacted version of "Prosecution's Submissions on Reparations," ICC-01/12-01/15-192, 2 December 2016) ICC-01/12-01/15 (6 December 2016) [14]–[18].
[74] See *Al Mahdi* (n 74) [18], [24]–[29], [62]–[63].
[75] *Al Mahdi* (n 7) [40].
[76] ibid [46].

In terms of the gravity of Al Mahdi's crime, a central calculus in sentencing, the trial chamber observed that he is unlike other accused the ICC has convicted in that he was never charged with crimes against persons.[77] Although the judges noted that crimes against property "are generally of lesser gravity than crimes against persons,"[78] they also underscored the symbolic value, religious salience, and affective attachment generated by the Timbuktu shrines.[79] They were quite responsive to Prosecutor Bensouda's argument, delivered initially in the confirmation of charges hearing, that "[w]hat is at stake here is not just walls and stones."[80] Judges hovered around the UNESCO designation: attacking such designated sites was found to be of particular gravity. On this note, perhaps, the judges not only valued UNESCO assessments as to what kind of culture is worth protecting, but also saw Al Mahdi's attacks as aimed against the international community and its organizations. The judges toggled back to the national one, however, underscoring that "the population of Mali, who considered Timbuktu as a source of pride, were indignant to see these acts take place."[81] The trial chamber also separately identified Al Mahdi's "discriminatory religious motive" as additional evidence of the gravity of the impugned conduct.[82]

In terms of the second step of sentencing, the individualization stage, judges found no aggravating circumstances. They however acknowledged five mitigating factors: admission of guilt; cooperation with prosecutors; demonstration of remorse and empathy; Al Mahdi's initial reluctance to carry out the destruction and the fact that he stopped the use of bulldozers at all but one of the shrines, which thereby limited overall damage; and his good behavior in detention.[83] Al Mahdi had (after the fact) issued a formal statement that "begged" the people of Timbuktu for forgiveness and that affirmed that he had lost his way when he had joined the *jihadist* group.[84]

[77] ibid [77].
[78] ibid.
[79] ibid [78].
[80] *Prosecutor v Ahmad Al Faqi Al Mahdi* (Transcript) ICC-01/12-01/15 (1 March 2016) 13.
[81] *Al Mahdi* (n 7) [80]. The trial chamber relied on the testimony of two witnesses (a Malian expert in cultural matters and a UNESCO witness). See Uzma S. Bishop-Burney, "International Decisions: Prosecutor v Ahmad Al Faqi Al Mahdi" (2017) 111 American Journal of International Law 126, 131.
[82] *Al Mahdi* (n 7) [81].
[83] ibid [109].
[84] Simons (n 7). At trial, Al Mahdi stated: "I am really sorry. I am really remorseful and I regret all the damage that my actions have caused": Ellis (n 8) 29; for the original statement see *Prosecutor v Ahmad Al Faqi Al Mahdi* (Transcript) ICC-01/12-01/15 (22 August 2016) 8.

The reparations order—issued approximately one year later—found Al Mahdi liable for 2.7 million euros in expenses for individual and collective reparations for (a) the damage caused by the attack on nine mosques and the Sidi Yahia Mosque door; (b) the economic loss caused to the individuals whose livelihoods depended upon the tourism and maintenance of these protected buildings and to the community of Timbuktu as a whole; and (c) the moral harm caused by the attacks.[85]

The trial chamber identified three sets of "victims": the inhabitants of Timbuktu (the direct victims of the crime), the population of Mali, and the international community. The reparations order echoed some of the themes pertinent to assessing the value of cultural property that previously suffused the criminal conviction. That said, when it comes to tensions between internationalist justifications for protecting cultural property, on the one hand, and nationalist ones, on the other, the reparations order—while at times underscoring the value of international "interest" as a proxy for value[86]—also allocated considerable relevance to nationalist approaches. Interestingly, this order even transcends national approaches by referencing the reparative rights of local communities and populations.[87] The people of Timbuktu were able to assert reparative rights in the destruction of "their" cultural property and "their" cultural heritage and received nearly all the reparations for damage to protected buildings, consequential economic loss, and moral harm. The Malian State received one symbolic euro. The trial chamber also granted "one symbolic euro . . . to the international community, which is best represented by UNESCO."[88]

The Reparations Order of trial chamber VIII was subsequently amended to a limited extent by the appeals chamber only insofar as it concerned the trial chamber determination of eligibility for individual reparations and the disclosure of identifying information on applicants to Al Mahdi.[89] For the most part the appeals chamber confirmed the previous Reparations Order.

[85] Al Mahdi is impecunious. So the Trust Fund for Victims could step in. For a discussion on the reparations ordered in this case, see also Karolina Wierczyńska and Andrzej Jakubowski, "The Al Mahdi Case: From Punishing Perpetrators to Repairing Cultural Heritage Harm" in Anne-Marie Carstens and Elizabeth Varner (eds), *Intersections in International Cultural Heritage Law* (OUP 2020) 133, 145–56.

[86] *Al Mahdi* (n 52) [17] ("Greater interest vested in an object by the international community reflects a higher cultural significance and a higher degree of international attention and concern").

[87] ibid [14] ("[C]ultural heritage plays a central role in the way communities define themselves and bond together, and how they identify with their past and contemplate their future").

[88] ibid [107].

[89] *Al Mahdi* (n 53) [97]–[99].

On March 4, 2019, trial chamber VIII issued its decision on the Updated Implementation Plan from the Trust Fund for Victims, approving the selection of projects presented by the Trust Fund for Victims in its updated plan, subject to certain conditions.[90]

Elemental among debates within cultural property theory is whether the protective impulse is internationalist or nationalist in motivation.[91] The 1954 Hague Convention,[92] for example, reflects a cosmopolitan approach that envisions the primary significance of cultural property in that it contributes to the cultural heritage of all of humanity. For the internationalist vision, the term "heritage," in particular common heritage of humanity, is preferred over the term "property" with its connotations of material ownership and rights of exclusion. Another major international instrument on cultural property is the 1970 UNESCO Convention on the Means of Prohibiting and Preventing the Illicit Import, Export and Transfer of Ownership of Cultural Property.[93] This instrument deals with the different context of looting and sale. It ties the importance of cultural property to individual States because that property expresses "the collective genius of . . . the State concerned."[94] This instrument

[90] *Prosecutor v Ahmad Al Faqi Al Mahdi* (Decision on the Updated Implementation Plan from the Trust Fund for Victims) ICC-01/12-01/15 (4 March 2019).

[91] John H Merryman, "Two Ways of Thinking about Cultural Property" (1986) 80 American Journal of International Law 831. See also ibid 853 (contrasting retentive nationalism with cultural internationalism; Merryman favors cultural internationalism owing to its emphasis on "preservation, integrity and distribution/access"). For critique of Merryman's views, see Lyndel V Prott, "The International Movement of Cultural Objects" (2005) 12 International Journal of Cultural Property 225.

[92] Hague Convention of 1954 (n 10). This Convention descends from the 1863 Lieber Code (Instructions for the Government of Armies of the United States in the Field, General Orders No. 100, adopted 24 April 1863), the 1899 Hague Conventions (adopted 29 July 1899, entered into force 4 September 1900) and 1907 Hague Conventions (adopted 18 October 1907, entered into force 26 January 1910), and the 1935 Roerich Pact (Treaty on the Protection of Artistic and Scientific Institutions and Historic Monuments, adopted 15 April 1935, entered into force 26 August 1935). In art 1, it defines cultural property as "moveable or immovable property of great importance to the cultural heritage of every people" and, in its preamble, affirms that "damage to cultural property belonging to any people whatsoever means damage to the cultural heritage of all mankind, since each people makes its contribution to the culture of the world." Destruction of a culture's property, therefore, is seen as eliminating part of the biodiversity of humanity. This Convention requires the affixing of a "distinctive emblem" (a blue and white shield), either three times or one time depending on the level of protection or identification, see Hague Convention of 1954 (n 10) arts 16, 17. Art 28 obliges States Parties to criminalize breaches of the Convention. See generally Patty Gerstenblith, "The Destruction of Cultural Heritage: A Crime against Property or a Crime against People?" (2016) 15 John Marshall Review of Intellectual Property Law 336, 346; Roger O'Keefe, "Protection of Cultural Property Under International Law" (2010) 11 Melbourne Journal of International Law 339 (noting that no charges have been laid within the meaning of art 28).

[93] Convention on the Means of Prohibiting and Preventing the Illicit Import, Export and Transfer of Ownership of Cultural Property (adopted 14 November 1970, entered into force 24 April 1972) 823 UNTS 231.

[94] ibid art 4(a).

thereby reflects a sense of cultural nationalism in that it attributes national character to the property in question, seeks its retention in its place of origin and traditional setting, and its repatriation in the case of illicit removal.[95] *Al Mahdi* offers little in the way of mindful reference to either of these overarching theories. In the end, the judgment—without assignation and with oscillation—places the Rome Statute provision somewhere between these two poles of cultural property theory: though inclining more toward the internationalist justification for protection in the case of the penal sanction and toward the nationalist justification in the reparations order. The reparations decision could in fact be read to impliedly gesture toward a third approach, namely a "localist" vision of cultural property protection in that nearly all the ordered funds were intended for the population of Timbuktu.

Al Mahdi was transferred to a Scottish prison on August 29, 2018, to serve his sentence.[96] As *per* art. 103 of the ICC Statute, accused convicted by the ICC will serve their sentences in a State designated by the Court from a list of states which have previously indicated their willingness to accept those persons to serve their sentence.[97] Accordingly, Al Mahdi's transfer was conducted pursuant to the Agreement between the Government of the United Kingdom of Great Britain and Northern Ireland and the International Criminal Court on the enforcement of sentences imposed by the International Criminal Court.[98]

IV. OTP Policies and Goals

The ICC is composed of four primary organs: the Presidency, the Judicial Divisions (an Appeals Division, a Trial Division, and a Pre-Trial Division), the OTP, and the Registry.[99] Part 4 of the Statute concerns the composition and administration of the Court and also its organs' tasks and mandates.[100]

[95] Merryman (n 94) 832, 846.

[96] See Press Release, "Ahmad Al Faqi Al Mahdi Transferred to UK Prison Facility to Serve Sentence" (3 May 2019) <https://www.icc-cpi.int/Pages/item.aspx?name=pr1451> accessed 30 May 2020.

[97] ICC Statute (n 4) art 103(1)(a).

[98] Agreement between the Government of the United Kingdom of Great Britain and Northern Ireland and the International Criminal Court on the enforcement of sentences imposed by the International Criminal Court, ICC-PRES/04-01-07 (adopted 8 November 2007, entered into force 8 December 2007) <https://www.icc-cpi.int/Pages/item.aspx?name=icc-uk> accessed 30 May 2020.

[99] ICC Statute (n 4) art 34.

[100] ibid Part 4, arts 34–52.

According to art. 42 of the ICC Statute,[101] the OTP is a separate organ of the court, entrusted with the mandate of receiving referrals, examining them, and investing and prosecuting the crimes within the Court's jurisdiction.[102] It is composed of the prosecutor, who acts as the head of the office, and one or more deputy prosecutors.[103] Other sub-paragraphs of the same provision deal with procedural aspects of the functioning of the OTP, such as, inter alia, the competence of the prosecutor and of the Deputy Prosecutors, their election, independence, impartiality, and disqualification.[104]

In particular, the ICC website explains that three main Divisions form the OTP, namely, the Jurisdiction, Complementarity and Cooperation Division, the Investigation Division, and the Prosecution Division.[105] The main functions of each Division entail, respectively, the conduct of preliminary examinations, the offer of advice on matters such as jurisdiction, admissibility, and cooperation, the coordination of judicial cooperation, and the management of the OTP's external relations; the direction of investigations, the endorsement of security plans and protection policies, and the examination of the relevant information and evidence; the preparation of litigation strategies and carrying out of prosecution, which might include applying for an arrest warrant or summons to appear as a first stage.[106]

There are three ways in which a case may be brought before the ICC and all of them involve the OTP prosecutor, to a different extent: (i) a State Party may refer to the prosecutor a situation where crimes within the ICC jurisdiction have allegedly been perpetrated;[107] (ii) the UN Security Council may act under Chapter VII of the UN Charter[108] and refer a situation to the prosecutor;[109] or (iii) the Prosecutor may initiate investigations *proprio motu* on the basis of the information received by the Court.[110] In all such cases, the role of the Prosecutor is focal for the exercise of the ICC jurisdiction.

[101] ibid art 42(1).

[102] For an analysis see Schabas (n 30) 736–48. See also Fatou Bensouda, "Looking Back, Looking Ahead - Reflections from the Office of the Prosecutor of the ICC" (2012) 11 Washington University Global Studies Law Review 437.

[103] ICC Statute (n 4) art 42(2).

[104] ibid art 42(3)–(9).

[105] ICC website <https://www.icc-cpi.int/about/otp> accessed 30 May 2020.

[106] ibid.

[107] ICC Statute (n 4) arts 13(a) 14. This was the case for Democratic Republic of the Congo, Uganda, Central African Republic on two occasions, and Mali; see <https://www.icc-cpi.int/about/otp> accessed 30 May 2020.

[108] Charter of the United Nations (adopted 26 June 1945, entered into force 24 October 1945) 1 UNTS XVI.

[109] ICC Statute (n 4) art 13(b). This was the case for Darfur and Libya, see <https://www.icc-cpi.int/about/otp> accessed 30 May 2020.

[110] ICC Statute (n 4) art 13(c), 15. This was the case for Kenya, Côte d'Ivoire, and Georgia; see <https://www.icc-cpi.int/about/otp> accessed 30 May 2020.

A. The OTP Approach to Crimes against Cultural Heritage

The posture of the OTP toward crimes concerning cultural heritage can be appreciated following at least three directives. First, the policy papers published by the OTP must be taken into account in order to properly identify the public commitment that the OTP has undertaken with respect to such category of crimes. Second, the conduct of the OTP must be addressed with regard to the big picture, that is, in its cooperation with other UN agencies. Third, and more importantly, the OTP attitude must be assessed in practice, through a detailed analysis of how the Office dealt with cultural heritage crimes in the cases brought before the ICC. Finally, this section also ponders the stance of the OTP toward this category of crimes and anticipates its future developments.

1. The Approach of the OTP through its Policy Papers

The increasing interest crimes against cultural property have been attracting in the last decades has also been reflected in the OTP policy paper on case selection and prioritisation[111] and in the ICC Strategic Plan 2019–2021.[112] As to the former, the OTP explains that it will pay particular attention to, among others, crimes against cultural objects.[113] The latter document clarifies that the OTP aims at finalizing its current work "toward the adoption of a comprehensive policy on the protection of cultural heritage within the Rome Statute legal framework, which will also cover the important issue of victimization."[114]

Furthermore, it might be useful to recall that the ICC has issued a code of conduct for the office of the prosecutor, entered into force on September 5, 2013.[115] Fundamental rule n. 4 and art. 8(h) of this code place respect for human rights and fundamental freedoms recognized by international law at the heart of the OTP action.[116] While this human rights-friendly standpoint

[111] OTP policy paper on case selection and prioritisation (15 September 2016) <https://www.icc-cpi.int//Pages/item.aspx?name=policy-paper-on-case-selection-and-prioritisation> accessed 30 May 2020.

[112] ICC Strategic Plan 2019–2021 (17 July 2019) <https://www.icc-cpi.int/Pages/item.aspx?name=20190726-otp-sp> accessed 30 May 2020.

[113] OTP policy paper on case selection and prioritisation (n 114) 15 [46].

[114] ICC Strategic Plan 2019–2021 (n 115) 5, Strategic goal 4; see also ibid 24 [37].

[115] ICC, code of conduct for the office of the prosecutor (entered into force 5 September 2013) <https://www.icc-cpi.int/Pages/item.aspx?name=Code-of-Conduct> accessed 30 May 2020. For an examination see Lawrence Pacewicz, "International Criminal Court Code of Conduct for the Office of the Prosecutor" (2014) 53 International Legal Materials 397.

[116] ICC, code of conduct for the office of the prosecutor (n 118) Introduction, Fundamental Rule n 4 and art 8(h).

remains a general trait of the overall functioning of the OTP, it does in fact also apply to the prosecution of the crimes here at stake.

2. The Approach of the OTP through Its Cooperation with Other Bodies

Specifically tailored developments in the OTP approach toward crimes against or affecting cultural heritage still have to see the light. Having said this, it is also commendable that the ICC OTP and UNESCO have joined their forces in order to strengthen cooperation in response to cultural cleansing and prevention of attacks on culture. In particular, they co-organized panels and events eventually leading to the drafting and signing of a Letter of Intent on November 6, 2017.[117] Arguably, mutual respect and synergy between different UN organs implies stronger funds and combined efforts toward the accomplishment of shared mandates.

3. The Approach of the OTP through the ICC Case Law

Some aspects of the OTP approach in *Al Mahdi* have already been analyzed in Section III of the present chapter. The OTP had a central role in the effort of making attacks directed against cultural property war crimes under the ICC jurisdiction. And indeed, cultural property possesses a special trait which differentiates it from the realm of goods and rights which international law aims at defending for at least two reasons. On the one hand, the protection of cultural heritage and property surpasses the idea that only tangible goods can be the object of safeguard. In this sense, logically, cultural property deserves to be shielded from any sort of jeopardy for the material and manifest significance it carries, for the aesthetic value it embodies, and for the technical advancement it encourages. But relics must also be preserved for the emotional weight they bear, for their symbolic essence, and their evocative power.[118] On the other hand, over and above, culture as a generic term is what ultimately brings individuals together, for its ability to create bonds and entrench enduring relationships. Cultural cleansing undermines the

[117] For the panel see <https://en.unesco.org/events/responding-cultural-cleansing-preventing-violent-extremism> and <https://en.unesco.org/news/unesco-and-partners-stand-against-cultural-cleansing-and-violent-extremism>; for the letter of intent see <http://www.unesco.org/new/media-services/single-view/news/international_criminal_court_and_unesco_strengthen_cooperati/>; <https://en.unesco.org/news/international-criminal-court-and-unesco-strengthen-cooperation-protection-cultural-heritage>and <https://www.icc-cpi.int/Pages/item.aspx?name=171106_OTP_Unesco> all accessed 30 May 2020.

[118] See on this point: *Al Mahdi* (n 7) [79].

associative existence of society whose pillars ground themselves upon cultural ties.

Especially with respect to reparations, the role of the OTP in *Al Mahdi* has been pivotal in the identification of the victims (direct and indirect, natural and legal persons, individual and group victims),[119] in the assessment of the harm suffered by those very victims (material, physical or psychological, direct or indirect),[120] in the ascertainment of the appropriate standard of proof and causation,[121] and in the establishment of the types and modalities of reparations.[122] Particularly on this latter point, the OTP strongly encouraged the issuance of collective reparations, "including modalities of reparation of preventive, transformative and symbolic value."[123]

An impending case is *Al Hassan*.[124] According to the information made available on the ICC website,[125] Al Hassan was an alleged member of Ansar Eddine and de facto chief of Islamic police and he is alleged to have been involved in the work of the Islamic Court in Timbuktu.[126] On September 30, 2019, the ICC pre-trial chamber I issued a confidential decision whereby it concluded that there were substantial grounds to believe that Al Hassan had performed, among others, an intentional direction of attacks against buildings dedicated to religion and historic monuments.[127] As noted earlier in this chapter, the pre-trial chamber decision was confirmed by the appeals chamber,[128] a trial chamber has been constituted at the end of 2019,[129] and the trial opened on July 14, 2020.[130]

119 *Al Mahdi* (n 76) [6]–[11].

120 ibid [14]–[18].

121 ibid [19], [20].

122 ibid [25]–[27].

123 ibid [26].

124 *Prosecutor v Al Hassan Ag Abdoul Aziz Ag Mohamed Ag Mahmoud*, ICC-01/12-01/18. For the developments of the case see <https://www.icc-cpi.int/mali/al-hassan> accessed 30 May 2020.

125 ibid.

126 For the facts of the case, please refer to the case information sheet: https://www.icc-cpi.int/mali/al-hassan accessed 30 May 2020.

127 ibid.

128 *Al Hassan* (Rectificatif à la Décision relative à la confirmation des charges portées contre Al Hassan Ag Abdoul Aziz Ag Mohamed Ag Mahmoud) (n 12). This decision was confirmed by the ICC Appeals Chamber in early 2020: *Al Hassan* (Judgment on the appeal of Mr Al Hassan against the decision of pre-trial chamber I entitled "Décision relative à l'exception d'irrecevabilité pour insuffisance de gravité de l'affaire soulevée par la défense') (n 12).

129 *Prosecutor v Al Hassan Ag Abdoul Aziz Ag Mohamed Ag Mahmoud* (Decision constituting trial chamber X and referring to it the case of The Prosecutor v. Al Hassan Ag Abdoul Aziz Ag Mohamed Ag Mahmoud) ICC-01/12-01/18 (21 November 2019).

130 *Prosecutor v Al Hassan Ag Abdoul Aziz Ag Mohamed Ag Mahmoud* (Decision Setting the Commencement Date of the Trial) ICC-01/12-01/18 (6 January 2020). On April 23, 2020, ICC pre-trial chamber I issued a confidential decision partially granting the Prosecutor's request to modify

As a suspect of crimes against humanity and war crimes allegedly committed in Timbuktu, Mali, between 2012 and 2013, Al Hassan is currently being kept in ICC custody.[131]

As regards attacks against cultural property, the OTP gives special attention to the examination of the term "attack" within the meaning of art. 8(2)(e)(iv) which, in its opinion, "has a 'special meaning' in the sense of the Vienna Convention, which differs from other uses of the term 'attack' in article 8."[132]

Besides this, the OTP arguably endorses a subtended link between the destruction of the sites concerned and the identity and dignity of the city of Timbuktu and its inhabitants.[133] While the OTP underscores the relevance of such sites for the religious, social, and cultural life of the people of Timbuktu,[134] it also stresses the much more extended grievance of Africa and the international community as a whole for the destruction of cultural objects which embodied memories of the past that should have been handed down to future generations.[135] Furthermore, this suggests a flexible interpretation of terms such as "religious"[136] or "historic"[137] buildings, which basically rejects a restrictive approach to the aforementioned criteria.[138]

In addition to the cases of Al Mahdi and Al Hassan, also in other cases the ICC had to deal with attacks against protected objects within the meaning of art. 8(2)(e)(iv) of the Statute (i.e., a category which requires a higher threshold than the mere nonmilitary nature of the attacked objects) in the context of NIACs, but none of them concerned attacks against cultural heritage as such.[139]

the charges against the accused to include additional facts: *Al Hassan* (Version publique expurgée du Rectificatif de la Décision portant modification des charges confirmées le 30 septembre 2019 à l'encontre d'Al Hassan Ag Abdoul Aziz Ag Mohamed Ag Mahmoud, 23 avril 2020, ICC-01/12-01/18-767-Conf) (n 14). See also Press Release (n 14).

[131] See <https://www.icc-cpi.int/mali/al-hassan> accessed 30 May 2020.

[132] *Prosecutor v Al Hassan Ag Abdoul Aziz Ag Mohamed Ag Mahmoud* (Public redacted version of the "Prosecution's final written observations regarding confirmation of the charges", 24 July 2019, ICC-01/12-01/18-430-Conf) ICC-01/12-01/18 (10 October 2019) [143]. See also *Procureur c Al Hassan Ag Abdoul Aziz Ag Mohamed Ag Mahmoud* (Version publique expurgée de la "Version amendée et corrigée du Document contenant les charges contre M. Al Hassan Ag Abdoul Aziz Ag Mohamed Ag Mahmoud," ICC-01/12-01/18-335-Conf-Corr, 11 mai 2019) ICC-01/12-01/18 (2 juillet 2019) (available in French only) [687–[703].

[133] *Al Hassan* (Version publique expurgée de la "Version amendée et corrigée du Document contenant les charges contre M. Al Hassan Ag Abdoul Aziz Ag Mohamed Ag Mahmoud," ICC-01/12-01/18-335-Conf-Corr, 11 mai 2019) [685].

[134] ibid.

[135] ibid [686].

[136] ibid [705]–[708].

[137] ibid [709]–[713].

[138] See, particularly: ibid [709].

[139] See *Ntaganda* (n 30) and *Prosecutor v Patrice-Edouard Ngaïssona et al.* (Public redacted version of "Document Containing the Charges", ICC-01-14/01-18-282-Conf-AnxB1, 19 August 2019) ICC-01/14-01/18 (18 September 2019).

B. The OTP Approach *in fieri*: Toward a Human Rights Approach to Crimes against or Affecting Cultural Heritage?

As it has been underpinned by the UN Special Rapporteur in the field of cultural rights, Karima Bennoune, in various instances,[140] only a "human rights approach to cultural heritage obliges one to go beyond preserving and safeguarding an object or a manifestation in itself to take into account the rights of individuals and groups in relation to such object or manifestation and to connect cultural heritage with its source of production."[141] Turning to the context of international criminal law, a human rights approach[142] enhances accountability and the fight against impunity,[143] justly because it allows for a focus on the cultural rights defenders[144] and on the victims' rights,[145] which, when violated, merit to be repaired.[146] In the words of Judge Cançado Trindade of the International Court of Justice: "the ultimate *titulaires* of the right to the safeguard and preservation of their cultural and spiritual heritage are the collectivities of human beings concerned, or else humankind as a whole."[147] Along this line, the Special Rapporteur welcomed the initiative of the ICC OTP in the *Al Mahdi* case to charge such crimes as "stand-alone war crime[s],"[148] rather than mere auxiliary ones.[149] Hence, the prioritization of such crimes enables their prosecution, by the OTP and the judges alike, with a deeper pivot on the victims' perspective: on their rights which have been

[140] See among others: UNGA, Report of the Special Rapporteur in the field of cultural rights, Karima Bennoune, UN Doc A/71/317 (9 August 2016) [52]–[58].

[141] ibid [53], also referring to UNGA, Report of the independent expert in the field of cultural rights, Farida Shaheed, UN Doc A/HRC/17/38 (21 March 2011) [2].

[142] See also, for example: UNGA, Report, Karima Bennoune (August 2016) (n 144) [6]–[13], [52]–[75]; UNGA, Report of the Special Rapporteur in the field of cultural rights, Karima Bennoune, UN Doc A/HRC/31/59 (3 February 2016) [47]–[51], [69]–[85]; UNGA, Report, Farida Shaheed (March 2011) (n 145) [4]–[8]; Brief by Ms Karima Bennoune, UN Special Rapporteur in the field of Cultural Rights, Expert Appointed by the International Criminal Court in the Case of The Prosecutor v. Ahmad Al Faqi Al Mahdi, ICC-01/12-01/15, Reparations Phase (27 April 2017) 11–18, 36–37. See also UN Human Rights Council, Resolution 33/20, UN Doc A/HRC/RES/33/20 (adopted 30 September 2016).

[143] UNGA, Report, Karima Bennoune (August 2016) (n 144) [54].

[144] UNGA, Report, Karima Bennoune (February 2016) (n 146) [74]–[75] and, more generally: UNGA, Report, Karima Bennoune (August 2016) (n 144) [68]–[75]; Brief by Ms Karima Bennoune (n 146) 17.

[145] On the identities of the victims see Brief by Ms Karima Bennoune (n 146) 25–28.

[146] On the reparation of the victims' rights see ibid 36–46.

[147] *Request for Interpretation of the Judgement of 15 June 1962 in the Case Concerning the Temple of Preah Vihear (Cambodia v Thailand) (Cambodia v Thailand)*, Order of 18 July 2011, Separate Opinion of Judge Cançado Trindade [2011] ICJ Rep. 566 [114] (emphasis in original), also quoted in: UNGA, Report, Karima Bennoune (February 2016) (n 146) [48].

[148] UNGA, Report, Karima Bennoune (August 2016) (n 144) [54]. See also, previously, UNGA, Report, Karima Bennoune (February 2016) (n 146) [78].

[149] (n 36) 125, 132.

infringed and on the restoration which will have to follow.[150] Accordingly, a holistic strategy,[151] which takes into account and, to some extent, promotes the viewpoint of those whose rights have been offended, shall be favored.

In the brief she submitted in the *Al Mahdi* case as an appointed expert of the ICC,[152] Prof. Bennoune highlighted that the harm caused by intentional destruction of property of cultural significance transcends the mere material damage[153] and endorsed the need for an overarching approach toward this type of crime, which takes into consideration the human rights impact of the acts at stake.[154] As a consequence, this widens the number and categories of victims affected by the above-mentioned crime, which cease to be limited to those who can claim direct and material damage and extends to the local, national, regional, and international communities in a broad sense.[155] Naturally, this will also carry implications on the reparations phase.[156]

V. Some Normative Takeaways

A. Anthropocentrism

The *Al Mahdi* judgment (notably on the matter of sentencing and reparations order) measured the gravity of the harm from the perspective of how much that property meant to people in real time. The usual premise is that crimes against persons are more "serious" than crimes against objects and things. Hence, when it came to the seriousness of the attacks in Timbuktu, judges emphasized that these attacks affected human beings and triggered suffering in the lives they live. The trial chamber thereby adopted a somewhat anthropocentric model of culture and loss. It measured the value of heritage in a relational sense and not in an intrinsic sense. On the one hand, this move seems natural, self-evident, and textually faithful to the language of the Rome Statute and approaches to gravity that are commonplace within the criminal

[150] Cf: UNGA, Report, Karima Bennoune (August 2016) (n 144) [54], quoting, at ft 42, Richard Goldstone, "The War Crime of Destroying Cultural Property" (*International Judicial Monitor*, Summer 2016) <http://www.judicialmonitor.org/summer2016/globaljudicialperspective.html> accessed 30 May 2020.

[151] UNGA, Report, Karima Bennoune (August 2016) (n 144) [57].

[152] Brief by Ms Karima Bennoune (n 146).

[153] ibid 23–25.

[154] ibid 24–25.

[155] See eg ibid 25–28.

[156] See eg ibid 36–49 and, specifically, 37–38.

law. On the other hand, this shift also belies far thicker and richer questions as to how to value cultural property and what exactly to protect.

Central to the *Al Mahdi* case, therefore, is that nearly all of the destroyed sites also had been routinely used by the residents of Timbuktu for religious purposes.[157] But what if the property was no longer being used? What if it served no religious or worship purpose? What if the property was ugly, unappreciated, ignored, dusty, dismal, and forlorn? Privately owned? What if a local population declared by democratic vote to reject the property as "cultural" in nature? Ironically the more that cultural property is loved and used, the higher the likelihood that it would be rebuilt. The gravest harms, after all, tend to befall the unloved and unappreciated and unkempt. While observers may quibble about whether cultural property ever can be truly rebuilt,[158] the fact remains that property that is marginal is more likely not to be rebuilt and therefore may simply disappear. What is more, if the will of the local community not (or no longer) to present something as cultural property is to be respected, so too must the will of the community to affirmatively designate something as cultural property. Such protective moves are commonplace. The Dutch, for example, have officially placed the Sinterklaas Festival and Black Pete on the National Inventory of Intangible Cultural Heritage.[159]

What about cultural property from a culture that no longer exists? Or a culture that moved away, leaving its property behind? Marina Lostal ties these questions to the *Al Mahdi* judgment's reasoning, which she chides as anthropocentric. Lostal specifically identifies as an example the destruction of the Bamiyan Buddhas by the Taliban in 2001. The Bamiyan Buddhas were two enormous statues built around the fifth to seventh century in a valley in what is now Afghanistan. The statues oversaw a community of Buddhist monasteries. Roughly 1,500 years later, the Taliban (who controlled Afghanistan) decreed these statues as the product of an infidel religion and dynamited them. The Bamiyan Buddhas, unlike the mausoleums in Timbuktu, were

[157] Interestingly, the emphasis on religion was less singular in the Hague Convention of 1954 (n 10), art 1(a) of which explicitly protected property "whether religious or secular."

[158] Prosecutor Bensouda, in her opening statement in Al Mahdi, submitted that, "Once destroyed, as noted by the UN International Criminal Tribunal for the former Yugoslavia, the restoration of cultural heritage never brings back its inherent value": Statement of the Prosecutor of the International Criminal Court, Fatou Bensouda, at the opening of Trial in the case against Mr Ahmad Al-Faqi Al Mahdi (22 August 2016) <https://www.icc-cpi.int/Pages/item.aspx?name=otp-stat-al-mahdi-160822> accessed 30 May 2020.

[159] Lucas Lixinski, "Confederate Monuments and International Law" (2018) 35 Wisconsin International Law Journal 549, 578, noting "'Black Pete' (*Zwarte Piet*)" as a 'Christmas tradition which includes a "helper" of Santa Claus as a black-face or just black person, who was once historically Santa Claus's African slave" (emphasis in original).

not used by local populations in religious practices— “there are no records indicating the presence of Buddhism in Afghanistan after 1336.”[160] Hence, according to Lostal, “their destruction could not affect the social practices and structures or the cultural roots of the local people.”[161] She adds: “It would lack what the Chief Prosecutor has pointed to as the common denominator of all crimes detailed by the ICC Statute—that is, that ‘[t]hey inflict irreparable damage to the human persons [*sic*] in his or her body, mind, soul and identity.’ ”[162] Palmyra in Syria constitutes a similar example.[163] So, too, does the ancient city of Sabratha: “once a jewel of the Roman Empire,” currently pockmarked with mortar and small arms fire from armed conflict in Libya and which is now “used” (in real-\ time) as a chaotic camp of departure for refugees—chased by smugglers and militias—fleeing across the Mediterranean.[164]

B. UNESCO and Its Lists

In *Al Mahdi*, the human “value” of the shrines could be established with relative ease through deployment of proxies. Nearly all of the shrines were protected by UNESCO as heritage sites (inscribed on the World Heritage List).[165] The UNESCO designations weighed heavily in the minds of the judges (and in the OTP submissions).[166] Within the umbrella of UNESCO,

[160] Lostal (n 54) 56.

[161] ibid 56–57

[162] ibid 57 (citation omitted).

[163] See eg Helga Turku, “When Cultural Property Becomes a Tool of Warfare: Law, Politics, and International Security” (2017) 1 Inter Gentes - The McGill Journal of International Law & Legal Pluralism 3, 16 (“Questions can be raised as to whether the pre-Islamic Roman Era ruins of Palmyra or the Assyrian city of Nimrud have anything in common with the predominantly Arab population that inhabits the region today. . . . Or do these historical sites partly represent the heritage of some people who lived there once in the past?”). ISIS also has targeted the ancient city of Dura Europos, located on the banks of the Euphrates river near the Syrian and Iraqi border.

[164] “ ‘Jewel of Roman Empire’ Faces Libya Dangers’ (France 24, 3 October 2018) <https://www.france24.com/en/20181003-jewel-roman-empire-faces-libya-dangers> accessed 30 May 2020.

[165] For the up-to-date list see <https://whc.unesco.org/en/list/> accessed 30 May 2020.

[166] *Al Mahdi* (n 7) [46]. The fourth sentence of the Prosecutor’s Opening Statement begins: “They were a major part of the historic heritage of this ancient city. They were also more generally a part of the heritage of Mali, of Africa and of the world. All, except one, were inscribed on the World Heritage List,” Statement of the Prosecutor at the opening of Al Mahdi Trial (n 162). In ICTY proceedings for destruction or willful damage of cultural property (rather than attacks), individuals were charged with and convicted for the destruction of the old town of Dubrovnik, also listed as a UNESCO World Heritage Site, and charged with but ultimately acquitted regarding the Stari Most bridge (as civilian property), which became formally listed with UNESCO in 2005 but had been listed as a “UN World Heritage Site” at the time of the attacks: Bishop-Burney (n 84) 130.

the World Heritage Committee has the final say on whether a property is inscribed on the World Heritage List. This Committee meets once a year. It consists of representatives from twenty-one of the States Parties to the World Heritage Convention.[167] Pursuant to art. 11(1) of this Convention, the Committee shall establish, keep up to date, and publish this list of properties forming part of the cultural heritage and natural heritage which it considers as having outstanding universal value in terms of such criteria as it shall have established. Outstanding universal value means cultural and/or natural significance which is so exceptional as to transcend national boundaries and to be of common importance for present and future generations of all humanity.[168] As of August 2020, the twenty-one States on the World Heritage Committee are Australia, Bahrain, Bosnia and Herzegovina, Brazil, China, Egypt, Ethiopia, Guatemala, Hungary, Kyrgyzstan, Mali, Nigeria, Norway, Oman, Russian Federation, Saint Kitts and Nevis, Saudi Arabia, South Africa, Spain, Thailand, Uganda.[169]

In many quarters, however, the UNESCO listing process "has been viewed as notoriously politicised and biased toward particular forms of heritage."[170] On this note, one observer has called for the "identification of objective criteria independent of UNESCO designation."[171] UNESCO has nonetheless been energized by the *Al Mahdi* judgment. As recalled in the above,[172] on November 6, 2017, its director-general, Irina Bokova, signed a letter of intent with Chief Prosecutor Bensouda to continue to collaborate including on a new policy initiative on cultural heritage.[173] The stakes for what UNESCO determines therefore seem to be rising. So, if UNESCO expert designations now are key elements of gravity in the application of international criminal law, perhaps the process by which UNESCO "experting" is developed should become split open or spruced up.

167 Convention for the Protection of the World Cultural and Natural Heritage (n 55).

168 See the Operational Guidelines for the Implementation of the World Heritage Convention, Guideline 49 <https://whc.unesco.org/en/guidelines/> accessed 30 May 2020 (all of which also provide details on procedures).

169 See <https://whc.unesco.org/en/committee/> and https://whc.unesco.org/en/sessions/44COM/ accessed 29 August 2020.

170 Sophie Starrenburg, "Who Is the Victim of Cultural Heritage Destruction? The Reparations Order in the Case of the Prosecutor v Ahmad Al Faqi Al Mahdi" (*EJIL: Talk!*, 25 August 2017).

171 Bishop-Burney (n 84) 132.

172 See section IV(A)(2) of this chapter (The approach of the OTP through its cooperation with other bodies).

173 Press Release, "International Criminal Court and UNESCO Strengthen Cooperation on the Protection of Cultural Heritage" (6 November 2017) <https://whc.unesco.org/en/news/1742> accessed 30 May 2020.

C. Whither Protection? Whither Deterrence? Questions of Legalisms and Legalities

An ongoing issue within the protection of cultural heritage in armed conflict is that international criminal law can only provide for ex post facto measures, rather than preventative mechanisms.[174] But can it function also as a deterrent for future violations, dissuading the condemned to repeat the crime (specific deterrence) and discouraging everyone else from engaging in similar conducts (general deterrence)?[175] This section analyzes the deterrent value of the international crime against cultural heritage at the ICC along two lines. First, it posits the shortcomings of the Rome Statute itself and suggests feasible areas of improvement. Secondly, it formulates several challenges to the ICC's preventative capacity.

Albeit declaring its consciousness that "[a]ll peoples are united by common bonds, their cultures pieced together in a shared heritage and concerned that this delicate mosaic may be shattered at any time,"[176] and as recalled in the above, the Statute does not employ the term "culture" in any of its declinations when identifying war crimes against cultural heritage. Rather, it replicates the terminology of the 1907 Hague Convention and the 1949 Geneva Conventions.[177] Hence, the drafters of the Statute missed the opportunity to sanction offences against "culture" per se[178] and to dignify cultural property by according it a stronger degree of protection than that afforded to any other type of civilian property.[179]

[174] See, inter alia, Erin Collins, "Preventing Cultural Heritage Destruction and the Responsibility to Protect" (2018) 13 Intercultural Human Rights Law Review 299, 300.

[175] For a brief survey on specific and general deterrence see, for example, *Al Mahdi* (n 7) [67]; David Wippman, "Atrocities, Deterrence, and the Limits of International Justice" (1999) 23 Fordham Internatial Law Journal 473, 476; Payam Akhavan, "Justice in the Hague, Peace in the Former Yugoslavia - A Commentary on the United Nations War Crimes Tribunal" (1998) 20 Human Rights Quarterly 737, 746–47.

[176] ICC Statute (n 4) first preambular paragraph; Knut Dörmann, "War Crimes under the Rome Statute of the International Criminal Court, with a Special Focus on the Negotiations on the Elements of Crimes" in Armin von Bogdandy and Rüdiger Wolfrum (eds), *Max Planck Yearbook of United Nations Law* (Brill 2003) vol 7, 341, 356–63, 377–78, 396–98, 400.

[177] The Hague Conventions of 1907 (n 95); Geneva Conventions of 1949 (n 31); Gottlieb (n 45) 865, also mentioning *Strugar* (n 17) [229].

[178] See Schabas (n 30) 268.

[179] ibid 267–68, quoting Michael Bothe, "War Crimes" in Antonio Cassese, Paola Gaeta, and John RWD Jones (eds), *The Rome Statute of the International Criminal Court* (OUP 2002) 379, 410; Carcano (n 16) 86–87. See also *Kordić et al* (Judgment) IT-95-14/2-A (17 December 2004) [92], where the ICTY ultimately accepted the destruction of schools as constituting, in any event, destruction of enemy property found in the Hague Convention (IV) of 1907 (n 29) art 23(g). Compare the provisions with the war crime of attacking civilian objects under ICC Statute (n 4) art 8(2)(b)(ii).

Moreover, it must be observed that the provisions on the table are limited in scope to immovable cultural properties,[180] that is, to edifices or constructions capable of being used, in principle, for military purposes. Articles. 8(2)(b)(ix) and 8(2)(e)(iv) do not cover movable cultural objects, nor do they provide for any legal nor logical rationale to justify such difference in treatment.

The Statute omits to penalize the conduct of those who use cultural property in support of military action or for any other criminal goal[181] and, even more so, the acts of those who turn such very property into a military objective and, by consequence, deprive it of legitimate protection.[182]

On a final note, it can also be pointed out that the Statute does not shed any light on whether crimes against cultural property could amount to crimes against humanity, which is a recurring question within international criminal law.[183] In this respect, the Statute is of little avail in allowing the ICC to align (or not) with the practice of the ICTY.[184]

Let us now turn to the deterrent efficacy of the ICC as regards attacks on cultural property. Whether international criminal law, in this case through the ICC, serves a deterrent function is a hotly debated and largely unsettled question.[185] In *Al Mahdi*, ICC judges were pithily confident in the deterrent

[180] Gottlieb (n 45) 866; Frulli (n 42) 212–13.

[181] Gottlieb (n 45) 867; compare the provision with the much broader scope of Second Protocol to Hague Convention of 1999 (n 10) art 15, with Additional Protocol I to the Geneva Conventions (n 29) art 53, with Additional Protocol II to the Geneva Conventions (n 29) art 16 and with Rule 39 and Rule 41 of the ICRC Database on Customary IHL <https://ihl-databases.icrc.org/customary-ihl/eng/docs/v1_rul_rule39> and <https://ihl-databases.icrc.org/customary-ihl/eng/docs/v1_rul_rule41> all accessed 30 May 2020.

[182] Frulli (n 42) 215–16.

[183] See, on this point, Sebastián A. Green Martínez, "Destruction of Cultural Heritage in Northern Mali: A Crime Against Humanity?" (2015) 13 Journal of International Criminal Justice 1073; McGeorge (n 15) 214, 222–23. See also Lenzerini (n 16) 63–64; Gottlieb (n 45) 888–91; Gerstenblith, (n 95) 390.

[184] McGeorge (n 15) 219; *Blaškić* (n 41) [227]; *Prosecutor v Krajišnik* (Judgement) IT-00-39-T (27 September 2006) [840]; *Prosecutor v Kordić et al.* (Judgment) IT-95–14/2-T (26 February 2001) [207]. See also *Prosecutor v Brđanin*, (Judgment) IT-99–36-T (1 September 2004) [1050]; *Prosecutor v Martić* (Judgment) IT-95-11-T (12 June 2007) [399]; *Prosecutor v Milutinović et al.* (Judgment) IT-05–87-T (26 February 2009) [205]; *Prosecutor v Đorđević* (Judgment) IT-05–87/1-T (23 February 2011) [1771]. See also *Prosecutor v Blaskić* (Judgment) IT-95-14-A (29 July 2004) [144]–[149] and *Prosecutor v Gotovina et al* (Judgment) IT-06–90-T (15 April 2011) [1830]. See also O'Keefe, "Protection of Cultural Property under International Criminal Law" (n 95) 380–85.

[185] For a few examples see Mark A. Drumbl, *Atrocity, Punishment, and International Law* (CUP 2007); Sang-Hyun Song, "Preventive Potential of the International Criminal Court" (2013) 3 Asian Journal of International Law 203; Jan Klabbers, "Just Revenge - The Deterrence Argument in International Criminal Law" (2001) 12 Finnish Yearbook of International Law 249; Christopher W Mullins and Dawn L Rothe, "The Ability of the International Criminal Court to Deter Violations of International Criminal Law: A Theoretical Assessment" (2010) 10 International Criminal Law Review 771. On specific and general deterrence see, for example, *Al Mahdi* (n 7) [67].

value of the conviction in the specific area of protection of cultural property. In the determination of the *Al Mahdi* sentence, the ICC mentioned retribution and deterrence "as the primary objectives of punishment at the ICC."[186] It referred to the necessity that the sentence be adequate "to discourage a convicted person from recidivism (specific deterrence), as well as to ensure that those who would consider committing similar crimes will be dissuaded from doing so (general deterrence)."[187] Interestingly enough, trial chamber VIII also considered Al Mahdi's admission of guilt as being potentially capable to deter others tempted to engage in similar crimes "in Mali and elsewhere."[188] The OTP too, on its part, made reference to deterrence as one of the two primary functions of sentencing at the ICC (the other one being retribution) and pushed forward with its two-tiered nature of special and general deterrence.[189] Furthermore, the OTP claimed the deterrent role of collective measures such as the wide dissemination of the Judgment and Sentence.[190] Its most vocal point on deterrence remains, in any event, its invocation of other conflict scenarios where cultural heritage is under particular threat. In the OTP's words: "[d]estruction of cultural property during armed conflict is not only inherently very serious; it is also an issue of current and ongoing concern. The desecration of ancient sites in Syria and Iraq is only the most recent reminder that cultural heritage remains at risk, particularly in conflict zones. Hence the need for a sentence in this case that furthers general as well as specific deterrence."[191]

It is also perplexing to ponder whether the categorization of cultural property as "international" or "cosmopolitan" might paradoxically trigger violence. In Al Mahdi's case, for example, there is evidence that he was able to rally some support around the attacks because he mocked the fact that "UNESCO jackasses"[192]—the distant international community—designated the shrines as worthy of protection. Al Mahdi in a sense galvanized some support around notions of international intervention, colonial

[186] *Al Mahdi* (n 7) [66]. The Court also referred to *Prosecutor v Germain Katanga* (Decision on Sentence pursuant to article 76 of the Statute) ICC-01/04-01/07 (23 May 2014) [37]–[38]; *Prosecutor v Jean-Pierre Bemba Gombo*, (Decision on Sentence pursuant to Article 76 of the Statute) ICC-01/05-01/08 (21 June 2016) [10].

[187] *Al Mahdi* (n 7) [67].

[188] ibid [100]

[189] *Al Mahdi* (n 74) [11].

[190] *Al Mahdi* (n 76) [27]. The OTP also referred, at ft 74, to: *Prosecutor v Thomas Lubanga Dyilo* (Order for Reparations (amended)) ICC-01/04-01/06 (3 March 2015) [43].

[191] *Al Mahdi* (n 74) [20].

[192] *Al Mahdi* (n 7) [46].

favoritism,[193] and perceptions of elite preferentialism of supposed aesthetics over actual religious content and meaning.

A final note arises within the reparations phase of the case of Al Mahdi and the human rights approach adopted by the OTP and the ICC more broadly.[194] Among other things, the ICC put emphasis on the aspect of guarantees of non-repetition, on the heels of the jurisprudence of the Inter-American Court of Human Rights.[195] In this sense, then, the reparative elements of the Rome Statute might also be connectable to preventative goals. Once again, however, deterrence is extremely hard to establish. It implies an evaluation of what "has been prevented from happening" or of what "has happened but with less intensity than it could have had." Both assessments weigh the "unknown," which, at least to some extent, goes beyond a strictly legalistic perspective. But, upon the uncertain assumption that the ICC judgment in *Al Mahdi* does have a deterrent effect, then, a set of unanticipated consequences might emerge. In its conclusion, which immediately follows, this chapter gestures toward some of those tricky questions.

D. Victimology: Who, Exactly, Is Hurt When Cultural Property Is Attacked?

The institutional regime created by the Rome Statute aspires to deliver justice for victims.[196] A comprehensive framework is established in this regard. The inclusion of reparations, for example, in the Rome Statute was intended to remedy a gap insofar as preexisting international criminal tribunals did not or were not able to pursue these restorative goals.

[193] See generally Charlotte L. Joy, *The Politics of Heritage Management in Mali: From UNESCO to Djenné* (Routledge 2013).

[194] See section IV(B) of this chapter (The OTP Approach *in fieri*: Towards a Human Rights Approach to Crimes against or Affecting Cultural Heritage?).

[195] Francesca Capone, "An Appraisal of the Al Mahdi Order on Reparations and Its Innovative Elements. Redress for Victims of Crimes against Cultural Heritage" (2018) 16 Journal of International Criminal Justice 645, 656–59.

[196] ICC Statute (n 4) preamble ("during this century millions of children, women and men have been victims of unimaginable atrocities that deeply shock the conscience of humanity"). See also the Statement of the Prosecutor of the International Criminal Court, Fatou Bensouda, at the opening of the trial in the case against Mr Al Hassan Ag Abdoul Aziz Ag Mohamed Ag Mahmoud (14 July 2020) <https://www.icc-cpi.int/Pages/item.aspx?name=200714-otp-statement-al-hassan> accessed 28 August 2020.

Paradoxically, the victimology of international crimes remains one of the most undertheorized areas of international criminal law.[197] Who is the victim? All sorts of distinctions abound—direct victims, indirect victims, natural persons, the international community as a whole.[198] Are these victims to be constructed as all equal or, perhaps inevitably, will hierarchies arise, to wit: Are some categories of victims more deserving of protection than other categories of victims?

The *Al Mahdi* proceedings demonstrate just how complex these categorizations of victims may become. As a starting point, all judgments and decisions in the *Al Mahdi* proceedings insist that the harm of his intentional attacks in Timbuktu is grave, serious, and severe: these trigger emotional, spiritual, and mental harm. The harm to victims, then, pushes cultural property crimes into the conceptual space of massive crimes physically committed against individuals and their bodies. At this point, however, the victimology becomes more muddied. As mentioned earlier, in the case of cultural property destruction, cosmopolitan approaches see the principal victim as the international community while retentionist approaches see the principal victim as the national or local community. Tensions among these approaches particularly arise in the context of reparations orders, since some individuals or some entities have to actually receive any funds that are awarded and disbursed. On this latter note, in the *Al Mahdi* case a localist approach was pursued in that nearly all the funds went to the population of Timbuktu. If affected victims are to be measured from the perspective of to whom a perpetrator apologizes, well, in Al Mahdi's case his apology extended to a broader spectrum: from the international community down to the local population.

If international war crimes are seen mostly as affecting local populations, then ostensibly this suggests that primary places (and ways) where and how these crimes are to be punished and remedied should also empower local communities and be run by locals. If international war crimes are seen mostly as affecting the global community, then ostensibly internationals should be the ones prosecuting in the hegemonic places and spaces

[197] See generally Drumbl (n 189).

[198] The baseline definition of "victim" is found in ICC Rules of Procedure and Evidence, Rule 85: "(a) "Victims" means natural persons who have suffered harm as a result of the commission of any crime within the jurisdiction of the Court; (b) Victims may include organizations or institutions that have sustained direct harm to any of their property which is dedicated to religion, education, art or science or charitable purposes, and to their historic monuments, hospitals and other places and objects for humanitarian purposes."

of globalism. Cultural property crimes, therefore, might help (re)situate the question of who should decide and enforce based on who has principally been hurt. On this note, however, the scattered and divergent approaches of the *Al Mahdi* sentencing judgment and the reparations order fail to offer a coherent approach.

This scenario becomes even more entangled in light of the latest developments in the *Al Mahdi* and *Al Hassan* cases. As evidenced by the ICC Prosecutor, applicants for reparations in the former case might include prosecution witnesses in the latter case precisely "due to the linkage between the two cases regarding the war crime of attacks against cultural property."[199] The "dual function" of the same individuals as victims and prosecutorial witnesses in two separate but related cases is very likely to raise due process concerns for the defendants in the first place. But what can this suggest in the context of crimes against cultural property? While the "dual function" of certain subjects of criminal proceedings cannot be limited to the limb of crimes against cultural heritage, it does acquire an outstanding significance in this area, for the primary role played by the identification of victims of those crimes, as this chapter posits.

The ICC has certainly made a step toward the acknowledgment that offenses to cultural heritage entail international crimes. As the above discussion has shown, however, more can ensue from this starting point so that victims are effectively repaired and dignified, the crime is more steadily and consistently interpreted, and justice is done.

VI. Conclusion

The discussion of the war crime against cultural heritage in the context of the ICC prompts a series of interrelated issues, one of which concerns the determination of which culture to protect and another one of which refers to the limits and exceptions to this very protection.

[199] *Prosecutor v Ahmad Al Faqi Al Mahdi* (Prosecution's Request regarding applications for individual reparations) ICC-01/12-01/15 (20 February 2020) [2]. See also *Prosecutor v Ahmad Al Faqi Al Mahdi* (Public redacted version of "Trust Fund's response to the "Prosecution's Request regarding applications for individual reparations" (ICC-01/12-01/15-345)") ICC-01/12-01/15 (25 March 2020) [10]. Trial chamber VIII delivered a decision on this request; see *Prosecutor v Ahmad Al Faqi Al Mahdi* (Decision on Prosecution's Request for Provision of Certain Individual Reparations Applications) ICC-01/12-01/15 (28 February 2020).

Activists assume that cultural property is attractive (or at a minimum benign) and comforting for people. The UNESCO Constitution proclaims that "the wide diffusion of culture, and the education of humanity for justice and liberty and peace are *indispensable* to the dignity of man and constitute a sacred duty which all the nations must fulfil."[200] A "culture is great" narrative justifies the entire content of cultural property protection. Hence, cultural property and heritage deserves to be shielded from destruction. But, at least to some extent, this is a naïve assumption. Oppressive cultures have their heritage and property and monuments too: a lot of monuments, statues, commemorations, and sites of worship are awful reminders to people of their own subordination. If prosecuting Al Mahdi deters destruction of cultural property, a question arises as to whether it would not do so ostensibly across the board, unless the judges appointed to international tribunals hoist upon themselves the tremendous power to determine which "cultures" are worthy of protection and which are not?

Outside the discussion of the ICC's deterrent effect, protection of cultural property may also come to interface awkwardly with transitional justice. Posner notes that "The history of iconoclasm is long: Are all iconoclastic movements to be condemned because they destroy cultural property?"[201] When Lemkin initially proposed the crime of "vandalism" in 1933, Aron Trainin, professor of criminal law at Moscow University, denounced this suggested crime because "revolutionary fighting was incompatible with the protection of historical monuments."[202] How to distinguish intentional attacks on Sufi shrines by Salafists, declared a crime in *Al Mahdi* and condemned in The Hague? How to analogize? Who to convict? Who not to charge? Following the *Al Mahdi* case, it may be that the international legal imagination offers less in the way of support for toppling and destroying cultural property which comes to be seen in the prevailing *Zeitgeist* as offensive, degenerate, or abusive. What is the interplay between criminalizing the destruction of cultural property, on the one hand, and transitional justice, on the other?

[200] Constitution of the United Nations Educational, Scientific and Cultural Organization (adopted 16 November 1945, entered into force 4 November 1946) 4 UNTS 275, fourth preambular paragraph (emphasis added). See also Prosecutor Bensouda's invocation that "[c]ulture is who we are": Statement of the Prosecutor at the opening of Al Mahdi Trial (n 162).

[201] Eric A Posner, "The International Protection of Cultural Property: Some Skeptical Observations" (2006) University of Chicago Public Law & Legal Theory, Working Paper No. 141, 9.

[202] Anton Weiss-Wendt, *The Soviet Union and the Gutting of the UN Genocide Convention* (University of Wisconsin Press 2017) 14. For discussion rooted in the South African experiences of colonialism and apartheid, see Lucas Lixinski, "Cultural Heritage Law and Transitional Justice: Lessons from South Africa" (2015) 9 International Journal of Transitional Justice 278.

Developments within international criminal law therefore link to the broader philosophical concerns that Duncan MacIntosh raises in this volume. Somewhat like Trainin, MacIntosh posits that, under certain circumstances, destruction and plundering may constitute morally reasonable acts such that the protection of cultural heritage should not be absolute. It may well be, MacIntosh argues, that theft and destruction of cultural property may be a weapon of self-defense or liberation by the oppressed facing unjust and oppressive cultures and, hence, that destruction could be constructed as "morally appropriate."[203] The work of the ICC, notably *Al Mahdi*, hardens the protection of cultural property, but a question emerges as to whether the law might allow some exceptionalism and suppleness, for example, when it comes to acts of resistance to cultural oppression, and a necessary injection of judgmentalism in terms of whose cultural property to protect and whose cultural property to permit to be deliberately pummeled. Or else, as I have extensively argued elsewhere,[204] the law may be used in assistance of those who seek to protect cultural property that lords over others and that entrenches hierarchy and exclusion. The law then may impede rather than ease transitional justice movements. Examples abound in the context of settler colonialism and "lost causes" (like Confederate memorials in the United States).

In a certain sense, it all comes down to the essential queries of "what is culture?" and "whose culture to protect from what?" This chapter explores these questions from the legal perspective. This perspective, however, must also connect to a variety of interdisciplinary angles so that law can be harmonized with and sensitive to a wider set of aspirations and remain mindful of far-flung concerns.

Any such perspective, moreover, must also adjust to two dynamics. First: the way in which people "view," "enjoy," or "appreciate" cultural property. Here, norms may rapidly be changing. Second: to recognize rapid technological developments such that cultural property may become indestructible through digitization and virtualization while remaining always accessible. If COVID-19 (or other pandemics) mean that, at least for a while, it no longer is safe to visit cultural property in real time, if it no longer is

[203] MacIntosh additionally contends that "since cultural objects can be both tools and symbols of unjust oppression, their theft and destruction ought to be seen as appropriate when this would be a means of overcoming oppression.": Duncan MacIntosh, Chapter 4 of this volume ("Weaponizing Culture: A Limited Defense of the Destruction of Cultural Heritage in War").

[204] Drumbl (n 2).

possible to worship onsite, if it is no longer possible to walk through a museum or look at a sculpture three-dimensionally with one's own eyes, if the musky scent of a chapel housing an ancient fresco can no longer be experienced, what does that imply for the gravity of destroying the actual original physical site assuming it has been digitized? It seems less grave, no? If re-created holograms, virtual tours, and couch-based online sessions determine the social practices of how humans, for their own safety, now interact with cultural property, including religious devotion, then whether the original physical cultural property is destroyed in a war becomes far less consequential or far less existential. For those who care about suddenly lonely "old-fashioned" cultural property that can be sat in, walked around, touched, and gazed upon, well, to some extent the anthropocentric approach developed by the ICC in *Al Mahdi* may indeed prove worrisome.

10
Training for Cultural Property Protection

Laurie W. Rush[1]

I. Introduction

Effective implementation of the values and rules enshrined in the 1954 Hague Convention for the Protection of Cultural Property in the Event of Armed Conflict and its Protocols requires civil-military cooperation. A precondition for successful implementation is an understanding of the relationship between civilian leadership, military leadership, those in charge of planning of military operations, military archaeologists, and subject matter experts. The process of first identifying an archaeological site or museum in a conflict zone to ensuring its survival is both long and arduous. On the one hand, it requires that proper and timely information and expertise reach commanders. On the other hand, it requires that the military has prepared these commanders by providing basic tools for cultural property awareness, opportunities for professional military education on cultural property protection (CPP), the inclusion of CPP scenarios during exercises and field training, and specialized instruction during preparation for deployment. This chapter offers a practitioner's perspective from the US Military on this process.

First, the chapter describes the background of the CPP program within the Department of Defense (DOD) and US Military. It then describes the approach that has been developed on the US side, bringing in cases and lessons identified from operations that serve as examples for building best practices. Finally, it offers recommendations on how to strengthen existing work through policy development.

[1] This chapter is written in her personal capacity and does not reflect the opinions of the US federal government, the US Army, Fort Drum, or the 10th Mountain Division.

Laurie W. Rush, *Training for Cultural Property Protection* In: *The Preservation of Art and Culture in Times of War.* Edited by: Claire Finkelstein, Derek Gillman, and Frederik Rosén, Oxford University Press. © Oxford University Press 2022. DOI: 10.1093/oso/9780197610565.003.0011

II. Origins of Modern Efforts to Establish a Cultural Property Protection (CPP) Program within the Department of Defense

A. Civilian Control over the US Military

In the United States, the duly elected president serves as the Commander-in-Chief of the US Military, a position Commander-in-Chief designed to ensure that the military serves under the control of the elected representatives of the American people. This structure means that a civilian with no previous military experience can give a military order that must be followed by the highest military leaders. The only acceptable reason for failing to follow an order from the Commander-in-Chief would be if the order were illegal. In January 2020, the Commander-in-Chief's declaration that the United States would target cultural sites in Iran brought this relationship into focus on the global stage.[2] There was almost no debate that a military order of this nature would be illegal, and the Secretary of Defense issued a clear statement on the matter within a 48-hour period,[3] making it clear that the Law of Armed Conflict (LOAC) prohibits the targeting of cultural sites and that the US Military would continue to abide by these rules.

It is within this framework of governance that military and academic heritage professionals have endeavored to work together to establish a meaningful cultural property protection program in DOD. It is important to remember that responsible military personnel have traditionally taken great pride in the fact that the US military reports to civilians, considering the chain of command structure to be both a matter of honor and a matter of law.

Recent efforts to establish a CPP Program in DOD began with the US invasion of Iraq in 2003. Not only did the looting of the Iraq Museum generate international criticism of the United States, but global reports of damage done by US Marines and Polish forces at Babylon further characterized Americans and the US military as having little knowledge, appreciation, or respect for the ancient world. Detailed documentation of the damage at Babylon

[2] Laurel Walmsley, "Trump Says He'll Target Iran's Cultural Sites. That's Illegal" (*NPR All Things Considered*, 6 January 2020) <https://www.npr.org/2020/01/06/794006073/trump-says-hell-target-iran-s-cultural-sites-that-s-illegal> accessed 11 February 2020.

[3] Peter Baker and Maggie Haberman, "Pentagon Rules out Striking Iranian Cultural Sites, Contradicting Trump" *The New York Times* (6 January 2020) <https://www.nytimes.com/2020/01/06/us/politics/trump-esper-iran-cultural-sites.html> accessed 16 June 2020.

submitted by John Curtis, then Keeper of the Middle East Department at the British Museum, worsened international condemnation of US troops.[4]

During the media outcry, academic archaeologists, especially those who specialized in ancient Mesopotamia and who were concerned about military damage in the region, made it clear they were unaware the DOD and UK Ministry of Defence had robust domestic cultural resource protection programs, which would help uniformed personnel fulfill their international law obligations to safeguard cultural property during operations.

1. Military Archaeologists and Cultural Property Protection

The United States has hundreds of highly qualified archaeologists, historic preservation architects, and heritage professionals serving as civilians on military payroll. US military archaeologists, most of whom trained first as anthropologists, manage vast acreages of military lands along with heritage professionals who care for historic structures; together, they are responsible for keeping US military installations in compliance with the National Historic Preservation Act (NHPA). NHPA requires inventory of cultural property under Section 110 and provides the opportunity for stakeholder consultation under Section 106 when proposed ground-disturbing activities risk damaging or destroying an archaeological site. In this respect, military land is managed to the same standards as all US federally owned land, including the National Parks. Since military training and construction often result in significant ground disturbance to these lands, the DOD invests millions of dollars annually conducting archaeological surveys, site evaluation, and stakeholder consultation. All military land that is subject to disturbance from military training as well as all new construction footprints require thorough archaeological review.

Given the scale of these activities and the diversified responsibilities they involve, hundreds of archaeologists are employed as civilians in the military, defense contractors, university recipients of military funds, field technicians, research fellows, and field school participants. Millions of acres have been surveyed, and there are currently tens of thousands of archaeological

[4] John E Curtis, "Report on Meeting at Babylon 11–13 December 2004" (The British Museum 2004) < https://www.academia.edu/35729613/Report_on_meeting_at_Babylon_11_13_December_2004_In_M_van_Ess_and_J_E_Curtis_eds_Final_Report_on_Damage_Assessment_in_Babylon_International_Coordination_Committee_for_the_Safeguarding_of_the_Cultural_Heritage_of_Iraq_UNESCO_Paris_2009_Annex_3 _ project/babylon_report_2004-5.aspx> no longer available.

sites in the DOD inventory. Thousands have been designated for permanent protection.

The UK Ministry of Defence has a similarly robust site protection program in place with full-time archaeologists and heritage professionals and has carefully inventoried its military training areas. Few people realize that Stonehenge, the world-famous heritage site, is immediately adjacent to the Salisbury Defence Estate, acreage that features some of the best-preserved archaeological properties in the United Kingdom.[5]

As an invasion of Iraq seemed imminent, US archaeologists and those with an interest in antiquities became increasingly alarmed by the possible destruction of Iraq's cultural heritage and attempted to warn US political and military leadership.[6] In January, 2003, a meeting took place between McGuire Gibson, Director of the University of Chicago Oriental Institute; Maxwell Anderson, President of the Association of Art Museum Directors; Ashton Hawkins, President of the American Council for Cultural Policy' and Joseph Collins, Deputy Assistant Undersecretary of Defense for Stability Operations, and his staff. After discussing the overall risks and concerns, Gibson stayed behind to clarify that there were thousands, rather than dozens, of sites to consider. He shared his data with the Defense Intelligence Agency, which was used in the development and implementation of the "no-strike" list for Iraq. In his interview with Cogbill,[7] Collins described the minimal destruction and damage due to direct US military attack as an "underreported success story."

This point has never been substantively challenged. The preponderance of damage to heritage in Iraq was nevertheless due to two types of problems—looting and construction impacts. The construction impact damage, more specifically, occurred during the post-conflict establishment of forward operating bases and expansion of military facilities. Current US military CPP efforts are still grappling with the challenge of effectively applying the data and success of the "no-strike" process to the planning and implementation of ground operations.

[5] Martin Brown, "Archaeology and Heathland on the Defence Estate" in HDV Prendergast (ed), *Heathlands—Past, Present, and Future* (East Sussex County Council 2005); Martin Brown, "Good Training and Good Practice: Protection of the Cultural Heritage on the UK Defence Training Estate" in Laurie Rush (ed), *Archaeology, Cultural Property and the Military* (Boydell and Brewer 2010).

[6] James Cogbill, "Protection of Arts and Antiquities during Wartime: Examining the Past and Preparing for the Future" (January–February 2008) Military Review 30–36; McQuire Gibson, "Diary" (2009) 31 (1.1) London Review of Books 42–43; Andrew Lawler, "Mayhem in Mesopotamia" (2003) 301 Science 582–88.

[7] Cogbill (n 6) 30–36.

We also saw an internal divide in responses among US archaeologists between anthropologists who serve on military bases and classicists and art historians who study the ancient world. While all are archaeologists, there is a simple explanation for the delayed partnership between the two communities in protecting cultural property in conflict zones. Although both professions use archaeological field excavation techniques, archaeologists who study the Americas and generally work on North American military land train first as anthropologists and continue their careers within the framework of the Society for American Archaeology (SAA). Archaeologists who work in the ancient world generally begin their careers learning ancient languages and/or studying ancient objects before applying archaeological excavation techniques to objects, ancient structures and communities, and the historical record. These professionals often work in museums and academic settings; their collegial organization is the Archaeological Institute of America (AIA). It is unusual for members of these two groups to collaborate as students, in journal publications, or at professional meetings.

2. The Iraq Experience

Both communities of archaeologists were deeply concerned after hearing about looting at the Iraq Museum and damage at Babylon. AIA archaeologists approached the military once again, while military archaeologists reached out to their academic and military colleagues to explore the possibilities for training troops. The goal was to offer expertise to deploying personnel, so they could identify and appropriately respond to the cultural property they encountered in the host nation environment or conflict zone. Archaeologists who choose to participate in military education and training serve as interlocutors between the academic and military communities, a position of great responsibility. Not only do these advisors have an obligation to be competent subject matter experts within their areas of expertise, but they also require a thorough understanding of military culture, training, and operations. Individuals who risk their lives to support a military mission deserve accurate and pertinent information that will contribute to a successful mission outcome. LOAC is important; however, if the ultimate goal is the protection of cultural property in armed conflict, then it is critical to develop an understanding of how effectively identifying and responding to cultural property on the battlefield will contribute to mission success. This process requires effective cross-cultural communication between the predominantly civilian academic community, who can provide knowledge, training, and education; and military personnel, who will benefit from access to critical information and the opportunity to practice their skills in the field.

Initial attempts from 2004 to 2006 to establish civil-military partnerships to improve military readiness included the AIA Soldier Lecture program and archaeologists working with the Army and Air Force Environmental Programs who provided lectures and developed archaeology awareness materials for soldiers. Brian Rose, then President of the AIA, along with Major (retired) Corine Wegener put together a multidisciplinary team that provided lectures at Camp LeJeune, Fort Bragg, and Fort Dix. Rose also offered soldiers an opportunity for behind-the-scenes visits at the University of Pennsylvania Museum. Major Wegener, the Founding President of United States Committee of Blue Shield, was the Civil Affairs Officer who reported to the National Museum of Iraq to assist after the looting. She is one of the few US Army Monuments Officers to serve since World War II, and among her significant accomplishments was the successful evacuation of the Iraq Jewish Archives from a sewage filled basement in Saddam Hussein's Intelligence Headquarters in Baghdad. Not only did Major Wegener provide lectures to soldiers, she also retired from the Army and devoted her energy to establishing the US Committee of the Blue Shield. This organization played a critical role in the ratification of the 1954 Hague Convention for the Protection of Cultural Property in the Event of Armed Conflict (1954 Hague) by the Senate in 2009.

DOD archaeologists received funding from 2006–2009 from the DOD Legacy Resources Management Program and from Air Combat Command to initiate the "In Theater Heritage Training Program for Deploying Personnel." The program approached the challenges related to heritage in operational areas from three directions: education and awareness training, mapping and planning, and establishing stronger military regulations and guidelines for cultural property protection. Since then, they have added a fourth initiative: research designed to better understand the strategic and tactical costs without CPP and better appreciate the mission benefits when CPP is implemented successfully during global operations. "In Theater" project components included informational websites about the heritage of Iraq, Afghanistan, and Egypt. (Egypt was included to assist in preparation for US involvement in the Bright Star War Games.) The project also developed archaeology awareness playing cards for the same three countries. The playing cards received widespread media coverage, and this publicity played a key role in helping the AIA archaeologists to find and partner with US military archaeologists.

The timing was rather fortuitous. As it would happen, First Lady Laura Bush was interested in historic preservation, making cultural property protection one of the top five environmental priorities for the US Central Command Environmental Program. The increased visibility of the issue encouraged the Office of the Secretary of Defense Environmental International Cooperation (DEIC) Program to support project initiatives, such as archaeology awareness materials to be used during the Bright Star War Games and opportunities for cultural property protection discussions at environmental meetings in Jordan, Abu Dhabi, Qatar, and Afghanistan. Participation by a US Army archaeologist in partnership with Abdul Wasey Feroozi, Director General of Afghan Heritage at environmental shuras in Kabul, resulted in one million dollars of support managed by the Army Corps of Engineers for construction of a warehouse to store recovered artifacts from the rescue archaeological excavations at Mes Aynek, the ancient Buddhist site threatened with destruction by a Chinese copper mine.

III. Cultural Property Protection as a Force Multiplier

All discussions concerning military implementation of cultural property protection begin with customary international law and the 1954 Hague Convention and its Protocols. During the Senate ratification process of the 1954 Hague in 2009, DOD supported ratification with the observation that, for the most part, DOD policies and practices were already in compliance with the commitments outlined in the Convention. However, that interpretation was based on a narrow interpretation of the 1954 Hague regarding the use of kinetic force. It did not consider the delicate political field challenges related to navigating missions in heritage rich areas, including sacred places and places of worship.

Lessons identified and shared by 10th Mountain Division soldiers and other units returning from recent operations indicate that, from the perspective of fighting units heading into a conflict zone, CPP can be critical to mission success. This relationship is best understood through the lens of the US-defined phases or general groups of military activities of a military operation, which are "shape [the military environment], deter [the enemy], seize initiative, dominate [the enemy], stabilize, and enable civil authorities."[8] These phases are often condensed into three phases, which are planning, execution, and enabling civil authority. The cultural property protection activities corresponding to these phases are *Avoidance, Minimization, Recovery, and Maximization*. The US military's working definitions of these concepts are the following:

Avoidance—Avoid adverse effects to cultural property if possible. Successful implementation of the no strike list is a perfect example.

Minimization—If avoidance is not an option, minimize direct impacts and collateral damage. Proportional force is critical to minimization if cultural property is put in play by hostile forces. If there is a determination of military necessity and cultural property is affected during kinetic operations, minimization still applies when stabilizing the environment. At this point, damage to cultural property can be minimized during the occupation of, base operations on, or in the immediate vicinity of an archaeological site or historic structure. Planning is also a key component of minimization: adequate information operations and mapping can minimize inadvertent damage to cultural property during the execution phase, humanitarian operations, and disaster response.

Recovery—This concept of "mea culpa" applies to situations where cultural property has been damaged, either as the result of first use or inadvertently. This concept outlines appropriate responses and reactions in these situations.

Maximization—This term refers to opportunities when respect for and protection of cultural property result in greater mission success. Maximization should offer examples of the strategic and potential tactical value of cultural property protection.

The following section will draw on examples from US operations to outline these dimensions of the relationship between CPP and military operations. The purpose is to give the reader a sense of the emerging perspective in the US military regarding how to address new challenges related to cultural property.

[8] "Joint Publication 3-0, Joint Operations, 17 January 2017, Incorporating Change 1, 22 October 2018" (US Joint Chiefs of Staff).

A. The Planning Phase: Avoidance and Minimization

Military considerations for operational planning for cultural property protection include identifying cultural properties and working with information operations, intelligence, and geospatial analysts to ensure that commanders in various branches get the necessary information to consider cultural property as part of the military environment. To achieve avoidance, the Defense Intelligence Agency and military planners need to know the nature and locations of property at risk. For the kinetic or active conflict phase, avoidance takes the form of providing the targeting or fires team with the non-lethal or "no strike" target list along with operational maps to enable effective cultural property protection during ground operations. Responsible planning for establishment of military Forward Operating Bases (FOBs), Command Outposts (COPs), and other forms of infrastructural improvement also require survey and evaluation processes to identify cultural property that could be affected by construction and occupation. In that regard, a key lesson for the United States is that these information, mapping, and assessment activities require workable partnerships between the military and subject matter experts who possess intimate knowledge of the mission area and can provide the most granular information possible.

The ideal solution is to avoid military activities in the immediate vicinity of significant cultural property; the next best option is to take cultural property into account in any planning activity. The ability to identify and respond appropriately to the presence of cultural property on the battlefield may enable commanders to take the necessary precautions. One oft-mentioned example is the case of Babylon in Iraq. The damage at Babylon, which stemmed from the US and Polish forces posted there to protect the site, could have been completely avoided if responsible commanders had called in archaeologists familiar with Babylon to agree on placement and construction methods for defensive perimeters. Significant damage to the site was caused by digging trenches and scooping soil to fill sandbags, so-called "Hesko™-bags." Filling Hesko-bags with local soil is a typical approach to preparing a secure wall in a dangerous environment, although the amount of soil required in such a construction can be enormous. The trouble with Heskos in archaeologically sensitive areas is that digging destroys archaeological material, removes it from its original context, and deposits it in completely different locations.

In addition to violating the 1954 Hague Convention, the damage at Babylon makes it clear that inattention to cultural property may complicate the mission politically. The damage caused at Babylon, an iconic property in the Middle East, had the secondary effects of causing the US military to lose respect among coalition military personnel in the Islamic world and generating substantial negative news coverage. From a Middle Eastern perspective, the mistakes made by US personnel at Babylon were due to either ignorance or indifference, neither of which are admirable qualities. This situation could have been avoided with minimal awareness and the involvement of archaeologists to advise military activities. The lesson identified is the importance of educational and accountability structures as well as the presence of an environmental compliance officer trained in CPP.

B. Avoidance and Minimization, Ancient Infrastructure

World heritage sites and other spectacular cultural sites are obvious and easy to identify. When soldiers travel to countries where the culture is unfamiliar, however, cultural property may be difficult to identify in the landscape, such as sophisticated water systems and other forms of ancient infrastructure. Oftentimes these systems remain in use and may form critical components of community and economic life at the local level. One example is the qanat system of the ancient Persians. Also known as "karez" in Afghanistan and "foggaras" in North Africa, karez can run for miles connecting the village irrigation system to the nearby hillsides where the system originates, tapping the water table. The subterranean karez channel can be large enough for men to travel long distances underground with the cleaning holes—the ones visible on the aerial imagery—offering access to the surface.

These systems have distinctive signatures in aerial imagery. When the lines of holes appear on the images, the ability to map and analyze the system offers a wealth of useful military intelligence. Following the water system on an image will lead to the irrigation outlet for the community, thus revealing both the family who controls this irrigation and local power dynamics. It is also critical to appreciate the nature of the system and the associated holes because any structure built on top is vulnerable to incursion from below.

Forward Operating Base (FOB) Wolverine in Afghanistan offers a case in point. As the United States began to expand FOB Wolverine, the Taliban went to the elders of the surrounding villages and told them the United States was going to destroy their water supply. The water supply in question was being provided by a viable karez system that had been functioning for at least two thousand, if not three thousand years. Imagery analysts noted the holes indicating the presence of the system; however, they had no idea what they were and chose to ignore their presence. In addition to the presence of the underground tunnel compromising force protection for the FOB, the Taliban were proven correct when the US project destroyed the water supply to four of the five villages surrounding FOB Wolverine. To add insult to injury, sewage from the FOB was entering the system, causing deep resentment in the affected villages where military personnel at the base were supposed to be "winning hearts and minds." Similar to the Babylon case, cultural property protection and military operational objectives go hand in hand. The FOB Wolverine example further illustrates the potential value of partnership with archaeologists for identification and analysis of critical features in host nation landscapes using remote sensing and aerial imagery.

C. Avoidance and Minimization, Warrior Base Kirkuk

As the United States occupied Iraq in 2003, coalition personnel found themselves on cultural property where Iraqi forces had placed military bases. It is true that from a landscape perspective, many defensible positions thousands of years ago are considered prime military real estate today. It remains unclear whether Saddam Hussein deliberately built up military bases on or adjacent to ancient sites, although the conventional wisdom assumes he did, especially in the placement of Talil Air Base adjacent to the Ziggurat of Ur. There is no question that building on or adjacent to an ancient site offers a strategic advantage in terms of the passive protection offered when the adversary must abide by LOAC. As a result, when the US coalition needed to secure Talil Air Base, its proximity to the Ancient City of Ur and its iconic ziggurat had to be taken into consideration by the fires team to minimize the risk of collateral damage.

Warrior Base Kirkuk is the US name for Al Hurriya Air Base established by the Iraqis at the summit of a tell with occupation dating back at least six thousand years as evidenced by Ubaid pottery found in the vicinity. The highest point on the installation conceals the remains of the temple area of the ancient Assyrian capital, Arrapha, dating to approximately 600 BCE. The nearby Citadel of Kirkuk was once the city of Arraphka in Sargon's Akkadian Empire dating to over 2300 BCE. Saddam Hussein's regime destroyed most of the historic homes on the Citadel in its attempts to Arabianize Kirkuk.

When the United States assumed responsibility for the base at Kirkuk, they found themselves occupying a significant archaeological site, which to many Western military personnel may have looked like an ordinary hill. The first mission impact resulted in delays for establishment of an air traffic control radar facility at the summit of the tell. The radar itself was mounted on a military vehicle that was able to navigate to the summit with a minimum of ground disturbance, and the Air Force completed its due diligence in terms of consulting with the Director of the Kirkuk Museum about placement of this equipment. The problem, however, arose when the Air Force needed to complete a fence along one of the terraces of the tell in order to provide additional security. Artifacts spilled out of the fence post excavations, delaying construction until the objects were recovered. Recognizing that the process was damaging archaeological deposits, fence construction was further delayed as the installation commander worked with the Iraqi site inspector and local museum representatives to find a solution for taking care of the artifacts that had been disturbed and a plan for minimizing further disturbance as the fence was installed. In terms of mission consequences, the supply line into FOB Warrior was seriously affected by the inability to safely land aircraft that were going to be relying on operable air traffic control. Interruption to the food supply meant that soldiers already living on base had to rely on powdered food known as "Meals Ready to Eat" or MREs for six additional weeks.[9]

The archaeological challenges continued for the duration of the US occupation at Warrior Base Kirkuk. In addition to remains of the ancient city, use of the area by Iraqi personnel had resulted in construction of mosques and interments of Iraqi soldiers who had been killed in previous conflicts. Every time the United States attempted any form of infrastructure improvement requiring ground disturbance, such as installation of electrical conduit or trenching for better drainage, they encountered archaeological material.

Would there have been an option to ignore the archaeological issues and expressions of Iraqi concerns? According to LOAC, the answer is no. In addition, stirring up discontent among the citizens of Kirkuk could easily have escalated into a force protection issue. Given the negative global media resulting from damage at Babylon along with looting of the

[9] Joseph (Sepp) Scanlin, "Personal Communication with Laurie Rush," ROTC Presentation (Fort Drum, NY 2017).

National Museum of Iraq, angry Iraqis in Kirkuk would have found journalists more than happy to share their story with a global audience creating further difficulties for the US military. Could the radar at Kirkuk been installed without delay? If the planners had been aware of the site and its implications to the operation and called in due expertise, they could have been ahead of the situation.

The lessons identified from Kirkuk, as well as from Babylon, make clear that when military necessity forces commanders to construct military installations in archaeologically sensitive areas, precaution for the sake of law and strategy greatly benefits from an awareness of the archaeological challenges *prior* to initiation of planning and construction. It furthermore benefits from speedy reach-back capability to archaeologists with regional expertise; maps of the affected archaeological property; ongoing consultation with host nation archaeological inspectors; and access to engineering techniques and specifications that minimize ground disturbance. Compared to the construction costs of military infrastructure, these items are low-cost-high-gain measures to fulfill LOAC obligation, navigate cultural and environmental sensitivities in mission areas, and safeguard international reputation.

Without institutionalized measures in place, cultural property protection becomes coincidental. In the case of Warrior Base Kirkuk, it was sheer good fortune that First Sergeant Darrel Pinckney, a NY Air National Guardsman and professional archaeologist, happened to be assigned to the base. 1SG Pinckney volunteered to act as a Cultural Resources Manager in addition to his regular duties during his tour at Kirkuk. With support from the Central Command Environmental Engineer, 1SG Pinckney established a Cultural Resources planning map of the base so that future excavations could be planned while minimizing adverse effects on the archaeology there. In addition, his availability as an immediate responder when projects uncovered artifacts made it possible for the challenges to be resolved quickly and effectively. As a First Sergeant with critical responsibilities unrelated to archaeology, the dual commitment was a challenge. There is no question, however, that an individual in uniform with background expertise is invaluable in these situations. Airman Pinckney's contributions at Kirkuk offer a model for effective and efficient cultural resources management going forward.[10]

[10] Darrell Pinckney, "Time Not On My Side, Cultural Resources Management in Kirkuk, Iraq" in Laurie Rush (ed), *Archaeology, Cultural Property and the Military* (Boydell & Brewer 2010) 117–25.

IV. The Execution Phase

A. Destruction of Cultural Property and Strategic Messaging

When military advisors focus on ideological explanations for deliberate or "performance" destruction of cultural property by an adversary, it prevents the military from gaining any analytical insights if the actions were instead studied as a form of military strategic messaging. Well-known cases include the Taliban's destruction of the Bamiyan Buddhas and ISIS's destruction at Palmyra.

One hypothesis that needs to be rigorously tested is whether there was a correlation between setbacks for ISIS and demonstrations of power in the form of deliberate destruction of iconic properties. For example, was the destruction of the Tomb of Jonah, Nebi Yunus, in Mosul on July 24, 2014, timed in response to the Delta Force prison raid on July 4, 2014, which killed multiple ISIS personnel? In any case, such intended cultural property destruction should be understood as a declaration of power and a military strategic move rather than a religious act.

For example, in June 2015, US forces were preparing for deployment to Iraq for an "Aid and Assist" mission where they would work with Iraqi forces in preparation for retaking of ISIS controlled territory. At this point in time, Iraqis, many of whom had lost family members or had family trapped within ISIS held territory, were anxious to begin their offensive. One of the main goals of the coalition was to encourage patience. It was critically important that the coalition not advance until there was confidence that all Iraqis involved were trained to the point where they would not only fight with courage but also be victorious. At the same time, ISIS had moved into the iconic Syrian City of Palmyra. In contrast to some previous episodes of destruction, ISIS took a hostage approach to Palmyra. At first, they said they would not do damage. Then they publicly assassinated the 82-year-old Director of the Museum who would not reveal the location of the antiquities they wished to steal and sell. After this atrocity, when ISIS again had the world's full attention, they began to select the monuments for destruction one by one. While the coalition was encouraging patience in the service of readiness, European commanders were receiving pressure from the court of public opinion that it was time to move. There was some similar sentiment in the United States, but not nearly to the extent of the feelings expressed in Western Europe. Was ISIS hoping that by holding Palmyra hostage in such a public way they could goad the coalition into moving too soon? Given the potential outcome of a 2015 anti-ISIS invasion of northern Iraq and Syria, this question deserves serious consideration. More importantly, if the United States is faced with similar circumstances in the future, the potential military messaging component of the behavior should, given the significant political role of cultural property in ethnic conflicts, be taken seriously by intelligence analysts.

B. Cultural Property and the Operational Landscape: "Vineyards Are the Worst"

Detailed understanding of cultural modifications to the landscape also provides valuable tactical intelligence for operations planning. For example, one form of typical construction for a vineyard in Afghanistan is excavation of deep trenches for planting the vines. The grapes grow up the sides of the trench, and the design maximizes access of the root stock to available water. A deeply trenched vineyard is not only a major obstacle for efficient movement across the landscape, but if a force is unfamiliar with the nature of the design, a trenched vineyard in full foliage can conceal hundreds of unexpected adversarial personnel. Improved vineyard real estate is highly prized in Afghanistan, and property lines are not straight and well defined. When Canadian forces attempted to build a straight road across vineyard property they had acquired by the North American legal process of eminent domain, they put the vineyard owners in the untenable position of either fighting to regain their honor or losing status within their local community.[11] The consequence was the creation of adversaries in places where there may have been prior support for the NATO mission.

C. Use of Proportional Force, Khan Neshin, Afghanistan

Khan Neshin is a fortification in the Helmand province that was originally constructed by the forces of Genghis Khan. As a strategic defensive position, Khan Neshin has possibly been in continuous use for military purposes since its construction approximately 900 years ago. In more

[11] Carlotta Gall and Ruhullah Khapalwak, "Winning Hearts While Flattening Vineyards Is Rather Tricky" *The New York Times* (11 March 2011) <https://www.nytimes.com/2011/03/12/world/asia/12panjwai.html> accessed 13 June 2020.

recent times, the fortification was an Afghan military installation before being occupied by the Taliban. In the spring and summer of 2009, US Marines moved into Khan Neshin, ousting the enemy forces located there. The taking of Khan Neshin is a good example of how military necessity may override international protection obligations, minding also how the strong evidence of Taliban forces contributed to the decision to take action. Recognizing the historical value of the site, the USMC judiciously used proportional force to minimize the damage.

Once secure, the international forces decided to establish their own base at Khan Neshin. The 1954 Hague Convention does not prohibit such use if deemed necessary and due precaution is taken. The cultural property protection challenge then became one of minimizing impacts to the historic structure and adjacent archaeological deposits during the occupation and possible expansion of the installation. An environmental inspection team documented the condition of the property relatively early in the infrastructure improvement construction phase. Careful documentation can support the mission by clarifying the condition of a property at the moment US forces take responsibility. As a result, the likelihood of the United States being held responsible for damage that occurred to a historic site prior to US troop presence diminishes. In comparison, failure to document conditions at Babylon made it easy to blame the United States for all damage observed there, even though Saddam Hussein had been "improving" the site for many years via "restoration" and palace construction prior to US occupation. Inclusion of documentation of historic structures by the environmental team at Khan Neshin helped to prevent the United States from being held responsible for damage to the structure from previous Afghan Army and Taliban occupation. However, post-occupation establishment of a larger modern military base adjacent to the historic Khan Neshin fortification with the associated damage to archaeological deposits is problematic.[12]

D. Use of Proportional Force, Sniper in the Date Palm

Lessons identified from US military operations also show how cultural property plays a role during the kinetic phase. During US operations in Iraq,

[12] Elena Leoni, "CPP Afghanistan Study," paper presented at NATO Capstone Workshop (San Remo, Italy 2016).

the proverbial "sniper in the date palm" story emerged. Whether or not a specific case can be documented, it serves as a useful cautionary tale for the inexperienced warfighter in an insurgency situation. The scenario is as follows: US forces begin to take sniper fire and recognize that the firing position is in the crown of a date palm located in a larger grove. From the ground it is impossible to identify the precise tree where the sniper is hiding. The force commander on the ground decides that the most expedient solution in terms of force protection is to cut down all the date palms in the vicinity. In some versions of the story, after destruction of the entire grove, the soldiers or Marines realize they still have not accurately identified the sniper's location. They later discover that an insurgent had covertly entered the grove belonging to a wealthy leader of a powerful extended family in the area. This individual had been appreciative of Saddam Hussein's removal and was somewhat sympathetic to US forces. The grove represented a major portion of his worldly assets; symbolized his power; was his legacy to his sons; and would take decades to recover. Destruction of this property would encourage him to organize the family and entire kinship network to ally with the insurgency. Destruction of cultural property can have the power to ignite an entire community of enemies.

E. Stabilization: Protection of the Ancient City of Ur and Return to Iraqi Stewardship

As the advantages of avoidance and minimization are considered, it quickly becomes clear that when cultural property is spared in conflict, some of the foundations for community recovery remain in place. The ancient City of Ur, putative birthplace of the Old Testament prophet Abraham, is another example where Saddam Hussein placed an Iraqi military installation, Talil Air Base, on or adjacent to an important archaeological site, perhaps hoping that Western forces would be reluctant to risk the collateral damage that could result from aerial bombardment. Ur of the Chaldees is one of the most important cities of ancient Mesopotamia and biblical birthplace of Abraham. Dating back at least six thousand years, the City of Ur covers an area of fourteen square kilometers and is surrounded by ancient suburbs that now contribute to archaeological deposits that extend beyond the immediate city area. Western archaeologists have been excavating at Ur since the late nineteenth and early twentieth centuries with eminent investigators like Sir

Leonard Woolley from the United Kingdom guiding a sustained presence from the British Museum and the University of Pennsylvania. The local community, prior to establishment of the air base, relied upon the archaeology as a critical component of the economy, providing laborers, food, hospitality, transportation, and a wide range of additional incidental supplies.

Archaeological site looting first emerged as a source of income as the West began to impose economic sanctions against the Hussein regime. Looting increased and reached epidemic proportions in the immediate aftermath of the 2003 invasion. As looters ravaged the ancient cities of Mesopotamia, the proximity of Ur to the air base played a critical role in saving the site. When the United States and coalition assumed responsibility for Talil, they extended the base perimeter and fence to incorporate the ancient city, preventing access by anyone other than Western military forces. Because of its biblical significance and the looming presence of the ziggurat that had been reinforced with modern mud brick, chaplains even organized tours to the site. A grandson of one of the original archaeological laborers who worked with Leonard Woolley and who lived in the immediate area was even hired to provide guided tours.

By 2008, however, the provincial site inspector had been denied access to the site by security guards, and Iraqis who lived in the area were becoming increasingly frustrated by the experience of looking through the fence and watching Americans in uniform visiting their heritage. Their complaints eventually reached US Commanding General David Petraeus. Fortunately, by that time, the region had stabilized to the point where Abdulamir Hamdani,[13] the Provincial Site Inspector, felt confident that it was safe for the site to return to Iraqi stewardship. Transfer of the site required installation of fencing closer to the military airfield with the associated construction of a new visitor's center checkpoint. Hamdani was concerned about potential site damage from these projects, so State Department Heritage Liaison Diane Siebrandt, brought in Brian Rose, then President of the AIA and a trusted authority, to inspect the construction excavations. There had been minor damage related to a borrow pit area, but the consensus was that the benefit of returning the ancient city outweighed damage on the outskirts. On May 13, 2009, the ancient city of Ur was returned in excellent condition to the stewardship of the Iraqi people. Foreign visitors in tour buses had even begun

[13] Now Dr. Abdulamir Hamdani, Minister of Culture, Iraq.

to arrive, and over 300 Iraqi people attended the celebration that included a rock concert using the steps of the ziggurat as a stage.

F. Maximization, Tourist Amenities at Aqar Quf

When US Forces entered Aqar Quf, Iraq, it was immediately clear that the tourist amenities had been damaged during civil unrest. Prior to US intervention, the ziggurat at Aqar Quf had been an important destination for tourists and pilgrims who contributed to the local economy. Given its location near Baghdad, the tourists to Aqar Quf were almost all Iraqi citizens, so this destination also represented an important and pleasant recreational opportunity for local communities that did not require extensive travel. In his civilian life, Reserve Officer 1LT (now Major) Benjamin Roberts was a historic preservation professional with an advanced degree in historic preservation from Georgia Tech University. LT Roberts used his expertise to analyze the potential economic contributions of the tourist site to the community and envision repairs to the tourist café. He encouraged his commanding officer to allocate Commander's Emergency Response Program (CERP) funds to support his idea. Representatives of US forces met with local officials to plan for restoration of the site. The rehabilitation project was a success, and tourists were able to return and enjoy the site.[14] This example underscores the potential value of cultural property expertise among uniformed personnel. LT Roberts's contribution is similar to the positive accomplishments of the Monuments Fine Arts and Archives (MFAA) officers of World War II.

While protecting the ancient City of Ur and the tourist amenities at Aqar Quf serve as both iconic and pragmatic examples, together they show how the presence of intact property, infrastructure, and heritage makes it easier to rebuild a community emerging from conflict or disaster. When the date palm groves, vineyards, pomegranate orchards, ancient water systems, places of worship, and even tourist lunch counters are intact or relatively undamaged, the fabric of community life has a much better opportunity to mend.

[14] Benjamin A Roberts and Gary B Roberts, "A Case Study in Cultural Heritage Protection in a Time of War" in James Zeidler and Joris Kila (eds), *Cultural Heritage in the Crosshairs* (Brill 2013) 169–93.

V. Civil-Military Relations and Cultural Property Protection

The earlier examples show how the implementation of the values and rules enshrined in the 1954 Hague Convention, as well as military handling of strategic and tactical issues related to the presence of cultural property in operational areas, requires cooperation between military leadership, military archaeology programs, and civilian subject matter experts during all phases of military operations. Lessons from the US military show that such cooperation on several occasions prevented and ameliorated serious operational errors that could have compromised military missions or caused them to fail. Once military archaeologists partnered with subject matter experts for host nation regions, both sides worked to establish a flow of information that could support continued information development, training opportunities, and education projects. Military archaeologists worked hard to bring warfighters directly into the partnerships. Initially, these efforts were organized in a structure called the Combatant Command Cultural Heritage Action Group or CCHAG, currently known as the Military Cultural Heritage Action Group or MILCHAG. This unofficial organization met on an annual basis at Central Command Headquarters and then in Washington and established a website where heritage information for conflict zones was made readily available for military personnel. Members of the academic community and NGOs also encouraged protection of cultural property in conflict zones by preparing cultural property inventories for areas of the world where cultural property is at risk.

The second Protocol of the 1954 Hague Convention suggests that each country that has ratified the convention could establish a Committee of the Blue Shield to assist the nation in meeting its ratification responsibilities. The United States and United Kingdom both have incredibly active Blue Shield Committees. These committees have worked to encourage ratification of the Convention by their respective countries, successfully in the United States and United Kingdom, and have been actively working to provide education, training, and mapping information to military personnel.

In the United States, in addition to the US Committee of the Blue Shield (USCBS), a consortium led by the Smithsonian Heritage Preservation Officer in partnership with the University of Pennsylvania and the American Association for the Advancement of Science has also been actively educating military personnel; analyzing impacts to cultural property as seen on satellite imagery; initiating research into patterns of deliberate destruction of cultural property; working on the ground in Syria; and assisting with protection of immovable cultural property in situ.[15]

Inspired by the NATO Advanced Research workshop and Smithsonian/Penn project outcomes, other research groups began to develop data-driven analysis of cultural property treatment on the battlefield. For example, in a comparison between villages in Afghanistan where NATO vehicles avoided cemeteries and roadside shrines and villages where NATO vehicles parked in cemeteries and damaged roadside shrines, Jacob Aronson[16] discovered a 30% increase in attacks with improvised explosive devices (IEDs) in the latter locations. When cultural property issues have a direct effect on the lives of military personnel, training and education becomes increasingly important.

VI. Challenges for Academic Military Partners

The idea of having archaeologists working with or for the DOD did not become overtly controversial until the US invasion of Iraq in 2003. It is true that events surrounding US intervention in Vietnam and covert actions in other sovereign nations created a schism in the United States between the academic and military communities, especially in the realm of social sciences. Historic events like Project Camelot, proposed in 1964 and shut down in 1965 when scholars voiced their concerns, are often mentioned as examples of the schism between the military and social science communities. Carolyn Fluehr-Lobban's volume *Ethics and Anthropology: Ideas and Practice*[17] offers a detailed and thoughtful history of the strained and complex relationship between the military and anthropology. David Price's volume *Weaponizing Anthropology*[18] also provides a detailed discussion of and historical context for issues surrounding US military efforts to incorporate knowledge of culture into planning, strategy, and preparation of deploying personnel. (Price[19] also provided historical context for relationships between archaeologists

[15] <https://culturalrescue.si.edu/what-we-do/research/culture-conflict-research-network/>.

[16] Jacob Aronson, "Identifying the Impact of Heritage Site Damage in Afghanistan" (The University of Maryland unpublished paper 2016).

[17] (AltaMira Press 2013).

[18] (Counterpunch and AK Press 2011).

[19] David Price, "Cloak and Trowel, Should Archaeologists Double as Spies?" (September/October 2003) 5 (56) Archaeology Magazine.

and the military in his article "Cloak & Trowel.") Susan Allen's *Classical Spies: American Archaeologists in the OSS in World War II Greece*[20] offers contrasting historical examples as she discusses archaeologists who served in a wide range of capacities in World War II.

It is important to note that there is no historic relationship between past employment of anthropologists by the DOD for intelligence and strategic purposes and the military archaeologists who are employed by defense to keep military installations in compliance with the National Historic Preservation Act. Installation archaeology is part of the Installation Management Command (IMCOM) Public Works Environmental portfolio. This component of the military is a completely different command from the fighting commands and distinct from the Defense Intelligence Agency. Installation archaeology and cultural resources management programs emerged in all the services for every large acreage military installation during the mid-1980s. Since then, judicial actions in favor of Native Hawaiian, Native Alaskan, and Native American ancestral and sacred places located on military land have reinforced the importance of cultural resources management and archaeological expertise for managing military land. For example, the Native Hawaiians secured a court injunction against military training at Makua on Oahu because of the sacred nature of the Makua valley.[21]

A major contributor to the controversy was the "Human Terrain System" (HTS), a misguided attempt to provide social science and cultural analysis support to deployed personnel, which the US Military experimented with in Iraq and Afghanistan. Perhaps the most tragic component of this program was that it was premised on the concept that military personnel could not be taught effective cross-cultural analytical or communication skills. As the controversy surrounding HTS unfolded, a portion of the anthropological community failed to distinguish between archaeologists trained as anthropologists who were working with defense to educate and plan for the protection of archaeological sites, and other forms of social science participation in conflict zones like HTS. In addition, there were archaeologists who politicized their colleagues' support of cultural property protection efforts, characterizing those efforts as an attempt to "legitimize" US actions in Iraq,

[20] (University of Michigan Press 2011).

[21] Megan Shute, "The History of Hawaii's Sacred Makua Valley Is Terribly Heartbreaking" (*Only in Your State*, 21 July 2011) <https://www.onlyinyourstate.com/hawaii/malama-makua-hi/> accessed 14 June 2020.

especially in the days following news of the military damage at Babylon and the looting of the Iraq National Museum in Baghdad.

A. The Importance and Benefits of Partnerships

In 2015, the State Department established a program for protecting members of religious minorities and religious minority communities located in conflict zones. Quickly recognizing that protection of sacred places, features, and structures provides an essential component of religious protection, this program also reached out to the US military, the USCBS, and the Smithsonian/Penn consortium. Establishment of these partnerships played a key role in development of training initiatives for coalition forces participating in the liberation of Mosul and the region of northern Iraq and Syria from ISIS. Another NGO that has contributed to this effort is the Iraq Conservation Institute at Irbil. The long-term goal of this institution is to provide continuing education to Iraqi heritage professionals. Given the challenges in the region, however, faculty and students alike are contributing to the goal of cultural property awareness and education for coalition personnel. All these organizations worked together to create trilingual guides to cultural property in Mosul and Raqqa (mentioned before) for distribution to friendly forces.

Increasing investment in expanding academic and military partnerships has made it possible for a US Army archaeologist to spend a year at the American Academy in Rome, meeting European counterparts and developing ideas for military cultural property protection curricula. Fellows of the American Academy in Rome served as Monuments Officers during World War II, and the Academy is proud of its contribution to saving cultural heritage in Europe and conflict zones around the world. In the fall of 2011, with funding from the Getty, the Council of American Overseas Research Centers, the Andrew Mellon Foundation, and the Academy hosted a symposium entitled, "Saving Archaeology in Crisis Areas." Delegates from over the world including Bosnia-Herzegovina, Palestine, Afghanistan, Aceh, and Libya were among the speakers. During his presentation on Libya, Hafed Walda recounted his inspection tour of the condition of archaeological sites after the NATO intervention in that country. Walda reported that the cultural property inventory for Libya provided by Susan Kane and Andrew Wilson to the Defense Intelligence Agency had been used effectively to spare features within the ancient Roman cities along the Mediterranean Coast of his country. Walda even offered a compelling specific example where the Gaddafi regime had placed a military radar installation on top of an ancient Roman fortification called Ras Almergrib. NATO forces had been able to use precision weaponry to remove the radar with minimal damage to the structure. Ultimately, NATO bombardiers flew over seventeen thousand sorties over Libya with only minor bullet ricochets on one archaeological feature as collateral damage.

Frances D'Emilio of the Associated Press was present and covered the symposium.[22] The news story she submitted concerning the success in Libya was picked up all over the world. This media coverage might have been one of the best good news stories in the history of the Defense Intelligence Agency. The positive effects on the analysts involved were immeasurable. The good press showed them that cultural property is valued and that their work was genuinely appreciated and made a difference on the ground. The NATO Public Affairs office picked up on the positive publicity and developed its own news story. Later, the NATO Joint Analysis and Lessons Learned Centre (JALLC) studied the Libya case as a positive lesson for the Alliance (JALLC 2012). The positive publicity associated with successful CPP during the Libya mission was instrumental in bringing the importance of heritage to the attention of the 29 NATO member countries.

Another contributing factor toward increased attention to CPP is that cultural heritage is emerging as an international human right issue. The UN Special Rapporteur in the field of Cultural Rights included issues of deliberate destruction versus preservation of cultural property in her reports to the UN.[23] In addition, NATO has adopted a policy for Protection of Civilians in which CPP serves as a sub-theme and thus is considered to be an aspect of NATO's Human Security Framework. Once cultural property protection is codified in military policy and guidance statements, professional staff and military personnel are empowered to further implement meaningful programming.

[22] Frances d'Emilio, "Expert: NATO Raids Spared Libyan Antiquities" (*Associated Press*, 4 November 2011).

[23] Karima Bennoune, *2016 Report of the U.N. Special Rapporteur for Cultural Rights*, prepared for the United National General Assembly <http://www.ohchr.org/Documents/Issues/CulturalRights/A-HRC-31-59_en.doc> accessed 16 June 2020.

VII. Cultural Property Protection Awareness Tools

Even as the preservation community works to address issues at the ongoing conflict/crisis level, long-term initiatives to institutionalize policy, doctrine, and best practices for cultural property protection continue to be important. In 2014, NATO member states approved a NATO Science for Peace and Security program aimed at supporting NATO with decisions regarding cultural property protection in NATO-led missions.

Over the course of its three-year duration, the project hosted a series of advanced research workshops with the purpose of supporting NATO organizations and allied nations to develop policy, doctrine, and capacities, including training and exercises, to accommodate the challenges of cultural property during NATO-led operations. The project included research activities, network-building, briefings to senior HQ staff and commanders, NATO delegations and national level institutions, and advocacy for cultural property considerations at a series of meetings for Civil Military Cooperation or CIMIC, the European version of US Military "Civil Affairs." The NATO Advanced Research Workshops on CPP and their products represent progressive thinking and offer the most comprehensive guidance on the issue in the world today.

Over the years, the CPP program within DOD developed information sharing as well as education and training activities to support the implementation of the 1954 Hague Convention. Military professional education and field training methods have ranged from distribution of graphic training aides and formal classroom sessions to offering soldiers in the field the opportunity to solve a cultural property protection challenge.

Sometimes, protection of cultural property only requires a minimal increase in awareness among those serving in its vicinity. To this purpose, it has proved effective to furnish troops and commanders with small Graphic Training Aids (GTAs) in the form of playing cards with images of cultural property and key rules of the 1954 Hague Convention.[24] The US "archaeology awareness" playing cards have been extremely well received and duplicated by additional NATO countries. Training aids have also included small, one-page, durable documents designed to fit in a soldier's pocket that outlines "do's and don'ts" when operating in the immediate vicinity of cultural

[24] James Zeidler and Laurie Rush, "In Theater Heritage Training through Cultural Heritage Playing Cards" in Laurie Rush (ed), *Archaeology, Cultural Property and the Military* (Boydell & Brewer 2010) 86–97.

property. Another successful model for GTAs is the Mali, Mosul, and Raqqa Cultural Property Passports. These multilingual booklets offer maps with images that share information on key cultural properties and sacred sites found in important and contested urban conflict zones.[25]

Military mapping of cultural property on operational maps not only offers a practical field tool, but also recognizes and represents the physical dimension of cultural themes that human terrain mapping aims to provide. The addition of a cultural property geospatial data layer to a human terrain map provides a didactic tool for changing the awareness and mentality around cultural property. Sometimes a graphic asset is all that is needed to ensure proper precautions are taken and the necessary legal and archaeological expertise is called in to support decision-making.

Such mapping still, and surprisingly, lags behind. As "human terrain mapping" emerged as a military intelligence asset, there was a fundamental flaw in the geographers' selection of terrain themes to be featured on the maps. Despite its focus on cultural themes like language, ethnicity, religion, and political affiliations, the human terrain mappers completely neglected to include cultural property as the material expression of such cultural themes. As a result, the military began to rely on intelligence mapping assets that lacked any mention of cultural property, including sacred sites.

When the US and NATO allies first entered Afghanistan after 9/11, understanding of ancient Afghan infrastructure was incredibly limited. As mentioned in the FOB Wolverine example, there were reports of Taliban disappearing into "tunnels" or "caves," but little recognition that these features were elements of ancient water systems. Yet when base expansion went awry, according to one informant, there was no one "in the room" who recognized the aerial imagery signature of a karez.[26] Hence, a properly identified feature on a map can sometimes make a world of difference.

VIII. Professional Military Education and Field Training

Effective implementation of the values and rules enshrined in the 1954 Hague Convention requires that proper and timely information and expertise find

[25] The Mali passport was developed by UNESCO, and the Mosul and Raqqa Passports were developed by a consortium led by the Smithsonian and the University of Pennsylvania.

[26] Laurie Rush, "Personal Communication SOUTHCOM Cultural Property Training Event" (Miami, SOUTHCOM HQ 2014).

its way to commanders, and that commanders possess the knowledge and institutional readiness to absorb it into their modus operandi. CPP, as recognized by NATO, is a boundary-crossing topic, which is essential to many levels and functions. There is a wide range of opportunities throughout the professional military education system to introduce the topic of CPP, from service academies, the Reserve Officer Training Corps (ROTC), war colleges, and language programs, to specialized forms of pre-deployment and in-mission training. The current challenge is that there is limited high-level support for scaling up the cultural property protection program within the DOD. There have only been two courses offered in CPP at the War Colleges, one at Air University and the other at Naval War College. The Army has been notably absent. Another critical absence occurs at the University of Virginia course for military legal advisors, where CPP should be introduced as a critical component of compliance with LOAC.

As already discussed, there are nonmilitary partners and academics who are willing to assist in cultural property protection education and training for the United States and other Western military organizations. The challenge is finding partners who are willing to develop a nuanced understanding of and appreciation for military culture in order to be effective. Ideally, academic CPP advisors have military experience, are willing to deploy to conflict zones if needed, will be available 24/7 for reach-back during the deployments they are supporting, and, most importantly, understand the relative priorities of the military mission versus any heritage agenda they may have. It is also critical that CPP educators are able to convey a comprehensive understanding of the relationship between successful implementation of CPP and mission success.

A key lesson identified at Fort Drum with regard to bridging the civil-military gap is the importance of field experience. Many civilians, particularly those coming from academic branches, have a difficult time understanding that the military is not a scholarly culture. Manuals and lectures will only get you so far; it is a practice and skill-oriented organizational culture that relies heavily on shared experiences. For that reason, Fort Drum, New York, home of the US Army's 10th Mountain Division, offers soldiers opportunities to train on actual archaeological sites. In 1940, a series of major US military bases expanded under the aegis of eminent domain in order to meet the military training needs required by World War II. As a result, over 350 families lost their farms, and citizens of five villages had to leave their homes to make room for tanks and soldiers. The remains of these properties are now archaeological sites found across the training installation. These properties are coming back to life, serving to teach soldiers how to look for and anticipate insurgent use of cultural features in a historic landscape. The crossroads at the Historic Village of Sterlingville, a nineteenth-century iron furnace community, can serve as anything from an insurgency stronghold to an ancient sacred site during modern training scenarios. In addition, the archaeology field team constructs replicas of archaeological sites and cultural properties in the training areas for soldiers to use.

Currently, over ten thousand soldiers per year train at Historic Sterlingville for exercises of all sizes using a wide range of scenarios, including counterinsurgency, checkpoints, inspections, and displaced person operations. Regardless of how the historic village is used, the soldiers occupying it learn to minimize the impacts of their presence on the site and to never dig into the remains. Even if the troops do not receive specific CPP training, they leave with an understanding of operations in an archaeologically rich environment.

The 10th Mountain Division has been the Army's leading Division in incorporating meaningful CPP into mission planning and operations. This is a result of the "in-house" training facilities at Fort Drum combined with the fact that the 10th Mountain Division is the most deployed division in the US military, which has allowed its personnel to gain mission experience in reading and responding to sacred sites and features of value in cross-cultural landscapes.

The 10th Mountain Division is also demonstrating increased success with implementation of "injects" on CPP into actual field training experiences. An inject is a special challenge built into a field scenario that makes the training experience more realistic in ways that mirror unexpected challenges a soldier may encounter in the deployed environment. The Fort Drum CPP injects are designed to involve as many types of soldiers as possible in addition to senior leaders. Injects offer the opportunity to use actual cultural property found in military training areas as training assets. At Fort Drum, all the protected archaeological properties are incorporated into major exercise scenarios and offered to the scenario writers and mission planners as the cultural property inventory for the no strike list. The archaeology team serves as role players, and Fort Drum's LeRay Mansion Historic District is an ideal venue for Key Leader Engagements (KLEs) as it provides a setting that soldiers might expect in foreign embassies and provincial palaces.

Active participation of subject matter experts enables implementation of realistic scenarios, such as iconic or sacred cultural property targeted for destruction by terrorists; theft or smuggling of objects from museums, places of worship, and cultural institutions; and/or first use of cultural property for strategic or tactical advantage. A typical inject could begin with theft of cultural objects by the adversary, continue with a KLE between the host nation Minister of Culture and the Brigade Commander where the host nation expresses concern about the potential presence of iconic property on the battlefield, transition to the recovery of critical objects by military personnel, and culminate with successful repatriation and associated positive strategic communication messages. Kristoffer Mills and Laurie Rush have written in detail about how to implement CPP injects.[27]

Exercises in deployed environments also offer opportunities for "on site" training. Just as Western monuments officers offered educational opportunities in sites like Leptis Magna and Cyrene Libya during World War II, subject matter experts have offered on-site training in conjunction with the Egyptian Bright Star War Games at sites like Saqqara, Giza, and El Alamein. The overwhelming consensus is that offering military personnel the opportunity to experience world heritage sites is a unique and powerful way to convey the significance of cultural property.

IX. Conclusion: The Future of CPP in the Department of Defense

The monuments officer program of World War II demonstrated unequivocally that success requires support, policy, and advocacy at the highest levels. The legislation that funds the DOD, the National Defense Authorization Act or NDAA (NDAA 2018), recently specified that the DOD must report to Congress their efforts to implement the requirements under the 1954 Hague, including appointment of an individual responsible for "(. . .) coordinating the existing obligations of the Department of Defense for the protection of cultural heritage, including the 1954 Hague Convention for the Protection of Cultural Property in the Event of Armed Conflict, and other obligations for the protection of cultural heritage"[28] Even though the Pentagon designated

[27] Kristoffer Mills and Laurie Rush, "Integration of Cultural Property Protection into a Decisive Action Training Exercise" (November–December 2017) Military Review 2–12.

[28] Cultural Heritage Protection Coordinator SEC. 1279C. "National Defense Authorization Act for Fiscal Year 2018," 115th US Congress, 2017–2018, Public Law No: 115-91 (12/12/2017) https://www.congress.gov/bill/115th-congress/house-bill/2810/text.

an office of responsibility and appointed an individual to handle the portfolio, a robust DOD wide program as yet to be realized. In the third decade of the new millennium, the DOD is shifting its emphasis to hybrid warfare, including cyberthreats, in an environment where there is concern about "near peer" conflict: the United States versus major powers like Russia and China. As a result, focus on preparation for war is shifting away from Phases 5 and 6, namely "Stabilize the Environment and Enable Civil Authority." Yet current deployments still place US military personnel in situations where they face asymmetric conflict and encounter host nation communities that are desperately striving for peace.

Another complication is enduring confusion within the US military about cultural awareness and the reality of CPP. Courses on behavioral "do's and don'ts" that cover topics like not showing the soles of your feet and how to drink tea, have traditionally been presented with minimum context. Typical cultural awareness pre-deployment courses feature a PowerPoint presentation with superficial lists of customs and ethnic groups likely to be encountered in the host nation, but this information is never connected to implementation of mission goals. When soldiers have experienced this type of training over the course of multiple deployments, it is easy to understand why they no longer see the value in cultural information. The failure to make a distinction between this sort of information in training and the potential value of cultural property intelligence has undermined the opportunity to introduce cultural property protection as a force multiplier. Overall, most pre-deployment programs related to any form of culture are currently undergoing cuts across all the services in the United States.

A main assumption underlying international approaches to protecting cultural property during violent conflicts is that sparing sacred places, agricultural infrastructure, traditional gathering spaces, and other elements of cultural life, a host nation community may have a greater chance of peace in the future.[29] A key lesson from the CPP program within the DOD and US military is that when CPP information is used wisely during the planning and kinetic phases of an operation, prepared military personnel will be less likely inadvertently to damage cultural property. This, in turn, reduces the probability of exacerbating conflict unnecessarily and works to avoid losses

29 Emma Cunliffe and Marina Lostal, "Cultural Heritage That Heals: Factoring in Cultural Heritage Discourses in the Syrian Peacebuilding Process" (The Historic Environment Policy & Practice 2016) 7, 1–12.

of reputation resulting from damages to valued property in host nation communities. The ultimate goal is to leave intact as much of the cultural fabric of a community as possible, thus facilitating the final phases of military operations, which are designed to transition that community back to civil society. Military personnel who have served in mission areas and have experience with cultural property in the host nation setting will often be extremely receptive to and appreciative of heritage professionals and academic personnel providing CPP information and training that have direct applications for future military operations. The most critical lesson that can be drawn from the CPP program within the US military is that cultural property matters to military operations because it matters to people all across the globe.

PART III

HEALING THE PAST: REPATRIATION OF STOLEN ART AND CULTURE

11

Wartime Loot in American Museums

Lessons from the Museum of Fine Arts, Boston

Victoria Reed

I. Introduction

> We the American museums have a deep interest in preserving the integrity of the free art market, for without it the future development and growth of our collections will virtually cease. Private individuals might continue to operate in a "black market" of antiquities in which no questions would be asked, but public institutions disposing of trust funds could not very well connive in the liquidation of the artistic patrimony of Europe and act as public receivers of stolen goods.
>
> —Francis Henry Taylor, 1943

Since 2014, the world has been shocked by reports of the widespread damage to cultural heritage under the Islamic State (ISIS, or Da'esh) in Iraq and Syria. While overseeing the destruction of antiquities, ISIS officials have also ordered the plunder of archaeological artifacts, issuing looting permits, and appropriating at least 20% of the value of the finds as *khums*, in Islamic tradition, a 20% tax collected on the spoils of war.[1] Reports of this activity have sounded alarm bells, causing justifiable concern over ISIS-looted antiquities circulating on the art market. Participants in the trade must be vigilant when there are reports of increased looting in certain areas. Indeed, the appearance of unprovenanced Middle Eastern objects on the market has given

[1] Amr Al-Azm, Salam al-Kuntar, and Brian I Daniels, "ISIS' Antiquities Sideline" (*New York Times*, 4 September 2014) A27; Jason Felch, "Twenty Percent: ISIS 'Khums' Tax on Archaeological Loot Fuels the Conflicts in Syria and Iraq" (*Chasing Aphrodite* blog, 14 August 2014) <https://chasingaphrodite.com/2014/08/14/twenty-percent-isis-khums-tax-on-archaeological-loot-fuels-the-conflicts-in-syria-and-iraq/>.

Victoria Reed, *Wartime Loot in American Museums* In: *The Preservation of Art and Culture in Times of War*. Edited by: Claire Finkelstein, Derek Gillman, and Frederik Rosén, Oxford University Press. © Oxford University Press 2022.
DOI: 10.1093/oso/9780197610565.003.0012

rise to fears that so-called "blood antiquities" are in the hands of established dealers and, potentially, in museum collections.[2]

It is not difficult to imagine ISIS-looted artifacts slipping through the cracks of the legitimate art market. Despite a widely shared goal of eliminating the circulation of stolen cultural property, illicit antiquities from all areas of the world routinely appear in the trade. Accompanied by scant paperwork or unverifiable collecting histories, plundered archaeological objects are usually identified as stolen only after they are acquired by a museum or advertised by an auction house or commercial gallery. In recent years, galleries, auction houses, and nonprofit institutions including The Metropolitan Museum of Art; the J. Paul Getty Museum; and the Museum of Fine Arts, Boston, have repatriated considerable numbers of demonstrably stolen Mediterranean, Southeast Asian, and African antiquities to their countries of origin.[3] These acts of restitution serve as a reminder that looted archaeological objects continue to tarnish the art trade as well as public and private collections. The challenge to any collector or museum who wishes to acquire antiquities is how to avoid inadvertently purchasing such looted artifacts, a concern that has become acute with the knowledge that archaeologically rich countries in the Middle East are more vulnerable than ever.

If art museums are to avoid acquiring stolen objects today, then it is instructive for them to consider how stolen art has entered their collections historically in order not to repeat their past mistakes. The acquisition of looted art in the aftermath of World War II undoubtedly offers the most comprehensive set of experiences from which to learn. The art collections of Europe, both

[2] Minor archaeological finds from the area have been documented for sale through nontraditional platforms, like online marketplaces and social media. See Amr Al-Azm and Katie Paul, "The Middle East's Other Facebook Revolution: Antiquities Trafficking in the Digital Age" (*World Politics Review*, 14 August 2018). In March 2018, two antiquities dealers were arrested in Spain for allegedly smuggling Libyan artifacts looted by ISIS. See Georgi Kantchev, "Suspected Traders of Ancient Art Linked to Islamic State Are Detained" (*Wall Street Journal*, 29 March 2018). The American dealership Phoenix Ancient Art was also reportedly investigated for connection with ISIS looting, an allegation the dealers have denied. See Benoit Faucon and Georgi Kantchev, "Prominent Art Family Entangled in ISIS Antiquities-Looting Investigations" (*Wall Street Journal*, 31 May 2017); Barry Meier, "Antiquities Dealer Sues Wall Street Journal over ISIS Article" (*New York Times*, 19 July 2017) C3.

[3] Each museum has publicly available information on these returns. See, for the J Paul Getty Museum <http://www.getty.edu/news/antiquities.html>; for the Metropolitan Museum of Art <https://www.metmuseum.org/press/news/2006/statement-by-the-metropolitan-museum-of-art-on-its-agreement-with-italian-ministry-of-culture> and <https://www.metmuseum.org/press/news/2013/cambodian-returns>; for the Museum of Fine Arts <https://www.mfa.org/collections/provenance/antiquities-and-cultural-property>. On February 15, 2019, the Metropolitan Museum of Art announced that it had transferred to the Manhattan District Attorney's Office an Egyptian gold coffin purchased in 2017, which was looted in 2011. See the online press release <https://www.metmuseum.org/press/news/2019/metropolitan-museum-of-art-returns-coffin-to-egypt>.

private and public, were plundered on an unprecedented scope during World War II. This looting activity was well-known at the time, it is copiously documented, and the US government sought to address the problem of looted art on the market before the war had even ended. In spite of this broad awareness and these strenuous efforts, however, stolen art changed hands easily after the war and has continued to circulate to this day. Attentiveness to the problem of looted art was clearly not sufficient to prevent its circulation. Similarly, an awareness of the current problem of looting in the Middle East alone will not be adequate to halt the acquisition of illicit antiquities from that region.

In this chapter, I examine case studies of works of art that were offered to the Museum of Fine Arts, Boston (MFA) during and immediately after World War II. Many of the MFA's postwar acquisitions had been plundered and needed to be returned, or otherwise have their ownership legally resolved. Since the Washington Conference on Holocaust-Era Assets (1998), the MFA has deaccessioned or reached settlements for no fewer than sixteen individual works of art that changed hands illicitly during the Nazi era and World War II, more than is known for any other American art museum.[4] To understand how these looted works of art made their way to the MFA in the first place I consider, first, the general knowledge of art looting within the museum community during and after the war. I examine the role of the US government to prevent the circulation of looted art. Finally, I look at the actions of individual MFA staff members in exercising due diligence when making acquisitions. Though there are obvious differences between the looting of Europe during World War II and the plunder of archaeological material today, it is hoped that the lessons afforded by previous wartime experiences can be applied to the present, as museums strive to build their collections diligently during periods of unrest.

II. American Knowledge of European Looting, 1933–1945

During the 12 years that constitute the Nazi era (1933–45) and World War II (1939–45), the American museum community developed a general, if

[4] For the MFA resolutions, see <https://www.mfa.org/collections/provenance/nazi-era-provenance-research/>. For resolutions reached by other American institutions, see <https://aamd.org/object-registry/resolution-of-claims-for-nazi-era-cultural-assets/browse>. The AAMD registry is not necessarily comprehensive, but it is the only known centralized resource on Nazi-era claims at American institutions.

incomplete, knowledge of the functioning of the art world under National Socialism. The purging of "degenerate art"—modern, avant-garde and abstract artwork—from Germany's state museums in 1937 quickly captured the attention of American museum personnel.[5] Galerie Fischer of Lucerne, which sold off some of the most marketable "degenerate" paintings, wrote to American collecting institutions in advance of the sale with the assurance that, in contradiction to the "vehement propaganda" that was circulating, proceeds from the sale would not go to the German government for the purposes of armament, and therefore the "sensational public sale" should not be boycotted.[6] While the MFA did not purchase any works of art through Fischer, curators were well aware of German museums disposing of some of their greatest modern masterpieces at this time.[7]

In February 1941, *The New York Times* reported that, according to British sources, fourteen Old Master paintings held by the state museums of Berlin were being sent through Siberia to the United States, where "it is hoped by the Germans that their sale will yield much-needed dollar exchange."[8] By this time, World War II had begun in Europe, and *The Times* commented on fears that any revenue brought in by the paintings would go toward Nazi propaganda efforts. Nevertheless, the article commented, these paintings would "be prized items for collectors" in the United States and were estimated to be an investment collectively worth $10,000,000.

[5] For background, see Stephanie Barron (ed), "Degenerate Art": The Fate of the Avant-Garde in Nazi Germany (Los Angeles, LA County Museum of Art 1991). On the American response, see Vivian Endicott Barnett, "Banned German Art: Reception and Institutional Support of Modern German Art in the United States, 1933–45" in Stephanie Barron (ed), *Exiles and Emigrés: The Flight of European Artists from Hitler* (Los Angeles, LA County Museum of Art 1997) 273–84.

[6] Letter from the Galerie Fischer, Lucerne, to the MFA (3 June 1939), kept inside the museum's copy of the auction catalogue (Hunt Library; call no SPA Fis 1939), transferred in 2007 to the Museum Archives. See also Stephanie Barron, "The Galerie Fischer Auction" in Barron (ed), "Degenerate Art" (n 5) 135–46, esp 139 on the letter from Fischer and transfer of funds to the Reich.

[7] An undated letter in the MFA Archives (Paintings Department Files, Correspondence: Germany, 1937–1961), intended for the Nationalgalerie, Berlin, urged the German museum to "consider dealing directly with a Museum such as the Boston Museum" in selling or exchanging paintings from its collection. A typed memorandum entitled "Paintings in German Galleries said to be for sale" listed Van Gogh's *Wheat Field* from the Folkwang Museum, Essen; and Cezanne's *Man with a Pipe* from the Kunsthalle, Mannheim, neither of which was sold or exchanged. In 1939, the Institute of Modern Art in Boston drew attention to the plight of modern artists in the exhibition "Contemporary German Art" (November 2–December 9, 1939). Curator (and future Monuments, Fine Arts and Archives officer) James Plaut wrote in the introduction to the catalogue about the "racial consolidation of all artistic pursuits under the Reich Chamber of Culture," the removal of degenerate art from State museums, and the Lucerne sale, from which many examples in the catalogue came. Exhibiting "degenerate art" at this time was certainly intended as an anti-Nazi political statement. See Barnett (n 5).

[8] "Paintings from Berlin Museums Reported Coming to US for Sale" (*New York Times*, 13 February 1941) 3.

Unlike the works of German modernism that had been sold from state collections in the late 1930s, for which there was no strong American market, paintings by Botticelli, Raphael, Rembrandt, and Velazquez had long been appreciated in the United States, and the possibility of their sale was tantalizing. *The Times* reported, however, that should the Nazis plunder the museum collections of occupied countries like France, Belgium, and the Netherlands, those works of art "would most certainly meet a storm of protest if they were offered for sale in New York."[9]

It is possible, therefore, that in the early years of World War II the displacement of art in Europe became synonymous in the American consciousness with the despoiling of public museums. In March 1942, by which time the United States had entered into the war, *The Times* followed up on its earlier report to state that the shipment of paintings from Berlin had either been intercepted or turned back. This comment was made as an aside in an article that otherwise reassured its readers that the museums of the Netherlands had escaped large-scale Nazi looting.[10] In July 1942, *The Times* again reported on fears that the museums of Western Europe would "lose their treasures when Hitler sees the second front near."[11] Yet the possibility that looted artwork would end up on American soil was presented as unlikely for two reasons. First, the British had formed a naval blockade of German goods in December 1939, and it was improbable that any "important" work of art would have made it through the blockade. Indeed, as early as 1940, the British detained a shipment of artwork bound for the United States that was believed to be intended for sale to benefit Nazi Germany.[12] Second, *The Times* reported, even if works of art were making their way to the United States, whether through European trade channels or in the possession of refugees, they were "works of no great value."[13] Readers were encouraged to be vigilant about masterworks looted from museums, or stolen art objects that had tremendous financial value, rather than lower-value items that may have been taken from private collections.

[9] ibid.

[10] David Anderson, "Dutch Art Escapes Big-Scale Looting" (*New York Times*, 15 March 1942) 23.

[11] "Germans Are Still Pilfering Art from Netherlands, Belgium, France" (*New York Times*, 27 July 1942) 17.

[12] The shipment belonged to the French art dealer Martin Fabiani. See Lynn H Nicholas, *The Rape of Europa: The Fate of Europe's Art Treasures in the Third Reich and the Second World War* (New York, Vintage 1994) 92–93; Nancy Caron Karrels, "Reconstructing a Wartime Journey: The Vollard-Fabiani Collection, 1940–1949" (2015) 22 (4) International Journal of Cultural Property 505–26.

[13] Anderson (n 10).

III. The Role of the Roberts Commission

As the war progressed, American art historians became increasingly concerned about the safety of monuments and works of art in areas of combat. In 1943, members of the American Council for Learned Societies (ACLS) formed the Committee for the Protection of Cultural Treasures in War Areas. They worked with the subcommittee of a coalition known as the American Defense-Harvard Group, led by Paul Sachs (1878–1965), Associate Director of the Fogg Art Museum at Harvard University. Together the two groups prepared lists of monuments at risk, generated manuals on safeguarding and conserving artwork, and generated names of qualified American personnel to conduct this work.[14] That same year, the federal government officially responded to concerns about cultural heritage in war zones. On August 20, 1943, the State Department established the American Commission for the Protection and Salvage of Artistic and Historic Monuments in Europe (the "Roberts Commission"). Its functions were to work with the Army to protect works of cultural value as well as to compile lists of property, both public and private, that had been looted by Axis forces. At the time of the Armistice, it was to urge the restitution of this looted property.[15] The Commission worked with both the ACLS and the Harvard Group. The committee on personnel was headed by Sachs and William George ("W.G.") Constable (1887–1976). Constable was a colleague of Sachs in the Boston area, serving as Curator of Paintings at the Museum of Fine Arts since 1937. The MFA curatorial staff therefore had a direct involvement in the Roberts Commission's efforts.

The formation of the Commission led to an increased awareness of the realities of art looting in Europe among museum staff as well as the public more generally. Francis Henry Taylor (1903–57), Director of The Metropolitan Museum of Art and one of the driving forces behind the creation of the Commission, penned a long article for *The Times* on Sunday, September 19, 1943, entitled "Europe's Looted Art: Can It Be Recovered?"[16] Rather than focus on museum objects and valuable, recognizable masterpieces, Taylor went into detail about how the financial persecution of Europe's Jewish

[14] The American Defense-Harvard Group formed shortly after the fall of France. Its initial goal was to alert Americans to the dangers posed by Axis powers. The records are held by the Harvard University Archives (*Records of the American Defense-Harvard Group, 1940–1945*, HUD 3139) and the online library record contains discusses the formation of the group. See also Michael J Kurtz, *America and the Return of Nazi Contraband: The Recovery of Europe's Cultural Treasures* (CUP 2006) 51.

[15] *Report of the American Commission for the Protection and Salvage of Artistic and Historic Monuments in War Areas* (Washington, DC 1946) 1–5.

[16] Francis Henry Taylor, "Europe's Looted Art: Can It Be Recovered?" (*New York Times*, 19 September 1943) SM 18–19, 42–43.

population fed National Socialist collecting habits. He noted that the Nazis made Jewish residents register their belongings and then confiscated their possessions, including works of art. Even in plundering Jewish collections, he wrote, the Nazis adhered to the letter of the law, which was why sales to German buyers in occupied countries were considered forced and would be invalidated at the conclusion of hostilities.[17] Most presciently, Taylor speculated that in the years immediately following the war, works of looted art would be offered for sale in the West:

> [W]e will see come out of hiding in the years immediately following the war objects of great intrinsic worth, held for the most part under fictitious names, and representing the real assets of the Nazi officials who are lucky enough to escape temporarily the justice of the invading armies. These works will be offered for sale primarily to the collectors of the Western Hemisphere. How can we prevent this from happening and becoming ourselves party to the looting of Europe?[18]

To answer his own question, Taylor advised that "a quarantine should be placed upon all works of art leaving European countries."[19]

Less than a year later, this quarantine on works of art was implemented by the US Treasury Department. Treasury Directive (TD) 51072, issued June 8, 1944, specified that no art object worth at least $5,000 or, regardless of value, having artistic, historic, or scholarly interest could be imported from any foreign country except Great Britain and its territories. Any work of art that had been imported after March 12, 1938 (the date of the *Anschluss*) and was still held by customs would not be released. Exceptions to these import restrictions were subject to the approval of the Treasury Department's Office of the Foreign Funds Control after completion of a two-page questionnaire (fig. 1).[20] The purpose of TD 51072 was to block and ultimately "restore art objects of

[17] The Inter-Allied Declaration Against Acts of Dispossession Committed in Territories Under Enemy Occupation or Control ("Declaration of London"), 5 January 1943, affirmed the rights of the Allied governments to "declare invalid any transfers of . . . property . . . taking the form of open looting or plunder, or of transactions apparently legal in form, even when they purport to be voluntarily effected." See Elizabeth Simpson (ed), *The Spoils of War: World War II and Its Aftermath: The Loss, Reappearance, and Recovery of Cultural Property* (New York, Abrams 1997) 287, App 9.

[18] Taylor (n 16) 42.

[19] ibid 43.

[20] RG 239, Records of the American Commission for the Protection and Salvage of Artistic and Historical Monuments in War Areas (The Roberts Commission), 1943–1946; Reports, compiled 1944–1946; Customs. National Archives and Records Administration, College Park, MD; Microfilm Publication M1944, Roll 7. For further on the Treasury Directive, see Marc Masurovsky, "TD 51072" (*plundered art* blog, 23 May 2018) <https://plundered-art.blogspot.com/2018/05/td-51072.html>.

(a)

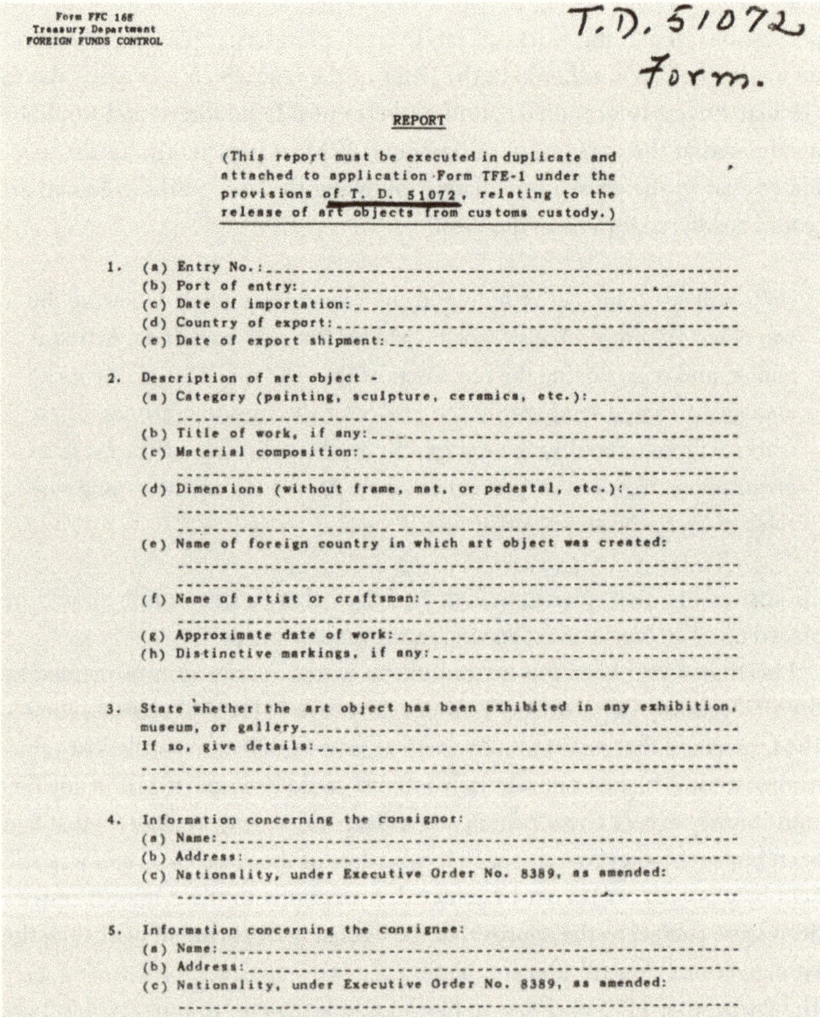

Form FFC 168
Treasury Department
FOREIGN FUNDS CONTROL

T.D. 51072
Form.

REPORT

(This report must be executed in duplicate and attached to application Form TFE-1 under the provisions of T. D. 51072, relating to the release of art objects from customs custody.)

1. (a) Entry No.:
(b) Port of entry:
(c) Date of importation:
(d) Country of export:
(e) Date of export shipment:

2. Description of art object -
(a) Category (painting, sculpture, ceramics, etc.):
(b) Title of work, if any:
(c) Material composition:
(d) Dimensions (without frame, mat, or pedestal, etc.):
(e) Name of foreign country in which art object was created:
(f) Name of artist or craftsman:
(g) Approximate date of work:
(h) Distinctive markings, if any:

3. State whether the art object has been exhibited in any exhibition, museum, or gallery
If so, give details:

4. Information concerning the consignor:
(a) Name:
(b) Address:
(c) Nationality, under Executive Order No. 8389, as amended:

5. Information concerning the consignee:
(a) Name:
(b) Address:
(c) Nationality, under Executive Order No. 8389, as amended:

Fig. 1 U.S. Treasury Department, Foreign Funds Control, FFC Form 168.

(b)

- 2 -

6. Names of countries in which article has been located since March 12, 1938: ______________________________

7. If the art object has been imported from any country in the Western Hemisphere, except one which constitutes a part of the United Kingdom, British Dominions, or British Colonies, state whether it has been continuously in the Western Hemisphere since March 12, 1938. ______________________________

8. Name, address, and nationality under Executive Order No. 8389, as amended, of every person having an interest in the art object, direct or indirect, since March 12, 1938, including every person now having any interest. Indicate period of time during which each person had an interest. ______________________________

9. Manner in which present owner acquired art object, and date and place of such acquisition. If by purchase, indicate price and currency in which payment was made. ______________________________

10. State purpose of importation or exportation. ______________________________

11. Have any similar importations or exportations been made by you since September, 1939? ______________________________

____
Signature of person signing report

____
Date

Fig. 1 Continued.

value... appropriated by the Axis powers or individuals acting under their authority or consent." Though the United States had taken specific measures as early as 1940 to freeze foreign assets, and tightly monitored foreign securities during the war, the Treasury Directive was the most purposeful step the government took to prevent Nazi-looted art from entering the country.[21]

[21] In April 1940, after Germany invaded Denmark and Norway, the United States began freezing foreign assets belonging to the nationals of occupied countries to prevent their use by Axis powers. In 1942, the government re-established the Office of the Alien Property Custodian, which vested enemy

Finally, as the war drew to a close, the Roberts Commission sought to ensure that American soldiers did not bring home any works of art as spoils of war. A circular letter drafted in 1945 was addressed to "Museums, Art and Antique Dealers and Auction Houses." The Commission had numerous reports of objects being offered to museums and the art trade by members of armed forces. If such circumstances arose, the Commission asked to be informed, so that it could work with the Customs Bureau and Foreign Funds Control officials to recover and return the objects. The letter urged:

> It is, of course, obvious that no clear title can be passed on objects that have been looted from public or private collections abroad. . . . [A]ny specific examples of looting of works of art or cultural materials [should] be brought to light as soon as possible.[22]

The United States had refused to sanction war plundering since it signed the Hague Conventions of 1899 and 1907, and the Roberts Commission did its best to ensure that the art world was aware of this fact.[23] By 1945, employees of American museums were on notice, thanks to general news sources and such specialized memoranda, to be diligent about works of art looted by Nazi forces and Allied troops and to work with the government for their return.

IV. Museum Acquisitions During Wartime: Two Case Studies

Despite the assurances provided by TD 51072 and efforts of the Roberts Commission, works of looted art came into the United States in contravention of the law before the close of World War II. In Boston, MFA staff were aware of their responsibilities under the wartime import restrictions

assets in the United States. For background, see *Plunder and Restitution: The US and Holocaust Victims' Assets*, Staff Report (Washington, DC, December 2000) 43–83.

[22] Art Looting and Nazi Germany: Records of the Fine Arts and Monuments Adviser, Ardelia Hall, 1945–1961, Part 2: Subject Files. Microfilm Publication, Reel 1, *Circular Letters to Universities and Museums, January 1948–December 1950*. The letter is annotated, "Provisional circular letter sent out by American Commission in 1945."

[23] The Hague Conventions of 1899 and 1907 are virtually identical in their prohibition of looting and pillage, but the 1945 circular cited the more recent, 1907 Convention, articles 3, 46, 47, and 56. Article 28 also discusses pillage. Simpson (n 17) 278–79, App 3.

and acted quickly when presented with obvious examples of looted property. For example, in the fall of 1945, Mrs. Fred Cooper of Edna, Kansas, wrote to the MFA offering "a collection of 1400 coins which came out of one of Germany's large museums."[24] Her husband had brought them back from the European theater of war. She continued: "We are wondering if you would be interested in them. We will appreciate hearing from you in regard to their value, etc." Director George Harold Edgell (1887–1954) responded on the Museum's behalf. He had no intention of accepting the coins, but asked somewhat disingenuously for more details and photographs so that he could come to a decision about them. He told Mrs. Cooper, "I am taking the liberty of sending your letter to the National Gallery in Washington in case there is an interest there." Edgell then alerted Huntington Cairns, General Counsel at the National Gallery of Art and Secretary-Treasurer of the Roberts Commission. He knew that Cairns would contact the proper authorities. Indeed, Cairns informed the Commissioner of Customs about the offer to the MFA. Eventually, the coins—which had not been imported properly under the Treasury Directive—were seized and in 1949 were given over to the Office of the Military Government for restitution.[25]

Precautions were in place to keep out Axis-owned property and spoils of war, but it was nearly impossible, especially before World War II began, to prevent the entry of artwork that had been sold or transferred under duress by private Jewish collectors. Hitler had been chancellor of Germany since January 1933, and as the result of racial persecution, Jewish residents of Europe were forced to part with their property for years before fighting even started in Europe. Works of art that were sold under duress during this time could cross international borders relatively easily. The MFA's *Portrait of a Man and Woman in an Interior* (ca. 1665–67) by Eglon van der Neer is one such example (fig. 2). It was purchased by the Museum in early December 1941 from Silberman Galleries of New York, which had held it since at least the spring of that year. It is not known when or how the painting arrived on American soil, but it seems likely to have been brought in with someone's

24 The correspondence pertaining to the coins is held by the Archives, Museum of Fine Arts, Boston. DIR AC3, National Gallery of Art (Washington, DC), folder 2/4; National Archives and Records Administration, College Park, MD, Microfilm Publication M 1944, roll 14, Roberts Commission: Correspondence, 1943–1946. Importation by Members of Armed Forces—Memorandum to Museums About Questionable Importation of Art Objects. See also National Archives and Records Administration, Ardelia Hall Subject Files, Reel 1, "949 Coins."

25 RG 59, Ardelia Hall Subject Files, Reel 1, Objects Returned May 1946–June 1959, "Works of Art Recovered in the United States, List of Cases, 1944–1961," pp 1–2, only notes that the coins were transferred to OMGUS in 1949, presumably for return to West Germany.

Fig. 2 Eglon van der Neer (Dutch, 1634–1703), *Portrait of a Man and Woman in an Interior*, 1665–1667. Oil on panel. Museum of Fine Arts, Boston, Seth K. Sweetser Fund. Photograph © Museum of Fine Arts, Boston

personal possessions. When curator W.G. Constable asked the dealer about the painting's provenance in 1942, he was told simply that it was "brought to this country by a refugee some time ago."[26]

Recent research has shown that the painting belonged to an art dealer named Walter Westfeld of Wuppertal, Germany, who owned it in May

[26] Letter from A Silberman to WG Constable (3 June 1942). Museum of Fine Arts (MFA), Art of Europe Department, Curatorial file 41.935.

1936. At that time, Westfeld was forced to close his gallery because he was Jewish. With no other means of income due to the racial persecution he faced in Nazi Germany, Westfeld had to have either sold or given away the painting under duress. It was no longer in his possession in November 1938, when he was arrested and imprisoned. Years later, Walter Westfeld was killed at Auschwitz. After uncovering these facts, the MFA reached a financial settlement with the Westfeld estate and heirs in 2011, and the painting remains at the Museum today.[27]

Not all of these critical details were discovered recently; some information had been available to MFA staff in the 1940s. In 1943, Robert Lebel (1901–86), a French art dealer spending the war years in the United States, visited the MFA and told Constable that he had sold the Eglon van der Neer to Walter Westfeld in the mid-1930s. Constable recorded their conversation for the curatorial files:

> Westfeld was arrested by the ~~Nazi~~ German government in 1938, sent to a concentration camp, and his property seized. This was sold by the German govt. through Lempertz, auctioneer, of Cologne, some time before the fall of France. Whether the picture had previously been sold by Westfeld, or was in the sale, Lebel does not know.[28]

Several months later, in February 1944, Westfeld's brother, Dietrich Westfield, who had immigrated from Germany to Nashville, Tennessee, also contacted the MFA. He had learned about the Van der Neer from Lebel. Westfield's letter to the Museum details the persecution his brother suffered in Germany and the confiscation of his art collection by the Nazis. He asked about the ownership history of the Van der Neer: "You will, no doubt, agree that, if the painting were found to be one of those the Nazis have stolen from my brother it would be only just to call to account the criminals and claim indemnification from them at the proper time."[29]

[27] For a full discussion, see Victoria Reed, "Walter Westfeld and the van der Neer *Portrait* in Boston: The Case Study of a Jewish Art Dealer in Düsseldorf" in Andrea Bambi and Axel Drecoll (eds), *Der Kunsthändler Alfred Flechtheim im Kontext von Kunstraub und Restitution* (Berlin, Walther de Gruyter 2015) 179–88.

[28] 8 October 1943 memorandum by WG Constable. MFA, Art of Europe, curatorial object file 41.935.

[29] Letter from Dietrich Westfield to the Director of the MFA (6 February 1944). A copy of this letter is in the MFA, Art of Europe, curatorial object file 41.935.

By 1944, Edgell was certainly familiar with the plunder of artwork in Nazi Germany. If he did not know the exact details of the painting's provenance, he nevertheless was aware that it could have been confiscated by National Socialist forces or sold under duress. Yet, in response to Dietrich Westfield's letter, Edgell wrote simply, "I cannot give you any information about its previous history nor from whom Silberman purchased it."[30] There is no evidence of further correspondence between the two men. The question of the painting's Holocaust-era provenance lay dormant from that time until the early 2000s, after those individuals who had firsthand knowledge of Westfeld's life and career had passed away, and precise information about the events of the 1930s and 1940s had become much harder to find.

These two case studies, the German coins and the Eglon van der Neer, exemplify divergent responses on the part of the same museum director within the span of only a year and a half. Today, one might wonder how Edgell could fail to act upon evidence of Nazi persecution and expropriation in 1944, but diligently report a museum theft to the authorities in 1945. It is only possible to speculate. First, the coins were offered to the MFA but never purchased, while the Van der Neer had been paid for and accessioned by the time new provenance information came in. Second, Edgell had specific information to act upon in the coins case, while for the Van der Neer he had, it could be argued, an indication—but no proof—of loss. Indeed, the danger of acquiring another museum's object (where legal ownership could be proven) probably carried greater moral weight in Edgell's mind than that of acquiring a painting that had been privately owned (where ownership could be argued, but was much harder to document), an unfortunate double standard that will be revisited later in this chapter.

V. Restitution in the Postwar Period

Once World War II ended, the process of recovering Nazi-looted art began immediately. Officers in the Monuments, Fine Arts, and Archives (MFA&A) section of the Army, working under the authority of the Allied Military Government, took control over looted property that they found in the US zones of Germany and Austria. They blocked transactions involving property

[30] George Harold Edgell to Dietrich Westfield (16 February 1944). MFA, Art of Europe, curatorial object file 41.935. The correspondence between Edgell and Westfield could not be located in the Museum Archives. Copies of these letters were kindly provided by Fred Westfield to the MFA.

that had been transferred under duress, or otherwise wrongly, under the Nazi regime. Works of art the Nazis had stored in salt mines and other repositories were taken to collecting points set up at Munich, Wiesbaden, Marburg, and elsewhere in West Germany; and once they were inventoried, identifiable objects were released to the nations from which they had been taken for restitution to individual owners.[31] The scope of the National Socialist looting of Europe became a matter of widespread knowledge with the reports of the Nuremberg Trials. In late 1945 and early 1946, *The New York Times* and other major news outlets detailed the machinations of the Einsatzstab Reichsleiter Rosenberg, the Nazi party's primary art looting organization, in plundering Europe's Jewish population through forced sales. *The Times* noted that the Germans sometimes "purchased" works of art "from private non-Jewish owners at ridiculously low prices . . . the price being not unconnected with the ever-present shadow of the concentration camp."[32]

By 1946, a vast amount of looted and displaced art had been recovered through the collecting points.[33] Recognizable masterworks like Jan van Eyck's *Ghent Altarpiece*, Michelangelo's *Bruges Madonna*, and Veit Stoss's celebrated altarpiece from Krakow were quickly located and returned. The art collections of well-known Jewish victims of Nazi plunder, like the Rothschild banking family and David David-Weill, were also largely recovered and restituted. Press accounts proudly seized upon these accomplishments. On November 29, 1946, the *Boston Globe* reported that more than two hundred thousand works of art had already been returned to their prewar owners, and the MFA&A Officers were nearing completion of their work.[34] At the end of the year, an exhibition of masterpieces recovered from Dutch collections began touring venues in the United States, further reinforcing the impression that the heavy lifting had been finished.[35] Nevertheless, work continued for several years; the Office of Military Government, United States, reported returning over 1.6 million cultural items by the end of 1948; the Munich

[31] On the collecting points, see Nicholas, *Rape of Europa* (n 12) 327–67; Kurtz, *Nazi Contraband* (n 14) 125–50. On the Munich Central Collecting Point, see Craig Hugh Smyth, *Repatriation of Art from the Collecting Point in Munich After World War II* (Maarssen, Gary Schwartz 1988); Iris Lauterbach, *The Central Collecting Point in Munich: A New Beginning for the Restitution and Protection of Art* (Los Angeles, Getty Research Institute 2019).

[32] Tania Long, "German Key Plan Details Art Thefts" (*New York Times*, 19 December 1945) 6; Drew Middleton, "British to Start Hess' Case Today" (*New York Times*, 7 February 1946) 16.

[33] Works of art that belonged to Germany and had not been looted, but were been put into storage for safekeeping, also passed through the collecting points.

[34] "Army Collects Nazi Art Loot" (*Boston Globe*, 29 November 1946) 34.

[35] *Paintings Looted from Holland, Returned through the Efforts of the United States Armed Forces* (7 December 1946–1 January 1948).

Central Collecting Point, which remained active until the fall of 1951, alone returned some 80,000 individual objects.[36]

VI. The Role of the State Department

Once hostilities were over, the wartime provisions that had been in place in the United States were no longer in force. Treasury Directive 51072, which had been effected through the Trading with the Enemy Act, was revoked on June 13, 1946. The Roberts Commission met for the last time just a few days later on June 20, 1946. The minutes from their final meeting reveal their thoughts about the problem of looted art coming into the United States. Francis Taylor, who had publicly called for the embargo on art from abroad, was the most outspoken in favor of revoking the Treasury Directive. He reported that since nothing "of consequence" had been brought into the United States at that point, only "souvenirs," there was no longer a need for the Directive. By July 1, he anticipated, "all the identifiable loot will be returned to countries of origin."[37] With the Roberts Commission about to go out of existence, responsibility for overseeing the return of looted art discovered in the United States was taken over by the Department of State.[38]

In 1946, Ardelia Ripley Hall (1899–1979), Consultant in the State Department's Division of Cultural Cooperation, served as a liaison among the Roberts Commission, the MFA&A, and the Department of State for matters pertaining to art restitution in the Pacific theater. When the Roberts Commission ceased, its files on art looting—both in the Pacific and European theaters—were transferred to her, and she assumed the role of Fine Arts and

[36] Kurtz, *Nazi Contraband* (n 14) 144; *Plunder and Restitution* (n 21) SR-144. The final report of the Munich Central Collecting Point from February 1952 stated that almost forty-nine thousand numbers had been registered, totaling around eighty thousand objects; Lauterbach (n 31), 207–08 (Lauterbach, however, notes the difficulty in establishing precise figures,, as for example, whether a cup and saucer together are one object or two).

[37] National Archives and Records Administration, College Park, MD. RG 239, Records of the American Commission for the Protection and Salvage of Artistic and Historical Monuments in War Areas (The Roberts Commission), 1943–1946. Microfilm Publication M1944, Roll 6, Minutes of Final Meeting, 20 June 1946.

[38] As pointed out by Ely Maurer, the State Department "does not have the legal power to seize stolen cultural property and return it to a victimized country or individual. . . . To compensate for our lack of legal power, we can suggest the application of legal powers held by sister agencies in the US Government. I am referring here to the Justice Department, the Customs Service, the Defense Department, and the Internal Revenue Service." See Ely Maurer, "The Role of the State Department Regarding National and Private Claims for the Restitution of Stolen Cultural Property" in Simpson (ed), *Spoils of War* (n 17) 142–43.

Monuments Adviser to the State Department.[39] Over the summer and fall of 1946, Hall and her colleagues expressed anxiety over the revocation of the Treasury Directive so soon after the end of the war. They wished to see import restrictions reimplemented, if even in a modified form, to ensure a system of Customs controls and clearance for artwork. They were unsuccessful. Lamont Moore, former administrative officer of the Roberts Commission, reported in July 1946 that any concerns expressed by the State Department were unfounded because "the bulk of looted art has [already] been discovered in Germany"; keeping import restrictions in place only encouraged art dealers to break the law; and during peacetime the government should not exert control over a private industry like the art trade. Moreover, even during the war, handling the cases sent to the Roberts Commission took only a quarter of a secretary's time, so in the postwar period it should not be a burdensome job.[40] (This last argument proved the most erroneous; Hall would work full-time on art restitution issues until her retirement in 1962). The reasoning was circular: there was no evidence of looted art at the border; therefore, the import restrictions that were enacted to keep looted art out of the country were not necessary.

It was up to the State Department to circulate lists of works of art known to be looted and to coordinate with other departments of the government, drawing upon existing legal remedies that would stop the circulation of stolen art within the United States. In 1947, the *Department of State Bulletin* published a memorandum on "The Return of Looted Objects of Art to Countries of Origin," reminding its readers:

> The introduction of looted objects of art into this country is contrary to the general policy of the United States and to the commitments of the United States under the Hague Convention of 1907 and in case of objects of a value of $5,000 or more is a contravention of Federal law [National Stolen Property Act].[41]

[39] On Hall's career, see Victoria Reed, "Ardelia Hall: From Museum of Fine Arts to Monuments Woman" (2014) 21 International Journal of Cultural Property 79–93.

[40] Memorandum of Telephone Conversation with Lamont Moore (19 July 1946). National Archives and Records Administration, RG 59, Records of the Fine Arts and Monuments Adviser, Ardelia Hall, 1945–1961, part 2: Subject Files, Reel 1: T[reasury] D[epartment] Documents—Regulations [on Art Objects], October 1945–December 1946.

[41] "Return of Looted Objects of Art to Countries of Origin," *Department of State Bulletin* (23 February 1947) 16 (359) 358–60. The National Stolen Property Act of 1934 (18 USC §2314 *et seq*) prohibits the foreign or interstate commerce of any movable property with a minimum value of five thousand dollars that is known to be stolen.

The State Department worked with the Customs Bureau to seize items that were smuggled into the country. An internal State Department memorandum from 1947 served as a reminder that "FALSE DECLARATION CAN BE USED AS A BASIS OF ACTION OF FORFEITURE" (emphasis in original) when an art object is imported.[42] Today, the art world is familiar with the ability of the government to seize artwork on the basis of a mis-declaration with Customs or a violation of the National Stolen Property Act, but in the 1940s, there was no established body of case law pertaining to stolen or smuggled art to rely upon when Nazi-looted art entered the country.

VII. Postwar Museum Acquisitions: Case Studies, 1945–1955

Despite the great successes achieved at the Allied collecting points, not all works of art that had been stolen, looted, or forcibly sold between 1933 and 1945 were recovered in Europe. Many wartime thefts were not reported, or in some cases were not even noticed, for years following the conclusion of hostilities. Other works of art changed hands privately and, like the Eglon van der Neer, surreptitiously crossed international borders. Non-unique items like prints, decorative arts, and furniture were (and remain) difficult if not impossible to track down. Finally, despite all best attempts at circulating lists of stolen objects in the postwar years, doing so in a comprehensive and timely manner proved difficult.[43] For all these reasons, plundered art continued to circulate.

The first looted work of art known to come into the MFA after World War II was registered with the Museum on June 28, 1946. The art dealer Arturo Grassi, who had addresses in Brooklyn and London, brought in a fourteenth-century embroidery, which he said belonged to an owner in Italy (fig. 3). It is not known when the embroidery was imported.[44] Curator Gertrude Townsend inquired about the subject and provenance of the embroidery and

[42] Department of State memorandum, Telephone Conversation with Mr Julian Simpson (12 February 1948). RG 59, Ardelia Hall subject files, Reel 1: Objects Returned, May 1946–June 1959.

[43] Even in 1946, State Department officials conceded that lists of stolen art could not "be distributed to all customs officials. Some central government agency would have to review and mimeograph the lists." Ralph Stimson, "The Problem of United States Customs Control of the Importation, Exportation, and Intransit Shipment of Looted or Axis-Owned Cultural Objects" (14 October 1946). Ardelia Hall Subject Files, Reel 1, T[reasury] D[epartment] Documents—Regulations [on Art Objects], October 1945–December 1946.

[44] Grassi traveled from Naples to New York from 25 September to 9 October 1945. Ancestry.com. New York, Passenger and Crew Lists (including Castle Garden and Ellis Island), 1820–1957 (database

Fig. 3 *Burial of Saint Vigilius and Delivery of his Acts to the Pope and Emperor*, 14th century. Linen plain weave, embroidered with silk and metal-wrapped thread. Museo Diocesano Tridentino, Trent (formerly Museum of Fine Arts, Boston, Otis Norcross Fund). Photograph © Museum of Fine Arts, Boston

was told only that "this piece—together with many other textiles of [an] early period—was part of a large collection of antique objects, which [the owner] has inherited, but he was unable to find any information specifically referring to this piece."[45] The MFA took the dealer at his word and voted to purchase the embroidery at the Collections Committee meeting of November 14, 1946.

Today, the embroidery is no longer in the Museum collection. The MFA deaccessioned it and returned it to the Diocesan Museum, Trent, Italy, in 2010, after learning that it had been stolen from Trent's cathedral sacristy sometime after 1939.[46] It is not known exactly when or by whom, nor for whom Grassi was

online). Provo, UT, USA: Ancestry.com Operations, Inc., 2010. Microfilm Serial T715, 1897–1957; Microfilm Roll 7015; line 29; p 152.

[45] Museum of Fine Arts, Textiles and Fashion Arts Department, Curatorial File 46.1198.

[46] See Victoria Reed, "Il ricamo di San Vigilio fra Trento e Boston: Ricerche sulla provenienza delle opere d'arte e restituzioni nella prassi del Museum of Fine Arts" in Domenica Primerano (ed), *Una Storia a Ricamo: La ricomposizione di un raro ciclo boemo di fine Trecento* (Trent, Museo Diocesano Tridentino 2011) 24–33.

Fig. 4 Herri Met De Bles (Netherlandish, 1480–1550), *Landscape with Burning City*, about 1500. Oil on panel. Museum of Fine Arts, Boston, Seth K. Sweetser Fund. Photograph © Museum of Fine Arts, Boston

selling it. In fact, the theft was not discovered until the 1950s, when Trent's museum collection was moved to its present home in the Palazzo Pretorio. The embroidery was never included on international databases of stolen art, although it was listed as "missing" and "location unknown" in numerous postwar catalogues and scholarly publications. Back in Trent, it today completes the narrative series of embroideries depicting the life of Vigilius, the city's patron saint, the rest of which survived World War II intact.

At the same November 14, 1946, Collections Committee meeting, the MFA voted to purchase two paintings from New York dealers: *The Good Samaritan* by Domenico Fetti offered by Schaeffer Galleries and a small Flemish landscape (fig. 4) offered by Aram Gallery. The next day, Constable wrote to each dealer to inquire about provenance. Siegfried Aram responded, "I hope to be able to give you further details about the [landscape] painting very soon . . . However, I heard that the picture is unknown to the art trade."[47] Dealer Hans Schaeffer sent Constable complete cataloguing information for the Fetti. The ownership history included Gustav Rochlitz, a notorious dealer of Nazi-looted art, and the German collector Fritz Haussmann. The painting had been exhibited in Berlin in 1927 and published in 1931 by Hermann Voss, later the director of Hitler's Führermuseum.[48]

[47] Museum of Fine Arts, Art of Europe Department, Curatorial file 46.1143.

[48] Museum of Fine Arts, Art of Europe Department, Curatorial file 46.1145. The painting is now titled *Parable of the Good Samaritan*.

For much of the twentieth century, it was typical to request provenance information for a work of art after its acquisition was finalized, as Constable did, rather than before. Provenance was considered privileged information, and in most cases, buyers assumed that they could take good title from any reputable seller.[49] While such a system is indisputably gentlemanly, it nevertheless burdens the buyer with nearly all the legal, financial, and reputational risk in the event that rightful ownership to that artwork is challenged in the future. Purchasing a work of art before asking about its provenance is nothing short of a gamble. Indeed, with the information provided, one could place reasonable bets on which of these two paintings the MFA acquired in November 1946 had been looted during the war.

Recent research has clarified that Fetti's *Good Samaritan* has an unbroken provenance during the Nazi era, having been in Haussmann's possession from at least 1931 until 1946, when he sold it through Schaeffer Galleries. The Flemish landscape is a different matter. On July 24, 1948, Jan Gerrit van Gelder of the Kunsthistorisch Instituut der Rijksuniversiteit te Utrecht wrote to Constable about the painting, referring to it as a work by Herri met de Bles:

> Herewith I send you the photograph of the picture by Herry met de Bles? formerly in the collection Koenigs in the Boymans Museum at Rotterdam. The picture was taken away by the Germans and belonged to . . . the Koenigs collection [which was] sold to Göring. All the pictures of the Koenigs collection are recuperated, but the picture by Herry met de Bles could not be traced till yet. The [D]utch government had claimed already in 1945 for [*sic*] this picture.[50]

The landscape hung at Carinhall, Hermann Göring's country estate. It was among the paintings from the collection of Franz Koenigs of Haarlem, which had been sold to Göring in 1940. In early 1945, Göring attempted to safeguard his collection by shipping it to Berchtesgaden. The train carrying the artwork was intercepted by the Allies, and the contents of the shipment were scattered. Most of the art was recovered, but numerous objects, including the

[49] In the first American case to be litigated over a work of Nazi-looted art, *Menzel v List* (Supreme Court, New York, 1966; 267 NYS2d 804), the defendant argued that "amongst such [reputable] galleries the offer of sale of any painting is in and of itself, in the custom of the trade as between galleries, warranty of title. Art galleries of such standing assume, without the necessity of inquiry, that an offer of sale constitutes a representation of authenticity and good title . . ."

[50] Museum of Fine Arts, Art of Europe Department, Curatorial file 46.1143.

landscape, were looted.[51] Other paintings that had been sold by Koenigs to Göring in 1940 were returned to the Netherlands at the end of the war and became the part of the "Netherlands Art Property" (Nederlands Kunstbezit) collection of unclaimed or otherwise unrestituted artwork.[52] If the landscape had been found, it too would have been returned to the Netherlands, but by the fall of 1946 it had already made its way to New York. Like the embroidery, it is not known exactly when the painting entered the United States, but it could either have come in contravention of wartime import restrictions or been imported shortly after they were revoked.

Upon receipt of the letter from Van Gelder, Constable pressed Siegfried Aram for further details on the landscape's history. The response was that it had come to Julian Acampora (a New York restorer) from the New York dealer Enzo d'Urbania; before that it was with a firm called Devany's Auction Galleries, and prior to that a Chicago private collection.[53] Whether there was any truth in these statements is unknown. On October 21, 1948, the MFA Trustees voted to return the Met de Bles to the Netherlands if need be. They stopped just short of deaccessioning it, since the Museum had not yet received an official restitution claim. A representative of the Dutch government should have been in touch with the MFA to formally request its return, but no request was made. The painting remains in the collection of the MFA, subject to an ongoing ownership dispute between the Dutch government and the Franz Koenigs heirs, both of whom claim to be its rightful owner.[54]

The State Department was involved in other issues of looted art that arose at the Museum of Fine Arts in the postwar period. Ardelia Hall had begun her career at the MFA, working for 11 years under Edgell's leadership before leaving the Museum in 1941 and, several years later, joining the Office of Strategic Services and then the State Department. Hall maintained many of her professional and personal relationships with the curatorial staff at the MFA, including her friend Dows Dunham, Curator of Egyptian Art. On August 24, 1951, Dunham wrote to Hall on a business matter:

[51] For further on the shipments from Carinhall, see Nancy H Yeide, *Beyond the Dreams of Avarice: The Hermann Goering Collection* (Dallas, Laurel Publishing 2009) 16, for information on the Met de Bles 292, cat. no. A452.

[52] On November 3, 2003, the Dutch Restitutions Committee issued a recommendation to deny the restitution of works of art from the NK Collection that had belonged to Franz Koenigs <https://www.restitutiecommissie.nl/en/summary_rc_16.html>. Also see Christine F Koenigs, "Under Duress: The Sale of the Franz Koenigs Collection" in Simpson (n 17) 237–40.

[53] Siegfried Aram to WG Constable (20 September 1948). Museum of Fine Arts, Art of Europe Department, Curatorial file 46.1143.

[54] See the online record <https://www.mfa.org/collections/object/landscape-with-burning-city-32987>.

Fig. 5 *Shield Ring*, 1st century BC. Gold, fused glass. Meroë, Pyramid N 6. Ägyptisches Museum und Papyrussammlung, Berlin, inv. no. 22871. © SMB Ägyptisches Museum und Papyrussammlung. Photo: Sandra Steiß

> A week ago today a former chaplain in the US Army brought to me a piece of gold jewelry for identification with the story that it had been given to him, as a token of gratitude, in Berlin in the spring of 1946 by German civilians whom he had helped with food and clothing . . . We identified the piece as one of the items of the famous Ferlini Treasure from Meroe (Meroitic, 1st century AD) from the Berlin Museum, and by reference to published catalogues, with photographs, found that it bore the Inventory No. 22871 of the Aegyptische Abteiling der Staatlichen Museen. . . . I persuaded the former chaplain to leave it with us . . . after explaining to him that we could not buy it since it appeared to be the property of a German national collection, and that the whole question of its status would have to be looked into.[55] (fig. 5)

[55] Dows Dunham to Ardelia Hall (24 August 1951). RG 59, Ardelia Hall Subject Files, Microfilm Reel 2, Egyptian Gold Ring from Meroe. The ring was registered with the MFA on August 17, 1951 (loan no

The chaplain in question was Joseph Shubow (1899–1969), a prominent rabbi and leader in Boston's Jewish community. He had voluntarily enlisted in the Army, served as a chaplain in Europe during World War II, and worked to reunite displaced persons in Berlin at the end of the war. For his activities, he was awarded a Bronze Star.[56] As he would later explain:

> While I was chaplain in Berlin I had the extraordinary privilege to feed hundreds of people, D[isplaced Pt[erson]s and native Germans, who had been oppressed and terrorized by the Nazi regime. . . . A number of them insisted on showing me their personal gratitude by bringing me a Bible or a book of one kind or another or some family heirloom or trinket . . . Among the various tokens of gratitude that I received from a family was a ring . . . I took it for its face value as the heart-rending expression of a broken family in gratitude for the kindness I showed them as an American officer and as a clergyman. This particular ring looked to me rather peculiar—it seemed so different from other such trinkets. I brought it back with me when I returned to this country [in] the latter part of May 1946.[57]

Shubow, who was not an art expert, had no knowledge of the value of the ring. In the years that followed his return to the United States, visitors to his home advised him that it was Egyptian, so he sought a professional opinion. Hall suggested to Dunham that he should reassure Shubow that "US policy is diametrically opposed to the official acts of Nazi Germany"; nevertheless, the ring was looted and therefore "in the category of cultural property which was strictly controlled in the United States Zone of Germany" by Army directives and military government laws.[58] Moreover, it had been brought into the country just before the wartime restrictions were revoked. After some contentious back and forth through the fall of 1951 with Shubow and his attorney, Lee Friedman, US Customs in Boston took possession of the ring for restitution to Berlin.[59] It was subject to forfeiture because it had not been

88.51). Its identification was probably facilitated by Bernard von Bothmer (1912–1993), formerly an assistant at the Egyptian Museum in Berlin; he had left Germany in 1938 because of his anti-Nazi sentiments and, beginning in 1946, worked as an assistant at in the Egyptian Department at the MFA.

[56] Rabbi Shubow's papers are held by the Leo Baeck Institute, New York, which has published a biography and finding aid online: <http://digifindingaids.cjh.org/?pID=1216160>.

[57] Joseph Shubow to James F Malone, US Customs Department, Boston (12 November 1951). Ardelia Hall Subject Files, Reel 1, Egyptian Gold Ring (as above).

[58] Ardelia Hall to Dows Dunham (29 August 1951). Subject files (as above).

[59] Hall received the ring at the National Gallery of Art on 11 January 1952. ibid.

declared at the border, but the ring was also obviously stolen property. It had probably been taken while it was in storage at Berlin's Tiergarten Flakturm (one of several anti-aircraft blockhouse towers in the city, which were used to store museum collections) before Soviet trophy brigades carried the rest of the treasure off.[60] As with the embroidery and the Met de Bles landscape, the details of precisely when and by whom it was stolen are no longer known.

The example of the Egyptian ring would be extraordinary enough on its own, but at the time that the MFA facilitated its return, the staff encountered yet another instance of looted art. In May 1950, the Museum voted to purchase a thirteenth-century Limoges enamel relief of the *Baptism of Christ* from Wildenstein Galleries, New York, for $28,000 (fig. 6). In January 1951, the MFA acquired a twelfth-century enamel showing the *Three Worthies from the Fiery Furnace*, also from Wildenstein, for $30,000 (fig. 7). Both pieces came from the illustrious Czartoryski collection of Poland and were, according to the curatorial recommendation for their purchase, "long known and now unexpectedly sold."[61] Georg Swarzenski (1876–1957) was the curator in charge of their acquisition. Swarzenski, perhaps more than anyone else at the MFA, had firsthand knowledge of the art world under National Socialism. He had directed the Städelsches Institut in Frankfurt, but was dismissed from his position and forced to flee because of his Jewish heritage. In 1939, he joined the MFA as Fellow for Research in Decorative Arts and Sculpture. A meticulous researcher, Swarzenski was keenly attuned to the details of publication, exhibition, and ownership history for each of his acquisitions, and it is tempting to surmise that he believed that the enamels were, like so many works of art on the market in the 1950s, being sold by a family disposing of its art collections after the war.[62]

[60] Konstantin Akinsha and Grigorii Kozlov, *Beautiful Loot: The Soviet Plunder of Europe's Treasures* (New York, Random House 1995) 172.

[61] This statement comes from the recommendation to purchase the *Baptism of Christ*, accessioned 13 April 1950 (accession no 50.858). The *Three Worthies in the Fiery Furnace* was accessioned 11 January 1951 (accession no 51.7).

[62] While at the MFA, Swarzenski maintained or resumed many of the professional relationships he had in Germany, particularly as art dealers and collectors fled and relocated their professions and collections to England and the United States. As early as 1940, he borrowed for the MFA works of art from Eugene Garbáty, a Jewish collector and businessman from Berlin, who had recently arrived in New York with his vast collection of Old Master paintings, sculptures, and decorative arts. Following the war, Swarzenski acquired objects that had been looted and subsequently restituted to the families of European collectors like Alphonse de Rothschild, Oscar Bondy, and Maximilian von Goldschmidt-Rothschild, or that had survived Nazi depredations entirely. In 1951, he purchased an Ottonian wooden Corpus from the heirs of Harry Fuld (MFA accession no 51.1405). In 1954, he helped acquire a sixteen-foot long, fifteenth-century tapestry depicting the battle between Wild Men and Moors from the collection of Ottmar Strauss (accession no 51.1431). Both objects he had known from his time in Frankfurt. On Georg Swarzenski, see Museum of Fine Arts Bulletin 55 Autumn–Winter 1957) 301–02.

Fig. 6 Limoges (France), *Baptism of Christ*, mid-13th century. Champlevé enamel and gilding on copper. Museum of Fine Arts, Boston, Bartlett Collection—Museum purchase with funds from the Francis Bartlett Donation of 1912. Photograph © Museum of Fine Arts, Boston

Both enamels, however, had been plundered from the Czartoryski family during World War II. Shortly after it was acquired, the *Baptism of Christ* was illustrated and discussed in the MFA *Bulletin* and Prince Wladyslaw Czartoryski (1918–78) saw the article.[63] On October 23, 1951, his attorney,

[63] Georg Swarzenski, "A Masterpiece of Limoges," Museum of Fine Arts Bulletin (February 1951) 49, no 275, 17–25.

Fig. 7 *Three Worthies in the Fiery Furnace*, about 1150–75. Champlevé enamel and gilding on copper. Museum of Fine Arts, Boston, William Francis Warden Fund. Photograph © Museum of Fine Arts, Boston

Thomas R. Webb of Coudert Brothers, Paris, wrote to the Museum, notifying the Director that Goluchow Castle had been looted by the Germans and most of the family's art collection was still missing. He asserted that the prince was the legal owner of the *Baptism*. Upon receipt of the claim, Edgell wrote to dealer Felix Wildenstein:

> I remember when we bought it, you said it was from the Czartoryski collection, and I cannot see why, if that collection were looted, they should try five years later to trace individual pieces. Would they not have been returned by the Army and the Government like all other works of looted art? Moreover, I cannot imagine a firm like Wildenstein getting caught on a looted object. Can you shed any light on the matter?[64]

[64] George Harold Edgell to Felix Wildenstein (27 October 1951). Museum of Fine Arts, Art of Europe Department, Curatorial files 50.858 and 51.7.

Wildenstein assured Edgell that the gallery had checked the enamels against the available lists of looted property and found no match. Edgell in response confirmed his suspicions about the claim, stating, "I have enough confidence not only in the integrity of Wildenstein and Company, but in their shrewdness to feel confident that they would never handle a dubious object."[65] The gentlemen's agreement by which artwork changed hands in the 1950s was, he felt, sufficient to assure the MFA that it had good title.

Representing the MFA, Harold Davis of the Boston law firm of Nutter, McClennan and Fish, responded to Webb's letter on November 30, 1951. "Some years ago," he wrote, the Baptism relief

> was acquired from a reputable dealer of long standing, after investigation of both authenticity and title. It is accordingly something of a surprise to learn that any claim for the article is being made, especially after such a long lapse of time. The dealer from whom the object was acquired is making further investigation, and I shall write you again when I have further information.[66]

In response, Webb responded that he, in turn, was

> surprised to learn from your letter that the relief was acquired by the Museum some years ago. The Bulletin of the Museum for February 1951, from which the Prince learned the whereabouts of the relief, states on page 17 that the object had been "recently purchased."[67]

The MFA was caught in a half-truth. Again, there is an unavoidable and uncomfortable disconnect in the attitude of the museum director. Having just confronted the wartime history of the Herri met de Bles landscape and Meroitic ring, Edgell was understandably exasperated to receive yet another claim, but there was no reason for him to be astonished. He surely knew that "all works of looted art" had not yet been returned, but were continuing to circulate and surface as many as five years after the end of the war.

[65] George Harold Edgell to Felix Wildenstein (2 November 1951); Museum of Fine Arts, Art of Europe Department, Curatorial files 50.858 and 51.7.

[66] Harold Davis to Thomas R. Webb (30 November 1951); Museum of Fine Arts, Art of Europe Department, Curatorial files 50.858 and 51.7.

[67] Thomas R. Webb to Harold Davis (nd); Museum of Fine Arts, Art of Europe Department, Curatorial files 50.858 and 51.7.

What prompted Edgell's defensive attitude when faced with the Czartoryski claim? Several explanations are possible. First, the Met de Bles had been a relatively minor, though not negligible, acquisition at $3,200, and the ring was never purchased by the Museum. Neither represented a significant financial loss for the MFA when they were claimed. The enamels had already cost the Museum $58,000, an astronomical sum in 1951, particularly for decorative arts.[68] Second, neither the Met de Bles nor the ring was offered with any paper trail or publication history. The enamels, however, were accompanied by publication, exhibition, and collecting history, and as such they were, or at least seemed, less likely to have slipped through the cracks of an illegal trade. Third, Wildenstein, unlike Siegfried Aram or Joseph Shubow, was a familiar entity to the MFA, and the name and reputation of the seller were considered an assurance of legitimacy. Finally, and perhaps most strikingly, the Met de Bles could be claimed by a nation (the Netherlands) and the ring by a state museum (in Berlin). The enamels were claimed by a private individual. It is inevitably harder for a private collector to prove legal ownership than it is for governments and accredited institutions, which often maintain ledgers, accession cards, and photographic documentation of their collections. The ethos of the 1940s was certainly to see the absence of evidence of looting as proof of clear title. Similarly, in 1945, Edgell had been quick to act diligently upon the offer of stolen German museum coins, yet in 1944 was remarkably passive when responding to Walter Westfeld's brother, who like Prince Czartoryski, was a private claimant.

The matter of the enamels went unresolved, and on September 14, 1952, *The New York Times* reported that the Prince Czartoryski was suing the MFA.[69] In 1953, Ardelia Hall wrote to her former director, asking Edgell on behalf of the State Department for photographs of the enamels and for further information about their history, which he supplied. By 1955, however, the claim had still not been resolved, and Hall wrote again, this time to Edgell's successor as director, Perry Rathbone (1911–2000), formally

[68] Also in 1951, the MFA purchased what proved to be a highlight of the decorative arts collection, a rare Renaissance bronze statuette of Saint Christopher (accession no 51.412) for $16,000. In 1950, Dirck van Baburen's 1622 painting *The Procuress* was purchased for only $1,960 (accession no 50.2721).

[69] "Takes Museum to Court" (*New York Times*, 14 September 1952) 60. Edgell is quoted in the article boasting that "never during my eighteen years as director of the museum have we bought any 'hot stuff' for the Museum."

requesting the surrender of the enamels to the State Department. This request prompted a litigious response from the Nutter law firm challenging her authority on the matter, to which Hall somewhat sarcastically replied, "It was assumed that the Museum would wish to uphold the principles of respect for the ownership of cultural property looted and dispersed since the war, in the present instance as it has done in the past."[70] Finally, in July 1955, all three parties—the MFA, Wildenstein, and Czartoryski—reached an agreement out of court, and title to both enamels passed fully to the MFA.

The two enamels are on permanent view in the MFA's medieval galleries. What is now known is that Wildenstein had bought them from a certain Pollock (or Pollack), a dealer in Switzerland. They were shipped by Schoeni, a Swiss company, whose representatives attested they had received the enamels on October 29, 1949, from a Mr. Vala in Zurich.[71] Unlike Rabbi Shubow's ring, the enamels had not entered the country in violation of Customs law. Hall obtained copies of the consular invoice for the pieces, which showed that they had been imported through Geneva from Vaduz on November 15, 1949, and were described and declared correctly with Customs. They were stolen, but there was nothing to prevent them from entering the United States freely, since there were no import controls on works of fine art at that time.

VIII. Museum Acquisitions in the 1960s: A Case Study

Hall retired from the State Department in 1962, having overseen dozens of cases and the restitution of hundreds, if not thousands, of objects.[72] By the 1960s, the subject of Nazi-era looting no longer seemed to be a significant concern to most participants in the art trade. Several members of museum staff who had firsthand involvement with the Roberts Commission retired. Both Georg Swarzenski and W.G. Constable left the Museum 1957; Swarzenski passed away later that year. Much of the MFA's curatorial staff in the 1960s was newly hired, and under Perry Rathbone's enthusiastic

[70] Ardelia Hall to Nutter, McClennan, and Fish (1 June 1955). MFA curatorial files.

[71] RG 59, Ardelia Hall Subject Files, Reel 6, St. Patroclus Shrine (Kaiser Friedrich Musuem) in Flakturm Fire (November 1951–March 1961).

[72] By 1954, she had overseen 66 cases and the restitution of nearly 1,600 items. Ardelia R Hall, "US Program for Return of Historic Objects to Countries of Origin, 1944–1954" *Department of State Bulletin* 31 (4 October 1954) 493.

leadership, they acquired ambitiously.[73] Yet the old ethos of collecting—to trust the reputation of the seller and ask few questions—persisted.

With the era of Nazi looting some twenty years in the past, and the tendency not to ask many questions about an object's provenance, it was almost certain that museums would continue to make problematic acquisitions. Even those who had experienced Nazi persecution appeared unconcerned by indications of looting. Hanns Swarzenski (1903–1985), Georg's son, likewise fled Germany in the late 1930s and assisted the Roberts Commission during the war; he joined the staff of the MFA in 1948.[74] In 1954, he worked with Hall to ensure the return of five silver-gilt statuettes from the Saint Patroclus shrine, a fourteenth-century reliquary that had gone missing from the Berlin museums during the war. The figures were offered by the art dealer Ernest Brummer and had caught Swarzenski's immediate attention when he saw them in New York.[75] More than a decade after their return, however, in 1966, Hanns showed himself to be far less diligent when he proposed the acquisition of a medieval stone spandrel with an angel (fig. 8). In his recommendation for its purchase, he wrote the following:

> The relief was discovered in a German collection in Paris during the German occupation in World War II and bought by Mr. Schwartz, today the most active private collector of Gothic sculpture in the Rhineland. Of its previous history, nothing is known.[76]

The Museum purchased the spandrel on September 21, 1966, from Hermann Schwartz of Mönchengladbach, Germany.

[73] See Belinda Rathbone, *The Boston Raphael: A Mysterious Painting, an Embattled Museum in an Era of Change and a Daughter's Search for the Truth* (Boston, David R. Godine 2014) esp 95–115.

[74] On Hanns Swarzenski, see ibid 116–36.

[75] RG 59, Ardelia Hall Subject files, Reel 6, St. Patroclus Shrine (as above). Like the Meroitic Ring, the shrine had been placed in storage during the war, but was burned. Hanns Swarzenski noted that the silver-gilt figures showed signs of fire damage in 1953. He reported this information to Brummer, advising him to contact the restitution officials. He also confided his concerns to Charles Kuhn of the Fogg Art Museum, who put him in direct touch with Hall. Following Hall's investigation, the figures were returned to Berlin in 1956 with relatively little fanfare. Hall reported at the time (7 November 1956) that the MFA "had already assisted several times in the recovery of works of art, [and] I was anxious that the museum should receive every consideration" not to receive undue or unwanted publicity. Ernest Brummer had acquired the figures from the French dealer Brimo de Laroussilhe, who purchased them at an auction held at Hotel Drouot, Paris, in 1951. The figures were seized in light of US military government regulations that had prohibited the trafficking of artwork in occupied zones; like the Czartoryski enamels, they had not been imported in violation of Customs law.

[76] Recommendation for purchase (21 September 1966). Museum of Fine Arts, Art of Europe Department, Curatorial file 66.438.

Fig. 8 *Spandrel with an Angel*, third quarter of the 12th century. Stone; limestone with polychromy. Museum of Fine Arts, Boston. Charles Amos Cummings Bequest Fund. Photograph © Museum of Fine Arts, Boston

The information provided in Hanns's recommendation raises a number of critical questions about the spandrel's Nazi-era history, in particular, who the German collector in Paris was and how he had obtained it. If these details were available in 1966, they were not recorded. The MFA has since learned that the sculpture belonged at one time to Alphonse Kann (1870–1948), a Jewish collector in France and victim of Nazi looting. It has not been determined precisely when Kann owned the spandrel, and no evidence has been found that it was plundered from him. It therefore remains in the collection of the MFA, where it is a high priority for ongoing provenance research.[77] In retrospect, it seems extremely unlikely that Hanns Swarzenski wanted to acquire a tainted object; it is almost certain, however, that he wanted to acquire a stunning object, and in order to do so, he ignored obvious signs of Nazi expropriation. Like Edgell, he had vigilantly reported stolen museum objects when they surfaced on the market, but in the absence of proof of looting from a private owner, he expressed no reservations about acquiring

[77] See the online record <https://www.mfa.org/collections/object/spandrel-with-an-angel-61936>.

the possibly-stolen spandrel. Thus, another object with a questionable wartime history entered the museum collection.

IX. Lessons for the Present Day

There are obvious differences in responses to the looting of Nazi-occupied Europe and the present-day plundering of archaeological sites in the Middle East and elsewhere. The identification and restitution of stolen art in wartime and postwar America was aided by the fact that the United States had been at war with Nazi Germany. Wartime import restrictions helped prevent the entry of looted art into the United States, though once they were lifted, there was little to stop illicit art (like the Czartoryski enamels or the figures from the Patroclus Shrine) from entering the country. Following the war, the State Department maintained a centralized role to oversee the restitution of looted property from conflict zones that surfaced in the United States, which lasted until Hall's retirement in 1962. Today, the State Department is still able to assist with Holocaust-era claims.[78] If a work of art comes into the country from a war zone, however—for example, from Afghanistan or Yemen—it is not necessarily clear which government office to contact or who should be responsible for coordinating its return.[79]

As of 2020, the United States is not formally at war and as a result is unable to implement the kinds of controls over art assets it did during the 1940s. Nevertheless, the government has demonstrated its commitment to preventing the circulation of stolen art by implementing the 1970 UNESCO Convention on the Means of Prohibiting and Preventing the Illicit Import, Export and Transfer of Ownership of Cultural Property. This has been

[78] On the State Department's ongoing role in this area, see Maurer (n 38) 142–44. In 1999, the State Department established the Office of the Special Envoy for Holocaust Issues.

[79] In 2015, the Association of Art Museum Directors issued Protocols for Safe Havens for Works of Cultural Significance from Countries in Crisis. The protocols allow for US museums to take possession—though not ownership—of works of art that come into the country and are "in danger of damage, destruction or looting as a result of war, terrorism or natural disasters" in their home countries. Museums are authorized to hold these objects transparently until such a time that they may be safely returned. The protocols were promulgated just before Congress passed the Protect and Preserve International Cultural Property Act (2016), the law that implements emergency import restrictions with Syria. The law makes specific provision for safe haven: "The President may waive such import restrictions for specified cultural property if the President certifies to Congress that: (1) the foreign owner or custodian of the specified cultural property has requested that the property be temporarily located in the United States for protection purposes, (2) the property shall be returned upon request to the foreign owner or custodian, and (3) the grant of a waiver will not contribute to illegal trafficking in cultural property or financing of criminal or terrorist activities."

achieved through bilateral agreements, or Memoranda of Understanding (MOUs), with twenty countries vulnerable to theft and looting.[80] The agreements restrict the importation of archaeological and ethnological materials from those nations. As unrest in the Middle East increased, the United States has also adopted emergency import restrictions on ancient artifacts from Iraq, Syria, and Yemen. All of these import restrictions require that cultural property be accompanied by a valid export permit in order to enter the United States. Lacking a permit, the object needs to have a documented provenance outside its country of origin for a certain period of time, usually since the time the import restriction was enacted.

When bilateral agreements are introduced or come up for renewal, they are frequently opposed by representatives of the art market, private collectors, and even museum associations. These groups have suggested that it is unfair for the government to try to control art commerce (an argument that was offered at the end of World War II) or, more often, that the MOUs are not actually helping stop the problem of looting, and for that reason no import restrictions should be implemented.[81] Drawing on the lessons of World War II, however, a counterargument can be made. If looting continues to be a problem, and plundered artifacts are circulating, then it is entirely reasonable for the government to try to prevent these objects from tainting the American market by regulating their import. Even if, as it was argued in 1946, no plundered artifacts were showing up at the border, it follows that there would be no harm in implementing sensible precautions in the event that they do.

Another significant difference between the art world of postwar America and today is the relative feasibility of identifying stolen art. The looting of

[80] The United States implements the UNESCO Convention, and enacts the Memoranda of Understanding, through the Convention of Cultural Property Implementation Act (HR 4566) of 1983. The countries (in 2020) include Algeria, Belize, Bolivia, Bulgaria, Cambodia, China, Colombia, Cyprus, Ecuador, Egypt, El Salvador, Greece, Guatemala, Honduras, Italy, Jordan, Libya, Mali, Nicaragua, and Peru.

[81] These arguments are typically offered as part of broader concerns that the criteria for the MOU are not being met by the source country. Ricardo St. Hilaire often reports on the State Department hearings on the Memoranda of Understanding on his blog, *Cultural Heritage Lawyer*. See Ricardo St. Hilaire, "Opposition to MoU's: A Change in Policy for the Association of Art Museum Directors?" (*Cultural Heritage Lawyer*, 22 January 2015) <https://culturalheritagelawyer.blogspot.com/2015/01/opposition-to-mous-change-in-policy-for.html> and related blog posts. Peter Tompa, an advocate for private collectors, is a frequent opponent of the Memoranda of Understanding, as he reports on his blog, *Cultural Property Observer* <http://culturalpropertyobserver.blogspot.com/search/label/Import%20Restrictions>. The Committee for Cultural Property has argued incorrectly that the result of the MOUs is to "completely block all art from 16 nations into the US" <https://culturalpropertynews.org/get-the-facts/#what-is-an-mou>.

Nazi Europe was vast, but much of it was orchestrated, and geographically it was limited to a group of contiguous countries. The objects that were taken or forcibly sold in Nazi-occupied Europe could be documented and reported as stolen; at least in theory, their ownership was traceable to a time before the theft. The present-day plundering of archaeological artifacts is, by contrast, a worldwide problem, and its scope virtually impossible to gauge or report reliably. Additionally, when an ancient object is illicitly removed from the ground, its collecting history begins anew. There is little way to report what is taken during an illegal excavation—and, without a paper trail, little way for subsequent owners to know for sure how long an archaeological object has been in circulation. For that reason, due diligence today must mean more than simply ensuring a work of art has not been reported as stolen.

Despite these differences, the wartime case studies from the Museum of Fine Arts offer lessons that remain applicable today. For instance, it was not then and is not now realistic to think that every looted work of art will be reliably documented. After World War II, the hard-copy lists of missing works of art that circulated were incomplete and frequently out of date by the time they reached museums and other stakeholders.[82] Photographs did not exist of many stolen objects, especially those from private collections. Even if a museum or gallery diligently checked the lists that were available, as Wildenstein said it did, it was in most cases difficult, if not impossible, to know for sure whether or not a particular work of art had been looted.

Today, the art world is in a more advantageous position, with the ability to digitize images of stolen art and upload and distribute information quickly and easily through the internet. Nonetheless, not all thefts are reported to law enforcement, and those that are still may not be included in online databases or registered with the most frequently used services like the Art Loss Register or Artive. Archaeological thefts are nearly impossible to trace and report. If there is a temptation to put faith into the absence of evidence of looting, today as in 1946, there is still inherent risk in doing so. Diligent buyers should take into account the full, documented history of an object (or lack thereof) when deciding whether to pursue an acquisition. Ultimately, however, there may be no way to rule out completely the possibility that a work of art was stolen.

[82] As, for example, the *Repertoire des Biens Spoliées en France durant la Guerre, 1939–1945* (Berlin, 1947), which issued several supplements; Austria's *Verzeichnisse gesuchter Kunstwerke aus Österreichischem Besitz* (nd, [1950?]).

X. Building Museum Collections Diligently

The task of making judicious decisions about museum acquisitions has always fallen to its personnel, usually curators and directors. For most of the twentieth century, buyers—including the MFA curators discussed earlier—did not ask questions about provenance before making a purchase, and then were caught off-guard when the museum's ownership was challenged. Fortunately, this system has changed drastically, and buyers know they have no excuse for not making inquiries before paying for a new acquisition. Yet stolen works of art continue to be identified in museum collections, only to be claimed, deaccessioned, and returned to their previous owners. If the ethos of collecting has changed, why does this problem persist?

One reason may be a natural inclination, today as in the postwar period, to be vigilant about the most egregious risk factor to the exclusion of others. During World War II, the threat of National Socialist forces taking masterpieces out of European museums justifiably alarmed journalists, museum directors, and curators. The forcible sale of Jewish property and the transportation of works of art of more modest value into the country, however, seemed negligible by comparison. As a result, curators were alert to museum thefts but relatively complacent about thefts from private individuals. Today, it cannot be disputed that awareness of the problem of ISIS looting is critical. Yet it would be a mistake to conclude that the greatest problem facing the art world is that of terrorist-financed "blood antiquities" and not looting from other parts of the Middle East or indeed the rest of the world. Participants in the art trade may be on the lookout for Syrian antiquities, but should also be attuned to the risk of archaeological plunder elsewhere, not to mention thefts from museums and private homes, smuggling, and other illegal activities.

Even more critical than awareness is personal responsibility. Museum staff did not want to acquire or hold onto stolen art during and after World War II, and they do not wish to do so now. Nevertheless, in spite of numerous examples of MFA personnel working with authorities to return plundered objects in the 1940s and 1950s, those same individuals concurrently turned a blind eye to other, arguably equally problematic acquisitions. The difference lay in the fact that the works of art they accepted bore no explicit proof of looting. As long as curators chose not to ask additional questions about provenance, they certainly would not turn up that proof. The same situation can arise today, particularly with archaeological acquisitions, which are not easily identified as lost or stolen.

It has always been the curator's job to identify and acquire outstanding works of art for their museum collection, particularly before other buyers can discover them. It can be tempting to accept a minimal amount of due diligence—for example, an art loss certificate, a plausible story from the seller, or just the absence of evidence of a theft—in the rush to make an exciting new addition to the collection. Curators should be thrilled by new discoveries, but they should also be unceasingly curious about where these stellar objects come from. Museum staff know that they must ask questions of their sellers, but there is little point in asking questions if the answers provided are accepted at face value. Curators must also do their best independently to verify provenance information provided by sellers and donors, especially when it is verbal or anecdotal, in order to avoid burdening their institutions with fake or stolen objects and, ultimately, losing these objects from the collection.

Since 2010, the Museum of Fine Arts, Boston, has required curatorial staff to fill out provenance questionnaires for nearly every potential acquisition and incoming loan (fig. 9). The forms, not unlike the questionnaires required by the Treasury Department during World War II, ask a series of factual questions about the object's previous ownership, publication history, international shipments, and legislation that would govern its ownership and export. The forms ask the curator to justify the acquisition based on the factual information provided. They are completed in collaboration with the Curator for Provenance and are subject to approval by the Director of Collections. This system ensures checks and balances in the acquisition process: no work of art is considered by just one staff member. It also compels curators to consider what is demonstrable about an object's history, as opposed to what is believed (or hoped) to be true. The process of completing a questionnaire does not rule out the possibility of acquiring a stolen work of art, but it does prompt a consideration of relevant issues and ensures a transparent and thoughtful acquisition process. Given the MFA's collecting mistakes of the past, the forms represent a proactive step that incentivizes active due diligence going forward.

XI. Conclusion

Museums like the MFA cannot undo their past acquisition decisions, but staff can address the legacy that has been left to them by their predecessors. Curators must study the history of their collections, particularly those works of art that changed hands during periods of conflict, and resolve potential ownership disputes whenever possible. Museums must also learn from the

BOSTON

MUSEUM OF FINE ARTS, BOSTON
Short-Form Diligence Questionnaire

BOSTON

For potential acquisitions and incoming loans:

1. **Title or Description, Medium and Dimensions (please insert or attach image if available):**

2. **Artist (if known):**

3. **Period or Date:**

4. **Approximate value/purchase price of object:**

5. **Where was the object created? If unsure, please list all possible countries, or explain in terms of historical geography . Use modern borders.**

6. **Where was the object discovered or excavated? If unsure, please list all possible countries, or explain in terms of historical geography. Use modern borders.**

7. **Who is selling, donating, or lending the object? What is their address?**

8. **Who owns the object?**

9. **Where, from whom and how did the current owner acquire the object? Please refer to the warranty, deed of gift, or other information provided by the owner.**

10. **Who owned the object before the current owner acquired it? What else have you been able to find out about the ownership history of the object? In addition to literal ownership history, provide all anecdotal information that adds to your knowledge of the object's history.**

11. **When and by whom was the object imported into the U.S.? What do the import documents state as the object's value and country of origin? Attach import documents.**

12. **When was the object exported from its country of modern discovery? Attach any export documents available.**

CONFIDENTIAL: FOR INTERNAL USE ONLY

Fig. 9 Cultural Property Questionnaire, Museum of Fine Arts, Boston

mistakes of their past and apply those lessons to their present-day collecting practices. In 1943, Francis Henry Taylor urged museums not to "operate in a 'black market' of antiquities in which no questions would be asked," lest they contribute to the circulation of Nazi-looted art.[83] The same exhortation must

[83] Taylor (n 16) 43.

13. Where else has the object been since that time and when was it exported from any other countries?

14. Exhibition history (venues, dates, and lender, if known:

15. Publication history (titles, dates, and any provenance or ownership information included):

16. What databases, websites, or other resources did you check to assure title of the object? (UNESCO, Interpol, Art Loss Register, websites maintained by countries with cultural heritage)

17. Are you aware of any claims to the object?

18. Are there any physical characteristics, individuals involved or other circumstances that might indicate looting, theft or other inappropriate past?

19. In MFA standard format, please list the provenance as you would have it appear in documentation and on the website.

20. What are the laws that might govern the ownership (i.e., national or cultural patrimony), export, or import of this object? Insert summary of relevant laws below, including year of implementation. Refer to http://www.ifar.org/art_law.php (for the current legislation of many countries) and/or http://www.unesco.org/culture/natlaws/index.php (for earlier and additional legislation).

21. Why is this acquisition or loan acceptable under the laws listed above and the MFA's Collections Policy?

22. Additional information:

CONFIDENTIAL: FOR INTERNAL USE ONLY

Fig. 9 Continued

be made even more forcefully today. Museum staff must ask questions of their sellers and verify the answers; know the legislation that could affect the acquisition of every object; and require correct shipping paperwork, warranties, and other critical documentation. Only by taking these steps will museums play an active role in discouraging the circulation of recently looted materials on the global art market, and avoid the collecting mistakes that were made after World War II.

12

Nazi Looting and Internal and External Colonial Plundering

Differences in Responses

Jos van Beurden

I. Introduction

The issue of return, restitution, and repatriation of looted cultural heritage is in the spotlight.[1] Many analyses of this new trend focus on one of three categories of loot in which Europeans were involved: cultural property looted by the Nazi regime from occupied areas in Europe; human remains and disputable objects from internal colonialism in Australia, Canada, New Zealand, and the United States; or the same from Europe's colonialism in Latin America, Asia, and Africa. Comparing issues of return for each of the three categories in a helicopter overview, the chapter notes serious inequality among the three ways. At an abstract level, cultural heritage is often spoken of in universal terms. That should make it immune to narrow political agendas and require a certain neutrality in the politics of return, restitution, and repatriation. But the chapter argues that, in practice, preferences

[1] Note on terminology. This chapter uses the word "return" as a rather neutral term, "restitution" for conveying a presupposition that a claim was based on an unjust acquisition. "Repatriation" is most frequently used for human remains and funerary objects. Lyndel V Prott (ed), *Witnesses to History—Documents and Writings on the Return of Cultural Objects* (Paris, UNESCO Publishing 2009) XXI–XXIV. Sometimes, the term "colonial contexts" is preferred above "colonies," as it covers also countries that were never colonized—such as China and Ethiopia—but felt the impact of European colonialism. Deutscher Museumsbund, *Guidelines on Dealing with Collections from Colonial Contexts* (Berlin, German Muesums Association May 2018) <https://www.museumsbund.de/publikationen/guidelines-on-dealing-with-collections-from-colonial-contexts-2/> accessed 13 November 2019. Some use the term "colonial framework" when writing about "colonial contexts." Felwine Sarr and Bénédicte Savoy, *The Restitution of African Cultural Heritage. Toward a New Relational Ethics* (Paris, Ministère de la Culture, 2018) <http://restitutionreport2018.com/sarr_savoy_en.pdf> accessed 13 November 2019.

Jos van Beurden, *Nazi Looting and Internal and External Colonial Plundering* In: *The Preservation of Art and Culture in Times of War.* Edited by: Claire Finkelstein, Derek Gillman, and Frederik Rosén, Oxford University Press. © Oxford University Press 2022. DOI: 10.1093/oso/9780197610565.003.0013

in the return discussion are easily politicized. There is no neutrality in the politics of return.[2]

II. New Phase in an Old Discussion

The extent of the Nazi loot has been brought into the open.[3] There is certain agreement about dealing with Nazi-looted works of art. General principles have been formulated, which enjoy broad international support. Although claimants of internal colonial loot have a way to go, they have gained the support of the 2007 UN Declaration on the Rights of Indigenous Peoples and of laws and programs developed by the four former settler colonies. More complicated are the chances to retrieve loot, war booty, and other displaced objects resulting from external colonial contexts. From their independence onward, countries in the Global South have knocked on the doors of former European colonial powers, but they lacked the means to support their claims and have achieved meager results. Currently, several countries that suffered under Europe's colonialism—Nigeria, the Republic of Benin, Ethiopia, and China—are intensifying their return claims. Some former colonial powers are seeking new ways to look at these claims—Germany, France, Sweden, Belgium, and the Netherlands. An example is the Benin Dialogue Group of representatives from ethnographic museums in several European countries and representatives from Nigeria and the Benin Kingdom, who together discuss the maldistribution of Benin objects between Europe and the African countries. The former hunters of the cultural heritage from colonial contexts acknowledge that they no longer have a monopoly on its possession. They are slightly opening the door. Could an adaptation of the principles, which exist for dealing with Nazi-looted art, to dealings with colonial loot be helpful? Does the new wave in the debate indicate a real change, or will it ebb away and die as a candle in the night? At this moment, the chapter concludes, increased talking about return has not resulted in many returns. Return is a multilayered, complicated trajectory.[4] It is difficult to determine the start of

[2] See eg Ana F Vrdoljak, *International Law, Museums and the Return of Cultural Objects* (CUP 2008). Prott (n 1); Jos van Beurden, *Treasures in Trusted Hands-Negotiating the Future of Colonial Cultural Objects* (Leiden, Sidestone 2017).

[3] See eg Lynn H Nicholas, *The Rape of Europe: The Fate of Europe's Treasures in the Third Reich* (New York, Vintage Books 1995); Tom Bower, *Blood Money-the Swiss, the Nazis and the Looted Billions* (London, Macmillan 1997).

[4] See eg Jeanette Greenfield, *The Return of Cultural Treasures* (CUP 2007); Vrdoljak (n 2); Prott, (n 1); Beurden (n 2). Some returns can be studied at *Arthemis* (University of Geneva, Art Law Centre) <https://plone.unige.ch/art-adr?set_language = en> accessed 14 November 2019.

the discussion about the transfer of disputed cultural heritage and human remains. Did the end of the Cold War and the fall of the Berlin Wall in 1989 give an impetus to families, which had been deprived of their land, houses, factories, and works of art, to submit claims? Did they, in turn, inspire claimants of Nazi-looted works of art to speed up efforts to retrieve their treasures? Or was it the growing strength of organizations of First Nations in the old settler colonies—Australia, Canada, New Zealand, and the United States? Was it the change in global power relations and ethics that led to a revival of the debate about disputed collections, which European colonial powers had shipped back from their colonial possessions? Maybe we are too much in the middle of events to determine the precise start.

With more certainty, we can argue that Europeans played a central role in each of the three "loot categories" and that this burdens them with a responsibility. They took human remains and objects from their new possessions in Latin America, Asia, and Africa on a massive scale. European settlers in North America, Australia, and New Zealand did the same in relation to the peoples they encountered in the new territories, peoples that had lived there long before their arrival. Between 1933 and 1945, the Nazis robbed Jewish people, political opponents, and other groups detested by them of art works, archives, and other cultural heritage.

Despite the remarkable upswing in the debate about disputed objects, it is not new. It is as old as the moment of their involuntary loss and forced seizure. In some instances, it remained limited to that moment; in others it has continued, always with ups and downs. Often the history of problematic acquisitions has remained covered and is now lost. The history of some is known, or we can get to know it by diving into books and archives.

Diving into early sixteenth-century Aztec chronicles teach us how Spanish conquistadores entered the palace premises of Aztec Emperor Montezuma Xokoyotzim II and took everything that gleamed, whether it came from the treasure room or Montezuma's parental house. The looting aroused profound dismay among Aztec eyewitnesses.[5] Since 1880, a precious Aztec headdress has been a centerpiece in the Weltmuseum in Vienna. In spite of regular Mexican requests, the museum will not return it, arguing that the crown is too fragile to be transported. Moreover, the museum doubts whether it really belonged to the Emperor. As a saving grace, it offers Mexican visitors

[5] Rudolf Van Zantwijk (ed), *De oorlog tegen de Goden - Azteekse kronieken over de Spaanse Verovering* (Amsterdam, Meulenhoff 1992) 99–100.

free access.[6] Among the centerpieces of the refurbished Africa Museum in Brussels is a nail statue. In 1878, it was captured by a Belgian trader from a community in the Boma region. Its leaders and population had opposed its removal. After independence in 1960, the Democratic Republic Congo claimed the statue. Belgium did not give in. When, in 2016, a historian from the Africa Museum showed a picture of the statue to the inhabitants of Boma, they recognized it and were deeply moved. According to a local chief, "the powers of the *kitumba* (statue) could be revived after restitution, and the object could thus be reused." In the new presentation, the Africa Museum leaves this historical background unmentioned.[7]

From the start of Europe's colonial expansion early in the fifteenth century, the destruction and seizure of cultural and historical treasures, human remains, and burial items were part of it. With obvious differences in periods and places of expansion and between colonial powers and colonial possessions, it can be stated that destruction and seizure were part of the violence and policies of Europeans in the distant areas to exploit local labor and resources and impose unequal treaties and trade monopolies. Countries of origin have experienced this loss of their cultural heritage as a form of injustice. They want this to be undone, and reclaim usually only some of their treasures. It is not hard to find comparable situations behind claims related to lost relics resulting from internal colonialism or from the pillage by the Nazis. Not long after the start of Europe's external colonialism, European settlers took comparable control over indigenous peoples in Australia, Canada, New Zealand, and the United States. These peoples had often lived there for millennia. The situation in North America became more complicated when the European newcomers had enslaved Africans brought as cheap labor. From the start, these immigrants and, at a later stage, collectors and scientists coming from Europe confiscated numerous treasures and remains. They remained in private collections or ended up in museums in the settler colonies and Europe. Similarly, part of the Nazi extinction policy toward Jews, Roma, Sinti, homosexuals, and political opponents was the seizure of their paintings, sculptures, ancient books, and other cultural properties. It began in 1933 and ended with their defeat in 1945. The Nazi loot has been documented by far the best.

[6] Weltmuseum Wien, "Quetzal feathered headdress" <https://www.weltmuseumwien.at/en/object/531234/?offset = 46&lv = list> accessed 4 October 2019.

[7] Maarten Couttenier, "EO.0.0.7943" (2018) 133(2) BMGN - Low Countries Historical Review 79–90 <https://www.bmgn-lchr.nl/articles/10.18352/bmgn-lchr.10553/> accessed 28 October 2019. This chapter's author visited the Africa Museum on 18 September 2018.

This brings us to the differences in these three specified categories of plunder of cultural heritage. These will be explored by comparing their context, the nature of the objects at stake, issues of provenance research, and who the rightful claimants are.

The Nazis developed special laws to justify their policy of confiscating and destroying millions of valuable objects, books, and archives, be it by the regime itself or its members for their own benefit. Settled laws in the occupied countries, where the loot took place, made *all* these expropriations criminal acts, which were part of an industrialized, *genocidal* policy toward specific population groups. This gives families that claim lost objects a strong position. Colonial looting was part of a systematic *exploitation* policy, although for some Native Americans, Aboriginal peoples, Herrero and Nama in Namibia, and millions of people in Belgian King Leopold II's Congo Free State, this policy bordered on genocide. European colonial powers and the European settlers considered the appropriation of cultural and historical treasures as legally and morally justified. They were sovereign in their new possessions and their new laws outweighed indigenous laws and customs, even if these strongly opposed the alienation of ritual and ceremonial objects.[8] In the view of local people the confiscations were criminal acts, but in the view of the Europeans they were not. They saw them as part of a civilizing mission and effort to save old civilizations. Nowadays, with changing ethics, Europe is replacing this civilizing discourse and salvage paradigm with a discourse in which the presence of *some* objects and collections is questioned.

To explain this, three types of objects from external and internal colonial contexts are distinguished. The first covers war booty, objects destroyed, confiscated or smuggled by colonial administrators and soldiers, missionaries, traders, scientists, explorers, and others. These objects are subject to dispute as they were instances of involuntary loss.[9] A second type consists of objects that were acquired in a situation in which local craftsmen and traders and Europeans who acquired such works agreed about the exchange of an object for another item or for money. They acted at a relatively equal level. There was a win-win situation. Between these two extremes exists the third type, a large gray area of objects which we do not know the circumstances of

[8] See, for instance, Evelien Campfens, "The Bangwa Queen: Artifact or Heritage?" (2019) 26 International Journal of Cultural Property 80–81.

[9] There were no *smuggled* objects among the loot resulting from internal colonialism, as the acquisitions occurred inside the borders of one state.

how they ended up in Western public or private collections.[10] To know more about this type requires extensive provenance research and the opening of unofficial archives such as diaries and letters.

In the current debate about return, the first type is most prominent, and inside this type war booty captured during external European raids—loot from the Old Summer Palace in Beijing (1860), the palace of Emperor Tewodros and nearby churches in Ethiopia (1868), the royal city of Abomey in the present-day Republic of Benin (1892), the royal palace on the island of Lombok in Indonesia (1894), the royal city of Benin in Nigeria (1897), and the Boxer revolt (circa 1900), to name a few. In their advice to President Emmanuel Macron, Senegalese writer Felwine Sarr and French art historian Bénédicte Savoy plea to focus more on another category in this first type: objects acquired during scientific expeditions in Africa, such as the Dakar-Djibouti mission (1931–33). They plea even for a reversion of the burden of proof. Objects should be returned "unless there is explicit evidence or information witnessing to the full consent on the part of the owners or initial guardians of the objects at the moment when the objects were separated from them." The principle of a reversed burden of proof is not new but also appears in the 1995 UNIDROIT Convention, adopted by the European directive 2014/60/UE of May 15, 2014.[11] The trio of objects is not valid for Nazi-looted cultural properties as the acquisition of all of them is considered criminal. National Restitution Committees in a number of European countries advised whether there had been involuntary loss or not.

Quite a number of treasures looted as a result of internal or external colonialism originally had a religious or ceremonial function. They symbolized the power of the defeated: flags, ceremonial weapons, royal crowns, certain masks, small sanctuaries, and so on. For Nazi-looted works this was rare. The Nazis were usually after works of art, precious books, and particular archives because of their beauty, the fame of their creator, or their meaning. An exception to this rule was objects confiscated from synagogues or religious objects coming from individual families with a sacred function in the owners' houses.[12] For instance, during the Kristallnacht pogrom on November 9, 1938, Nazi troops looted Torah rolls, hanukiahs, and

[10] Beurden (n 2) 41.

[11] Sarr and Savoy (n 1) 58, fn 71.

[12] This observation is based on annual reports of the Dutch Restitution Committee. Advisory Committee on the Assessment of Restitution Applications for Items of Cultural Value and the Second World War <https://www.restitutiecommissie.nl/en/publications.html> accessed 10 October 2019.

other objects from 1,400 synagogues: many of which German museum directors since laid their hands on.[13]

In the comparison of the three categories of loot, more differences appear. Some are obvious. The looting by the Nazi regime occurred during a relatively brief and recent period of history in a limited number of countries, mostly in Europe. Internal and external colonialism was, with strongly varying intensity, spread over a much larger area and period (five centuries). Nazi looting took place after the acceptance of the Hague Conventions of 1899 and 1907, which prohibited the seizure of cultural and other properties from the territories occupied by Member states. Much of the colonial plunder took place before 1900 and European powers considered themselves sovereign in their colonial possessions.

A complicated difference, with far-reaching consequences, is that the seizure of cultural property by colonizers is much less documented than that by the Nazis, and thus it is harder to track down whether a colonial object is disputable. Germans had a habit of extensively documenting activities, which included looting activities. Moreover, many claimants of Nazi-looted works of art had been able to keep documentation, such as a list of their properties, a photograph of the original owner and their painting, or title deeds, although many had lost all documentation after a rushed flight. Biographies of most disputable colonial objects are heavily amputated. We will never know who created them, who were their first possessors or their community of origin.[14] Many countries claiming them lack the instruments and know-how for thorough provenance research. In the earlier-mentioned examples of looted chronicles of the Aztec people and the confiscated nail statue of a community in Congo Free State, the chronicles themselves and the diary of a Belgian colonial have been helpful in offering other perspectives on these acquisitions. The chronicles can be defined as colonized records, the diary as an unofficial archival piece. Colonized and unofficial records complement official colonial records. Recently, attention for their value has been growing. They tell much about the disputable collecting by museums and private possessors. They rarely recorded data on all they received, let alone on how it was acquired.[15] Due to amputated biographies, it happens that Western institutions holding

[13] Monika Griebeler, "What the Nazis Stole from Synagogues during the November 1938 Pogrom" (*Deutsche Welle*, 9 November 2018) <https://www.dw.com/en/what-the-Nazis-stole-from-synagogues-during-the-november-1938-pogrom/a-46215426> accessed 9 October 2019.

[14] Sarr and Savoy (n 1) 75–76.

[15] Johannes Fellmann, "Gesammelt – erbeutet – erworben? - Ob Offizier, Gouverneur, Wissenschaftler, Händler oder Missionar: In den deutschen Kolonien herrschte die Gier nach

objects and human remains without documentation do not know the original region or source, and consequently where to offer them for repatriation.

The rightful owners of works of art looted by the Nazis are mostly private people and institutions such as synagogues and therefore relatively easy to identify. Restitution has a direct, personal interest for them insofar as personal property was stolen. As a result, many works of art looted by the Nazis have been returned to these owners. Out of a total of six hundred thousand paintings which are said to have been looted from Jewish owners, one hundred thousand are said to be still missing.[16] For colonial loot the question of ownership is much harder to resolve. Many ethnic groups that lost them have merged into larger units. To whom should the earlier-mentioned nail statue from the DR Congo be returned: to the chief and the community, the government, or the new national museum to be built in Kinshasa? A recent example shows how complicated the answer to the question "to whom to return" can become. It is about a claim of the Yaqui people to the National Museums of World Culture in Sweden.[17]

The Yaqui in Sonora in present-day northern Mexico number some 25,000 people. They had always tried to remain autonomous, but a century ago had to bow to the Mexican army. Because of all the violence, a number of them moved to Arizona. Initially considered migrant workers, they became a federally recognized tribe later in 1974, and since 1991 they have enjoyed the cultural and economic rights that other indigenous peoples have in the United States. Yaqui in Arizona are generally better educated and wealthier than their fellow tribesmen in Sonora. They run a casino that brings in money and employment.[18] The Yaqui in northern Mexico are poor but receive scarcely any government support. In 1934, a Swedish expedition visited

ethnographischen Objekten" (Berlin, *Kulturstiftiung der Länder*, 2015) <https://www.kulturstiftung.de/gesammelt-erbeutet-erworben/> accessed 9 October 2019; "In deutschen Völkerkundemuseen herrscht totales Chaos" (München, *Süddeutsche Zeitung*, 9 July 2019) <https://www.sueddeutsche.de/kultur/ethnologisches-museum-raubkunst-1.4516193-2> accessed 10 October 2019.

[16] Stuart E Eizenstat, "Art Stolen by the Nazis Is Still Missing. Here's How We Can Recover It" (*The Washington Post*, 2 January 2019) <https://www.washingtonpost.com/opinions/no-one-should-trade-in-or-possess-art-stolen-by-the-Nazis/2019/01/02/01990232-0ed3-11e9-831f-3aa2c2be4cbd_story.html> accessed 10 October 2019 and 20 February 2020; "Nazi-Looted Art: Why Are Restitutions Still the Exception?" (*Deutsche Welle*, 3 December 2018) <https://www.dw.com/en/Nazi-looted-art-why-are-restitutions-still-the-exception/a-46507241> accessed 10 October 2019.

[17] The author collected information about the Yaqui case from Adriana Muñoz, archaeologist of the National Museums of World Culture in Sweden, 10 October 2019, and built on this for further research.

[18] "Pascua Yaqui Tribe" (*Casino del Sol*) <https://www.casinodelsol.com/pascua-yaqui-tribe> accessed 28 October 2019.

Sonora and met with two Danish-Mexican Protestant missionaries who were close with the Yaqui. The two helped the Swedes to be allowed to participate in a religious ceremony. Thus, they acquired a *Maaso Kova* or deer mask and some other items that had been made for them and had probably never been ritually used. These objects ended up in the National Museums of World Culture in Sweden. In 2003, the Swedes received a claim for the objects. The claimant was not the Yaqui in northern Mexico but rather in Arizona. The Swedish institution made inquiries about the acquisition of the objects, and although it found nothing illegal or unethical it was willing to return them. Next, the question came up as to whether they should go to the Yaqui in the United States or to their birth ground in Mexico. The Yaqui in Mexico and the United States are divided on the issue, and a decision has not yet been made. The Yaqui in Arizona are unwilling to discuss the "to whom to return" question and avoid their fellow tribesmen in Sonora. They want the objects back and criticize the Swedish museum for not doing this. The museum argues that although the claim came from Arizona, their home is not there but in Mexico.[19]

In all three categories of looting, a variety of actors was involved. For colonial looting, administrators, soldiers, missionaries, scientists, collectors, and others have already been mentioned. It was a diffuse and scarcely organized group. Already before the independence of colonies, missionaries had begun to show more respect for local religions. And, from independence onward, European administrators and military disappeared as actors. But, certainly in the first decades thereafter, the looting continued and old actors were joined by new ones, both local and foreign. For Nazi looting, the Nazi regime and a number of high-ranking Nazi individuals were responsible. The organization of this group was much clearer. On the closing days of World War II, one more actor was added: the Soviet Union, which shipped millions of treasures from East Germany and other East European countries.[20]

[19] National Museums of World Culture in Goteborg, "Seminar: Yaqui People" <http://www.varldskulturmuseerna.se/varldskulturmuseet/pa-gang/kalendarier/program/yaqui-people/> accessed 9 October 2019; Adriana Muñoz, "From Oblivion to Conflict: The Case of a Yaqui Mask in Sweden" (unpublished 2019).

[20] A minor actor were members of the Allied Forces. In 2015, *The New York Times* reported that "thousands of works, among them masterpieces by Dürer, Cranach and Hals, crossed the Atlantic in footlockers and mail parcels in the 1940s" and that "very few have trickled back." Tom Mashberg, "Returning the Spoils of World War II, Taken by Americans" (*The New York Times*, 5 May 2015) <https://www.nytimes.com/2015/05/06/arts/design/returning-the-spoils-of-world-war-ii-taken-by-our-side.html> accessed 14 February 2020. In 2020, the exhibition "Occupied, Liberated &

Except for Germany and Italy, European countries were not involved in looting during World War II, whereas they were directly responsible for looting during colonialism. For these European countries, negotiating with other states about return forces them to confront their looting activities. For these countries, it is easier to deal with issues of Nazi loot than of colonial loot. Finally, descendants of Jewish and other families who lost assets to Nazi looting, and who are seeking help with restitution, have the support of such bodies as the World Jewish Congress and the World Jewish Restitution Organization, the latter set up in 1992, whereas those who wish to claim for loot taken during colonialism have no equivalent organizations to lobby for them.[21]

In spite of these obvious differences, the three categories of loot have one thing in common. Both external colonialism, internal colonialism, and the Nazis operated through institutionalized brutal inequality and injustice. Colonizers and Nazis had in common that they considered themselves superior to the peoples and groups they subjugated, thus creating an artificial and racist hierarchy among peoples. The varied group of internal and external colonizers—the conquistadores in Latin America, the British in South Asia, or the Japanese in China—had in common that they applied their own value interpretations on objects and scarcely considered values attached to them by source communities. This imposition of their own value hierarchies legitimated the appropriation of the cultural and historical objects from these other groups and peoples. In spite of these commonalities, the ways to undo the injustice surrounding each category differ considerably, especially when it comes to the return of objects. Before this chapter summarizes these ways to undo injustice, a remark has to be made about a hierarchy in the size of suffering, damage, and losses sustained. Each category has advocates claiming that "their" period saw the worst of all. This chapter does not follow them. Objective means to measure this are missing and, even if they were there, it would not solve the absence of objects below the top of the hierarchy.

Looted - Allied Looting in the Nijmegen Region, 1944–1945" in the *Freedom Museum in Groesbeek*, the Netherlands, showed looting from private houses of paintings, graphics, drawings and table- and church-silver. Visit by this chapter's author on 4 February 2020. See also Paul Klinkenberg Thissen and Paul van der Heijden, *Bezet, bevrijd & geplunderd - Geallieerde plunderingen in de region Nijmegen, 1944–1945* (Nijmegen, Vantilt 2020) 68.

21 World Jewish Restitution Organisation <https://wjro.org.il/> accessed 20 February 2020.

III. Displaced Objects Resulting from External Colonialism, the Least Returns

Apart from the increasing number of colonies, first in Asia, then in Africa, which gained independence after World War II, another important development was the setting of supranational rules. The 1948 Universal Declaration of Human Rights (UDHR) became central in the international order that made outside scrutiny possible of sovereign states maltreating their citizens. Conventions, other declarations, and rules were built on it. Among these was the 1970 UNESCO Convention on the Means of Prohibiting and Preventing the Illicit Import, Export and Transfer of Ownership of Cultural Property.[22] Although it lacked retroactive power and was unsuitable for claiming lost colonial objects, the role of former colonies in its creation makes it relevant for this chapter.

Newly independent states wanted the same treatment while claiming lost objects as had been applied after World War I (1914–1918) and was being discussed for claimants of Nazi loot.[23] Two former Spanish colonies, Mexico and Peru, played a prominent role in the initiative for the Convention. They did not want to "differentiate between objects removed before and after independence." China proposed the inclusion of a retroactive clause stipulating that each State party shall endeavor to restore cultural objects that were "illicitly acquired, inalienable to, and inseparable from the history and civilization of another State" to that State party. For European and North American countries this was unacceptable. In turn, the latter presented a proposal for the blanket recognition of ownership vested in a State of cultural objects acquired before 1970. This was unacceptable for former colonies.[24] Their proposal echoed in the 2002 Declaration on the Importance and Value of Universal Museums of eighteen major Western museums, which stated that "objects acquired in earlier times must be viewed in the light of different sensitivities and values, reflective of that earlier era," as the conditions then were "not comparable with current ones."[25] For decades, former colonial powers

[22] "UNESCO Convention on the Means of Prohibiting and Preventing the Illicit Import, Export and Transfer of Ownership of Cultural Property" (Paris, UNESCO 14 November 1970) <http://portal.unesco.org/en/ev.php-URL_ID = 13039&URL_DO = DO_TOPIC&URL_SECTION = 201.html> accessed 29 October 2019.

[23] Prott (n 1) 12.

[24] Vrdoljak (n 2) 207, 208.

[25] "Declaration on the Importance and Value of Universal Museums" (Paris, ICOM 2004) <http://archives.icom.museum/pdf/E_news2004/p4_2004-1.pdf> accessed 10 October 2019.

have remained hesitant to accept the convention, fearing—in spite of the Convention's non-retroactivity—claims from former colonial possessions. Earlier signatories were former colonies. The first European country to accede was Italy in 1978. It suffered itself under the ongoing illicit trade in art and antiquities. Portugal, Spain, and France followed in 1980s, Great Britain, Germany, Belgium, and the Netherlands only after the turn of the century.[26]

To meet the wishes of former colonies, Art. 15 opened up the possibility for bilateral agreements on the return of cultural objects removed *before* the Convention came into force. Although many bilateral agreements have been concluded, even those with former colonies do not cover colonial loot, only the ongoing illicit trade.[27] Former colonies continued to lobby for returns in the United Nations. In 1973, the DR Congo submitted Resolution 3187 (XXVIII) on the Restitution of Works of Art to Countries Victim of Expropriation in the UN General Assembly. It deplored the involuntary loss of objects "frequently as a result of colonial or foreign occupation" and asked Member states for their "prompt restitution." A large majority voted in favor, but most former colonial powers voted against.[28] Another compensation was made in 1978 when UNESCO created the Intergovernmental Committee for Promoting the Return of Cultural Property to its Countries of Origin or its Restitution in case of Illicit Appropriation (ICPRCP).[29] In the event that two states were unable to solve their dispute about important objects lost as a result of colonial or foreign occupation or illicit appropriation, the ICPRCP was supposed to come to help. Return of colonial cultural objects thus became a central task.[30]

The ICPRCP has never become known for its support of former colonies. Their claims easily got stuck, as is shown with respect to a 1980 claim

[26] "UNESCO Convention 1970 - States" (Paris, UNESCO 2019) <http://www.unesco.org/eri/la/convention.asp?KO = 13039&language = E> accessed 16 October 2019.

[27] The United States concluded twenty-two bilateral agreements, China eighteen, Switzerland eight. For the United States, see Bureau of Educational and Cultural Affairs <http://eca.state.gov/cultural-heritage-center/cultural-property-protection/bilateral-agreements> accessed 10 October 2019; People's Republic of China, "National report on the implementation of the 1970 convention on the means of prohibiting and preventing the illicit import, export and transfer of ownership of cultural property 2011–2015" (Paris, UNESCO 2015) <http://www.unesco.org/new/fileadmin/MULTIMEDIA/HQ/CLT/pdf/Rapport_Chine.pdf> accessed 10 October 2019; Swiss Government, Federal Office of Culture, "Bilateral Agreements" (Berne, 2019) <https://www.bak.admin.ch/bak/en/home/cultural-heritage/transfer-of-cultural-property/bilateral-agreements.html> accessed 10 October 2019.

[28] Prott (n 1) 27–28.

[29] Intergovernmental Committee for Promoting the Return of Cultural to its Countries of Origin or its Restitution in case of Illicit Appropriation <http://www.unesco.org/new/en/culture/themes/restitution-of-cultural-property/intergovernmental-committee/> accessed 29 October 2019.

[30] Prott (n 1) 16.

of Sri Lanka. In 1975, Sri Lanka had finished a book with fifteen thousand objects of cultural interest, found in Austria, Belgium, France, Germany, the Netherlands, Switzerland, the United Kingdom, and some other countries.[31] The claim covered a small selection of these.[32] The 1980 meeting, however, did not deal with it as Sri Lanka's submission had come in too late. In 1983, the claim was put again on the agenda again, but rejected as Sri Lanka had failed to fill in the standard forms sufficiently, through which it had to prove that the objects had "a fundamental significance from the point of view of spiritual values and cultural heritage of a people."[33] One object on the list had been the ceremonial canon of the King of Kandy, captured by soldiers of the Dutch East India Company in 1765 and placed in the Rijksmuseum Amsterdam (RMA) in 1880. That the 1980 claim was not unreasonable is shown by the 2017 initiative of the RMA to include the canon into a provenance research pilot project. The outcome might be that the Netherlands returns it to Sri Lanka. Sri Lanka has expressed its desire for it.[34] Although it is broadly agreed upon that the canon is war booty, the RMA claims it needs more time for a final report. This has been met with incomprehension in Sri Lanka.[35]

A glance at the approximately thirty UN General Assembly declarations about return and restitution, adopted between 1973 and 2017, reveals that the ICPRCP's contribution to the return of disputed objects from colonial contexts has remained minimal.[36] Discussions about colonial treasures largely disappeared and were replaced by disputes about cases of recent theft and smuggling, especially in conflict areas such as Iraq and Syria. It made former colonies avoid the ICPRCP road.

In the 1970s, four former colonizers and five former colonies concluded return agreements.[37] Most contained measures for the strengthening of the

[31] PHDH de Silva, *A Catalogue of Antiquities and Other Cultural Objects from Sri Lanka (Ceylon) Abroad* (Colombo, National Museums of Sri Lanka 1975).

[32] Government of Sri Lanka, "Statement concerning the restitution of significant cultural objects from Sri Lanka" UNESCO/ICPRCP, CC-79/CONF.206/6, 5–9 May 1980 (Paris, UNESCO/ICPRCP 1980).

[33] ICPRCP, "Letter to the government of Sri Lanka" CLT/CH/SP/4.5/7.2./388.2/YRI/cv-71.83, 15 June 1983 (Paris, UNESCO/ICPRCP 1983).

[34] This author's notes from symposium "'Who Owns Heritage?' The Historical, Moral, Commercial and Legal Issues," organized by Foundation Netherlands Sri Lanka, 5 November 2019.

[35] Communication with Martine Gosselink, chief historian Rijksmuseum Amsterdam, and with Sanuja Kasthuriarachchi, Director General, Department of National Museums, Sri Lanka, 5 November 2019.

[36] Resolutions adopted by the United Nations General Assembly about Return and Restitution of Cultural Property (Paris, UNESCO) <http://www.unesco.org/new/en/culture/themes/restitution-of-cultural-property/united-nations/> accessed 29 October 2019.

[37] For this section, the author leans on earlier research, Beurden (n 2) chs 7–d12.

former colonies' museum infrastructures. In 1970, the DR Congo asked Belgium for the return of two hundred internationally known treasures. Belgium agreed to *donate*[38] a wooden statue representing a Kuba King and 114 other objects from the storerooms of the Africa Museum in Tervuren. In 2000, an anthropologist of the museum concluded, after putting the donated objects under a microscope, that almost none of the two hundred claimed objects were included among these and that the Africa Museum had replaced them with items of often inferior quality.[39] Apparently, the Congolese had lacked the expertise to study the donation. While the media in Belgium and Europe hardly paid attention to this, they focused on the disappearance of many of the donated objects from the unstable African country. In 1971, Denmark came to an agreement with its former "cold" colony Iceland about the transfer of two thousand ancient manuscripts which were linked to Iceland's history and culture. Iceland had been asking for them since 1830. More general manuscripts remained in the Royal Library of Copenhagen. In 1975, Indonesia and the Netherlands agreed on "Joint Recommendations . . . concerning Cultural Cooperation in the field of Museums and Archives including Transfer of Objects." Of Indonesia's wish list of ten thousand objects, the Netherlands *donated* a few hundred. For Indonesia, the most important one was an ancient Prajñaparamita statue, sometimes called the Mona Lisa of Java. In addition, objects and a painting related to national hero Prince Diponegoro, objects from the Lombok treasure, and archival material went back. Also, in 1975, Australia agreed with its nearby former colony Papua New Guinea to return around 3,500 objects. Most had belonged to the so-called MacGregor collection. William MacGregor was a colonial administrator at the end of the nineteenth century. While collecting over ten thousand objects, he had observed strict rules. At the end of his term, he had agreed with the Queensland Museum in Brisbane to store his collection until there would be a safe place for it in Port Moresby. In 1975, the National Museum in Port Moresby had reached that stage. Earlier, Australia and Papua New Guinea had agreed upon the return of ancient archives to Port Moresby. Finally, in 1983, the directors of the national museums of Denmark and its former "cold" colony Greenland agreed to repatriate thirty-five thousand archaeological and ethnographic items to Nuuk. It was about one-third of all Greenlandic items in Denmark.

[38] Belgium refused the term "return" as it might associate with illegal appropriations. In 1975, the Dutch would refuse to talk about "return" for the same reason.

[39] Boris Wastiau, *Congo - Tervuren. Aller-retour* (Tervuren, Africa Museum 2000).

The repatriation enabled the two museums to hold Greenlandic collections of equal importance. After these agreements had been reached, no more substantial returns have taken place.

In the last few years, some countries in the North and the South have begun to search for new ways of dealing with colonial loot. Beginning in Europe, Germany seems the most active. In 2017, the German Museums Bund published *Guidelines on Dealing with Collections from Colonial Contexts*.[40] The federal government is funding provenance research and several museums are intensifying this type of manpower and time-consuming research. In 2019, the Linden Museum in Stuttgart returned—after six years of negotiations—a Bible and a whip of Namibia's national hero, Hendrik Witbooi. Namibia had difficulty in deciding whether they were to be returned to the national archive, the Nama ethnic group, or the Witbooi royal family, but found a compromise. The handover of the two items took place in Gibeon, the Witbooi family's place of residence since the 1840s, after which they were brought to the national archive where they will be kept.[41] The storm about a radically new French restitution policy, aroused by President Macron in Burkina Faso in November 2017, has subsided again. Macron asked Felwine Sarr and Bénédicte Savoy for advice. Their report continues to inspire the global return debate, while in France it has resulted in few concrete measures. Until late 2019, the main commitment has been the return of twenty-six pieces of war booty to the Republic of Benin. In public speeches the term "restitution" is competing with the term "circulation" of objects. In January 2020, a diaspora group interrupted the auction of twenty-eight other pieces of war booty from the Republique of Benin in the French city of Nantes, after which they were withdrawn from auction. French antiquarians put the money together and had them sent back to Cotonou.[42] In the Netherlands, the Rijksmuseum Amsterdam started the earlier-mentioned pilot project for provenance research of ten possibly disputable objects in 2017, the aim being the development of a methodology for provenance research. In 2018, the National Museum of World Cultures published a repatriation framework, "Return

[40] Museumsbund (n 1).

[41] "Namibia: Dispute over Return of the Witbooi Bible" (*Deutsche Welle*, 27 February 2019) <https://www.dw.com/en/namibia-dispute-over-return-of-the-witbooi-bible/a-47712784> accessed 14 November 2019; Brigitte Weidlich, "Witbooi Bible Returned to Namibia" (Windhoek, *Gondwana's Newsroom*, 6 March 2019) <https://www.gondwana-collection.com/news/article/2019/03/06/witbooi-bible-returned-to-namibia/> accessed 20 February 2020.

[42] "French Group Returns Colonial-Era Royal Artefacts to Benin" (*The Local*, 19 January 2020) <https://www.thelocal.fr/20200119/french-group-returns-colonial-era-royal-artefacts-to-benin> accessed 26 August 2020.

of Cultural Objects: Principles and Process," in which it outlines the procedure that a claimant country has to follow.[43] So far, no claims have been submitted. Since 2019, the Dutch government promotes provenance research of colonial loot. There has been only one return of a disputable object by the Netherlands recently, the keris (dagger) of Indonesia's national hero, Diponegoro. Indonesia had been asking for it since 1975, but only in 2017 a solid research traject was started, in cooperation with the Indonesian authorities.[44]

Former colonies show an upsurge in their activities too. The French offer of returning twenty-six objects to the Republic of Benin was a reaction on a Beninese claim for some five thousand war booty objects, captured by French soldiers in 1892. Ethiopia wants the Maqdala treasures, looted by British soldiers from Emperor Tewodros in 1868 to be returned. Among the objects that China is eager to retrieve are those that British and French soldiers took from the Old Summer Palace in Beijing in 1860, those that military of the Eight Nations Alliance took during the Boxer Rebellion around 1900, and the objects confiscated by Japan during World War II. Chile is after objects removed from Eastern Island. Ivory Coast and Senegal have presented wish lists to France. Apart from the exceptional Nefertiti bust in the Neues Museum in Berlin, which Egypt has repeatedly claimed, Africa's most iconic collection claimed by its country of origin is that of the Benin objects.

Since 2010, the National Commission for Museums and Monuments (NCMM) of Nigeria, the Royal Court of Benin, and the Edo State Government have been in dialogue with museum directors and delegates from Austria, Germany, the Netherlands, Sweden, and the United Kingdom about the future of the Benin objects that British soldiers had confiscated in 1897 after defeating the army of the Edo Kingdom. At the opening of the exhibition *Benin Kings and Rituals: Court Arts from Nigeria* in the Weltmuseum in Vienna in 2007, Mono N'Oba Erediauwa, king of Benin, had prayed, in a note in the catalogue, "that the people and the government of Austria will show humaneness and magnanimity and return

[43] National Museum of World Cultures, *Return of Cultural Objects: Principles and Process* (Leiden, 2018) <https://www.volkenkunde.nl/sites/default/files/2019-05/Claims%20for%20Return%20of%20Cultural%20Objects%20NMVW%20Principles%20and%20Process.pdf> accessed 27 May 2020.

[44] National Museum of World Cultures, *Kort verslag over de keris van Prins Diponegoro* (Leiden, 2020) <https://easaonline.org/downloads/networks/hoan/HOAN_Newsletter_16p_Provenance_Leiden_2020.pdf> accessed 26 August 2020.

to us some of these objects which found their way to your country."[45] The Weltmuseum, itself the possessor of 167 Benin treasures, flatly answered "no" as the objects were "state-property" and could not be alienated.[46] For decades, Nigeria had expressed its desire to retrieve a number of these "pages" in the history of the kingdom.[47]

After the exhibition, the "no" inspired the responsible curator of the Vienna museum, Barbara Plankensteiner, and the NCMM to initiate a dialogue on the accessibility of the treasures of the Benin Kingdom for the Nigerian public. It was the start of what was going to be called the Benin Dialogue Group. In 2010, the group met for the first time and discussed exchange of information, cooperation, and return. In the years thereafter, the return aspect disappeared into the background. During its meeting in Benin City in 2019, the Benin Dialogue Group discussed the establishment of a museum in Benin City for a permanent display reuniting Benin works from around the world.[48] European museums are willing to lend Benin objects temporarily for it. Nigerians have their doubts about the process. Folarin Shyllon, who attended most sessions of the Group as legal expert, argues: "Restitution is the proper solution to the return of iconic cultural objects wrongfully acquired in colonial times and in war. Whatever the legal basis of these acquisitions in international law, the usurpation of the identity and history of a people should be seen as intolerable and genuine efforts made to reverse the supremacy of the rule of plunder."[49]

For the time being, there is much talk about returns in Europe, but returns have taken place only incidentally. In the coming years, the rise of the Black Lives Matter movement and diaspora groups might affect this slow trend.

[45] Mono N'Oba Erediauwa, "Introductory Note" in Barbara Plankensteiner (ed), *Benin Kings and Rituals - Court Arts from Nigeria* (Wien, Weltmuseum 2007) 13.

[46] Interview with Barbara Plankensteiner, then Weltmuseum Wien, 21 July 2014.

[47] Staffan Lundén, *Displaying Loot: The Benin Objects and the British Museum* (Gothenburg University 2016) 436–39; Peji Layiwola, "The Benin Massacre" in Barbara Plankensteiner (ed), *Benin—Kings and Rituals* (2007) 88; Peji Layiwola, "Walker and the Restitution of Two Benin Bronzes" (*Premium Times*, 20 June 2014); Folarin Shyllon, "Museums and Universal Heritage: Right of Return and Right of Access" (*Black Herbal Review Blogs*, 2007) <http://www.blackherbals.com/museums_and_universal_heritage.htm> accessed 21 August 2014.

[48] Benin Dialogue Group, "Press Statement" (Benin City, 5–7 July 2019) <https://www.tropenmuseum.nl/nl/press-statement-meeting-benin-dialogue-group-1> accessed 18 November 2019.

[49] Folarin Shyllon, "Benin Bronzes: Something Grave Happened and Imperial Rule of Law Is Sustaining it!" (October 2019) 24 (3) Art, Antiquity and Law 274–84.

IV. Massive Losses Resulting from Internal Colonialism, Remedies for Returns

Worldwide there are between 350 to 500 million indigenous peoples or First Nations. They represent some 90% of the world's cultural diversity, their traditions and customs deeply embedded within the environment.[50] Through the centuries, they lost objects on a large scale. Compared with the means for claiming loot resulting from external colonialism, their supranational and national means to support claims are more effective. This chapter limits itself to those nation-states where European settlers came to dominate First Nations. Their legal frameworks and programs constitute a rather varied palette. In some, a philosophy of repatriation is outweighing the legal frameworks.

Of the supranational rules related to lost relics of indigenous peoples, the 2007 United Nations Declaration on the Importance of Indigenous Peoples (UNDRIP) is the most important. UNDRIP is a normative agreement of the international community that was created "to address the wrongs of the past that continue to affect Indigenous peoples' lives today."[51] It took three decades to finalize it. Unlike the 1970 UNESCO Convention, which addresses Western norms of property rights, UNDRIP focuses more on human rights and international customary norms for indigenous rights.[52] Some of its principles relate to cultural and historical objects and return issues. The first three principles of the declaration establish the right of indigenous people to the full enjoyment of all human rights and fundamental freedoms. They are equal to all other peoples and individuals and have the right to self-determination and to pursue their economic, social, and cultural development. Art. 11 and Art. 12 relate to claims for cultural and historical objects. Art 11.1. gives indigenous peoples the right to practice and revitalize their cultural traditions and customs. Art 11.2. obliges states to provide "redress through effective mechanisms, which may include restitution, developed in conjunction with indigenous peoples, with respect to their cultural, intellectual, religious and

[50] Rawiri Taonui, "UNDRIP at 10: Are We Making Progress in the Global Fight for Indigenous Rights?" (Canadian International Council, *OpenCanada*, 13 September 2017) <https://www.opencanada.org/features/undrip-10-are-we-making-progress-global-fight-indigenous-rights/> accessed 15 October 2019.

[51] Australian Human Rights Commission, "The Community Guide to UNDRIP" (Sydney, 2010) <https://www.humanrights.gov.au/sites/default/files/declaration_abridged_community_guide.pdf> accessed 16 October 2019.

[52] Lynda Knowles, "International Repatriation of Human Remains of Indigenous Peoples" (Paris, *ICOM News*, 8 August 2018) <https://icom.museum/en/news/international-repatriation-of-human-remains-of-indigenous-peoples/> accessed 15 October 2019.

spiritual property taken without their free, prior and informed consent or in violation of their laws, traditions and customs." Art 12.1. gives indigenous peoples the right to manifest and practice their spiritual and religious traditions and ceremonies and to the use and control of their ceremonial objects and the repatriation of human remains. Art 12.2. asks states to seek to enable the access and/or repatriation of ceremonial objects and human remains in their possession through fair, transparent, and effective mechanisms developed in conjunction with indigenous peoples concerned.[53]

UNDRIP is a UN declaration (and not international law) and a normative agreement of the international community. Of the 158 Member states (out of 193) that voted on the declaration in the UN General Assembly, 143 voted in favor, eleven abstained, and four countries voted against. The latter were Australia, Canada, New Zealand, and the United States. Each of them had to harmonize its own legislative framework and program for dealing with claims from indigenous groups with the declaration. Currently, the four have adapted their positions. In 2017, the Expert Mechanism on the Rights of Indigenous Peoples of the UN Human Rights Council concluded that UNDRIP is "the most far-reaching comprehensive instrument concerning indigenous peoples . . . It has been overwhelmingly recognized as reflecting a global consensus on the rights of indigenous peoples, individually and collectively," but the question of its implementation remains. Some have praised its "strong status"[54] or its "tremendous political and practical influence."[55] Balancing this praise is the observation that discrimination and violation of human rights of indigenous people still occurs.[56] Looking at the four countries dealt with in this chapter, some progress can be reported.

A. Australia

The government of Australia changed its reluctant position in 2009, stating that it considers the declaration "a comprehensive statement of Australia's

[53] United Nations, "United Nations Declaration on the Rights of Indigenous Peoples" (New York, 2007) <https://www.un.org/esa/socdev/unpfii/documents/DRIPS_en.pdf> accessed 15 October 2019.

[54] Campfens (n 8) 102.

[55] Patrick J O'Keefe and Lyndel V Prott (eds), *Cultural Heritage Conventions and Other Instruments. A Compendium with Comments* (Crickadarn, Institute of Art and Law 2011) 334.

[56] UN Human Rights Council, Expert Mechanism on the Rights of Indigenous Peoples, "Ten years of the implementation of the United Nations Declaration on the Rights of Indigenous Peoples: Good practices and lessons learned—2007–2017" (preliminary draft, Geneva, July 2017) <https://www.

existing human rights obligations to Aboriginal and Torres Strait Islander peoples. Although it does not create new rights, it provides a comprehensive framework for action."[57] It set up implementation instruments. Critics doubt whether much has changed. Indigenous peoples made "considerable advancements between the 1960s and early 1990s," they observe, while there has been "a stall in any progress, as statements and apologies were not followed by policies."[58] In 1984, Australia introduced the Aboriginal and Torres Strait Islander Heritage Protection Act. Since, the National Museum of Australia in Canberra has advised indigenous groups about how to retrieve lost remains and relics. In 2000, it set up a Repatriation Unit. Until the acceptance of UNDRIP in 2009, the National Museum itself returned the remains of 405 individuals to Aboriginal peoples.[59] Also, long before 2009, the government of Queensland developed laws for the protection and repatriation of human remains, including burial objects and associated material such as bark coffins.[60] The South Australian Museum in Adelaide embraced UNDRIP when announcing new partnerships with Aboriginal communities and its intention to return the almost five thousand remains and four thousand funerary objects in its storerooms. They "are in a secure Keeping Place with restricted access . . . until these old people are returned to Country and a final resting place."[61] The repatriation of Aboriginal human remains from abroad is intensifying. Until 2019, some 1,500 ancestors have been repatriated from Austria, the Czech Republic, Germany,[62] Great Britain, and the

ohchr.org/Documents/Issues/IPeoples/EMRIP/Session10/A.HRC.EMRIP.2017.CRP.2.pdf> accessed 16 October 2019.

[57] ANTaR, *Campaigns and Issues* (Strawberry Hills, 2017) <https://www.antar.org.au/campaigns/un-declaration-rights-indigenous-peoples> accessed 16 October 2019.

[58] Marie Lamensch, "Australia's Slow Progress on Indigenous Rights" (Canadian International Council, *OpenCanada*, 1 May 2019) <https://www.opencanada.org/features/australias-slow-progress-on-indigenous-rights/> accessed 16 October 2019.

[59] National Museum of Australia, "The Return of Indigenous Human Remains and Sacred Objects—Annual Report 2002–2003" (Canberra, 2003) <https://www.nma.gov.au/about/corporate/annualreports/02_03/part_2/performance_commentaries_output_group_1.1/the_return_of_indigenous_human_remains_and_sacred_objects> accessed 16 October 2019.

[60] Queensland Government, Department of Aboriginal and Torres Strait Islander partnerships, "Guidelines for the discovery, handling and management of human remains" (last modified 1 September 2019) <https://www.datsip.qld.gov.au/resources/datsima/people-communities/cultural-heritage/guidelines-human-remains.pdf> accessed 17 May 2020.

[61] South Australian Museum, "Aboriginal Heritage and Repatriation" (Adelaide, 2019) <http://www.samuseum.sa.gov.au/learn/aboriginal-heritage-and-repatriation> accessed 21 October 2019.

[62] Australian government, "Record number of Indigenous ancestors returned from Germany" (Canberra, 19 April 2019) <https://www.minister.communications.gov.au/minister/mitch-fifield/news/record-number-indigenous-ancestors-returned-germany#> accessed 21 October 2019. The remains came from the Five Continents Museum, Munich, the Linden Museum, Stuttgart, the University of Freiburg, the State Ethnographic Collections, in Saxony, and the Martin Luther University in Halle-Wittenberg.

United States. According to the Australian government, these repatriations contribute to "healing and reconciliation."[63] The impression one gets is that hard and soft law measures are less important than the intensifying cooperation with indigenous peoples. It is making the Australian repatriation experience "a reliance on a *philosophy* of repatriation."[64]

B. New Zealand

New Zealand is developing a similar attitude. In 2010, it signed on to UNDRIP in relation to Maori and Moriori communities. But the impact of UNDRIP on repatriation is hard to assess here. In 2019, the government began developing a plan for its implementation long before repatriation measures had been taken. In 1975, the country had introduced the Protected Objects Act with provisions relating to the return of *ngā taonga tūturu,* objects related to Maori communities.[65] Art. 19 of the Act gives the Maori Land Court jurisdiction to decide who should be given custody of remains and property recovered from any Maori burial sites. Art. 20 requires any person who finds Maori remains or artifacts to turn them over to the government. Through the centuries, foreigners had acquired large numbers of preserved, tattooed Maori heads. In 1831, the British had imposed a ban on the export of these heads. Until 2003, the remains of thirty-seven ancestors had been returned. That year, New Zealand set up a program for the international and domestic repatriation of preserved Maori and Moriori human remains. The government does not claim ownership of the remains and objects but facilitates and empowers indigenous communities and appointed the Museum of New Zealand Te Papa Tongarewa as the organization to lead the repatriation process. By now, the Museum of New Zealand has secured the cooperation of over forty foreign museums and "420 Māori and Moriori ancestral remains from overseas institutions," including from countries such as Australia, Austria,

[63] Australian government, "International repatriation highlights" (Canberra, 2019) <https://www.arts.gov.au/what-we-do/cultural-heritage/indigenous-repatriation/international-repatriation/recent-international> accessed 21 October 2019.

[64] Michael Pickering and Phil Gordon, "Repatriation: The End of the Beginning" in *Understanding Museums* (Canberra, National Museum of Australia 2011) <https://nma.gov.au/research/understanding-museums/MPickering_PGordon_2011.html> accessed 17 October 2019.

[65] Government of New Zealand, *Protected Objects Act 1975* (Wellington, 1975) <http://www.legislation.govt.nz/act/public/1975/0041/latest/DLM432116.html?search = ts_act_protected%2Bobjects_resel&p = 1&sr = 1> accessed 29 October 2019.

Canada, France, Germany, the Netherlands, Sweden, the United Kingdom, and the United States. The organization estimates that "there are over 600 still awaiting their homecoming."[66] In each instance, the Museum of New Zealand has located the appropriate Maori or Moriori tribe and discussed with the tribe the ceremonies to be conducted. If need be, the government of New Zealand pays for the transportation costs of the repatriation.

A lesson of the New Zealand experience is that concerted cooperation between First Nations, the relevant national museum, and government can enhance the chances of a repatriation program. The three stakeholders have developed procedures which respect traditions and are professional with clearly defined tasks. The repatriation program, one of the most effective in the world, has enabled the Maori and Moriori communities to shake off the helplessness under which indigenous peoples elsewhere can be weighed down when they face authorities and museums at home or abroad. In this case, the repatriation has a healing impact on the communities once affected. A practical advantage for Western institutions that have to let human remains and funerary objects go is that they no longer have to take care of remains and objects that they will not, with the current knowledge of sensitivities in communities of origin, any longer exhibit.

C. United States

The situation in the United States is more ambiguous. At the second White House Tribal Nations Conference in 2010, the American administration announced that "in response to the many calls from Native Americans," it would drop its opposition to UNDRIP. Representatives of 565 recognized American Indian tribes applauded the announcement. But soon it became clear that the concept of self-governance, applied by US lawmakers, was more limited than "the existing right of self-determination in international law."[67] A critic wrote, "Indigenous peoples domestically and presumably internationally must be held in perpetual tutelage under the control of each

[66] This part builds on the website of the program "The Karanga Aotearoa Repatriation Programme" (Wellington, Museum of New Zealand Te Papa Tongarewa, 2019) <https://www.tepapa.govt.nz/about/repatriation/karanga-aotearoa-repatriation-programme> accessed 16 October 2019 and 7 February 2020.

[67] US State Department, "Announcement of U.S. Support for the United Nations Declaration on the Rights of Indigenous Peoples" (2010) <https://2009-2017.state.gov/s/srgia/154553.htm> accessed 16 October 2019.

state's government."[68] Twenty years earlier, in 1990, the United States had introduced a hard law enabling native groups to recover Native American and Hawaiian human remains and funerary objects from federal agencies and federally funded museums, the Native American Graves Protection and Repatriation Act (NAGPRA). It had some remarkable stipulations. It was retroactive and required federal institutions to inventory and repatriate remains and objects, even if acquired before 1990. NAGPRA supports indigenous communities financially with search for human remains and objects. It criminalizes the trafficking of human remains and objects and provides guidelines for their excavation. It is difficult to assess whether the 14,449 sets of human remains and 334,318 associated burial objects, which were returned to Native Americans between 1990 and 2017, are impressive or dismaying figures.[69] For Native Americans it is only a fraction of what they lost. They complain that, in practice, they often have to carry the burden of proof, while museums claim not to have financial resources and personnel for thorough provenance research.[70] Since 2016, the US Senate has been discussing a new law, the Safeguard Tribal Objects of Patrimony Act of 2019 (STOP Act). Section 2.1. increases the maximum penalty for violations of NAGPRA. Section 2.3 makes NAGPRA internationally applicable. Section 2.4. enables the authorities "to access other countries' domestic laws and law enforcement mechanisms to facilitate international repatriation by explicitly prohibiting the exportation of Native American cultural items obtained in violation" of NAGPRA.[71] The new law might have inspired Finland's National Museum in 2019 to return its Mesa Verde collection of over six hundred items. The remains of some twenty individuals and twenty-eight funerary objects, which are part of it, were collected by a Swedish researcher from the Mesa Verde site in current Colorado in 1891. He passed them to the Finnish museum.[72]

[68] Rudolf Ryser, "US Government on UNDRIP: Yes but No" (*Center for World Indigenous Studies*, 18 December 2018) <https://www.cwis.org/2010/12/us-government-on-undrip-yes-but-no/> accessed 16 October 2019.

[69] US Department of the Interior, "Fiscal Year 2017 Report National NAGPRA Program" (2018) 6 <https://www.nps.gov/nagpra/DOCUMENTS/Reports/FY2017-National-NAGPRA-Program-Report.pdf> accessed 30 October 2019.

[70] Jos van Beurden, Kathleen M Adams, and Paul Catteeuw, "Return Unravelled" (2019) 120 (3) Volkskunde 305–40.

[71] US Congress, S 2165: Safeguard Tribal Objects of Patrimony Act of 2019 <https://www.govtrack.us/congress/bills/116/s2165/text/is> accessed 30 October 2019.

[72] US Department of the Interior, Press Release, "Secretary Bernhardt Commends President Trump, President Niinistö of Finland on Agreement to Repatriate Mesa Verde Puebloan Remains From Finland to the United States" (2 October 2019) <https://www.doi.gov/pressreleases/secretary-bernhardt-commends-president-trump-president-niinisto-finland-agreement> accessed 30 October 2019.

D. Canada

In 2007, Canadian critics of UNDRIP explained the broad support for it, that it was for most Member states "irrelevant to their own interests" and "high on principle but low on practical application." And some countries with large indigenous populations "had no intention of meeting its terms." The multi-interpretable Art 26.1. ("Indigenous peoples have the right to the lands, territories and resources which they have traditionally owned, occupied or otherwise used or occupied.") made the declaration the wrong basis for dealing with Canada's indigenous peoples.[73] In 2016, Canada declared itself "a full supporter of the declaration, without qualification."[74] Even hereafter, a cabinet minister called UNDRIP "unworkable" and "a political distraction" while disagreements about its legal impact remained.[75] But slowly, UNDRIP began to gain influence. In 2019, the Royal British Columbia Museum (RBCM) published *Indigenous Repatriation Handbook* that details the close cooperation between the RBCM and indigenous communities. It formulates how a community should handle a claim. It offers the repatriation of five hundred Haida and the making of an inventory of twelve thousand Haida objects in museums around the world as a best practice. While the healing effect of repatriation "cannot be measured, it is visible in the way we live our lives . . . the healing is not only ours." Taking their responsibility enables "Western museums to become voluntary agents of change, rather than the physical evidence of Canada's genocide against Indigenous Peoples . . . it helps museum staff address or heal from the shame of colonialism many carry." It is "not quick, easy or pretty; it is complicated, powerful and transformative."[76] Also in 2019, Canada initiated an Indigenous Human Remains and Cultural Property Act and a National Strategy on Indigenous Human Remains and Cultural Property Repatriation. By promoting the

[73] Daniel Livermore, "UNDRIP: The Wrong Basis for Canada's International Indigenous Agenda" (Ottawa, *Center for International Policy Studies*, 17 November 2011) <https://www.cips-cepi.ca/2011/11/17/undrip-the-wrong-basis-for-canadas-international-indigenous-agenda-2/> accessed 15 October 2019.

[74] "Canada Officially Adopts UN Declaration on Rights of Indigenous Peoples" (Toronto, *CBC News*, 10 May 2016). <https://www.cbc.ca/news/indigenous/canada-adopting-implementing-un-rights-declaration-1.3575272> accessed 15 October 2019.

[75] James Wilt, "Implementing UNDRIP Is a Big Deal for Canada. Here's What You Need to Know" (*The Narwhal*, 12 December 2017) <https://thenarwhal.ca/implementing-undrip-big-deal-canada-here-s-what-you-need-know/> accessed 17 October 2019.

[76] Royal BC Museum and the Haida Gwaii Museum at Kay Llnagaay, *Indigenous Repatriation Handbook* (Victoria BC, 2019) 61, 68–70, 72 <https://royalbcmuseum.bc.ca/sites/default/files/indigenous_repatriation_handbook_v01_screen_jw_20190327.pdf> accessed 13 September 2019.

repatriation of indigenous human remains and cultural property "wherever situated," the act runs parallel to the STOP Act in the United States and repatriation programs in Australia and New Zealand.[77] Like the approach in Australia, the Canadian approach represents more a philosophy of repatriation than a legal framework. This is closer to how indigenous peoples like to deal with the repatriation issue.

V. Massive Losses Under the Nazi Regime, Relatively Most Returns

During World War II, 600,000 paintings and 4.4 million other precious items are estimated to have changed hands illegally.[78] After the war, the Allied forces recaptured many and handed them over to the governments of the countries from which the Nazi regime had taken them. Most recipient countries kept them for themselves and their museums and did not look for the rightful owners. At the end of the twentieth century, some newspapers and Jewish advocacy groups questioned this approach, which in a country such as the Netherlands had resulted in "financial and bureaucratic obstacles" for the original owners and their descendants.[79] At that time, the latter were still recovering from the war and lacked the means for submitting claims. Hard law possibilities were "limited, if not non-existent," non-binding declarations would be developed later.[80] As was mentioned earlier, the fall of the Berlin Wall in 1989 might have been the start of a process of claims for properties, which were lost during occupation or oppression.

In 1998, the US State Department and the US Holocaust Memorial Museum hosted a conference, where forty-four countries, including the unified Germany, adopted the Washington Conference Principles on Nazi-Confiscated Art.[81] Principle IV asks for consideration for "unavoidable gaps

[77] House of Commons Canada, *National Strategy on Indigenous Human Remains and Cultural Property Repatriation* (Ottawa, 19 February 2019) <https://www.parl.ca/DocumentViewer/en/42-1/bill/C-391/third-reading> accessed 12 September 2019.

[78] "Nazi-Looted Art: Why Are Restitutions Still the Exception?" (*Deutsche Welle*, 3 December 2018) <https://www.dw.com/en/Nazi-looted-art-why-are-restitutions-still-the-exception/a-46507241> accessed 23 October 2019.

[79] A country such as the Netherlands received over four thousand, often precious, artworks. Ekkart Committee, *Origins Unknown, Final Report* (Zwolle, Waanders 2006) 9.

[80] Evelien Campfens, "Sources of Inspiration: Old and New Rules for Looted Art" in E Campfens (ed), *Fair and Just Solutions? Alternatives in Nazi-Looted Art Disputes: Status quo and New Developments* (The Hague, Eleven International Publishing 2015) 38.

[81] Commission for Looted Art in Europe, *Washington Conference Principles on Nazi-Confiscated Art* (London, 1999) <https://www.lootedartcommission.com/Washington-principles> accessed 23 October 2019.

or ambiguities in the provenance in light of the passage of time and the circumstances of the Holocaust era." Principle IX advocated a "just and fair solution" for claims. If prewar owners or their descendants cannot be identified, it asks that "steps should be taken expeditiously to achieve a just and fair solution." Principle XI recommends "alternative dispute resolution mechanisms," thus avoiding complicated and expensive court cases. The acceptance of the principles contributed to the establishment of national restitution committees in several European countries and North America.[82]

The set of Washington principles were followed by others. In 1999, the Parliamentary Assembly of the Council of Europe translated the Washington Conference Principles in Resolution No. 1205 concerning Looted Jewish Cultural Property. It handled a broader concept of cultural property than the Washington Conference Principles, a concept that went "beyond a concentration on high-profile objects of significant monetary value."[83] It declared in Principle 8 that restitution should enable "the reconstitution of the place of the Jewish culture in Europe." Principles 13.I and 13.II stated that restitution should be facilitated by "extending or removing statutory limitation periods" and "removing restrictions on alienability." Principle 16 favored out-of-court approaches.[84]

Building on the Washington principles and European resolution, thirty-eight governments of the Council of Europe adopted the Vilnius Forum Declaration in 2000. It was a wake-up call to intensify research, exchange of information, and other measures for the restitution "of the massive and unprecedented looting and confiscations of art and other cultural property owned by Jewish individuals, communities and others." Principle 1 asked governments to maximise their efforts. Principle 2 asked "governments, museums, the art trade and other relevant agencies to provide all necessary information."[85]

The year 2009 saw two efforts to strengthen the position of claimants. UNESCO formulated a set of principles relating to Cultural Objects Displaced in Connection with the Second World War, but there was no

[82] Annemarie Marck and Eelke Muller, "National Panels Advising on Nazi-Looted Art in Austria, France, the United Kingdom, the Netherlands and Germany" in E Campfens (ed), *Fair and Just Solutions?* (Eleven 2015) 41–89; Douglas Davidson, "Just and Fair solutions: A View from the United States" in E Campfens (ed), *Fair and Just Solutions?* (Eleven 2015) 91–101.

[83] Patrick O'Keefe, "A Comparison of the Washington and Vilnius Principles and Resolution 1205," in Prott (n 1) 158.

[84] Council of Europe, *Resolution 1205 Calling for the Restitution of Looted Jewish Cultural Property in Europe* (Strasbourg, 5 November 1999) <https://www.lootedartcommission.com/council-of-europe> accessed 23 October 2019.

[85] Vilnius International Forum on Holocaust Era Looted Cultural Assets, *Vilnius Forum Declaration* (2000) <https://www.lootedartcommission.com/vilnius-forum> accessed 23 October 2019.

majority for accepting it.[86] The other was the adoption in the Czech Republic of the Terezin Declaration on Holocaust Era Assets and Related Issues. Next to confiscations, it mentioned "forced sales and sales under duress of property" and applied a broad concept of cultural property, including "sacred scrolls, synagogue and ceremonial objects as well as the libraries, manuscripts, archives and records of Jewish communities." Its focus was on Jewish cultural property. Worried about the slow progress, it stressed "the importance for all stakeholders to continue and support intensified systematic provenance research" and "the establishments of mechanisms to assist claimants and others in their efforts."[87]

The four sets of principles have in common that restitution is "the primary way of achieving justice"[88] and they work retroactively. They focus more on lost cultural properties of Jewish people than on those of other victims of the Nazi regime. They ask governments and other possessors to do active provenance research, publish this research so potential claimants can use it, and look for fair and just solutions. The definition of cultural properties was slowly expanding from "art" in the Washington Conference Principles and includes "burial sites . . . ceremonial objects, libraries, manuscripts, archives and records of Jewish communities" in the Tereza Declaration. All stakeholders involved were asked to understand problems with evidence. They were urged to avoid going to court and to look for alternative dispute resolution mechanisms.

It is hard to measure the effectiveness of all these principles. There are doubts and there is support for them. The first doubt concerns the implementation of the principles at a national level. Of the forty-four signatory countries of the Washington Conference principles, only five, that is, Austria, Germany, France, the Netherlands, and the United Kingdom, have set up advisory panels or restitution committees, while five others, that is, Hungary, Italy, Russia, Poland, and Spain, have not made any progress.[89] Even in the

86 "Draft UNESCO Declaration of Principles Relating to Cultural Objects Displaced in Connection with the Second World War" (Paris, UNESCO 2009) <https://www.lootedartcommission.com/OVNKN480270> accessed 23 October 2019.

87 The Holocaust Era Assets Conference, *Terezin Declaration on Holocaust Era Assets and Related Issues* (Terezin, 30 June 2009) <https://www.lootedartcommission.com/NPNMG484641> accessed 23 October 2019.

88 Campfens (n 80) 37.

89 Sarah Cascone, "It's Been 20 Years Since the Creation of the 'Washington Principles' to Return Nazi-Looted Art. But How Effective Have They Been?" (*ArtNet News*, 27 November 2018) <https://news.artnet.com/art-world/washington-principles-Nazi-looted-art-agreement-turns-20-1403614> accessed 24 October 2019; Wesley A Fisher and Ruth Weinberger, "Holocaust-Era Looted Art: A

active countries, there is concern about the lack of sufficient and thorough provenance research. In 2014, "only one-third of German museums" was said to have undertaken provenance research to identify Nazi-looted art in their collections.[90] Moreover, the principles have mainly impacted public institutions. Private possessors have been called to account much less. This led a member of the Holocaust Art Research Project to consider the principles "a failure."[91] In 2018, Germany and the United States emphasized the need of "improved databases, more detailed provenance research, and more readily available genealogical information" to locate heirs.[92]

The second doubt concerns the lawsuits that are taking the place of hoped-for settlements and alternative dispute resolutions, especially in the United States.[93] *The Republic of Austria v. Altmann*, 541 U.S. 677 lawsuit over five paintings stolen by the Nazis in a government museum in Austria is an example. Thanks to a discovery by a journalist, the case began in 1998. A court case was started, but claimant Maria Altmann stopped, since she thought she would have a better chance with a civil action against Austria in a US federal district court. In 2004, she won the lawsuit.[94]

A third doubt concerns the large number of Nazi-looted art works in private possession. The discovery, in 2012, of over 1,400 artworks by painters such as Chagall, Matisse, Munch, Picasso, and Klee in the private collection of the late German art dealer Hildebrandt Gurlitt in Munich renewed the spotlight on this. Not much has been achieved in respect to Nazi-looted art works in private possession. Many art works with a contestable background

Current World-Wide Overview" (St. Petersburg, ICOM Museum & Politics Conference, September 2014) <http://art.claimscon.org/wp-content/uploads/2014/11/Worldwide-Overview.pdf> accessed 24 October 2019.

[90] "Nazi-Looted Art: Why Germany Hasn't Dealt with It" (*Deutsche Welle*, 24 November 2014) <https://www.dw.com/en/Nazi-looted-art-why-germany-hasnt-dealt-with-it/a-18079662> accessed 23 October 2019.

[91] "Nazi-Looted Art: Why Are Restitutions Still the Exception?" (*Deutsche Welle*, 3 December 2018) <https://www.dw.com/en/Nazi-looted-art-why-are-restitutions-still-the-exception/a-46507241> accessed 23 October 2019.

[92] The Federal Government Commissioner for Culture and the Media of the Federal Republic of Germany and the Expert Adviser for Holocaust-Era Issues to the US Department of State, "Germany-USA Joint Declaration Concerning The Implementation of the Washington Principles from 1998" (26 November 2018) <https://www.lootedartcommission.com/TDRUEB99814> accessed 23 October 2019.

[93] Judith Bresler, "United Kingdom: Holocaust-Looted Art: A Changing Legal Landscape" (*LootedArt.com*, June 2011) <https://www.lootedart.com/OW91H4689161> accessed 24 October 2019.

[94] US Government Local Services Reports, "Republic of Austria v. Altmann, 541 U.S. 677 (2004)" <http://cdn.loc.gov/service/ll/usrep/usrep541/usrep541677/usrep541677.pdf> accessed 30 October 2019.

will only appear if they are offered for sale through a gallery or auction house. "The end of the restitution problem will not appear on the horizon" as long as these private owners are not involved in its solution.[95]

Some scholars emphasize the principles' effectiveness because of "the moral imperative that they state: regardless of the strict application of property law, the issue must be grappled with." The terminology underlying the principles of Nazi-confiscated art "evokes the most overt kind of theft."[96] It is a reminder of other peoples (on other continents, and in other periods) that were persecuted or fled and had to sell cultural objects out of necessity.[97]

Occasionally, dealings with Nazi looting and colonial looting have coincided. One example is the Great Zimbabwe Bird. In 1889, a South African trader had taken the sacred object from the ruined city of Great Zimbabwe to Germany, thereby neglecting protests of local Shona people. One-half of the bird ended up in Berlin, the other half remained in Zimbabwe. When withdrawing from Germany in 1945, the Soviet Union took it. After the fall of the Berlin Wall in 1989, it handed it back to Germany. In 2004, Germany returned it to Zimbabwe where it was reunited with the other half.[98] Another example concerns the claim of the descendants of Hans Meyer. Between 1900 and 1930, Meyer had acquired some objects captured by British soldiers from the Edo Kingdom in Nigeria in 1897. Under communist rule, they had gone to the University of Leipzig. After the fall of the Berlin Wall, Meyer's descendants claimed the Benin objects. The museum argued that restitution "would be almost as tragic as the original removal of the objects of the Oba's palace nearly a century ago." It was allowed to keep the objects.[99] Since 2018, the Weltmuseum Frankfurt has been doing provenance research into objects with a mixed history from East Africa and Indonesia.[100]

[95] Dutch Restitution Committee, *Annual Report 2013* (The Hague, Restitution Committee 2014) 5, 6 <https://www.restitutiecommissie.nl/sites/default/files/Report%202013.pdf> accessed 24 October 2019.

[96] Nicholas M O'Donnell, "Are the Principles Set Out for Identifying Nazi-Looted Art Fit for Purpose?" (*Apollo*, 29 October 2018) <https://www.apollo-magazine.com/are-the-principles-set-out-for-identifying-Nazi-looted-art-fit-for-purpose/> accessed 24 October 2019.

[97] Kwame Opoku, "Parzinger's Misconceptions and Misrepresentations of the Restitution of African Artefacts" (*Modern Ghana*, 3 March 2018) <https://www.pambazuka.org/land-environment/parzinger%E2%80%99s-misconceptions-and-misrepresentations-about-restitution-african> accessed 24 October 2019.

[98] C Renold, AL Bandle, and A Chechi, "Case Great Zimbabwe Bird—Zimbabwe and Prussia Cultural Heritage Foundation, Germany" (*Platform ArThemis*, 2013) <http://unige.ch/art-adr> accessed 1 November 2019.

[99] Beurden (n 2) 25.

[100] Julia Friedel and Vanessa von Gliszczynski, "Collected. Bought. Looted? Provenance Research at the Weltkulturen Museum in Frankfurt" (2018) 2 (2) Journal for Art Market Studies <https://www.fokum-jams.org/index.php/jams/article/view/39/81> accessed 1 November 2019.

VI. Convention, Declaration of Principles for Dealing with Colonial Loot

The countries and communities that claim loot from external colonialism have few means to support their claims. This raises the question whether such means should be developed. Whether the ongoing intensified contacts between former colonizers and colonies make such means superfluous will be known only later. The history of returns and slow pace of current negotiations make it doubtful. Suppose that former colonies can choose one of the means used in the two other categories of loot, which one would be suitable? Should they go for a new convention aimed at the return of colonial loot? An advantage would be that it is binding and offers general backing for claims. A disadvantage would be that it will take many years, if not decades, to get it accepted widely (as was the case with the 1970 UNESCO Convention), and that the momentum of former colonizers being willing to return colonial collections might be lost. Is a more pragmatic approach to be preferred? One in which former colonizers and their museums make inventories of disputable objects in their collections and discuss their return with countries of origin? It could lead to returns, but with the three stages of restitution distinguished by Sarr and Savoy—recognition of the illegitimacy of the property, an attempt to open a pathway toward establishing new cultural relations, and a return of objects[101]—these might remain rather meager. This approach differs from those for dealing with Nazi loot about which there is now a vast literature on the injustice that was at its root. Would then the sort of principles developed for dealing with Nazi loot be a helpful means? Is it thinkable that nations, which once were colonizers or colonized and which want to decolonize, sit together to define principles for healing and reconciliation through returns? Broadly but clearly formulated principles that guide their bilateral return negotiations?

How should such principles be? When, after World War II, the decision was made to assert universal human rights and, in the second half of the 1990s, principles for dealing with Nazi loot, it took only a few years to formulate them. A mixed group of influential people from all corners in the world was responsible for the declaration of human rights and for the principles about Nazi loot, countries that until then had failed to return works of art to the rightful owners. Below the author has adapted the

[101] Sarr and Savoy (n 1) 29.

1998 Washington Conference Principles for external colonial loot. It has required several adjustments. "Art" in Nazi-confiscated art has become "objects of cultural or historical importance," a term also used in several bilateral return agreements concluded in the 1970s. "Confiscated" has been reworded as "taken without just compensation or involuntarily lost," as the former colonizers were—according to European law—entitled to confiscate objects from their colonial possessions. In Principle 1, "restitution" has become "return," a more neutral word. In Principle 5, "Pre-War owners" has been replaced by "rightful claimants," as the term owner or ownership is better avoided because of legal complexities. "Rightful" is not so much being used in the legal sense but more in terms of justice. The "central register," mentioned in Principle 6, is unsuitable for colonial objects, as many disputes are between states. Registers should be made at a bilateral basis and in close cooperation with source countries.[102]

Table 12.1 Washington Conference Principles

Washington Conference Principles on Nazi-Confiscated Art	Principles on objects of cultural or historical importance, taken without just compensation or involuntarily lost in the European colonial era
In developing a consensus on non-binding principles to assist in resolving issues relating to Nazi-confiscated art, the Conference recognizes that among participating nations there are differing legal systems and that countries act within the context of their own laws.	In developing a consensus on non-binding principles to assist in resolving issues relating to objects of cultural or historical importance, taken without just compensation or involuntarily lost in the European colonial era, it is recognized that among participating nations, there are differing legal systems and that countries act within the context of their own laws.

[102] Beurden, (n 2) 252–53.

Table 12.1 *Continued*

Washington Conference Principles on Nazi-Confiscated Art	Principles on objects of cultural or historical importance, taken without just compensation or involuntarily lost in the European colonial era
1. Art that had been confiscated by the Nazis and not subsequently restituted should be identified.	1. Objects of cultural or historical importance, taken without just compensation or involuntarily lost in a territory controlled by European, American, or Asian colonial powers and not subsequently returned should be identified.
2. Relevant records and archives should be open and accessible to researchers, in accordance with the guidelines of the International Council on Archives.	2. Relevant records and archives should be open and accessible to researchers, in accordance with the guidelines of the International Council on Archives.
3. Resources and personnel should be made available to facilitate the identification of all art that had been confiscated by the Nazis and not subsequently restituted.	3. Resources and personnel should be made available to facilitate the identification of all objects of cultural or historical importance taken without just compensation or involuntarily lost in the European colonial era and not subsequently returned.
4. In establishing that a work of art had been confiscated by the Nazis and not subsequently restituted, consideration should be given to unavoidable gaps or ambiguities in the provenance in light of the passage of time and the circumstances of the Holocaust era.	4. In establishing that an object of cultural or historical importance had been taken without just compensation or had been lost involuntarily in the European colonial era and not subsequently returned, consideration should be given to unavoidable gaps or ambiguities in the provenance in light of the passage of time and the circumstances of the European colonial era.

Continued

Table 12.1 *Continued*

Washington Conference Principles on Nazi-Confiscated Art	Principles on objects of cultural or historical importance, taken without just compensation or involuntarily lost in the European colonial era
5. Every effort should be made to publicize art that is found to have been confiscated by the Nazis and not subsequently restituted in order to locate its pre-War owners or their heirs.	5. Every effort should be made to publicize objects of cultural or historical importance that are found to have been taken without just compensation or were lost involuntarily during the European colonial era and not subsequently returned in order to locate its rightful claimants.
6. Efforts should be made to establish a central registry of such information.	6. Efforts should be made to establish a registry of such information on a bilateral basis.
7. Pre-War owners and their heirs should be encouraged to come forward and make known their claims to art that was confiscated by the Nazis and not subsequently restituted.	7. Rightful parties should be encouraged to come forward and make known their claims to objects that were taken without just compensation or lost involuntarily in the European colonial era and not subsequently returned.
8. If the pre-War owners of art that is found to have been confiscated by the Nazis and not subsequently restituted, or their heirs, can be identified, steps should be taken expeditiously to achieve a just and fair solution, recognizing this may vary according to the facts and circumstances surrounding a specific case.	8. If the rightful claimants can be identified, steps should be taken expeditiously to achieve a just and fair solution, recognizing this may vary according to the facts and circumstances surrounding a specific case.

Table 12.1 *Continued*

Washington Conference Principles on Nazi-Confiscated Art	Principles on objects of cultural or historical importance, taken without just compensation or involuntarily lost in the European colonial era
9. If the pre-War owners of art that is found to have been confiscated by the Nazis, or their heirs, cannot be identified, steps should be taken expeditiously to achieve a just and fair solution.	9. If no rightful claimants can be identified, steps should be taken expeditiously to achieve a just and fair solution.
10. Commissions or other bodies established to identify art that was confiscated by the Nazis and to assist in addressing ownership issues should have a balanced membership.	10. Commissions or other bodies established to identify objects of cultural or historical importance that are found to have been taken without just compensation or to have been lost involuntarily in the European colonial era and to assist in addressing ownership issues should have a balanced membership.
11. Nations are encouraged to develop national processes to implement these principles, particularly as they relate to alternative dispute resolution mechanisms for resolving ownership issues.	11. Nations, including the minorities and indigenous peoples in these nations, are encouraged to develop national and international processes to implement these principles, particularly as they relate to alternative dispute resolution mechanisms for resolving ownership issues.

VII. Conclusion

In three waves of looting the cultural heritage of subjugated peoples, Europeans have played a central role: Nazi-looted cultural property, human remains and disputable objects from internal colonialism, and the same from external colonialism. All waves were built on the presumption of the superiority of one civilization above others. The seizure of objects was often against the will of the source communities. It damaged their identity. The hierarchy, thus created by the Europeans, has not been lifted by the independence or self-determination of oppressed peoples. It continues in the minds of both the descendants of the colonizers and the colonized.

All three waves have become subjects of international debate, and there have been returns of displaced objects for all three. Claimants of Nazi-looted works of art have had the best chances and most support to retrieve lost treasures. Relatively speaking, many works of art have been restituted. Claimants of looted objects resulting from external colonialism have made the least progress as relatively few objects have been returned. So far, there have been two periods of returns to former external colonies. The first, in the 1970s, was based on extensive claims of former colonies. But most former European colonizers did not move. Exceptions were some relatively small returns by Belgium to DR Congo and by the Netherlands to Indonesia. They were motivated by the desire to maintain economic relations with their former colony and to protect their financial interests. Countries such as France, the United Kingdom and Germany made only incidental returns.

The first indications of a new period came with the end of the Cold War and the fall of the Berlin Wall in 1989. The new period certainly started in 2003, the year that a number of major European museums declared themselves universal museums and adopted the Declaration on the Importance and Value of Universal Museums. It was a new defense wall against claims, but some African contacts considered it their last line of defense. They have been proven right. The present period is part of a general decolonization movement. Organizations of indigenous peoples in Australia, Canada, New Zealand, and the United States, where European settlers once subjugated the First Nations, have helped as much as the Black rights movement in the United States and anti-colonial civil organizations in Europe. Moreover, many academics and museum professionals in Western countries are changing their nationalist for more cosmopolitan ethics. Much of the war booty in Western museums has a universal value, but this does not mean that they are the best places to keep it and that they can impose their values and practices upon the ways countries of origin are dealing with returned objects.

This chapter shows that there is no neutrality in the politics of return. Return is a multilayered and complicated trajectory. There remain striking differences between the ways of enforcing a claim for an object that was lost during one of these waves. Europe's former external colonies lack hard laws or sets of principles to retrieve lost objects. Their efforts in the 1970s and 2010s to establish a return lobby remained short-lived. The participating countries differed in their drive to retrieve lost treasures and claims were not multilateral, but bilateral matters. UNESCO's ICPRCP has scarcely been an instrument supporting them. So far, UN declarations and a bilateral agreement with former colonizer have been their only remedy. For a number of years, the governments and heritage institutions of former colonizing states such as Germany, France, and the Netherlands have begun developing return principles or policies. But these have scarcely resulted in returns. To fill the gap between talking about returns and actual returning, this chapter has formulated "Principles on objects of cultural or historical importance, taken without just compensation or involuntarily lost in the European colonial era."

A major theme in these principles is provenance research. Two questions linger around this: one concerning practice, the other principle. The practical question recognizes that provenance research is time-consuming and requires experts and money. Much documentation has disappeared, if it existed at all. Most object biographies are amputated. The example of the research into the provenance of the canon of the King of Kandy shows this. This touches the second question concerning principle. The Rijksmuseum Amsterdam will spend several years gathering sufficient provenance information about the canon. In turn, Sri Lanka has informed the museum about its serious interest in the return of the canon. The canon is one object, but Western museums have such vast collections from colonial contexts that it is necessary to organize and prioritize provenance research. The principle question is, who decides what the priorities are? Are these the countries of origin? Are these the museums that hold disputable objects? Or a combination of the two? So far, the spirit of a coproduction is mostly felt in two documents: the advice of Sarr and Savoy to President Macron and *Indigenous Repatriation Handbook* of the Royal

British Colombia Museum and the Haida Gwaii Museum at Kay Llnagaay. In most other efforts, the initiative has remained in a European country that consulted counterparts in former colonial contexts. This touches the issue of equality between partners in the global village, one of which used to consider itself superior to the other.

13

Syrian and Iraqi Opinion on Protecting, Promoting, and Reconstructing Heritage after the Islamic State

Benjamin Isakhan and James Barry

I. Introduction

From November 2013, the Syrian city of Raqqa was transformed into the capital of a new Caliphate that would become known as the Islamic State of Iraq and Syria (ISIS).[1] In 2014, ISIS burst into Iraq capturing several significant cities such as Mosul in June. Upon conquering such a vast swathe of territory, ISIS imposed their strict interpretation of sharia law, enacted mass genocidal pogroms, and created a sequence of geopolitical and humanitarian challenges to regional stability and the global order.[2] They also undertook a sustained campaign to target the sites and artifacts that embody the rich and complex heritage of the region, including the mass looting of archaeological zones; the razing of ancient buildings and statues; the destruction of scores of religious sites that did not conform to their strict doctrine; as well as the desecration of what might be called "secular" state institutions such as museums, art galleries, and libraries.[3]

[1] This article uses the simplified English name of "Islamic State" for the jihadist terrorist group known in Arabic as *Da'esh* and alternatively in English as the Islamic State of Iraq and Syria (ISIS).

[2] Benjamin Isakhan (ed), *The Legacy of Iraq: From the 2003 War to the "Islamic State"* (Edinburgh UP 2015); David Kilcullen, *Blood Year: Islamic State and the Failures of the War on Terror* (Hurst 2016); Michael Weiss and Hassan Hassan, *ISIS: Inside the Army of Terror* (Simon and Schuster 2015).

[3] A significant body of recent scholarship has analyzed and examined various aspects of the heritage destruction conducted by the Islamic State. For a few key examples, see Neil Brodie, "Syria and Its Regional Neighbors: A Case of Cultural Property Protection Policy Failure?" (2015) 22 International Journal of Cultural Property; Salaam Al Quntar and Brian Daniels, "Responses to the Destruction of Syrian Cultural Heritage: A Critical Review of Current Efforts" (2016) 5 International Journal of Islamic Architecture; Benjamin Isakhan and Antonio González Zarandona, "Layers of Religious and Political Iconoclasm under the Islamic State: Symbolic Sectarianism and Pre-Monotheistic Iconoclasm" (2018) 24 International Journal of Heritage Studies; Ömür Harmanşah, "ISIS, Heritage, and the Spectacles of Destruction in the Global Media" (2015) 78 Near Eastern

Benjamin Isakhan and James Barry, *Syrian and Iraqi Opinion on Protecting, Promoting, and Reconstructing Heritage after the Islamic State* In: *The Preservation of Art and Culture in Times of War.* Edited by: Claire Finkelstein, Derek Gillman, and Frederik Rosén, Oxford University Press. © Oxford University Press 2022. DOI: 10.1093/oso/9780197610565.003.0014

The violence and heritage destruction unleashed by groups such as ISIS prompted international condemnation and saw various state parties, NGOs, and multilateral institutions launch a suite of initiatives designed to protect, promote, and reconstruct the heritage of Syria and Iraq. These can be broadly understood to have occurred along three key axes. The first concerns the role that the international community can or ought to play in protecting cultural property during times of conflict. The second concerns the extent to which the international community should engage in education programs and awareness-raising initiatives pertaining to heritage and heritage destruction issues in the Middle East. The third axis revolves around the extent to which a concerted international effort ought to be made to reconstruct heritage sites in Syria and Iraq. While such efforts are undoubtedly well-intentioned, they are occurring within a complex (post-)conflict environment in which ISIS and many other actors remain capable of unleashing new waves of horrific violence and iconoclastic attacks. More to the point, such efforts often rely on problematic assumptions about how the people of Syria and Iraq value and engage with their heritage, how they perceive and interpret its destruction, and the value they place on its reconstruction. Indeed, very little empirical data has been collected about how Syrians or Iraqis have perceived and experienced the cataclysmic events unleased by ISIS,[4] and there is even less on their attitudes toward heritage, heritage destruction, and its reconstruction.[5]

Archaeology; Kristy Campion, "Blast through the Past: Terrorist Attacks on Art and Antiquities as a Reconquest of the Modern Jihadi Identity" (2017) 11 Perspectives on Terrorism; Sofya Shahab and Benjamin Isakhan, "The Ritualization of Heritage Destruction Under the Islamic State" (2018) 18 Journal of Social Archaeology; Benajmin Isakhan, "The Islamic State Attacks on Shia Holy Sites and the 'Shrine Protection Narrative': Threats to Sacred Space as a Mobilization Frame" (2018) 32 Terrorism and Political Violence; Benjamin Isakhan and Sofya Shahab, "The Islamic State's Destruction of Yezidi Heritage: Responses, Resilience and Reconstruction after Genocide" (2020) 20 Journal of Social Archaeology; Benjamin Isakhan, Antonio González Zarandona, and Taghreed Jamal Al-Deen, "Cultural Cleansing and Iconoclasm under the Islamic State: Attacks on Yezidis and Christians and their Heritage" in Firat Oruc (ed), *Sites of Pluralism: Community Politics in the Middle East* (Hurst 2019); Chiari De Cesari, "Post-Colonial Ruins: Archaeologies of Political Violence and IS" (2015) 31 Anthropology Today; Marina Lostal and Emma Cunliffe, "Cultural Heritage That Heals: Factoring in Cultural Heritage Discourses in the Syrian Peacebuilding Process" (2016) 7 The Historic Environment: Policy and Practice; Benjamin Isakhan and Lynn Meskell, "UNESCO's Project to 'Revive the Spirit of Mosul': Iraqi and Syrian Opinion on Heritage Reconstruction after the Islamic State" (2019) 25 International Journal of Heritage Studies.

[4] For two notable exceptions see Adam Baczko, Gilles Dorronsoro, and Arthur Quesnay, *Civil War in Syria: Mobilization and Competing Social Orders* (CUP 2018); Charles Lister, *The Syrian Jihad: Al-Qaeda, the Islamic State and the Evolution of an Insurgency* (OUP 2017).

[5] Some preliminary empirical data documenting interviews with Syrians and Iraqis concerning the destruction of their heritage can be found in Isakhan and Meskell (n 3); Isakhan and Shahab (n 3).

This chapter seeks to address this lacuna by presenting the results of fifty-three in-depth semi-structured interviews with Iraqis and Syrians from various areas and ethnic and religious backgrounds.[6] It juxtaposes the above three axes of heritage engagement in Syria and Iraq against the opinions expressed by these Syrian and Iraqi interviewees. This is not to set up a false dichotomy between the opinions and efforts of experts in the "West" and the Syrian and Iraqi people. Indeed, the respondents often agree with and support key heritage initiatives. Instead, it is designed to demonstrate where ideas converge and diverge: representing opportunities for collaboration in the former and for further efforts to understand local opinion in the latter. It is also important to note that the responses given by these interviewees are not considered to be representative of broader Syrian or Iraqi opinion, but are instead designed to yield an array of qualitative insights into each individual's views on heritage protection, promotion, and reconstruction. The chapter concludes by noting that the new empirical insights gleaned from these interviews is a step toward enabling current and future (post-) conflict heritage projects to be cognizant of local sentiment and to tailor their initiatives to best meet the needs and respect the values of the local communities. It is hoped that such awareness will help prevent well-intentioned projects from being insensitive or unaware of the nuanced and divergent opinions, attitudes, and needs of the local populations whose heritage they seek to protect, promote, or reconstruct.

II. International Protection of Heritage in Conflict

The destruction of heritage sites in Syria and Iraq triggered several prominent debates as well as internationally backed initiatives focusing on the role that the international community can or ought to play in protecting cultural property during times of conflict. Such debates are far from new. Following

[6] This chapter draws on 53 in-depth semi-structured interviews conducted both in person and via Phone/Skype between March 2017 and October 2019. The interviewees represent a broad spectrum of different people from across Syria and Iraq. The majority were from across Iraq (35) and the remainder from Syria (18). The respondents identified as being part of an array of different ethnic and religious affiliations, including: Sunni Arab (22), Christian (17), Yezidi (6), Sunni Kurd (4), Shia Arab (3), and Druze (1). And just over one-quarter of the participants were women (15). These interviews were collected in accordance with the ethical standards of the Deakin University Human Research Ethics Committee, Australia. Informed consent was obtained for all participants, who remain anonymous and non-identifiable. Further details on the methodology can be found in Isakhan and Meskell (n 3); Isakhan and Shahab (n 3).

the mass devastation of both World War I and World War II,[7] the international community ratified a series of international conventions, including the first such document to address the topic of heritage protection during times of war, the Convention for the Protection of Cultural Property in the Event of Armed Conflict (1954, commonly known as the Hague Convention).[8] This document and its two subsequent protocols sought to establish an international framework for the legal obligations of militaries to avoid doing harm to cultural heritage and to actively preserve it during times of armed conflict and occupation.[9]

Despite the significance of the Hague Convention, cultural property continued to suffer through many of the key conflicts—both between and within states—of the second half of the twentieth century. This has ranged from major international military endeavors such as Vietnam[10] to civil wars such as that in Lebanon,[11] nationalist, and sectarian conflict like that in Northern Ireland,[12] and during mass cultural cleansing campaigns such as in China[13] and Cambodia.[14] Another prominent example is the Balkans conflicts of the 1990s. The ethno-religious and asymmetric nature of the war saw the "deliberate destruction of mosques, churches, museums, civil records, monuments and artifacts."[15] A key response from the international community

[7] Alan Kramer, *Dynamic of Destruction: Culture and Mass Killing in the First World War* (OUP 2007); Elizabeth Simpson (ed), *The Spoils of War: World War II and Its Aftermath: The Loss, Reappearance and Recovery of Cultural Property* (Harry N Abrams 1997).

[8] See Elizabeth Varner, "Non-party Obligations Underlying the 1954 Hague Convention for the Protection of Cultural Property in the Event of Armed Conflict, Protocol II" in this volume.

[9] Patty Gerstenblith, "The 1954 Hague Convention on the Protection of Cultural Property in the Event of Armed Conflict: Its Background and Prospects for Ratification in the United States" in Lawrence Rothfield (ed), *Antiquities under Siege: Cultural Heritage Protection after the Iraq War* (Alta Mira Press 2008); Patty Gerstenblith, "The Obligations Contained in International Treaties of Armed Forces to Protect Cultural Heritage in Times of Armed Conflict" in Laurie Rush (ed), *Archaeology, Cultural Property and the Military* (Boydell 2010); Joris Kila, *Heritage under Siege: Military Implementation of Cultural Property Protection Following the 1954 Hague Convention* (Brill 2012).

[10] Andrew Hardy, Mauro Cucarzi, and Patrizia Zolese (eds), *Champa and the Archaeology of My San* (National University of Singapore Press 2009).

[11] Caroline Sandes, "Urban Cultural Heritage and Armed Conflict: The Case of Beriut Central District" in Joris Kila and James Zeidler (eds), *Cultural Heritage in the Crosshairs: Protecting Cultural Property During Conflict* (Brill 2013).

[12] Graham Dawson, *Making Peace with the Past?: Memory, Trauma and the Irish Troubles* (Manchester UP 2007).

[13] Wang Liang, "The Confucius Temple Tragedy of the Cultural Revolution" in TA Wilson (ed), *On Sacred Grounds: Culture, Society, Politics, and the Formation of the Cult of Confucius* (Harvard UP 2002).

[14] Tim Winter, *Post-Conflict Heritage, Postcolonial Tourism: Culture, Politics and Development at Angkor* (Routledge 2007).

[15] Robert Layton and Julian Thomas, "Introduction: The Destruction and Conservation of Cultural Property" in Robert Layton, Peter G Stone, and Julian Thomas (eds), *Destruction and Conservation of Cultural Property* (Routledge 2001) 12.

was to use evidence of the deliberate targeting of cultural property in the trial of several important military figures, including Slobodan Milosevic, at the International Court of Justice and the International Criminal Tribunal.[16]

The early twenty-first century has also seen its share of heritage destruction in conflict. The cultural property of Afghanistan suffered terribly across successive decades of conflict, especially after the Soviet withdrawal of 1989 and the rise of the Taliban in 1996. War and looting ravaged the Old City of Herat and the National Museum, the latter of which also endured waves of Islamist iconoclasm under the Taliban.[17] Most famously, in 2001 the Taliban detonated explosives at the giant statues of the Buddha in the Bamiyan valley, reducing the early seventh-century CE monuments to rubble.[18] This was followed by a US-led military intervention in Afghanistan (2001 to present) which saw further damage to cultural property across the country, especially the systemic looting operations that ravaged ancient archaeological sites.[19] An even worse fate befell the cultural heritage of Iraq after the US-led intervention of 2003 (until 2011).[20] Immediately after the fall of Baghdad in 2003, a wave of looting spread across the country—most notably at the Iraq National Museum where looters set fires, smashed cabinets, and stole as many as fifteen thousand objects.[21] In addition, coalition forces set up a number of their key military bases at historically or culturally sensitive sites such as the ancient city of Babylon which was occupied from April 2003 until December 2004. The damage done during the military occupation of the site

[16] Andrew Herscher and András Riedlmayer, *The Destruction of Cultural Heritage in Kosovo, 1998–1999: A Post-War Survey. The Case of* Prosecutor v. Slobodan Milosevic (No. P486) (International Criminal Tribunal for the Former Yugoslavia 2002); András Riedlmayer, *Destruction of Cultural Heritage in Bosnia-Herzegovina, 1992–1996: A Post-War Survey of Selected Municipalities. The Case of* Prosecutor v. Slobodan Milosevic (No. P486) (International Criminal Tribunal for the Former Yugoslavia 2002); Helen Walasek, *Bosnia and the Destruction of Cultural Heritage* (Routledge 2016).

[17] Nancy Hatch Dupree, "Cultural Heritage and National Identity in Afghanistan" (2002) 23 Third World Quarterly; Gil J Stein, "The War-Ravaged Cultural Heritage of Afghanistan: An Overview of Projects of Assessment, Mitigation, and Preservation" (2015) 78 Near Eastern Archaeology.

[18] Jamal Elias, "The Taliban, Bamiyan, and Revisionist Iconoclasm" in Stacy Boldrick, Leslie Brubaker, and Richard Clay (eds), *Striking Images, Iconoclasms Past and Present* (Ashgate 2013); Barry Finbarr Flood, "Between Cult and Culture: Bamiyan, Islamic Iconoclasm, and the Museum" (2002) 84 The Art Bulletin.

[19] France 24/AFP, "Archaeologists Seek Protection for Afghan Treasures" (*Culture in Development*, 22 June 2010).

[20] Lawrence Rothfield (ed), *Antiquities Under Siege: Cultural Heritage Protection after the Iraq War* (Alta Mira Press 2008); Peter Stone and Joanne Farchakh Bajjaly (eds), *The Destruction of Cultural Heritage in Iraq* (Boydell 2008).

[21] Matthew Bogdanos, *Thieves of Baghdad: One Marine's Passion for Ancient Civilizations and the Journey to Recover the World's Greatest Stolen Treasures* (Bloomsbury 2005); Donny George Yukhanna, "The Looting of the Iraq National Museum" in Peter Stone and Joanne Farchakh Bajjaly (eds), *The Destruction of Cultural Heritage in Iraq* (Boydell 2008).

included that to the Ishtar Gate and the Procession Street of the ancient city.[22] In terms of religious sites, the most notable attack was the 2006 bombing of the Al-Askari mosque in Samarra by Al-Qaeda in Iraq. This site is highly revered by the Shia Arab population, and the bombing proved to be a catalyst for Iraq's descent into a brutal sectarian civil war.[23] As many have demonstrated, the failure of the US-led coalition to protect cultural property in both Afghanistan and Iraq contravene a vast body of international law.[24]

More recent conflicts have also proven devastating for cultural property. After conquering parts of northern Mali in March 2012, the Al-Qaeda linked terrorist group Ansar al-Dine went on to destroy ten historical Sufi shrines in Timbuktu. Five years later, a key leader of Ansar al-Dine, Ahmed Al-Mahdi, was sentenced to nine years in prison in a landmark case at the International Criminal Court for the destruction of the shrines.[25] In Yemen, the Saudi-led intervention from 2015 has not only unleashed mass human suffering, but has also led to the destruction of many significant cultural heritage sites across the country.[26] In this instance, however, the international community has proved reticent to confront the Saudi-led coalition and its US and UK backers over the destruction of heritage. As recent research has shown, even UNESCO has proven ineffective in lobbying powerful Member states to cease the suffering and destruction.[27]

With the onset of the Syrian civil war (2011–present) and the war against ISIS in Iraq (2014–17), the issue of the obligation to protect cultural property during conflict once again came to the fore. This was especially pronounced after Islamist factions such as Jabhat al-Nusra and ISIS captured significant territory and began to destroy various historical and religious sites from 2012

[22] Zainab Bahrani, "The Battle for Babylon" in Peter Stone and Joanne Farchakh Bajjaly (eds), *The Destruction of Cultural Heritage in Iraq* (Boydell 2008); Mariam Moussa, "The Damages Sustained to the Ancient City of Babel as a Consequence of the Military Presence of Coalition Forces in 2003" in Peter Stone and Joanne Farchakh Bajjaly (eds), *The Destruction of Cultural Heritage in Iraq* (Boydell 2008).

[23] Benjamin Isakhan, "Heritage Destruction and Spikes in Violence: The Case of Iraq" in Joris D Kila and James A Zeidler (eds), *Cultural Heritage in the Crosshairs: Protecting Cultural Property during Conflict* (Brill 2013).

[24] Gerstenblith, "The 1954 Hague Convention on the Protection of Cultural Property in the Event of Armed Conflict" (n 9); Gerstenblith, "The Obligations Contained in International Treaties of Armed Forces to Protect Cultural Heritage in Times of Armed Conflict" (n 9).

[25] Ana Filipa Vrdoljak, "Introductory Note to Prosecutor v Ahmad Al Faqi Al Mahdi: Judgment and Sentence and Reparations Order (International Criminal Court)" (2018) 57 International Legal Materials.

[26] Lamya Khalidi, "The Destruction of Yemen and Its Cultural Heritage" (2017) 49 International Journal of Middle East Studies.

[27] Lynn Meskell and Benjamin Isakhan, "UNESCO, World Heritage and Gridlock: Failing to Confront the Saudi-led Intervention in Yemen" (2020) 41 Third World Quarterly.

onward. Of the many significant historical and religious sites deliberately targeted and destroyed by these Islamist factions, that of the ancient archaeological site of Palmyra in Syria garnered perhaps the most attention.

In May 2015, Palmyra was the scene of heavy fighting between ISIS and Assad forces, and by the end of the month ISIS had captured the ancient city.[28] Between June and October 2015, ISIS went on to do a great deal of damage at Palmyra, including the destruction of seven funerary monuments dating to the first and second centuries CE; 2,000-year-old temples dedicated to pagan gods, the Baalshamin Temple, and the Temple of Bel; and the Arch of Triumph, an 1,800-year-old structure that framed the entrance to the city.[29] Such events were widely covered in the international media and UNESCO described the destruction at Palmyra as evidence of "how terrified by history and culture the extremists are . . . and exposes [their heritage destruction] as expressions of pure hatred and ignorance."[30] In March 2016, the Assad regime, backed by Russian air support, "liberated" Palmyra only to lose it to ISIS in December 2016. The following month, January 2017, ISIS destroyed the Roman-era Tetrapylon that dated back to the first century CE. In March 2017, the ancient city was retaken by the Syrian military, once again with Russian support.

The protracted battle in and around the ancient city of Palmyra prompted some to argue that the international community or state governments should engage in some form of military action to protect Palmyra. A storm of controversy erupted in Britain when Boris Johnson, then Mayor of London, opined that the United Kingdom must fight to save Palmyra, a site he claimed was emblematic of the "very idea of our Western civilization and what we stand for." He called upon British forces, already engaged in the fight against ISIS, to take action via "some kind of exclusion zone around the site, or at least for air strikes."[31] This call to use coordinated airstrikes to protect the ancient ruins received some support from the British press but did not materialize

[28] Mandie Sami, "Islamic State: Militants within Kilometres of Syria's Palmyra Raising Fear for Ancient City" (*ABC News*, 15 May 2015).

[29] Michael Danti and others, "American School of Oriental Research Cultural Heritage Initiatives: Planning for Safeguarding Heritage Sites in Syria and Iraq" (2–15 September 2015) Weekly Report 57–58; Michael Danti, Alison Cuneo, Marina Gabriel, Susan Penacho, Kyra Kaercher, Lee Ann Barnes Gordon, Emily Ham, and John O'Neill, "American School of Oriental Research Cultural Heritage Initiatives: Planning for Safeguarding Heritage Sites in Syria and Iraq" (30 September–13 October 2015) Weekly Report 61–62.

[30] Irina Bokova, "Director-General Condemns the Destruction of the Arch of Triumph in Palmyra" (*UNESCO Office in Beirut*, 5 October 2015).

[31] Boris Johnson, "We Must Save Palmyra or the Maniacs will Raze Civilization" (*The Telegraph*, 17 May 2015).

into military action.[32] Others framed their plea to protect Palmyra within the "Responsibility to Protect" doctrine, arguing it could be expanded from the protection of human life to those cultural assets that have shaped the history and identity of both local citizens and the global community.[33] This led to calls for some form of "Cultural Peacekeeping" (CPK) force to be integrated into international operations.[34] Along these lines, in 2016 UNESCO partnered with the Italian government to create a specialized unit designed to protect cultural property in conflict, later nicknamed the "Blue Helmets for Culture."[35]

The notion that the international community ought to use military force to protect heritage sites during the conflicts in Syria and Iraq received some support from the interviewees. As one Sunni Arab man from Baghdad put it: "I wish there was international guardianship over cultural heritage sites. There are international platforms and organizations which can set rules to protect the sites. They can put sites under international protection till the circumstances of violence change."[36] One respondent, a female Assyrian Christian from Dohuk, specifically named the "USA," "other Western countries," and the "Iraqi government"[37] as having some responsibility to protect heritage sites during conflict. Another interviewee focused on "international organisations like UNESCO," arguing that they "must take the role for protection of heritage sites. There must be international funds to support the protection of heritage sites."[38] Others were more specific, agreeing that some kind of international military deployment would be necessary to protect

[32] Rowan Moore, "Coalition Air Strikes Should Defend Palmyra—It Belongs to the Whole World" (*The Guardian*, 17 May 2015); Jonathan Jones, "Palmyra: Is Saving Priceless Antiquity as Important as Saving People?" (*The Guardian*, 19 May 2015).

[33] Federico Lenzerini, "Terrorism, Conflicts and the Responsibility to Protect Cultural Heritage" (2016) 51 The International Spectator: International Journal of International Affairs; Thomas Weiss and Nina Connelly, "Protecting Cultural Heritage in War Zones" (2019) 40 Third World Quarterly.

[34] Paolo Foradori and Paolo Rosa, "Expanding the Peacekeeping Agenda: The Protection of Cultural Heritage in War-Torn Societies" (2017) 29 Global Change, Peace & Security.

[35] UNESCO, Resolution 48 adopted by the General Conference at its 38th session, Paris, 3–18 November 2015, 41 accessed 9 March 2016; "UNESCO Director-General: 'Protecting Culture Is a Moral Responsibility and a Security Issue'" (*UNESCO Media Services*, 16 February 2016) <http://www.unesco.org/new/en/media-services/single-view/news/unesco_director_general_protecting_culture_is_a_moral_resp/> accessed 7 November 2018. However, at the time of writing, the unit had not been deployed due to a lack of operation guidelines.

[36] Interview via Phone (Amman, Jordan) with Male Sunni Arab from Baghdad now living in Ramadi (Ramadi, Iraq, July 2017).

[37] Interview via Phone/Skype (Amman, Jordan) Female Assyrian Christian from Dohuk (Dohuk, Iraq, May 2018).

[38] Interview via Phone/Skype (Melbourne, Australia) with Male Sunni Arab from Aleppo, Syria (Tubingen, Germany, December 2017).

heritage during times of conflict. As one Syriac Catholic man from Baghdad put it:

> It is always about protection—they need special forces to send to Iraq to keep guarding all these places, the churches and all the heritage in Iraq. And to protect it they should not be Iraqis. They should be a special force and they should be supported and not afraid of anyone.[39]

Some in the international community, however, have expressed grave reservations about the ethics of using international military forces to protect heritage sites in Syria and Iraq. One such concern was that these operations would fail unless they engaged with local civil society, heritage experts, and communities, thereby securing their active participation in the heritage protection process.[40] Another concern was the potential ethical dilemmas that such forces would face, including the privileging (or the perception of privileging) the protection of heritage sites over the loss of human life.[41] Not surprisingly, several respondents shared these ethical concerns about protecting heritage in the midst of such large-scale human suffering. As one Sunni Arab woman from Damascus put it:

> As long as there's conflict, there's going to be destruction of sites. Unless you deploy UN forces just to those sites. But then what are you saying to the people? People can die, that's okay, as long as you don't [destroy heritage]—that's awful. What kind of symbol are you trying to say then? The message that you're sending is that these heritage sites are more important than lives or hospitals or schools that are being destroyed.[42]

Beyond the deployment of military forces to protect heritage sites, another response from the international community concerning the protection of heritage sites in Syria and Iraq were various efforts to stanch the revenues raised by groups such as ISIS via the illicit looting of archaeological sites and

[39] Interview with Male Syriac Catholic Christian from Baghdad (Marka, Jordan, August 2018).

[40] Gabriele D'amico Soggetti, "Blue Helmets for Culture: Involving Communities in the Protection of their Heritage" in Evelyn Lagrange, Stefan Oeter, and Robert Uerpmann-Wittzack (eds), *Cultural Heritage and International Law: Objects, Means and Ends of International Protection* (Springer 2018).

[41] Erich Hatala Matthes, "'Saving Lives or Saving Stones?' The Ethics of Cultural Heritage Protection in War" (2018) 32 Public Affairs Quarterly; Helen Frowe and Derek Matravers, "Conflict and Cultural Heritage: A Moral Analysis of the Challenges of Heritage Protection" (2019) 3 J Paul Getty Trust Occasional Papers in Cultural Heritage Policy.

[42] Interview with Female Sunni Arab from Damascus (Melbourne, Australia, August 2017).

their sale on the international black market for antiquities. In an address at the UN General Assembly, UNESCO Director-General Irina Bokova referred to the looting as "taking place on an industrial scale."[43] Although the exact profits made by ISIS from such looting operations are difficult to determine, one report by the US State Department estimated that the minimum revenue generated by ISIS at just one archaeological site was $1.25 million. As a result, they calculated that in the twelve months following mid-2014, ISIS had "probably earned several million dollars from antiquities sales."[44] UNESCO's lobbying led to the adoption of UN Security Council Resolution 2199 in February 2015, which explicitly recognized the connection between the illegal looting of antiquities and regional security—and requested that UNESCO coordinate with Interpol to stem the flow of illicit antiquities onto the international black market. As Brodie has pointed out, however, the international community has largely failed to be effective in stopping the trade in antiquities because it has focused on protecting sites from looting or returning artifacts rather than on addressing the demand for relics and the shadowy black market that sates this demand.[45]

Despite such limitation, several respondents were in favor of international efforts to prevent the illegal looting of archaeological sites. One interviewee, a Sunni Arab man from Mosul, called upon the international community to do more to address the global black market in antiquities, stating that:

> I wish something can be done to stop illegal smuggling of antiquities in conflicts. Unfortunately there is no international support in this regard. The black market is shady and there are many antiquity traders who have great influence, some countries and even international museums are involved in this operation . . . We should, as Iraqis, protect our heritage. We should fight and prevent illegal excavation and smuggling of antiquities in Iraq so we can end this international web.[46]

[43] "Address by Irina Bokova, Director-General of UNESCO on the Occasion of the Conference "Conflict Antiquities: Forging a Public/Private Response to Save the Endangered Patrimony of Iraq and Syria" (*UN General Assembly*, New York, 29 September 2015).

[44] Andrew Keller, *Documenting ISIL's Antiquities Trafficking: The Looting and Destruction of Iraqi and Syrian Cultural Heritage: What We Know and What Can Be Done* (US Department of State 2015).

[45] Brodie (n 3).

[46] Interview via Phone/Skype (Melbourne, Australia) with Male Sunni Arab from Mosul (Istanbul, Turkey, November 2017).

Others proposed several new initiatives that would help to curtail the black market in antiquities. For example, one Shia Arab man from Baghdad not only recommended increased policing of the trade in antiquities, but that any recovered antiquities should be returned to their country of origin once the conflict had abated. As he put it:

> Perhaps the international community can put pressure on the international police or on the countries where the antiquities smuggle through. I think more scrutiny and surveillance are needed on illegal looting and smuggling. There should be also an agreement between Iraq, for example and the countries where the antiquities are found, to keep them in a safe place and return them to Iraq after the war has completely ended.[47]

Another response from the international community concerning heritage protection in Syria and Iraq consisted of global discussions pertaining to the relevant international legal frameworks used to prosecute those who commit acts of heritage destruction during times of conflict. As Cunliffe et al. point out, there are several relevant bodies of law—international customary law, various national laws, and treaty law (such as the Hague Convention)—under which perpetrators can be held to account for crimes against cultural property.[48] Despite the case of Ahmed Al-Faqi Al-Mahdi of Ansar al-Dine, it remains extremely difficult to apply these laws to non-state actors such as ISIS.

Nonetheless, the respondents were generally in agreement that there ought to be more robust international legal frameworks concerning cultural property protection in conflict and more effective ways of prosecuting the perpetrators on the international stage. As one Sunni Arab man from Mosul put it:

> The first advice is to make international laws to protect these sites and criminalize the perpetrators . . . Hatra, Nimrud and Palmyra in Syria . . . All people look at these as remains of civilization. I hope there are international

[47] Interview via Phone/Skype (Melbourne, Australia) with Male Shia Arab from Baghdad (Iraq). Now living in (Detroit, United States, November 2017).

[48] Emma Cunliffe, Nibal Muhesen, and Marina Lostal, "The Destruction of Cultural Property in the Syrian Conflict: Legal Implications and Obligations" (2016) 23 International Journal of Cultural Property.

> laws to preserve these as internationally recognized cultural sites not only local Iraqi or Syrian heritage.[49]

Others went even further, arguing that relevant international laws must not only prosecute the perpetrators of heritage destruction per se, but also the foreign powers that financed the rise of these non-state actors in the first place. As one Sunni Kurd man from Sulaymaniyah argued: "the countries who have exported or created ISIL or provided logistic support for ISIL acts should be punished by the international community. Otherwise, we will have different other versions of ISIL in the future."[50]

Despite broad agreement that the international community ought to protect heritage during conflict via military deployment, end looting and, prosecute the perpetrators, several other respondents expressed disappointment and cynicism concerning the failures to protect heritage sites in Syria and Iraq and across the broader Middle East. As one interviewee, a Greek Orthodox Christian man from Aleppo, put it:

> The international community did not do anything, for people and for heritage. The international community unfortunately failed in really fulfilling its responsibility towards the whole of humanity and history. The international community failed to safeguard the culture in Yemen, failed in preserving the culture in Palmyra, failed in protecting the heritage in Afghanistan . . . but this will return more negative impacts on the international society. Because people who lose everything and become hopeless, they will not have any incentive or any motivation to work for human justice or to work for social cohesion . . . When you see broken people, people who have really lost their dignity in life, you see them living in misery today. So I mean the international community is responsible for what happened, is responsible for what will happen in the future.[51]

More to the point, several respondents were very skeptical that there could be any kind of robust international protection of heritage sites during the ongoing conflicts in Syria and Iraq. They offered nuanced views and pointed

[49] Interview via Phone/Skype (Amman, Jordan) with Male Sunni Arab from Mosul (Mosul, Iraq, March 2017).

[50] Interview with Male Sunni Kurd from Sulaymaniyah (Sulaymaniyah, Iraqi Kurdistan, May 2017).

[51] Interview via Phone/Skype (Melbourne, Australia) with Male Greek Orthodox Christian from Aleppo (Beirut, Lebanon, October 2017).

out the various factors that limited the protection of heritage during complex asymmetric civil wars and the fact that many perpetrators were non-state actors. As one respondent, a Sunni Arab man from Mosul, pointed out: "international protection during ISIL rule is not practical because these people do not believe or deal with the international community and its institutions."[52] Another interviewee agreed, a Sunni Arab man from Mosul, stating that if ISIS "don't care about people how do you expect them to care about heritage?"[53]

III. Awareness Raising and Education Programs about Heritage

The second key response from the international community has been the launch of several awareness raising initiatives and education programs concerning heritage and heritage destruction issues in Syria and Iraq. Among the most prominent examples have been those run and promoted by the world's foremost multilateral institution concerned with the protection of heritage, UNESCO. Born of the horrors of World War II, UNESCO was established by the international community to foster global peace via various educational, scientific, and cultural initiatives and awareness raising programs. An essential component of UNESCO's mission has centered around heritage sites it deems to be of "outstanding universal value" in the belief that such sites hold the capacity to promote shared understandings of the past as a pathway to a tolerant and peaceful future.[54] To label a heritage site as being of "outstanding universal value," however, has proved contentious and politically charged. Critics have pointed to the problems inherent in imposing one overarching set of criteria that fails to acknowledge the unique and divergent ways in which heritage sites are valued by local communities.[55] Other scholars have

[52] Interview via Phone/Skype (Amman, Jordan) with Male Sunni Arab from Mosul (Mosul, Iraq, March 2017).

[53] Interview via Phone/Skype (Melbourne, Australia) with Male Shia Arab from Baghdad (Detroit, USA, November 2017).

[54] Lynn Meskell, *A Future in Ruins: UNESCO, World Heritage and the Dream of Peace* (OUP 2018).

[55] Chiara De Cesari, "World Heritage and Mosaic Universalism" (2010) 10 Journal of Social Archaeology; Sophia Labadi, *UNESCO, Cultural Heritage and Outstanding Universal Value* (Alta Mira Press 2013); Nathalie Peutz, *Islands of Heritage: Conservation and Transformation in Yemen* (Stanford UP 2018); Sarah Titchen, "On the Construction of "Outstanding Universal Value": Some Comments on the Implementation of the 1972 UNESCO World Heritage Convention" (1996) 1 Conservation and Management of Archaeological Sites.

accused the process of being Eurocentric,[56] reflected in the fact that a significant proportion of "world" heritage sites are located in Europe[57] and that UNESCO apparently views cultures and their heritage as monolithic, stagnant, and coherent.[58] Further literature has underscored the highly politicized process of inscribing sites,[59] including the fact that debates over inscription have become a proxy for broader geopolitical struggles and competing agendas between states.[60] Further debate has ensued over UNESCO's handling of conflict, particularly when it has involved the deliberate destruction of heritage sites, including those on the World Heritage List.[61]

The agency's awareness raising and advocacy function is best espoused by their vast program of media engagement, public statements made by the Director-General; the funding of exhibitions, workshops, and conferences; as well as its ever-growing online presence, all of which were mobilized in response to the wave of heritage destruction that swept across Syria and Iraq, especially at the hands of ISIS. For example, in March 2014, UNESCO launched the Emergency Safeguarding of Syrian Cultural Heritage Project with funding from the European Union. This was principally an awareness raising tool designed to monitor the destruction and disseminate information about it to national and international audiences.[62] Along similar lines, UNESCO also released several extensive damage assessment reports of key heritage sites in Syria and Iraq such as the Old City of Aleppo and the ancient archaeological site of Nimrud.[63] Significant awareness raising tools

[56] Trinidad Rico, "Negative Heritage: The Place of Conflict in World Heritage" (2008) 10 Conservation and Management of Archaeological Sites; Trinidad Rico, *The Making of Islamic Heritage: Muslim Pasts and Heritage Presents* (Palgrave Macmillan 2017).

[57] Henry Cleere, "The Concept of "Outstanding Universal Value" in the World Heritage Convention" (1996) 1 Conservation and Management of Archaeological Sites.

[58] Thomas Hylland Eriksen, "Between Universalism and Relativism: A Critique of the UNESCO Concept of Culture" in Jane Cowan, Maroie-Benedicte Dembour and Richard Wilson (eds), *Culture and Rights: Anthropological Perspectives* (CUP 2012).

[59] Marko Scholze, "Arrested Heritage: The Politics of Inscription into the UNESCO World Heritage List: The Case of Agadez in Niger" (2008) 13 Journal of Material Culture.

[60] Lynn Meskell, "Gridlock: UNESCO, Global Conflict and Failed Ambitions" (2015) 47 World Archaeology.

[61] Sigrid van der Auwera, "UNESCO and the Protection of Cultural Property during Armed Conflict" (2013) 19 International Journal of Cultural Policy; Sigrid van der Auwera, "'Culture for Development' and the UNESCO Policy on the Protection of Cultural Property during Armed Conflict" (2014) 20 International Journal of Cultural Policy; Cunliffe, Muhesen, and Lostal (n 48); Meskell and Isakhan (n 27).

[62] "The Emergency Safeguarding of the Syrian Cultural Heritage Project" (2014) Observatory of Syrian Cultural Heritage.

[63] "UNESCO Reports on Extensive Damage in First Emergency Assessment Mission to Aleppo" (*UNESCO News,* 19 January 2017) <http://whc.unesco.org/en/news/1619/> accessed 12 November 2018; "UNESCO Director General Sends Rapid Assessment Mission to the Nimrud Archaeological

deployed by UNESCO have included the catalogue of statements released by former Director-General Irina Bokova in which she condemned the ongoing heritage destruction in Syria and Iraq, especially that conducted by ISIS. These garnered wide media attention, particularly when she called for a UN Security Council meeting after ISIS attack on the Mosul Museum, describing it as "far more than a cultural tragedy—this is also a security issue as it fuels sectarianism, violent extremism and conflict."[64] She later referred to the destruction of the Assyrian city of Nimrud in Iraq as a "war crime"[65] and, following the destruction of the Arch of Triumph at Palmyra, threatened to work closely with the International Criminal Court "to ensure that the perpetrators of these acts of destruction are tried and punished."[66] A final example of a UNESCO-led awareness raising initiative is the "#Unite4Heritage" campaign. Launched in March 2015 by Bokova from Baghdad University, this social media campaign, consisting of a Twitter account and a website,[67] holds the lofty ambition of harnessing "the power of social networks to create a global movement to protect and safeguard heritage under threat."[68] While UNESCO's goal to raise awareness about heritage destruction and to mobilize people to protect it is admirable, the actual mechanisms by which it hopes to ensure that mission are largely digital and severely underfunded. More to the point, as Al Quntar and Daniels point out, the bulk of such awareness raising initiatives and education programs have been limited to the collection and dissemination of information about heritage destruction across Syria and Iraq with comparatively few projects raising awareness or implementing any form of heritage education inside the two countries.[69]

Despite such criticisms, most respondents felt that such education and awareness raising programs about heritage—its value, destruction, and reconstruction—were an effective way in which the international community could enact meaningful change. A few interviewees, however, offered

Site in Iraq" (*UNESCO News*, 14 December 2016) <https://whc.unesco.org/en/news/1611/> accessed 12 November 2018.

[64] Irina Bokova, "Director-General Requests UN Security Council Meeting in Destruction of Heritage in Mosul" (*UNESCO Press*, 26 February 2015).

[65] Irina Bokova, "UNESCO Director-General Condemns Destruction of Nimrud in Iraq" (*UNESCO Media Services*, 6 March 2015).

[66] Bokova (n 30).

[67] The Twitter handle is @Unite4Heritage and the URL is <http://www.unite4heritage.org>.

[68] "#Unite 4 Heritage campaign launched by UNESCO Director-General in Baghdad" (*UNESCO Media Services*, 28 March 2015).

[69] Salam Al Quntar and Brian I Daniels, "Responses to the Destruction of Syrian Cultural Heritage: A Critical Review of Current Efforts" (2016) 5 International Journal of Islamic Architecture.

generic advice to improve these types of programs. A typical response was given by one Shia Arab man from Baghdad:

> They [the international community] can also contribute to educating and raising awareness of our society. This is one of the priorities because our society is in dire need to be educated on the significance of cultural sites. They need to know about their history and civilization, which, if extinct, their identity will be extinct too.[70]

The respondents also pointed to the need for media campaigns,[71] community awareness programs,[72] and a reform of the education system[73] in order to raise awareness about the significance and value of Syria's and Iraq's rich cultural heritage. Along these lines, one Sunni Arab man from Mosul stated:

> . . . to minimize the destruction of heritage sites during conflicts and wars . . . [you need to] educate people. We should educate young people about the importance and value of these sites and how we can protect them . . . There is nothing in the curriculum, [even] in first and second year university, explaining the value of these sites as well as the way we [can] protect them during times of war and armed conflict. So I think education is the first step.[74]

Other interviewees also highlighted the need to understand the motives and ideologies that underpinned the violence and destruction wrought by ISIS. For example, another Sunni Arab man from Mosul stated that:

> [The international community can play a meaningful role] through educating young generations about the destruction that happened at the hands of *Da'esh*. The UNESCO, for example, with its amazing programs of education might be able to initiate something like this . . . Children should

[70] Interview via Phone/Skype (Amman, Jordan) with Male Shia Arab from Baghdad (Baghdad, Iraq, June 2017).

[71] Interview via Phone/Skype (Amman, Jordan) with Male Shia Arab from Baghdad (Baghdad, Iraq, June 2017).

[72] Interview via Phone/Skype (Melbourne, Australia) with Male Shia Arab from Baghdad (Detroit, USA, November 2017).

[73] Interview with Male Sunni Kurd from Qamishli, Syria (Sulaymaniyah, Iraqi Kurdistan, May 2017).

[74] Interview via Phone/Skype (Melbourne, Australia) with Male Sunni Arab from Mosul (Istanbul, Turkey, November 2017).

> always be reminded of what happened to the heritage sites. And I think the best way is through education. Each site destroyed should have a label and a story telling how it was destroyed so that the young generation will not forget.[75]

For other respondents, the issue was not so much educating people about *heritage per se*, but about fostering a broader cosmopolitan ethic that imbued respect for other cultures, religions, and traditions. As one Chaldean Christian man from Koya argued, the antidote to the manifold problems unleashed by ISIS,

> is raising awareness of the dangers of fundamentalism . . . raising awareness that this person is like you. He has a nose and two eyes like you and he is a human being. He has a heart, a family and he deserves to be respected . . . We must tackle the mind-set to have a civil mentality, to have a humanitarian way of thinking not military or religious.[76]

Many other respondents, however, were less concerned about awareness raising programs regarding heritage issues inside Syria and Iraq as they were the need to educate the outside world about the mass human suffering unleashed by ISIS. This was especially true of respondents belonging to those minority communities that were specifically targeted by ISIS, such as Yezidis and Christians. As one Yezidi woman from Bashiqa explained:

> Each story that happened with each member of the Yezidi and Christian community must reach to the world and the world should provide to the minorities international protection in their areas . . . I hope for the world and the UN to find solutions to satisfy everybody and to live and see each other as part of humanity before everything else, before resources and religions. There are children who became homeless, orphans were killed and raped. There are lost children and captive women, and families with no houses or money.[77]

[75] Interview via Phone/Skype (Melbourne, Australia) with Male Sunni Arab from Mosul (Amsterdam, the Netherlands, December 2017).

[76] Interview via Phone/Skype (Amman, Jordan) with Male Chaldean Christian from Koya, Iraqi Kurdistan (Erbil, Iraqi Kurdistan, May 2018).

[77] Interview via Phone/Skype (Amman, Jordan) with Female Yezidi from Bashiqa, Iraq (Bashiqa, Iraq, July 2018).

IV. Reconstructing Heritage Sites After Conflict

The third axis revolves around the extent to which a concerted international effort ought to be made to reconstruct heritage sites across Syria and Iraq. The reconstruction of heritage sites, however, is perhaps as politically charged as their destruction. Who decides what should be rebuilt, by whom, when, and for what purpose?[78] Should destroyed heritage sites be left in ruins to commemorate the horrors of war?[79] Could heritage reconstruction play a role in peacebuilding and a renewed sense of national solidarity after the end of hostilities?[80] Or would heritage reconstruction further the agenda of oppressive regimes or militant actors, thus exacerbating tensions and leading to renewed violence and iconoclasm?[81] Or is heritage reconstruction neither a positive or negative part of (post-)conflict renewal, but rather an inevitable process via which negotiations over the past play a vital role in the present?[82]

These questions are far from new. Following the Spanish Civil War of the second half of the 1930s, several heritage reconstruction projects were launched. Such projects have been criticized for underpinning the emergence of a new and repressive state identity.[83] Along similar lines, some research has suggested that the externally driven preservation of Angkor in Cambodia in the 1990s helped legitimize the brutal Khmer Rouge regime.[84] A different scenario played out in the post-civil war reconstruction of Beirut which was critiqued not for its political failures but for its privileging of renewed commercial and economic activity, appealing mostly to tourists and

[78] Chiara De Cesari and Rosita Dimova, "Heritage, Gentrification, Participation: Remaking Urban Landscapes in the Name of Culture and Historic Preservation" (2018) 25 International Journal of Heritage Studies.

[79] J John Lennon and Malcolm Foley, *Dark Tourism: The Attraction of Death and Disaster* (Continuum 2000); William Logan and Keir Reeves (eds), *Places of Pain and Shame: Dealing with "Difficult Heritage"* (Routledge 2009).

[80] Roha Khalaf, "A Viewpoint on the Reconstruction of Destroyed UNESCO Cultural World Heritage Sites" (2017) 23 International Journal of Heritage Studies; Lynn Meskell and Colette Scheermeyer, "Heritage as Therapy: Set Pieces from the New South Africa" (2008) 13 Journal of Material Culture.

[81] Nour Munawar, "Reconstructing Cultural Heritage in Conflict Zones: Should Palmyra be Rebuilt?" (2017) 2 EX NOVO: Journal of Archaeology; Dacia Viejo-Rose, *Reconstructing Spain: Cultural Heritage and Memory after Civil War* (Sussex Academic Press 2011).

[82] John Daniel Giblin, "Post-Conflict Heritage: Symbolic Healing and Cultural Renewal" (2014) 20 International Journal of Heritage Studies.

[83] Dacia Viejo-Rose, *Reconstructing Spain: Cultural Heritage and Memory after Civil War* (Sussex Academic Press 2011).

[84] Michael Falser, "Representing Heritage without Territory: The Khmer Rouge at the UNESCO in Paris during the 1980s and their Political Strategy for Angkor" in Michael Falser (ed), *Cultural Heritage as Civilizing Mission* (Springer 2015).

a few urban elites, over fostering social cohesion and a return to peace.[85] Following the Balkans conflict of the 1990s, several major initiatives were launched to reconstruct heritage sites. The reconstruction of sites such as the Stari Most bridge in Mostar, however, was criticized for not only failing to consult locals during the process,[86] but also that the UNESCO-led reconstruction was a staged affair for largely international audiences: the bridge a symbol of peace and stability in the center of a city still riven with tension.[87]

In Afghanistan, UNESCO has spearheaded a swathe of projects seeking to reconstruct various heritage sites across the country with the support of the US State Department and the Agha Khan Trust for Culture.[88] These include the reconstruction of several significant religious and historical buildings in the Old City of Herat and the National Museum of Afghanistan where they not only repaired the building but did extensive restorative work on many of the sculptures destroyed by the Taliban.[89] In terms of the Bamiyan Buddhas, UNESCO, Afghan authorities, and various other stakeholders have frequently disagreed over whether or not to reconstruct the statues. The Afghan government and some local residents of the Bamiyan Valley would like to see them reconstructed in the hope of rekindling tourism and a renewed sense of national solidarity in the wake of the crimes of the Taliban.[90] UNESCO, however, has frequently cautioned against the reconstruction on technocratic grounds, arguing that it would be extremely difficult given their size, location, and the fact that the original materials were almost entirely destroyed in the blasts.[91] This led to a collaboration between UNESCO and the German branch of ICOMOS to preserve the remains of the Buddhas and the niches where they once stood as best as possible.[92] In the absence of the physical reconstruction of the Buddhas, the project also included the creation of 3D

[85] Caroline A Sandes, "Remembering Beirut: Lessons for Archaeology and (Post-) Conflict Urban Redevelopment in Aleppo" (2017) 2 EX NOVO: Journal of Archaeology.

[86] Walasek (n 16).

[87] Susan Forde, "The Bridge of the Neretva: Stari Most as a Stage of Memory in Post-Conflict Mostar, Bosnia-Herzegovina" (2016) 51 Cooperation and Conflict.

[88] Brendan Cassar and Sara Noshadi (eds), *Keeping History Alive: Safeguarding Cultural Heritage in Post-Conflict Afghanistan* (UNESCO 2015).

[89] Stein (n 17); Aga Khan Trust for Culture in Afghanistan, "The Herat Old City Area Development Programme: Public, Religious and Residential Buildings in the Historic Quarter" in Brendan Cassar and Sara Noshadi (eds), *Keeping History Alive: Safeguarding Cultural Heritage in Post-Conflict Afghanistan* (UNESCO 2015).

[90] Kiko Itasaka, "Should Afghanistan's Bamiyan Buddhas be Rebuilt?" (*NBC News*, 29 November 2017).

[91] Bokova (n 30).

[92] Michael Petzet, "Preserving the Fragments of the Buddha's of Bamiyan and their Future Preservation" in Brendan Cassar and Sara Noshadi (eds), *Keeping History Alive: Safeguarding Cultural Heritage in Post-Conflict Afghanistan* (UNESCO 2015).

digital models of the Buddhas which were re-created in an immersive virtual reality environment at a university in Aachen in 2009.[93] In 2015, a Chinese couple managed to project a life-size laser 3D model of the Buddhas onto the cavities left by the destruction with the approval of UNESCO.[94]

Following the initial wave of heritage destruction during the Iraq War, several heritage reconstruction projects were launched. At the Iraq National Museum, UNESCO partnered with key Iraqi, American, Italian, and other national governments to refit the museum, including restoring collections and storage facilities, laboratories and equipment, as well as the restoration of certain objects damaged during the war.[95] After nearly twelve years, the site was officially reopened in February 2015.[96] In 2008, the World Monuments Fund, in collaboration with Iraqi authorities and the US State Department, launched the "Future of Babylon" project to preserve and reconstruct the fragile archaeological remains at the ancient city.[97] This extensive project also saw evaluation, restoration, and reconstruction work done to the Ishtar Gate from 2017.[98] Finally, UNESCO led a project sponsored by the Iraqi Government and the European Union to rehabilitate and reconstruct the Al-Askari mosque over a four-year period from 2008.[99] The project not only included Iranian academics who were commissioned to document the damage done to the site,[100] it also used hundreds of local Iraqi contractors to do much of the clearing and reconstruction work. More importantly, UNESCO is said

[93] Georgios Toubekis and others, "Preservation and Management of the UNESCO World Heritage Site of Bamiyan: Laser Scan Documentation and Virtual Reconstruction of the Destroyed Buddha Figures and the Archaeological Remains" (2009) Proceedings XXII CIPA Symposium.

[94] Edward Delman, "Afghanistan's Buddhas Rise Again" (*The Atlantic*, 10 June 2015).

[95] Priscilla Singer, "The New American Approach to Cultural Heritage Protection: Granting Foreign Aid for Iraqi Cultural Heritage" (2010) 11 Chicago-Kent Journal of International and Comparative Law 27; "Restoring Conservation Labs of the Iraq National Museum" (*UNESCO Office for Iraq*) <http://www.unesco.org/new/en/iraq-office/culture/museum-sector/conservation-labs/> accessed 6 November 2018; Centro Ricerche Archeologiche e Scavi di Torino, "The Iraq Museum in Baghdad" accessed 6 November 2011.

[96] "Looted Iraqi Museum in Baghdad Reopens 12 years On" (*BBC News*, 28 February 2015).

[97] Singer (n 95).

[98] "The Future of Babylon" (*World Monument Fund*) <https://www.wmf.org/project/future-babylon> accessed 6 November 2018.

[99] "Restoration of Samara Al Askari Shrine" (*UNESCO Multimedia Archives*, 2011) <http://www.unesco.org/archives/multimedia/?pg=33&s=films_details&id=2801> accessed 6 November 2018; "UNESCO to Help Iraq Reconstruct Revered Al-Askari Shrine in Samarra" (*UN News*, 26 June 2007); "Samarra Shrine Restoration" (*UNESCO Office for Iraq*) <http://www.unesco.org/new/en/iraq-office/culture/samarra-shrine-restoration/> accessed on 6 November 2018.

[100] Mohammad Yekrangnia and Alireza Aghababai Mobarake, "Restoration of Historical Al-Askari shrine I: Field Observations, Damage Detection and Material Properties" (2016) 30 Journal of Performance of Constructed Facilities; Mohammad Yekrangnia and Alireza Aghababai Mobarake, "Restoration of Historical Al-Askari Shrine II: Vulnerability Assessment by Numerical Simulation" (2016) 30 Journal of Performance of Constructed Facilities.

to have regularly consulted with local civil society actors and with religious leaders who were regularly briefed on progress.[101] By April 2009, the mosque had been partially rebuilt and was reopened to visitors.[102]

Another UNESCO-led heritage reconstruction project followed the destruction of Sufi shrines in Timbuktu in Mali. Here, funds from the European Union enabled UNESCO to reconstruct the sites.[103] A crucial difference to earlier projects was the involvement of local people in the process which UNESCO claims has contributed to broader peacebuilding and reconciliation processes.[104] The project, however, has been criticized for privileging heritage reconstruction over addressing the extreme poverty and ongoing violence that has left both the local people and their heritage sites vulnerable to further waves of violence and iconoclasm.[105]

Despite the ongoing and asymmetric nature of the conflicts across both Syria and Iraq, several significant heritage reconstruction projects have already begun. These projects, however, have largely been developed and deployed to serve specific political agendas. For example, following the "liberation" of Palmyra from ISIS by the Assad regime with Russian air support in March 2016, several proposals to rebuild Palmyra were put forward including those by German and British institutions, while a replica of the Arch of Triumph was erected in London's Trafalgar Square in April 2016.[106] A storm of controversy followed UNESCO's support for Syrian and Russian plans to reconstruct parts of Palmyra. Upon capturing the site, Syrian and Russian authorities immediately began assessing the damage done across Palmyra and prepared detailed plans for reconstructing structures such as the Arch of Triumph.[107] Bokova endorsed the plans and offered UNESCO support for the reconstruction after talking with Russian President Vladimir Putin and Syrian counterparts.[108] Not surprisingly, UNESCO was heavily criticized for not only having failed to consider the potential ramifications of restoring such a significant site in the midst of the ongoing conflict, but also

[101] Usam Ghaidan, *Rebuilding the Al-Askariyyain Shrine in Samarra—Iraq* (UNESCO 2008).

[102] Martin Chulov, "Bombed Iraq Shrine Reopens to Visitors" (*The Guardian*, 17 April 2009).

[103] "Reconstruction of Timbuktu Mausoleums nears Completion" (*UNESCO News*, 2015) <http://whc.unesco.org/en/news/1307/> accessed 19 August 2017.

[104] "Director-General Praises the People of Timbuktu for the Reconstruction of the City's Mausoleums" (*UNESCO News*, 2015) accessed 19 August 2017.

[105] Charlotte Joy, "Crimes against Cultural Heritage in Timbuktu" (2018) 34 Anthropology Today.

[106] Lauren Turner, "Palmyra's Arch of Triumph Recreated in London" (*BBC News*, 19 April 2016).

[107] "Hope in Our Hearts": Syrian Antiquities Chief says Experts to Assess Damage in Palmyra within Days" (*Russia Today*, 27 March 2016).

[108] "UNESCO Director-General and President Vladimir Putin Discuss the Protection of Palmyra's Cultural Heritage" (*UNESCO*, 27 March 2016).

for taking a partisan position that could be perceived to celebrate the military victories of the Assad regime and the Russian military.[109] Apparently impervious to such criticisms, the Russian symphony orchestra performed a classical music concert at Palmyra in May 2016.[110] The following March, a joint Syrian and Russian project saw some restoration work at the site, including clearing it of mines and preparing it for tourists, which they expected to receive from mid-2019.[111]

In Iraq, 2017 saw UNESCO partner with the Iraqi Government to launch the Response Plan for Safeguarding of Cultural Heritage in the Liberated Areas of Iraq.[112] The following year, in February 2018, the Kuwait International Conference for the Reconstruction of Iraq saw some $30 billion donated, falling well short of Baghdad's appeal of $88 billion.[113] The largest donors were from across the Middle East: Saudi Arabia, Kuwait, Qatar, the UAE, and Turkey each contributed significant sums to the reconstruction and redevelopment of Iraq after the country was ravaged by ISIS. UNESCO's new Director-General, Audrey Azoulay, used the Kuwait conference to launch a new flagship project to "Revive the Spirit of Mosul."[114] According to her, the project was specifically designed to coordinate several initiatives to reconstruct the Old City of Mosul and other key religious and historical sites in and around the city.[115] The first and perhaps the largest such project began in April 2018 when an agreement was signed between Iraq, the UAE, UNESCO, and ICCROM in the Assyrian Hall of the Iraq National Museum in Baghdad.[116] The UAE provided $50.4 million over five years for the reconstruction of the Great Mosque of al-Nuri and its famous leaning minaret, known locally as *al-Hadba* (the hunchback).[117] In June 2014, IS leader Abu Bakr al-Baghdadi had used the mosque to announce the creation of his

[109] Florence Evin, "The Politics and Poetry of Restoring War Ruins" (*Gulf News*, 29 June 2016).

[110] Luka Harding, "Palmyra Hosts Russian Concert after Recapture by Syrian Forces" (*The Guardian*, 6 May 2016).

[111] Anna Sansom, "Syria's Palmyra to be Ready for Tourists by Summer 2019" (*The Art Newspaper*, 24 August 2018).

[112] "Revive the Spirit of Mosul" (*UNESCO*) <https://en.unesco.org/projects/the-spirit-of-mosul> accessed 6 November 2019.

[113] Maher Chmaytelli and Ahmed Hagagy, "Allies Promise Iraq $30 Billion, Falling Short of Baghdad's Appeal" (*Reuters*, 14 February 2018).

[114] "UNESCO Launches Flagship Initiative to Revive the Spirit of Mosul" (*UNESCO World Heritage Centre*, 14 February 2018).

[115] Audrey Azoulay, "Reviving the Spirit of Mosul" (*Asharq al-Awsat*, 17 February 2018).

[116] Mina al-Oraibi, "UAE Launches Greatest Cultural Restoration Project in Iraq to Revive Al Nuri Mosque" (*The National*, 23 April 2018).

[117] "UAE, UNESCO and Iraq Conclude Historic $50m Partnership to Reconstruct Mosul's Iconic Al-Nouri Mosque and Al-Hadba Minaret" (*UNESCO*, 23 April 2018).

new Caliphate. Three years later, in June 2017, during the final stages of the battle for Mosul, ISIS destroyed the site by detonating explosives inside it and reducing much of the twelfth-century CE mosque to rubble. The reconstruction plan not only includes a reconstruction of the mosque and its famous minaret—including its lean—but also the creation of a memorial and a museum on the site to document its history, including its destruction.[118] As with earlier projects, UNESCO has claimed that they will work closely with the people of Mosul to ensure that they are not only employed as part of the reconstruction team where possible but are also consulted throughout the project.[119] The project began in December 2018 with a symbolic ceremony to celebrate the laying of the mosque's foundation stone, attended mostly by political and religious dignitaries.[120]

These and other ongoing international efforts to reconstruct heritage sites in Syria and Iraq, however, received mixed reactions from the interviewees. Several respondents provided generic support for the notion that the international community should play a prominent role in reconstructing Syria's and Iraq's significant heritage sites that had been damaged or destroyed during the ongoing conflict. As one Sunni Arab man from Mosul noted, "The main demand of the masses is the restoration and rehabilitation of the religious places, mosques and churches which were attacked."[121] Indeed, many respondents saw great value in reconstructing key heritage sites moving forward. For example, some participants made statements like, "Of course, they [the international community] should play a role in restoration and reconstruction of key sites. The value of preserving and restoring these heritage sites is self-evident. They are the key symbols of human civilization and Syrian history."[122] Another respondent, a Kurdish man from Qamishli in Syria, urged institutions from within the "US, Australia and Europe working on cultural heritage [to] get involved in preserving the cultural heritage in these countries [Syria and Iraq] in coordination with the UN . . . These can do a great job."[123] Others focused on specific existing projects and agreed that

[118] Rebecca Spong, "UAE Backs Restoration of 'Symbolic' Mosul Mosque after Destruction by Daesh" (*Arab News*, 10 July 2018).
[119] ibid.
[120] "Foundation Stone Ceremony of the Al-Nouri Mosque in the Old City of Mosul" (*UNESCO Office for Iraq*, 17 December 2018).
[121] Interview via Phone/Skype (Amman, Jordan) with Male Sunni Arab from Zummar, Iraq (Mosul, Iraq, June 2017).
[122] Interview with Male Sunni Arab from Damascus, Syria (Bar Elias, Lebanon, October 2018).
[123] Interview with Male Sunni Kurd from Qamishli, Syria (Sulaymaniyah, Iraqi Kurdistan, May 2017).

they would succeed both in reconstructing the site and restoring peace. As one Shia Arab man from Baghdad put it:

> I think that it is important for Iraq to rebuild some of the heritage sites like the Al-Nuri Mosque. I think UNESCO and the international community will do a good job and the reconstruction will be a positive sign of peace for Iraq.[124]

Despite their being some support for international efforts to reconstruct heritage, other respondents were very clear that it ought to be Syrians or Iraqis who are ultimately responsible for the reconstruction of their heritage sites. One respondent, a Sunni Arab man from Homs, put it succinctly: "We don't want others to just come and rebuild it all for us. We destroyed it so we should rebuild it together."[125] To do so, some respondents called on the international community to invest not so much in reconstructing the sites themselves, but in teaching the relevant technical and trade skills to Syrians and Iraqis so that they could rebuild their own heritage. Typical of such responses, one Sunni Arab man from Zummar stated that: "whether in Iraq, Lebanon or Yemen . . . the international community can provide the technical support to scholars to repair damaged antiquities, develop and re-excavate heritage sites."[126] As another respondent put it:

> We cannot rebuild all this quickly. We need to be taught the right skills and need international support to get it right. But if we can rebuild it properly it would be very good for tourism and the economy. This is about the future of Syria—by rebuilding the past we can rebuild the future.[127]

For some, the very process of Syrians and Iraqis rebuilding their heritage could help to re-establish inter-community solidarity and herald a move toward a more peaceful future. As one Sunni Arab woman from Homs explained:

[124] Interview with Male Shia Arab from Baghdad (Amman, Jordan, October 2018).
[125] Interview with Male Sunni Arab from Homs, Syria (Mufraq, Jordan, October 2018).
[126] Interview via Phone/Skype (Amman, Jordan) with Male Sunni Arab from Zummar, Iraq (Mosul, Iraq, June 2017).
[127] Interview with Male Sunni Arab from Homs, Syria (Mufraq, Jordan, October 2018).

> The most important thing is security. To get security in Syria, you need to rebuild the relationships between different communities, to rebuild the trust. There is not much trust left between the different communities. Heritage can play a role—if we rebuild the Christian and Sunni and Alawi places together then we can rebuild the country.[128]

Other respondents were more concerned about the ethics of taking money from countries who had played problematic roles in the conflicts across Syria and Iraq and in some cases funded the rise of ISIS. For example, each of the Middle East states who donated funds for the reconstruction of Iraq at the February 2018 Kuwait Conference has been accused of either directly or indirectly funding ISIS militants. Both Kuwait and Qatar were accused of lax financial regulation, which enabled their citizens, as well as wealthy private donors from other Gulf states such as Saudi Arabia and the UAE, to send funds through to jihadists groups such as ISIS.[129] For its part, Turkey has been complicit in weapons, money, and foreign fighters flowing across its borders into Syria to bolster the efforts of various militant groups.[130] In other words, UNESCO is now taking funds to reconstruct Iraqi heritage sites from those who directly or indirectly funded the militants who destroyed the sites in the first place. While UNESCO has not commented publicly on this ethical dilemma, it was front of mind for some of the respondents. As one Syrian Orthodox Christian man from Mahardah put it:

> [In both Iraq and Syria, the] government wants to reconstruct many of these heritage and historical places. They have even been giving some of the contracts to Qatar and Turkey—these are the people responsible for the destruction. They funded different groups and let them come across the border. They caused the destruction and now they want to be paid to rebuild it. They should pay us.[131]

[128] Interview with Female Sunni Arab from Homs, Syria (Mufraq, Jordan, October 2018).

[129] Lori Plotkin Boghardt, *Saudi Funding of ISIS* (The Washington Institute for Near East Policy 2014); Lori Plotkin Boghardt, *The Terrorist Funding Disconnect with Qatar and Kuwait* (The Washington Institute for Near East Policy 2014).

[130] "Islamic State: Where Does Jihadist Group get its Support?" (*BBC News*, 1 September 2014).

[131] Interview with Male Syrian Orthodox Christian from Mahardah, Syria (Beirut, Lebanon, October 2018).

Focusing specifically on the UAE funding the UNESCO led-project to reconstruct the Great Mosque of al-Nuri and the *al-Hadba* minaret, one Sunni Arab woman from Khanaqin made her objections very clear:

> The reconstruction of the al-Nuri mosque is just politics. The UAE want to fund it because some of them are Wahhabi's and they funded *Da'esh* to do all this terrible destruction. It is Wahhabi ideology to kill Christians or Yezidis and to destroy historical sites and cultural sites. But now the Gulf countries are embarrassed by what *Da'esh* did so they want to show that they are for peace and don't believe in this violence. But they funded it, they created it . . . They gave money to *Da'esh* to make them powerful. But then they went crazy and so now the Gulf wants to pay some money to fix up the mess they made. I don't want their dirty money. I want them to leave us alone to live in peace.[132]

It is also worth noting that several respondents criticized the international emphasis on restoring ancient archaeological sites such as Palmyra over local religious sites. For example, one Sunni Arab man from Mosul stated that:

> I don't think we can rebuild the archaeological sites like Hatra or Nimrud but [instead] . . . All heritage sites of Yazidis, Christians should be rebuilt. All mosques should be rebuilt. We need to build a society where each ethnic and religious community heritage sites and traditions be respected and embraced.[133]

Other respondents, however, raised questions about who would use these minority religious sites if they were rebuilt. They pointed to the tension between rebuilding sites for Christian, Yezidi, and other minority communities and the fact that these same minorities were leaving their ancient homelands in large numbers. One stated: "They raise these buildings [churches] but Christians are fleeing, I do not know who will be using them. Only those who stay [which are] very few."[134]

[132] Interview with Female Sunni Arab from Khanaqin, Iraq (Beirut, Lebanon, October 2018).

[133] Interview via Phone/Skype (Melbourne, Australia) with Male Sunni Arab from Mosul (Amsterdam, the Netherlands, December 2017).

[134] Interview via Phone/Skype (Amman, Jordan) with Male Chaldean Christian from Koya, Iraqi Kurdistan (Erbil, Iraqi Kurdistan, May 2018).

Finally, it is important to mention that several respondents argued that reconstructing heritage sites simply was not an important priority given the complex set of political and humanitarian challenges facing contemporary Syria and Iraq. As one Sunni Arab man from Homs put it: "The most important thing we need is security and safety . . . Then we can begin to reconstruct and rebuild Syria."[135] Others went even further, questioning how heritage reconstruction could be considered a priority given the monumental humanitarian challenges. As one Sunni Kurdish man from Kirkuk put it:

> I am from Kirkuk and there is a huge need there. We have tension with Kurds and Arabs. We have sectarian violence. We have people starving, we have ladies who have been raped, we have kids with no school and all they have seen is violence and terror. Children raised on death and destruction. They need help: hospitals, schools, roads, psychology, jobs, food, water, electricity, education. We need hygiene and security and work. We don't need an old minaret. It was useless anyway . . . Heritage is not a priority for us.[136]

V. Conclusion

International projects to protect, promote, and reconstruct the heritage of Syria and Iraq are important and meaningful initiatives that could have a profound and positive impact on the future of the two countries. If these projects are to be successful, they must expand their efforts to create an ongoing dialogue with the local populations—despite their divergent and competing views—and create opportunities for their participation in and ownership over the future of heritage in Syria and Iraq. As this chapter has demonstrated, however, this is not an easy task. Understandably, the people of Syria and Iraq have difficult and divergent views of how to approach heritage protection, promotion, and reconstruction.

In terms of the first axis—namely, the role that the international community can or ought to play in protecting cultural property during times of conflict—the participants had nuanced views. Many argued that the international community should (and was obliged to) play a pivotal role in protecting key heritage sites in conflicts such as those in Syria and Iraq, because

[135] Interview with Male Sunni Arab from Homs, Syria (Mufraq, Jordan, October 2018).
[136] Interview with Male Sunni Kurd from Kirkuk, Iraq (Beirut, Lebanon, October 2018).

they were embroiled in the broader conflict and had the military and financial resources to do so. Some participants, however, were concerned about the ethics of using international forces to protect heritage sites, arguing that it must not come at the cost of saving human lives. The respondents also broadly supported international efforts to end the looting of archaeological sites and stanch the global trade in illicit artifacts—but also suggested that more ought to be done to police the antiquities trade and to return stolen objects to their country of origin. The respondents also agreed that more needed to be done to promulgate and utilize international legal frameworks to prosecute the perpetrators of heritage destruction, but also called for similar laws to be extended to hold the countries that supported the rise of ISIS to account for their crimes. Finally, the interviewees also expressed deep disappointment and cynicism about the role of the international community in Syria and Iraq to date, especially as it pertained to the protection of heritage.

The respondents were generally very supportive of initiatives that fall under the second axis—the role that the international community should engage in education programs and awareness-raising programs concerning heritage. Many respondents also argued that while education about heritage and its destruction was valid, there were three further knowledge gaps that the international community could help to address: raising awareness about the motives and ideologies that drove ISIS to destroy heritage sites in the first place; educational programs about the myriad ethnic and religious peoples of Syria and Iraq with a view to fostering inter-communal understanding and social cohesion; and the need to inform those in the West about the ongoing human suffering unleashed by ISIS.

Finally, initiatives under the third axis—the extent to which a concerted international effort ought to be made to reconstruct heritage sites in Syria and Iraq—were seen as largely misplaced by many of the respondents. On the one hand, there was some support for international involvement in the reconstruction of key heritage sites. On the other hand, however, many respondents raised concerns about the foreign funding of such reconstruction projects and the prioritizing of ancient archaeological sites over local places of worship. However it is done, most respondents thought that any reconstruction ought to be led by Syrians and Iraqis who urgently needed to be taught the relevant skills and trades to do it themselves. By doing so, as some respondents argued, the international community could not only facilitate heritage reconstruction, but foster a unique opportunity for different communities to work together toward a common goal. By literally rebuilding

Syria or Iraq together, the respondents hoped they could also rebuild the social structures and mutual understandings that had once underpinned their sense of a common national identity. Others did not agree, arguing that the heritage reconstruction, no matter who did it or with what intentions, was simply not a priority given the ongoing humanitarian crises facing contemporary Syria and Iraq.

These results point to the urgent need for further research to document the ways in which people in complex (post-)conflict environments such as Syria and Iraq value and engage with their heritage, how they perceive and interpret its destruction, and the role they envisage for the international community in protecting and then reconstructing their heritage sites. Engaging with the opinions of the various peoples across Syria and Iraq—even when their opinions are difficult, divergent or derisive—is perhaps the only way that international efforts to protect and restore heritage can have a meaningful long-term impact in the region. This would enable current and future heritage protection and reconstruction projects in (post-)conflict environments to be cognizant of local sentiment and to tailor their initiatives to best meet the needs and respect the values of the local communities. Failing to listen to and heed these opinions ultimately undermines the broader mission to foster stability and promote peace, and can fuel the propaganda machinery of Islamist groups such as ISIS.

14

The Geopolitical Context of Cultural Heritage Destruction

Carsten Paludan-Müller

I. Introduction

> *Es bleibt ein unumstößliches Gesetz der Geschichte, daß sie gerade den Zeitgenossen versagt, die Große Bewegungen, die ihre Zeit bestimmen, schon in ihren ersten Anfängen zu erkennen.*
>
> —Stefan Zweig[1]

In the quotation above, Stefan Zweig refers to our blindness to the significance of new phenomena emerging in our own time. Phenomena that only in hindsight will reveal their seminal character. The blindness goes the other way as well, when we fail to look back from our own time to better discern important origins of how we live today. We may have been lured and blinded by the vast global changes during the nineteenth and twentieth centuries that seemed to be heralding a new era of globalized modernity by rolling back non-Western and premodern cultures toward obliteration. So, we were unprepared for their deep-rooted perseverance and resonance, for instance where modernity and globalization have failed their promises to improve people's lives.

Cultural heritage constitutes a strong symbolic link between cultural/ethnic groups, territory, and history. Geopolitics is about the relationship between polities, geography, and cultural/ethnic groups through time. Geopolitics is therefore relevant for examining how values ascribed to cultural heritage relate to space, territory, and power on a global to local scale

[1] "It remains an irrefragable law of history that contemporaries are denied a recognition of the early beginnings of the great movements which determine their times." Stefan Zweig, *Die Welt von Gestern* (44. Auflage Berlin 2019) 406.

Carsten Paludan-Müller, *The Geopolitical Context of Cultural Heritage Destruction* In: *The Preservation of Art and Culture in Times of War*. Edited by: Claire Finkelstein, Derek Gillman, and Frederik Rosén, Oxford University Press. © Oxford University Press 2022. DOI: 10.1093/oso/9780197610565.003.0015

across the ages. Heritage together with the understanding of its origins and meanings (in plural) for the same reason becomes a factor in our understanding of and approach to contemporary conflicts.

This chapter will first present an overview of the contexts in which the destruction of cultural heritage in conflict takes place. It will do so by discussing the symbolic meanings and connotations attached to cultural heritage. Then it will discuss the complex mix of cultural contributions that usually have been brought together in what is too often misrepresented as the autonomous product of one single culture. The discussion will move on to the cultural complexity found in regions that used to be part of multiethnic empires, since this is where many of today's armed conflicts take place. It is a context in which identity politics becomes a prominent and manipulative factor, which involves cultural heritage as one of its constituting elements.

To offer a conceptual framework for understanding the complex interplay between history, geography, cultural identity/heritage, and conflict, we then turn to geopolitics. The chapter presents and discusses the development of geopolitics as a set of particular approaches or schools, each of which reflect different contexts in time and space. We discuss the particular importance ascribed by French geopoliticians to the cultural dimension—an approach of obvious relevance to the subject of this chapter.

With this background we move on to discuss the multicultural empires of the past and their legacies and impact in today's world. Our particular focus will be on the Ottoman Empire, since it included most of the territories in the European perimeter from the Black Sea to Algeria that were recently, or are at this moment, theaters of conflict; it is often referred to as "Europe's ring of fire." After a presentation of the logic that guided the ethnic composition of the Ottoman Empire, we go on to discuss the long and painful process of its unraveling and subsequent transformation into nation-states. The aim is to offer a framework for understanding how these nation-building processes have conditioned many recent and current conflicts. Through the lens of both the recent and the more distant history of the region, we will better understand why it contains such an abundant diversity of cultures and cultural heritage, and why that diversity becomes important in the context of conflict. The final sections of this chapter will discuss the communicative aspects of heritage destruction and also the potential role of cultural heritage in a post-conflict situation.

II. The Link Between Cultural Heritage and Geopolitics

Built cultural heritage has two important properties: First, it is located at a particular place. And second, it is a product of both past and present. It is in its origins a product of social and cultural[2] processes that happened at a specific place in the past, that is, it has a geographic and historic context. But not all material products of the past are regarded as cultural heritage. There is a selection process—formal or informal—guided by values of the present, which gives some of them a formal or informal status of "cultural heritage." That again may provide them with a degree of—sometimes official—attention and protection. The values that guide the present in its selection of these objects as heritage have to do with their semantic value for people in today's world. Often it is a meaning that refers to the identity of those who live in and around that heritage. It can also be a meaning for people living somewhere else, who may even be willing to travel far, as visitors to that heritage. In some cases, it is both. From a nation-state perspective cultural heritage, with its interpretation, may provide fix points for the national narrative about origins, rights, achievements, sufferings, and triumphs.

It is the ascribed meaning or meanings of cultural heritage together with its territorial embeddedness that makes it relevant in the context of contemporary conflict. When the Taliban destroyed the Bamyan Buddhas, and when ISIS destroyed monuments in Palmyra, it was exactly because they were aware of the meaning of these monuments to an international audience, whose attention they wanted to catch, while also making a statement aimed at the local population about Western preferences for heritage instead of people.

When ISIS destroyed inconspicuous burial grounds in Syrian village communities, and when the parties to the Yugoslav Wars destroyed humble local community mosques, churches, and monasteries, it was done in order to negate the historic ties between people and territory. When Myanmar's army destroyed all physical traces of Rohingya villages fled by their inhabitants, it was not only to destroy the economic basis for an eventual return of the

[2] The term cultural is used here in a narrow sense, covering language, religion, and historicity (narratives about and understandings of the groups past). These are considered the most frequent markers of group identity. The term social refers broadly to living conditions ie, equality/inequality, healthcare, security, education, and obviously the means to provide for yourself and those who rely on you, issues that are key to the stability of a social contract between the rulers and the ruled.

refugees, but also to rewrite the historic script on the landscape to say, "your history was never here."

When some of Israel's best-known archaeologists and generals were exercising both professions, it was because they sought archaeological evidence and monuments to "prove" that the territory they took from Palestinians was in fact merely reconquered ancient and exclusive Jewish land, and hence a historically justified takeover.[3] History provides many more examples to illustrate the point: cultural heritage is also about territory and historic rights to it. It is about documenting the story we want to tell about ourselves and how we see things.

III. When History Gets Complex

In the examples already listed we have made the point that cultural heritage carries important meanings to particular people, who see it as an expression of their belonging to a particular place. But in many instances, there will be multiple and sometimes dissonant relations between a particular cultural heritage and different groups. A stately manor or house may be seen by some as the historic home of a great national figure, by others as the manifestation of wealth appropriated through exploitation of slaves and/or workers. Many monuments have a long history of appropriation and modification by different and sometimes competing groups, the descendants of which may claim the same monument as proof of their narrative or their right to the territory in which it is situated.

The existence of such dissonances should not surprise us. It is in the very nature of the objects, that we classify as cultural heritage, that they are products of historic processes. Processes that can be long and complicated by the involvement of actors with a variety of identities and affiliations through time. Often a building classified as cultural heritage will already in its original shape consist of elements drawn not from one single, but from a variety of cultures. Afterwards a succession of actors will have shaped, altered, and used a historic building, town or landscape in a variety of ways through its

[3] See, for instance, Ben-Yehuda Nachman, *The Masada Myth: Collective Memory and Mythmaking in Israel* (University of Wisconsin Press 1995). See also Rachel Havrelock, *The Joshua Generation: Israeli Occupation and the Bible* (Princeton UP 2020).

history.[4] Each of these, or their descendants, will have a different story to tell about that particular heritage, and each of them will emphasize as proof of their "ownership" a particular selection of elements such as certain building techniques, decorations, inscriptions, garden layout, or a particular selection of previous inhabitants or users.[5]

The longer the history of a particular monument, the more complex and diverse its affiliation with and meanings to different groups can be. Even within the same group, understandings and attitudes toward a particular cultural heritage may change with time. There are for instance marked developments in how the battlefields around Verdun were perceived and presented immediately after World War I and then with the passing of time and generations until today. Verdun was at first seen as hallowed ground, a monument of French honor and patriotic sacrifice in an epic struggle with the German enemy. Today it has become a common ground of commemoration for the two nations and a place of recognition for the many different nations, whose young people lost their lives there.[6] A similar process has transformed the way the battlefield Dybbøl, from the Danish-German war of 1864, is commemorated.[7]

IV. When Complexity Becomes Conflictual

In many cases a long and complex history of changing inhabitants in a particular town or street need not be much more than diverse and colorful. The transformation of New York's Little Italy into a Chinese neighborhood or the change of London's Brick Lane from an Irish and Jewish neighborhood to today's "Banglatown" could serve as examples. But the same can hardly be said of the transformation of Haifa from a Palestinian to a Jewish-Israeli city. Or of the change of the Jewish quarter in Łódź to a purely Polish

[4] Carsten Paludan-Müller, "Actors and Orders: The Shaping of Landscapes and Identities" in Tom Bloemers, Henk Kars, Arnold Van der Valk, and Mies Wijnen (eds), *The Cultural Landscape & Heritage Paradox* (Amsterdam UP 2010) 53–66.

[5] Carsten Paludan-Müller, "Postscript 2: When Memory Takes Place" in Marie Louise Stig Sørensen and Dacia Viejo-Rose (eds), *War and Cultural Heritage: Biographies of Place* (CUP 2015) 261–67.

[6] Jean-Paul Amat, Paola Filippucci, and Edwige Savouret, "The Cemetery of France: Reconstruction and Memorialisation on the Battlefield of Verdun (France)" in Marie Louise Stig Sørensen, and Dacia Viejo-Rose (eds), *War and Cultural Heritage: Biographies of Place* (CUP 2015) 46–68.

[7] Marie Louise Stig Sørensen, and Inge Adriansen, "Dybbøl: The Construction and Reconstruction of a Memorial Landscape" in Marie Louise Stig Sørensen and Dacia Viejo-Rose (eds), *War and Cultural Heritage: Biographies of Place* (CUP 2015) 18–45.

neighborhood as a consequence of the Holocaust of the mid-twentieth century. Nor could it be said about the many cities, towns, and villages in today's India, Pakistan, and Bangladesh, from which either Muslims or Hindus had to flee in 1947, when the British Raj transformed into some sort of nation-states, partly defined along religious lines, and hence denying the long and complex history of cultural cross-fertilization between Persianate-Muslim culture and Hindu culture.

We tend to think of our own time as being characterized by a particularly high degree of globalization and cross-cultural encounters. This may (still) be true for some Western countries. But what we see, coming out of today's many armed conflicts, is a reduced capacity for cohabitation of different cultures within a shared geographical space, whether it be a state, a province, or a town. What remains of the multicultural fabric from earlier empires (see later in the chapter) risks becoming an antagonistic and destabilizing factor in political struggles within many of those nation-states, that grew from the ashes of former multiethnic empires. This is not to claim that ethnic differences are in themselves the cause of confrontations between citizens. But cultural differences are easily abused as rallying points in a situation of severe scarcity, when people struggle for their own survival and that of their closest kin. Thus, many of today's conflicts appear to be all about identity, while in fact their deeper causes are poverty, inequality, and the absence of hope for a better future under the prevailing circumstances. In order to better appreciate the long lines and deeper logic behind today's many conflicts, we need to turn to geopolitics.

V. Geopolitics in Short

Geopolitical thinking originated as an analytical approach to the late nineteenth-century's increasing imperial competition for and redistribution of territories and resources. It is the study of the interplay through time between politics and geography, both physical and human. The scale or perspective is global and goes deep in time.

The late nineteenth century was a period of instability, characterized by declining, collapsing, and ascending powers, not unlike the times we are living through in the early decades of the twenty-first century. Geopolitics became a way for the competing powers of understanding the implications of control over certain territories and seas, and of analyzing how best to position themselves in the competition.[8] Some of the pioneers of early geopolitics are briefly introduced here to provide a sense of early geopolitical thinking:

Friedrich Ratzel (1844–1904) was a German geographer occupied with the scientific understanding of the geographical dimensions of politics. His engagement was inspired by the Bismarckian and Wilheminian striving for supremacy in Europe and in the world, and by Darwinism. He coined the ill-famed term "Lebensraum" (1897) to designate the space necessary for the survival of an organism/state.

Karl Haushofer (1869–1946) was a German officer and geographer. As a student he was inspired by his professor, Friedrich Ratzel. But he took a more radical stance in the analyses of Germany's geopolitical position, which he saw as threatened. He saw Germany alongside USA, Japan, and Russia as destined to dominate each of their zones of the Globe. Haushofer, who was the teacher of Rudolf Hess, has been seen as an inspirator of Hitler's "Großdeutsche" geopolitical project.

Halford Mackinder (1861–1947) was a British Oxford geographer whose main contribution (1904) is expressed in his Mercator-projection that defines the world in terms of three zones: Heart Land/Pivot Area (the central Euro-Asian Continent), Inner Crescent (the non-Arctic coastal and insular perimeters of the Euro-Asian Continent and their hinterland), and Outer Crescent (The Americas, Australia and Oceania). Mackinder's thesis was that whoever controlled the "Heartland, controlled the World"—the so-called "The Heartland-theory." Mackinder's work belongs to the school of "Realpolitik."

Alfred Thayer Mahan (1840–1914) was an American admiral. In 1897, he published "The Interest of America in Sea Power." He outlined a grand strategy for the achievement of global US naval supremacy following the example of Great Britain. The main element was a network of harbors, naval bases, and points of solid control with major sea routes. Mahan's ideas clearly contributed to the actual strategy followed by the United States.

Nicholas John Spykman (1893–1943) was an American journalist. He was critical toward the approach of Haushofer, which he regarded as

[8] Johannes Paulmann, *Globale Vorherrschaft und Fortschrittsglaube: Europa 1850–1914* (CH Beck 2019) 415–420; Gearóid Ó Tuathail, Simon Dalby, and Paul Routledge (eds), *The Geopolitics Reader* (Routledge 2006) 17–30; Aymeric Chauprade and François Thual, *Dictionaire de Géopolitique* (ELLIPSES 1999) 587–633.

too deterministic. He also distanced himself from Mackinder's emphasis on the central role of the Heartland/Pivot Area. For Spykman the most important zone is Mackinder's "Rimland" (Inner Crescent), of the Eurasian continent. This is where the confrontation of the major players takes place.

Jacques Ancel (1879–1943) was a French geographer and geopolitician, particularly occupied with the role of borders and the formation of nations. In his writings he criticizes the German, Ratzel-Haushofer approach to geopolitics for being both too physically deterministic and too ideologically obsessed with pan-Germanism. Instead of physical determinants Ancel stresses the role of cultural similarities and differences as the crucial factors that decide which role is ascribed to physical barriers or links.

After World War II geopolitics vanished out of focus in the broader public discussion partly due to its association with the thinking of "The Third Reich," and partly due to the reordering of the world into a relatively stable bipolar system controlled by the two new hegemons, USA and USSR. In this system most conflicts seemed understandable in the light of the "East-West" competition. Still geopolitics was present in the thinking of the hegemons, as exemplified by The Containment Strategy developed by the American diplomat and historian George F. Kennan and implemented by the Truman administration to counter the expansionist drive of the USSR.[9] When that bipolar system collapsed around 1989, old patterns of conflict and regional interests, previously held in check by the two hegemons, began to re-emerge. They made themselves increasingly felt as the brief moment of near-absolute American hegemony gave way to a still emerging new pattern of multipolarity.

From a superficial perspective, other lines of conflict, now relating to opposing cultures and identities, have substituted the economic, social, and ideological lines visibly dominant during the Cold War Era. This is what has famously been dubbed "The Clash of Civilizations," a term coined by Samuel P. Huntington in his paper of the same name.[10] The new lines of conflict were in fact not so new. They often followed regional territorial logics well known from history. These re-emerging logics have brought about a renewed interest

[9] Tuathail, Dalby, and Routledge (n 8) 1–12.
[10] Samuel P Huntington, "The Clash of Civilizations" (1993) 72 (3) Foreign Affairs 22.

in geopolitics to help a better understanding of the themes and dynamics of conflicts, new as well as old. Thus, geopolitics again became a common word in the public discussion about international affairs.

As was the case in the period from the late nineteenth century until the end of World War II, there is today no such thing as a unified geopolitical perspective, and as with any other discipline within the historic-socio-political field, there are different schools of thought, with varying emphasis on physical, cultural, economic, and political aspects and with varying ideological inclinations. Those leaning mainly toward the political dimension also show stronger affiliations with International Relations Theory, which reaches back to Thucydides, Machiavelli, and Hobbes and continues into our own times with scholars like Kenneth Waltz.

For the purpose of understanding the relationship between cultural heritage, history, and today's pattern of conflict, however, the historic-geographical approaches are better suited exactly because of their combined cultural and spatial perspective. Today, with the post-Cold War resurgence of geopolitics there is a plethora of scholars and trends. Some of the most interesting are found in France, maybe also because of the strong French tradition, initiated by Louis XVI's diplomat François Callières (1645–1717), for clinical analysis of interests, actions, and options on the international arena. What unites the thinking of several otherwise diverging French geopoliticians is their interest in the formation of culture in a spatio-economic context and its role in geopolitical dynamics. The importance ascribed to culture is particularly prominent in French approaches to understanding the world, as exemplified within the Annales School of historians, which has influenced contemporary geopoliticians. For them it has obviously been easy to relate to the strong emphasis on geography characteristic of the Annales School. The cultural approach of the French geopoliticians is highly relevant to our attempt to understand the historic roots and contexts of contemporary conflicts, and their symbolic entanglement with culture and cultural heritage. Through this widened approach geopolitics demonstrates an academic maturity emancipating it from its origins in the colonial and imperial thinking of the late nineteenth and early twentieth centuries.

Yves Lacoste (1929–) is a French geographer and geopolitician closely linked with the anti-colonial movement. He is strongly critical of the German "Geopolitik" for its services to the imperial projects of Germany. As was the case with Jacques Ancel, culture and identity are important for Lacoste. He understands them as significant factors in the shaping of history, though basically he regards them as false representations of other more fundamental physical and socioeconomic issues. The historic background for the present is important but rarely analytically detailed in his work. Among his most influential publications and famous for its analytical maps is "Géopolitique, La longue histoire d'aujourd'hui" 2009/2012.

François Thual (1944–) is a French historian influenced by the Annales School and by Realpolitik. He refuses deterministic or monocausal explanations and offers analysis where socioeconomic issues and geography remain key, behind the screen of other issues such as religion. He lectured at the Military Academy and has in his writings analyzed a variety of topics, many of which have to do with the role of religion in contemporary conflicts. One of his most influential books is *Les conflits identitaires* from 1995 in which he analyzes the post-bipolar pattern of conflicts and their causes.

Aymeric Chauprade (1969–) is a French political scientist and geopolitical thinker with a strong *souverainiste* engagement for the nation against any imperial projects. Chauprade's approach belongs to the realist tradition, and is deeply rooted in history, inspired by the "longue durée" approach of the Annales School (F. Braudel). Chauprade rejects the position of Lacoste on culture as superficial. Chauprade's textbook *Geopolitique, constantes et changements dans l'histoire* (2003/8) has been used by the French military academy. Chauprade is also a controversial figure due to his engagement on the French far right. Still he is regarded as one of today's leading geopolitical thinkers. With his scholarly approach heavily influenced by the Annales School and little by his ideological position he offers important insights and considerations, not least in the textbook mentioned.

VI. A Geopolitical Perspective on Empire and Diversity

The main benefit of a geopolitical approach to cultural heritage in contemporary conflict is that it provides a framework for understanding the geohistory of the affected region, which has also layered itself in the cultural heritage and in the meanings ascribed to it. It invites a focus on the basic features of the landscapes: their diversities, connections, and barriers; and their resources, demography, cultures, and political history. And also, how these have interacted through history to shape the current stage of conflicts and alliances, so that we may better understand how the structures of contemporary politics relate to those of the past. Hence we will better understand how narratives and meanings may become attached to cultural heritage in ways that makes it emblematic for the parties to a conflict.

In the following, we shall look into the geopolitical logics of early modern empires and their internal functioning in order to understand how they differed from modern nation-states in ways that affect the transition from empire to nation-state. Because of its relevance to the understanding of some of today's most dangerous conflicts we will in particular focus on the Ottoman Empire.

Many contemporary conflicts occur in regions that through long spans of history were under some sort of imperial rule. That goes both for continental empires such as the Ottoman, the Safavid, the Mughal, the Chinese, the Habsburgian or the Russian/Soviet; and for overseas colonial empires such as the Spanish, Portuguese, Dutch, British, and French. It is important to understand the complex and diverse demographics of these empires. They encompassed under one ruler a wide variety of people and cultures, layered in complex mosaics through history. Difference in culture and religion could have many origins. A difference in economic strategies could be one, migrations could be another, and differences in relations to the ruling power leading to religious conversion could be a third. The coherence of the empire was dependent not on demographic homogeneity, but on the loyalty of its segments and subjects to the common ruler. Often, as in the Ottoman Empire, the different groups were allowed some degree of autonomy in their own religious and intra-communal legal affairs, the so-called Millet-system,[11] whereas the Ottoman rulers were mainly handling inter-communal disputes. Tax collecting (tax farming) would in some cases also be handled by leaders of the millets.

The ability to legitimize the ruling of a diversity of populations within an empire was not linked to the construction of a unified "national" identity. The success or failure of the rulers was mainly dependent on their ability to sufficiently balance the interests and strengths of the different groups, and thus remain in control as the supreme coordinating link between them, and to uphold control over tax collection and external borders. The latter two were closely connected, with the revenue from the taxes used to finance the upholding of the garrisons necessary for border

[11] Karen Barkey, *Empire of Difference: The Ottomans in Comparative Perspective* (CUP 2008) 130–31.

defense or expansion.[12] For the imperial ruler these purposes could be pursued in a variety of ways. One of them would be to sometimes shift population groups around in order to avoid too large regions settled by one homogenous group. Having groups with different languages, religions, and historical narratives next to each other, there would always be differences of identity to exploit for the ruler. This strategy was actively pursued both during Ottoman times and for a variety of reasons not least under the Turkish Republic as the successor state of the Ottoman Empire, especially in the Kurdish, Syriac, and (former) Armenian parts of Eastern Anatolia.

For the understanding of the present situation in the Kurdish regions, a historic perspective is important. The Kurds are linguistically part of the Iranian sphere (not the Turkish). Nevertheless, for the Ottomans they provided an important semiautonomous ally in the disputed mountainous region bordering the (Iranian) Safavid Empire.[13] The border in itself was not well defined, and the border region, because of its mountainous topography, was difficult to access and control. For that reason, it served the Ottoman interests to accept a high degree of autonomy and local rule for the Kurds in return for their loyalty and services to the Sultan in major confrontations with the Safavids. This was a low-cost investment in securing the border, compared to the resources required—if at all possible—to establish full and permanent control over this part of Eastern Anatolia. For the Sunni Kurds, sandwiched between two major empires, it made sense on those terms to lean toward the Sunni Ottomans rather than toward the Shia Safavids. This historic and geographical background is important for our ability to understand today's issues in and around Kurdistan. Aymeric Chauprade offers an analysis of the special geopolitical role of mountainous regions in general with observations that also have relevance for the understanding of the Kurdish issue.[14]

When we look at the former Ottoman territories outside of the Turkish Republic, such as Iraq, Syria, Lebanon, and Israel/Palestine, it is obvious that also in these lands a diversity of different cultural groups has cohabited.[15] Just as within Turkey, it is a demographic composition that has a variety of

[12] Gábor Ágoston, "Defending and Administering the Frontier. The Case of Ottoman Hungary" in Christine Woodhead (ed), *The Ottoman World* (Routledge 2012) 220–36.

[13] Nelida Fuccaro, "The Ottoman Frontier in Kurdistan in the Sixteenth and Seventeenth Centuries" in Christine Woodhead (ed), *The Ottoman World* (Routledge 2012) 237–50.

[14] Aymeric Chauprade, *Géopolitique. Constantes et changements dans l'histoire* (3rd edn, Paris, ELLIPSES 2008) 183–89.

[15] Baki Tezcan, "Ethnicity, Race Religion and Social Class: Ottoman Markers of Difference" in Christine Woodhead (ed), *The Ottoman World* (Routledge 2012) 159–70.

explanations. First of all, the ethnic composition within a given area does not necessarily fall into clearly segregated major territories and cannot merely be explained as the result of the policies of a single empire. For the whole of the Levant, the Caucasus, the Balkans, and well into Central and Eastern Europe we are in territories where for millennia a succession of competing empires with shifting borders between them has been in control from Antiquity until the twentieth century. In the Balkans the Habsburgian and the Ottoman Empires fought for centuries to push their mutual border further away from their own center. The Habsburgians employed an active settlement policy to secure their hold on their territories: for instance, by resettling on their side of the border Christian Serbs, who fled Ottoman territories.[16] The Ottomans on their side recruited both Christians and Muslims from their Balkan provinces to help man garrisons at the Habsburgian borders. During much of Ottoman rule, segments of Christian populations for a variety of reasons converted to Islam, thus establishing a religious (i.e., cultural) distinction between themselves and their (former fellow) Christian neighbors: a distinction that lasts until today.[17]

An important factor in the mixing of cultural groups in the Ottoman Empire was the vastness of its territory. At its height during the seventeenth century it reached from Algeria in the West to Basra in the East, and from Aden in the South to Budapest in the North. It controlled two-thirds of the Mediterranean Coast and reached deep down the coasts of the Red Sea and the Persian Gulf. For traders, artisans, sailors, and others this offered a vast economic space ruled more or less by the same laws—and communicating with a shared language (Turkish). Thus, communities of various cultural groups settled around the empire bringing their special trade to cities, where Arabs, Greeks, Jews, Armenians, Albanians, Berbers, Kurds, Bulgars, and of course Turks in different constellations cohabited with many others.

In sum, the Ottoman Empire functioned during much of its history reasonably well on this basis of balanced diversity. But that does in no way imply that all subjects were treated equally. First of all, it was only the non-Muslims who were taxed with the special cizye tax, until it was abandoned shortly before the downfall of the empire. There was also a distinction between inner and outer provinces and the ways in which they were ruled.[18]

[16] Marie-Janine Calic, *Südosteuropa, Weltgeschichte einer Region* (München 2016) 153–58.
[17] Barkey (n 11) 125–28.
[18] Ibid 86.

VII. The Erosion and Collapse of Cultural Coexistence in the Ottoman Empire

During the nineteenth century the Ottoman Empire began its decline.[19] It was a process with two major causes, both related to a wider geopolitical shift. This shift is essential to bear in mind because it still influences today's geopolitical dynamics in the wider South Eastern Mediterranean region, and because it can help us understand parallels in other regions of the world, where an imperial legacy struggles with the logics of the nation-state.

On the ideological side, there was a marked influence from the European revolutions of 1789 and 1848, which established the idea of the nation and of the citizen, instead of the monarch, as the two basic conceptual pillars on which a modern state should build. On the political side, the nineteenth century saw a culmination of a worldwide territorial competition between the major, now industrialized, European powers. Inside of the Ottoman Empire a national awakening took place among many of the Christian minorities. Most prominently, and first, among the Greeks, led by the Phanariotes—a name given to the Greek-Ottoman elite families living in the Phanar quarter of Constantinople.[20] The Greek aspirations for national independence were hailed and supported by European intellectuals as a rebirth of the classical Greek culture and thus a point of contact between modern European culture and its acclaimed deepest roots, from which it could hopefully rejuvenate.[21] Philhellenes like Chateaubriand, Hölderlin, Wilhelm von Humboldt, Pushkin, Shelley; and most prominent of them all, Byron, in speech, writing, and action supported the Greeks in their war of independence (1821–28) against the Ottoman Empire. The Philhellenes fostered an understanding of the Greeks as the natural inheritors of the achievements of classical Greece, struggling to unshackle themselves from a supposedly inferior, despotic Oriental rule in order to resume their cultural leadership of Europe.[22] By

[19] Martin Kröger, "Spielfeld der Mächtigeren. Das Osmanische Reich und der europäische Kolonialismus" in Charlotte Trümpler (ed), *Das Grosse Spiel. Archäologie und Politik zur Zeit des Kolonialismus* (Essen 2010) 28–33; Ussama Makdisi, "The Problem of Sectarianism in the Middle East in an Age of Western Hegemony" in Nader Hashemi and Danny Postel (eds), *Sectarianization: Mapping the New Politics of the Middle East* (OUP 2017) 23–34.

[20] Georges Corm, *L'Europe et l'Orient. De la balkanisation à la libanisation. Histoire d'une modernité inaccomplie* (Paris 2002) 97.

[21] Constanze Güthenke, *Placing Modern Greece: The Dynamics of Romantic Hellenism 1770–1840* (OUP 2008).

[22] Fani-Maria Tsigakou, *The Rediscovery of Greece: Travelers and Painters of the Romantic Era* (London 1981) 42–78; David Roessel, "Philhellenism" in Anthony Grafton, Glenn W Most and Salvatore Settis (eds), *The Classical Tradition* (Harvard UP 2010) 710–12.

casting classical Greek heritage as Occidental and opposed to Oriental, the Philhellenes (even if some of them had doubts about this genealogy) ignored both the classical and the Byzantine heritage internalized into Ottoman and Muslim culture and the Byzantine and Ottoman heritage internalized into contemporary Greek culture.[23] This line of thought is significant for how East and West have been thinking of each other and of their heritage and belonging for the last couple of centuries.

After that of the Greeks, came the nationalist independence movements, of among others, the Serbs and the Bulgars. And, with the weakening of the Ottomans came, preluded by Napoleon's Egyptian Campaign in 1798–1801, an increased effort on the side of the major European powers in mutual competition to secure their slice of the waning Empire before the others got hold of it. Sometimes one of the European players would support the Ottomans in an effort to stop the expansion of another. This was the rationale on the side of France, Britain, and Sardinia when they engaged in the Crimean War (1853–56) to stop Russia's Southward push in the Black Sea Region and the Caucasus. This was also part of the so called "Great Game" in which Russia and Britain competed for control over land and sea routes from Europe to India. But in spite of the occasional support from other powers, the Ottomans lost more and more territory to the national independence movements as well as to the Russians, the Austro-Hungarians, the British, the French, and the Italians. Particularly grave was the gradual loss of almost all of the Balkan provinces, which were the richest and for centuries among the best integrated in the Ottoman Empire.

No less important was the effect the losses had on the demographic composition of the remaining geographic core of the Ottoman Empire. With the ongoing territorial losses in the Black Sea region, the Caucasus, and especially the Balkans came an enormous influx of mainly Muslim refugees, because the new Balkan nation-states defined themselves as Christian, with little tolerance for Muslims. They emigrated to and were resettled in Anatolia. This huge Muslim immigration combined with the loss of all of the Christian Ottomans in the Balkans also affected the overall balance between the different segments in the (remaining) Ottoman population. During the years 1878–1907 the Muslim population changed from a share of 60% to 74% of the total population.[24] This demographic shift was further accelerated by the

[23] Maurizio Bettini, *Radici: Tradizione, identitá, memoria* (Bologna 2016) 93–99.
[24] Makdisi (n 19) 30.

fatal loss in 1912 of the Bulgarian territories and the influx of refugees from there. When World War I broke out almost 40% of the Anatolian population were immigrants from the lost provinces.[25]

At the same time, as the Ottoman government tried militarily to defeat the national liberation movements and resist the attacks from competing European powers, they also pursued a strategy of European inspired reforms, designed to strengthen both the Empire's civilian coherence and its military capacity, but also to gain legitimacy by accommodating European demands for nondiscrimination against Christian minorities. Hence the Tanzimat reforms (1839–76) were also a response to pressure from the European powers, who imposed themselves as protectors of the Christian minorities under Ottoman rule. By abolishing the uneven distribution of privileges and duties among the different segments of the population, the Sultanate put the members of religious minority communities on an equal footing with the Muslim majority. This was a gradual move from a de facto recognition of equal rights for all in 1839 to a formalized transformation in 1869 of the Ottoman populations from subjects to citizens, confirmed in the 1876 constitution.[26] It was a dramatic ideological shift away from an Ottoman Empire that had defined itself as Muslim and accordingly ascribed higher status to its Muslim subjects than to non-Muslims. This reshuffle of prestige, rights, and duties between the different religious communities also provoked violent conflict, with Muslim attacks against the Christian populations. For the Muslim population the loss of position added to the general animosity and mistrust against the Christian communities for being under the watchful protective eyes of foreign powers to whom the Ottoman had lost territory.

In 1903 the so-called Mürzsteg Scheme was forced upon the Ottomans to solve the "Macedonian Question," which, in short, referred to the breakdown of order in the Ottoman Balkan province devoured by uprisings against the Ottomans, combined with interethnic conflict between the insurgent Greeks, Albanians, Bulgarian, Serbians, and Rumanians and between Christians and Turkish-speaking Muslims.[27] The Mürzsteg Scheme gave the control over provincial police authorities in Macedonia to an international police commission appointed by European powers. The acceptance of the Mürzsteg Scheme, however reluctantly, by the Ottoman government was a humiliation that infuriated and stimulated the growing movement(s) of Turkish reformists, usually

[25] Barkey (n 11) 286.
[26] Makdisi (n 19) 27.
[27] Calic (n 16) 352–53.

referred collectively to as "The Young Turks." They wanted to halt the gradual collapse of the Turkish-led state around them in its ongoing confrontation with major European powers and with domestic national insurrections. They found hope in two observations. One was the recent (1905) victory of Japan over the Russian Empire in the naval battle of the Tsushima Strait, whereby a European (Russian) imperial power in North East Asia was thwarted and humiliated by a newly modernized non-European power.

The other observation was that nationalism and the nation-state constituted an apparently invincible enemy for their own state in its current multiethnic imperial configuration. Out of these two observations came the aspirations of leading members of the Young Turks: to combine modernization and ethnic cleansing. In 1913 the nationalist fraction took control over the Party of Union and Progress (CUP), previously formed as the Committee of Union and Progress jointly by the liberal and the nationalist Young Turks. CUP remained in government without interruption from 1923 until 1950.

VIII. Demographic Engineering and Genocide

The increasing influx of Muslim refugees from lost Balkan provinces, the abolition of special privileges and status for Ottoman Muslims, the sense of humiliation imposed by the interventions and assaults of European powers, the questions about the loyalty of Christian citizens, now under some sort of protection by foreign powers—all of this combined with the experience of the failure of the multiethnic empire to resist the national liberation movements and the European nation-states—had since the end of the nineteenth century given impetus to a growing conviction among leading actors (first of which were those within "The Young Turks") that the only valid response to the nationalist movement and the nation-states would be to follow their lead by abandoning the multicultural empire and transform it into a culturally Turkish-Muslim nation-state centered in Anatolia. The dynamics of the processes leading up to and through the transformation of the Ottoman Empire into the Turkish Republic is thoroughly detailed and analyzed in two publications by Uğur Ümit Üngör.[28] It is, however, a process that is difficult to study because important Ottoman and Turkish archival material relating to

[28] Uğur Ümit Üngör, "Turkey for the Turks: Demographic Engineering in Eastern Anatolia 1914-1945" in Ronald Suny, Fatma Müge Göçek, and Norman M Naimark (eds), *A Question of*

the decisions about the fate of the non-Turkish minorities, and their land and properties, remain classified. The new concept of Turkishness as *the* identity basis for a future state in the remaining Ottoman core territory spelled disaster for populations with other cultural belongings, populations that for thousands of years had inhabited the Anatolian landscapes, villages, and cities.

The spread of the nation-states can be likened to a process of crystallization, where the transformation of one part of a free-flowing liquid into the firm and bounded structure of a crystal provokes a similar process to take place "next door." After the sequential formation of new nation-states in the former Ottoman provinces in the Balkans, this was then what happened in Anatolia in the period from 1913 and up until the mid-twentieth century, with a thoroughly considered and radical project of demographic and cultural engineering. It served the double purpose of making room for the many Muslim refugees from the Balkans and at the same time of homogenization through Turkification.[29] The Christian populations of Greeks, Syriacs, and Armenians were considered unsuited for Turkification, whereas non-Turkish-speaking Muslim populations (Arabs and Kurds for instance) were subjected to harsh demands of abandoning their mother tongue. The Kurds were seen by the Young Turks as an especially difficult population element. As previously described, they had held a relatively independent role as buffers in the mountainous zone between the Ottoman and the Safavid (Iranian) Empires. The new Turkish leadership wanted to bring Eastern Anatolia under full control by moving some of the Kurds from their Eastern Anatolian homeland to Western Anatolia, in order to dilute their otherwise dominant regional presence by resettling immigrants from the lost Ottoman provinces in former Kurdish villages.

The Greek communities that had been living on Anatolia's Aegean Coast for millennia were exposed to pogroms until 1923, when an internationally sponsored exchange of populations between the nation-states of Greece and Turkey took place. For the Armenian population, mainly settled in Eastern Anatolia, the effect of the demographic engineering was even more disastrous. The tragedy of the genocide has been described many

Genocide: Armenians and Turks at the End of the Ottoman Empire (OUP 2011) 287–305; Uğur Ümit Üngör, *The Making of Modern Turkey: Nation and State in Eastern Anatolia 1913–1950* (OUP 2011).

[29] Üngör, "Turkey for the Turks" (n 28) 287–305.

times—most recently by Benny Morris and Dror Ze'evi,[30] by Heghnar Zeitlan Watenpaugh,[31] and by Makdisi.[32] The Armenian genocide is the best known of the ethnic cleansings, which targeted the non-Muslim minorities in the pursuit of a "purely" Turkish nation-state in Anatolia after the loss of most of the European and Arab territories of the Ottoman Empire.

With a peak in 1915 the Armenian communities were systematically destroyed by mass killing and expulsion. Entire towns and villages were burned and property confiscated or simply plundered. Up to 1.5 million Armenians are estimated to have lost their lives, and many more were exiled. Their towns, villages, and remaining houses were subsequently used for the resettling of Muslim refugees from the lost provinces in the Balkans, the Black Sea, and the Caucasus. The territory was literally cleared from its historic inhabitants and prepared for accommodating the new inhabitants.

IX. Cultural Engineering and Culturicide

What still remained to be accomplished in the building of a new Turkish nation-state following the genocide, ethnic cleansing, and resettling was some sort of legitimization of the new facts on the ground. Now this was no longer about shifting people, but about shifting the memories embedded in cultural heritage—material as well as immaterial. Therefore, the next phase, after the demographic engineering, was the construction of the identity of the new Turkish nation-state by giving it roots also in the places that used to belong to Armenians, Greeks, Kurds, and Syriacs. This was about the construction of narratives and the editing of memories. Besides the enforcement of Turkish as the only language for hitherto non-Turkish-speaking Muslims, a new law was passed that Turkified family names. Also, thousands of place names, especially in Eastern Anatolia, were changed from Armenian, Greek, Arab, and Kurdish into Turkish sounding names. Even Turkish place names referring to a local Armenian history were changed. New publications of local history were systematically produced. They took out the history of the Christian minorities and played down that of the Kurds, and obviously avoided any

[30] Benny Morris and Dror Ze'evi, *The Thirty-Year Genocide: Turkey's Destruction of Its Christian Minorities 1894–1924* (Harvard UP 2019).

[31] Heghnar Zeitlan Watenpaugh, *The Missing Pages: The Modern Life of a Medieval Manuscript from Genocide to Justice* (Stanford UP 2019).

[32] Ussama Makdisi, *Age of Coexistence: The Ecumenical Frame and the Making of the Modern Arab World* (University of California Press 2019) 80–84.

mention of genocide or other forms of ethnic cleansing. Everywhere the purpose was the same, namely, to sink the recent non-Turkish past and the Ottoman ethnic diversity into oblivion.

It would be wrong, however, to see the erasing of non-Turkish identities as the only effort in the ideological nation-building effort. No less important were the development of an active preservation policy and new architectural language that referred back to the golden age of the Ottoman Empire during the sixteenth century.[33] So, the nation-building was a combined process of modernization, historic revival, and monocultural Turkification.

It is in this context that we should understand one of history's clearest examples of systematic heritage destruction, the one following the genocide on the Armenian population during World War I in the territories that were to become the Turkish Republic.[34] Up until the 1960s the Turkish state conducted, encouraged, and tolerated an extensive, sometimes systematic destruction of medieval monasteries and churches that remained visible in the landscapes after they had lost their Armenian congregations. Many were targeted with artillery rounds or dynamited. Others were converted into mosques, used as barns or quarried for building materials. The idea was to eradicate all traces of the Armenian communities that used to belong there until 1915. In other places the Armenian character of particular monuments was disputed and competing interpretations introduced. The destruction of Armenian heritage in Turkey was a removal of evidence of the historic Armenian presence and meant to rewrite the history of the territory. The eradication of Armenian heritage from the territory of the Turkish Republic corresponds with the still-closed governmental archives from the period, and the official denial of the genocide and punishment for mentioning it.

Today eradication of Kurdish heritage is taking place, as historic towns and villages in Eastern Anatolia are being inundated and demolished in the context of the Tigris dam projects. Hasankey is one of them and, in spite of international attempts to save the town, by early 2020 it was completely inundated by the waters from the Ilisu Dam. Officially the destruction of Hasankey is a pure technical necessity. But if it had been important for the Turkish government to reach out to its Kurdish citizens, this pattern of heritage destruction

[33] Mesut Dinler, *Modernization through Past: Cultural Heritage during the Late-Ottoman and the Early-Republican Period in Turkey* (Pisa 2019) 47–67.

[34] Alan Kramer, *Dynamics of Destruction: Culture and Mass Killing in the First World War* (OUP 2007) 147–50; Robert Bevan, *The Destruction of Memory: Architecture at War* (London 2006) 53–60.

might have been avoided.[35] The same goes for the extensive destruction of Sur, Diyarbakir's historic center, during the 2016 war against PKK.[36] That destruction can also be read into the context of a long-standing ambition within the Turkish government to radically redo the impoverished Sur in order to turn it into a place for tourists and well-situated residents. This would at the same time re-engineer the demography of the city and probably reduce the number Kurdish residents.

It is a thought that international appeals and pressures directed against the Turkish Republic in favor of its minorities and their cultures might be seen as falling into a historic pattern of often ruthless European interventions into the domestic politics of the late Ottoman Empire. They are seen in Turkey as leading up to the Sèvres Treaty of 1920 forced upon the Ottoman government by the victorious Western powers. That treaty completely split the Anatolian territories between Greeks, Armenians, Kurds, French, British, and Italians leaving only a semiautonomous Turkish rump state at the Black Sea Coast. This was what then fueled the Turkish war of liberation and the formation and international recognition in 1923 of the Turkish Republic within its present borders (treaty of Lausanne). Europeans and North Americans often fail to recognize the long-term effect of this chain of events. For many Turks, any foreign attempt to weigh in on Turkish politics fits a pattern that is linked to the humiliation and eventual downfall of the Empire, and therefore foreign appeals are often too easily discarded and even instrumentalized with an assertion of Turkish sovereignty. Especially in periods of heightened domestic problems and tensions, when beating the national drums can serve to divert attention and rally support. In 2020 the reconversion of Istanbul's Hagia Sophia from museum to mosque and the international row it has fueled offered a good case in point to illustrate that cultural heritage has a huge symbolic value that can be instrumentalized in both domestic and international politics. The international protests against the reconversion are easily cast as another reminder of the times when the waning Ottoman Empire was forced to comply with demands and conditions imposed by major European powers. It is worth keeping in mind that the 1934 conversion of Hagia Sophia into a museum by Kemal Atatürk was already then criticized

[35] "Hasankeyf" (*World Monuments Fund*) <https://www.wmf.org/project/hasankeyf> accessed 26 May 2020.

[36] "The Destruction of Sur: Is This Historic District a Target for Gentrification?" (*The Guardian*, 9 February 2016) <https://www.theguardian.com/cities/2016/feb/09/destruction-sur-turkey-historic-district-gentrification-kurdish> accessed 26 May 2020.

by some as a step too far in the pursuit of his Western-inspired secular modernization program for the new Turkish Republic. As such the reconversion can be seen as a symbolic expression of defiance that has matched Turkey's coinciding foreign military confrontations and postures in the wider Eastern Mediterranean region. Both of them have also been seen as intended to lead the focus away from a domestic social and economic crisis.

There is however also another recent trend, that especially since the beginning of the twenty-first century has led to a gradual shift in the Turkish policy toward the Armenian heritage in Turkey, most prominently with the Turkish nomination in 2012 of the Medieval Armenian city of Ani for UNESCO's world heritage list, onto which it was accepted in 2016 with the endorsement of the Armenian government. Someday this may lead to an ability for Turks and Armenians to come together in reconciliatory understanding of their common past.

X. The Ring of Fire and the Legacy of Imperial Collapse

The countries that were once part of the Ottoman Empire coincide more or less with what has been referred to as Europe's "ring of fire."[37] It borders the Southern and Eastern perimeters of the European Union, reaching from Ukraine in the East to Algeria in the West. The designation refers to present, recent, or potential conflicts that in the Western understanding seem hard to comprehend because of the difficulties we have with the role played by identity issues, which on the surface seem to drive most of them.

And many of them do appear in the guise of identity confrontations. It is important, however, to refuse a simplistic characterization of post-cold war conflicts as representing a transition from conflicts merely driven by socioeconomic issues to conflicts merely driven by identity issues, here understood as language, religion, and history. Many cold war conflicts were obviously cast as socioeconomic and ideological, reflecting the fact that, besides their local causes, they were also proxy wars between the competing Soviet and US hegemons, championing competing ideologies ("socialist-anti-imperialist/capitalist" against "liberal-democratic/free-world"). Still, below the

[37] "Ring of Friends—Ring of Fire?" (*Bertelsmann Stiftung*, 12 February 2014) <https://www.bertelsmann-stiftung.de/en/our-projects/abgeschlossene-projekte/strengthening-and-connecting-europe/news/ring-of-friends-ring-of-fire/> accessed 26 May 2020.

socioeconomic/ideological surface, old identity-related lines of division played important roles, and often coincided with existing socioeconomic divisions.

Likewise, post- cold war conflicts often have socioeconomic roots, as was also the case with the Syrian version of "the Arab Spring." It was then derailed and recast into a cultural or sectarian conflict by actors who found that easier to manipulate for their own purposes. Sectarian division of people and power can be an important way for ruling classes both to keep focus away from their pursuit of own interests and privileges, and at the same time legitimize the delimitations of their own "fiefdom." In this way there are strong interests for a regime to cultivate symbols and images that can support narratives of difference and division.

After the retreat of the colonial (including the mandatory) powers from the MENA region (Middle East North Africa), the former colonies and mandatory territories transformed into some sort of nation-states after the dominant Western model and mostly within the same borders that had been drawn by the United Kingdom and France to serve their own geopolitical interests. The idea guiding the political organization of the newly independent Arab territories was to build a state identity on a blend of modernization and Pan-Arabism.[38] The investments in modernization programs, however, did not in the long run compete well with the priorities given by authoritarian rulers and self-serving elites to secure power and privilege for themselves and their supporters in a strongly clientelist system.[39] The shortcomings of such a system was overwhelmingly exposed by the 2020 explosion that destroyed much of Beirut.

In the wake of the dysfunction and decline of many of the recently founded (postcolonial) nation-states as the primary organizers of identity and territorial belonging, combined with the *seemingly* identity-driven character of contemporary conflicts, cultural heritage (re-)emerges as a crucial reference for mooring collective identities to geography. And hence, cultural heritage has come into focus as symbolic rallying points for manifestations of identities and conflicts between them exactly because conflicts often relate to or thematize historicity.[40] This is why cultural heritage is so often purposefully

[38] In Israel the identity construction was built on the idea of reviving a territorial Jewish nation-state claimed to have been a historic reality in biblical times. Havrelock (n 3).

[39] Nader Hashemi and Danny Postel, "Introduction: The Sectarianization Thesis" in Nader Hashemi and Danny Postel (eds), *Sectarianization: Mapping the New Politics of the Middle East* (OUP 2017) 1–22.

[40] Aurel Croissant, Uwe Wagschal, Nicolas Schwank, and Christoph Trinn, *Kulturelle Konflikte seit 1945: Die kulturellen Dimensionen des globalen Konfliktgeschehens* (Baden-Baden 2009) 250.

destroyed during conflict, and this is why its eventual reconstruction may or may not help post-conflict reconciliation, depending on with whom, for whom, and how it is done.

But, as has been convincingly argued by Hashemi and Postel with others[41] and by François Thual,[42] the fact that for instance the sectarian division between Sunni and Shia goes back to the early days of Islam, immediately after the death of the Prophet, is being confused with the causes of what is now a geopolitical conflict between major regional powers for supremacy. This confrontation between (Shia) Iran and (Sunni) Saudi Arabia competing for supremacy in the Gulf and in the wider MENA region is being fought as proxy wars in other theaters, such as Syria, Iraq, Libya, and Yemen. In this struggle sectarian markers have been instrumentalized as rallying points by the two main proponents. But other regional actors such as Turkey have also showed their willingness to encourage sectarian violence as an instrument to serve their own geopolitical interests, for instance, in Syria.

So even if the causes of conflict are social and economic, sectarianism easily comes into play. For Saudi Arabia to characterize civil unrest at home as instigated by Shia fundamentalists, supported by Iran, leads attention away from or disqualifies a dangerous critique of the Saudi political order. For Iran the specter of Saudi-sponsored Wahabi terrorism can serve as a way of disqualifying domestic social unrest. In the West we fall into this conceptual trap when we characterize an entire region as a hopeless victim of an eternal, "dark-age" sectarian conflict. Still we should not underestimate the long-term effect within the region itself of using sectarian markers to distinguish friend from foe. When bitter conflicts over access to a decent life are fought for a sufficiently long time under the banners of religion, race, or language, these markers do become powerful factors in themselves. They will eventually influence the ability of the populations involved to deal with each other and solve their problems together in the future.

Atrocities perceived as committed in the name of religion will be remembered and memories reactivated in the future, as has been the case in the post-Yugoslav wars around the turn of the century. They drew on historic references, not only to the Balkan wars leading up to World War I or to the Croat-Serb conflict during World War II. They were reaching as far back as the battle of Kosovo Polje in 1389 between the Serbs (Christians) and

[41] Hashemi and Postel, "Introduction" (n 39).
[42] François Thual, *Les Conflits Idéntitaire* (Paris 1995).

the Ottomans (Muslims). This was not a religious war, but part of ongoing Ottoman imperial expansion that also targeted territories populated by Muslims. But in the narratives of Serb nationalism the battle of Kosovo Polje was presented as the heroic defeat of Christians (Serbs) against Muslims (Ottomans), helped by "treacherous" Bosniaks, who had abandoned their Christian faith to serve the Sultan.

XI. Destruction and Communication

Collateral damage is the technical term for the unintended killing and destruction that happens during armed conflict to civilians and to objects such as cultural heritage, that are not in themselves strategic or tactic targets. The international laws and conventions, intended to prevent or minimize destruction of cultural heritage, also by banning its use for military purposes,[43] do not have the same reach in a time when armed conflict often involves non-state combatants. Cultural heritage may become involved and targeted, because it is being used as a vantage position for snipers (a minaret or a belfry) or as a protected point from where access to a wider territory can be controlled (a castle). But it may also be destroyed to make a statement, as described at the beginning of this chapter.

"Communicative heritage destruction" is nothing new, and definitely not a prerogative of non-state actors. The sacking of Jerusalem and the Temple in 70 C.E., represented on the Titus Arch in Rome, is also an early example of the connection between ethnic cleansing and destruction and looting of heritage. A more recent example is the destruction of the historic city of Louvain/Leuven by the German army in 1914. The destruction was intended as a message to the Belgians not to oppose the occupation, and allegedly also driven by a strong animosity on the side of the German army against the catholic institutions of the city with its famous university and library.[44] The destruction of the Bamyan Buddhas by Taliban as well as the destructions by ISIS in Palmyra, or the Islamists' destruction of Sufi heritage in Timbuktu in 2012, were all meant to be seen by a wider audience. They were messages of

[43] See for instance chapters in this volume by Frederik Rosén, by Kristin Hausler and Andrzej Jakubowski, and by and Mark Drumbl.
[44] Kramer (n 34) 6–30.

defiance sent to subdue the local population, to discourage enemies, and to encourage sympathizers to join the ranks of the Islamists.

Some of these messages also target a Western audience. The destruction of heritage related to what is put on display in the major museums of Europe and North America is meant to hurt Western cultural identity, because European culture considers itself the rightful inheritor of the early civilizations of the MENA region and of the Graeco-Roman heritage so amply represented there. Alongside the equally scenographed cynical killings of captives, the spectacles of heritage destruction have been willingly distributed by international media, who thus help the perpetrators spread their propaganda and encourage repetition.

In contrast to the ISIS destruction in Palmyra, the Turkish destruction of Kurdish heritage is not an act meant to be seen in itself. It is the history of the Kurds in Anatolia that is meant not to be seen. The same goes for the ongoing "editing" of cultural heritage in Israel and the occupied territories. Here the effort is meant through selective excavation, accessibility, preservation, and interpretation to emphasize the Jewish, and to downplay the Palestinian history.[45]

XII. Intervention, Reconstruction, and Communication

The harm and hurt inflicted by the destruction of cultural heritage is considerable. It hurts the identity of people, their dignity, and pride. It damages future relations between the victims and the perpetrators. It damages important assets for the livelihood of local populations, because cultural heritage is a source of jobs and income from ongoing management and tourism, and through urban quality that attracts a diversity of economic activities and residents. The loss of heritage can therefore harm the socioeconomic recovery of affected areas and populations after war.

There can be many incitements for the international community to intervene when conflicts threaten such famous heritage sites as Palmyra or Bamyan; and the frustrations over the destructions run high also among heritage experts and scholars. But intervention is also a statement. It is a statement of priorities, in which we rank the value of stones above that

[45] For instance, Chiara de Cesari, *Heritage and the Cultural Struggle for Palestine* (Stanford UP 2019) 84–90.

of human lives, that we did not intervene to safeguard. It is also a statement about concern over the loss of those particular types of heritage that "we" want to see in our museums or to visit as tourists on location. If that concern is manifested at the same time as we seem un-agitated by the destruction of (in our eyes less spectacular) local community heritage such as the village mosque, chapel, or graveyard, it sends a message about indifference to the plight and dignity of local communities. This is heritage that matters to the local population and its sense of identity and belonging. By overlooking that, while concentrating all of our concerns and efforts on the monuments celebrated in the West, we risk creating or reinforcing a false distinction between "our heritage" and "theirs." That does no service in the long run to the preservation of either and wins few "hearts and minds" where we most need them.

When war ends comes a difficult and important phase of recovering some kind of a "normal" life for the populations in the war zone. In those conflicts, where sectarian violence has taken over as the apparent casus belli, that recovery will, among other issues, have to deal with damaged cultural heritage, whether the damage was collateral or meant to destroy important markers of identity.

A reconstruction effort is in itself a statement, that inevitably refers to an understanding of the conflict and in a positive or negative way is bound to affect the ability to heal wounds within and between people. Among the questions we might have about cultural heritage preservation are the following. Who decides what to restore, and how it is done? How do we assure a balanced representation in decision-making bodies from the local parties to the conflict? How to engage local communities in ways that foster "ownership"? What is the role of the international actors and institutions? How do we select an identity-balanced representation of monuments for reconstruction, so that we do not disproportionally favor one side in the conflict? How do we avoid competitive (re-)construction of monuments? How do we work with the interpretations and the narratives of the monuments, in a way that also highlights relatedness, and demotivates conflict? How do we encourage a shared interest across divides in the preservation efforts? How do we develop jobs for all on the basis of heritage projects? How do we avoid narrow investment and developer interests hijacking the post-conflict reconstruction, and add deepened socioeconomic segregation to the sectarian segregation, as it happened in Beirut after the civil war?

After the Yugoslav wars at the turn of the century, huge efforts were made by the international community to bring back lost and damaged monuments. There have been many laudable projects to also bring back the humbler monuments of minor communities. But one project stands out as almost iconic for the international effort, that of the reconstruction of the Mostar Bridge. The international community was captivated by the symbol of a bridge to unite a divided population. So, the bridge—an important monument from the Ottoman period—was to be rebuilt, even if the two banks to be reconnected were both part of Bosniak Mostar. The local Croat community in Mostar did not see the bridge as in any way *their* heritage, and somehow never became involved in its reconstruction. That was done mainly by specialists and entrepreneurs from Turkey and from the neighboring Croatian republic. After its reconstruction the bridge alongside other restored parts of the Bosniak town became destinations for one-day tourists bussed in for a few hours from the holiday resorts on Croatia's Dalmatian coast. This is a form of tourism that generates little income for the local population. The creation of jobs for all sides in the former conflict is among the most important factors in a successful healing process. That was ignored when the international community stepped in to help reconstruction of the bridge.

The Mostar Bridge was at least restored in accordance with the original. But in many other instances in post-war Bosnia there was a competitive (re-)construction of monuments that were emblematic for the parties to the conflict. Mosques were rebuilt in non-local style (reflecting foreign sponsors) and supplied with higher minarets than the previous ones just as churches were rebuilt with higher belfries than the originals. A similar pattern can be observed in post-civil war Beirut: a new grand mosque has supplanted a much humbler prewar place for prayers. The Saudi funded mosque has four towering minarets. Next door the Christian Maronites rebuilt their cathedral and fitted it with a long-desired new belfry of the same height as the minarets. The point to be made with these examples is that even if reconstruction at a first glance appears as an obvious and positive contribution to heal the scars of conflict, it may well without proper understanding of the deeper geopolitical context contribute to its continuation with other means, helping inter-sectarian antagonisms to live on—ready to fuel new armed confrontations.

XIII. Conclusion

In times of bewilderment and upheaval, when people look for hope, meaning, and direction for their lives and their future, cultural heritage is clearly moving into focus. It becomes of particular importance, along with questions of identity, rights, and roots in time and space. The examples are many in the early decades of the twenty-first century. We have already mentioned the reconversion of Istanbul's Hagia Sophia as an example of a historic revival that in this case was designed to suggestively remind a disaffected population of the golden age of the Ottoman Empire.

Another example could be the initiation of construction work in 2020 of a new temple for Lord Ram (one of the avatars of the Hindu god Vishnu) at the very site where a large group of Hindus in 1992 tore down one of India's most historic mosques, Babri Masjid built in 1528–29 on the orders of India's first Mughal ruler, Babur—the founder of the Mughal Empire. Hindu nationalists claimed that the mosque had been built on that site after destruction and clearing of a temple marking the supposed birthplace of Lord Ram. The erection of a Hindu temple, on the spot from which the Babri Masjid (Babur's Mosque) stood, coincided with other moves challenging India's considerable Muslim minority.[46]

Indian Prime Minister Narendra Modi was leading the ceremony to celebrate the beginning of the temple construction, just as the Turkish President Recep Tayyip Erdoğan played a prominent ceremonial part in the first Friday prayer in the reconverted Hagia Sophia. In both cases religious heritage is used by leaders to bolster popular support for their political project by evoking the idea of a past "golden age" as an inspiration for the future. Both countries have strong antagonistic neighbor relations in which claims of historic rights and religious differences play important parts. In both India and Turkey there is an ongoing conflict between a secularist and a religious vision

[46] New laws granting rights to obtain citizenship only to non-Muslim illegal immigrants from neighboring countries were passed by the Indian parliament in 2019. The law has been seen as a redefinition of Indian citizenship as attached to religion, in this case by excluding Muslims. "Citizenship Amendment Bill: India's New 'anti-Muslim' Law Explained" (*BBC News*, 11 December 2019) <https://www.bbc.com/news/world-asia-india-50670393> accessed 9 February 2020. Earlier in 2019 new laws were passed by the Indian parliament opening for people from elsewhere in India to obtain permanent residence in Indian administered Kashmir. This has been seen by Kashmir's Muslims as threatening to shift the demographic balance of Kashmir to their disadvantage. "India's New Residence Law Triggers Fury In Kashmir" (*DW*, 4 April 2020) <https://www.dw.com/en/indias-new-residence-law-triggers-fury-in-kashmir/a-53015259> accessed 9 February 2020.

of what the state should be. These visions encompass the question of balance between minority right and majority might.

The explosive potential of heritage has also been demonstrated in the context of the Black Lives Matter movement that spread through United States and Europe during 2020. Conflicts, sometimes violent, have unfolded around the question of removal of monuments and statues of persons related to enslavement and colonialism. In all of these examples, we have clear demonstrations of why and how cultural heritage can become a potent element in a conflict between opposing groups. Once such conflicts spin out of control and turn violent, cultural heritage is bound to become not only a target but also theme that can drive further escalation.

In a contemporary context, where more wars are hybrid, involving non-state combatants (sometimes as proxies for foreign states), the effect of international conventions to protect heritage is limited. Furthermore, wars today are for a large part fought intensively in an urban environment, where heritage density is higher than in the open landscape. Contemporary armed conflicts, irrespective of their deeper socioeconomic roots, are frequently fought under the banner of cultural identity. Therefore, targeted destruction of cultural heritage with emblematic value for the warring parties almost inevitably becomes part of the conflict.

This chapter has focused on conflicts happening in the MENA region, because they have a considerable direct and indirect impact on Europe. But also, because these conflicts are insufficiently understood by policymakers and public opinion in the outside world, too often they are misrepresented as products of an archaic culture that keeps repeating century-old conflicts. Many of the observations made about the MENA region have relevance to other regions, where empires have ruled vast territories and a diversity of cultures.

From within a short time frame and Western nation-state perspective, we often fail to understand the long lasting and cataclysmic impact from the breakdown of the Ottoman Empire on the complex sociocultural and demographic fabric of its former territories. Many of the post-Ottoman state formations outside of Turkey carried with them much of the cultural diversity from the empire. That has been explicit in the Levant and Maghreb, but also in the Balkan region, where different empires for centuries competed for control over territory and populations.[47] That diversity did not necessarily sit easy with the post-imperial nation-states, which represented an entirely

[47] Oliver Jens Schmitt, *Der Balkan im 20. Jahrhundert, Eine postimperiale Geschichte* (Stuttgart 2019).

different logic of statehood and identity. In times of conflict, whether domestic or international, ethnic diversity constituted a potential powder keg. This was the case in Yugoslavia, when local elites from the different parts of the federal republic failed to agree on the principles of power sharing after the death of the post-World War II leader, Josip Broz Tito. That coincided with the breakdown of the rigid bipolar international order, which had dominated Europe since 1945, and kept local and regional conflicts in check.

In these situations, identity issues have been exploited to pursue or defend interests, positions, and privileges. At that moment cultural heritage would also become part of the conflict. Once a conflict has reached that stage, it will be difficult for outside parties to justify intervening to safeguard cultural heritage without also aiming at stopping the carnage on the populations. As demonstrated by recent conflicts, intervention without coherent viable goals and an exit plan is a course fraught with dangers of creating more problems than solutions. The best protection of cultural heritage from becoming part of a conflict for symbolic reasons is to deconstruct divisive interpretations and narratives that exploit heritage as a vehicle for sectarian or nationalistic propaganda.

In fact, cultural heritage is seldom the exclusive product of a single culture. Cultures interact and borrow inspirations from each other. They share architectural solutions, decorative motives, and techniques in buildings. They also share music, tales, and food across today's closed borders, physical as well as mental. Such shared cultural heritage needs to be exposed, recognized, and understood also before war breaks out. And afterward, when the difficult post-conflict healing begins, it should be an important focus for any international effort to help.

But most essential, cultural heritage has importance far beyond itself. After conflicts, in which identity and sectarian diversity has been instrumentalized to generate or manipulate the conflict, it is essential to work in the cultural dimension to rebuild dialogue, dignity, and mutual respect between the affected groups. Creating jobs from restoring heritage and from showing it to the outside world is an essential part of bringing people together in shared pride of where they come from and who they are. Thus, working together across identity borders to reclaim damaged heritage, to share it, and to appreciate what we have in common will be one of the most important efforts to help post-conflict reconciliation. It is at the same time essential not to deny the existence and value of difference. It is the variation in the ways we do things that enriches us and fosters innovation. We may well draw on many of the same elements when we build, sing, or cook. But we select, process, and combine them differently and probably add some ideas and elements particular to us. With a common social contract to regulate our interactions, we should cherish our neighbor's way of doing things differently, while also taking pride in our own.

The involvement of neutral agents from the outside world is likely to be necessary to facilitate the opening of dialogue and cooperation between the parties to a recent conflict. But the facilitation must be respectful, guided by sensitivity to the deep-rooted feelings in people traumatized by war. The external involvement will have to provide resources without imposing solutions and choices. These should be found and made with the local communities and their authorities. This will be the only way to turn culture and cultural heritage into an asset for the long process of overcoming conflict.

Index

For the benefit of digital users, indexed terms that span two pages (e.g., 52–53) may, on occasion, appear on only one of those pages.

Note: Tables and figures are indicated by *t* and *f* following the page number